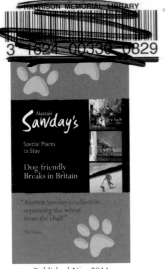

Published Nov 2011

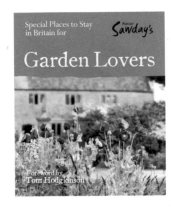

Alastair

Sawday's

Special Places to Stay

Sixteenth edition
Copyright © 2011
Alastair Sawday Publishing Co. Ltd
Published in September 2011
ISBN-13: 978-1-906136-53-6

Alastair Sawday Publishing Co. Ltd,
The Old Farmyard, Yanley Lane,
Long Ashton, Bristol BS41 9LR, UK
Tel: +44 (0)1275 395430
Email: info@sawdays.co.uk
Web: www.sawdays.co.uk

The Globe Pequot Press,
P. O. Box 480, Guilford,
Connecticut 06437, USA
Tel: +1 203 458 4500
Email: info@globepequot.com
Web: www.globepequot.com

Series Editor Alastair Sawday
Editor Wendy Ogden
Assistant to Editor Lianka Varga
Editorial Director Annie Shillito
Content & Publishing Manager
Jackie King
Writing Wendy Ogden, Alex Baker, Tom
Bell, Jo Boissevain, Nicola Crosse,
Monica Guy
Inspections Jan Adam, David Ashby,
Mandy Barnes, Neil Brown, Anne
Coates, Angie Collings, Gillian Cooper,
Trish Dugmore, Alison Harper, Jemima
Lewis, John MacLean, Vickie MacIver,
Margot Rawson, Aideen Reid, Nicky
Tennent, Jacqui Vallis, Caro Woods,
Mandy Wragg
*And thanks to those people who did an
inspection and write-up or two.*
Sales & Marketing & PR
01275 395433

*We have made every effort to ensure the accuracy
of the information in this book at the time
of going to press. However, we cannot accept any
responsibility for any loss, injury or
inconvenience resulting from the use of
information contained therein.*

Maps: Maidenhead Cartographic Services
Printing: Butler, Tanner & Dennis, Frome
UK distribution: Penguin UK, London
Production: The Content Works

Cover photo credits. 1. © Loupe Images/Jan Baldwin 2. © istockphoto.com/whitemay
3. Lesley Chalmers

Alastair
Sawday's

Special Places
to Stay

British
Bed & Breakfast

4 Contents

Front	Page
A word from Alastair Sawday	6
Introduction	7
How we choose our Special Places	9
Inspections	9
Feedback	9
Subscriptions	10
Disclaimer	10
Using this book	11
Finding the right place for you	11
Maps	11
Ethical Collection	11
Sawday's Travel Club	11
Symbols	11
Quick reference indices	12
Practical matters	13
Types of places	13
Rooms	13
Meals	14
Prices and minimum stays	14
Booking and cancellation	16
Payment	16
Tipping	16
Arrivals and departures	16
Closed	16
Maps	17–39

Guide entries	Entry	Map
England		
Bath & N.E. Somerset	1-7	3
Bedfordshire	8	9
Berkshire	9-10	3,4
Brighton & Hove	11	4
Bristol	12	3
Buckinghamshire	13-15	8, 9
Cambridgeshire	16-20	9
Cheshire	21-25	7, 8
Cornwall	26-68	1, 2
Cumbria	69-93	11, 12
Derbyshire	94-101	8, 12
Devon	102-151	2
Dorset	152-192	3
Durham	193	12
Essex	194-199	9, 10
Gloucestershire	200-232	3, 7, 8
Hampshire	233-245	3, 4
Herefordshire	246-260	7
Isle of Wight	261-262	4
Kent	263-291	5
Lancashire	292-294	11, 12
Leicestershire	295-297	8, 9
Lincolnshire	298-310	9, 13
London	311-337	22
Middlesex	338	22
Norfolk	339-364	9, 10
Northamptonshire	365-368	8, 9
Northumberland	369-381	12, 16
Nottinghamshire	382-383	9
Oxfordshire	384-399	3, 4, 8
Rutland	400	9
Shropshire	401-423	7
Somerset	424-470	2, 3
Staffordshire	471-473	8
Suffolk	474-498	9, 10
Surrey	499-504	4
Sussex	505-528	4, 5
Warwickshire	529-542	8

Guide entries	Entry	Map
England contd.		
Wiltshire	543-569	3
Worcestershire	570-575	8
Yorkshire	576-613	12, 13
Channel Islands		
Guernsey	614	4
Scotland		
Aberdeenshire	615-621	19
Angus	622-623	19
Argyll & Bute	624-631	14, 17
Ayrshire	632	14
Clackmannanshire	633	15
Dumfries & Galloway	634-639	11, 14, 15
Dunbartonshire	640-641	14, 15
Edinburgh & Lothians	642-657	15, 16
Fife	658-660	15, 16, 19
Highland	661-674	17, 18, 21
Moray	675	18
Perth & Kinross	676-682	15, 18
Scottish Borders	683-688	15, 16
Stirling	689-692	15
Western Isles	693-695	20
Wales		
Anglesey	696	6
Carmarthenshire	697-701	6, 7
Ceredigion	702-703	6
Conwy	704-705	7
Denbighshire	706	7
Flintshire	707-708	7
Gwynedd	709-714	6, 7
Monmouthshire	715-717	7
Pembrokeshire	718-724	6
Powys	725-735	7
Swansea	736	2
Wrexham	737	7

Back	Page
Sawday's Travel Club	413
Sawday's Gift Cards	414
Quick reference indices	415
Wheelchair-accessible	415
Stay all day	415
Singles	416
On a budget?	417
ASP - a green company	418
Ethical Collection	420
Other titles from Sawday's	424
Index by town	426
What's in each entry?	432

Photo: Tom Germain

generally do it all with panache. These lovely people are rarely slaves to fashion.

I have often written glowingly of the integrity of our owners, of the way they insist on the finest food — growing their own and supporting local producers. Chickens strut their stuff at more and more of our B&Bs. Homemade bread supports layers of homemade marmalade. This is more encouraging than it might seem, for we are approaching a food crisis in the UK.

In 2004 there were, much to the alarm of many of us, 19 major supermarkets in the South West. There are now over 80. In Bristol, the 'riot' over Tesco's new branch near the city centre was based upon a genuine fear for the future of local food producers, the future of food in general. The fear is well-founded, for the commercial model behind supermarkets demands continual growth; where is that to come from if not overseas and from the erosion of the independent sector? Our food-producing B&B owners are taking a stand and contributing positively to the well-being of the UK.

I don't want you to think that I do this often, but every time I leaf through a magazine about interiors, houses, hotels and holidays, I am struck by the surreptitious way we are inveigled into thinking along similar lines. Advertising still works a treat on the gullible and also on the less gullible. Who isn't thinking about roll top baths? Or painted furniture and floorboards?

So I am especially delighted that our collection of B&Bs continues to celebrate the personality of individuals, their differences and their idiosyncrasies. Many of them will have those roll top baths and paint their floors, but will

We are proud of the enterprise, imagination and kindness within these pages. Our owners are bottomless stores of intelligence on their areas. By staying in a Special Place you are plugging into lovely people and great ideas. This remains one of the great treats of life in the UK.

Alastair Sawday

Sizzling home-cured bacon in Somerset, eggs from Clarissa the chicken in Dorset, tawny owls in Dumfries & Galloway, campfires in Wales... Settle down with this brand new edition and find your Special Place to Stay for a night, a mid-week break, a long weekend, a sabbatical.

One of our Derbyshire owners mentioned to me that some happy guests left hers saying, "We use Sawday's as a stepping stone: we choose a Sawday place that we feel we'd like, stay a few days and explore the area round about. We're now moving on to Lincolnshire, followed by Cambridgeshire, to do the same." What a great way to use the guide.

Some new owners to this edition spent months travelling round the UK in a camper van looking for their own special place – they found a lovely old Welsh slate cutting mill in Gwynedd and opened their doors to B&B guests. Whether you're a city lover, peace seeker, walker, biker, birdwatcher or you believe strongly in Slow Food, our wonderfully varied B&Bs and their owners are waiting to be discovered.

Bath is splendid with its Roman Baths, Georgian theatre and interesting shops. Head off into the surrounding country-side and find a wealth of interest: cathedrals, concerts and Gregorian chants, arboretum, bird song and country peace. Dip your toes in history in Oxford and Cambridge and stay in one of the colleges, with their candle-lit

Photo: Alec Studerus

chapels and gorgeous walled gardens. In Cornwall and Devon plenty of our B&Bs are within strolling distance of the spectacular coast; mackerel fishing and boat trips are on tap.

Herefordshire and Shropshire will surprise you with their beauty; the walks and views, Black Mountain and streams are stunning. These areas are brimming with literary festivals, lively food markets and festivals, cider makers and cottage industries. We have over forty B&Bs to choose from in Wales – from pretty Pembrokeshire to wild Anglesey – where you'll find secret sandy beaches and rambling farmhouses, cockles and lavabread, lakes, miles of Snowdonia National Park and spectacular walks.

In Wiltshire and the surrounding counties discover thatched cottages on little lanes, colourful period homes in extensive grounds or walled town gardens and seclusion in your own little house. Suffolk and Norfolk have festivals, seals and beautiful old pink houses aplenty. In Sussex and Kent find barns, potteries, elegant and inviting town houses, theatre and Glyndebourne, Shetland sheep...

London gleams with choice: super central but peaceful pads, mansion flats, handsome terraces and sweet gardens — great value here too.

Yorkshire has rural bliss, village gems and chic town houses, whilst Cumbria and Northumberland are wonderfully un-spoilt with wild walks, wildlife and banks of daffodils. In Scotland we have over 75 peaceful, special places with lochs and glens, a herb garden with 200 varieties, fishing on the Tweed, grand estates and bays in the isles bursting with boats.

On your travels enjoy bedrooms that are sumptuous or simple, bathrooms state of the art or spartan. Some homes are splendid old places big enough to swallow hordes; others are little cottages with one guest bedroom. You will find smart boutique styles, rustic simplicity, elegance and grandeur, eccentric and quirky touches, roses and wisteria... home from home, but better.

Our owners are an eclectic group too: jazz enthusiasts, professional chefs, organic farmers and inspired gardeners, artists, peach growers and bee keepers, wedding cake makers, solar power producers and rare breed and Slow Food aficionados... to name a few.

The list of breakfast ingredients is mouthwateringly endless: the full free-range Monty with proper sausages, kippers and kedgeree, porridge and pancakes with maple syrup, home-smoked salmon, homemade breads and jams, orchard compotes and juices. Many places do a delicious dinner too or have good pubs and restaurants close by — from more than 100 entries it's a walk to your dinner table, and from most of the others it's just a short drive.

So get your maps out or fire up the satnav, invite friends... then book your stays and set off armed with happy anticipation. The authenticity, gentle unstuffy feel and delightful welcome at these Special Places will remain as a warm memory long after you've returned home. Enjoy!

Wendy Ogden

Photo: Lesley Chalmers

It's simple. There are no rules, no boxes to tick. We choose places that we like and are fiercely subjective in our choices. We also recognise that one person's idea of special is not necessarily someone else's so there is a huge variety of places, and prices, in the book. Those who are familiar with our Special Places series know that we look for comfort, originality, authenticity, and reject the insincere, the anonymous and the banal. The way guests are treated comes as high on our list as the setting, the architecture, the atmosphere and the food.

Inspections

We visit every place in the guide to get a feel for how both house and owner tick. We don't take a clipboard and we don't have a list of what is acceptable and what is not. Instead, we chat for an hour or so with the owner and look round. It's all very informal, but it gives us an excellent idea of who would enjoy staying there. If the visit happens to be the last of the day, we sometimes stay the night. Once in the book properties are re-inspected every four years or so, to keep things fresh and accurate.

Feedback

In between inspections we rely on feedback from our army of readers, as well as from staff members who are encouraged to visit properties across the series. This feedback is invaluable to us and we always follow up on comments. So do tell us whether your stay has been a joy or not, if the atmosphere was great

Photo: Alec Studerus

or stuffy, the owners cheery or bored. The accuracy of the book depends on what you, and our inspectors, tell us. A lot of the new entries in each edition are recommended by our readers, so keep telling us about new places you've discovered too. Please visit our site, www.sawdays.co.uk/recommend to tell us about your discoveries.

However, please do not tell us if the bedside light was broken, or the shower head was scummy. Tell the owner, immediately, and get them to do something about it. Most owners are more than happy to correct problems and will bend over backwards to help.

Far better than bottling it up and then writing to us a week later!

Subscriptions

Owners pay to appear in this guide. Their fee goes towards the high costs of inspecting, of producing an all-colour book and of maintaining our website. We only include places that we like and find special for one reason or another, so it is not possible for anyone to buy their way onto these pages. Nor is it possible for the owner to write their own description. We will say if the bedrooms are small, or if a main road is near. We do our best to avoid misleading people.

Disclaimer

We make no claims to pure objectivity in choosing these places. They are here simply because we like them. Our opinions and tastes are ours alone and this book is a statement of them; we hope you will share them. We have done our utmost to get our facts right but apologise unreservedly for any mistakes that may have crept in.

You should know that we don't check such things as fire regulations, swimming pool security or any other laws with which owners of properties receiving paying guests should comply. This is the responsibility of the owners.

Photo: Union Place, entry 604

Finding the right place for you

All these places are special in one way or another. All have been visited and then written about honestly so that you can take what you like and leave the rest. Those of you who swear by Sawday's books trust our write-ups precisely because we don't have a blanket standard; we include places simply because we like them. But we all have different priorities, so do read the descriptions carefully and pick out the places where you will be comfortable. If something is particularly important to you then do check when you book: a simple question or two can avoid misunderstandings.

Maps

Each property is flagged with its entry number on the maps at the front. These maps are a great starting point for planning your trip, but please don't use them as anything other than a general guide – use a decent road map for real navigation. Most places will send you detailed instructions once you have booked your stay.

Ethical Collection

We're always keen to draw attention to owners who are striving to have a positive impact on the world, so you'll notice that some entries are flagged as being part of our "Ethical Collection". These places are working hard to reduce their environmental footprint, making significant contributions to their local community, or are passionate about serving local or organic food. Owners

have had to fill in a very detailed questionnaire before becoming part of this Collection – read more on page 420. This doesn't mean that other places in the guide are not taking similar initiatives – many are – but we may not yet know about them.

Sawday's Travel Club

We've launched a Travel Club, based around the Special Places to Stay series; you'll see a 📷 symbol on those places offering something extra to Club members, so to find out how to join see the inside front cover.

Symbols

Below each entry you will see some symbols, which are explained at the very back of the book. They are based on the information given to us by the owners. However, things do change: bikes may be under repair or a new pool may have been put in. Please use the symbols as a guide rather than an absolute statement of fact and double-check anything that is

Photo: Munden House, entry 188

don't like them but because they may have a steep stair, an unfenced pond or they find balancing the needs of mixed age groups too challenging.

Pets – Our 🐕 symbol shows places which are happy to accept pets. It means they can sleep in the bedroom with you, but not on the bed. Be realistic about your pet – if it is nervous or excitable or doesn't like the company of other dogs, people, chickens, children, then say so. Do let the owners know when booking that you intend to bring your pet – particularly if it is not the usual dog!

Owners' pets – The 🐈 symbol is given when the owners have their own pet on the premises. It may not be a cat! But it is there to warn you that you may be greeted by a dog, serenaded by a parrot, or indeed sat upon by a cat.

important to you – owners occasionally bend their own rules, so it's worth asking if you may take your child or dog even if they don't have the symbol.

Children – The 🧒 symbol shows places which are happy to accept children of all ages. This does not mean that they will necessarily have cots, high chairs, etc. If an owner welcomes children but only those above a certain age, we have put these details at the end of their write-up. These houses do not have the child symbol, but even these folk may accept your younger child if you are the only guests. Many who say no to children do so not because they

Quick reference indices

At the back of the book you'll find a number of quick-reference indices that will help you choose the place that is just right for you.

In this edition you'll find listings of properties where

- at least one bedroom and bathroom is accessible for wheelchair-users.
- a double costs £70 or less.
- you can stay all day.
- owners have a single room, or they let a double bedroom to guests travelling alone for half the double occupancy or less.

Photo: The Old Manor House, entry 541

Types of places

Some houses have rooms in annexes or stables, barns or garden 'wings', some of which feel part of the house, some of which don't. If you have a strong preference for being in the throng or for being apart, check those details. Consider your surroundings when you are packing: large, ancient country houses may be cooler than you are used to; city places and working farms may be noisy at times; and that peacock or cockerel we mention may disturb you. Light sleepers should pack ear plugs, and take a dressing gown if there's a separate bathroom (though these are sometimes provided).

Some owners give you a front door key so you may come and go as you please; others like to have the house empty between, say, 10am and 4pm. If you would prefer not to wander far during the day then look for the places that have the 'Stay all day' quick reference at the back of the book.

Rooms

Bedrooms – We tell you if a room is a double, twin/double (ie with zip and link beds), suite (with a sitting area), family or single. Most owners are flexible and can juggle beds or bedrooms; talk to them about what you need before you book. Staying in a B&B will not be like staying in a hotel; it is rare to be given your own room key and your bed will not necessarily be made during your stay, or your room cleaned. Make sure you are clear about

the room that you have booked, its views, bathroom and beds, etc.

Bathrooms – Most bedrooms in this book have an en suite bath or shower room; we only mention bathroom details when they do not. So, you may get a 'separate' bathroom (yours alone but not in your room) or a shared bathroom. Under certain entries we mention that two rooms share a bathroom and are 'let to same party only'. Please do not assume this means you must be a group of friends to apply; it simply means that if you book one of these rooms you will not be sharing a bathroom with strangers. If these things are important to you, please check when booking. Bath/shower means a bath with shower over; bath and shower means there is a separate shower unit.

Sitting rooms – Most B&B owners offer guests the family sitting room to share, or they provide a sitting room specially for

Photo: Cothelstone Manor, entry 432

guests. If neither option is available we generally say so, but do check. And do not assume that every bedroom or sitting room has a TV.

Meals

Unless we say otherwise, a full cooked breakfast is included. Some owners – particularly in London – will give you a good continental breakfast instead. Often you will feast on local sausage and bacon, eggs from resident hens, homemade breads and jams. In some you may have organic yogurts and beautifully presented fruit compotes. Some owners are fairly unbending about breakfast times, others are happy to just wait until you want it, or even bring it to you in bed.

Apart from breakfast, no meals should be expected unless you have arranged them in advance. Although we don't say so on each entry – the repetition a few hundred times would be tedious – all

owners who provide packed lunch, lunch or dinner need ADVANCE NOTICE. And they want to get things right for you so, when booking, please discuss your diet and meal times. Meal prices are quoted per person, and dinner is often a social occasion shared with your hosts and other guests.

Do eat in if you can – this book is teeming with good cooks. And how much more relaxing after a day out to have to move no further than the dining room for an excellent dinner, and to eat and drink knowing there's only a flight of stairs between you and your bed. Very few of our houses are licensed, but most are happy for you to bring your own drink.

Prices and minimum stays

Each entry gives a price PER ROOM for two people. We also include prices for single rooms, and let you know if there is a supplement to pay should you choose to loll in a double bed on your own.

The price range for each B&B covers a one-night stay in the cheapest room in low season to the most expensive in high season. Some owners charge more at certain times (during regattas or festivals, for example) and some charge less for stays of more than one night. Some owners ask for a two-night minimum stay at weekends and we mention this where possible. Most of our houses could fill many times over on peak weekends and during the summer; book early, especially if you have specific needs.

Photo left: Rock Cottage, entry 256
Photo right: Edington House, entry 441

Booking and cancellation

You may not receive a reply to your booking enquiry immediately; B&Bs are not hotels and the owners may be away. When you speak to the owner double-check the price you will pay for B&B and for any meals.

Requests for deposits vary; some are non-refundable, especially in our London homes, and some owners may charge you for the whole of the booked stay in advance. Some cancellation policies are more stringent than others. It is also worth noting that some owners will take the money directly from your credit/debit card without contacting you to discuss it. So ask them to explain their cancellation policy clearly before booking to avoid a nasty surprise.

Payment

All our owners take cash and UK cheques

Photo: Cothelstone Manor, entry 432

with a cheque card. Few take credit cards but if they do, we have given them the appropriate symbol. Check that your particular credit card is acceptable.

Tipping

Owners do not expect tips. If you have been treated with extraordinary kindness, write to them, or leave a small gift. Please tell us, too – we love to hear, and we do note, all feedback.

Arrivals and departures

Say roughly what time you will arrive (normally after 4pm), as most hosts like to welcome you personally. Be on time if you have booked dinner; if, despite best efforts, you are delayed, phone to give warning.

Closed

When given in months this means the whole of the month stated.

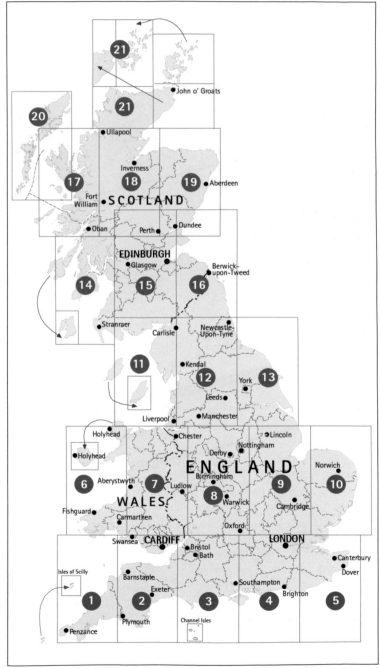

©Maidenhead Cartographic, 2011

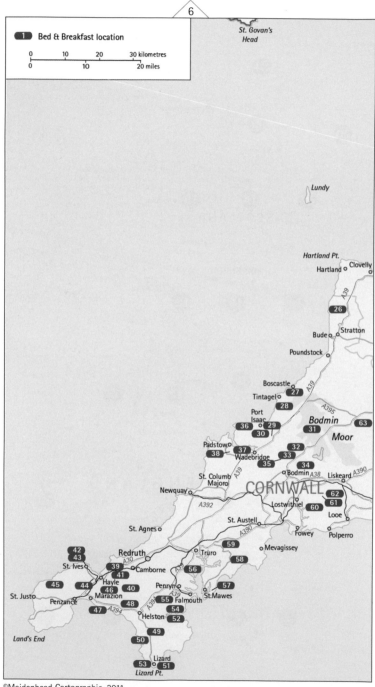

©Maidenhead Cartographic, 2011

Map 2   19

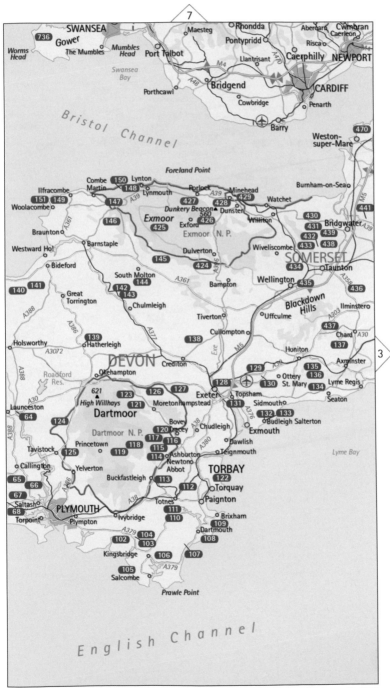

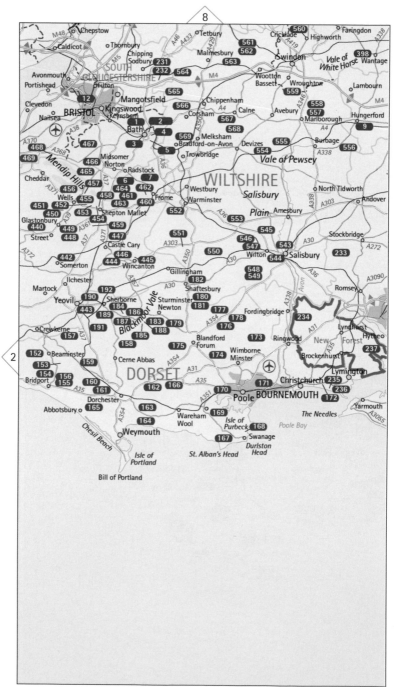

Map 4

21

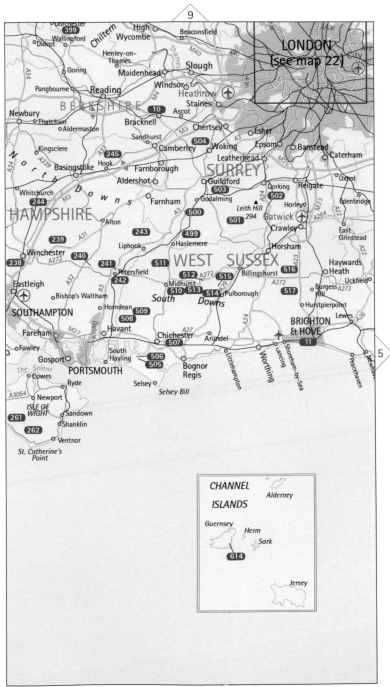

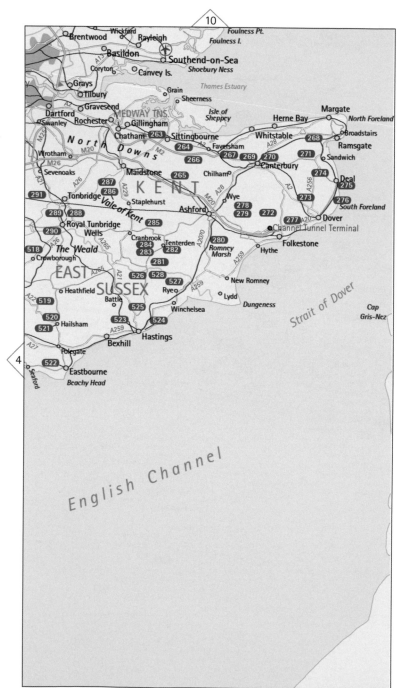

Map 6

23

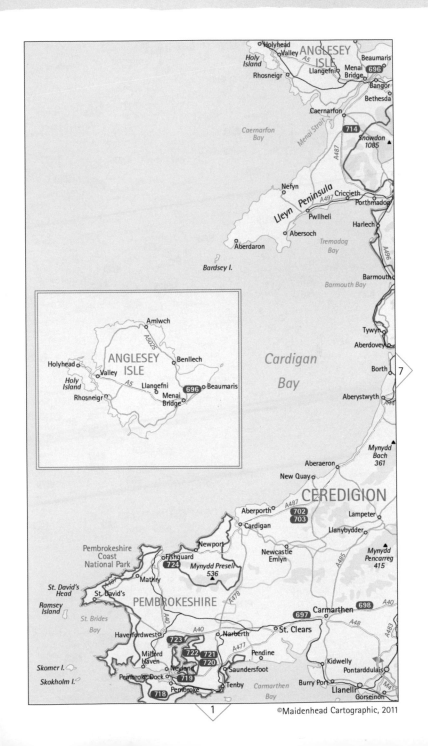

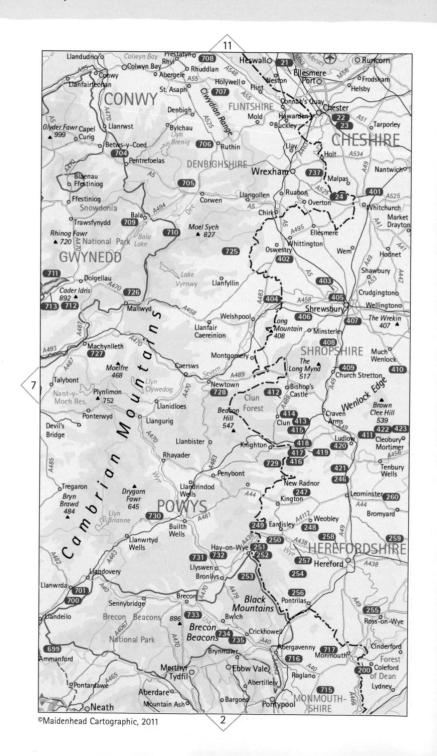

Map 8   25

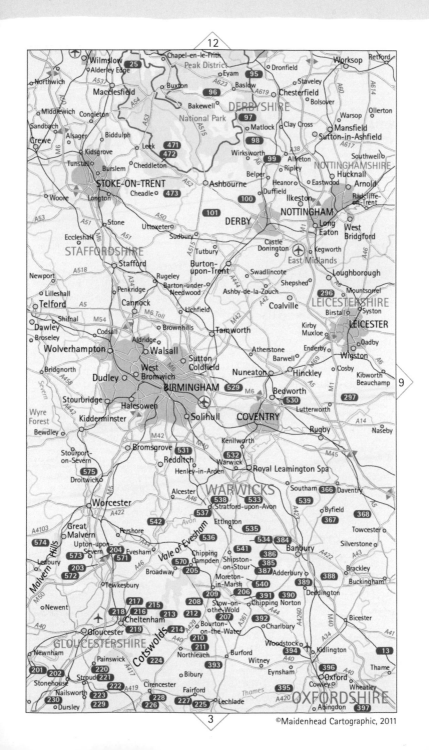

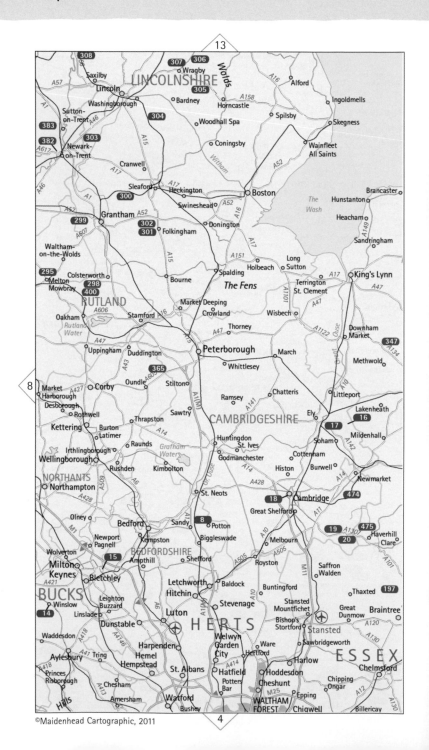

Map 10

27

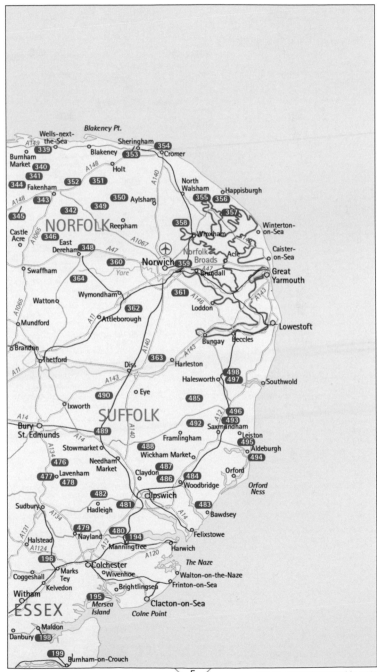

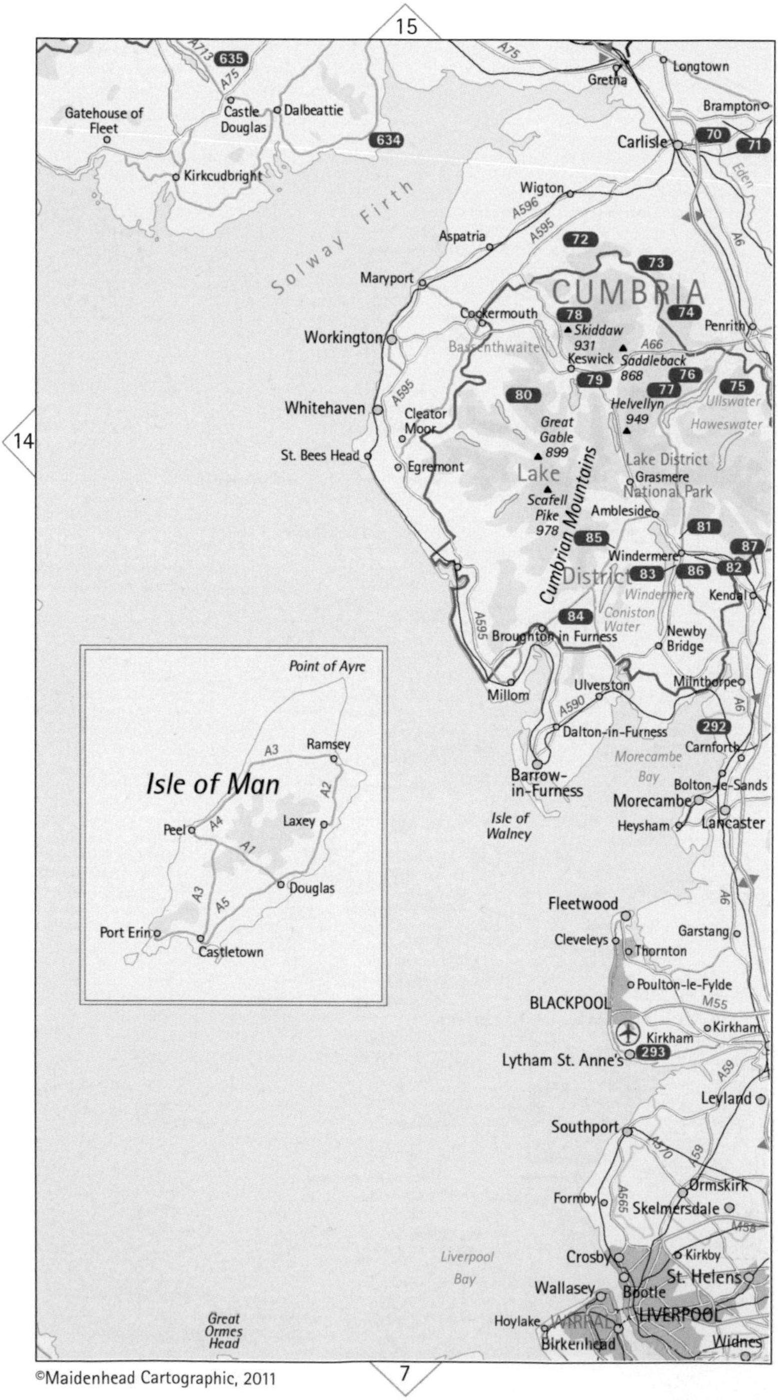

15

A713
635
A75

Gatehouse of Fleet
Castle Douglas
Dalbeattie
634

Kirkcudbright

Longtown

Gretha
Brampton
Carlisle
70
71

Eden

Solway Firth

Wigton
A596

Aspatria
A595
72

Maryport
73

CUMBRIA
74
Penrith

Cockermouth
78
Skiddaw 931
A66
Saddleback 868
76
75

Workington
Bassenthwaite
Keswick
79
77
Ullswater
Haweswater

Whitehaven
A595
Cleator Moor
80
Great Gable 899
Helvellyn 949

St. Bees Head
Egremont
Lake
Scafell Pike 978
Lake District National Park
Grasmere
Ambleside
81

14

Cumbrian Mountains
District
85
Windermere
83
86
82
87
Kendal

84
Broughton in Furness
Coniston Water
Windermere
Newby Bridge

A595
Millom
Ulverston
A590
Dalton-in-Furness
Milnthorpe
Carnforth
292
A6

Point of Ayre

A3
Ramsey
A2

Isle of Man

Peel
A4
Laxey

A1
Douglas

A3
A5
Port Erin
Castletown

Barrow-in-Furness
Morecambe Bay
Bolton-le-Sands
Morecambe
Isle of Walney
Heysham
Lancaster

Fleetwood
Garstang
Cleveleys
Thornton
Poulton-le-Fylde
M55
BLACKPOOL
Kirkham
Kirkham
293
Lytham St. Anne's

A59
Leyland
A6

Southport
A570
A59

Formby
Ormskirk
A565
Skelmersdale
M58

Liverpool Bay
Crosby
Kirkby
St. Helens
Wallasey
Bootle
LIVERPOOL
Great Ormes Head
Hoylake
ARRIVAL
Birkenhead
Widnes

7

Map 12   29

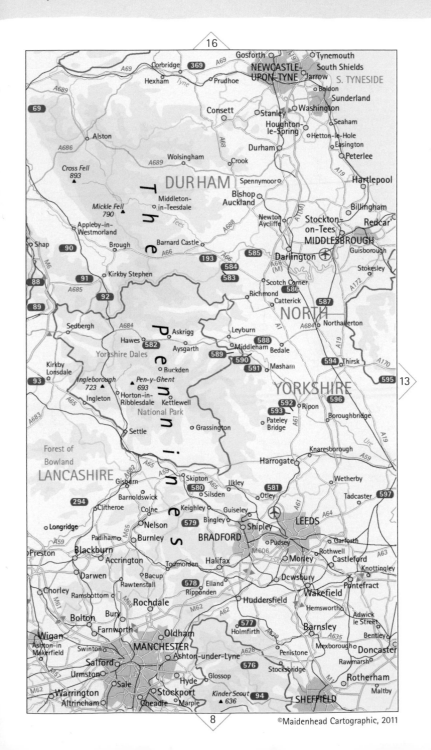

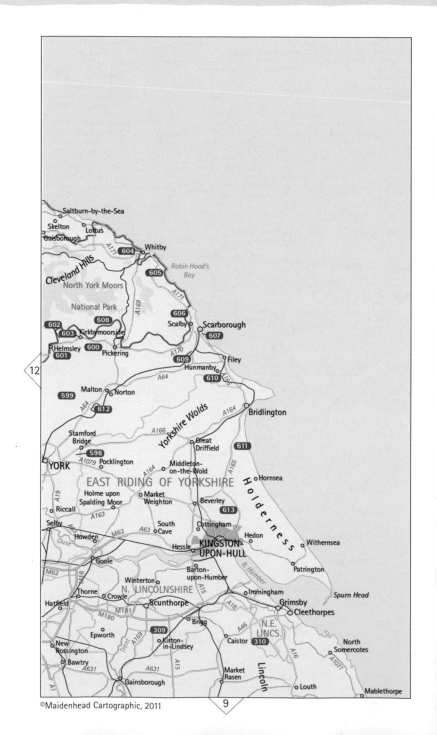

Map 14

31

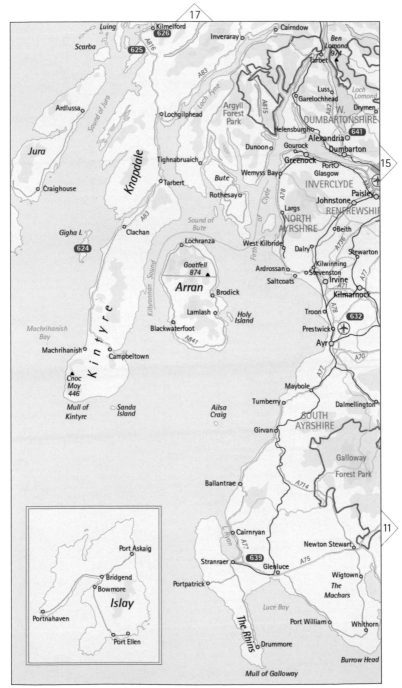

17

15

11

Luing
Scarba
Kilmelford
626
625
A816
Inveraray
Cairndow
Ben Lomond 974
Tarbet

Ardlussa
Sound of Jura
Lochgilphead
Argyll Forest Park
A83
Loch Fyne
A815
Luss
Garelochhead
Drymen
W. DUMBARTONSHIRE
Loch Lomond
A82
641

Jura
Knapdale
Helensburgh
Dunoon
Gourock
Alexandria
Dumbarton

Craighouse
Tighnabruaich
Tarbert
Bute
Rothesay
Wemyss Bay
Greenock
Port Glasgow
INVERCLYDE
Paisley
Johnstone
RENFREWSHIRE

Gigha I.
624
Clachan
A83
Sound of Bute
Largs
NORTH AYRSHIRE
Beith
Dalry
Stewarton
A736

Lochranza
West Kilbride
Kilwinning
A77

Kilbrannan Sound
Goatfell 874
Arran
Brodick
Ardrossan
Saltcoats
Stevenson
Irvine
A71
Kilmarnock
A78

Machrihanish Bay
Lamlash
Holy Island
Troon
632

Machrihanish
Blackwaterfoot
A841
Prestwick
Ayr

Kintyre
Campbeltown
A70

Choc Moy 446
Mull of Kintyre
Sanda Island
Ailsa Craig
Maybole
Turnberry
Dalmellington
SOUTH AYRSHIRE

Girvan

Galloway Forest Park

Ballantrae
A714

Islay inset:
Port Askaig
Bridgend
Bowmore
Islay
Portnahaven
Port Ellen

Cairnryan
Loch Ryan
A77
Newton Stewart
Stranraer
639
Glenluce
A75
Portpatrick
Wigtown
The Machars

The Rhins
Luce Bay
Port William
Whithorn
Drummore
Burrow Head
Mull of Galloway

©Maidenhead Cartographic, 2011

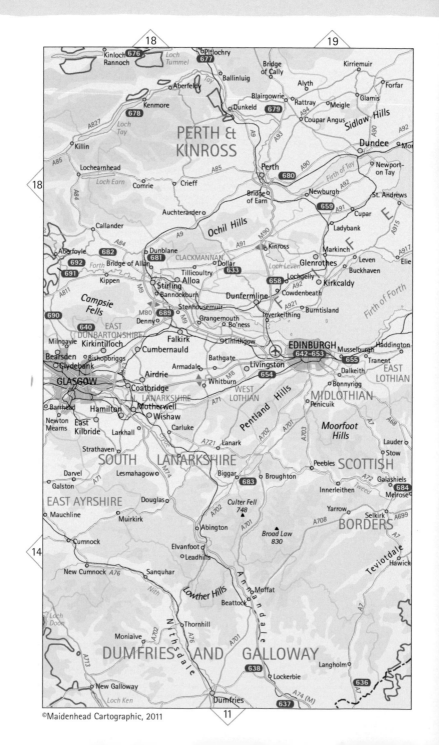

Map 16

33

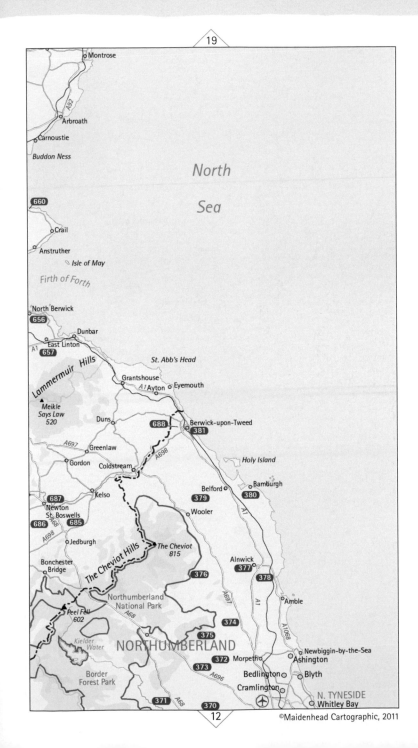

Montrose

A92

Arbroath

Carnoustie

Buddon Ness

North

Sea

660

Crail

Anstruther

Isle of May

Firth of Forth

North Berwick

656

Dunbar

East Linton

A1

657

Lammermuir Hills

St. Abb's Head

▲ Meikle
Says Law
520

Grantshouse

A1 Ayton Eyemouth

Duns

688

Berwick-upon-Tweed

381

A697

Greenlaw

A698

Gordon

Coldstream

Holy Island

687

Kelso

Belford

Bamburgh

Newton
St. Boswells

379

380

686 685

Wooler

A1

A698

Jedburgh

The Cheviot Hills

The Cheviot
815

Bonchester
Bridge

376

Alnwick

377

378

The Cheviot Hills

Northumberland
National Park

A697

A1

Amble

Peel Fell
602

A68

374

A1068

Kielder
Water

375

NORTHUMBERLAND

Newbiggin-by-the-Sea

372

Morpeth Ashington

Border
Forest Park

373

A696

Bedlington

Blyth

Cramlington

371

A68

370

N. TYNESIDE

Whitley Bay

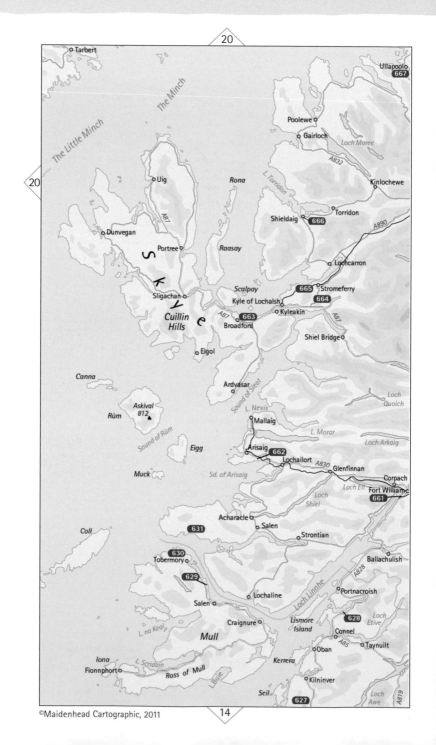

⬦ 20

⬦ 20

Tarbert ○

Ullapool ○
667

The Minch

The Little Minch

Poolewe ○

Gairloch ○

Loch Maree

A832

Uig ○

Rona

L. Torridon

Kinlochewe ○

A87

Torridon ○

Dunvegan ○

Shieldaig ○   666

A890

Portree ○

Raasay

Lochcarron ○

S
k
y
e

Scalpay

Stromeferry ○   665

Sligachan ○

Kyle of Lochalsh ○   664

Cuillin
Hills

A87   663

Kyleakin ○

Broadford ○

Shiel Bridge ○

Elgol ○

Canna

Ardvasar ○

Sound of Sleat

Loch
Quoich

Askival
812 ▲

Rùm

L. Nevis

Mallaig ○

Sound of Rùm

L. Morar

Eigg

Loch Arkaig

Arisaig ○   662

Muck

Sd. of Arisaig

Lochailort ○   A830   Glenfinnan ○

Corpach ○

Loch Eil   Fort William ○

661

Loch
Shiel

Coll

Acharacle ○   631

Salen ○

Strontian ○

Tobermory ○   630

Ballachulish ○

A828

629

Portnacroish ○

Loch Linnhe

Salen ○

Lochaline ○

Lismore
Island   628   Loch
Etive

Craignure ○

Connel ○

Iona
Fionnphort ○

L. na Keal

Mull

Kerrera

Oban ○   A85   Taynuilt ○

L. Scridain   Ross of Mull

L Buie

Kilninver ○

Seil

627

Loch
Awe

A819

©Maidenhead Cartographic, 2011   ⬦ 14

Map 18   35

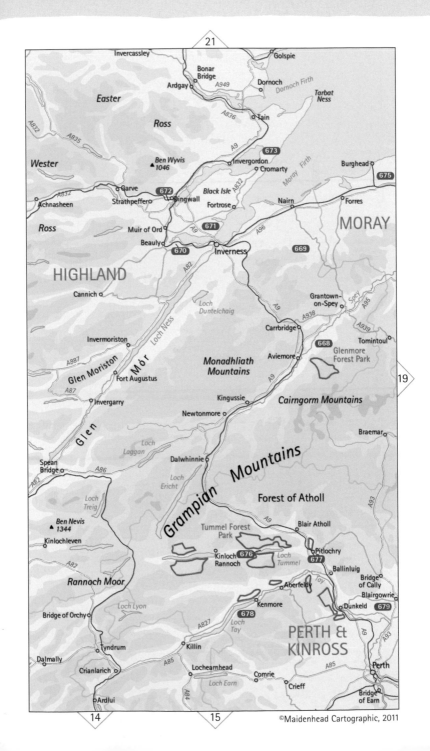

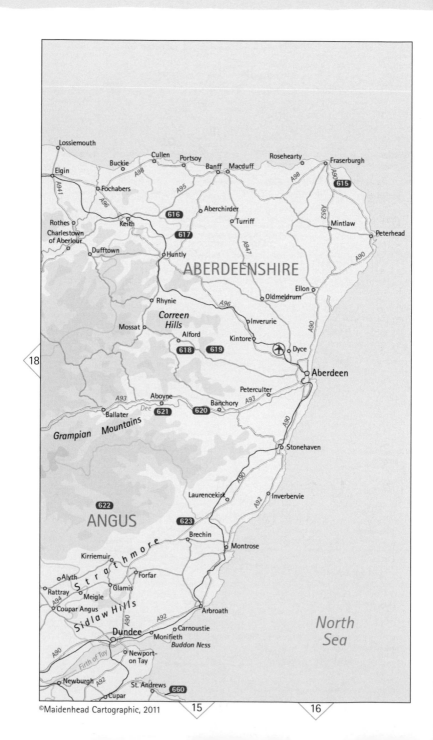

Map 20

37

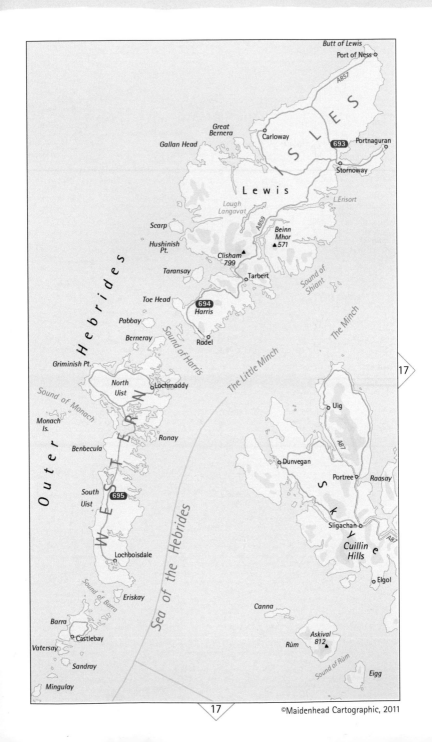

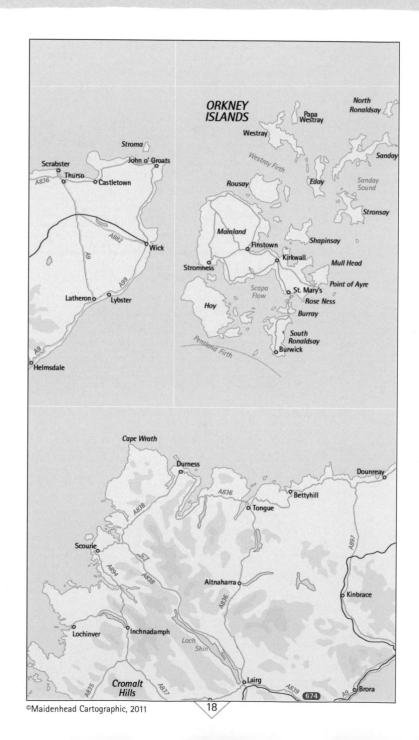

ORKNEY
ISLANDS

North
Ronaldsay

Papa
Westray

Westray

Stroma

John o' Groats

Scrabster

Thurso

Castletown

A836

A882

A9

A99

Wick

Latheron

Lybster

A9

Helmsdale

Rousay

Westray Firth

Eday

Sanday

Sanday
Sound

Stronsay

Mainland

Finstown

Shapinsay

Kirkwall

Mull Head

Stromness

Point of Ayre

Scapa
Flow

St. Mary's

Rose Ness

Hoy

Burray

South
Ronaldsay

Pentland Firth

Burwick

Cape Wrath

Durness

Dounreay

A836

Bettyhill

A838

Tongue

A897

Scourie

A894

A838

Altnaharra

A836

Kinbrace

Lochinver

Inchnadamph

Loch
Shin

Cromalt
Hills

A835

A837

Lairg

A839

674

A9

Brora

Map 22   39

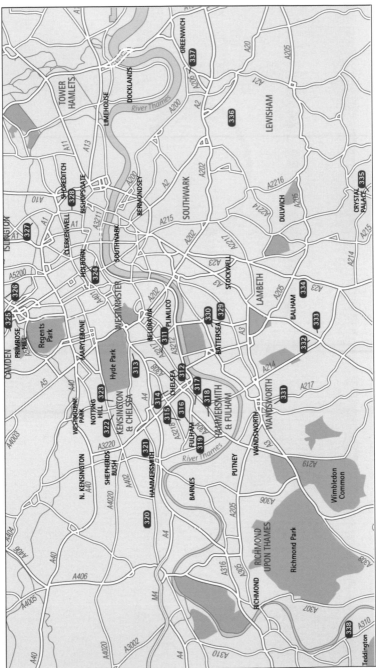

©Maidenhead Cartographic, 2011

England

Bath & N.E. Somerset

77 Great Pulteney Street

Elegant stone steps lead down past exotic ferns to a spacious garden flat in this broad street of grand Grade I-listed houses. Inside all is pale wood, modern art, bergère chairs and palms. Downstairs is a large, smart bedroom and bathroom with loads of books and its own door to a delightful small sunny garden. On fine mornings you breakfast here, or choose the gorgeous upstairs dining room: fine local bacon and sausages and fruit from the allotment. Ian is a keen cook so dinner will also be special, but there are lots of good places to eat – and shop – nearby. Henry may play the Northumbrian pipes for you if you ask nicely...

Price	£75–£100. Singles from £55.
Rooms	1 double.
Meals	Dinner £25. Packed lunch from £5.
Closed	Rarely.
Directions	A4 into centre of Bath. Last house before Laura Place on south side of Great Pulteney St. Parking by arrangement; 7-minute walk from station.

Ian Critchley & Henry Ford
77 Great Pulteney Street,
Bath BA2 4DL

Tel	+44 (0)1225 466659
Email	critchford@77pulteneyst.co.uk
Web	www.77pulteneyst.co.uk

Entry 1   Map 3

Bath & N.E. Somerset

Sir Walter Elliot's House

The period, hand-printed wallpaper is just one of the remarkable features of this elegant Grade I-listed house: Julian is an expert. The house, in one of Bath's finest Regency terraces, has been so beautifully restored that the BBC used its rooms for Jane Austen's *Persuasion*. Bedrooms are flooded with light and views are stunning; one stylish bathroom has marquina marble, cherrywood and ebony. Have breakfast in the family kitchen, or in the conservatory; for the adventurous, Mechthild serves up an Austrian alternative of cold meats and cheeses, fresh rye breads and homemade cakes. Herrlich! *Min. stay two nights weekends.*

Price	£95–£135. Singles £85.
Rooms	3 twins/doubles.
Meals	Pub/restaurant 300 yds.
Closed	Rarely.
Directions	A46 to Bath, then A4 for city centre. Left onto A36 over Cleveland Bridge; follow signs to Holburne Museum. Directly after museum, left. House on right.

 3 nights for the price of 2 Mon-Thurs. Homemade Austrian cakes in room.

Mechthild Self von Hippel
Sir Walter Elliot's House,
95 Sydney Place, Bath BA2 6NE

Tel	+44 (0)1225 469435
Mobile	+44 (0)7737 793772
Email	visitus@sirwalterelliotshouse.co.uk
Web	www.sirwalterelliotshouse.co.uk

Entry 2   Map 3

Bath & N.E. Somerset

14 Raby Place

A listed Regency house within walking distance of one of Europe's most beautiful cities. Muriel likes modern art and has filled the elegant rooms with stunning pictures and objects, antique chairs and lovely fabrics. Beautifully proportioned double bedrooms are graceful and spotless with laundered linen; one on the top (third) floor has fabulous views over the city to the Abbey, the small single has a piano in case you get the urge. Breakfast is organic, delicious, and eaten at a communal table in the dining room; chat to Muriel or bury your head in a paper. *Free parking permit for road outside.*

Price	£70-£75. Singles £35. Family room £80.
Rooms	5: 2 doubles, 1 family room; 1 twin with separate shower; 1 single with separate bath. Cot available.
Meals	Restaurants 8-minute walk.
Closed	Rarely.
Directions	Bathwick Hill is turning off the A36 towards Bristol; look for signs to university. No. 14 on left as you go uphill, before left turn into Raby Mews.

Muriel Guy
14 Raby Place,
Bathwick, Bath BA2 4EH
Tel   +44 (0)1225 465120
Email   murieljeanguy@gmail.com

Entry 3   Map 3

Bath & N.E. Somerset

Tolley Cottage

Breakfast on the patio on fine days and watch the barges pass the bottom of the gorgeous garden; raise your eyes to Bath Abbey on the skyline. This Victorian house is a ten-minute walk from city centre, spa and fine Georgian theatre. Sunny and bright, rooms are a comfortable mix of contemporary and classical; books, art and interesting glass pieces catch the eye. Bedrooms are small, calming and charming with elegant furnishings and long views; bathrooms sparkle. Judy does outstanding breakfasts; James, Master of Wine, can arrange tastings. Both are warm and relaxed, give attention to every detail and love sharing their home.

Ethical Collection: Food; Community.
See page 420.

Price	From £110. Singles from £100.
Rooms	2: 1 double, 1 twin.
Meals	Pubs/restaurants 10-minute walk.
Closed	Christmas.
Directions	Follow signs for American Museum & University up Bathwick Hill. Take 1st turn right to Sydney Buildings. House 200 yds on right. Free parking.

Judy & James John
Tolley Cottage,
23 Sydney Buildings, Bath BA2 6BZ
Tel   +44 (0)1225 463365
Mobile   +44 (0)7703 534331
Email   jj@judyj.plus.com
Web   www.tolleycottage.co.uk

Entry 4   Map 3

Bath & N.E. Somerset

55a North Road

Prepare yourself for a surprise. A short hop from Capability Brown-designed Prior Park, hidden down a narrow drive off one of Bath's less remarkable streets, is an architectural novelty — only the roof tiles give away the 1980s origins. Energetic owners Natalie and Guy offer you two completely private self-contained studios each with its own entrance, delightful small kitchen and elegant furniture. Find a charming mix of ultra-chic and traditional: oak floors, wool carpets, limestone tiles, old Irish bedheads and pure cotton linen. Natalie bring a very delicious breakfast to your room. *Ask about beauty & massage therapies.*

Bath & N.E. Somerset

Melon Cottage Vineyard

Interesting, friendly hosts who are entirely natural and unbusinesslike make this place special; it's excellent value, too. The ancient Mendip-style 'long cottage' with mullioned windows and beams made of ships' timbers, fronted by a small vineyard, is temptingly close to Babington House, the treasures of Bath and Wells, the gardens and concerts at Stourhead, and Gregorian chant in Downside Abbey. The rooms are old-fashioned and cosy, the jams are homemade and the hosts the kindest you may meet. No sitting room, but tea in the walled garden is rich compensation. *Children over five welcome. Minimum two nights.*

Price	From £110. Singles from £90.
Rooms	2 studios: 1 double, 1 twin, each with kitchen.
Meals	Pubs/restaurants within 1 mile.
Closed	Rarely.
Directions	Turn off North Road in Combe Down between (and on same side as) Farrs Lane and Hadley Road into wide driveway. Keep left. 55a is behind number 55.

10% off stays of 2 or more nights.

Price	£65-£70. Singles £30.
Rooms	1 double/family.
Meals	Pubs 2 miles.
Closed	Rarely.
Directions	From Bath A367, Wells road, through Radstock. After 3 miles, at large r'bout, B3139 for Trowbridge. After 1.1 miles, and Charlton sign, right up 2nd driveway on right. Pink house at top, visible from road.

 Late checkout (12pm).

Natalie & Guy Woods
55a North Road,
Combe Down, Bath BA2 5DF
Tel   +44 (0)1225 835593
Mobile   +44 (0)7977 904931
Email   info@55anorthroad.co.uk
Web   www.55anorthroad.co.uk

Entry 5   Map 3

Virginia & Hugh Pountney
Melon Cottage Vineyard,
Charlton, Radstock, Bath BA3 5TN
Tel   +44 (0)1761 435090
Email   meloncottage@hotmail.co.uk
Web   www.meloncottage.co.uk

Entry 6   Map 3

Bath & N.E. Somerset

Hollytree Cottage

Meandering lanes lead to this 16th-century cottage, with roses round the door, a grandfather clock in the hall and an air of genteel tranquillity. The cottage charm has been updated with Regency mahogany and sumptuous sofas. The bedrooms have views over undulating countryside; pretty bathrooms have oils and lotions. On sunny days breakfast is in the lovely garden room looking onto a colourful ornamental patio, sloping lawns, a pond, flowering shrubs and trees. A place to come for absolute peace, birdsong and walks; the joys of elegant Bath are 20 minutes away and Julia knows the area well; let her help plan your trips.

Price	£75–£90. Singles £45–£50.
Rooms	3: 1 double, 1 twin, 1 four-poster.
Meals	Pub/restaurant 0.5 miles.
Closed	Rarely.
Directions	From Bath, A36 to Wolverton. Just past Red Lion, turn for Laverton. 1 mile to x-roads; towards Faukland; downhill for 80 yds. On left, just above farm entrance on right.

 10% off room rate Mon-Thurs.

Julia Naismith
Hollytree Cottage,
Laverton, Bath BA2 7QZ
Tel   +44 (0)1373 830786
Mobile   +44 (0)7564 196703
Email   jnaismith@toucansurf.com
Web   www.hollytreecottagebath.co.uk

Bedfordshire

Warren Farm Lodge

Horses run to greet you at the field gate. Their owners, the delightful Deirdre and husband Robert, have transformed the old stables and cowsheds of this red-brick dairy farm into a beautiful home. The stunning 'long room' is the hub of the house: reclaimed beams over the Aga, a wood-burner for chilly evenings, worn leather sofas on terracotta tiles. The rest of the house is a joy to explore: the sun room, the lounge with its grand piano, the library on the mezzanine. Masses of space, light, and comfy corners at every turn; big bedrooms have views of the lovely gardens. Bring the kids, stay the weekend.

Price	£65–£95. Singles £55–£85. Family suite £80–£130.
Rooms	3: 1 double, 1 suite, 1 family suite, each with separate bath.
Meals	Lunch £8–£9. Dinner £20. Pubs/restaurants within 3 miles.
Closed	Rarely.
Directions	From r'bout on A1M, take B1042 thro' Sandy dir. Potton. After approx. 2.8 miles right to Sutton into Carthagena Rd; approx. 50 yds on, then right at sign for Warren Farm.

10% off stays of 2 or more nights.

Deirdre Evans
Warren Farm Lodge, Carthagena Road,
Sutton, Sandy SG19 2NQ
Tel   +44 (0)1767 262927
Email   deirdre.evans@warrenfarmlodge.co.uk
Web   www.warrenfarmlodge.co.uk

Berkshire

Wilton House

With its handsome Queen Anne frontage, "the most ambitious house in Hungerford" (Pevsner) conceals medieval origins – and the roofline is pure Dickens. A classic townhouse in a charming market town, its interior is a panelled, soft-painted delight. Light floods through sash windows onto paintings and prints, books, antiques and wide, inviting sofas; bedrooms are understatedly elegant and relaxing; bathrooms are a good size. So is your (almost all local or organic) breakfast in the 18th-century dining room: the Welfares, and their labradors, look after you perfectly. *Children over eight welcome.*

Price	From £78. Singles from £65.
Rooms	2: 1 double, 1 twin/double.
Meals	Packed lunch £5. Pub 100 yds.
Closed	Christmas.
Directions	M4 exit 14; A338 to A4; right for Marlborough, turning at Bear Hotel onto Salisbury road (A338). Over canal bridge into High St. House 200 yds past Town Hall on right.

Deborah & Jonathan Welfare
Wilton House,
33 High Street,
Hungerford RG17 0NF

Tel	+44 (0)1488 684228
Email	welfares@hotmail.com
Web	www.wiltonhouse-hungerford.co.uk

Entry 9 Map 3

Berkshire

Whitehouse Farm Cottage

Beyond the housing estates of Bracknell, an idyllic find: a 17th-century farmhouse with a gorgeous garden, and two charmingly converted buildings. Garden Cottage has a beamed drawing room downstairs and an immaculate gallery bedroom with a cast-iron bed. The Forge – deliciously cosy – keeps the blacksmith's fireplace and overlooks an atmospheric courtyard garden with pebble mosaics. The single is in the house with its own cosy sitting room. Fabulous locally sourced breakfasts with freshly baked bread are served in the house by delightful Keir and Louise, film prop makers by profession. Just perfect!

Price	£80-£100. Singles £70-£90.
Rooms	3: 1 single & sitting room. The Forge: 1 double & summerhouse. Garden Cottage: 1 double & sitting room.
Meals	Pubs/restaurants within 1 mile.
Closed	Christmas & occasionally.
Directions	From A329, B3408 to Binfield. At 2nd traffic lights left into St Marks Rd. Then 2nd left Foxley Ln, 1st left Murrell Hill Ln. House immed. on right. Do not use postcode for satnav.

Keir & Louise Lusby
Whitehouse Farm Cottage,
Murrell Hill Lane, Binfield,
Bracknell RG42 4BY

Tel	+44 (0)1344 423688
Mobile	+44 (0)7711 948889
Email	garden.cottages@ntlworld.com

Entry 10 Map 4

Brighton & Hove

4-5 Palmeira Square

Drift along Brighton seafront, and emerge into the Regency splendour of Palmeira Square. Susie with the twinkling eyes welcomes you into a fun, bohemian, ground-floor flat in Hove. Rooms are flooded with light, ceilings are high, furnishings have pizzazz (kilims on bamboo floors, funky chandeliers). Your bedroom is deep lilac and lovely, your bathroom (big shower, stylish toiletries) is Susie's. She has lived in Portugal, Brazil, Bordeaux, works from home and delivers a delicious breakfast to your door. Or, at a pretty seat in the window bay; turn your head and you'll catch the sea. *Minimum stay two nights.*

Price	£80-£90.
Rooms	1 double with shared bath.
Meals	Continental breakfast. Pub/restaurant 500 yds.
Closed	Rarely.
Directions	Seafront towards Hove. Right onto Adelaide Crescent (white Regency buildings) then immediate right, following road up into Palmeira Square. No 5 is just after Crescent becomes Square.

10% off room rate Mon-Thurs. Bottle of wine in room for returning guests.

Susie de Castilho
4-5 Palmeira Square,
Flat 1, Hove BN3 2JA
Tel   +44 (0)1273 719087
Mobile   +44 (0)7917 562771
Email   stay@2staybrighton.co.uk
Web   www.2staybrighton.co.uk

Entry 11   Map 4

Bristol

9 Princes Buildings

A super city base with jolly comfortable beds, charming owners and, without a doubt, the best views in Clifton. You are a short hop from the elegant Suspension Bridge, good restaurants, shops and pubs of the village and a ferry to whisk you to town or the station; yet all is quiet, green and leafy. Walk in to a big square hall, a drawing room with a peaceful feel and a veranda for gazing in fine weather. Your bedroom is fresh, light and traditional, one downstairs overlooks the garden. Best of all, Simon and Joanna are easy-going and give you a breakfast cooked to order with homemade jams and marmalade.

Price	From £80. Singles from £55.
Rooms	4: 2 doubles, 1 twin/double; 1 twin/double with separate bath.
Meals	Pub/restaurant 100 yds.
Closed	Rarely.
Directions	In Bristol signs to Clifton and Clifton Suspension Bridge, just before bridge left down Sion Hill, past Avon Gorge hotel on right. House next to hotel with double red front doors.

Simon & Joanna Fuller
9 Princes Buildings,
Clifton, Bristol BS8 4LB
Tel   +44 (0)117 973 4615
Email   info@9pb.co.uk
Web   www.9princesbuildings.co.uk

Entry 12   Map 3

Buckinghamshire

Long Crendon Manor

Masses of history and oodles of character in this timbered listed house with high chimneys, dating from 1187. No wonder TV companies are keen to get through the arched entrance and into the courtyard! The vast dining room is a dramatic setting for breakfast: sausages and black pudding from Sue's pigs, home-baked bread, and plum and mulberry jam from the gardens. Windows on both sides bring light into the fire-warmed drawing room with leather sofas, gleaming furniture, family bits and bobs, pictures galore. Sleep soundly in comfortable, country-house style bedrooms (one with gorgeous yellow panelling). Peaceful.

Price	£100. Singles £80.
Rooms	2: 1 double; 1 double with separate bath.
Meals	Supper £25. Pubs/restaurants 3-minute walk.
Closed	Christmas.
Directions	M40 junc. 8a, A418 Aylesbury. On outskirts of Thame at services' roundabout take B4011 to Long Crendon; 1st left in village at square and continue straight down Frogmore Lane. Stone archway 50 yards on left.
🧳	Free pick-up from local bus/train station. Late checkout (12pm).

	Sue Soar
	Long Crendon Manor, Frogmore Lane, Long Crendon, Aylesbury HP18 9DZ
Tel	+44 (0)1844 201647
Email	sue.soar@longcrendonmanor.co.uk
Web	www.longcrendonmanor.co.uk

Entry 13   Map 8

Buckinghamshire

Brook Hall

Delicious smells emanate from this handsome red-brick Queen Anne house — Stephen (who ran Raymond Blanc's cookery school at Le Manoir) and Joanna offer cookery courses here. Bedrooms have pretty bed covers, books and magazines; one bathroom has a huge period bath. Downstairs find a fine drawing room, polished wooden floors with rugs, interesting antique kitchen pieces and cookbooks galore. Dinner with other guests in the elegant dining room is a highlight— perhaps braised lemon sole with crab and Asian greens, or pigeon with celeriac and madeira. A scrumptious place for all who appreciate good local food and a friendly feel.

Price	£90-£110. Singles £60-£75.
Rooms	3: 1 twin/double; 1 double, 1 twin/double with shared bath.
Meals	Continental breakfast included, full English £5. Dinner, 3 courses, £28.50. Pub/restaurant across the road.
Closed	Christmas; two weeks mid-July & one week Easter.
Directions	A413 between Buckingham (6 miles) and Aylesbury (12 miles), just off Market Square in Winslow, opposite car park to The Bell Hotel.
🧳	10% off stays of 2 or more nights. 10% off one-day cookery courses.

	Joanna Bulmer
	Brook Hall, 9 Sheep Street, Winslow, Buckingham MK18 3HL
Tel	+44 (0)1296 712111
Email	info@brookhall.net
Web	www.brookhall.net

Entry 14   Map 9

Buckinghamshire

South Lodge

Handy for the M1, this interestingly developed single-storey building appears pleasant enough. But clever Julia has introduced modern English art, dramatic lighting and contemporary furniture. A dark slate corridor lit by fluorescent multicoloured ceiling sticks leads to big airy bedrooms (one is as large as a suite) with memory mattresses and hi-spec bathrooms; all generous, all different. Velux blinds are solar-powered, heating is underfoot, rainwater is harvested for loos. You have your own patio overlooking a colourful garden, you can walk to the Stables Theatre, and Woburn Abbey is nearby. Great for house parties.

Cambridgeshire

The Old Vicarage

Tug the bell pull and step inside a 19th-century parsonage with a labyrinth of rooms. Homemade flapjack and chocolates await, peaceful bedrooms are countrified and classy with stylish bathrooms – one a lovely en suite. Original artwork peppers every wall and is mostly for sale online. Take breakfast overlooking a big mature garden and brace yourself for a wonderful full English. Cats, dogs and chickens roam freely and if you're lucky you'll spot a proud peacock or muntjac deer within the trees. Explore Cambridge, walk Wicken Fen with its Konik ponies and birdlife, then stroll to one of the locals. *Ask about creative courses.*

Price	£126-£148. Singles from £63.	Price	£80-£90. Singles £45-£55.
Rooms	3: 2 doubles, 1 suite/family room.	Rooms	2: 1 twin/double; 1 double with separate bath.
Meals	Supper, 2 courses, £18. Pubs/restaurants within 0.5 miles.	Meals	Pubs in village.
Closed	Occasionally.	Closed	Christmas & New Year.
Directions	Directions on website.	Directions	A14, junc. 37 A142 to Ely. At 3rd r'bout right onto B1102 for 0.8 miles, right onto River Lane, then Collins Hill and Isleham Rd. House opp. church next to social centre; iron gates.

 20% off 2 night stays (Fri/Sat or Sat/Sun). Free pick-up from local bus/train station.

	Julia Cox		Gill Pedersen
	South Lodge,		The Old Vicarage,
	33 Cross End, Wavendon,		7 Church Street, Isleham,
	Milton Keynes MK17 8AQ		Ely CB7 5RX
Tel	+44 (0)1908 582946	Tel	+44 (0)1638 780095
Email	info@culturevultures.co.uk	Email	gill@pedersen.co.uk
Web	www.culturevultures.co.uk	Web	www.oldvicarageisleham.co.uk

Entry 15   Map 9   Entry 16   Map 9

Cambridgeshire

The Old Hall

You'll feel spoilt in this stunning house, transformed phoenix-like by the charming Morbeys, who look after guests in style. Arrive to tea and homemade cake in the beamed sitting room with paintings, photographs, fresh flowers, soft places to unwind and a dreamy view of the cathedral. Sleep well in smart, large bedrooms (cleverly planted trees disguise any road noise) and wake to Ely sausages, hot waffles with maple syrup, or smoked salmon and scrambled eggs on ciabatta toast. Cambridge is a short train ride away but there is history galore here, a formal garden and 15 acres of parkland with lakeside walks. Excellent value.

Price	From £110. Singles from £85.
Rooms	3: 2 doubles, 1 twin.
Meals	Pub/restaurant 1 mile.
Closed	Christmas & New Year.
Directions	From Ely A142 towards Newmarket, under railway bridge. After 1 mile entrance gates on left, signed. Do not use satnav.

Anthony & Alison Morbey
The Old Hall,
Stuntney, Ely CB7 5TR

Tel   +44 (0)1353 663275
Email   stay@theoldhallely.co.uk
Web   www.theoldhallely.co.uk

Entry 17   Map 9

Cambridgeshire

Cambridge University

Buses, bicycles and punting on the Cam: huge fun when you're in the heart of it all. Enter the Great Gate Tower of Christ's College – as did John Milton in 1625 – to be wooed by tranquil, beautiful quadrangle gardens, breakfasts beneath portraits of hallowed masters, and a serene chapel. At smaller Sidney Sussex –1598-old with additions – you can play tennis in gorgeous gardens, picnic on perfect lawns and start the day with rare-breed sausages. More charm, and a candlelit chapel, at St Catherine's on King's Parade. Bedrooms and lounges are functional; well-informed porters are your first port of call. *12 colleges in total.*

Price	Doubles £80-£90. Twins £75-£120. Singles £41-£77.
Rooms	Sidney Sussex: 267 twins & singles. St Catherine's: 347 twins & singles. Christ's College: 150 singles/twins/doubles. Some share showers.
Meals	Breakfast included. Christ's College: no breakfast Sundays. St Catherine's: supper £6.
Closed	Mid-Jan to mid-March; May/June; Oct/Nov; Christmas. A few rooms available throughout year.
Directions	Website booking. Limited parking at a few colleges.

University Rooms
Cambridge University,
Cambridge

Web   www.cambridgerooms.co.uk

Entry 18   Map 9

Cambridgeshire

Springfield House

The former school house hugs the bend of a river, its French windows opening to delightful rambling gardens with scented roses, a yew garden, and a mulberry tree providing fruit for breakfast. Find interesting items from American history, maps and paintings; the conservatory, draped with a huge mimosa, is an exceptional spot for summer breakfasts. Bedrooms are large and comfortable, with interesting books, flowers and garden or river views; one is reached by narrow stairs and has steps to the garden too. This is an old-fashionedly elegant home and Judith is a thoughtful hostess. Good value and peaceful, yet close to Cambridge.

Price	£70–£80. Singles £45–£60.
Rooms	3: 2 doubles; 1 double with separate bath.
Meals	Pubs 150 yds.
Closed	Rarely.
Directions	A1307 from Cambridge, left into High St. 1st right after The Crown (on left) into Horn Lane. House on right next to chapel, before ford. Or bus no. 13 and 13A from Cambridge.

	Judith Rossiter
	Springfield House,
	14-16 Horn Lane, Linton CB21 4HT
Tel	+44 (0)1223 891383
Email	springfieldhouselinton@gmail.com
Web	www.springfieldhouse.org

Entry 19   Map 9

Cambridgeshire

Westoe Farm

Immerse yourself in miles of waving wheat, woodlands and sugar beet. The house is a flint-knapped oasis of deep comfort: find traditionally comfortable bedrooms and a large and attractive hall with your own huge sitting room. Generous Tim and Henrietta are a capable pair and you are well looked after; they produce their own organic pork, jams and honey, eggs are home-laid, breakfasts are award-winning and their home is self-sustaining in solar electricity. There's a fine, rose-filled garden, woods and fields; stroll around to your heart's content before a delicious dinner of home-grown vegetables and local game in season.

Ethical Collection: Environment. See page 420.

Price	£100. Singles £65.
Rooms	2 twins/doubles.
Meals	Dinner, 2 courses, £27.50. BYO. Pub/restaurant 1 mile.
Closed	Christmas & New Year.
Directions	A1307 to Linton, right at Bartlow crossroads through Bartlow, then 1 mile from village, house signed, 3rd farm track on right.

10% off stays of 2 or more nights Mon–Thurs.

	Henrietta Breitmeyer
	Westoe Farm,
	Bartlow CB21 4PR
Tel	+44 (0)1223 892731
Mobile	+44 (0)7776 258666
Email	enquire@bartlow.u-net.com
Web	www.westoefarm.co.uk

Entry 20   Map 9

Cheshire

Goss Moor

Crunch up the gravelled drive to the big white house, a beautifully run family home. Bedrooms are light, bright and decorated in creams and blues; bathrooms are spotless and warm. Be cosseted by fluffy bathrobes, biscuits, decanters of sherry – all is comfortable and inviting. After a day's exploring the Wirral and Liverpool, historic Chester and the wilds of north Wales – a short drive all – return to a kind welcome from Sarah. Expect a generous and delicious breakfast by the sunny bay window; in the summer, you are free to enjoy the garden, tennis court and pool.

Price	£80-£85. Singles £50-£55.
Rooms	2: 1 twin/double; 1 double with separate bath.
Meals	Occasional dinner with wine, £25. Pub/restaurant 2 miles.
Closed	Rarely.
Directions	From Chester, A540 north. After about 7 miles turn right to Willaston. Right at T-junc., then first left into Mill Lane. House is 9th on left.

Bottle of wine in your room.

Chris & Sarah White
Goss Moor, Mill Lane,
Willaston, Neston CH64 1RG
Tel   +44 (0)1513 274000
Mobile   +44 (0)7771 510068
Email   sarahcmwhite@aol.com
Web   www.gossmoor.co.uk

Entry 21   Map 7

Cheshire

Cotton Farm

Only a four-mile hop from Roman Chester and its 900-year-old cathedral is this sprawling, red-brick farmhouse. Elegant chickens peck in hedges, ponies graze, lambs frisk and cats doze. The farm, run by conservationists Nigel and Clare, is under the Countryside Stewardship Scheme – there are wildflower meadows, summer swallows and 250 acres to roam. Farmhouse bedrooms are large, stylish and cosy with lovely fabrics, robes, a decanter of sherry and huge bath towels, but best of all is the relaxed family atmosphere. Breakfasts, with homemade bread, are delicious and beautifully presented. *Stabling available. Over tens welcome.*

Price	£80. Singles £50.
Rooms	3: 2 doubles, 1 twin.
Meals	Pub 1.5 miles.
Closed	Rarely.
Directions	A51 Chester-Nantwich. 1.5 miles from outskirts, after golf course on left, right, down Cotton Lane, signed Cotton Edmunds; 1.5 miles, left on sharp right-hand bend; 2nd drive on right.

3 nights for price of 2 for arrivals on Sun, Mon, Tue (Oct-Apr, excluding bank holidays).

Clare & Nigel Hill
Cotton Farm,
Cotton Edmunds, Chester CH3 7PG
Tel   +44 (0)1244 336616
Mobile   +44 (0)7840 682042
Email   information@cottonfarm.co.uk
Web   www.cottonfarm.co.uk

Entry 22   Map 7

Cheshire

Greenlooms Cottage

This pretty cottage was where the estate's chief hedger and ditcher lived. The smallholding has gone but the walnuts, quinces and garden pump remain – and the views still reach to the Peckforton Hills. Now it is a stylishly simple and fun place to stay, thanks to Deborah – traveller, ex-potter, fabulous cook – and Peter, furniture-maker and restorer. Follow your nose to the Aga-cosy kitchen where the best black pudding and bacon are waiting to fuel you for a day on the Cheshire cycle route. Return to two sweet bedrooms, one up one down: crisp white duvets, Floris soaps in simple walk-in showers, ethnic touches.

Price	£75. Singles from £50.
Rooms	2: 1 double, 1 twin.
Meals	Dinner, with wine, £25. Pub 3 miles.
Closed	Rarely.
Directions	A41 Whitchurch; south from Chester. After petrol station, 2nd left at antiques shop. On for 1.5 miles thro' village, right into Martins Lane; 1 mile on right.

 10% off stays of 2 or more nights.

Deborah Newman
Greenlooms Cottage, Martins Lane,
Hargrave, Chester CH3 7RX
Tel   +44 (0)1829 781475
Mobile   +44 (0)7791 014231
Email   dnewman@greenlooms.com
Web   www.greenlooms.com

Cheshire

Mulsford Cottage

Delicious! Not just the food (Kate's a pro chef) but the sweet whitewashed cottage with its sunny conservatory and vintage interiors, and the green Cheshire countryside that bubble-wraps the place in rural peace. Chat – and laugh – the evening away over Kate's superb dinners, lounge by the sitting room fire, then sleep deeply in comfy bedrooms: cane beds, a bright red chair, a vintage desk. The double has a roll top bath, the twin a tiny shower-with-a-view. Step out to birdsong and the 34-mile Sandstone Trail to Shropshire. Wales starts just past the hammock, at the bottom of the large and lovely garden.

Price	£80. Singles £45.
Rooms	2: 1 twin; 1 double with separate bath.
Meals	Dinner, 2-3 courses, £18-£25. Pub/restaurant 1.5 miles.
Closed	Rarely.
Directions	From Malpas B5069 to Worthenbury. After 5 miles left into Mulsford Lane. After 1 mile Mulsford Cottage on left.

 10% off room rate Mon-Thurs. Bottle of wine with dinner on first night.

Kate Dewhurst
Mulsford Cottage,
Mulsford, Sarn, Malpas SY14 7LP
Tel   +44 (0)1948 770414
Email   katedewhurst@hotmail.com
Web   www.mulsfordcottage.co.uk

Cheshire

Harrop Fold Farm

Artists, foodies and walkers adore this antique-filled farmhouse with soul-lifting views. On the edge of the Peak District, the oldest building on the farm dates from 1694 (Bonnie Prince Charlie visited here). The B&B part has a warm peaceful breakfast room, a stone-flagged sitting room, a spectacular studio. Fresh flowers, antique beds, fine fabrics, hot water bottles with chic covers, bathrooms with fluffy robes: you get the best. Gregarious Sue and daughter Leah hold art and cookery courses so the food too is outstanding. Bedrooms have stupendous views – and flat-screen TVs and DVDs just in case they pall.

Ethical Collection: Food; Community.
See page 420.

Price	£95. Singles £60.
Rooms	2 doubles.
Meals	Dinner £30. Supper £15. Cookery demo & dinner £55. Packed lunch available. Pub 0.25 miles.
Closed	Rarely.
Directions	B470 Macclesfield to Whaley Bridge. After 4 miles Highwayman pub; 0.25 miles further down track (rutted at top); on left, immed. before sharp right bend.

Local food/produce in your room.

Sue Stevenson
Harrop Fold Farm,
Rainow, Macclesfield SK10 5UU
Tel   +44 (0)1625 560085
Email   stay@harropfoldfarm.co.uk
Web   www.harropfoldfarm.co.uk

Entry 25   Map 8

Cornwall

The Old Vicarage

The first sight of quirky chimneys – the spires of former owner Reverend Hawker's parish churches – sets the scene for a huge house packed with interest and steeped in Victoriana. Jill and Richard, both delightful, know the local history – and the cliff-top walks, which are glorious. Rooms are casually grand, dotted with *objets* – brass gramophone, magic lantern, eccentric Hawker memorabilia. Browse books in the study, play the grand piano, sip brandy over billiards. Bedrooms are country-house pretty, with bathrooms refurbished, lawns well tended and views to the sea. Blissfully, mobiles don't work.

Price	From £80. Singles from £40.
Rooms	3: 1 double, 1 twin, 1 single.
Meals	Pub/tea rooms 5-10 minute walk.
Closed	December/January.
Directions	From A39 at Morwenstow, follow signs towards church. Small turning on right, just before church, marked 'public footpath'. Drive down to house.

Jill & Richard Wellby
The Old Vicarage,
Morwenstow EX23 9SR
Tel   +44 (0)1288 331369
Email   jillwellby@hotmail.com
Web   www.rshawker.co.uk

Entry 26   Map 1

Cornwall

The Old Parsonage

A spellbinding coastline, secret coves, spectacular walks. All this and a supremely comfortable Georgian rectory — with a drying room for wet togs to return to. Morag and Margaret have transformed the interior. Superb pitch pine floors and original woodwork add warmth and a fresh glow, the big engaging bedrooms (including one on the ground floor) have a quirky, upbeat mix of furniture and furnishings, and the bathrooms are pampering. In front of the house the land slopes away to the Atlantic, just a five-minute walk across a SSSI. There are plans afoot for the garden, which already has some pleasant corners.

Ethical Collection: Environment; Food.
See page 420.

Price	From £85. Singles from £68.
Rooms	5 twins/doubles.
Meals	Packed lunch £5.95. Pub/restaurant 600 yds.
Closed	November-January.
Directions	In Boscastle head towards Tintagel on B3263. 500 yds after garage on left turn right into Green Lane. After bend, house 3rd on right.

 Bottle of champagne for bookings of 2 or more nights.

 Use your Sawday's Gift Card here.

Morag Reeve & Margaret Pickering
The Old Parsonage,
Forrabury, Boscastle PL35 0DJ
Tel   +44 (0)1840 250339
Mobile   +44 (0)7890 531677
Email   morag@old-parsonage.com
Web   www.old-parsonage.com

Entry 27   Map 1

Cornwall

Upton Farm

A restored farmhouse set back from the rugged coastline with unrivalled views, from Tintagel to Port Isaac and beyond… the sunsets are sublime. There's a games room and safe storage for surfers, slate slabs in the hall, gentle colours throughout, and bedrooms smart and traditional. From the depths of the sea-green sofa in your drawing room, breathe in those AONB views. Such seclusion, yet ten minutes across fields is the coastal path and, nearby, serious surfing, a great pub, a restaurant and more. Kick-start your day with Ricardo's signature muesli. *Minimum two nights. Children over eight welcome.*

Price	From £95.
Rooms	3: 2 doubles, 1 twin.
Meals	Pub/restaurant 1 mile.
Closed	Rarely.
Directions	South thro' Delabole, right into Treligga Downs Rd; right at T-junc. towards Trebarwith; Farm on right after 1 mile.

Elizabeth & Ricardo Dorich
Upton Farm,
Trebarwith, Delabole PL33 9DG
Tel   +44 (0)1840 770225
Mobile   +44 (0)7975 710833
Email   ricardo@dorich.co.uk
Web   www.upton-farm.co.uk

Entry 28   Map 1

Cornwall

Tremoren

Views stretch sleepily over the Cornish countryside. You might feel inclined to do nothing more than wander the lovely garden or snooze by the pool, but the surfing beaches, the Camel Trail and the Eden Project are so close. The stone and slate former farmhouse has been smartly updated and your airy ground-floor bedroom comes with soft colours, pretty china, crisp linen, a comfortable bathroom. And its own cosy sitting room, full of books and interesting maps, leading to a flower-filled terrace — perfect for a pre-dinner drink. Lanie, bubbly and engaging, runs her own catering company; your dinner will be delicious!

Price	£90-£100.
Rooms	1 double & sitting room.
Meals	Dinner, 4 courses, £26. Inns 0.5 miles.
Closed	Rarely.
Directions	A39 to St Kew Highway through village; left at Red Lion. Down lane, 1st left round sharp right-hand bend. 2nd drive on right; signed.

Philip & Lanie Calvert
Tremoren,
St Kew,
Bodmin PL30 3HA
Tel   +44 (0)1208 841790
Email   la.calvert@btopenworld.com

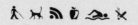

Entry 29   Map 1

Cornwall

The Corn Mill

This restored mill in a quiet Cornish valley is a relaxed and friendly home. Step inside and find a country cottage medley of flowers and family furniture, antique rugs and interesting market finds. Artist Suzie has her studio in a folly in the pretty garden; ducks and chicks wander in the orchard. Cosy bedrooms have flowery fabrics, antique eiderdowns, warm blankets and good cotton; bathrooms are simple and fresh with fluffy towels. Breakfast well in the farmhouse kitchen on locally sourced food and bread fresh from the Rayburn. Exceptional coastal walking, music festivals, great beaches and Port Isaac are all nearby.

Price	£75.
Rooms	2: 1 double, 1 family room.
Meals	Pub/restaurant 2 miles.
Closed	Christmas & New Year.
Directions	A39 Wadebridge towards Camelford. Left at St Kew Highway towards Trelill. Left at crossroads for Pendoggett, then 300 yds down hill. House on right.

Susan Bishop
The Corn Mill,
Port Isaac Road, Trelill,
Bodmin PL30 3HZ
Tel   +44 (0)1208 851079

Entry 30   Map 1

Cornwall

The Barn at The Old Stables

The closer you inch down the lane to The Barn, the greener the fields become, the louder the bleating lambs. But that's all the noise here: this converted hay barn is a hubbub–free hideaway. Find a lavish double bedroom with fine touches: vast bathroom, sublime sink in' mattress and contemporary furniture made by Judith's son. Judith lives opposite and is most at home by her Aga, whipping up a delicious breakfast with local bacon or preparing extraordinary three-course suppers: after a day's walking or cycling the Camel Trail and Cornish coast, you can eat in the candlelit dining room, the valley unfolding beyond.

Price	£80-£95.
Rooms	Barn: 1 double.
Meals	Dinner, 3 courses, £25. Pub/restaurant 5 miles.
Closed	Christmas & New Year.
Directions	From A30 follow road to Helland. Over crossroads; after 0.5 miles right by large grass verge with sign Coldrenick Farm Offices. Follow signs to The Old Stables.

Free pick-up from local bus/train station.

Judith Argent
The Barn at The Old Stables,
Helland,
Bodmin PL30 4QE
Tel   +44 (0)1208 75543
Email   juargent@hotmail.com
Web   www.thebarnincornwall.co.uk

Entry 31   Map 1

Cornwall

Higher Lank Farm

Families rejoice: you can only come if you have a child under five! Celtic crosses in the garden and original panelling hint at the house's 500-year history; bedrooms, newly decorated, have pocket sprung mattresses and large TVs. Nursery teas begin at 5pm, grown-up suppers are later and energetic Lucy will cheerfully babysit while the rest of you slink off to the pub. Farm-themed playgrounds are covered in safety matting and grass, there are piglets and chicks, eggs to collect, pony and trap rides, a sand barn for little ones and cream teas in the garden. Oh, and real nappies are provided!

Price	From £100. Singles by arrangement.
Rooms	3 family rooms.
Meals	Supper £20. Nursery tea £7. Pub 1.5 miles.
Closed	November-Easter.
Directions	A30 past Launceston. Right to St Breward 4 miles. Across moor through Bradford, then take first right. Humpback bridge and crossroads, turn left (no sign & not straight on to St Breward). Follow road to bottom of hill; house signed opposite.

Lucy Finnemore
Higher Lank Farm,
St Breward,
Bodmin PL30 4NB
Tel   +44 (0)1208 850716
Email   lucyfin@higherlankfarm.co.uk
Web   www.higherlankfarm.co.uk

Entry 32   Map 1

Cornwall

Lavethan

A glorious house in the most glorious of settings: views sail down to the valley. It rambles on many levels and is part 15th-century: walls are stone, floors are flagged, stairs are oak. The sunny bedroom in the house is best, with its panelled walls and smart bathroom; bedrooms across the courtyard are very private with their own entrances and have pretty quilted bedspreads. Catherine, a warm hostess, has decorated in country style; the guest sitting room is hugely welcoming with books, flowers and piano. All this and acres of ancient woods, Celtic crosses and a heated pool in the old walled garden. *Children over ten welcome.*

Price	£90. Singles £50.
Rooms	3: 2 twins/doubles, 1 double.
Meals	Pub 0.25 miles.
Closed	Rarely.
Directions	From A30, turn for Blisland. There, past church on left & pub on right. Take lane at bottom left of village green. 0.25 miles on, drive on left (granite pillars & cattle grid).

10% off stays of 2 or more nights.

Christopher & Catherine Hartley
Lavethan,
Blisland, Bodmin PL30 4QG
Tel   +44 (0)1208 850487
Email   chrishartley@btconnect.com
Web   www.lavethan.com

Entry 33   Map 1

Cornwall

Cabilla Manor

There's a treasure round every corner and an opera house in one of the barns. Instant seduction as you enter the old manor house out on the moor, brimful of interest and colour. Rich exotic rugs and cushions, artefacts from around the world, Louella's sumptuous hand-stencilled quilts, huge beds, coir carpets, garden flowers. There's a dining room crammed floor to ceiling with books, many of them Robin's (a writer and explorer) and a lofty conservatory for meals overlooking a semi-wild garden – with tennis and elegant lawns. The views are heavenly, the hosts wonderful and the final mile thrillingly wild.

Ethical Collection: Environment; Community. See page 420.

Price	£90. Singles £45.
Rooms	4: 1 double; 1 double with separate bath; 1 double, 1 twin, sharing bath (let to same party only).
Meals	Dinner, 3 courses with wine, £35. Pub 4 miles. Restaurant 8-10 miles.
Closed	Christmas.
Directions	6 miles after Jamaica Inn on A30, left for Cardinham. Through Millpool & straight on, ignoring further signs to Cardinham. After 2.5 miles, left to Manor 0.75 miles; on right down drive.

Robin & Louella Hanbury-Tenison
Cabilla Manor,
Mount, Bodmin PL30 4DW
Tel   +44 (0)1208 821224
Mobile   +44 (0)7770 664218
Email   louella@cabilla.co.uk
Web   www.cabilla.co.uk

Entry 34   Map 1

Cornwall

Menkee

From this handsome Georgian farmhouse there are long views towards the sea; you're 20 minutes away from the coastal path and wild surf but you may not want to budge. Gage and Liz are deliciously unstuffy and look after you well: newspapers and a weather forecast appear with a scrumptious breakfast, your gorgeously comfortable bed is turned down in the evening and walkers can be dropped off and collected. The elegant house is filled with beautiful things, gleaming furniture, fresh flowers, roaring fires and pretty fabrics – all you have to do is slacken your pace and wind down. *Minimum stay two nights in high season.*

Ethical Collection: Food. See page 420.

Price	£80–£90. Singles from £40.
Rooms	2 doubles.
Meals	Pub/restaurant 1.3 miles.
Closed	Rarely.
Directions	A389 Bodmin-Wadebridge; 2.5 miles, then fork right on B3266; on for 2 miles for Camelford; 600 yds after St Mabyn turn-off, left down drive.

Arrangement for St Enodoc golf (green fee excl.). Talk on Cornish gardens or coastal & moor walks over glass of wine.

Gage & Liz Williams
Menkee,
St Mabyn, Wadebridge PL30 3DD
Tel   +44 (0)1208 841378
Mobile +44 (0)7999 549935
Email   gagewillms@aol.com
Web   www.cornwall-online.co.uk/menkee

Cornwall

Porteath Barn

A converted 'upside-down' barn in an exquisite valley setting, elegantly uncluttered inside. Downstairs bedrooms – not vast – have fresh flowers, quilted bedspreads and beautiful bathrooms, and French windows that open onto a large and lovely garden. From here a path leads down to Epphaven Cove and the beach – fabulous. Continue further for wonderful walks on the coastal path if you're feeling hearty, return to a sitting room with seagrass flooring and a wood-burner. Jo and Michael are gracious and delightful and their breakfasts (kedgeree, kippers, pancakes, home-made jams) are superb. *Over 12s by arrangement.*

Price	From £90. Singles by arrangement.
Rooms	3: 2 twins/doubles, each with separate bath or shower; 1 double sharing bath (let to same party only).
Meals	Pub 1.5 miles.
Closed	Rarely.
Directions	A39 to Wadebridge. At r'bout signed for Polzeath, then to Porteath Bee Centre. Through Bee Centre shop car park, down farm track; house signed on right after 150 yds.

Use your Sawday's Gift Card here.

Jo & Michael Bloor
Porteath Barn,
St Minver, Wadebridge PL27 6RA
Tel   +44 (0)1208 863605
Email   m.bloor17@btinternet.com

Cornwall

Roskear

Drive down the fields to this 17th-century working farmhouse, a blissfully peaceful escape. A large sitting room with log fire, a warm and smiling hostess, happy dogs, comfortable bedrooms, a cheerful Aga, fabulous estuary views – country life at its most charming. Delicious breakfasts are served on blue china, doors open to the garden on sunny days and there are acres of woodland and grassland to explore. Good restaurants include Rick Stein's, the ferry takes you to Rock, surfing is a short drive and the Camel cycle trail is nearby (hire bikes locally). Uncomplicated, good value B&B.

Cornwall

Molesworth Manor

It's a splendid old place, big enough to swallow hoards of people, peppered with art and interesting antiques. There are palms and a play area in the garden, a drawing room with an honesty bar and an open fire for cosy nights, a carved staircase leading to bedrooms that vary in style and size – His Lordship's at the front, the Maid's in the eaves – and bathrooms that are lovely and pampering. The whiff of homemade muffins lures you downstairs in the morning, the Cornish Riviera and its food scene will ravish you later – you're in the heart of it all. A superb bolthole run by Geoff and Jessica, youthful and fun.

Price	From £70. Singles £35.
Rooms	2: 1 double with separate bath; 1 twin/double sharing bath (let to same party only).
Meals	Pubs/restaurants 0.5-6 miles.
Closed	Rarely.
Directions	Bypass Wadebridge on A39 for Redruth. Over bridge, pass garage on left, straight over roundabout, filter 1st right to Edmonton. By modern houses turn immed. right to Roskear over cattle grid.

Price	£70-£115. Singles from £52.50.
Rooms	9: 7 doubles, 1 twin/double; 1 twin with separate shower.
Meals	Pubs/restaurants 2 miles.
Closed	November-January. Open off-season by arrangement for larger parties.
Directions	Off A389 between Wadebridge & Padstow. Entrance clearly signed; 300 yds from bridge in Little Petherick.

10% off stays of 2 or more nights.

Rosina Messer-Bennetts
Roskear,
St Breock, Wadebridge PL27 7HU
Tel   +44 (0)1208 812805
Mobile   +44 (0)7748 432013
Email   rosina@roskear.com
Web   www.roskear.com

Geoff French & Jessica Clarke
Molesworth Manor,
Little Petherick, Padstow PL27 7QT
Tel   +44 (0)1841 540292
Email   molesworthmanor@aol.com
Web   www.molesworthmanor.co.uk

Entry 37   Map 1

Entry 38   Map 1

Cornwall

Calize Country House

Beneath wheeling gulls and close to blond beaches, the big square 1870 guest house has amazing views of skies and sea. Virginia Woolf's lighthouse is in the bay and winter seals cavort at the colony nearby. A fresh, uncomplicated décor brings the tang of the sea to every room. Artworks recall a world of surf; deckchair stripes clothe the dining table and dress the window; traditional sofas call for quiet times with a book. Upstairs, patterned or pale walls, practical bath or shower rooms, perhaps a sea view. Jilly and Nigel are testament to the benefits of sea air and look after you beautifully.

Ethical Collection: Environment; Food.
See page 420.

Price	£80–£90. Singles £60.
Rooms	4: 2 doubles, 1 twin, 1 single.
Meals	Packed lunch £5. Pub 350 yds.
Closed	Rarely.
Directions	Exit A30 at Camborne (west) A3047. Left, then right at r'bout. Right on entering Connor Downs, then on for 2 miles. House on right after sign for Gwithian.

 Use your Sawday's Gift Card here.

Jilly Whitaker
Calize Country House,
Gwithian, Hayle TR27 5BW
Tel   +44 (0)1736 753268
Email jilly@calize.co.uk
Web   www.calize.co.uk

Entry 39   Map 1

Cornwall

Drym Farm

Rural, but not too deeply: the Tate at St Ives is a 15-minute drive. The 1705 farmhouse, beautifully revived, is surrounded by ancient barns, a dairy and a forge, fascinating to Cornish historians. Jan arrived in 2002, with an enthusiasm for authenticity and simple, stylish good taste. French limestone floors in the hall, eclectic art on the walls, a roll top bath, a *bateau lit*, an antique brass bed. Paintwork is fresh cream and taupe. There are old fruit trees and young camellias, a TV-free sitting room with two plump sofas and organic treats at breakfast. Charming and utterly peaceful.

Price	£80–£100. Singles from £60.
Rooms	2 doubles.
Meals	Pubs/restaurants within 1-4 miles.
Closed	Rarely.
Directions	From A30 to Hayle; through Hayle to r'bout, left to Helston. At Leedstown, left towards Drym. Follow road until right turn to Drym. Farm fourth on lane, on right after Drym House.

 Local food/produce in your room.

Jan Bright
Drym Farm, Drym, Praze-an-Beeble,
Camborne TR14 0NU
Tel   +44 (0)1209 831039
Email drymfarm@hotmail.co.uk
Web   www.drymfarm.co.uk

Entry 40   Map 1

Cornwall

House at Gwinear

An island of calm – it sits, as it has for 500 years, in its own bird-trilled acres a short drive from St Ives. The Halls are devoted to the encouragement of the arts and crafts which is reflected in their lifestyle. There's no stuffiness – just fresh flowers on the breakfast table, a piano in the corner, rugs on polished floors and masses of books. In a separate wing you have a cosy bedroom and sitting room and a fine view of the church from the bath. The big lawn-filled gardens are there for bare-footed solace, and you can have breakfast in the Italianate courtyard on sunny days.

Cornwall

11 Sea View Terrace

In a smart row of Edwardian villas, with stunning harbour and sea views, is a delectable retreat. Sleek, softy coloured interiors are light and gentle on the eye – an Italian circular glass table here, a painted seascape there. Bedrooms are perfect with crisp linen and vistas of whirling gulls from private terraces; bathrooms are state of the art. Rejoice in softly boiled eggs with anchovy and chive-butter soldiers for breakfast – or continental in bed if you prefer. Grahame looks after you impeccably and design aficionados will be happy. *Free admission to Tate Gallery & Barbara Hepworth Museum. Over 12s welcome.*

Price	From £75.
Rooms	1 twin/double with separate bath & sitting room.
Meals	Dinner, with wine, from £29. Supper, with glass of wine, £22.50. Pub 1.5 miles.
Closed	Rarely.
Directions	From A30 exit Hayle (Loggans Moor r'bout); 100 yds left at mini r'bout; 400 yds left for Gwinear; 1.5 miles, top of hill, driveway on right, just before 30mph Gwinear sign.
	Talk about St Ives artists with a glass of wine.

Price	£90–£125. Singles from £65.
Rooms	3 suites.
Meals	Dinner, with wine, from £25 (groups only). Packed lunch from £15. Pubs/restaurants 5-minute walk.
Closed	Rarely.
Directions	At Porthminster Hotel, signs for Tate; down Albert Rd, right just before Longships Hotel. Limited parking.

	Charles & Diana Hall House at Gwinear, Gwinear, St Ives TR27 5JZ
Tel	+44 (0)1736 850444

	Grahame Wheelband 11 Sea View Terrace, St Ives TR26 2DH
Tel	+44 (0)1736 798440
Mobile	+44 (0)7973 953616
Email	info@11stives.co.uk
Web	www.11stives.co.uk

Entry 41   Map 1

Entry 42   Map 1

Cornwall

Organic Panda B&B & Gallery

A five-minute walk from busy St Ives, with a panoramic view of the bay, boutique B&B in perfect harmony with this artistic spot; enjoy vibrant modern art throughout and dine at a ten-seater rustic table. Spacious contemporary bedrooms have a laid-back style with organic linen, bamboo towels, chunky beds, white walls and raw-silk cushions. Shower rooms are small but perfectly formed. Andrea is an artist and theatre designer, Peter a photographer and organic chef; the food is delicious and bread home-baked. The most beautiful coastal road in all England leads to St Just. *Min. stay three nights Christmas, Easter, July & August.*

Ethical Collection: Environment; Food.
See page 420.

Price	£80–£150.
Rooms	3: 2 doubles, 1 twin.
Meals	Packed lunch £10. Restaurants nearby.
Closed	Rarely.
Directions	A3074 to St. Ives. Follow leisure centre sign; house on corner of Talland Rd and Albert Rd. Train station 5-minute walk.

Bottle of Cornwall's finest Camel Valley wine or bottle of Polgoon Juice & hand-made truffles.

Peter Williams & Andrea Carr
Organic Panda B&B & Gallery,
1 Pednolver Terrace, St Ives TR26 2EL

Tel	+44 (0)1736 793890
Mobile	+44 (0)7787 854380
Email	info@organicpanda.co.uk
Web	www.organicpanda.co.uk

Entry 43   Map 1

Cornwall

The Old Vicarage

Artists will be inspired, not just with the proximity to St Ives but with Jackie's dazzling collection of her own and other artists' work. This is an airy welcoming house whose big sash windows and elegant sitting room overlook a fabulous subtropical garden; wander at will after a grand breakfast of fresh fruit and local bacon and sausages. Bedrooms have soft coloured walls, deeply comfortable beds, period furniture and more lovely artwork adding spots of colour; bathrooms are gleaming and fresh. There's a sandy beach 20-minutes' walk away and you can join the coastal path just up the road. Wonderful house, lovely owners.

Price	From £80. Singles from £50.
Rooms	3: 1 twin; 1 double with separate bath, 1 single sharing bath (let to same party only).
Meals	Pubs within 8-minute walk. Restaurants in St Ives 2.5 miles.
Closed	November, December & March.
Directions	A30 Penzance. At 2nd Hayle r'bout, A3074 St Ives. After Wyvale Garden Centre, over mini r'bout; right at next; into Lelant. Brush End on left after Elm Farm sign. House at end.

Free pick-up from local bus/train station.

Jackie & Howard Hollingsbee
The Old Vicarage,
Brush End, Lelant, St Ives TR26 3EF

Tel	+44 (0)1736 753324
Mobile	+44 (0)7841 522021
Email	bookings@oldvicaragelelant.co.uk
Web	www.oldvicaragelelant.co.uk

Entry 44   Map 1

Cornwall

Keigwin Farmhouse

Off the glorious coast road to St Ives, in two walled acres overlooking the sea, is a very old farmhouse lived in by Gilly. Walk to the beach at Portheras Cove, dine well at Gurnard's Head, return to little whitewash-and-pine bedrooms with views that make you want to get out your paints, and a big shared bathroom with a massive old bath, fresh with organic cotton towels. A treat: Gilly's scones on arrival, eggs from the neighbour's farm, stacks of books above the stairs and an arty feel – wide floorboards, creamy colours, family pieces, sculptures, ceramics, glass. A relaxed, delightful – and musical instrument-friendly – B&B.

Cornwall

Ennys

Prepare to be spoiled. A fire smoulders in the sumptuous sitting room, tea is laid out in the Aga-warm kitchen, bedrooms are luxurious (a king-size bed, an elegant modern four-poster, a powerful shower) and breakfasts are served at separate tables. The stylishness continues into the suites and everywhere there are fascinating artefacts from Gill's travels, designer fabrics and original art. The road ends at Ennys, so it is utterly peaceful; walk down to the river and along the old towpath to St Ives Bay. Or stay put: play tennis (on grass!) and swim in the heated pool sunk deep into the tropical gardens. *Yoga weekends.*

Price	From £60. Singles from £30.
Rooms	3: 2 doubles, 1 single, sharing bath/shower.
Meals	Pub 3 miles.
Closed	Rarely.
Directions	Coast road from St Ives, B3306, dir. St Just. Keigwin between Morvah & Bojewyan. Turn off road at Yew Tree Gallery sign. Farmhouse next to the Gallery.

Price	£95-£175. Singles from £75.
Rooms	5: 3 doubles; 2 suites (twins/doubles) each with kitchenette.
Meals	Pub 3 miles.
Closed	25 October-1 April.
Directions	2 miles east of Marazion on B3280, look for sign & turn left leading down Trewhella Lane between St Hilary & Relubbus. On to Ennys.

	Gilly Wyatt-Smith
	Keigwin Farmhouse,
	Keigwin, Morvah, Penzance TR19 7TS
Tel	+44 (0)1736 786425
Email	gilly@yewtreegallery.com
Web	www.keigwinfarmhouse.co.uk

	Gill Charlton
	Ennys,
	St Hilary, Penzance TR20 9BZ
Tel	+44 (0)1736 740262
Email	ennys@ennys.co.uk
Web	www.ennys.co.uk

Entry 45   Map 1

Entry 46   Map 1

Cornwall

Ednovean Farm

There's a terrace for each fabulous bedroom (one truly private) with views to the wild blue yonder and St Michael's Mount Bay, an enchanting outlook that changes with the passage of the day. Come for peace, space and the best of eclectic fabrics and colours, pretty lamps, Christine's sculptures, fluffy bathrobes and handmade soaps. The beamed open-plan sitting/dining area is an absorbing mix of exotic, rustic and elegant; have full breakfast here (last orders nine o'clock) or continental in your room. A footpath through the field leads to the village; walk to glorious Prussia Cove and Cudden Point, or head west to Marazion.

Price	£95–£115.
Rooms	3: 2 doubles, 1 four-poster.
Meals	Pub 5-minute walk.
Closed	Christmas & rarely.
Directions	From A30 after Crowlas r'bout, A394 to Helston. 0.25 miles after next r'bout, 1st right for Perranuthnoe. Farm drive on left, signed.

Christine & Charles Taylor
Ednovean Farm,
Perranuthnoe, Penzance TR20 9LZ
Tel +44 (0)1736 711883
Email info@ednoveanfarm.co.uk
Web www.ednoveanfarm.co.uk

Entry 47   Map 1

Cornwall

The Gardens

Two old miners' cottages combine to create this small, cosy, charming home. Irish Moira, a retired midwife and passionate gardener, brightens every corner with posies of flowers; Goff is a potter and both are friendly, helpful and kind. Snug bedrooms with patchwork quilts, cotton sheets and plenty of books look out onto the pretty cottage gardens; one is on the ground floor, two are up a narrow stair. Enjoy Moira's welcoming tea and homemade cakes by the wood-burner in the comfy guest sitting room; delicious Aga-cooked breakfasts and homemade jams are served in the sun-streamed conservatory. Great value.

Price	£70–£78. Singles £40.
Rooms	3: 2 doubles; 1 twin/double with separate bath.
Meals	Packed lunch from £8. Pubs/restaurants 10-minute drive.
Closed	Christmas & New Year.
Directions	A394 Helston to Penzance, 2nd right after Lion & Lamb pub in Ashton for Tresowes Green. After 0.25 miles, sign for house on right.

10% off stays of 2 or more nights.

Moira & Goff Cattell
The Gardens,
Tresowes, Ashton, Helston TR13 9SY
Tel +44 (0)1736 763299
Mobile +44 (0)7881 758191
Email moira.cattell@gmail.com

Entry 48   Map 1

Cornwall

Halzephron House

The coastal path runs through the grounds and the view is to die for – you can see St Michael's Mount on a clear day. Be greeted by homemade biscotti and organic coffee roasted in Cornwall: lovely Lucy and Roger – foodies, designers – have a café and shop in the cottage next door. Bedrooms, contemporary, quirky and full of charm, are super-private; 'Tower' is in the house, with a velvet sofa and a French bed. Elsewhere: recycled wooden floors, art on white walls, bowls of wild flowers. You can walk to three amazing beaches, a 13th-century church, a golf course and a gastropub. Heaven. *Dogs welcome in Observatory & Cabin.*

Price	£80–£130.
Rooms	3: 1 suite. Cabin: 1 suite. Observatory: 1 double.
Meals	Pub 0.25 miles.
Closed	Rarely.
Directions	From Helston head towards the Lizard. After 2 miles, right signed Gunwalloe. In village lane towards Church Cove passing Halzephron Inn on left. House at top of hill overlooking the sea.
🧳	Key to 'secret' clifftop garden.

Lucy & Roger Thorp
Halzephron House,
Gunwalloe, Helston TR12 7QD
Tel   +44 (0)1326 241719
Email   lucy@halzephronhouse.co.uk
Web   www.halzephronhouse.co.uk

Entry 49   Map 1

Cornwall

Halftides

Hugely enjoyable and special, surrounded by three acres with dazzling views down the coast and out to sea. Fresh funky bedrooms, not huge but filled with light, have gorgeous fabrics, crisp bedding, dreamy views; bathrooms (one a small pod-shower in the room) are sleek in glass and chrome. Susie is great fun, an artist and chef and gives you a delicious organic breakfast in the pretty, airy dining room. Take the coastal path north or south, visit the working harbour in the village, head for a swim down the private path to the beach below. A perfect place to relax and unwind. *Min. stay two nights. Over threes welcome.*

Price	£95–£120. Singles £60–£75.
Rooms	3: 1 double; 1 double, 1 single sharing separate bath.
Meals	Dinner, 2-3 courses with wine, £30–£35. Pub 0.5 miles.
Closed	February.
Directions	A3083 to Lizard, right to Cury, 5 miles; past Poldhu beach & into Mullion. Right into Laflouder Lane, past 'No Through Road' sign. Ignore side road on right. House 1st on right.

Charles & Susie Holdsworth Hunt
Halftides, Laflouder Lane,
Mullion, Helston TR12 7HU
Tel   +44 (0)1326 241935
Email   halftides@btinternet.com
Web   www.halftides.co.uk

Entry 50   Map 1

Cornwall

Bay House

Perched on the edge of the map, high on rugged, seapink-tufted cliffs, Bay House is as close to the sea as you can get. Rooms are spacious (one with a bay window), the dining room defers to stunning sunsets and the attention to detail is immaculate. Expect fine original artwork and antiques, Ralph Lauren dressing gowns, designer linen, Molton Brown lotions, iPod docks and DVD players. Scramble down to secluded beaches, take a short stroll to the famous Lizard Lighthouse or relax to the sound of the surf in the beautiful garden under rustling palms and hovering kestrels. Breakfast, by the way, is outstanding.

Price	£120-£150.
Rooms	2 twins/doubles.
Meals	Dinner, 2 courses, £35. Pub/restaurant 100 yds.
Closed	Christmas.
Directions	Left in Lizard village, then past playing fields. Take 1st right and at end of road right into Bay House.

  Free pick-up from local bus/train station.

Use your Sawday's Gift Card here.

Carla Caslin
Bay House,
The Lizard, Helston TR12 7PG
Tel +44 (0)1326 290235
Mobile +44 (0)7740 168805
Email carla.caslin@btinternet.com
Web www.mostsoutherlypoint.co.uk

Entry 51   Map 1

Cornwall

The Hen House

Greenies will be delighted: Sandy and Gary, truly welcoming, are passionately committed to sustainability and happy to advise on the best places to eat, visit and walk; there are OS maps on loan too. Enlightened souls will adore the spacious colourful rooms, the bright fabrics, the wildflower meadow with inviting sun loungers, the pond, the tai chi, the fairy-lit courtyard at night, the scrumptious locally sourced breakfasts, the birdsong. There's even a sanctuary room for reiki and reflexology set deep into the earth in this generous, peaceful retreat. *Min. two nights. Over 12s welcome. Self-catering in Barn available.*

Ethical Collection: Environment; Food. See page 420.

Price	From £80. Singles £70.
Rooms	3: 2 doubles. Barn: 1 double.
Meals	Pub/restaurant 1 mile.
Closed	Rarely.
Directions	A3083 from Helston, then B3293 to St Keverne; left to Newtown-in-St Martin. After 2 miles, right at T-junc. Follow road for 2.3 miles then left fork. Round 7 bends then right at triangulation stone for Tregarne.

  Reiki or reflexology therapy session per room on minimum stay of 7 nights.

Sandy & Gary Pulfrey
The Hen House, Tregarne,
Manaccan, Helston TR12 6EW
Tel +44 (0)1326 280236
Mobile +44 (0)7809 229958
Email henhouseuk@aol.com
Web www.thehenhouse-cornwall.co.uk

Entry 52   Map 1

Cornwall

Carmelin

The setting of this bungalow is sensational, gazing straight out to sea from the Lizard, England's most southerly point. Your peaceful bedroom shares the views, and leads into a sun room just for you: a sofa, a log-effect fire, a private entrance, more beautiful views. Breakfast – a spread of breads and pastries, fruits, freshly made yogurt and homemade jams – fights for your attention against the breaking waves and sparkling sea. John and Jane are gentle dog-loving people, seasoned B&B providers who enjoy their guests. Walk the coastal path, stroll to the pub for a meal. *French & German spoken.*

Price	From £90. Singles by arrangement.
Rooms	1 double with separate bath/shower & sitting room.
Meals	Pub/restaurant within walking distance.
Closed	Rarely.
Directions	From Helston to the Lizard; at Lizard Green, right, opp. Regent Café (head for Smugglers Fish & Chips); immed. right, pass wc on left. Road unmade; on for 500 yds; double bend; 2nd on right.

Bottle of wine in your room. Discounts on Jane & John's books.

Jane & John Grierson
Carmelin,
Pentreath Lane, The Lizard TR12 7NY
Tel +44 (0)1326 290677
Email pjcarmelin@gmail.com
Web www.bedandbreakfastcornwall.co.uk

Entry 53   Map 1

Cornwall

Trerose Manor

Follow winding lanes through glorious countryside to find the prettiest, listed manor house, a warm family atmosphere and welcoming tea in the beamed kitchen. Large, light bedrooms, one with floor-to-ceiling windows, sit peacefully in your own wing and have views over the stunning garden. All are dressed in pretty colours, have comfy seats for gazing and smartly tiled bathrooms. A sumptuous breakfast can be taken outside in summer, there are lovely walks over fields to river or beach, stacks of interesting places to visit and lots to read in the library for the lazy. Lovely. *French, German & Italian spoken.*

Ethical Collection: Community. See page 420.

Price	£105–£125. Singles £80.
Rooms	3 doubles.
Meals	Pubs/restaurants within walking distance.
Closed	Rarely.
Directions	Left at Red Lion in Mawnan Smith. After 0.5 miles right down Old Church Road. After 0.5 miles house on right through white gate immediately after Trerose Farm.

Use your Sawday's Gift Card here.

Tessa Phipps
Trerose Manor,
Mawnan Smith, Falmouth TR11 5HX
Tel +44 (0)1326 250784
Email info@trerosemanor.co.uk
Web www.trerosemanor.co.uk

Entry 54   Map 1

Cornwall

Bosvathick

A huge old Cornish house that has been in Kate's family since 1760, along with all the art, heavy furniture, Indian rugs, ornate plasterwork, pianos and even a harp. Historians will be in their element: pass three Celtic crosses dating from the 7th century before the long drive finds the imposing house (all granite gate posts and lions) and a rambling garden with grotto, lake, pasture and woodland. Bedrooms are simple and traditional, full of books and antiques; bathrooms are spick and span, one plain and functional, one new. Come to experience a 'time warp' and charming Kate's good breakfasts; close to Falmouth University too.

Cornwall

Trevilla House

Come for the position: the sea and Fal estuary wrap around you, and the King Harry ferry gives you an easy reach into the glorious Roseland peninsula. Inside find comfortable airy bedrooms with homemade quilts on the beds — the twin with a sofa and old-fashioned charm, the double with stunning sea views. Jinty rustles up delicious locally sourced breakfasts and homemade jams, and you eat in the sunny conservatory that looks south over the sea. Trelissick Gardens and the Copeland China Collection are just next door; the Maritime Museum, Eden, Tate, cycling, watersports and coastal walks are all close by.

Price	From £80. Singles £40-£60.
Rooms	4: 1 twin/double, 1 twin sharing bathroom; 2 singles sharing bathroom. Each party has sole use of a bathroom.
Meals	Supper, with wine, £25. Packed lunch £5-£10. Pubs 2 miles.
Closed	Rarely.
Directions	From Constantine, signs to Falmouth. 2 miles, pass Bosvathick Riding Stables, next entrance on left. Drive thro' gateposts & green gate. A map can be sent to visitors.

Price	From £85. Singles £50.
Rooms	3: 1 twin, 1 double; 1 single sharing bath (let to same party only).
Meals	Restaurants/pubs 1-2 miles.
Closed	Christmas & New Year.
Directions	A390 to Truro; A39 to Falmouth. At double r'bout with garage, left off 2nd r'bout (B3289); pass pub on left; at x-roads, left (B3289); 200 yds on, fork right to Feock. On to T-junc., then left; 1st on right.

Kate & Stephen Tyrrell
Bosvathick,
Constantine, Falmouth TR11 5RD

Tel	+44 (0)1326 340103
Email	kate@bosvathickhouse.co.uk
Web	www.bosvathickhouse.co.uk

Jinty & Peter Copeland
Trevilla House,
Feock, Truro TR3 6QG

Tel	+44 (0)1872 862369
Mobile	+44 (0)7791 977621
Email	jinty@trevilla.com
Web	www.trevilla.com

Cornwall

Nearwater

St Mawes is gorgeous, a tiny town on the Roseland peninsula that paddles in the sea. In summer sailing boats flutter on the water, dodging the ferry as it nips across to Falmouth. Nearwater matches the mood perfectly, its airy interiors filled with seaside chic. White walls soak up the light, a driftwood mirror hangs above the fire, there are maps for walkers, a sofa to sink into, games and books aplenty. Uncluttered bedrooms have blond wood furniture, blue and white blankets, crisp linen, fantastic bathrooms. Delicious breakfasts set you up for the day, so pull on your walking boots or hire a kayak in town.

Price	£95-£105. Singles from £85.
Rooms	3: 2 doubles, 1 twin/double.
Meals	Pubs/restaurants in village.
Closed	24-27 December.
Directions	A3078 south into St Mawes. Keep left and house signed on left in village.

Tim & Amelia Whitaker
Nearwater, Polvarth Road,
St Mawes, Truro TR2 5AY
Tel   +44 (0)1326 279278
Email   bookings@nearwaterstmawes.co.uk
Web   www.nearwaterstmawes.co.uk

Entry 57   Map 1

Cornwall

Hay Barton

Giant windows overlook many acres of farmland and Jill and Blair look after you well. Breakfasts are special with the best local produce, homemade granola, yogurt and more. Arrive for tea and lovely home-baked cake, laid out in the comfortable guest sitting room with a log fire and plenty of books and maps. Bedrooms are fresh and pretty with garden flowers, soft white linen on big beds and floral green walls. Gloriously large panelled bathrooms have long roll top baths and are painted in earthy colours. Guests can use the tennis court; you are near to good gardens and plenty of places to eat. *Min. stay two nights in summer.*

Price	£80. Singles £50.
Rooms	3 twins/doubles.
Meals	Pubs 1-2 miles.
Closed	Rarely.
Directions	A3078 from Tregony village towards St Mawes. After 1 mile, house on left, 100 yds down lane.

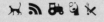   Fruit bowl in your room.

Jill & Blair Jobson
Hay Barton,
Tregony, Truro TR2 5TF
Tel   +44 (0)1872 530288
Mobile   +44 (0)7813 643028
Email   jill@haybarton.com
Web   www.haybarton.com

Entry 58   Map 1

Cornwall

Creed House

The beautiful Georgian rectory is surrounded by one of Cornwall's loveliest gardens. Light pours into every elegant corner and your warm, gracious hosts give you fresh, traditional bedrooms in a peaceful wing with stunning views over bluebell woods. Sheets are crisp, colours are serene and flowers are from the garden. Local breads and jams, fruit salads and a full English await you at breakfast – enjoyed in the cosy guest sitting room or handsome dining room. A perfect place from which to explore Cornwall's wonderful gardens and coast. *NGS garden.*

Price	£90.
Rooms	2: 1 double, 1 twin.
Meals	Pub/restaurant 1 mile.
Closed	Christmas & New Year.
Directions	From St Austell, A390 to Grampound. Just beyond clock tower, left into Creed Lane. After 1 mile, left at grass triangle opp. church. House behind 2nd white gates on left.

Jonathon & Annabel Croggon
Creed House,
Creed, Grampound, Truro TR2 4SL

Tel	+44 (0)1872 530372
Email	jrcroggon@btinternet.com
Web	www.creedhouse.co.uk

Entry 59   Map 1

Cornwall

Collon Barton

Come for the lofty position on a grassy hillside, the heartlifting views over unspoiled countryside and the pretty creekside village of Lerryn. This 18th-century house is a working sheep farm and an artistic household (sculptures galore). Interesting and generous Anne and Iain give you eggs from their free-range chickens, traditional airy bedrooms in pink or blue and an elegant drawing room. Anne sells huge dried hydrangeas and, on sunny days, welcomes you with tea in the summer house. Wonderful riverside and coastal walks and good gardens; the Eden Project is 20 minutes away. *Children & pets by arrangement.*

Price	£80. Singles £40.
Rooms	2: 1 twin/double, 1 twin/double with dressing room & extra beds.
Meals	Pub 10-minute walk.
Closed	Rarely.
Directions	A390 to Lostwithiel. After Lostwithiel sign 1st left, signed Lerryn. 200 yds, left at 1st x-roads for Lerryn. After 2 miles, at top of hill, hard left signed Bodmin & Liskeard. Immed. right by 5-bar gate, stone farm lane.

Anne & Iain Mackie
Collon Barton,
Lerryn, Lostwithiel PL22 0NX

Tel	+44 (0)1208 872908
Mobile	+44 (0)7721 090186
Email	annemackie@btconnect.com

Entry 60   Map 1

Cornwall

Cornwall

Botelet

The farmhouse at the end of the wild-flowered lane is an inspired synthesis of stone, wood, Shaker simplicity and comfy old chairs: the chicest of shabby chic. Rustic bedrooms reached by a steep stair have planked floors, antique beds and beautiful linen; the bathroom is below. Breakfasts – organic, home-baked, home-picked, vegetarian – are enjoyed at a scrubbed table by the Rayburn. Drink in the pure air, explore the farm, walk the wooded valley; return to a therapeutic massage in your room. Botelet has been in the family since 1860 and is quirky, friendly, artistic, huge fun. The yurts are amazing. *Over tens welcome.*

Ethical Collection: Environment; Food; Community. See page 420.

Trussel Barn

Jo and Mike look after you beautifully: large, light bedrooms with super views, squashy pillows, sumptuous quilts, state-of-the-art bathrooms, your own hidden-away fridge. They're keen on reducing their carbon footprint, too; drink water from their borehole, wander down to the wildlife pond, admire the vegetable and strawberry beds, tuck into a locally sourced breakfast cooked in an eco-Aga, ask about their plans for off-grid electricity – it's fascinating stuff. Explore acres of garden running down to a wildlife pond, drive the five miles to the coast, and come home to a roaring fire in the guest sitting room.

Ethical Collection: Environment; Food. See page 420.

Price	From £70. Yurt £170 (2 nights).
Rooms	2: 1 double, 1 twin/double (with extra single), sharing bath. Yurts: each 1 double.
Meals	Continental breakfast (£10 for yurt). Pub 2 miles.
Closed	December to Easter.
Directions	A38 bypassing Liskeard. At next r'bout take 2nd exit signed St Austell. After East Taphouse left onto B3359 dir. Looe. After 2 miles right signed Botelet.

Price	From £85. Singles from £55.
Rooms	2 doubles.
Meals	Pubs/restaurants within 2 miles.
Closed	Rarely.
Directions	A38 Plymouth–Liskeard, then B3254 to St Keyne for 1.5 miles. Climb steep hill; at bend, 1st left into Trussel Barn. Or train to Liskeard, 2 miles.

	The Tamblyn Family Botelet, Herodsfoot, Liskeard PL14 4RD
Tel	+44 (0)1503 220225
Email	stay@botelet.com
Web	www.botelet.com

	Jo Lawrence Trussel Barn, St Keyne, Liskeard PL14 4QL
Tel	+44 (0)1579 340450
Email	trusselbarn@me.com
Web	www.trusselbarn.com

Cornwall

Hornacott

The garden, in its lovely valley setting, has seats in little corners poised to catch the evening sun — perfect for a pre-dinner drink. The peaceful house is named after the hill and you have a private entrance to your airy suite: a room with a large bed plus a lofty sitting room with a balcony and windows that look down onto the wooded valley. With CD player, music, chocolates and magazines you are truly self-contained. Jos, a kitchen designer, and Mary-Anne love having guests and living the slow life — busily! — and give you top-notch local produce and free-range eggs for breakfast.

Price	From £80. Singles £50.
Rooms	2: 1 suite; 1 twin with separate shower.
Meals	Dinner, 3 courses, £20. BYO. Pubs/restaurants 4.5 miles.
Closed	Christmas.
Directions	B3254 Launceston-Liskeard. Through South Petherwin, down steep hill, last left before little bridge. House 1st on left.

Cornish produce. Luxury toiletries.

Jos & Mary-Anne Otway-Ruthven
Hornacott,
South Petherwin, Launceston PL15 7LH
Tel   +44 (0)1566 782461
Email   otwayruthven@btinternet.com
Web   www.hornacott.co.uk

Entry 63   Map 1

Cornwall

St Leonards House

Enjoy gardens, history, riding, fishing? John runs tailormade tours for groups and individuals, and knows Cornwall like the back of his hand; Jane is an embroiderer whose curtains add colour to the rooms. The twin, downstairs, overlooks the garden; the doubles are up; expect good mattresses, anti-allergic duvets, bath oils and waffle robes. Breakfast is served in a low-ceilinged dining room whose beams attest to the house's age and whose tiled floor is elegantly rugged. You are on the edge of Launceston, quaint capital of Cornwall, and close to the great beaches of Widemouth Bay, Crackington Haven and Bude.

Price	£80. Singles £50.
Rooms	3: 2 doubles, 1 twin.
Meals	Dinner £22. Cream tea £3.50. Pub/restaurant 2 miles.
Closed	Christmas & New Year.
Directions	From Launceston A30 towards Polson. Opposite rugby club take road to St Leonards. After 150 yds house is next to the Equitation Centre.

10% off stays of 2 or more nights.

John & Jane Marshall
St Leonards House,
Polson, Launceston PL15 9QR
Tel   +44 (0)1566 779195
Email   enquiries@stleonardshouse.co.uk
Web   www.stleonardshouse.co.uk

Entry 64   Map 2

Cornwall

Cadson Manor

This Georgian manor, with spectacular views across the Lynher valley, has been in the Crago family for generations. Chatty and friendly, Brenda and John look after you well and have been doing B&B for years. Everything shines, from the slate hall floor and antique furniture to the pretty china and talkative parrot. Fish in the lake, picnic in the grounds or wander further afield to find Highland cattle. Bedrooms and bathrooms have hotel comfort, rich drapes and curtains, thoughtful extras and Cornish biscuits. National Trust's Cadson Bury, the Eden Project and the coast are all close, and the walks and wildlife are sublime.

Price	£96. Singles £60.
Rooms	4: 2 doubles; 1 double, 1 twin sharing bath (2nd room let to same party only).
Meals	Pub/restaurant 3 miles.
Closed	Occasionally.
Directions	From Callington, A390 Liskeard road. House signed on left just after going over the river Lynher.

 4 nights for the price of 3.

Brenda Crago
Cadson Manor,
Callington PL17 7HW
Tel +44 (0)1579 383969
Email brenda.crago@btclick.com
Web www.cadsonmanor.co.uk

Entry 65 Map 2

Cornwall

Pentillie Castle

So many temptations: woodland gardens that tumble down to the Tamar, a walled Victorian kitchen garden still being restored, a magnificent Victorian bathing hut… and Pentillie beef cattle, uniquely theirs, grazing either side of the great drive up to the handsome house. Bedrooms are smart, spacious and deeply comfortable, bathrooms pamper. Ted and Sarah, with daughter Sammie, have mastered that delicate balancing act between luxury and stuffiness, bringing out one and banishing the other. It's the sort of place where you gasp at the perfection of it all and then throw your shoes off before diving into the sofa.

Price	£105–£197.
Rooms	9: 8 twins/doubles, 1 four-poster suite.
Meals	Dinner, 3 courses, £25 (for groups of 6+). Pubs/restaurants 15-minute drive.
Closed	Rarely.
Directions	Cross Tamar River into Cornwall on A38. Right onto A388. 3.1 miles, then right at Paynters Cross. Entrance within 100 yds.

10% off room rate.

Sammie Coryton
Pentillie Castle,
St Mellion, Saltash PL12 6QD
Tel +44 (0)1579 350044
Email contact@pentillie.co.uk
Web www.pentillie.co.uk

Entry 66 Map 2

Cornwall

Lantallack Farm

You will be inspired here, in this heart-warming old Georgian farmhouse where generous Nicky runs one-to-one courses in landscape painting and sculpture. Find a straw-yellow sitting room with a log fire, books to read, a grand piano and bedrooms with deliciously comfortable beds; views are breathtaking across countryside, streams and wooded valleys. Breakfast in the walled garden on fine days: apple juice from the orchard and bacon and sausages from down the road. There are 40 acres to explore, a leat-side trail and a heated outdoor pool; marvellous. *Minimum stay two nights at weekends. Self-catering cottages available.*

Ethical Collection: Environment; Food; Community. See page 420.

Price	From £100. Singles by arrangement.
Rooms	2: 1 double; 1 double with separate bath.
Meals	Pubs/restaurants 1 mile.
Closed	Rarely.
Directions	A38 thro' Saltash, continue 3 miles. At Landrake 2nd right at West Lane. After 1 mile, left at white cottage for Tideford. House 150 yds on, on right.

A bottle of Lantallack apple juice on checkout.

Nicky Walker
Lantallack Farm,
Landrake, Saltash PL12 5AE
Tel   +44 (0)1752 851281
Email   enquiries@lantallack.co.uk
Web   www.lantallack.co.uk

Entry 67   Map 2

Cornwall

Buttervilla Farm

Gill and Robert are so good at growing vegetables (organically) they supply the local restaurants. They're pretty good at looking after you too, in a relaxed fashion, delivering breakfasts of rare-breed bacon, eggs from their own chickens and sweet home-grown tomatoes. No sitting room but bedrooms are comfortable and cared for with modern furniture, flat screen TVs and fresh coffee; bathrooms are smart with solar-powered showers and thick towels. Explore these 15 beautiful eco acres, spot woodpeckers and kestrels, stride the coastal path or head for the surf. *Soil Association certified organic smallholding.*

Ethical Collection: Environment; Food. See page 420.

Price	£75-£95.
Rooms	3 doubles.
Meals	Restaurants within 3 miles.
Closed	Rarely.
Directions	Turn by Halfway House at Polbathic for Downderry. House 400 yds up hill from inn, on left; signed before lane.

10% off stays of 3 or more nights except Jul & Aug. Advance purchase Eden Project tickets.

Gill & Robert Hocking
Buttervilla Farm, Polbathic,
St Germans, Torpoint PL11 3EY
Tel   +44 (0)1503 230315
Mobile   +44 (0)7787 124878
Email   info@buttervilla.com
Web   www.buttervilla.com

Entry 68   Map 2

Cumbria

Sirelands

Sirelands, once a gardener's cottage, stands among rhododendrons and spreading trees on a sunny slope, a stream trickling by: a stunning spot. The Carrs have lived here for years and the house has a relaxed and homely feel. Enjoy home-grown produce at dinner on a polished table, then retire to the sitting room, delightful with log basket, honesty bar, flowers and books. Sash windows overlook the wooded garden, visited by roe deer and a wide variety of birds. Bedrooms and bathrooms are pleasant, peaceful and spotless; one loo has an amazing view! Friendly Angela loves cooking and treats you to tea and homemade cake.

Price	£90.
Rooms	2: 1 twin; 1 double with separate bath/shower.
Meals	Dinner, 2-3 courses, £22-£27.50. Pubs within 5 miles.
Closed	Christmas & New Year.
Directions	M6 north to junc. 43; A69 Newcastle; 3 miles to traffic lights. Right, on to Heads Nook; house 2 miles after village.

Bottle of wine with dinner per couple.

David & Angela Carr
Sirelands, Heads Nook,
Brampton, Carlisle CA8 9BT
Tel   +44 (0)1228 670389
Mobile   +44 (0)7748 101513
Email   carr_sirelands@btconnect.com

Entry 69   Map 12

Cumbria

Warwick Hall

The position here is magnificent, a slice of English heaven. The house stands resplendently in 260 acres on the banks of the river Eden, one of the best salmon beats in the country; a two-mile stroll hugs the water. Inside, everything is gorgeous: vast windows that flood the place with light; a wonderful drawing room with sofas in front of the fire; a dining room with views of hill and river. Delightful country-house bedrooms have high ceilings, beautiful fabrics, super bathrooms; one has its own fire. Bonnie Prince Charlie once stayed, though not in the comfort you can expect. Delicious food and a great atmosphere, too.

Price	£120. Suites £180. Catered house party rates available.
Rooms	8: 6 twins/doubles; 2 suites with kitchenettes.
Meals	Dinner, 3 courses, £30. Restaurant 1 mile.
Closed	Rarely.
Directions	M6, junc. 43, then A69 east. After 2 miles, pass town sign and on left down hill before bridge.

Val Marriner
Warwick Hall,
Warwick-on-Eden, Carlisle CA4 8PG
Tel   +44 (0)1228 561546
Mobile   +44 (0)7818 448756
Email   info@warwickhall.org
Web   www.warwickhall.org

Entry 70   Map 11

Cumbria

Chapelburn House

Yomp in the most dramatic scenery close to the best bits of Hadrian's Wall, then head for Chapelburn House. Matt and Katie are young, charming, unflappable, food is reared happily then cooked with more flavour than fuss. Honey is from their bees, bread is home-baked. You have a sitting room with an open fire, lots of books and squishy sofas, *and* a south-facing garden room for summer dreaming. Bedrooms are deeply comfortable and bathrooms (one definitely not for fatties!) brand spanking new. Children are more than welcome to join in. This would delight exhausted refugees from London, too.

Price	£70–£90. Singles £55.
Rooms	2 doubles.
Meals	Dinner, 3 courses, £25. Packed lunch £5–£7.50. Restaurant 5 miles.
Closed	Christmas & New Year.
Directions	From Newcastle, A69 west for 40 miles. Right to RAF Spadeadam; next left to Low Row. Chapelburn House 1 mile on left.

🧳 10% off stays of 2 or more nights.

Matthew & Katie McClure
Chapelburn House,
Low Row, Brampton CA8 2LY
Tel +44 (0)1697 746595
Email stay@chapelburn.com
Web www.chapelburn.com

Entry 71   Map 11

Cumbria

Boltongate Old Rectory

The setting of this lovely old rectory could hardly be more pastoral; many of its rooms face south and have superb fells views. Furniture is a beautiful mix of antique and contemporary – handmade Harris mattresses, big chunky sofas – in a house whose roots go back to 1360. The treats continue at table: Gill is passionate about sourcing organic and local ingredients for her kitchen, David knows his wines and you eat by candlelight in a 16th-century room. They're relaxed and charming and, when the place is full, create a fabulous house-party feel. Outside: red squirrels and well-fed rabbits, a croquet lawn and stunning Skiddaw.

Ethical Collection: Environment; Food; Community. See page 420.

Price	From £120. Singles from £105.
Rooms	3: 1 double, 1 twin/double; 1 double with separate bath.
Meals	Dinner, 3 courses, £33. Pub 10-minute drive.
Closed	Sundays & Mondays. December/January.
Directions	B5305 to Wigton; at A595, left. After 5 miles, left to Boltongate. Left at T-junc.; in village, signs for Ireby; down hill, last driveway on left.

🧳 Free pick-up from local bus/train station.

Gill & David Taylor
Boltongate Old Rectory,
Boltongate, Wigton CA7 1DA
Tel +44 (0)1697 371647
Mobile +44 (0)7763 242969
Email boltongate@talk21.com
Web www.boltongateoldrectory.com

Entry 72   Map 11

Cumbria

Daffodil & Daisy

Who wouldn't love it here? Teen and David, young and friendly, live in a bright-white-and-pale-green farmhouse in soaring countryside with the waggiest dog, wandering hens, ducks and geese, their own pigs. They also care about feeding you well: homemade cakes, mouthwatering breakfasts and delicious suppers. Through your own entrance find private suites with enormous, pillow-filled beds, fresh flowers, pink bubbly, fruit and cosy robes; there's an adjoining door for families. Bathrooms are spanking new; outside are a wood-fired hot tub and pizza oven. Generous and fun. *£10 discount if you come without a car.*

Price	£150. Singles £110.
Rooms	2 doubles.
Meals	Packed lunch from £9. Supper from £15. Pub within 1 mile.
Closed	Rarely.
Directions	M6 exit 41, take B5305 to Wigton. 7 miles then left Hesket Newmarket, 2nd right Hallfield. Pass farm in dip, at brow of hill turn right in front of dry stone wall into lane to house.

25% off stays of 2 or more nights.

David & Teen Fisher
Daffodil & Daisy, Banks Farm,
Hesket Newmarket, Wigton CA7 8HR
Tel +44 (0)1697 478137
Email banksfarm@mac.com
Web www.daffodilbanksfarm.co.uk

Cumbria

Johnby Hall

You are ensconced in the quieter part of the Lakes and have independence in this Elizabethan manor house – once a fortified Pele tower, now a family home. Two suites (one in the converted granary) are fresh and light: each has its own sitting room with lots of books and pictures, squashy sofas, pretty fabrics and whitewashed walls. Beds have patchwork quilts, windows have stone mullions and there is absolute quiet. Henry gives you sturdy breakfasts, and good home-grown suppers by a roaring fire in the great hall; he and Anna can join you or leave you in peace. Walks from the door are sublime.

Price	£100–£110. Singles £75–£80.
Rooms	2: 1 twin/double & sitting room. Granary: 1 family suite.
Meals	Supper, 2 courses, £20. Pub 1 mile.
Closed	Rarely.
Directions	M6 Penrith junc. 40. A66 west approx. 2 miles; right-hand exit signed Greystoke. At T-junction left to Greystoke. At Greystoke follow signs right then left to Johnby. Hall on left after 1 mile.

10% off stays of 2 or more nights.

Henry & Anna Howard
Johnby Hall,
Johnby, Penrith CA11 0UU
Tel +44 (0)17684 83257
Email bookings@johnbyhall.co.uk
Web www.johnbyhall.co.uk

Cumbria

Whitbysteads

Swing into the yard of a gentleman's farmhouse at the end of a drive lined with gorse, stone walls and sheep. It's a working farm, so lots going on with four-wheel drives, dogs, busy hens and relaxed bustle. Victoria does styles and periods well: warm rugs, flowery sofas with plain linen armchairs, modern family paintings. The main bedroom is sumptuous and stylish, the smaller room simpler; bathrooms are wonderfully vintage, eclectic and big. Great hosts who make you feel instantly at home here; enjoy the breathtaking views over the fells – easy for the M6 too. Dress up in the evening for dinner at Sharrow Bay. *Garden open for NGS.*

Price	£100–£110.
Rooms	3: 1 double; 1 double, 1 twin with shared bath.
Meals	Children's tea £5. Pub 0.5 miles.
Closed	Rarely.
Directions	Exit 39 M6. A6 north, through Askham village, turn left up the hill past postbox, over cattle grid and fork left. House is about 1 mile up here – on the top of the hill to the left.

	Victoria Lowther
	Whitbysteads,
	Askham, Penrith CA10 2PG
Tel	+44 (0)1931 712284
Mobile	+44 (0)7976 276961
Email	info@gnap.fsnet.co.uk
Web	www.whitbysteads.org

Entry 75   Map 11

Cumbria

Greenah

Tucked into the hillside off a narrow lane, this 1750s smallholding is surrounded by fells, so is perfect for walkers. Absolute privacy for four friends or family with your own entrance to a beamed and stone-flagged sitting room with wood-burning stove, creamy walls and cheery floral curtains. Warm bedrooms have original paintings, good beds, hot water bottles, bathrobes and a sparkling bathroom with a loo with a remarkable view. Malcolm is a climber; Marjorie is totally committed to organic food so you get a fabulous breakfast and good advice about the local area. Fell walking is not compulsory!

Ethical Collection: Food. See page 420.

Price	£85–£95. Singles £55-60.
Rooms	2: 1 double; 1 twin sharing shower (let to same party only).
Meals	Pubs/restaurants 3 miles.
Closed	Rarely.
Directions	M6 junc. 40 follow A66 west. Left for Matterdale; after 1.5 miles, left signed Dacre. Up the hill, right fork to Lowthwaite, house 100 yds on right.

	Marjorie & Malcolm Emery
	Greenah,
	Mattterdale, Penrith CA11 0SA
Tel	+44 (0)1768 483387
Mobile	+44 (0)7767 213667
Email	info@greenah.co.uk
Web	www.greenah.co.uk

Entry 76   Map 11

Cumbria

Lowthwaite

Leave your worries behind as you head up the lanes to the farmhouse tucked into the fell. Jim, ex-hiking guide, and Danish Tine moved back from Tanzania with their daughters in 2007 and give you four peaceful bedrooms in the view-filled barn wing. Handsomely chunky twin beds are of recycled dhow wood, crisp light bathrooms sport organic soaps and you wake to the smell of homemade bread; breakfasts are fine Scandinavian and English inspired spreads. In a garden full of bird feeders and pheasants a stream trickles through one of the guest terraces, and there are endless fells to explore. A treat for peace-seekers and families.

Price	£60-£90. Singles £40-£70.
Rooms	4: 2 twins/doubles, 2 family rooms.
Meals	Packed lunch £6. Dinner £18-£27. Pubs 2.5 miles.
Closed	Christmas.
Directions	Penrith M6 junc. 40, A66 towards Keswick. Left opposite B5288 onto Matterdale road. After 1.25 miles, left after Walloway Farm. Up hill, then right signed 'Lowthwaite 1'.

Tine & Jim Boving Foster
Lowthwaite,
Matterdale, Penrith CA11 0LE

Tel	+44 (0)1768 482343
Email	info@lowthwaiteullswater.com
Web	www.lowthwaiteullswater.com

Entry 77   Map 11

Cumbria

Willow Cottage

Gaze across rooftops through tiny windows towards the towering mass of Skiddaw, the Lakes' third highest mountain. Here is a miniature cottage garden with sweet peas, herbs, vegetables and flowers... all suitably rambling. Roy and Chris have kept most of the old barn's features: wooden floorboards, wonderful beams. Dried flowers, pretty china, antique linen, glowing lamps and patchwork quilts, a collection of christening gowns... dear little bedrooms have panelled bathrooms and old pine furniture. TV is delightfully absent, classical music plays and you are in the heart of a farming village.

Price	£65-£70. Singles £50.
Rooms	2: 1 double, 1 twin.
Meals	Packed lunch £5. Pub 300 yds.
Closed	December/January.
Directions	From Keswick A591 towards Carlisle (6.5 miles) right for Bassenthwaite village (0.5 miles). Straight on at village green, house on right.

Roy & Chris Beaty
Willow Cottage,
Bassenthwaite, Keswick CA12 4QP

Tel	+44 (0)1768 776440
Email	chriswillowbarn@googlemail.com
Web	www.willowbarncottage.co.uk

Entry 78   Map 11

Cumbria

Howe Keld

Dismiss all thoughts of the chintzy Keswick guest house: David and Val have swept through with carpets made of Herdwick sheep wool, bedroom furniture made by a local craftsman, gorgeous fabrics, striking wallpaper and smart bathrooms with green slate. It's luxurious but not flashy, and there's a cosy sitting room in primary colours crammed with local info; theatre, shops and restaurants are all strolling distance (choose rooms at the front if you need total quiet). Fill up at breakfast on home-baked bread, freshly made smoothies or a jolly good fry-up. *Minimum stay two nights at weekends, three on bank holidays.*

Ethical Collection: Environment. See page 420.

Price	£80–£130. Singles £45-60.
Rooms	14: 13 doubles, 1 single.
Meals	Pub/restaurant 300 yds.
Closed	Part December including Christmas. Most of January excluding New Year.
Directions	Penrith M6, junc. 40; W A66. 18 miles; r'bout with A591. Left towards Keswick; 800 yds, left at junc. On to mini r'bout in high street, then right. After 600 yds right into The Heads.

 A bottle of wine in your room for stays of 3 or more nights Sun-Thurs.

	David Fisher
	Howe Keld,
	5/7 The Heads, Keswick CA12 5ES
Tel	+44 (0)1768 772417
Email	david@howekeld.co.uk
Web	www.howekeld.co.uk

Entry 79   Map 11

Cumbria

New House Farm

The large comfy beds, the extravagant baths, the linen, the fabrics, the pillows – comfort par excellence! The renovation is impressive, too; the plasterwork stops here and there to reveal old beam, slate or stone. A trio of the bedrooms are named after the mountain each faces; Swinside brings the 1650s house its own spring water. The breakfast room has a wood-burner, hunting prints and polished tables for Hazel's breakfasts to fuel your adventures, the sitting room sports fireplaces and brocade sofas, and walkers will fall gratefully into the hot spring spa. Luxurious, and huge fun. *Children over six welcome.*

Price	£140–£180. Singles £70–£120.
Rooms	5: 2 doubles, 1 twin/double. Stables: 2 four-posters.
Meals	Lunch from £6 (April-November). Dinner, 3-5 courses, £30-£37. Packed lunch £8. Afternoon tea £3. Pubs 2.5 miles.
Closed	Rarely.
Directions	A66 to Cockermouth, then B5289 for Buttermere. Signed left 2.5 miles south of Lorton.

Bottle of Moët champagne for bookings of 2 or more nights.

	Hazel Thompson
	New House Farm,
	Lorton, Cockermouth CA13 9UU
Mobile	+44 (0)7841 159818
Email	hazel@newhouse-farm.co.uk
Web	www.newhouse-farm.com

Entry 80   Map 11

Cumbria

Fellside Studios

Off the beaten tourist track, a piece of paradise in the Troutbeck valley: seclusion, stylishness and breathtaking views. Prepare your own candlelit dinners, rise when the mood takes you, come and go as you please. The flower beds spill with heathers, hens cluck, and there's a decked terrace for continental breakfast in the sun – freshly prepared by your gently hospitable hosts who live in the attached house. In your studio apartment you get oak floors, slate shower rooms, immaculate kitchenettes with designer touches, DVD players, comfy chairs, luxurious towels. Wonderful. *Minimum stay two nights.*

Price	£70–£90. Singles from £45.
Rooms	2 studios: 1 double, 1 twin/double & kitchenette each.
Meals	Pub/restaurant 0.5 miles.
Closed	Rarely.
Directions	From Windermere, A592 north for 3 miles; after bridge, immed. before church, left signed Troutbeck; 300 yds, 1st house on right.

Monica & Brian Liddell
Fellside Studios,
Troutbeck, Windermere LA23 1PE
Tel +44 (0)1539 434000
Email brian@fellsidestudios.co.uk
Web www.fellsidestudios.co.uk

Entry 81   Map 11

Cumbria

Gillthwaite Rigg

All is calm and ordered in this light, airy and tranquil Arts and Crafts house. Come for nature and to be surrounded by countryside – you may spot a badger or deer. Find panelled window seats, gleaming oak floors, leaded windows, wooden latched doors and motifs moulded into white plaster. Homely bedrooms with large beds, reached via a spiral staircase, have an uncluttered simplicity and mountain and lake views. Banks of books, wood-burners and kind, affable hosts add cheer. Rhoda and Tony are passionate about conservation and wildlife in their 14 acres of garden and woodland. *Babies & children over six welcome.*

Price	£70–£85. Singles £55.
Rooms	2: 1 double, 1 twin/double.
Meals	Pubs/restaurants 1 mile.
Closed	Christmas & New Year.
Directions	M6 junc. 36; A590 & A591 to r'bout; B5284 (signed 'Hawkshead via ferry') for 6 miles. After golf club, right for Heathwaite. Bear right up hill past nursery. Next drive on right; central part of manor.

Guided woodland walks & badger watching. Maps loaned & help planning local trips.

Rhoda M & Tony Graham
Gillthwaite Rigg, Heathwaite Manor,
Lickbarrow Road, Windermere LA23 2NQ
Tel +44 (0)1539 446212
Email tony_rhodagraham@hotmail.com

Entry 82   Map 11

Cumbria

Low Fell

Steve and Louise are great fun, their warmth is infectious and their well-orchestrated house is packed with maps, lists, books and guides. Bedrooms are bright, sunny, pretty, with elegant patterned or checked fabrics, heavenly big beds, plump pillows, warm towels; the suite up in the loft is a super hideaway and you overlook trees animated with birds. Tuck into warm homemade bread and Aga pancakes at breakfast, warm your toes by the fire in winter, relax in the lovely secluded garden with a glass of wine in summer. The house is a five-minute stroll from the lake and bustling Bowness. *Children over ten welcome.*

Price	£78–£104. Half price for children.
Rooms	2: 1 double, 1 family suite (1 double, 1 twin).
Meals	Pubs/restaurants 200 yds.
Closed	Christmas.
Directions	Directions sent on confirmation of booking.

20% off dinner at Lindeth Howe Hotel (includes use of leisure facilities). 20% off Mountain Goat Tours.

	Louise & Stephen Broughton
	Low Fell, Ferney Green, Bowness-on-Windermere, Windermere LA23 3EW
Tel	+44 (0)1539 445612
Mobile	+44 (0)7921 057552
Email	louisebroughton@btinternet.com
Web	www.low-fell.co.uk

Entry 83   Map 11

Cumbria

Cockenskell Farm

The house and hill farm garden with its wild rhododendrons and damson orchard sits at the southern end of Lake Coniston and the views are glorious. Inside find beamed rooms, art and antique pine; bedrooms have pretty patchwork covers and lovely wallpapers. Relax with a book in the conservatory, stroll through the magical, bird-filled garden or tackle a bit of the Cumbrian Way which meanders through the fields to the back. On sunny days Sara will give you breakfast in the conservatory. History seeps from every pore, the place glows with loving care and to stay here is a treat. *Children over 12 welcome.*

Price	£90. Singles from £45.
Rooms	2: 1 twin; 1 twin with separate bath.
Meals	Packed lunch £7.50. Pubs 2-4 miles.
Closed	November-February.
Directions	In Blawith, opp. church up a narrow lane, through farmyard. Right after cattle grid, over fell, right at fork through gates & up drive.

Late checkout (12pm). Free picnic and maps for walkers.

	Sara Keegan
	Cockenskell Farm, Blawith, Ulverston LA12 8EL
Tel	+44 (0)1229 885217
Mobile	+44 (0)7909 885086
Email	keegan@cockenskell.fsnet.co.uk
Web	www.cockenskell.co.uk

Entry 84   Map 11

Cumbria

Yew Tree Farm

Everything here is special: 600 acres of sheep and cattle, a farmhouse once owned by Beatrix Potter, a spinning gallery on the side of the barn, one of the best known buildings in the Lakes. Jon farms the rising hills, Caroline (a member of the Mountain Rescue team) looks after guests with great warmth. Inside, ancient panelling, vast flagstones and William Morris wallpaper shine. There's a fire at breakfast (home-cured bacon, home-laid duck eggs), Ms Potter's furniture, letters from Wordsworth and Ruskin in a cabinet. Bedrooms are traditional with original wood, smart fabrics and views of the valley. Unmissable.

Cumbria

Gilpin Mill

Come to be seriously spoiled. Down leafy lanes is a pretty white house by a mill pond, framed by pastures and trees. Steve took a year off to build new Gilpin Mill, and Jo looks after hens, labs and guests – beautifully. In the country farmhouse sitting room young oak beams span the ceiling and a slate faux-lintel sits above the log fire. Bedrooms are equally inviting: beds are topped with duck down, luscious bathrooms are warm underfoot. Alongside is a lovely old barn where timber was made into bobbins; in the mill pond is a trout ladder and dam, soon to provide power for the grid. And just six cars pass a day!

Price	£104–£124. Singles £70.
Rooms	3: 1 double, 1 four-poster; 1 four-poster with separate bath.
Meals	Dinner, 3 courses, £30. Supper £15 (min. 6).
Closed	Rarely.
Directions	From M6 junc. 36, then A591 signed Windermere. 17 miles then outside Ambleside left at lights, then left onto A593 signed Coniston. After 5 miles house signed on right.

10% off stays of 4 nights.

Jon & Caroline Watson
Yew Tree Farm,
Coniston LA21 8DP
Tel   +44 (0)1539 441433
Mobile   +44 (0)7732 757043
Email   info@yewtree-farm.co.uk
Web   www.yewtree-farm.com

Entry 85   Map 11

Price	£78–£98. Singles £54–£64.
Rooms	3 twins/doubles.
Meals	Pub 2.5 miles.
Closed	Christmas.
Directions	Kendal to Windermere, 1st round-about B5284 to Crook. Left at Crook church, follow signs to Winster; house is on the river.

10% off room rate Mon-Thurs off season.

Jo & Steve Ainsworth
Gilpin Mill,
Crook, Kendal LA8 8LN
Tel   +44 (0)1539 568405
Email   info@gilpinmill.co.uk
Web   www.gilpinmill.co.uk

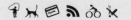

Entry 86   Map 11

Cumbria

Summerhow House

In four acres of fine landscaping and fun topiary is a large and inviting home of flamboyant wallpapers and shades of aqua, lemon and rose. Stylish but laid-back, grand but unintimidating, both house and hosts are a treat. Bedrooms have gilt frames and marble fireplaces, Molton Brown goodies and garden views, there are two sitting rooms to retreat to and breakfasts to delight you – fruits from the orchard, eggs from Sizergh Castle (John's family home). Two miles from Kendal: hop on the train to the Lakes. Walkers, sailors, skiers, food-lovers, dog-lovers will be charmed... aspiring actors too (talk to Janey!).

Price	£80–£120. Singles £50–£69.
Rooms	2: 1 double, 1 twin.
Meals	Pub/restaurant 1.5 miles.
Closed	Occasionally.
Directions	M6, junc. 36 for Kendal. Then follow signs for A6 Shap & on outskirts of Kendal, as 40mph zone ends, immediate next right at white gates. House signed on wall next to gate.

 10% off room rate Mon-Thurs. Free pick-up from local bus/train station.

Janey & John Hornyold-Strickland
Summerhow House,
Shap Road, Kendal LA9 6NY
Tel +44 (0)1539 720763
Email stay@summerhowbedandbreakfast.co.uk
Web www.summerhowbedandbreakfast.co.uk

Entry 87 Map 11

Cumbria

Low Jock Scar

You will be made to feel completely at home here: a cheerful greeting from John and Roslyn comes with homemade cake in the garden, or the guest sitting room with its books and maps, and a log fire for chilly days. Roslyn is a keen cook and spoils you with seasonal and local produce in the sun room with its lovely garden views. Gloriously peaceful and comfortable bedrooms have pretty fabrics; all are a good size and filled with light. Stride those hills, explore Kendal with its interesting shops and theatre, or just find a seat in the garden by the river, watch the wildlife go by and unruffle yourself.

Price	£68–£95. Singles £46–£65.
Rooms	5: 3 doubles, 2 twins.
Meals	Dinner £23. Pubs/restaurants 6-8 miles.
Closed	Rarely.
Directions	From Kendal, A6 to Penrith. After 6 miles, sign on left for Low Jock Scar. From north M6 junc. 39 to A6 south; after 9 miles sign on right for Low Jock Scar.

John & Roslyn Flackett
Low Jock Scar,
Selside, Kendal LA8 9LE
Tel +44 (0)1539 823259
Email info@lowjockscar.co.uk
Web www.lowjockscar.co.uk

Entry 88 Map 12

Cumbria

Lapwings Barn

In the back of most-beautiful-beyond, down narrow lanes, this converted barn is a gorgeous retreat for two – or four. Delightful generous Gillian and Rick give you privacy and an upstairs sitting room with log stove, sofa and a balcony with views. Bedrooms (separate entrances) are elegantly rustic with sweeping beams and modern, stone-tiled bathrooms. Breakfast is delivered: sausages and bacon from their Saddlebacks, eggs from their hens, superb homemade bread and marmalade. Stroll along lowland tracks, watch curlews and lapwings, puff to the top of Whinfell. Ambleside and Beatrix Potter's house are near. One of the best.

Ethical Collection: Food. See page 420.

Price	£50–£90. Singles from £35.
Rooms	Barn: 2 twins/doubles & sitting room.
Meals	Packed lunch £5. Pub/restaurant 3.5 miles.
Closed	Rarely.
Directions	A685 Kendal–Appleby. After 500 yds, left signed Mealbank; over hill after Mealbank, after 2nd bridge at Patton, middle road of 3. After Borrans Farm, left fork; 0.25 miles on left.

20% off purchase of our marmalades, sausages, bacon & eggs.

Use your Sawday's Gift Card here.

Rick & Gillian Rodriguez
Lapwings Barn,
Whinfell, Kendal LA8 9EQ
Tel   +44 (0)1539 824373
Mobile   +44 (0)7901 732379
Email   stay@lapwingsbarn.co.uk
Web   www.lapwingsbarn.co.uk

Entry 89   Map 12

Cumbria

Drybeck Hall

Looking south to fields, woodland and beck this Grade II* listed, 1679 farmhouse has blue painted mullion windows and exposed beams. Expect a deeply traditional home with good furniture, an open fire and pictures of Anthony's predecessors looking down on you benignly; the family has been in the area for 800 years. Comfortable bedrooms have pretty floral fabrics and oak doors; bathrooms are simple but sparkling. Lulie is relaxed and charming and a good cook: enjoy a full English with free-range eggs in the sunny dining room, and home-grown vegetables and often game for dinner. A genuine slice of history.

Price	£90. Singles £45.
Rooms	2: 1 double, 1 twin.
Meals	Dinner, 3 courses, £25. Pub/restaurant 4 miles.
Closed	Rarely.
Directions	From A66 south on B6260. After Hoff take 2nd left signed Drybeck, left at bottom of hill, then left at fork. House on left.

Free pick-up from local bus/train station.

Lulie & Antony Hothfield
Drybeck Hall,
Appleby-in-Westmorland CA16 6TF
Tel   +44 (0)1768 351487
Email   lulieant@aol.com
Web   www.drybeckhall.co.uk

Entry 90   Map 12

Cumbria

Coldbeck House

An old mill leat runs through the garden — elegant with trees, populated by woodpeckers and red squirrels; at breakfast they feed by the window. Belle's forte is her cooking and Richard assists with walks; both are natural hosts. The dignified 1820s house with Victorian additions has sanded and polished floors, antiques and splendid stained glass, a guest sitting room with a log-burning stove and a country-house feel. Bedrooms are delightful: fresh flowers, homemade biscuits, towels to match colourful walls. It's peaceful here, on the edge of a village with a green, and you are in unsurpassed walking country.

Price	£95–£105. Singles £60–£65.
Rooms	3: 2 doubles, 1 twin.
Meals	Dinner for groups, 2–4 courses, £20–£30. Pubs within 5-minute walk.
Closed	Christmas.
Directions	M6 exit 38; A685 to Kirkby Stephen; 6 miles, then right to Ravenstonedale. 1st left opp. Kings Head pub; drive immed. on left.

 10% off stays of 2 or more nights.

Use your Sawday's Gift Card here.

Belle Hepworth
Coldbeck House, Ravenstonedale,
Kirkby Stephen CA17 4LW
Tel   +44 (0)1539 623407
Mobile +44 (0)7966 799171
Email   belle@coldbeckhouse.co.uk
Web   www.coldbeckhouse.co.uk

Entry 91   Map 12

Cumbria

A Corner of Eden

In this Georgian farmhouse, set in a glorious valley with infinite sky and distant Cumbrian hills, tradition and comfort luxuriously combine. The sitting room has a cosy log fire and delicious candlelit breakfasts are served in the beamed dining room. Bedrooms glow with original fireplaces, polished wooden floors and rich fabrics. Engaging Richard and Debbie live in the byre and show a passion for detail: robes and slippers for shared bathrooms, sloe gin in the rooms, barbours by the door, an honesty bar and home-bakes in the dairy. Offset any indulgence by a walk to the pub across the fields. *Self-catering available.*

Ethical Collection: Environment. See page 420.

Price	£120.
Rooms	4: 2 doubles, 1 four-poster, 1 twin, all sharing 2 bathrooms. Max 3 rooms let at any one time (unless whole house let).
Meals	Dinner, 3 courses, £30 (only for house parties). Pub 1 mile.
Closed	Christmas.
Directions	M6 junc. 38, Brough A685. Right into Ravenstonedale; through village until The Fat Lamb, then right. After 0.5 miles left to Stennerskeugh, keep bearing left.

Bottle of wine with stays of 2 nights.

Debbie Temple & Richard Greaves
A Corner of Eden, Low Stennerskeugh,
Ravenstonedale, Kirkby Stephen CA17 4LL
Tel   +44 (0)1539 623370
Mobile +44 (0)7759 469059
Email   enquiries@angelbarn.co.uk
Web   www.acornerofeden.co.uk

Entry 92   Map 12

Cumbria

Lavender House

An 1850s house – the local vet's for many years – a comfortable stroll from the centre of the bustling little market town with its interesting shops and pubs; John can collect you if you come by train. Tea and homemade cake are served in the yellow sitting room – admire Diana's lovely paintings on the walls – with comfy chairs and a fire on chilly days. Bedrooms are bright, with vibrant cushions and antique furniture; bathrooms have big mirrors, thick towels and plenty of soaps and bubbles. On sunny mornings try a Manx kipper on the roof terrace with its 'Mary Poppins' views and smart potted plants. *Minimum stay two nights at weekends.*

Ethical Collection: Food. See page 420.

Price	£75-£85. Singles from £40.
Rooms	2: 1 double; 1 twin/double with separate bath.
Meals	Packed lunch £6. Pub/restaurant 150 yds.
Closed	Rarely.
Directions	M6 junc. 36; A65 Kirkby Lonsdale. After 6.5 miles, left at r'bout. Pass Booth's supermarket. Right at junc. House 50 yds on left; park in drive.

Bottle organic wine 2-night stay. 10% off stays 2 or more nights.

Use your Sawday's Gift Card here.

John & Diana Craven
Lavender House, 17 New Road,
Kirkby Lonsdale LA6 2AB

Tel	+44 (0)1524 272086
Mobile	+44 (0)7775 564157
Email	info@lavenderhousebnb.co.uk
Web	www.lavenderhousebnb.co.uk

Entry 93   Map 12

Derbyshire

Underleigh House

A Derbyshire longhouse in Brontë country built by a man called George Eyre. The position is unbeatable – field, river, hill, sky – but the stars of the show are Philip and Vivienne, dab hands at spoiling guests rotten. There's a big sitting room with maps for walkers, a dining room hall for hearty breakfasts, and tables and chairs scattered about the garden. Back inside, bedrooms vary in size, but all have super beds, goose down duvets and good views; a couple have doors onto the garden, the suites have proper sitting rooms. Fantastic walks start from the front door, Castleton Caves are on the doorstep, Chatsworth is close.

Price	£85-£105. Singles from £65.
Rooms	5: 3 doubles, 2 suites.
Meals	Packed lunches £5. Pubs/restaurants 0.5 miles.
Closed	22 December-5 February.
Directions	A6187 west into Hope. Right for Edale opposite church. Left onto Lose Hill Lane after 0.6 miles, then house on right in 0.25 miles.

Free pick-up from local bus/train station.

Philip & Vivienne Taylor
Underleigh House, Lose Hill Lane,
Hope, Hope Valley S33 6AF

Tel	+44 (0)1433 621372
Email	Info@underleighhouse.co.uk
Web	www.underleighhouse.co.uk

Entry 94   Map 12

Derbyshire

Horsleygate Hall

Hens and guinea fowl animate the charming old stable yard, and the gardens are vibrant and fascinating, with stone terraces and streams, hidden patios, modern sculptures and seats in every corner... the Fords, attentive and kind, encourage you to explore. Inside the 1783 house, Margaret has created yet more charm. There is a warm, timeless, harmonious feel, with worn kilims on pine boards, striped and floral wallpapers, deep sofas and pools of light. Breakfast is served round a big table in the old schoolroom – homemade jams and oatcakes, garden fruit, eggs from the hens. Special. *Children over five welcome.*

Price	£75-£85. Singles from £50.
Rooms	3: 1 double; 1 family room, 1 twin sharing bath.
Meals	Pubs/restaurant 1 mile.
Closed	23 December-4 January.
Directions	M1 exit 29; A617 Chesterfield. 4th exit, 1st r'bout A61, dual c'way; 2nd exit at 3rd r'bout B6050. 2 miles then right at T-junc., B6051 to Barlow & Millthorpe; 1 mile to Horsleygate Lane on right. House at bottom of lane.

 5% off each night for stays of 2 or more nights.

Robert & Margaret Ford
Horsleygate Hall, Horsleygate Lane,
Holmesfield S18 7WD
+44 (0)1142 890333

Entry 95   Map 8

Derbyshire

River Cottage

Well-travelled Gilly and John have restored their large house – built in the 1740s – and given it a fresh modern twist. Interiors are light and airy; modern wallpapers, soft furnishings, mirrors and antiques give each room a charm of its own. There's the little village to explore and a lovely, tiered garden with the duck-and-trout-filled river Wye idling past; easy to forget the busy A6 when settled here with a cup of tea or glass of wine. Fishing can be arranged and you are ten minutes from Chatsworth. Many guests come by bus: it stops outside the house. *Minimum two nights at weekends Easter-October.*

Price	£90-£125. Singles from £75.
Rooms	4: 3 doubles; 1 double with separate bath.
Meals	Pubs 600 yds.
Closed	Rarely.
Directions	On northern edge of Ashford village, 1.5 miles N of Bakewell on A6. Buses from Nottingham, Matlock, Manchester & Buxton stop outside the door.

 Bottle of wine in your room Apr-Oct. 3 nights for the price of 2 Nov-March.

Gilly & John Deacon
River Cottage, Buxton Road, Ashford-in-the-Water, Bakewell DE45 1QP

Tel	+44 (0)1629 813327
Email	info@rivercottageashford.co.uk
Web	www.rivercottageashford.co.uk

Entry 96   Map 8

Derbyshire

Tinkersley Cottage

Sarah has painstakingly reassembled two run-down cottages at the very top of a hill, with the giddiest views over the Peak district's loveliest parts. You can tell she's a stylist: here are pretty stripes and florals, painted wood panelling, chandeliers and shabby chic, Farrow and Ball colours. The comfy and restful bedroom, with antique linen, painted French bed and the fantastic views, is gloriously private with its own entrance up steps from the pretty terraced garden. Sarah is bright and bubbly and loves having guests: breakfast comes from Chatsworth farm shop (you can walk there) or Bakewell farmers' market.

Price	£85.
Rooms	1 suite.
Meals	Pubs/restaurants within 1 mile.
Closed	Rarely.
Directions	A6 Bakewell to Matlock. Through Rowsley, East Lodge Hotel on left, after 0.5 miles Barn Lane on left. House at top of hill.

£80 per night for 2 or more nights.

	Sarah Copley
	Tinkersley Cottage,
	Tinkersley, Rowsley, Matlock DE4 2NJ
Tel	+44 (0)7802 494814
Email	sarahcopley16@hotmail.co.uk
Web	www.tinkersleycottage.co.uk

Entry 97   Map 8

Derbyshire

Manor Farm

Between two small dales, close to great houses (Chatsworth, Hardwick Hall, Haddon Hall), lies this cluster of ancient farms and church; welcome to the 16th century! Simon and Gilly, warm, delightful and fascinated by the history, have restored the east wing to create big, beamy rooms in the old hayloft and a pretty garden room on the ground floor; a cosy and quaint bedroom overlooks the church. Wake to a scrumptious organic breakfast in the atmospheric Elizabethan kitchen. There's a 'book exchange' in the old milking parlour and a lovely garden with sweeping views across the valley and distant hills. *Children over six welcome.*

Ethical Collection: Environment; Food; Community. See page 420.

Price	£80-£90. Singles £55-£70.
Rooms	4: 1 double, 3 twins/doubles.
Meals	Pubs within 10-minute drive.
Closed	Rarely.
Directions	M1 exit 28. A38, then A615 dir. Matlock. Thro' Wessington, after 1 mile, past Plough pub on right. Take 3rd turning on left after Plough (Dethick Lane). Down lane for 1 mile to Dethick.

10% off stays of 2 or more nights Sun-Thurs Nov to mid-Mar (excluding Christmas & New Year).

	Simon & Gilly Groom
	Manor Farm,
	Dethick, Matlock DE4 5GG
Tel	+44 (0)1629 534302
Mobile	+44 (0)7944 660814
Email	gilly.groom@w3z.co.uk
Web	www.manorfarmdethick.co.uk

Entry 98   Map 8

Derbyshire

Mount Tabor House

On a steep hillside between the Peaks and the Dales, a chapel with a peaceful aura and great views. Enter a hall where light streams through stained-glass windows – this is a relaxed, easy place to stay with a distinctive and original interior and a log-burner to keep you toasty; Fay is charming and generous. Breakfast, served in a dining room with open stone walls, is delicious, mainly from the village shops and as organic as possible; you can eat on the balcony in summer. Walk to the pub for dinner, then retire to your inviting, big comfortable bed. *Usually minimum stay two nights at weekends.*

Derbyshire

Park View Farm

An extravagant refuge after a long journey, run by hospitable hosts. Daringly decadent, every inch of this Victorian farmhouse brims with flowers, sparkling trinkets, polished brass, plump cushions and swathes of chintz. The rooms dance in swirls of colour, frills, gleaming wood, lustrous glass, buttons and bows; eggs from the hens, fresh fruits, homemade breads and their own rare-breed sausages accompany the grand performance. Have afternoon tea on the vine-covered terrace, roam the 370 organic acres. Kedleston Hall Park provides a stunning backdrop. *Children over eight welcome.*

Ethical Collection: Food. See page 420.

Price	£85. Singles £60.
Rooms	1 twin/double.
Meals	Occasional dinner £25. Pub 100 yds.
Closed	Rarely.
Directions	M1 exit 26; A610 towards Ripley. At Sawmills, right under r'way bridge, signed Crich. Right at marketplace onto Bowns Hill. Chapel 200 yds on right. Can collect from local stations.

Price	£80-£90. Singles £60.
Rooms	3: 2 four-posters; 1 four-poster with separate bath.
Meals	Pub/restaurant 1 mile.
Closed	Christmas.
Directions	From A52 & A38 r'bout west of Derby, A38 north, 1st left for Kedleston Hall. House 1.5 miles past park on x-roads in Weston Underwood.

10% off room rate Mon-Thurs. 10% off any 3 or more nights (not bank holidays, Christmas, Easter).

10% off stays of 2 or more nights Mon-Thurs.

	Fay Whitehead
	Mount Tabor House,
	Bowns Hill, Crich, Matlock DE4 5DG
Tel	+44 (0)1773 857008
Mobile	+44 (0)7813 007478
Email	mountabor@msn.com

	Linda Adams
	Park View Farm, Weston Underwood,
	Ashbourne DE6 4PA
Tel	+44 (0)1335 360352
Mobile	+44 (0)7771 573057
Email	enquiries@parkviewfarm.co.uk
Web	www.parkviewfarm.co.uk

Entry 99   Map 8

Entry 100   Map 8

Derbyshire

Hungry Bentley Barn

Off a lane in the tranquil Dales, a beautiful, light-filled, modern interpretation of a barn conversion, renovated by Jane and Brian. Genial and relaxed, she breeds dressage horses and walls are hung with equine prints and oils; his passion is vintage cars… a spin in the Bentley may be offered. Find pale chintzy sofas by a huge fireplace, and a grand piano on a toasty warm floor. Up handcrafted oak stairs is a small library of books and maps: a lovely spot to read. Uncluttered cream bedrooms have high ceilings, oak timbers and sandstone floors; bathrooms are fabulous. Wake to rare breed sausages and homemade preserves.

Price	From £78.
Rooms	3: 1 double, 2 four-posters.
Meals	Pubs/restaurants 1.5 miles.
Closed	Christmas, New Year & January.
Directions	From A50 take A515 to Ashbourne. After 4 miles right at crossroads. House 1 mile on right, next to Bentley Hall.

 10% off second and subsequent nights.

Jane Boothroyd
Hungry Bentley Barn, Derby Lane,
Alkmonton, Ashbourne DE6 3DJ
Tel   +44 (0)1335 330296
Mobile   +44 (0)7931 564985
Email   bandb@hungrybentleybarn.co.uk
Web   www.hungrybentleybarn.co.uk

Entry 101   Map 8

Devon

Orchard Cottage

Tucked into a quiet village corner, this is the last cottage in a row of three. Walk through the pretty garden, past seats that bask in the English sun and around to your own entrance and terrace… you may come and go as you please. Your bedroom is L-shaped and large, with a comfortable brass bed and a super en suite shower; it is both rustic and spotless. The Ewens are friendly and fun – their spaniel equally so. Modbury has an eclectic mix of shops and you're brilliantly positioned for Dartmoor, Plymouth and sandy beaches. Breakfasts in the beamy light-filled dining room are generous and delicious. This is excellent value B&B.

Price	From £60. Singles £45.
Rooms	1 double.
Meals	Pubs 300 yds.
Closed	Christmas.
Directions	A379 from Plymouth for Modbury. On reaching Church St at top of hill, before Modbury, fork left at Palm Cross, then immed. 1st right into Back St. Cottage 3rd on left, past village hall.

Maureen Ewen
Orchard Cottage, Back Street,
Palm Cross Green, Modbury PL21 0R
Tel   +44 (0)1548 830633
Mobile   +44 (0)7979 558568
Email   moewen@talktalk.net

Entry 102   Map 2

Devon

Annapurna

Rural bliss: the garden of this pretty, cream-painted longhouse surrounded by munching cows and happy hens looks down the folded valley to the steeple of Modbury Church. Inside, Carol and Peter spoil you with blueberry pancakes, organic home-baked bread and home-laid eggs for breakfast. Charming bedrooms with a fresh country feel have garden flowers, sparkling bathrooms and wonderfully comfortable beds. The views stretch for miles, fabulous walking starts from the door and you are close to the watery delights of Salcombe and Dartmouth. Readers love this place: "Carol & Peter are perfect hosts!"

Ethical Collection: Food. See page 420.

Price	£70-£75. Singles £30-£40.
Rooms	2: 1 twin/double; 1 single with separate bath.
Meals	Pubs/restaurants 1 mile.
Closed	Rarely.
Directions	A38 Modbury & Ermington. After 1.5 miles approx. Kittaford Cross straight on, thro' California Cross. After 2.4 miles left down unmarked lane. House 300 yds on right.

 A 'spoil yourself' day: massage, seaweed bath & scented candles (reduced rate of £25).

	Carol Farrand & Peter Foster
	Annapurna,
	Mary Cross, Modbury PL21 0SA
Tel	+44 (0)1548 831299
Mobile	+44 (0)7977 200324
Email	carolfarrand@tiscali.co.uk
Web	www.annapurna-devon.co.uk

Entry 103   Map 2

Devon

High Barn

A quiet spot among rolling hills with artist Nick, cook Jill, two pointers, an inquisitive cat and roaming chickens. This is a warm, generous household with an easy-going atmosphere: large sofas round a wood-burner, big art and a snooker table. Comfy bedrooms with colourful quilts are downstairs, one opens onto the sunken courtyard. At breakfast you get freshly squeezed juice, homemade preserves, local bacon and just-laid eggs; suppers can be simple or elaborate, or a barbecue in the garden. Explore Dartmoor, walk the coastal paths or head for the beaches; there's plenty of space for your dingy, boards and sandy wetsuits.

Price	£60-£65. Singles £40.
Rooms	3: 1 twin/double; 2 family rooms (extra bed/cots available).
Meals	Dinner, 2 courses, from £15. Pubs within 2 miles.
Closed	Rarely.
Directions	A379 west from Kingsbridge to Aveton Gifford. Thro' village, then right past church. Continue 2 miles to Chillaton Cross, then left (after Lixton turning). House 1st on left.

	Nick & Jill Bremer
	High Barn, Chillaton,
	Loddiswell, Kingsbridge TQ7 4EG
Tel	+44 (0)1548 550838
Email	stay@highbarndevon.co.uk
Web	www.highbarndevon.co.uk

Entry 104   Map 2

Devon

Rafters Barn

A delightful, peaceful, 300-year-old barn along the narrowest of lanes, with far-reaching valley views. This is big sailing country but mostly agricultural so you will avoid the madding crowds. You can relax and read in an outdoor picnic spot or by the wood-burner in a comfy guest sitting room; a large choice at breakfast is served in the open hallway. Neat bedrooms have bright colours and pretty touches: two with beams are upstairs, the suite is downstairs. Tiled bathrooms gleam. Kind, thoughtful, smiling Elizabeth can steer you towards the best beaches and places to eat in Salcombe; her two dogs will welcome yours, too.

Price	£70-£85.
Rooms	3: 1 double, 1 twin; 1 suite with separate bath.
Meals	Dinner from £20 (Oct-Mar only). Pubs/restaurants 4 miles.
Closed	Christmas & New Year.
Directions	A381 dir. Salcombe. Just before Hope Cove sign, right to Bagton & S. Huish. Follow lane for 1 mile; 30 yds past saw mill, right up farm lane; at bottom on left.

Bottle of wine in your room.

Elizabeth Hanson
Rafters Barn, Holwell Farm,
South Huish, Kingsbridge TQ7 3EQ

Tel	+44 (0)1548 560460
Mobile	+44 (0)7971 293288
Email	raftersdevon@yahoo.co.uk
Web	www.raftersdevon.co.uk

Entry 105   Map 2

Devon

Washbrook Barn

Hard not to feel happy here – even the blue-painted windows on rosy stone walls make you want to smile. Inside is equally sunny. The barn – decrepit until Penny bought it nine years ago – rests at the bottom of a quiet valley. She has transformed it into a series of big light-filled rooms with polished wooden floors, pale beams and richly coloured walls lined with fabulous watercolours: the effect is one of gaiety and panache. No sitting room as such, but armchairs in impeccable bedrooms from which one can admire the rural outlook. The beds are divinely comfortable and the fresh bathrooms sparkle.

Price	From £80. Singles from £55.
Rooms	3 doubles.
Meals	Dinner occasionally available in winter. Pubs/restaurants 10-minute walk.
Closed	Christmas & New Year.
Directions	From Kingsbridge quay to top of Fore St; right into Duncombe St; on to T-junc.; left to Church St. Right into Belle Cross Rd; 150 yds, right into Washabrook Lane; 250 yds left; at bottom on right.

10% off room rate Mon-Thurs.

Penny Cadogan
Washbrook Barn, Washabrook Lane,
Kingsbridge TQ7 1NN

Tel	+44 (0)1548 856901
Mobile	+44 (0)7989 502194
Email	penny.cadogan@gmail.com
Web	www.washbrookbarn.co.uk

Entry 106   Map 2

Devon

Strete Barton House

Contemporary, friendly, exotic and exquisite: French sleigh beds and Asian art, white basins and black chandeliers, and a garden with sofas for the views. So much to love, and the coastal path right outside the door. Your caring hosts live the dream, running immaculate B&B by the sea, in an old manor house at the top of the village. Breakfasts are exuberantly local (village eggs, sausages from Dartmouth, honey from the bay), there's a wood-burner in the sitting room and Kevin and Stuart know exactly which beach, walk or pub is perfect for you. *Minimum stay two nights in summer. Pets in cottage only.*

Ethical Collection: Food; Community. See page 420.

Price	£100–£150.
Rooms	6: 3 doubles, 1 twin; 1 twin with separate shower. Cottage: 1 suite & sitting room.
Meals	Pub/restaurant within 50 yds.
Closed	Rarely.
Directions	From Dartmouth, A379 to Kingsbridge. At mini r'bout, left onto A379 signed Stoke Fleming. A379 to Strete, then right into Totnes Rd. House 20 yds up hill on right.

Free pick-up from local bus/train station.

Use your Sawday's Gift Card here.

Stuart Litster & Kevin Hooper
Strete Barton House, Totnes Road, Strete, Dartmouth TQ6 0RU
Tel +44 (0)1803 770364
Email info@stretebarton.co.uk
Web www.stretebarton.co.uk

Entry 107   Map 2

Devon

Nonsuch House

The photo says it all! You are in your own crow's nest, perched above the flotillas of yachts zipping in and out of the estuary mouth: stunning. Kit and Penny are great fun and look after you well; ex-hotelier Kit smokes his own fish fresh from the quay and produces brilliant dinners. Further pleasures lie across the water, and a five-minute walk brings you to the ferry that transports you (and your car) to the other side. Breakfasts in the conservatory are a delight, bedrooms are big and comfortable, and fresh bathrooms sparkle. *Over tens welcome. Min. two nights at weekends. Disabled ramps available.*

Ethical Collection: Food. See page 420.

Price	£110–£150. Singles £85–£125.
Rooms	4: 3 twins/doubles, 1 double.
Meals	Dinner, 3 courses, £37.50. (Not Tues/Wed/Sat.) Pub/restaurant 5-minute walk & short boat trip.
Closed	Rarely.
Directions	2 miles before Brixham on A3022, A379. Right at r'bout, 100yds on fork left (B3205) downhill, through woods, left up Higher Contour Rd, down Ridley Hill. At hairpin bend. Parking nearby.

Bottle of wine with dinner on first or second night. Late checkout (12pm).

Kit & Penny Noble
Nonsuch House, Church Hill, Kingswear, Dartmouth TQ6 0BX
Tel +44 (0)1803 752829
Email enquiries@nonsuch-house.co.uk
Web www.nonsuch-house.co.uk

Entry 108   Map 2

Devon

Kaywana Hall

With glossy modern lines and sparkling glass in its own wooded valley, this is a 'Grand Designs' project in the making. All is smart and contemporary from the great oil paintings and slate and wooden floors to the ultra-crisp bed linen and immaculate bathrooms. The bedrooms are separate from the main house and up steps; one has views over the pool, and its own terrace. The feel is spacious and uncluttered but warm and cosy, too. Friendly Tony gives you delicious locally sourced choices at breakfast, you can hop on the ferry for Dartmouth and close by are regattas, gardens to visit, beaches and steam train and river trips.

Price	£125–£145. Singles £135.
Rooms	3: 2 doubles, 1 twin/double.
Meals	Pub/restaurant 0.5 miles.
Closed	February.
Directions	Torquay towards Brixham; 1 mile from Brixham, turn towards Kingswear. Pass cemetery on left. House next on left.

Bottle of wine in your room.

Anthony Pithers & Gordon Craig
Kaywana Hall, Higher Contour Road,
Kingswear, Dartmouth TQ6 0AY
Tel   +44 (0)1803 752200
Email res@kaywanahall.co.uk
Web   www.kaywanahall.co.uk

Entry 109   Map 2

Devon

Riverside House

The loveliest 18th-century house with the tidal river estuary bobbing past with boats and birds; dip your toes in the water while sitting in the garden. Felicity, an artist, and Roger, a passionate sailor, give you pretty bedrooms with paintings, poetry, little balconies, wide French windows and binoculars; spot swans at high tide, herons (perhaps a kingfisher) when the river goes down. Stroll to the pub for quayside barbecues and jazz in summer; catch the ferry from Dittisham to Agatha Christie's house; discover delightful Dartmouth. Kayaks and inflatables are welcome by arrangement. *Min. two nights at weekends.*

Price	From £75. Singles from £60.
Rooms	2: 1 double; 1 double with separate shower.
Meals	Pubs 100 yds.
Closed	Rarely.
Directions	In Tuckenhay, pass Maltsters Arms on left to 2nd thatched house on left, at right angle to road. Drive past, turn at bridge and return to slip lane.

Bottle of wine in your room for stays of 2 or more nights. Use of slipway.

Felicity & Roger Jobson
Riverside House,
Tuckenhay, Totnes TQ9 7EQ
Tel   +44 (0)1803 732837
Mobile +44 (0)7710 510007
Email felicity.riverside@hotmail.co.uk
Web   www.riverside-house.co.uk

Entry 110   Map 2

Devon

Avenue Cottage

The tree-lined approach is steep and spectacular; the cottage sits in 11 wondrous acres of rhododendron, magnolia and wild flowers with a lily-strewn pond, grassy paths and lovely views over the river. Find a quiet spot in which to read or simply sit and absorb the tranquillity. Richard is a gifted gardener, and the archetypal gardener's modesty and calm have penetrated the house itself – it is uncluttered, comfortable and warmed by a log fire. The old-fashioned twin room has a big, faded bathroom with a faux-marble basin and a balcony with sweeping valley views; the pretty village and pub are a short walk away.

Price	£60–£80. Singles £40–£50.
Rooms	2: 1 twin/double; 1 double sharing shower.
Meals	Pub 0.5 miles.
Closed	Rarely.
Directions	A381 Totnes to Kingsbridge for 1 mile; left for Ashprington; into village, then left by pub ('Dead End' sign). House 0.25 miles on right.

Richard Pitts
Avenue Cottage,
Ashprington, Totnes TQ9 7UT
Tel +44 (0)1803 732769
Mobile +44 (0)7719 147475
Email richard.pitts@btinternet.com
Web www.avenuecottage.com

Entry 111   Map 2

Devon

Manor Farm

Sarah is a happy gardener, producing vegetables that will find their way into your (excellent) dinner, and raspberries for your muesli. She keeps bees and hens too, so you can have honey and eggs for breakfast, served in a super red dining room. The farmhouse, facing a communal courtyard, twists and turns around unexpected corners thanks to ancient origins, and its good traditional bedrooms in bright farmhouse colours are reached via two separate stairs – nicely private. Sarah and Michael's labs are charming and the village is pure Devon: surrounded by apple orchards and with two good pubs for eating out.

Price	From £70. Singles £45–£50.
Rooms	2: 1 double; 1 twin with separate bath/shower.
Meals	Dinner £17–£23. Packed lunch £5. Pubs 500 yds.
Closed	Rarely.
Directions	From Newton Abbot, A381 for Totnes. After approx. 2.5 miles, right for Broadhempston. Past village sign, down hill & 2nd left. Pass pub on right & left after high stone wall into courtyard.

Sarah Clapp
Manor Farm,
Broadhempston, Totnes TQ9 6BD
Tel +44 (0)1803 813260
Email mandsclapp@btinternet.com

Entry 112   Map 2

Devon

Kilbury Manor

You can stroll down to the Dart from the garden and onto their little island, when the river's not in spate! Back at the Manor – a listed longhouse from the 1700s – are four super-comfortable bedrooms, the most private in the stone barn. Your genuinely welcoming hosts (with dogs Dillon and Buster) moved to Devon to renovate a big handsome house and open it to guests. Julia does everything beautifully so there's organic smoked salmon for breakfast, baskets of toiletries by the bath, the best linen on the best beds and a drying room for wet gear – most handy if you've come to walk the Moor. Spot-on B&B.

Price	£75-£90. Singles from £55.
Rooms	4: 2 doubles. Barn: 1 twin/double; 1 double with separate bath.
Meals	Pubs/restaurants 1.5-4 miles.
Closed	Rarely.
Directions	Leaving A38, left for Totnes. After 0.5 miles, right over river on narrow bridge; follow lane over railway bridge then immed. left into Colston Rd. House 0.25 miles on left.

Julia & Martin Blundell
Kilbury Manor,
Colston Road, Buckfastleigh TQ11 0LN
Tel +44 (0)1364 644079
Email info@kilburymanor.co.uk
Web www.kilburymanor.co.uk

Entry 113   Map 2

Devon

Agaric Rooms at Tudor House

A merchant's townhouse now happily given over to rooms for the Agaric Restaurant. Sophie and Nick are young, fun and very clever: in these mostly large, individually styled rooms, fabrics are plush, colours rich and bathrooms have roll tops, robes and smart towels; the ground floor double has a striking wet room. A breakfast room is cool with leather and palms; full English or anything else you want is served here. Don't come without booking into the restaurant for fabulous modern British cooking – then stagger two steps down the street to your well-earned bed. Ashburton bustles with good food shops, antiques and books.

Price	£110-£130. Singles £50.
Rooms	4: 2 doubles, 1 family, 1 single.
Meals	Owners' restaurant next door. Packed lunch from £10 for 2.
Closed	Rarely.
Directions	From A38 follow signs to Ashburton. North Street is the main street, house is on the right after the Town Hall.

 10% off room rate Mon-Thurs. 10% off stays of 2 or more nights.

Sophie & Nick Coiley
Agaric Rooms at Tudor House,
36 North Street, Ashburton TQ13 7QD
Tel +44 (0)1364 654478
Email eat@agaricrestaurant.co.uk
Web www.agaricrestaurant.co.uk

Entry 114   Map 2

Devon

Penpark

Clough Williams-Ellis of Portmeirion fame did more than design an elegant house; he made sure it communed with nature. Light pours in from every window and the views are long, across rolling farmland to Dartmoor and Hay Tor. The big double has a comfy sofa and its own balcony; the private suite has arched French doors to the garden and an extra room for young children. Antiques and heirlooms, African carvings, silk and fresh flowers – it is deeply traditional and comforting. Your generous hosts have been doing B&B for years; they and their two springer spaniels look after you well.

Price	From £76. Singles by arrangement.
Rooms	3: 1 family suite; 2 twins/doubles, each with separate bath/shower.
Meals	Pub 1 mile.
Closed	Rarely.
Directions	A38 west to Plymouth; A382 turn off; 3rd turning off r'bout, signed Bickington. There, right at junc. (to Plymouth), right again (to Sigford & Widecombe). Over top of A38 & up hill; 1st entrance on right.

 10% off room rate Mon-Thurs. Lift to local pub.

Madeleine & Michael Gregson
Penpark,
Bickington, Ashburton TQ12 6LH
Tel   +44 (0)1626 821314
Email   maddy@penpark.co.uk
Web   www.penpark.co.uk

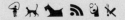

Entry 115   Map 2

Devon

Hooks Cottage

At the end of a long bumpy track, the hideaway mine captain's house may have few original features but the woodland setting is gorgeous. Mary and Dick have a finely judged sense of humour; labradors Archie and Cobble will charm you. It is simple, rural, close to the Moors, with woodland birds and a gentle river to unwind stressed souls. Carpeted bedrooms have a faded floral charm and pretty stream views; bathrooms are plain. Enjoy local sausages and Mary's marmalade for breakfast, a lovely garden and amazing bluebells in spring; walks from the house are sublime. Your horse is welcome too. *Dogs no charge.*

Price	From £65. Singles from £40.
Rooms	2: 1 double en suite (wc across landing); 1 twin with separate bath.
Meals	Pub/restaurant 2 miles.
Closed	Rarely.
Directions	From A38, A382 at Drumbridges for Newton Abbot; 3rd left at r'bout for Bickington. 2.7 miles on, down hill, right for Haytor. Under bridge, 1st left & down long, bumpy track, past thatched cottage to house.

10% off stays of 2 or more nights. Late checkout (12pm).

Mary & Dick Lloyd-Williams
Hooks Cottage,
Bickington, Ashburton TQ12 6JS
Tel   +44 (0)1626 821312
Email   hookscottage@yahoo.com
Web   www.hookscottage.co.uk

Entry 116   Map 2

Devon

Bagtor House

What a setting! A ten-minute walk and you're on top of the moor. Enfolded by garden, fields and sheep, the 15th-century house with the Georgian façade is the last remaining manor in the parish. Find ancient beauty in granite flagstones, oak-panelled walls, great fireplaces glowing with logs, country dressers brimming with china. Sue looks after hens, geese, labs, guests, grows everything and makes her own muesli. She gives you a large and elegant double room with an antique brass bed, and an oak-panelled family room with a four-poster and adjoining twin. Warm, homely, spacious, civilised, and close to beautiful Hay Tor.

Ethical Collection: Environment; Food. See page 420.

Price	From £76. Singles by arrangement.
Rooms	2: 1 double; 1 family room with separate bath/shower.
Meals	Restaurants/pubs 1.5 miles.
Closed	Christmas.
Directions	From A38 to Plymouth, A382 turn off at r'bout, 3rd exit to Ilsington; up through village, 2nd left after hotel (to Bickington), 1st crossroads right to Bagtor, 0.5 miles, on right next to farm.

Late checkout (12pm). Lift to local pubs.

Sue & Nigel Cookson
Bagtor House,
Ilsington, Newton Abbot TQ13 9RT
Tel +44 (0)1364 661538
Email sawreysue@hotmail.com
Web www.bagtormanor.co.uk

Entry 117   Map 2

Devon

Corndonford Farm

An ancient Devon longhouse and an engagingly chaotic haven run by warm and friendly Ann and Will, along with their Shire horses and Dartmoor ponies. Steep, stone circular stairs lead to bedrooms: bright colours, a four-poster with lacy curtains, gorgeous views over the cottage garden and a shower room with a beam to duck. A place for those who want to get into the spirit of it all — maybe help catch an escaped foal, chatter to the farm workers around the table; not for fussy types or Mr and Mrs Tickety Boo! Delicious Aga breakfasts and good for walkers too — the Two Moors Way footpath is on the doorstep. *Over tens by arrangement.*

Ethical Collection: Food. See page 420.

Price	£70. Singles £35.
Rooms	2: 1 four-poster; 1 twin sharing bathroom.
Meals	Pub 2 miles.
Closed	Rarely.
Directions	From A38 2nd Ashburton turn for Dartmeet & Princetown. In Poundsgate pass pub on left; 3rd right on bad bend signed Corndon. Straight over x-roads, 0.5 miles, farm on left.

Late checkout (12pm). Drive in carriage with pair of Dartmoor Hill ponies.

Ann & Will Williams
Corndonford Farm,
Poundsgate, Newton Abbot TQ13 7PP
Tel +44 (0)1364 631595
Email corndonford@btinternet.com

Entry 118   Map 2

Devon

Heron Cottage

Folded into a valley in an idyllic corner of Dartmoor is a freshly renovated riverside B&B — one of two adjoining 18th-century cottages. You have complete privacy in your own Swedish style wooden house down by the water — a light, airy, roomy space with cosy triple-glazing and sparkling shower room. Your hosts — outgoing, musical, hospitable and well-travelled — bring you delicious breakfasts (local eggs and sausages, homemade bread and jams) at flexible times; in summer it's served beside the tumbling river with buzzards soaring above. The Two Moors Way runs right by the door and this magical haven is loved by all who stay.

Ethical Collection: Food. See page 420.

Price	£75. Singles £55.
Rooms	Garden house: 1 double.
Meals	Pub 2 miles.
Closed	Rarely.
Directions	Bovey Tracy to Widecombe, then Ponsworthy road for 1.2 miles, then 1st right and 1st left to Jordan. Left again, down to bottom of hill. Cottage on bend.

	Sue Bottomley
	Heron Cottage, Jordan, Widecombe-in-the-Moor, Newton Abbot TQ13 7PN
Tel	+44 (0)1364 631596
Email	sue@patrickgarvey.demon.co.uk
Web	www.heroncottagedartmoor.co.uk

Entry 119   Map 2

Devon

Highfield House

Come for complete peace in the Dartmoor National Park and be bowled over by the glorious garden. Helen is charming and her smart contemporary house gleams; light floods in through huge windows and the south-facing terrace runs the length of the house. Large bedrooms with armchairs are sumptuous, one has its own roof terrace with views of the moor; bathrooms are sparkling and modern. The birds sing, the pale oak floors are heated from underneath and the locally sourced breakfast is generous. Wonderful walks start at the end of the garden and the pretty village has a friendly pub serving good food.

Price	£75-£85. Singles £60-£70.
Rooms	3: 1 double, 2 twins/doubles.
Meals	Pub 300 yds. Restaurants within 5 miles.
Closed	Christmas, New Year & occasionally.
Directions	A382 past Bovey Tracey, then left to Lustleigh. Over railway bridge, into village; 3 bungalows & steep hill on right. Up hill & house 7th on left.

 10% off stays of 3 or more nights.

	Helen Waterworth
	Highfield House, Mapstone Hill, Lustleigh, Newton Abbot TQ13 9SE
Tel	+44 (0)1647 277577
Email	helen@highfieldhousedevon.co.uk
Web	www.highfieldhousedevon.co.uk

Entry 120   Map 2

Devon

Cyprian's Cot

A charming 16th-century terraced cottage filled with beams and burnished wood. The old stone fireplace is huge, the grandfather clock ticks, the views are stunning and Shelagh is warm and welcoming. Guests have their own sitting room with a crackling fire; up the narrow stairs and into cosy bedrooms – a small double and a tiny twin. Tasty breakfasts, served in the dining room, include free-range eggs, sausages and bacon from the local farm and garden fruits. Discover the lovely town with its pubs, fine restaurant and interesting shops. With the Dartmoor Way and the Two Moors Way on the doorstep, the walking is wonderful too.

Price	£60. Singles from £30.
Rooms	2: 1 twin; 1 double with separate bath.
Meals	Pubs/restaurants 4-minute walk.
Closed	Rarely.
Directions	In Chagford pass church on left; 1st right beyond Globe Inn opposite. House 150 yds on right.

10% off stays Mon-Thurs.

Shelagh Weeden
Cyprian's Cot, 47 New Street,
Chagford, Newton Abbot TQ13 8BB
Tel   +44 (0)1647 432256
Email   shelaghweeden@btinternet.com
Web   www.cyprianscot.co.uk

Entry 121   Map 2

Devon

Cary Court

Disraeli lived next door and Lily Langtry had a house around the corner, in the days when this was a popular seaside resort. You can still get the train here – Paul will pick you up from the station. Once up the steep drive you find yourself immersed in a proper 'plantation style' house, a short walk away from the bustle. Find a mix of antique and reproduction furniture, brocade pale-gold sofas, oriental side lamps, and smart colourful bedrooms. It is all squeaky clean and very comfortable, there's an exercise room, a heated pool and huge breakfasts. The garden is amazingly lush and exotic, your hosts are charming and affable.

Price	£65-£95. Singles £45-£57.50.
Rooms	10: 6 doubles, 2 twins, 2 four-posters.
Meals	Pubs/restaurants 0.25 miles.
Closed	December-February.
Directions	From harbour left at clock tower roundabout onto Babbacombe Road. Pass museum, then left into Braddon Hill Road East. At hill top right into Hunsdon Road. Second drive on left.

10% off mid-week stays. Earlier check-in by arrangement.

Linda & Paul Garwood
Cary Court,
Hunsdon Road, Torquay TQ1 1QB
Tel   +44 (0)1803 209205
Email   stay@carycourthotel.co.uk
Web   www.carycourthotel.co.uk

Entry 122   Map 2

Devon

Parford Well

Everything here is beautiful. The house – small but perfectly formed – is wrapped in peace and stands in an acre of trim gardens, with roses rambling across the walls and a willow dipping its branches into a passing stream. Inside you find fabulous art, regal busts, books everywhere and sofas in front of the sitting room fire. Bedrooms come with antique wood furniture, crisp linen, fresh flowers, beautiful views. Tim had a smart hotel in London and knows how to look after guests. Breakfast – served at an old oak table – is a treat; everything is brought to you. Walks start from the front door, Castle Drogo is close.

Price	£75-£95.
Rooms	3: 2 doubles; 1 double with separate bath.
Meals	Pub in village.
Closed	Occasionally.
Directions	A30 to Whiddon Down, then A382 south for Moretonhampstead. After three miles, left in Sandy Park and immediately on left.

Tim Daniel
Parford Well,
Sandy Park, Chagford TQ13 8JW

Tel	+44 (0)1647 433353
Email	tim@parfordwell.co.uk
Web	www.parfordwell.co.uk

Entry 123   Map 2

Devon

Burnville House

Granite gateposts, Georgian house, rhododendrons, beechwoods and rolling fields of sheep: that's the setting. But there's more. Beautifully proportioned rooms reveal subtle colours, elegant antiques, squishy sofas and bucolic views, stylish bathrooms are sprinkled with candles, there are sumptuous dinners and pancakes at breakfast. Your hosts left busy jobs in London to settle here, and their place breathes life – space, smiles, energy. Swim, play tennis, walk to Dartmoor from the door, take a trip to Eden or the sea. Or… just gaze at the moors and the church on the Tor and listen to the silence, and the sheep.

Price	From £80. Singles £55.
Rooms	3 doubles.
Meals	Dinner from £19. Pub 2 miles.
Closed	Rarely.
Directions	A30 Exeter-Okehampton; A386 dir. Tavistock. Right for Lydford opp. Dartmoor Inn; after 4 miles (thro' Lydford), Burnville Farm on left (convex traffic mirror on right).

Bottle of wine in your room.
Late checkout (12pm).

Victoria Cunningham
Burnville House,
Brentor, Tavistock PL19 0NE

Tel	+44 (0)1822 820443
Mobile	+44 (0)7881 583471
Email	burnvillef@aol.com
Web	www.burnville.co.uk

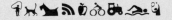

Entry 124   Map 2

Devon

Mount Tavy Cottage

Between Dartmoor and Tavistock, this 250-year-old former gardener's bothy has been made into a warm and welcoming home by Jo and Graham. Pretty bedrooms in the house have stripped floorboards, a four-poster or half-tester bed and free-standing baths. Two simpler bedrooms, each with a big shower, are across the courtyard in the garden studios; here you can be completely independent, or trot over to the house for a delicious breakfast. Lots to enjoy outside too: a cider orchard with beehives, a walled garden, rare breed pigs in the wood and a lake with a thatched dining spot. *Arrivals after 5pm, unless previously arranged.*

Ethical Collection: Food. See page 420.

Price	From £70. Singles from £35.
Rooms	4: 1 double, 1 four-poster, both with separate bath. 2 studios: 1 twin/double & kitchenette each.
Meals	Dinner, 3 courses, £20. Pub 2 miles.
Closed	Rarely.
Directions	From Tavistock B3357 towards Princetown; 0.25 miles on, after Mount House School, left. Drive past lake to house.

Bottle of wine with dinner on first night.

G H Moule
Mount Tavy Cottage,
Tavistock PL19 9JL
Tel   +44 (0)1822 614253
Mobile   +44 (0)7776 181576
Email   mounttavy@btinternet.com
Web   www.mounttavy.co.uk

Entry 125   Map 2

Devon

Higher Eggbeer Farm

Over 900 years old and still humming with life: pigs, cows, ponies, rabbits and chickens share the rambling gardens. Sally Anne, son Alistair and William are artistic, fun, slightly wacky and charming. It's an adventure to stay, so keep an open mind: the house is a historic gem and undeniably rustic. Huge fireplaces, interesting art, books, piano, wellies, muddle and lived-in charm. Your lovely hosts will take children to feed animals and collect eggs, and will babysit. Be wrapped in peace in one of two wings (with beautiful drawing room), immersed in a panorama of forest, hills and fields of waving wheat.

Price	£65-£75. Singles £42.
Rooms	East wing: 1 double, 1 twin sharing bath (let to same party only). West wing: 2 doubles, 1 twin, 1 single, all sharing bath & 2nd wc. Self-catering option.
Meals	Restaurants 5-minute walk.
Closed	Rarely.
Directions	A30 to Okehampton. After 10 miles left exit into Cheriton Bishop; 1st left after Old Thatch pub, signed Woodbrooke. Down & up hill; road turns sharp left but you don't. Right down private lane.

Sally Anne Selwyn &
Alistair Scott Lawson
Higher Eggbeer Farm,
Cheriton Bishop, Exeter EX6 6JQ
Tel   +44 (0)1647 24427
Mobile   +44 (0)7850 136131
Email   ascottlawson@gmail.com

Entry 126   Map 2

Devon

Brook Farmhouse

Tuck yourself up in the peace and quiet of Paul and Penny's whitewashed, thatched cottage, surrounded by glorious countryside. Inside find your own charming sitting room with a huge inglenook, good antiques, fresh flowers, and comfy sofa and chairs; breakfast here on homemade apple juice, eggs from the owners' hens and delicious local bacon and sausages. Up the ancient spiral stone stairs is your warm, beamed bedroom with smooth linen, chintzy curtains, lots of cushions. You are near Dartmoor and can reach the Devon beaches and the north Cornish coast; perfect for hearty walkers, birdwatchers, surfers and picnic-lovers.

Price	£80. Singles £45.
Rooms	1 double with separate bathroom.
Meals	Pub 2 miles.
Closed	Christmas & New Year.
Directions	In Tedburn village turn into North Park Rd opp. garage, then right at T-junc. after bridge. House on right after 1.4 miles at bottom of steep hill.

Paul & Penny Steadman
Brook Farmhouse,
Tedburn St Mary, Exeter EX6 6DS

Tel	+44 (0)1647 270042
Email	penny.steadman@btconnect.com
Web	www.brookfarmhouse.2day.ws

Entry 127   Map 2

Devon

The Garden House

Refulgent! An extraordinary restoration of a 1930s house, carried out with passion. Bedrooms are sumptuous: beds plump with cushions, fabrics smooth, colours vibrant, scents divine. The exuberance reaches the lovely garden; Jane's energy among the pots, quirky topiary and tulips is almost palpable and on sunny days it's a peaceful haven. A huge collection of books are stacked hither and thither, chandeliers sparkle, homemade cakes abound and there's a vast choice at breakfast – locally sourced and beautifully served. Deeply comfortable, generous to a fault, immaculate, good-humoured and an easy walk into the city.

Price	£85–£90. Singles £50–£60.
Rooms	2: 1 double; 1 twin with separate bath/shower.
Meals	Restaurant 8-minute walk. Pubs nearby.
Closed	Rarely.
Directions	M5 junc. 30 for city centre (Middlemoor Ln) & uni. Behind John Lewis, Longbrook St into Pennsylvania Rd. Thro' lights, 2nd left Hoopern Ave; house at end on left.

David & Jane Woolcock
The Garden House, 4 Hoopern Avenue,
Pennsylvania, Exeter EX4 6DN

Tel	+44 (0)1392 256255
Mobile	+44 (0)7968 374876
Email	david.woolcock11@virginmedia.com
Web	www.exeterbedandbreakfast.co.uk

Entry 128   Map 2

Devon

Larkbeare Grange

Expectations rise as you follow the tree-lined drive to the immaculate Georgian house... and are met, the second you enter. The upkeep is perfect, the feel is chic and the whole place exudes well-being. Sparkling sash windows fill big rooms with light, floors shine and the grandfather clock ticks away the hours. Expect the best: good lighting, goose down duvets, contemporary luxury in fabric and fitting, a fabulous suite perfect for a small family, flexible breakfasts and lovely views from the bedrooms at the front. Charlie, Savoy-trained, and Julia are charming and fun: you are in perfect hands.

Ethical Collection: Environment. See page 420.

Price	£98-£175. Singles £83-£110.
Rooms	4: 2 doubles, 1 twin/double, 1 suite.
Meals	Pub 1.5 miles.
Closed	Rarely.
Directions	From A30 Exmouth & Ottery St Mary junc. At r'bouts follow Whimple signs. 0.25 miles, right; 0.5 miles, left signed Larkbeare. Grange 1 mile on left.

 Upgrade when available or 10% off stays Sun-Thurs (phone booking).

 Use your Sawday's Gift Card here.

	Charlie & Julia Hutchings
	Larkbeare Grange,
	Larkbeare, Talaton, Exeter EX5 2RY
Tel	+44 (0)1404 822069
Email	stay@larkbeare.net
Web	www.larkbeare.net

Entry 129   Map 2

Devon

Lower Allercombe Farm

Horses in the paddock and no-frills bedrooms at this down-to-earth, very friendly B&B. Don't expect twinsets and pearls; Susie, ex-eventer, may greet you in two-tone jodhpurs instead. She and Lizzie (her terrier) live at one end of the listed longhouse, guests at the other. There's a sitting room with horsey pictures and wood-burner, and bedrooms upstairs that reflect the fair price. You'll feast on home eggs and tomatoes in the morning, and rashers from award-winning pigs. Very handy for Exeter, the south coast and Dartmoor; the airport is ten minutes away, the A30 is one mile. *Stabling available.*

Price	£60-£70. Singles £40-£50.
Rooms	3: 1 double, 1 twin; 1 double with separate bath.
Meals	Pub/restaurant 2 miles.
Closed	Rarely.
Directions	From Exeter junc. 29, M5. A30 towards Honiton. At Daisymount exit to Ottery St Mary, B3180 off r'bout. 200 yds, then right to Allercombe. 1 mile until x-roads, then right. House 50 yds on right.

	Susie Holroyd
	Lower Allercombe Farm,
	Rockbeare, Exeter EX5 2HD
Tel	+44 (0)1404 822519
Mobile	+44 (0)7980 255107
Email	holroyd.s@gmail.com
Web	www.lowerallercombefarm.co.uk

Entry 130   Map 2

Devon

Beach House

Lapping at the riverside garden is the Exe estuary, wide and serene. Birds and boats, the soft hills beyond, a gorgeous Georgian house on the river and interesting hosts who have been here for years. The garden is pretty with quirky rooster-shaped topiary and old apple trees; you may have a locally sourced breakfast in the conservatory or in the dining room, and there are raspberries and blackberries in season. Relax on comfy chairs in bedrooms with antique white bedspreads, charmingly old-fashioned, sparkling bathrooms and estuary views. Cycle into Exeter, for culture and cathedral; the RSPB reserve is five minutes away.

Price	From £80. Singles £50.
Rooms	2: 1 twin, 1 double.
Meals	Pubs/restaurants 8-minute walk.
Closed	December-March.
Directions	M5 exit 30; signs to Exmouth. After approx. 2 miles right at pub. After 1 mile, immed. left after level crossing. At mini r'bout, left down The Strand. House last on left by beach.

Trevor & Jane Coleman
Beach House, 45 The Strand,
Topsham, Exeter EX3 0BB
Tel   +44 (0)1392 876456
Email   janecoleman45@hotmail.com

Entry 131   Map 2

Devon

Simcoe House

In a gracious seaside setting, this 18th-century villa was the summer home of General Simcoe – look up the history in the local museum. There are stunning views from wide windows in the big inviting sitting room, so find a book and settle by the fire. Bedrooms, sunny and lovely, have good art, fresh flowers and fabulous vistas; the newest is in the coach house, open-plan, restful and reached via an outside spiral stair. Enjoy the terrace with its subtropical palms and beautiful sea views. A charming home with wonderful owners, in strolling distance from beach and town. *Children over ten welcome.*

Price	From £80. Singles from £70.
Rooms	3: 1 double, 1 twin. Coach house: 1 double & sitting area.
Meals	Pubs/restaurants 5-minute walk.
Closed	Christmas.
Directions	M5 junc. 30 onto A376. Then B3179 to Budleigh Salterton (approx. 8 miles). Into town centre then left opposite The Creamery, onto Fore Street Hill. 150 yds on right and through white gates into car park. Steps lead to front door.

Jane & John Crosse
Simcoe House, 8 Fore Street Hill,
Budleigh Salterton EX9 6PE
Tel   +44 (0)1395 446013
Mobile   +44 (0)7747 633060
Email   simcoehouse@hotmail.co.uk
Web   www.simcoehouse.co.uk

Entry 132   Map 2

Devon

Pebbles

Once owned by the Duchess of Westminster, this neat 1920s house has spectacular views of sea, surf and seagulls. Gentle, friendly Humfrey and Rosemary have mixed old with new, fun art with recycled pieces. Bedrooms, with big comfy beds, face the sea; spotless bathrooms sport robes and good lotions. The Sail Loft has two plantation chairs and a sweet extra room with twin beds; two rooms have their own little conservatories. Breakfast is a spread: compotes, homemade muesli, good bacon. Stride the coast path, visit castles, spot dolphins from the conservatory, soak up those huge views. *Min. two nights weekends April-Sept.*

Price	From £99. Singles from £89.
Rooms	3: 1 twin/double; 2 twins/doubles each with separate bath.
Meals	Pubs/restaurants within 100 yds.
Closed	Rarely.
Directions	From Exeter A30 or M5 to junc. 30. A365 signed Exmouth. Left on B3179 signed Budleigh Salterton. Into town, thro' high street. House on right next to tourist information centre.

Humfrey & Rosemary Temple
Pebbles, 16 Fore Street,
Budleigh Salterton EX9 6NG

Tel	+44 (0)1395 442417
Email	stay@bedandbreakfastbythebeach.com
Web	www.bedandbreakfastbythebeach.com

Entry 133   Map 2

Devon

Glebe House

Set on a hillside with fabulous views over the Coly valley, this late-Georgian vicarage is now a heart-warming B&B. The views will entice you, the hosts will delight you and the house is filled with interesting things. Chuck and Emma spent many years at sea – he a Master Mariner, she a chef – and have filled these big light rooms with cushions, kilims and treasured family pieces. There's a sitting room for guests, a lovely conservatory with a vintage vine, peaceful bedrooms with blissful views and bathrooms that sparkle. All this, two sweet pygmy goats, wildlife beyond the ha-ha and the fabulous coast a hike away.

Price	From £70. Singles £45.
Rooms	3: 1 double, 1 twin/double, 1 family.
Meals	Dinner, 3 courses £25. Pubs/restaurants 2.5 miles.
Closed	Christmas & New Year.
Directions	A375 from Honiton; left opposite Hare & Hounds on B3174 to Seaton. 2nd left to Southleigh, 1.5 miles. In village 1st left to Northleigh; 600 yds, drive on left.

 10% off stays of 3 or more nights. Evening meal by arrangement.

Use your Sawday's Gift Card here.

Emma & Chuck Guest
Glebe House,
Southleigh, Colyton EX24 6SD

Tel	+44 (0)1404 871276
Mobile	+44 (0)7867 568569
Email	emma_guest@talktalk.net
Web	www.guestsatglebe.com

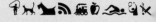

Entry 134   Map 2

Devon

West Colwell Farm

Devon lanes, pheasants, bluebell walks *and* sparkling B&B. The Hayes clearly love what they do; ex-TV producers, they have converted this 18th-century farmhouse and barns into a cosy, warm and stylish place to stay. Be charmed by original beams and pine doors, heritage colours and clean lines. Bedrooms feel self-contained, two have terraces overlooking the wooded valley and the most cosy is tucked under the roof. Linen is luxurious, showers are huge and breakfasts (Frank's pancakes, lovely bacon, eggs from next door) are totally flexible. A pretty garden in front, beaches nearby, peace all around. Bliss.

Price	From £80. Singles £60.
Rooms	3 doubles.
Meals	Restaurants 3 miles.
Closed	December/January.
Directions	3 miles from Honiton; Offwell signed off A35 Honiton-Axminster road. In centre of village, at church, down hill. Farm 0.5 miles on.

Frank & Carol Hayes
West Colwell Farm,
Offwell, Honiton EX14 9SL

Tel	+44 (0)1404 831130
Email	stay@westcolwell.co.uk
Web	www.westcolwell.co.uk

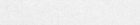

Entry 135   Map 2

Devon

Haye Farm

At the end of winding lanes bursting with spring flowers is a big stone farmhouse with sweeping views. Seven minutes from River Cottage HQ, this rare-breed farm is run by the warm, humorous Rumsbys whose passion for good husbandry is infectious; slow-grown beef and pork is their speciality. Find inside a chic, fabulous, eclectic décor: polished flagstone floors, vibrant textiles, country pine, French antiques, and a huge bed to dive into… your pink polka-dot mini fridge in the hall says it all! Chickens dot the yard, songbirds chirrup, buzzards soar and the breakfasts are generous and delicious.

Ethical Collection: Food. See page 420.

Price	From £85 pn.
Rooms	1 double with separate bath/shower.
Meals	Pub 3 miles.
Closed	Rarely.
Directions	Sent on booking.

 Free pick-up from local bus/train station. 10% off stays of 2 or more nights Mon-Thurs.

Susan Rumsby
Haye Farm,
Musbury, Axminster EX13 8ST

Tel	+44 (0)1297 551504
Email	susanrumsby@aol.com
Web	www.hectorshousecottage.co.uk

Entry 136   Map 2

Devon

Applebarn Cottage

A tree-lined drive leads to a long white wall, and a gate opening to an explosion of colour – the garden. Come for a deliciously restful place and the nicest, most easy-going hosts; the wisteria-covered 17th-century cottage is full of books, paintings and fresh flowers. Bedrooms – one in an extension that blends in beautifully – are large, traditional, wonderfully comfortable, and the views down the valley are sublime. Patricia trained as a chef and dinners at Applebarn are delicious and great fun. Breakfast, served in a lovely oak-floored dining room, includes a neighbour's homemade honey. *Minimum stay two nights.*

Price	£76–£80. Half-board option (dinner) £60–£63 p.p.
Rooms	2 suites.
Meals	Pub/restaurant 3 miles.
Closed	November to mid-March.
Directions	A30 Chard to Honiton. Left at top of hill, Wambrook & Stockland. Straight on at next x-roads (Membury); 0.75 miles, left, Cotley & Ridge. Past Hartshill Boarding Kennels; signed 2nd right.

Bottle of wine with dinner for stays of 3 or more nights. 5% off 2nd and subsequent stays.

Patricia & Robert Spencer
Applebarn Cottage,
Bewley Down, Axminster EX13 7JX
Tel +44 (0)1460 220873
Email paspenceruk@yahoo.co.uk
Web www.applebarn.wordpress.com

Entry 137   Map 2

Devon

Redyeates Farm

Alastair and Carol run this 17th-century, pretty farmhouse from a blissful spot where the night sky still twinkles and chickens roam free. Chill out in a sitting room with smart chesterfields, claret walls, a wood-burner for winter nights; retire to lovely, light, elegant bedrooms with big beds, sparkling bathrooms, beautiful linen. There's an orchard, a tennis court, sweeping lawns and a terrace with stunning views onto fields and distant villages. Best of all is the food and wine, served at one long friendly table, lovingly sourced and utterly delicious, from the smoked trout tian to the breakfast sausages. *Over eights welcome.*

Price	£85–£135. Singles by arrangement.
Rooms	5: 1 double, 1 twin. Old Dairy: 3 doubles.
Meals	Dinner £35 (Wed-Sat only). Occasional lunch. Pub 1 mile.
Closed	Mondays & rarely.
Directions	From Cadeleigh, 1.5 miles to Postbox Cross, turn left to Cheriton Fitzpaine. Follow road to Redyeates x-roads, then right; house is 150 yards on left down track.

10% off stays of 2 or more nights, Tues-Thurs. Bottle of house wine with dinner on Wed & Thurs.

Alastair & Carol Peebles
Redyeates Farm,
Cheriton Fitzpaine, Crediton EX17 4HG
Tel +44 (0)1363 866742
Email alastair@redyeatesfarm.co.uk
Web www.redyeatesfarm.co.uk

Entry 138   Map 2

Devon

Raymont House

Delightful to be in the heart of a historic little town with a Tuesday market and good pubs yet close to the wilds of Dartmoor. This is civilised B&B: your charming hosts give you one bedroom (or, if you're a party, three), peaceful, pretty and serene, and a wow of a bathroom that mixes period features with beautiful modern fittings. No guest sitting room but TVs, homemade biscuits, delicious breakfasts, dressing gowns and fresh flowers... The breakfast room is warmed by a wood-burner, there's a drying room for wet gear, you're on the Tarka Trail and near to RHS Rosemoor. Great value.

Devon

Leworthy Barton

Biscuits, scones, sweet vases of hedgerow flowers. Breakfasts are left for you to cook and come courtesy of Rupert's Tamworth pigs and happy hens; bread and jams are homemade, wellies and waxed jackets are on tap. Rupert is a busy farmer and designer who chooses to give guests what he would most like himself. So... you have the whole of the stables, tranquil, beautifully restored and with field and sky views. Downstairs is open-plan, with kitchen and log-burner; up are sloping ceilings, wooden floors, big bed, soft towels. It's cosy yet spacious, stylish yet homely, and the Atlantic coast is the shortest drive.

Ethical Collection: Food. See page 420.

Price	From £75. Singles £45-£55.	Price	£80. Singles £60.
Rooms	3: 2 doubles, 1 single all sharing bath (let to same party only).	Rooms	Barn: 1 double, sitting room & kitchen.
Meals	Pub/restaurant 50 yds.	Meals	Pub 3 miles.
Closed	Christmas & New Year.	Closed	Rarely.
Directions	From Okehampton, signs to Hatherleigh for 6 miles. At round-about, right thro' Hatherleigh to top of Market Street. House on left.	Directions	A39 to Woolfardisworthy. At T-junc. in village, left. 0.5 miles left to Stibb Cross. Over bridge bear right, then left. Uphill, right towards Leworthy & Mill; 0.5 miles; on left.

 Use your Sawday's Gift Card here.

	Jan & Alan Toogood		Rupert Ashmore
	Raymont House, 49 Market Street,		Leworthy Barton,
	Hatherleigh, Okehampton EX20 3JP		Woolsery, Bideford EX39 5PY
Tel	+44 (0)1837 810850	Tel	+44 (0)1237 431140
Email	info@raymonthouse.co.uk		
Web	www.raymonthouse.co.uk		

Entry 139 Map 2

Entry 140 Map 2

Devon

Beara Farmhouse

The moment you arrive at the whitewashed farmhouse you feel the affection your hosts have for the place. Richard is a lover of wood and a fine craftsman – every room echoes his talent; he also created the pond that's home to mallards and geese. Ann has laid brick paths, stencilled, stitched and painted, all with an eye for colour; bedrooms and guest sitting room are delectable and snug. Open farmland all around, sheep, pigs and hens in the yard, the Tarka Trail on your doorstep and hosts happy to give you 6.30am breakfast should you plan a day on Lundy Island. Readers love this place. *Minimum stay two nights June-September.*

Price	£70. Singles by arrangement.
Rooms	2: 1 double, 1 twin.
Meals	Pub 1.5 miles.
Closed	20 December-5 January.
Directions	From A39, left into Bideford, round quay, past old bridge on left. Signs to Torrington; 1.5 miles, right for Buckland Brewer; 2.5 miles, left; 0.5 miles, right over cattle grid & down track.

Ann & Richard Dorsett
Beara Farmhouse,
Buckland Brewer, Bideford EX39 5EH
Tel +44 (0)1237 451666
Web www.bearafarmhouse.co.uk

Entry 141   Map 2

Devon

Lower Hummacott

Charming decorative touches, antique furniture, fresh fruit and handmade chocolates: you'll find thoughtful extras in the bedrooms (one with a gorgeous king-size bed) and in the guest sitting rooms. Plus delicious organic and traditionally reared meat, vegetables and eggs, fresh fish, homemade cakes... As if that were not enough, the Georgian farmhouse has formal landscaped gardens in seven acres of grounds with woodland, streams, ponds, wildlife and orchard hens. Liz, a weaver, and Tony, a professional artist (there's a gallery by the house) are charming and friendly and look after you brilliantly. Great value.

Price	£68.
Rooms	2 doubles & sitting rooms.
Meals	Dinner £27 (Sunday only). Pub/restaurant 1.5 miles.
Closed	Rarely.
Directions	0.5 miles east of Kings Nympton village is Beara Cross; go straight over marked to Romansleigh for 0.75 miles; Hummacott is 1st entrance on left; down drive & 1st house on right.

Tony & Liz Williams
Lower Hummacott,
Kings Nympton, Umberleigh EX37 9TU
Tel +44 (0)1769 581177
Email tony@tonywilliamsart.co.uk
Web www.tonywilliamsart.co.uk

Entry 142   Map 2

Devon

Hillbrow House

This lovely 'house on the hill' has a deep veranda and glorious views over the Taw valley, Exmoor (and, on a clear day, to distant Dartmoor). The light, uncluttered rooms are neat as a pin with coordinated colours, thick fabrics, antiques and your own upstairs studio sitting room; bedrooms have feather pillows, proper blankets and luxurious bathrooms. Golfers and walkers will be in paradise, Highbullen Golf Club is a short walk, surfers can reach Croyde easily and many gentler beaches lie in the other direction. RHS Rosemoor is also within striking distance; stoke up on Clarissa's delicious homemade granola for breakfast.

Price	From £85. Singles £45.
Rooms	2: 1 double; 1 double with separate bath.
Meals	Dinner, 3 courses, £25. Pubs/restaurants within walking distance.
Closed	Christmas.
Directions	Take B3226 from South Molton for 5 miles. Turn right for Chittlehamholt, left at T-junc., then through village. House is last on right.

10% off stays Mon-Thurs. Free pick-up from local bus/train station. Bottle of wine with dinner on first night.

Clarissa Roe
Hillbrow House,
Chittlehamholt, Umberleigh EX37 9NS

Tel	+44 (0)1769 540214
Mobile	+44 (0)7774 784601
Email	clarissaroe@btinternet.com
Web	www.hillbrowhouse.com

Entry 143   Map 2

Devon

Catsheys

Folded into the Devon hills, this open 30-year-old house is full of light and surprises. Lovely likeable David and Rosie are designers and their home is a hymn to contemporary texture and colour. Bedrooms are superb – a French sleigh bed here, a chic 60s armchair there, new art, crisp linen, ethnic treasures. Bathrooms are pure delight. Surrounded by bluebell woods and badgers, the garden has flowers for your room and a solar-heated pool for summer swims. After breakfast of homemade granola and fresh-laid eggs, surf the north Devon coast, ramble the two moors, walk the Tarka Trail. Special. *Over 12s welcome. Min. two nights bank hols.*

Price	From £95. Singles from £60.
Rooms	2: 1 twin/double, 1 double.
Meals	Pubs within 3 miles.
Closed	Rarely.
Directions	From South Molton, B3137 for 4.5 miles; right at Odam Cross to Romansleigh; next left at Buckham Cross signed 'No Through Road'; steep hill, over ford, 2nd right, house on left at top of hill.

10% off room rate Mon-Thurs.

Rosie & David Ames
Catsheys, Romansleigh,
South Molton EX36 4JW

Tel	+44 (0)1769 550580
Email	rooms@catsheys.co.uk
Web	www.catsheys.co.uk

Entry 144   Map 2

Devon

Sannacott

On the southern fringes of Exmoor you're in peaceful rolling hills and hidden valleys. The Trickeys produce point-to-point and national hunt horses from their Georgian style farmhouse; find roaring log fires, antiques, pretty fabrics and a friendly relaxed feel. Bedrooms are traditional and comfortable, some have lovely views over the garden and countryside. Generous breakfasts include homemade bread and jams and organic or local goodies. There's a pretty bird-filled garden to wander, walkers can enjoy the North Devon coastal path nearby, birdwatchers and riders will be happy and there are well-known gardens to visit too.

Price	From £80. Singles £45.
Rooms	3: 1 double, 1 twin/double sharing bath/shower (let to same party only). Annexe: 1 twin & kitchenette.
Meals	Occasional dinner, 3 courses, £25. Pub 2.5 miles.
Closed	Rarely.
Directions	M5 junc. 27; A361 Barnstaple, past Tiverton, 15.5 miles; right next r'bout (Whitechapel). 1.5 miles to junc., right Twitchen & N. Molton; 1.5 miles to 3rd on left, black gates.

10% off stays of 2 or more nights. Local food/produce in your room.

Clare Trickey
Sannacott,
North Molton EX36 3JS
Tel +44 (0)1598 740203
Email mctrickey@hotmail.com
Web www.sannacott.co.uk

Entry 145   Map 2

Devon

Bratton Mill

Absolute privacy down the long lane to a thickly wooded and beautifully secluded valley: watch for dragonflies, red deer, buzzards and the flash of the kingfisher. Breakfast, locally sourced and superb, may be served in summer by the Exmoor trout stream – to deafening birdsong! To the backdrop of the rushing stream is the house, filled with treasure – including Marilyn, who spoils you with elegant china, flowers, embroidered bed linen and a decanter of port. Or choose independence in a prettily furnished folly in the garden, opening onto a terrace and just a hop from the water. Strolls and hikes from the door – wonderful.

Price	£95–£125. Singles £60.
Rooms	2: 1 double. Extra single available. Folly: 1 double and kitchen.
Meals	Pub within walking distance.
Closed	Rarely.
Directions	From Bratton Fleming High Street turn right into Mill Lane. Down road for 0.5 miles through railway cutting; turn right.

Free pick-up from local bus/train station.

Use your Sawday's Gift Card here.

Marilyn Jacobs Holloway
Bratton Mill, Bratton Fleming,
Barnstaple EX31 4RU
Tel +44 (0)1598 710026
Email contact@brattonmill.co.uk
Web www.brattonmill.co.uk

Entry 146   Map 2

Devon

Beachborough Country House

A gracious 18th-century rectory with stone-flagged floors, lofty windows, wooden shutters, charming gardens. Viviane is vivacious and spoils you with dinners and breakfasts straight from the Aga; dine in the kitchen or in the elegant dining room with twinkling fire. Hens cluck, horses whinny but otherwise the peace is deep. Ease any walker's pains away in a steaming roll top tub; big airy bedrooms are fresh as a daisy with Turkish rugs and great views – admire them from the window seats. There's a games room for kids in the outbuildings and Combe Martin is a short hop for a grand beach day. Huge fun. *Dogs £5 per stay.*

Ethical Collection: Food; Community. See page 420.

Price	From £75. Singles £50.
Rooms	3: 1 twin/double, 2 doubles.
Meals	Dinner, 2-3 courses, from £19. Pub 3 miles.
Closed	Rarely.
Directions	From A361 take A399 for 12 miles. At Blackmoor Gate, left onto A39. House 1.5 miles on right.

 Waived charge for dogs, or decanter of port.

 Use your Sawday's Gift Card here.

Viviane Clout
Beachborough Country House,
Kentisbury, Barnstaple EX31 4NH
Tel   +44 (0)1271 882487
Mobile   +44 (0)7732 947755
Email   viviane@beachborough.freeserve.co.uk
Web   www.beachboroughcountryhouse.co.uk

Entry 147   Map 2

Devon

North Walk House

Sea views, brass bedsteads and big rooms at this calm retreat, perfectly positioned on a clifftop path – super for walkers and foodies. Ian and Sarah welcome you with homemade cake in a cosy guest lounge, and give you light bedrooms with sparkling bathrooms and seductive beds. Enjoy the coastal and Exmoor walks, or genteel Lynton and Lynmouth; return to log fire and armchairs. Take your tea on a sea-view terrace, or be tempted by Sarah's four-course supper, seasonal and mostly organic. Everything here is thoughtful, from the welcome to the décor and the refreshments: arrive, unpack, unwind…

Ethical Collection: Food. See page 420.

Price	£80-£150. Singles £50-£100.
Rooms	5: 4 doubles, 1 twin.
Meals	Dinner, 4 courses, from £24. Pub/restaurant 0.25 miles.
Closed	Rarely.
Directions	A39 from Barnstaple to Lynton Town Hall. From there, left turn at the church down North Walk. Third hotel on left.

Bottle of wine with dinner on first night.

Ian & Sarah Downing
North Walk House,
North Walk, Lynton EX35 6HJ
Tel   +44 (0)1598 753372
Email   walk@northwalkhouse.co.uk
Web   www.northwalkhouse.co.uk

Entry 148   Map 2

Devon

Southcliffe Hall

An Argentinian chandelier, antique French radiators, a rediscovered Victorian garden; this is a grandly idiosyncratic house with inherited eccentric touches. Overlooking the sea and originally the Manor House, each floor resounds with history. Charming Kate and Barry will give you dinner in the panelled dining room, and local produce for a delicious breakfast. Bedrooms are vast with rich carpets, big beds, antique flourishes; bathrooms are unique – roll top baths to Victorian high-level cisterns. Spot deer in the woodland, walk to rock pools, hike to great beaches; the view of the bay is fabulous.

Ethical Collection: Food. See page 420.

Price	£100. Singles by arrangement.
Rooms	2 twins/doubles.
Meals	Dinner, 3 courses, £30. Pub 5-minute walk.
Closed	Rarely.
Directions	From A361, B3343 towards Woolacombe. Turn right, through Lincombe, into Lee. Long drive to house is on left, between village hall and red telephone box.

 Bottle of wine with dinner on first night.

Kate Seekings & Barry Jenkinson
Southcliffe Hall,
Lee EX34 8LW
Tel   +44 (0)1271 867068
Mobile   +44 (0)7910 473725
Email   stay@southcliffehall.co.uk
Web   www.southcliffehall.co.uk

Entry 149   Map 2

Devon

St Vincent House

Everything here is wonderful. Outside, an old wisteria fans out across the house, which was built by Captain Green with monies 'gained' at the battle of Cape St Vincent. Inside, stripped floors, smart rugs, gilt mirrors and polished brass are the order of the day. A fire smoulders in the sitting room, light pours into the breakfast room and delightful bedrooms offer comfy beds, warm colours, super little bathrooms. You're in the middle of town, but lush plants screen you from it. Jean-Paul is Belgian, as are his waffles, served at breakfast alongside free-range eggs and dry-cured bacon. He and Lin are stars, the place is a gem.

Price	£75–£80.
Rooms	4: 3 doubles, 1 twin.
Meals	Pubs/restaurants within walking distance.
Closed	November–Easter.
Directions	In Lynton, ignore 1st sign to left; follow signs for car parks. Up hill, see car park on left, thatched house on right; on left after car park, next to Exmoor Museum.

Jean-Paul Salpetier & Lin Cameron
St Vincent House, Market Street,
Castle Hill, Lynton EX35 6JA
Tel   +44 (0)1598 752244
Email   welcome@st-vincent-hotel.co.uk
Web   www.st-vincent-hotel.co.uk

Entry 150   Map 2

Devon

Victoria House

Beachcombers, surfers and walkers will be in their element in this Edwardian seaside villa where each bedroom has a magnificent view. Choose between the two in the main house (with sofas) and the beach-hut annexe with a big romantic deck facing the sea. Heather is lively and fun, she and David are ex-RAF and go out of their way to give you the best; bathrooms are state of the art, breakfasts are a tour de force – fruits, yogurts, waffles, eggs benedict or the full Monty. No garden but you are on the coastal road to Woolacombe (of surf and kite surfing fame) and the beach is a ten-minute walk. A top spot.

Ethical Collection: Food. See page 420.

Price	£90–£140.
Rooms	3: 1 double, 1 twin/double. Annexe: 1 double.
Meals	Pubs/restaurants 200 yds.
Closed	Rarely.
Directions	From B3343, right for Mortehoe. Through village & past the old chapel. Down steep hill, with the bay ahead; house 3rd on left.

 Late checkout (12pm).

	Heather & David Burke
	Victoria House, Chapel Hill, Mortehoe, Woolacombe EX34 7DZ
Tel	+44 (0)1271 871302
Email	heatherburke59@fsmail.net
Web	www.victoriahousebandb.co.uk

Entry 151   Map 2

Dorset

Crosskeys House

In previous lives a pub, a cobbler's shop and a smithy, this listed stone house, right on the village crossroads, is well settled into its B&B role. Robin and Liz offer you a fabulous breakfast menu and happily advise you on the glories of west Dorset (walks, pubs, stately homes): nothing is too much trouble. Their sitting room is softly traditional – plump sofas, family portraits and antiques, garden flowers, glossy magazines – while lovely cosy bedrooms have king-size beds and interesting books. The house is near the road but there's a courtyard garden for breakfast and water fresh from the well.

Price	From £90. Singles from £70.
Rooms	3: 1 double, 2 twins/doubles.
Meals	Pub 200 yds.
Closed	Rarely.
Directions	A35 to Bridport then A3066 to Beaminster. B3163 to Broadwindsor. House is at end of one-way system, the last on the right (just before crossroads).

5 nights for the price of 4 Mon–Thurs.

	Robin & Liz Adeney
	Crosskeys House, High Street, Broadwindsor, Beaminster DT8 3QP
Tel	+44 (0)1308 868063
Email	robin.adeney@care4free.net
Web	www.crosskeyshouse.com

Entry 152   Map 3

Dorset

Pear Tree Farm

Just four miles from bustling Bridport, this traditional pretty Dorset farmhouse is reached down secret narrow lanes and surrounded by deep valleys. A keen traveller and garden designer, Emma has created a vibrant home brimming with interesting art, good antique furniture, rugs, comfy old armchairs and books galore: there is an extraordinary collection of glass walking sticks. The garden is a delight and blissful views from flowery bedrooms will charm you. Wake to a breakfast of local bacon and home-laid eggs in the sunny kitchen. Close to River Cottage, Bridport Literary Festival and the coast; a walker's paradise.

Price	£75. Singles £50.
Rooms	2: 1 twin/double; 1 twin sharing bath (2nd room let to same party only).
Meals	Pubs/restaurants within 4 miles.
Closed	Christmas & Easter.
Directions	Bridport A3066 towards Beaminster. At Melplash right towards Loscombe; 0.25 miles right to Loscombe. 1 mile to bottom of hill; left at T-junc. House 2nd on left.

10% off room rate Mon-Thurs. Bottle of wine in the sitting room.

Emma Poë
Pear Tree Farm,
Loscombe, Bridport DT6 3TL
Tel   +44 (0)1308 488223
Email   poe@gotadsl.co.uk
Web   www.peartreefarmbedandbreakfast.co.uk

Entry 153   Map 3

Dorset

No 27

In Bridport – all seafood restaurants, market stalls and pretty façades – is a rambling 1780 artisan's house with steep stairs and an irresistible charm. Juliet has opened up walls then painted them chalky hues, revealed flagstones, laid floorboards and added kelims… and books, paintings, antiques and flowers. An orchard with hens at the end of the garden, a spacious drawing room, airy bedrooms – one with views to the hills – and bathrooms modern and elegant. All is uncluttered and calm. Juliet's passions are cooking, gardening and wild water swimming – you'll love her! *Ask about parking.*

Price	£85–£110.
Rooms	2: 1 double; 1 double with separate bath.
Meals	Supper from £15. Pubs/restaurants in town.
Closed	Rarely.
Directions	At Bridport r'bout on to A3066. Then 2nd left into St Andrews Road and forward into Barrack Street. No 27 is the tall house with a brick façade on right.

Juliet Lewis
No 27,
27 Barrack Street, Bridport DT6 3LX
Tel   +44 (0)1308 426378
Email   julietalewis@gmail.com
Web   www.no27.co

Entry 154   Map 3

Dorset

Knowle Farm

Find a classic Dorset Long House, fragrant with wisteria in May, and hosts with a passion for rare and special plants. Alison and John's garden is a peaceful place of gentle colours and careful structure; it's open for the National Gardens Scheme but all are welcome to stroll around the old cider orchard, rose walk, wildlife garden and greenhouse. Bedrooms are pretty in pinks and lilacs, one in a converted barn with private entrance; bathrooms are swish. Stroll past thatched cottages to the pub for a meal, wake to an Aga-cooked breakfast, browse gardening books, lounge in a lofty sitting room, savour the loveliness of it all. *Minimum stay two nights.*

Price	£80–£90. Singles £60.
Rooms	2: 1 double; 1 twin with separate bath.
Meals	Pub 200 yds.
Closed	December to mid-February.
Directions	Leave A35 two miles east of Bridport, following signs to Uploders. Left at Crown Inn, in village. House on right opposite white chapel.

	Alison & John Halliday
	Knowle Farm,
	Uploders, Bridport DT6 4NS
Tel	+44 (0)1308 485492
Email	info@knowlefarmbandb.com
Web	www.knowlefarmbandb.com

Entry 155   Map 3

Dorset

Orchard Barn

Immerse yourself in the Jurassic coast – a World Heritage Site with huge cliffs, fabulous seascapes and secret villages hiding in green folds. This is 'River Cottage' country and you will eat like kings – from the dazzling breakfast menu (try Jersey cream on your porridge) to delicious light suppers, all as local and organic as possible. Inside your own barn-like sitting room a fire burns brightly all day, bedrooms are nurturing and fresh, bathrooms awash with perfumed oils and fluffy towels. Nigel and Margaret are old hands at making everything very relaxing indeed. Sit on the terrace in summer and admire the lovely garden.

Price	£105–£139. Singles from £85.
Rooms	2 twins/doubles.
Meals	Light supper £7.50–£20.00. Pubs/restaurants within 1 mile.
Closed	Rarely.
Directions	From Dorchester on A35 east of Bridport within 30mph limit, right into Lee Lane (with 6' 6" width restriction). Over bridge, round bend & into Dead End Lane. On right.

	10% off stays of 3 or more nights Sun–Thurs.
	Use your Sawday's Gift Card here.

	Nigel & Margaret Corbett
	Orchard Barn,
	Bradpole, Bridport DT6 4AR
Tel	+44 (0)1308 455655
Email	corbett@lodgeatorchardbarn.co.uk
Web	www.lodgeatorchardbarn.co.uk

Entry 156   Map 3

Dorset

Wooden Cabbage House

Leafy lanes and a private drive lead you to Martyn and Susie's beautifully restored keeper's cottage, hidden deep in rolling West Dorset countryside. Leave the hubbub behind, savour the valley views, relax in this spacious stylish home, filled with fresh flowers, fine antiques and paintings, and country-house charm in cosy bedrooms. Enjoy delicious meals in the verdant garden room, or by the Aga in winter – homegrown fruits and vegetables, local eggs and sausages; relax on comfy sofas by the log fire. The Lees are fabulous hosts – nothing is too much trouble. Great local walks and the Jurassic coast is half-an-hour away.

Price	From £95. Singles from £70.
Rooms	3: 2 doubles, 1 twin.
Meals	Dinner, 3 courses with wine, £35. Supper, 2 courses with wine, £25. Pub/restaurants 3 miles.
Closed	Rarely.
Directions	3 miles S of Yeovil on A37, turn west to Closworth. Continue on this road, past turn to Halstock; 200 yds on right, over cattle grid. House down drive on left.

A jar of Susie's homemade marmalade or jam.

Martyn & Susie Lee
Wooden Cabbage House,
East Chelborough, Dorchester DT2 0QA
Tel +44 (0)1935 83362
Mobile +44 (0)7805 378583
Email relax@woodencabbage.co.uk
Web www.woodencabbage.co.uk

Entry 157 Map 3

Dorset

Holyleas House

This is a fabulous house, comfortable and easy; Tia and her two friendly dogs are genuinely welcoming. You breakfast by a log fire in the elegant dining room in winter: free-range eggs, bacon and sausages from the farmers' market, homemade jams and marmalade. Sleep in light, softly-coloured bedrooms with lovely views across the well-tended gardens, and spotless bathrooms. Walkers and explorers will be happy: return to a roaring fire and a good book in the drawing room. It's a short hop to the pub for supper and Tia is happy to babysit too. *Minimum stay two nights in high season & at weekends.*

Price	£80–£90. Singles £40.
Rooms	3: 1 double, 1 family room; 1 single with separate bath.
Meals	Pub a short walk.
Closed	Christmas & New Year.
Directions	From Dorchester, B3143 into Buckland Newton over x-roads; Holyleas on right opp. village cricket pitch.

Bottle of wine in your room.

Use your Sawday's Gift Card here.

Tia Bunkall
Holyleas House,
Buckland Newton, Dorchester DT2 7DP
Tel +44 (0)1300 345214
Mobile +44 (0)7968 341887
Email tiabunkall@holyleas.fsnet.co.uk
Web www.holyleashouse.co.uk

Entry 158 Map 3

Dorset

Fullers Earth

Such an English feel: the village with pub, post office and stores, the rose-filled walled garden with fruit trees beyond, the tranquil church view. This listed house – its late-Georgian frontage added in 1820 – is a treat: flowers and white linen, a lovely sitting room where you settle with tea and cake by the fire, roomy bedrooms with comfortable beds, books and views. At breakfast enjoy perfect compotes and jams from the garden, Fullers Earth muesli and local produce. Friendly Ian and Wendy will plan great walks with you in this AONB, the Jurassic coast is 20 minutes away and you walk to the pub through the garden.

Price	£85–£90. Singles from £60.
Rooms	2 doubles.
Meals	Pub 500 yds.
Closed	Christmas.
Directions	From A37 take Cattistock turning downhill to T-junc. Left through village. Pub on left. After 90 degree right-hand bend, 5th house on right.

5% off stays of 3 or more nights Mon-Thurs.

Wendy Gregory
Fullers Earth,
Cattistock, Dorchester DT2 0JL
Tel +44 (0)1300 320190
Mobile +44 (0)7792 654543
Email stay@fullersearth.co.uk
Web www.fullersearth.co.uk

Entry 159   Map 3

Dorset

Manor Farm

You are high up on the chalk hills that fall to the Jurassic Coast. Tessa's family have lived in the flint and stone house since 1860 and it is crammed with history: solid antiques, books galore, pictures, maps and photographs. From all the windows views soar to sheep-dotted hills. You share the family sitting room in soft pinks and greens, and have an Aga-cooked breakfast or supper in the handsome dining room, or the garden in summer; cooking is one of Tessa's passions. Bedrooms are without frills but clean and comfortable; the bathroom is large and sparkling. Outdoor heaven is yours; find a pet pig called Pork!

Price	From £65.
Rooms	2: 1 double, 1 twin sharing bath (let to same party only).
Meals	Dinner, 2-3 courses, from £15. Pub/restaurant 4 miles.
Closed	Rarely.
Directions	A35 direction: down hill, stone wall and gate on right. A37 direction: down hill, 3rd turning on left. Satnav does not always work.

10% off stays of 2 or more nights.

Tessa Russell
Manor Farm,
Compton Valence, Dorchester DT2 9ES
Tel +44 (0)1308 482227
Mobile +44 (0)7818 037184 (signal unreliable)
Email tessa.nrussell@btinternet.com
Web www.manor-farm.uk.com

Entry 160   Map 3

Dorset

Whitfield Farm Cottage

Jackie and David make light of the practicalities of B&B; they and their pretty thatched 18th-century cottage have much character and charm. Breakfast in the large, stone-tiled, beamed kitchen, or in the walled courtyard in summer. The twin with garden access and its own shower is immaculate in its fresh white and blue checks; the sitting room is cosy with comfy sofas and coral-checked cushions, inglenook fireplace and window seats. Minutes from the main road but with a rural feel; the Frome – beloved by local fishermen – is 150 yards away and you can fish here for £35 a day. *Minimum stay two nights at weekends.*

Price	£80–£85. Singles £50.
Rooms	1 twin/double. Extra room available.
Meals	Pubs/restaurants 1.25 miles.
Closed	Christmas & Easter.
Directions	From r'bout at top of Dorchester, west on B3150 for 100 yds. Right onto Poundbury Rd (before museum); 1 mile; over another road; 2nd track on right by house sign. Cottage set back from road.

Bottle of wine in your room. Free pick-up from local bus/train station.

Jackie & David Charles
Whitfield Farm Cottage,
Poundbury Road, Dorchester DT2 9SL
Tel +44 (0)1305 260233
Email dcharles@gotadsl.co.uk
Web www.whitfieldfarmcottage.co.uk

Entry 161   Map 3

Dorset

The White Cottage

Strolling distance from lovely old Athelhampton House and its gardens is this thatched cottage where Lindsay and Mark are slowly becoming self-sufficient. You will be well fed: home-grown vegetables, bacon from the pigs, eggs from Clarissa the chicken. It's a lively young-family household with gorgeous bedrooms, super linen, fresh flowers, plump pillows, chocolates; generous bathrooms have thick towels and eco-friendly lotions. The suite has its own entrance and a big comfortable sitting room. Help feed the animals and enjoy the river Piddle running through the garden – fish for brown trout but please put them back!

Price	£70–£120. Singles from £50.
Rooms	3: 1 double, 1 suite for 2-4 (with sofabed); 1 twin with separate bath.
Meals	Pubs 1 mile.
Closed	Rarely.
Directions	A35 exit Puddletown & Athelhampton; signs for Athelhampton House. Left at lights in Puddletown; house 200 yds on right, after Athelhampton House.

Lindsay & Mark Piper
The White Cottage,
Athelhampton, Dorchester DT2 7LG
Tel +44 (0)1305 848622
Mobile +44 (0)7788 166322
Email bookings@white-cottage-bandb.co.uk
Web www.white-cottage-bandb.co.uk

Entry 162   Map 3

Dorset

Yoah Cottage

Rosemary makes delicate, sometimes humorous, pieces, Furse creates bold works in clay; their thatched, cob-walled, rambling house is a jaw-dropping gallery of modern art, ceramics, tapestries. The cottage garden's colours complete the vibrant picture. A private guest wing holds a country-pretty double and a twin under the eaves, sharing a bathroom (with friends or family). Breakfast is next to the couple's studio; Rosemary will also whip up a Swedish-style supper on a tray if you can't bear to budge from the sitting room fire. Such enthusiastic, artistic owners — and you're deep in Hardy country. *Minimum stay two nights.*

Price	£65–£85. Singles £40–£50.
Rooms	2: 1 double, 1 twin sharing bath (let to same party only).
Meals	Supper on a tray £15. Pub next door.
Closed	Christmas & Easter.
Directions	A352 out of Dorchester towards Wareham. Thro' Whitcombe, then next turning left to West Knighton. Left again, to New Inn. House next to pub.

	Furse & Rosemary Swann
	Yoah Cottage,
	West Knighton, Dorchester DT2 8PE
Tel	+44 (0)1305 852087
Email	roseswann@tiscali.co.uk
Web	www.yoahcottage.co.uk

Entry 163 Map 3

Dorset

Marren

On the Dorset coastal path, with spectacular views of Portland, a blissfully tranquil and bird-rich spot. The owners have transformed their 1920s house, set in six acres of terraced and wooded garden, and their style reflects their penchant for natural materials, Slow Food and the country life. Bedrooms are pretty and comfortable: one has its own door onto the garden, and you can marvel at the sun setting over the sea from the other. Enjoy superb spreads of farm produce and homemade bread in the breakfast room, then head off for cliff-top hikes. Leave the low-slung Morgan at home: the track here is adventurously steep!

Price	£90–£110.
Rooms	2 doubles.
Meals	Pub 1 mile.
Closed	Rarely.
Directions	On A353 after Poxwell, left at Ringstead sign; up hill (not to Ringstead), over cattle grid into NT car park; cross & drive through gate 'No Cars'; 2 more gates; 100 yds after 3rd gate, sharp right down steep track.

	Peter Cartwright
	Marren,
	Holworth, Dorchester DT2 8NJ
Tel	+44 (0)1305 851503
Mobile	+44 (0)7957 886399
Email	marren@lineone.net
Web	www.marren.info

Entry 164 Map 3

Dorset

Waddon House

Don't be daunted when this magnificent Dorset manor house swings into view: it's grand yet gracious and Suzie is lovely. The house breathes 500 years of history and at every turn you'll discover a fine artefact or period feature, from white hounds at the courtyard entrance to silver tureens in a handsome oak dining room. Bedrooms are in the east wing, one a vision of fine yellow silk and antique pieces, the other a raftered art deco dream with stained glass windows and furniture from the Queen Mary. Formal gardens envelop the house, a maze of balustrades, finials, statues and steps, with stunning views to the Jurassic coast. Unique.

Price	£110–£150. Singles £90–£100.
Rooms	2: 1 twin/double; 1 four-poster with separate bath.
Meals	Dinner, 3 courses, £25. Pub/restaurant 2 miles.
Closed	Occasionally.
Directions	A30 from Dorchester; at Winterbourne Abbas take left towards Portesham. In Portesham take the left turning to Upwey. House 1 mile on left.

	Suzie Chaffyn-Grove
	Waddon House, Waddon,
	Portesham, Weymouth DT3 4ER
Tel	+44 (0)1305 871241
Mobile	+44 (0)7966 436420
Email	suzie@waddonhouse.co.uk
Web	www.waddonhouse.co.uk

Entry 165   Map 3

Dorset

Honeycombe Cottage

As dreamy as its name, the 16th-century cottage in the village, with deep walls, open fireplaces and flagged floors houses one dog, one cat and gentle, generous Heather. Now her children have flown the nest, she gives you a garden that blooms as wonderfully as the house and, up under the eaves, soft curtains, soothing colours, aromatic oils and delicious beds. Have breakfast (pancakes with maple syrup, bacon from up the road) in the homely kitchen, or outside on fine days, where lawns and borders drift effortlessly into orchard, fields and hills. An all-year-round delight. *Children over five welcome.*

Price	From £75.
Rooms	2: 1 twin/double; 1 twin/double with separate bath.
Meals	Pubs/restaurant 0.33 miles.
Closed	Rarely.
Directions	From A31 to Bere Regis on West Street. At end of village, left down 'No Through Road', over bridge. Thatched wall on left, cottage at end.

	Heather Loxton
	Honeycombe Cottage,
	Shitterton, Bere Regis BH20 7HU
Tel	+44 (0)1929 471660
Mobile	+44 (0)7717 783839
Email	info@honeycombecottage.com
Web	www.honeycombecottage.com

Entry 166   Map 3

Dorset

Lower Lynch House

On the glorious Isle of Purbeck, between the old stone village of Corfe Castle and Kingston atop a hill, this wisteria-strewn house sits at the end of a long woodland track. Aga-cooked breakfast is served at tables overlooking courtyard and garden; cosy, traditional bedrooms with pale colours and florals are as peaceful as can be. No sitting room, but a small sofa in the double. You are a five-minute drive from the coastal path: a great spot for walkers and peace-seekers. Bron and Nick are warm and friendly, their home a relaxing retreat with a mature garden to wander and wild deer roaming. *Minimum stay two nights.*

Price	£80.
Rooms	2: 1 twin; 1 double with separate bath.
Meals	Inn 0.75 miles.
Closed	Christmas & New Year.
Directions	A351 from Wareham to Corfe Castle. At end of village fork right on B3069 for Kingston. Left 0.5 miles down track (sign on roadside).

Bron & Nick Burt
Lower Lynch House,
Kingston Hill, Corfe Castle BH20 5LG
Tel +44 (0)1929 480089
Email bronburt@btinternet.com

Entry 167   Map 3

Dorset

The Old Post Office

The stunning coastal path comes past the front door of this restored bungalow on the cliff-top estate. Clamber down to a hidden beach and a short walk will take you to Swanage, or high over Ballard Down with views to the Isle of Wight. Bedrooms are comfortable and sunny, bathrooms are warmed by underfloor heating. Artist Rowena and rare-book dealer David give you much local food at breakfast, in the jolly kitchen (with piano), or on the terrace. Colours are strong and earthy, rugs and cushions bright and colourful, interesting books and art plentiful. Rocking chairs on the veranda are marvellous for a drink at sunset.

Price	£70. Singles £50.
Rooms	2: 1 twin; 1 double with separate bath.
Meals	Pub/restaurant 0.3 miles.
Closed	Rarely.
Directions	A351 to Swanage seafront, then left. Up hill, round one-way. Left into Ballard Way (corner shop on left). Through private estate barrier. House 2nd on right.

Bottle of wine in your room.

Rowena Bishop
The Old Post Office,
4 Ballard Estate, Swanage BH19 1QZ
Tel +44 (0)1929 422041
Mobile +44 (0)7976 356013
Email rowena@outwardbound.plus.com
Web www.oldpostofficeswanage.co.uk

Entry 168   Map 3

Dorset

Gold Court House

Anthea and Michael have created a mood of restrained luxury and uncluttered, often beautiful, good taste in their Georgian townhouse. Restful bedrooms have antiques, beams, linen armchairs, radios and TVs. There's an eye-catching collection of aqua marine glass, interesting art, and a large drawing room and pretty walled garden in which to relax after a day out. Views are soft and lush yet you are in the small square of this attractive town with cafes and galleries a short walk. Your hosts are delightful – "they do everything to perfection," says a reader; both house and garden are a refuge. *Over tens welcome.*

Price	£80. Singles £55.
Rooms	3: 1 double; 1 twin/double, 1 twin/double each with separate bathroom.
Meals	Restaurants 50 yds.
Closed	Rarely.
Directions	From A35, A351 to Wareham. Follow signs to town centre. In North St, over lights into South St. 1st left into St John's Hill; house on far right corner of square.

Free pick-up from local bus/train station.

Use your Sawday's Gift Card here.

Anthea & Michael Hipwell
Gold Court House,
St John's Hill, Wareham BH20 4LZ
Tel +44 (0)1929 553320
Email info@goldcourthouse.co.uk
Web www.goldcourthouse.co.uk

Entry 169   Map 3

Dorset

Bering House

Fabulous in every way. Renate's attention to detail reveals a love of running B&B: the fluffy dressing gowns and bathroom treats, the biscuits, fruit and sherry. She and John are welcoming, enthusiastic, delightful. Expect pretty little sofas, golden bath taps, a gleaming breakfast table, a big sumptuous suite with fine views across sparkling Poole harbour, Brownsea Island and the Purbeck Hills. Breakfasts are served on blue and white Spode china, among the birds and the breezes on summery days. Fresh fruit, Parma ham, smoked salmon, kedgeree: the choice is superb. An immaculate harbourside retreat.

Price	£80–£95. Singles £70–£85.
Rooms	2: 1 twin/double; 1 suite (twin/double) & kitchenette.
Meals	Pub 400 yds. Restaurant 500 yds.
Closed	Rarely.
Directions	From A35 & A350 at Upton, B3068 south to Hamworthy & Rockley Park. 1.5 miles on at pub on left, right into Lake Rd; under bridge; 2nd left down Branksea Ave. House last on left.

Late checkout (12pm). Free pick-up from local bus/train station. 10% off stays of 5 or more nights.

Renate & John Wadham
Bering House, 53 Branksea Avenue,
Hamworthy, Poole BH15 4DP
Tel +44 (0)1202 673419
Email johnandrenate1@tiscali.co.uk

Entry 170   Map 3

Dorset

7 Smithfield Place

Valerie adores large mirrors – which she paints and distresses herself – rich fabrics, real wood, dainty antiques. She also delights in looking after guests, so no detail is missed in her elegant home, from the gorgeous bathroom to a 'full works' breakfast – taken in the spanking new breakfast room or on a sunny patio. Built in 1880 as a worker's cottage, the house sits on a quiet cul-de-sac off Winton's thriving high street, two miles from Bournemouth town centre with easy public transport. The garden is lit up in spring by blooming camellias and cherry blossom, and the whole house sparkles – as does your charming hostess.

Price	£70. Singles £50.
Rooms	1 double.
Meals	Packed lunch £15. Pub/restaurant 100 yds.
Closed	Christmas.
Directions	M27 to New Forest, on to A31, then exit A338 Bournemouth. Exit to A3049, up to r'bout, 3rd exit still on A3049. 1.5 miles, right into Wimborne Rd, then left into Smithfield Pl.

10% off room rate Mon-Thurs.

Valerie Johns
7 Smithfield Place,
Winton, Bournemouth BH9 2QJ
Tel   +44 (0)1202 520722
Mobile +44 (0)7743 481671
Email   valeriejohns@btinternet.com
Web   www.smithfieldplace.co.uk

Entry 171   Map 3

Dorset

Sondela

All is leafy and sedate, with tall pines and rhododendrons hiding large houses: a short drive sweeps you to the front of this colonial style bungalow smothered in roses. Glynda and Selwyn, warm and intelligent, have filled their lovely light home with interesting antiques, textiles and artefacts from their years in South Africa; guests have their own sitting room in soft blues with a stone fireplace and fresh flowers. Bedrooms are quiet (the double is bigger and more contemporary) with pure white cotton sheets and splashes of colour from bedspreads or cushions; on sunny days you breakfast in the glorious garden.

Price	£70-£80. Singles £35-£50.
Rooms	2: 1 double, 1 twin.
Meals	Dinner by arrangement. Restaurant 5-minute walk.
Closed	Rarely.
Directions	After Lyndhurst follow A35 to Christchurch for 9 miles. Past East Close Hotel on left, 1 mile to junction, left to Walkford. Thro' Walkford, left Chewton Farm Road; 500 yards on left.

Bottle of wine in your room. Late checkout (12pm). Free pick-up from local bus/train station.

Glynda & Selwyn Morrison
Sondela, 20 Chewton Farm Road,
Highcliffe, Christchurch BH23 5QN
Tel   +44 (0)1425 270978
Mobile +44 (0)7734 991034
Email   morglyn@hotmail.com
Web   www.chewtonbedandbreakfast.com

Entry 172   Map 3

Dorset

Thornhill

This pretty thatched house has peaceful views from every window... of fields, woods and superb gardens. Sara and John are charming hosts and love having people to stay; they have lots of local knowledge too. Downstairs are pastel walls, polished antiques, beautiful cedar floors and interesting art. All is neat, tidy, spacious and spotless, and Sara pays great attention to detail: fruit, chocolates and a choice of teas in comforting bedrooms with an old-fashioned feel. You can spot deer on the lawn, stride out straight from the door, visit the Minster, drive to beaches. Come on a Thursday if you like to play bridge!

Price	From £64. Singles from £32.
Rooms	3: 1 double, 1 twin, 1 single, all sharing 2 baths. Possible use of separate bath.
Meals	Pub/restaurant 400 yds.
Closed	Rarely.
Directions	From Wimborne B3078 towards Cranborne. Right to Holt. After 2 miles Thornhill on right, 200 yds beyond Old Inn. Up straight drive, do not turn into Thornhill Cottage driveway.

John & Sara Turnbull
Thornhill,
Holt,
Wimborne BH21 7DJ
Tel +44 (0)1202 889434
Email scturnbull@lineone.net

Entry 173   Map 3

Dorset

Crawford House

Below, the river Stour winds through the valley and under the medieval, nine-arched bridge. Above, an Iron Age hill fort; between is Crawford House. It's an elegant Georgian house in an acre of walled garden, soft and pretty inside with an easy, relaxed atmosphere. Carpeted bedrooms are homely and warm, with long curtains; one room has four-poster twin beds with chintz drapes. The sun streams through the floor-to-ceiling windows of the downstairs rooms, and charming 18th- and 19th-century oil paintings hang in the dining room. Andrea is fun, and a great host, with lots of local knowledge. *Broadband available.*

Price	From £65. Singles £35.
Rooms	3: 1 twin/double; 1 twin with separate bath; 1 twin with separate shower.
Meals	Pub in village.
Closed	Mid-October to mid-April.
Directions	North on A350; after entering Spetisbury, 1st gateway immediately on left after crossroads (B3075).

10% off stays Mon-Thurs.

Andrea Lea
Crawford House,
Spetisbury,
Blandford Forum DT11 9DP
Tel +44 (0)1258 857338
Email andrea@lea8.wanadoo.co.uk

Entry 174   Map 3

Dorset

Stickland Farmhouse

Charming Dorset... and a soft, delightful thatched cottage in an enviably rural setting. Sandy and Paul have poured love into this listed farmhouse and garden, the latter bursting with lupins, poppies, foxgloves, clematis, delphiniums. Sandy gives you delicious breakfasts with homemade soda bread from the Aga. Cottagey bedrooms have crisp white dressing gowns and lots of books and pictures – one room opens onto your own seating area in the garden. You are in a village with a good pub, and Cranbourne Chase, rich in barrows and hill forts, is close by. *Children over ten welcome. Min. two nights at weekends in summer.*

Price	£70-£75. Singles £55.
Rooms	3: 2 doubles, 1 twin.
Meals	Pub 3-minute walk.
Closed	Rarely.
Directions	Leave Blandford for SW, cross river Stour. Hard right after Bryanston school for W. Stickland. Down North St, right signed W. Houghton. House 150 yds on left with 5-bar gate.

Sandy & Paul Crofton-Atkins
Stickland Farmhouse,
9 West Street, Winterborne Stickland,
Blandford Forum DT11 0NT

Tel	+44 (0)1258 880119
Email	sandysticklandfarm@tiscali.co.uk
Web	www.sticklandfarmhouse.co.uk

Entry 175   Map 3

Dorset

Launceston Farm

Farmhouse chic in the most glorious of surroundings. Sarah has named her bedrooms after the fields, and they are an exquisite marriage of contemporary and traditional: rococo beds and mirrors, curtains of iridescent silk, heavenly colours. Two rooms have roll tops in the room itself; every bathroom is seductive. Downstairs is an open-plan living area with a scattering of sofas, a charming bay window, an open fire, and candles for dinner – farm-sourced and deliciously rustic. Sarah, who was born in this listed house, is full of enthusiasm and ideas; son Jimi's farm tours are a must. Amazing value. *Children over 12 welcome.*

Ethical Collection: Food. See page 420.

Price	From £80. Singles from £55.
Rooms	6: 4 doubles, 2 twins.
Meals	Dinner, 2-3 courses, £20-£25 (Mon & Fri only). Pub 1 mile.
Closed	Rarely.
Directions	From Salisbury, A354 to Blandford Forum. Left at Tarrant Hinton. First village is Tarrant Launceston; house is on right.

 10% off double room rate Mon-Thurs.

Sarah Worrall
Launceston Farm,
Tarrant Launceston,
Blandford Forum DT11 8BY

Tel	+44 (0)1258 830528
Email	info@launcestonfarm.co.uk
Web	www.launcestonfarm.co.uk

Entry 176   Map 3

Dorset

The Old Rectory

Walk all day on Cranborne Chase, return for tea at The Old Rectory, then stroll off for a meal at the much-fêted pub down the road... What could be nicer? Vicky's brick-and-flint Victorian house is in the middle of the village, yet feels wonderfully peaceful in its ten-acre grounds. Bedrooms, with huge bathrooms, are traditional, comfortable and charming; Aga breakfasts are full and hearty. The drawing and dining rooms have the warm, gracious air of a much-loved and lived-in home, family portraits hang on the walls, the furniture is polished, the dogs are friendly and big windows overlook sweeping lawns and summer terrace.

Price	From £80.
Rooms	2: 1 double, 1 twin.
Meals	Pub within walking distance.
Closed	Christmas.
Directions	16 miles south west of Salisbury on A354 Blandford Forum road. Farnham is signed off main road; house is in Farnham opposite Museum pub.

10% off stays of 2 or more nights.

Vicky Forbes
The Old Rectory,
Farnham, Blandford Forum DT11 8DE
Tel   +44 (0)1725 516474
Email   forbescopper@compuserve.com
Web   www.theoldrectorydorset.co.uk

Entry 177   Map 3

Dorset

Sarunds Cottage

Steep lanes tumble down to wooded Farnham and the famous Museum Inn. A little further, up a gravelled driveway, are Josephine's interior design studio and elegant Georgian house. Through a gate, privately in its own lane, is a cottage housing your suite – spacious, luxurious, on the first floor and bliss for independent souls. Light-filled and beamy, with a rococo-esque bed and toile de Jouy curtains, it's a vision of cream, grey and soft ochre. The chandelier'd bathroom is stunning, breakfast in a basket is a cook-your own affair. Deer bound in the forests of Cranbourne Chase, Salisbury is 20 minutes away.

Price	£120. Singles £80-£100.
Rooms	Cottage: 1 suite with sitting room & kitchenette.
Meals	Pub/restaurant 200 yds.
Closed	Rarely.
Directions	A354 Blandford to Salisbury road. After 6 miles left to Farnham, 1.5 miles into village and past The Museum Inn. House 200 yds on left.

10% off room rate Mon-Thurs.
Local food/produce in your room.

Josephine Browning
Sarunds Cottage,
Farnham, Blandford Forum DT11 8DE
Tel   +44 (0)1725 552555
Email   jb@countryhouse-interiordesign.co.uk
Web   www.sarundscottage.co.uk

Entry 178   Map 3

Dorset

Manor Barn

What was once an L-shaped cow shed is now a rather smart, self-contained, one-storey barn – attached to the main house and with views to an Iron Age hill. Relax in a roomy, beamed sitting room looking onto a pretty courtyard garden, its squashy sofas and pastel colours enlivened by fabrics in rich earthy tones; down a corridor are two restful bedrooms with delightful linen and huge fluffy pillows. A generous breakfast is brought over to you. It's rustic-contemporary, nicely independent and perfect for friends or families. You're in one of Dorset's friendliest villages, and the circular walks are great. *Over eights welcome.*

Price	£98. Singles £70.
Rooms	Barn: 2 twins/doubles & sitting room.
Meals	Pub in village.
Closed	Rarely.
Directions	South on A350 from Shaftesbury; right at sign 'Child Okeford 3 miles'. Just before village, drive is on left, opposite 30 ft high hedge.

 Bottle of wine in your room.

Carolyn Sorby
Manor Barn, Upper Street, Child
Okeford, Blandford Forum DT11 8EF
Tel +44 (0)1258 860638
Mobile +44 (0)7973 595344
Email carisorby@btinternet.com
Web www.manorbarnbedandbreakfast.co.uk

Entry 179   Map 3

Dorset

Glebe Farm

You're in Dorset's highest village – views from the house sprawl for miles. Ian farms 1,000 acres, Tessa looks after the horses, ponies and chickens. Their home, newly built, comes with green oak, soaring ceilings and walls of glass that frame spectacular views ("Emmerdale meets Grand Designs" to quote a happy guest). Aga-cooked breakfasts include local bacon and home-laid eggs, while bedrooms, one up, one down, have warm colours, big beds, beautiful views, super bathrooms. The Wessex Ridgeway starts in the village, so follow it over to magnificent Hambledon Hill, an Iron Age hill fort. You can dine in summer on the terrace.

Price	£90–£100. Singles from £50.
Rooms	2 twins/doubles.
Meals	Dinner, 2 courses, £25. Pubs 2 miles.
Closed	Christmas & New Year.
Directions	A350 south to Fontwell Magna, then left at Crown Inn for Ashmore. Straight ahead, over x-roads, up hill to village. On left at pond.

Tessa & Ian Millard
Glebe Farm, High Street,
Ashmore, Salisbury SP5 5AE
Tel +44 (0)1747 811974
Mobile +44 (0)7799 858961
Email stay@glebefarmbandb.co.uk
Web www.glebefarmbandb.co.uk

Entry 180   Map 3

Dorset

The Old Forge, Fanners Yard

Step back in time in this beautifully restored forge: retro signs, museum pieces, ponies in the paddock and a simpler, slower way of life… Tim and Lucy's smallholding gives you a taste of harmonious living with the seasons, and they recycle everything. This includes Tim's classic cars, a cosy gypsy caravan and a vintage shepherd's hut. The attic bedrooms are snug — Lucy's quilts, country antiques, sparkling bathrooms, flowers — and their breakfasts are renowned: eggs from their hens, organic bacon and sausages, home-grown jams, apple juice straight from the orchard. A happy place, a tonic to stay. *Self-catering in the Smithy.*

Price	£75-£95.
Rooms	4: 1 double, 1 family. Gypsy caravan & shepherd's hut: 1 double each (each with shower/wc close by).
Meals	Pub/restaurant within 3 miles.
Closed	Rarely.
Directions	From Shaftesbury, A350 to Compton Abbas. House 1st on left before Compton Abbas sign. Left; entrance on left.

Local food/produce in your room. Homemade biscuits.

Tim & Lucy Kerridge
The Old Forge,
Fanners Yard, Compton Abbas,
Shaftesbury SP7 0NQ
Tel   +44 (0)1747 811881
Email   theoldforge@hotmail.com
Web   www.theoldforgedorset.co.uk

Entry 181   Map 3

Dorset

Rose Cottage

You are buried deep in a quiet corner here, just perfect for long walks: return to a wood-burner and a cup of tea in a beamed sitting room with plenty of sofas and books — no dull TV. Bedrooms are light and charming with chintzy curtains and fabulous views over the pretty garden; loll in big beds with cushions and crisp white sheets. Breakfast is a fairly flexible, mostly organic treat with Rose Cottage honey, served in an elegant yellow-walled dining room with gleaming furniture and dollops of morning sunshine; delicious supper includes home-grown vegetables. Amanda, warm and welcoming, looks after you very well indeed.

Price	From £70. Singles £45. Child £15.
Rooms	2: 1 twin/double; 1 twin/double with separate bath/shower.
Meals	Light supper & packed lunch available. Pub/restaurant 1 mile.
Closed	Christmas.
Directions	From Shaftesbury A350 north. Right signed Wincombe & Donhead St Mary. After 2 miles 2nd right. Watery Lane 100 yds on left, house 200 yds on right, drive thro' field gate.

Free pick-up from local bus/train station. 10% off stays of 2 or more nights.

Giles & Amanda Vardey
Rose Cottage,
Watery Lane, Donhead St Mary,
Shaftesbury SP7 9DF
Tel   +44 (0)1747 828449
Email   amanda@rosecottage.uk.com
Web   www.rosecottage.uk.com

Entry 182   Map 3

Dorset

Gorse Farm House

Wendy is a generous soul and throws open her lovely house; you are free to wander the garden, grab a book and laze in the sunny conservatory or settle into the snug and watch TV. Upstairs find light-filled, peaceful bedrooms with dreamy views over fields, a bowl of sweets, dainty china and more books; bathrooms are sparkling. Lee is a sculptor and his work peeps out from clever planting around the garden: find a seat on the veranda or near the natural pond and listen to the birds. Breakfast on local sausages, bacon and free-range farm eggs then tackle some fabulous walks and cycles straight from the door.

Price	From £60. Singles £40.
Rooms	2: 1 twin/double; 1 twin/double with separate bath.
Meals	Pub/restaurant 2 miles.
Closed	Christmas.
Directions	West of Sturminster Newton, south off A357 signed Hazlebury Bryan. 0.5 miles Rivers Corner, left signed Fifehead St Quintin. 0.5 miles bear right at sign for Fifeheads. House 0.25 miles on left.

 Free pick-up from Gillingham bus/train station (20-minute drive).

Wendy Dickenson
Gorse Farm House,
Fifehead St Quintin,
Sturminster Newton DT10 2AW
Tel   +44 (0)1258 475343
Email   contactus@gorsefarmhousebb.co.uk
Web   www.gorsefarmhousebb.co.uk

Entry 183   Map 3

Dorset

Blackrow Farm

In Hardy's 'Valley of the Dairies' is Blackrow Farm – immaculately thatched, beautifully converted and steeped in character. Annie, who practises kinesiology, has imbued the house with a deep sense of calm. There's a private stair to a pretty cottage-style bedroom in the wing, with thick silk curtains at mullioned windows, bedcovers in crewel and a big, cosy, carpeted bathroom stocked with lovely soaps. Paintings and antiques fill this rambling house, a fresh breakfast is served in a historic room with dark panelling and huge inglenook (old bread ovens intact) and the views spread over paddocks, orchards and fields.

Price	£80. Singles £50.
Rooms	Wing: 1 twin/double.
Meals	Pub 1 mile.
Closed	Rarely.
Directions	From Sturminster Newton A357 to Stalbridge. After Lydlinch left onto A3030. Just after the deer park left onto B3143. Farm approx. 350 yds on left.

 10% off stays of 2 or more nights.

Annie Coultas
Blackrow Farm,
Kings Stag,
Sturminster Newton DT10 2BE
Tel   +44 (0)1963 23156
Email   anniecoultas@gmail.com
Web   www.blackrowfarm.co.uk

Entry 184   Map 3

Dorset

Old Causeway Bakery

In an unpretentious village, a quirky gem. Inside, abundant flower arrangements and bold colours – deep green and cerise – glow alongside oils, prints and antiques dotted around; bookcases bow with the weight of walking guides. In the self-contained bakery wing is a theatrical boudoir (think gold drapes and chaise longue). The main house bedrooms are more serene though still eclectic, with antiques and tapestry-upholstered headboards; bathrooms are super throughout. Full English breakfasts are all locally sourced, and can be had whenever you like. Come prepared to cuddle Henry and Bertie – the friendly resident dogs.

Price	£85–£95. Bakery Wing £100–£120. Singles £75–£85.
Rooms	3: 2 doubles. Bakery Wing: 1 double.
Meals	Pub 30 yds.
Closed	Rarely.
Directions	From Sturminster Newton B3092 Blandford; right at lights, then left signed Hazelbury Bryan. 4 miles into village centre, right after pub. House immed. on left.

 Late checkout (12pm). £10 off room rate for stays of 3 or more nights.

Sandra Williams & Simon Boggon
Old Causeway Bakery, Hazelbury Bryan,
Sturminster Newton DT10 2BH
Tel   +44 (0)1258 817228
Mobile   +44 (0)7825 815796
Email   sandrasimonbw@btinternet.com
Web   www.oldcausewaybakery.co.uk

Entry 185   Map 3

Dorset

Golden Hill Cottage

Deep in the countryside lies Stourton Caundle and this charming thatched cottage. The sitting room, traditionally furnished with antiques, paintings and coal fire, is all yours if you stay, along with a carpeted twin room and small shower up a private stair. Anna, courteous and kind, brings you splendid platefuls of local bacon and sausage, homemade jams and Dorset honey for breakfast; nothing is too much trouble for these owners. There are glorious walks from the village, a good pub that serves food and real ales, and Sherborne, Montacute and Stourhead for landscape, culture and history. *Babes in arms welcome.*

Price	£70–£80. Singles £50.
Rooms	1 twin & sitting room.
Meals	Pubs/restaurants within 3 miles.
Closed	Rarely.
Directions	From Sherborne, A352 to Dorchester; after 1 mile, left onto A3030; on to far end of Bishops Caundle, left to Stourton Caundle; after sharp left into village street, house 200 yds on right.

 10% off stays of 2 or more nights Mon-Thurs.

Anna & Andrew Oliver
Golden Hill Cottage, Stourton Caundle,
Sturminster Newton DT10 2JW
Tel   +44 (0)1963 362109
Email anna@goldenhillcottage.co.uk
Web   www.goldenhillcottage.co.uk

Entry 186   Map 3

Dorset

Glebe House

Clematis and wisteria cover much of the mellow brickwork of this spacious and uncluttered 1950s house, down a quiet lane in a tiny hamlet in the heart of stunning Blackmore Vale. From the hall look right through to the mature pretty garden; it's open house and David and Barbara love having guests to stay. Enjoy tea and scones in the garden room, neat-as-a-pin bedrooms and bathrooms, and wide views from every window. Tuck into all sorts of tasty choices at breakfast, by the fire in the dining room. Magnificent castle and abbey are close, and walks from the door are outstanding — you could stay a week and never do the same one!

Price	£70–£80. Singles £50.
Rooms	2: 1 double, 1 twin/double.
Meals	Pub /restaurant within 1 mile.
Closed	Rarely.
Directions	A352 from Sherborne, then left to A3030 (dir. Sturminster Newton). After 1.5 miles at Alweston right to Folke. Glebe House 800 yds on left.

Reduced rate of £60 for 3 or more nights. Late checkout (12pm).

David & Barbara Fifield
Glebe House,
Folke, Sherborne DT9 5HP
Tel +44 (0)1963 210337
Mobile +44 (0)7980 864033
Email glebe.house@hotmail.com
Web www.glebehouse-dorset.co.uk

Entry 187　Map 3

Dorset

Munden House

This is a super B&B — a couple of farm cottages and assorted outbuildings beautifully stitched together. It's run with great warmth by Colin and Annie, who buy and sell colourful rugs and have travelled the world to do it. Outside, long views shoot off over open country; inside, airy interiors, pretty bedrooms and lots of colour. The garden studios are bigger and more private; one has a galleried bedroom above a lovely sitting room. Annie cooks fantastic food — local meat, fish from Brixham — but her vegetarian dishes will seduce die-hard carnivores. You eat at smartly dressed tables; breakfast is on the terrace in good weather.

Price	£80–£120. Singles from £70.
Rooms	7: 2 doubles, 1 twin/double, 1 four-poster, 3 garden studios.
Meals	Dinner, 3 courses, £25.
Closed	Christmas.
Directions	A352 south from Sherborne, then A3030, east to Alweston. In village, pass post office on right, then left into Mundens Lane before bakery.

10% off room rate Mon–Thurs. Late checkout (12pm). Free pick-up from local bus/train station.

Annie Fabbri & Colin Fletcher
Munden House, Mundens Lane,
Alweston, Sherborne DT9 5HU
Tel +44 (0)1963 23150
Email stay@mundenhouse.co.uk
Web www.mundenhouse.co.uk

Entry 188　Map 3

Dorset

Holt Cottage

The house stands on high ground and the views are fabulous and panoramic. Richard and Annabel give you a big welcome and two super suites in the cottage a step away. One upstairs, one down, each has its own sitting room, and private entrance too so you can come and go as you please. All is sparkling, light and inviting, with elegant prints on the walls. Bedrooms have wonderful mattresses, good linen and fresh flowers; find fluffy white towels and lots of potions in immaculate bathrooms. Breakfast by the Aga in the large beamed farmhouse kitchen: fresh fruit salad, local bacon and sausages and eggs from Annabel's wandering hens.

Ethical Collection: Food. See page 420.

Price	From £85. Singles £65.
Rooms	Cottage: 1 double & sitting room; 1 twin/double & sitting room.
Meals	Pub/restaurant 1 mile.
Closed	Rarely.
Directions	From Sherborne, A352 south. After 1 mile, left onto A3030 Blandford road. In Bishops Caundle, left at Murco garage. House 1 mile on left.

 10% off room rate Mon–Thurs. Free pick-up from local bus/train station.

	Richard & Annabel Buxton Holt Cottage, Alweston, Sherborne DT9 5JF
Tel	+44 (0)1963 23014
Mobile	+44 (0)7766 583344
Email	annabelbuxton@hotmail.com
Web	www.holtcottagedorset.com

Entry 189   Map 3

Dorset

Avalon Townhouse

You'll feel lucky to end up at Paul and Nicky's smart Edwardian townhouse just a few minutes' walk from the station. A large, high-ceilinged sitting room has a cosy fire, sash windows, paintings and prints, and a baby grand piano if you fancy showing off. Bedrooms nod to the contemporary and are as neat as a pin, with beech furniture and satin throws and cushions; bathrooms are spanking new and filled with pleasant things in bottles. Wander down in the morning to a menu bursting with local food and a bit of 'interactive time' with Paul and his Aga. Antiques, medieval buildings and music in the Abbey await. Perfect town B&B.

Price	£80–£90. Singles £70–£80.
Rooms	3 doubles.
Meals	Pub/restaurant 300 yds.
Closed	Rarely.
Directions	A30 to Sherborne. Come off A30 heading south for train station. House 300 yds from station.

 10% off room rate Mon–Thurs. 10% off stays of 2 or more nights.

	Paul & Nicky Aleman Avalon Townhouse, South Street, Sherborne DT9 3LZ
Tel	+44 (0)1935 814748
Email	enquiries@avalontownhouse.co.uk
Web	www.avalontownhouse.co.uk

Entry 190   Map 3

Dorset

Hound House

In a shy corner of Dorset where the village houses come in soft yellow ham stone, your own entrance leads to a private sitting/dining room with a Swedish cream wood-burner, lots of pictures, books and maps, easy chairs and a sofa in rose and aqua colours. Breakfast is a help-yourself affair during the week: Dorset cereals, local yogurt, homemade bread and fresh fruit. At weekends charming Claire gives you a locally sourced feast. Upstairs are two delicious bedrooms with deep window sills, sumptuous fabrics and gleaming antique furniture; the bathroom is large with eau-de-nil panelling. Serene, and delightfully independent.

Price	From £80.
Rooms	2: 1 double & sitting room; 1 twin sharing bath (let to same party only).
Meals	Pub 300 yds,
Closed	Rarely.
Directions	A352 from Sherborne towards Dorchester. Just south of Sherborne, right signed Thornford and Yetminster. Once in Yetminster, 2nd left into High Street. House 2nd on left.

 10% off stays of 2 or more nights. Local food/produce in your room.

Claire & Nick MacLeod-Ash
Hound House, High Street,
Yetminster, Sherborne DT9 6LF
Tel +44 (0)1935 872243
Email claire@macleod-ash.com
Web www.houndhousebandb.com

Dorset

Windrush Farm

Fun to eat in the light farmhouse kitchen with its Aga, polished oak table, and rag-rolled dresser full of colourful plates. Upstairs, too, is delightful – creaky floors, sloping ceilings and a maze of corridors brightened by new Zoffany wallpapers. Pretty bedrooms are in soft colours; everywhere there are paintings, prints and photos. On colder evenings, your charming hosts will light a fire for you in the guest sitting room – lived-in and snug with artwork and piles of books – while for summer there's a scented rambler-strewn garden and a terrace with the loveliest views. Bustling Sherborne is a ten-minute drive.

Price	From £75. Singles from £50.
Rooms	2: 1 double with separate bath; 1 twin sharing bath (2nd room let to same party only).
Meals	Dinner £25. Pub/restaurant 1 mile.
Closed	Christmas.
Directions	A357 Wincanton-Templecombe. Right at 2nd turn Stowell, opp. entrance to Horsington House. On for approx. 1 mile, then steep hill; pass church on left. House on left after 0.5 miles.

Richard & Jenny Gold
Windrush Farm,
Stowell, Sherborne DT9 4PD
Tel +44 (0)1963 370799
Email jennygold@hotmail.co.uk
Web www.windrushfarmbedandbreakfast.com

Durham

The Coach House

There's so much to gladden your heart – the cobbled courtyard that evokes memories of its days as a coaching inn, the river running through the estate, the drawing room's log fire, the delicious breakfasts, the blackberry crumbles with cream… and Peter and Mary, your kind, unstuffy, dog-adoring hosts (they have three well-behaved ones). All your creature comforts are attended to in this small, perfect, English country house: lined chintz, starched linen, cushioned window seats, cut flowers, heated towel rails. Friendly, delightful, and the perfect stepping stone to Scotland or the south.

Price	£85. Singles £50.
Rooms	2: 1 twin/double; 1 twin/double with separate bath.
Meals	Dinner, 3 courses, £25. Pub/restaurants within 3 miles.
Closed	Rarely.
Directions	A1(M) to Scotch Corner. A66 west for 8 miles until Greta Bridge turn-off. House on left just before bridge. Front door is near right-hand corner of courtyard.

Peter & Mary Gilbertson
The Coach House,
Greta Bridge, Barnard Castle DL12 9SD
Tel   +44 (0)1833 627201
Email   info@coachhousegreta.co.uk
Web   www.coachhousegreta.co.uk

Entry 193   Map 12

Essex

Emsworth House

Unexpectedly tranquil is this 1937 vicarage, with wide views over the Stour and some wonderful light for painting. Penny, an artist, is a flexible and generous host and you can laze or picnic in her two-acre garden. This is Constable country – great for walking; you are near to Frinton beach and golf, sailing and riding. Return to comfy sofas and chairs, open fires and good books, and redecorated bedrooms with a country feel and the odd African throw or splash of colour. There's heaps of lovely art and a garden full of birds. Penny has camp beds and high chairs and a can-do attitude. Great fun.

Price	From £60. Singles from £45.
Rooms	3: 1 double, 1 twin; 1 double with separate bath.
Meals	Pub/restaurant 0.5 miles.
Closed	Rarely.
Directions	A12-A120 (to Harwich) & left to B1035; right at TV mast to Bradfield, 2 miles; house on right. Manningtree Station 5 miles. A14-A137-B1352, house on left.

10% off room rate Mon-Thurs.

Penny Linton
Emsworth House, Ship Hill, Station Road, Bradfield, Manningtree CO11 2UP
Tel   +44 (0)1255 870860
Mobile +44 (0)7767 477771
Email   emsworthhouse@hotmail.com
Web   www.emsworthhouse.co.uk

Entry 194   Map 10

Essex

Bromans Farm

The island of Mersea is surprisingly secluded, and Bromans Farm is in a most tranquil corner; the sea murmurs across the Saltings where Brent geese wheel and Constable skies stretch. The house began in 1343 – nearly as old as the exquisite village church; the Georgians added their bit, but the venerable beams shine through. Ruth and Martin are charming and give you a very pretty bedroom in yellow and blue, a superb bathroom off the landing, log fires in the snug sitting room, homemade breakfast jams at a beautiful antique table, and tea from Grandmother's blue and white china. Wild walks beckon and the garden is much-loved.

Price	£70–£80. Singles £40.
Rooms	1 twin/double with separate bath.
Meals	Pub 0.5 miles.
Closed	Rarely.
Directions	From Colchester B1025, over causeway, bear left. After 3 miles, pass Dog & Pheasant pub; 3rd right into Bromans Lane. House 1st on left.

 Free pick-up from local bus/train station.

Ruth Dence
Bromans Farm,
East Mersea CO5 8UE
Tel   +44 (0)1206 383235
Email   ruth.dence@homecall.co.uk
Web   www.bromansfarm.co.uk

Entry 195   Map 10

Essex

Caterpillar Cottage

Traditional brick and clapboard, dormer windows, tall chimneys – this looks like the real thing. But the 'converted farm building' in the grounds of Patricia's former grand house is brand new! Filled with fine furniture, family photographs and *objets* from far-flung travels, it invites relaxation. The double-height, vaulted sitting room brims with sofas and books, logs crackle on chilly nights and bedrooms are simple and comfortable with decent-sized bathrooms. Patricia, a lively grandmother, adores children while her big garden promises home-grown fruit and tranquillity.

Price	From £65. Singles from £35.
Rooms	2: 1 triple; 1 double with separate bath/shower.
Meals	Packed lunch available. Pubs 50 yds.
Closed	Rarely.
Directions	A12 to A1124. In Fordstreet, cottage through gateway shared with Old House, opposite Old Queens Head pub. 88 bus stops at the gate.

 10% off stays 3 or more nights. Box handmade local chocolates.

 Use your Sawday's Gift Card here.

Patricia Mitchell
Caterpillar Cottage, Fordstreet,
Aldham, Colchester CO6 3PH
Tel   +44 (0)1206 240456
Mobile   +44 (0)7776 202713
Email   bandbcaterpillar@tiscali.co.uk
Web   www.caterpillarcottage.co.uk

Entry 196   Map 10

Essex

Brook Farm

Large low Georgian windows fill the house with light, unpretentious family pieces warm the bedrooms and the stunning carved crossbeam in the largest is late-medieval. Anne, country lover and B&B-er, has farmed here for over 30 years; outbuildings dot the yard, sheep and horses roam the acres. In Anne's sitting room logs fill the copper and hunting prints line the walls – no TV, but magazines and books aplenty – and you breakfast (deliciously) at a long table with fine antique benches. The handsome bright farmhouse oozes history and a faded country charm – yet is 30 minutes from Stansted.

Price	£70–£80. Singles £35–£45.
Rooms	3: 1 twin; 1 double, 1 family room, each with separate bath.
Meals	Packed lunch £3–£5. Pubs within 2 miles.
Closed	Rarely.
Directions	House on B1053, 500 yds south of Wethersfield.

Anne Butler
Brook Farm,
Wethersfield, Braintree CM7 4BX
Tel   +44 (0)1371 850284
Mobile   +44 (0)7770 881966
Email   abutlerbrookfarm@aol.com
Web   www.brookfarmwethersfield.co.uk

Entry 197   Map 9

Essex

32 The Hythe

The Thames barge in all her glory: the Gibbs' garden runs almost into the river Blackwater where these majestic old craft are moored and the mudflats are a birdwatcher's dream. Summer breakfast on the deck – local smoked kippers and free-range eggs – watching the barges sail up the river is a rare treat. Beneath wide limpid skies this sensitively extended fisherman's cottage looks out to 12th-century St Mary's at the back where Kim and Gerry ring the Sunday bells. It's immaculate and comfortable inside, an inspired mix of modern and antique lit by myriad candles, among other romantic touches. *Over 14s welcome.*

Price	£80. Singles £70.
Rooms	2: 1 double; 1 double with separate bath.
Meals	Pub 100 yds.
Closed	Christmas & Boxing Day.
Directions	From A12 to Maldon. House on The Hythe by river, signed for the river. Past St Mary's church then right at the bottom. House at end of road on right.

Kim & Gerry Gibbs
32 The Hythe,
Maldon CM9 5HN
Tel   +44 (0)1621 859435
Mobile   +44 (0)7753 135108
Email   gibbsie@live.co.uk
Web   www.thehythemaldon.co.uk

Entry 198   Map 10

Essex

Fourteen

White linen, white walls, nautical touches, a private sauna: a wow of a place for sybarites, walkers, watersporters and designers. Architects Mike and Diana have created a super-sleek home in boaty Burnham with gorgeous views across the marshes. Pull up through the tall white gates and enter the inner sanctuary. The blissful bedroom is privately on the ground floor, off its own sitting room with a large flat screen, and the indoor pool kept at a tempting 28 degrees; the lovely hosts live above. There's a fragrant patio – all yours – and a pontoon ahead, and at weekends you can be ferried across the river. Stupendous.

Price	£100. Singles £75.
Rooms	1 twin/double & sitting room.
Meals	Dinner, 2 courses with wine, £20. Pubs/restaurants 100 yds.
Closed	Christmas & Boxing Day.
Directions	B1010 into Burnham, from High St right into Shore Rd at clock tower. Left through Anchor Hotel car park & straight ahead at white gates into Fourteen.

10% off stays of 2 or more nights.

Mike Lewis & Diana Bailey
Fourteen, The Quay,
Burnham-on-Crouch CM0 8AT
Tel   +44 (0)1621 782002
Email   diana@baileylewis.co.uk

Entry 199   Map 10

Gloucestershire

Steep Meadow

An understated exterior belies the charm of Helen and John's modern home. Built into the hillside, bedrooms give a hare's-eye view of woods and wildlife; the guest sitting room above, with its wall of sliding glass, is a comfortable eyrie peering proudly over the Forest of Dean. Recycled local wood and bricks warm the light and generous bedrooms; gleaming bathrooms have homemade soaps. Meals from the Aga-top are a treat: eggs, bacon, sausages, pork, and honey from the Meadow's lively menagerie. There are wonderful walks from the door and Abergavenny, with its magnificent food festival in September, is a 30-minute drive.

Ethical Collection: Environment; Food.
See page 420.

Price	£78-£88. Singles £38.
Rooms	3: 2 doubles, 1 single.
Meals	Dinner, 2 courses, £14; 3 courses, £17. Pub/restaurant 400 yds.
Closed	Rarely.
Directions	A4136 Monmouth towards Coleford. Right immed. after Staunton 30mph signs. At fork in road (150 yds) right up steep hill; house 1st on left.

Local food/produce in your room. Pig and chicken keeping advice. Lifts to walking start points.

Use your Sawday's Gift Card here.

Helen Theophilus
Steep Meadow,
Staunton, Coleford GL16 8PD
Tel   +44 (0)1594 832316
Email   helen@steepmeadow.co.uk
Web   www.steepmeadow.co.uk

Entry 200   Map 7

Gloucestershire

Grove Farm

Boards creak and you duck, in a farmhouse of the best kind: simple, small-roomed, stone-flagged, beamed, delightful. The walls are white, the polished furniture is good and there are pictures everywhere. In spite of great age (16th century), it's light, with lots of pretty windows. The 400 acres are farmed organically and Penny makes award-winning cheese and a grand breakfast – continental at busy times. Stupendous views across the Severn estuary to the Cotswolds, the Forest of Dean on the doorstep, and woodland walks carpeted with spring flowers. And there is simply no noise – unless the guinea fowl are in voice.

Price	£70. Singles £40.
Rooms	2: 1 double; 1 twin/double with separate bath.
Meals	Packed lunch £5. Pub 2 miles.
Closed	Rarely.
Directions	2 miles south of Newnham on A48. Almost at bottom of hill right into a pull-in just after sign on left to Bullo Pill. There are two tracks, take the left one.

Penny & David Hill
Grove Farm,
Bullo Pill, Newnham GL14 1DZ
Tel +44 (0)1594 516304
Email davidandpennyhill@btopenworld.com
Web www.grovefarm-uk.com

Entry 201 Map 8

Gloucestershire

Frampton Court

Deep authenticity in this magnificent Grade I-listed house. The manor of Frampton-on-Severn has been in the family since the 11th century and although Rollo and Janie look after the estate, it is Gillian who greets you on behalf of the family and looks after you. There are exquisite examples of decorative woodwork and, in the hall, a cheerful log fire; perch on the Mouseman fire seat. Bedrooms are traditional with antiques, panelling and long views. Beds have fine linen, one with embroidered Jacobean hangings. Stroll around the ornamental canal, soak up the old-master views. An architectural masterpiece.

Price	£135–£170.
Rooms	3: 1 twin/double, 1 double, 1 four-poster.
Meals	Dinner £29. Pub across the green. Restaurant 3 miles.
Closed	Rarely.
Directions	M5 junc. 13 west A38 south, then B4071. Left down village green, 400 yds. 2nd turning left, between two chestnut trees & through ornamental gates in wall.

Rollo & Janie Clifford
Frampton Court, The Green, Frampton-on-Severn, Gloucester GL2 7EX
Tel +44 (0)1452 740267
Email framptoncourt@framptoncourtestate.co.uk
Web www.framptoncourtestate.co.uk

Entry 202 Map 8

Gloucestershire

Astalleigh House

The views from here to the Malvern Hills are worth the journey alone, but you also get bright, softly-coloured bedrooms with outrageously snuggly beds, the floatiest goose down, and compact bathrooms with generous towels and Body Shop goodies. There's a sitting room with pale walls, lots of books and magazines, jazzy striped cushions on a comfy sofa and interesting paintings of Northumberland – you can flop here happily. Affable Harriet gives you eggs from their hens and delicious sausages and bacon from the local butcher to set you up for grand walks; this is a good romantic escape for those with outdoor tastes.

Price	From £80. Singles £55. Child £15.
Rooms	2: 1 double, 1 family.
Meals	Pub/restaurant 0.5 miles.
Closed	Christmas & New Year.
Directions	M5, junc. 8, M50 junc. 1 north A38. Then 2nd left Ripple, Uckinghall, Equine Hospital, left at x-roads. House 1st on left. Train to Cheltenham, Gloucester or Pershore.

Harriet & Keith Jewers
Astalleigh House, School Lane,
Ripple, Tewkesbury GL20 6EU
Tel   +44 (0)1684 593740
Mobile   +44 (0)7530 144557
Email   jewers@jewers.freeserve.co.uk
Web   www.astalleighhouse.co.uk

Entry 203   Map 8

Gloucestershire

Ivydene House

A joy to arrive and a pleasure to stay, at this red-brick 1790s house a short hop from the Malvern Hills. Rosemary greets guests with tea and homemade cake by the fire, little Teddie (white and fluffy) shows you around the garden. Downstairs has been decorated in warm farmhouse style: old polished quarry tiles, cream walls, fresh flowers, wicker dining chairs, a great big inglenook. Fabulous bedrooms have an upbeat elegance with contemporary headboards, crisp linen and silk cushions – "just heavenly," say readers. Bathrooms sparkle, breakfasts are beautiful and Peter and Rosemary couldn't be nicer. Such value.

Price	From £75. Singles from £55.
Rooms	2: 1 twin/double, 1 double.
Meals	Pub within walking distance.
Closed	Christmas.
Directions	M5 junc. 8 onto M50. Exit junc. 1 onto A38 north, then 1st left to Ripple. Through to Uckinghall, over bridge, house at bottom on right.

 DVDs in bedrooms. Free pick-up from local bus/train station.

 Use your Sawday's Gift Card here.

Rosemary Gallagher
Ivydene House,
Uckinghall, Tewkesbury GL20 6ES
Tel   +44 (0)1684 592453
Mobile   +44 (0)7879 463291
Email   rosemary@ivydenehouse.net
Web   www.ivydenehouse.net

Entry 204   Map 8

Gloucestershire

The Court

Just off Chipping Campden high street this huge honey-hued Jacobean house has been in the family since it was built in 1624 by Sir Baptist Hicks. Dogs sound the alarm when you knock… step inside to find a relaxed faded splendour. Delicate ornaments sit on exquisite antiques, family portraits and spectacular oils line the walls; up winding stairs, bedrooms (some with TVs) have comfy beds, books, a mix of beautiful and functional furniture and breathtaking views of rooftops or gardens. Jane's friendly housekeeper cooks your Aga breakfast – eggs and jams are from the garden. The walking is superb, Hidcote and Kiftsgate are close.

Gloucestershire

The Old School

Comfortable, warm and filled with understated style is this 1854 Cotswold stone house. Wendy and John are generous, beds are enormous, linen is laundered, towels and robes are thick and fluffy. Your own mini fridge is carefully hidden and lighting is well thought-out. Best of all is the upstairs sitting room: a chic, open-plan space with church style windows letting the light flood in and super sofas, good art, lovely fabrics. A wood-burner keeps you toasty, Wendy is a grand cook and all is flexible. A gorgeous, relaxing place to stay – on the A44 but peaceful at night – where absolutely nothing is too much trouble.

Price	£40–£70.
Rooms	4: 2 family suites; 1 double, 1 family suite, each with separate bath.
Meals	Pub/restaurant 30 yds.
Closed	Christmas, Easter, Whitsun bank holiday & half term.
Directions	Oxford A34 to Moreton-in-Marsh & Chipping Campden, then right into High St, right signed Shipston. Round one way system left into Calf Lane; 1st house on left.

10% off stays of 2 or more nights.

Jane Glennie
The Court, Calf Lane,
Chipping Campden GL55 6JQ
Tel   +44 (0)1386 840201
Email   j14glennie@aol.com
Web   www.thecourtchippingcampden.co.uk

Entry 205   Map 8

Price	From £120. Singles from £96.
Rooms	4: 3 doubles, 1 twin/double.
Meals	Dinner, 4 courses, £32. Supper, 2 courses, £18. Supper tray £12. Pub 0.5 miles.
Closed	Rarely.
Directions	From Moreton, A44 for Chipping Norton & Oxford. Little Compton 3.5 miles; stay on main road, then right for Chastleton village. House on corner, immed. left into drive.

10% off room rate Mon-Thurs.

Use your Sawday's Gift Card here.

Wendy Veale & John Scott-Lee
The Old School, Little Compton,
Moreton-in-Marsh GL56 0SL
Tel   +44 (0)1608 674588
Mobile   +44 (0)7831 098271
Email   wendy@theoldschoolbedandbreakfast.co
Web   www.theoldschoolbedandbreakfast.com

Entry 206   Map 8

Gloucestershire

Trinity House

Meet Zelie: generous, charming, and passionate about the Cotswolds. Off a lane in dreamy Upper Oddington is a smart modern house with a crisp gravel drive and newly planted borders. Inside, a country elegance prevails. Antique furniture shines with care and polish, walls are covered with 20th-century art and splendid sofas front the fire. Bedrooms and bathrooms ooze comfort and joy: one with its own terrace, all with village views. But don't snuggle under the goose down for too long: breakfast verges on the sinful and is locally sourced and delicious. Prepare to be thoroughly spoiled!

Price	From £100. Singles from £60.
Rooms	3 twins/doubles.
Meals	Pubs within walking distance.
Closed	Rarely.
Directions	From Stow-on-the-Wold A436. Fork right dir. Bledington & Kingham, 0.75 miles left Upper Oddington. Drive immed. after phone box on right.

 10% off stays of 2 or more nights.

Zelie Mason
Trinity House, Upper Oddington,
Moreton-in-Marsh GL56 0XH

Tel	+44 (0)1451 831284
Mobile	+44 (0)7809 429365
Email	zelie.mason@talk21.com
Web	www.trinityhousebandb.co.uk

Entry 207   Map 8

Gloucestershire

Windy Ridge House

Everyone loves Windy Ridge. It's comfortable, it's cosy, it's run by a cheerful staff and it's well positioned for touring the Cotswolds. Nick's father was in construction and built this in traditional style using the finest timbers and stone; refurbishment sees brand-new carpets for bedrooms, stairs and landings. There's a green marble bathroom with mirrored walls, a proper four-man lift, a pine-panelled drawing room and polished things at every turn. Take a book to a velveteen sofa and help yourself from the honesty bar; visit the arboretum, the prize-winning gardens and the summer heated pool.

Price	From £90. Singles from £70.
Rooms	4: 2 doubles; 1 double, 1 twin/double each with separate bath.
Meals	Pub 100 yds.
Closed	Rarely.
Directions	From Stow, north for Broadway on A424 for 2 miles to Coach & Horses pub. Opp., right by postbox & 30mph signs down single-track lane. Entrance 100 yds down on left, bear left up drive.

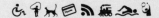 10% off stays of 3 or more nights Mon-Thurs.

Use your Sawday's Gift Card here.

Nick & Jennifer Williams
Windy Ridge House, Longborough,
Moreton-in-Marsh GL56 0QY

Tel	+44 (0)1451 830465
Email	nick@windy-ridge.co.uk
Web	www.windy-ridge.co.uk

Entry 208   Map 8

Gloucestershire

Wren House

Barely two miles from Stow-on-the-Wold, this peaceful house sits charmingly on the edge of a tiny hamlet. It was built before the English Civil War and Kiloran spent two years stylishly renovating it; the results are a joy. Downstairs, light-filled, elegant rooms with glowing rugs on pale Cotswold stone; upstairs, delicious bedrooms, spotless bathrooms and a doorway to duck. Breakfast in the vaulted kitchen is locally sourced and organic, where possible, and the well-planted garden, in which you are encouraged to sit, has far-reaching views. Explore rolling valleys and glorious gardens; Kiloran can advise.

Ethical Collection: Food. See page 420.

Gloucestershire

Clapton Manor

Karin and James's 16th-century manor is as all homes should be: loved and lived-in. And, with three-foot-thick walls, Persian rugs on flagstoned floors, sit-in fireplaces and stone-mullioned windows, it's gorgeous. The garden, enclosed by old stone walls, is full of birdsong and roses. One bedroom has a secret door that leads to a fuchsia-pink bathroom; the other room, smaller, has a recently revealed Tudor stone fireplace and wonderful garden views. Wellies, dogs, barbours, a comfy guest sitting room… and breakfast by a vast fireplace on homemade bread and jams and eggs from the hens. A happy, charming family home.

Price	£100–£110. Singles from £75.
Rooms	3: 1 twin/double; 1 twin/double with separate bath & shower; 1 twin with separate bath.
Meals	Pubs/restaurants 1 mile.
Closed	Rarely.
Directions	A429 between Stow & Moreton; turn to Donnington; 400 yds, left uphill; 150 yds, sign right in wall opp. 30mph sign. Enter between this and Granary Cottage; park at rear through 5-bar gate.

10% off stays of 3 or more nights Mon-Thurs.

Use your Sawday's Gift Card here.

Price	From £100. Singles £90.
Rooms	2: 1 double, 1 twin/double.
Meals	Pub/restaurants within 15-minute drive.
Closed	Rarely.
Directions	A429 Cirencester-Stow. Right signed Sherborne & Clapton. In village, pass grassy area to left, postbox in one corner; house straight ahead on left on corner, facing down hill.

10% off stays of 2 or more nights Mon-Thurs (Nov-Mar).

	Kiloran McGrigor
	Wren House, Donnington,
	Stow-on-the-Wold GL56 0XZ
Tel	+44 (0)1451 831787
Mobile	+44 (0)7802 676673
Email	enquiries@wrenhouse.net
Web	www.wrenhouse.net

Entry 209   Map 8

	Karin & James Bolton
	Clapton Manor,
	Clapton-on-the-Hill GL54 2LG
Tel	+44 (0)1451 810202
Mobile	+44 (0)7967 144416
Email	bandb@claptonmanor.co.uk
Web	www.claptonmanor.co.uk

Entry 210   Map 8

Gloucestershire

Sherborne Forge

You are in a quiet Cotswolds corner, in your own restored cottage across the garden from the owner's 17th-century house, and overlooking Sherborne Brook. Walk in to a large living space with a high beamed ceiling, comfy sofas, bright rugs, antiques, flowers, books and a dining table and chairs. You have your own small kitchen for toast and tea; Karen brings over a delicious organic breakfast, served on a private terrace on sunny mornings. Your bedroom has pretty fabrics and fine linen; the bathroom has a big tub for long soaks. Fish for trout in the brook, head off for glorious walks and bike rides... this is a sanctuary.

Price	From £98. Singles £75.
Rooms	Cottage: 1 double, sitting room & kitchenette.
Meals	Pub/restaurant 2.5 miles.
Closed	Rarely.
Directions	A429 at Northleach; A40 towards Oxford. 3 miles, left signed Clapton & Sherborne. After 1 mile, left signed Farmington & Turkdean. 400 yds past houses, right before 30mph exit sign. 100 yds down small lane to house.

	Karen Kelly
	Sherborne Forge, Number 1
	Sherborne, Cheltenham GL54 3DW
Tel	+44 (0)1451 844286
Mobile	+44 (0)7796 146130
Email	karen.j.kelly@btinternet.com
Web	www.sherborneforge.co.uk

Entry 211   Map 8

Gloucestershire

Rectory Farmhouse

Once a monastery, now a farmhouse with style. Passing a development of converted farm buildings to reach the Rectory's warm Cotswold stones makes the discovery doubly exciting. More glory within: Sybil, a talented designer, has created something immaculate, fresh and uplifting. A wood-burner glows in the sitting room, bed linen is white, walls cream; beds are superb, bathrooms sport cast-iron slipper baths and power showers and views are to the church. Your hosts are naturally friendly; Sybil used to own a restaurant and her breakfasts – by the Aga or in the conservatory under a rampant vine – are a further treat.

Price	From £96. Singles £70.
Rooms	2 doubles.
Meals	Pubs/restaurants 1 mile.
Closed	Christmas & New Year.
Directions	B4068 from Stow to Lower Swell, left just before Golden Ball Inn. Far end of gravel drive on right.

	Sybil Gisby
	Rectory Farmhouse,
	Lower Swell, Cheltenham GL54 1LH
Tel	+44 (0)1451 832351
Email	rectoryfarmhouse@yahoo.com
Web	www.rectoryfarmhouse.yolasite.com

Entry 212   Map 8

Gloucestershire

North Farmcote

Step back 50 years, to a solid 19th-century farmhouse high on the escarpment, and views falling away to the west; on a clear day you can see Hay Bluff. A brilliant spot for North Cotswolds' exploration, it is run by charming and gently self-deprecating David – farmer of cereals and sheep, keen walker, good shot. The exploits of his family decorate the walls (racing at Brooklands, hunting in Africa), there's a floral three-piece to sink into, a terrace with outstanding views, and a great pub you can stride to across fields. Bedrooms and bathrooms are old-fashioned, spacious, comfortable and spotless.

Price	From £70. Singles from £50.
Rooms	3: 1 double, 1 twin; 1 twin with separate bath.
Meals	Pub 2 miles.
Closed	Rarely.
Directions	B4077 from Stow-on-the-Wold. After Ford, left to Farmcote (signed). After 1.5 miles right. House at end on left.

David Eayrs
North Farmcote,
Winchcombe, Cheltenham GL54 5AU
Tel   +44 (0)1242 602304
Email   davideayrs@yahoo.co.uk
Web   www.northfarmcote.co.uk

Entry 213   Map 8

Gloucestershire

Fieldways

High in the Wolds, close to a sleepy village green, are a secluded house and garden where life ticks over beautifully inside and out. Rosewood mahogany, heaps of flowers, a pretty gazebo and a staircase lined with art – all this is the creation of Scottish-Canadian Alan, generous to a fault, a perfectionist in all he does. Marble bathrooms have heated floors while classic country bedrooms are full of deep-carpeted comfort. An immaculate, traditional drawing room and conservatory are yours to share. Wake to the prospect of a fine cooked breakfast, homemade jams, teas from all over the world. Marvellous.

Price	£80–£100. Singles £65–£75.
Rooms	3: 1 double, 2 twins.
Meals	Lunch £15–£20. Dinner from £40. Pub 50 yds.
Closed	Rarely.
Directions	From M40, exit at junc. 15 onto A429. At Bourton-on-the-Water take A436, then left at sign for Cold Aston. Ask for Fieldways or phone 07790 024532.

 Late checkout (12pm). Bottle of wine in your room.

Alan Graham
Fieldways, 12 Chapel Lane,
Cold Aston, Cheltenham GL54 3BJ
Tel   +44 (0)1451 810659
Mobile +44 (0)7790 024532
Email   cascadegroup@aol.com
Web   www.fieldways.com

Entry 214   Map 8

Gloucestershire

Westward

Susie and Jim are highly organised and efficient, juggling farm, horses and B&B. She's also a great cook (Leith trained). The grand, but cosy, house sits above Sudeley Castle surrounded by its own 600 acres; all bedrooms look west to long views. Colours, fabrics and furniture are in perfect harmony, beds and linen are inviting, and the easy mix of elegant living and family bustle is delightful. There's tea on the terrace in summer and by a log fire in winter... your hosts delight in sharing this very English home. Wonderful walks, Cheltenham, Cotswold villages, fabulous restaurants and pubs are near.

Price	From £90. Singles from £60.
Rooms	3: 1 double, 2 twins/doubles.
Meals	Pubs/restaurants 1 mile.
Closed	December/January.
Directions	From Abbey Sq., Winchcombe, go north; after 50 yds, right into Castle St. Follow for 1 mile; after farm buildings, right for Sudeley Lodge; follow for 600 yds. House on right; first oak door.

Susie & Jim Wilson
Westward, Sudeley Lodge,
Winchcombe, Cheltenham GL54 5JB
Tel   +44 (0)1242 604372
Email   westward@haldon.co.uk
Web   www.westward-sudeley.co.uk

Entry 215   Map 8

Gloucestershire

Detmore House

Down a private drive, surrounded by seven acres, this smart shiny house has been the home of poets, artists and writers. Gill carries on the creativity with her cooking, interior design, jewellery, gardening and chickens; she and Hugh are easy natural hosts. Supremely comfortable bedrooms have a smart hotel feel, bathrooms are immaculate and you and your dinner party guests will be spoiled with organic produce from the garden. There are wide lawns and mature trees and you can lap up the views across Charlton Hills from lots of lovely sitting spots. Cheltenham and the Cotswold Way are on the doorstep.

Price	From £85. Singles from £65.
Rooms	4: 2 twins/doubles, 1 family room for 3, 1 twin.
Meals	Dinner from £28.50 (for groups of 6+). Packed lunch £6. Pub 1 mile.
Closed	Christmas & New Year.
Directions	A40 from Cheltenham dir. Oxford, thro' Charlton Kings. After 1 mile BP garage on right, next left into Detmore Close. Driveway immed. on right (signed).

 10% off stays of 3 or more nights.

Gill Kilminster
Detmore House, London Road,
Charlton Kings, Cheltenham GL52 6UT
Tel   +44 (0)1242 582868
Email   enquiries@detmorehouse.com
Web   www.detmorehouse.com

Entry 216   Map 8

Gloucestershire

The Courtyard Studio

This smart first-floor studio, attractive in reclaimed red brick, is reached via its own wrought-iron staircase; you are beautifully private. The friendly owners live next door, and will cook you a delicious breakfast in the house, or leave you a continental one in your own fridge. Find a clever, compact, contemporary space with a light and uncluttered living area, a mini window seat opposite two very comfortable boutiquey beds, fine linen, wicker armchair, and a patio area for balmy days. A 20-minute walk brings you to the centre of Cheltenham and you're a two-minute canter from the races. *Minimum stay two nights.*

Price	£75.
Rooms	Studio: 1 twin.
Meals	Restaurants/pubs within 1 mile.
Closed	Rarely.
Directions	Racecourse r'bout, A435 dir. town centre, right Cleevelands Drive. 300 yards on left, thro' pillared gateway in front of mansion. Keep left, enter courtyard. No 1 in left corner.

10% off stays of 2 or more nights. Free pick-up from local bus/train station.

John & Annette Gill
The Courtyard Studio, 1 The Cleevelands Courtyard, Cleevelands Drive, Cheltenham GL50 4QF

Tel	+44 (0)1242 573125
Mobile	+44 (0)7901 978917
Email	courtyardstudio@aol.com

Entry 217   Map 8

Gloucestershire

5 Ewlyn Road

In a bustling suburb of Cheltenham, Barbara's red-brick villa remains firmly unmodernised. The whiff of beeswax fills the air and Barbara looks after you with old-fashioned ease; the front room has an open fire where you can read a book or chat. Your bedroom is peaceful, the bed is firm, and the white cotton sheets robustly pressed; the clean and purposeful bathroom is shared but not noticeably. In the warm parlour Barbara gives you freshly squeezed orange juice, best Gloucester Old Spot bacon, sausage and free-range eggs – have it outside the sunny back door in summer. Authentic, great value B&B.

Price	£60. Singles £30.
Rooms	1 twin sharing bath (& separate shower).
Meals	Pubs/restaurants 5-minute walk.
Closed	Rarely.
Directions	From A40, signs to Stroud. Up Bath Road past shops; at mini round-about bear left, then left signed Emmanuel Church. House 2nd on right; front door to side.

Barbara Jameson
5 Ewlyn Road,
Cheltenham
GL53 7PB

Tel	+44 (0)1242 261243

Entry 218   Map 8

Gloucestershire

Hanover House

The former home of Elgar's wife, in an early-Victorian terrace in Cheltenham's heart, is warm, elegant, inviting and surprisingly peaceful. There are big trees all around and the river Chelt laps at the foot of the garden. Inside, a graceful period décor is enlivened by golden retriever Sophie and exuberant splashes of colour; the delectable drawing room, with pale walls and a trio of arched windows, is the perfect foil for paintings, books and rugs. Bedrooms have vivid Indian throws, bathrooms are simply stylish, breakfasts are superb. Best of all are Veronica and James: musical, well-travelled, irresistible.

Price	£100–£110. Singles £70.
Rooms	3: 1 double; 1 double, 1 twin each with separate bath.
Meals	Pubs/restaurants 200 yds.
Closed	Rarely.
Directions	In Cheltenham town centre, 200 yds from bus & coach station; 800 yds from railway station. Parking available.

Veronica & James Ritchie
Hanover House,
65 St George's Road,
Cheltenham GL50 3DU
Tel   +44 (0)1242 541297
Email   info@hanoverhouse.org
Web   www.hanoverhouse.org

Entry 219   Map 8

Gloucestershire

St Annes

Step straight off the narrow pavement into a sunny hall and a welcome to match. Iris worked in tourism for years and lives here with antique restorer Greg, two smiling children and Rollo the dog. They've also made this pretty 17th-century house in the centre of a captivating village (some road noise) as eco-friendly as possible. Comfy bedrooms are charming; farmers' market breakfasts are a warm, cosy, stylish feast. As for Painswick, it is known as 'the Queen of the Cotswolds': enjoy superb walks through orchid meadows and beech woods carpeted with bluebells; great pubs on the way too. *Min. two nights at weekends April-Sept.*

Ethical Collection: Environment; Food. See page 420.

Price	£70. Singles £45.
Rooms	3: 1 double, 1 twin; 1 four-poster.
Meals	Packed lunch £5. Restaurants/pubs in village.
Closed	Rarely.
Directions	A46 Stroud to Painswick; in Painswick, left after lights; house 3rd door on right. Bus: from Cheltenham & Stroud. Parking within 100 yds.

Iris McCormick
St Annes,
Gloucester Street,
Painswick GL6 6QN
Tel   +44 (0)1452 812879
Email   greg.iris@btinternet.com
Web   www.st-annes-painswick.co.uk

Entry 220   Map 8

Gloucestershire

Nation House

Three cottages were knocked together to create this wisteria-clad, listed village house, now a terrific B&B. Beams are exposed, walls are pale and hung with prints, floors are close-carpeted, the sitting room is formally cosy and quiet. Smart, comfortable bedrooms have patchwork quilts, low beams and padded seats at lattice windows; the bathroom is spotless and the small shower room gleaming. In summer, breakfast in the conservatory on still-warm homemade bread, local bacon and sausages, Brenda's preserves. The village is a Cotswold treasure, with two good eating places and with many walks from the door.

Price	£75–£85. Singles £50.
Rooms	3: 1 family for 3; 2 doubles sharing bath (let to same party only).
Meals	Pubs 50 yds.
Closed	Rarely.
Directions	From Cirencester A419 for Stroud. After 7 miles right to Bisley. Left at village shop. House 50 yds on right.

 10% off stays of 2 or more nights. Bottle of wine in your room.

Use your Sawday's Gift Card here.

Brenda & Mike Hammond
Nation House,
George Street, Bisley GL6 7BB
Tel +44 (0)1452 770197
Email nation.house@homecall.co.uk
Web www.nationhouse.co.uk

Entry 221 Map 8

Gloucestershire

Well Farm

Perhaps it's the gentle, unstuffy attitude of Kate and Edward. Or the great position of the house with its glorious views across the valley. Whichever, you'll feel comforted and invigorated by your stay. It's a real family home and you get both a fresh, pretty bedroom that feels very private and the use of a comfortable, book-filled sitting room opening to a flowery courtyard: Kate is an inspired gardener. Sleep soundly on the softest of pillows, wake to the deep peace of the countryside and the delicious prospect of eggs from their own hens, local sausages and good bacon. The area teems with great walks — lovely pubs too.

Price	From £85.
Rooms	1 twin/double & sitting room.
Meals	Dinner from £20. Pubs nearby.
Closed	Rarely.
Directions	Directions on booking and on website.

Kate & Edward Gordon Lennox
Well Farm,
Frampton Mansell, Stroud GL6 8JB
Tel +44 (0)1285 760651
Email kategl@btinternet.com
Web www.well-farm.co.uk

Entry 222 Map 8

Gloucestershire

Forwood Farm

Strong old bones and quiet contemporary design make for a pale, restful atmosphere at Forwood, the oatmeal, cream and caramel base brightened by scatter cushions, patterned rugs and modern art. Rose has flair and is enjoying reviving the big garden and its stone terraces. Home-grown fruit and eggs are served with local bacon in the pale blue breakfast room: rustic chest on original oak floorboards, wood-burner and fresh flowers, French windows onto a pretty courtyard. Lovely bedrooms with super modern showers, too. Walk out onto National Trust common land or to pure-Cotswold Minchinhampton for pubs and other antique fleshpots.

Price	£85. Singles £75.
Rooms	3 twins/doubles.
Meals	Packed lunch for walkers £7. Pub/restaurant 0.5 miles.
Closed	Rarely.
Directions	Directions on booking.

10% off room rate Mon-Thurs.

Rose Evans
Forwood Farm, Forwood,
Minchinhampton, Stroud GL6 9AB
Tel +44 (0)1453 731620
Email rose@forwoodfarm.com
Web www.forwoodfarm.com

Entry 223   Map 8

Gloucestershire

The Guest House

You get your own new timber-framed house with masses of light and space, a terrace, and spectacular valley and woodland views. The living room has wooden floors, lovely old oak furniture and French windows onto the rose-filled garden. Sue brims with enthusiasm and is a flexible host: breakfast can be over in her kitchen or continental in yours. Look forward to the papers, eggs from the hens, delicious dinners with produce from the veg patch. The bedroom is a charming up-in-the-eaves room with oriental rugs, colourful linen and a big comfy bed; your fresh, simple wet room is downstairs. A peaceful, secluded place.

Price	From £120.
Rooms	Cottage: 1 double, sitting room, sofabed & kitchenette.
Meals	Dinner, 2 courses, from £12; 3 courses, from £20. Pub 1 mile.
Closed	Rarely.
Directions	From Cirencester, A435 dir. Cheltenham. Left after golf course; over x-roads; 1st left. Left in Bagendon after phone box, immed. left up steep hill signed 'No through Road'.

Bottle of wine with dinner on first night.

Sue Bathurst
The Guest House, Manor Cottage,
Bagendon, Cirencester GL7 7DU
Tel +44 (0)1285 831417
Email heritage.venues@virgin.net
Web www.cotswoldguesthouse.co.uk

Entry 224   Map 8

Gloucestershire

The Old Rectory

English to the core — and to the bottom of its lovely garden, with a woodland walk and plenty of quiet places to sit. You sweep into the circular driveway to a yellow labrador welcome. This beautiful 17th-century high gabled house is comfortably lived-in with an understated décor, antiques, creaky floorboards and a real sense of history. The bedrooms, one with a garden view, have very good beds, a chaise longue or an easy chair; bathrooms are vintage but large. Caroline is calm and competent and serves breakfasts with organic eggs and local bacon at the long polished table in the rich red dining room. A special place.

Price	£80–£95. Singles from £50.
Rooms	2: 1 double, 1 twin/double.
Meals	Pub 200 yds.
Closed	December/January.
Directions	South through village from A417. Right after Masons Arms. House 200 yds on left, through stone pillars.

Roger & Caroline Carne
The Old Rectory,
Meysey Hampton, Cirencester GL7 5JX
Tel +44 (0)1285 851200
Email carolinecarne@cotswoldwireless.co.uk
Web www.meyseyoldrectory.co.uk

Entry 225 Map 8

Gloucestershire

Ewen Wharf

Life, colour and warmth fill Fiona's pretty early 19th-century wharf keeper's cottage, snoozing in a tranquil corner of the Cotswolds. A log fire blazes in the cosy low-beamed sitting room, a little Norfolk terrier wags enthusiastically, porcelain marches proudly over shelves and you may recognise art by Fiona's father-in-law — creator of the famous Guinness advertisements. A pleasure to take tea in the well-tended garden, slumber deeply in plump, comfortable beds, chat to Fiona over bacon and eggs from the local farm. Stride out on the Thames Path or stroll to the village pub. Such a peaceful home — and good value too.

Price	£75–£80. Singles £50.
Rooms	2: 1 twin/double, 1 twin sharing bath (let to same party only).
Meals	Pub/restaurant 1 mile.
Closed	Christmas & New Year.
Directions	From Cirencester follow signs to south west and Tetbury. 2 miles, left onto A429 to Kemble signed Chippenham. After 1 mile, left to Ewen. House on right before bridge.

Fiona Gilroy
Ewen Wharf,
Kemble, Cirencester GL7 6BP
Tel +44 (0)1285 770469
Email fmgilroy@tiscali.co.uk
Web www.ewenwharf.co.uk

Entry 226 Map 8

Gloucestershire

Kempsford Manor

On the edge of the Cotswolds, this 17th-century village manor house is surrounded by hedges and mature trees. Crunch up the gravelled drive to find floor-to-ceiling windows, dark floors with patterned rugs, wood panelling, a piano and a library. Spacious bedrooms have super garden views; one comes with a Chinese theme, a mix of rugs and blankets and a pretty quilt. Bathrooms are functional and old-fashioned. Beautifully tended gardens (snowdrops are special here) lead to an orchard and canal walk; stoke up on Zehra's homemade muesli and bread and return for dinner — vegetables are home-grown. *NGS garden. Art exhibitions held.*

Price	£65–£70. Singles from £40.
Rooms	3: 2 doubles, 1 single sharing 2 bathrooms.
Meals	Dinner by arrangement. Pub 200 yds.
Closed	Rarely.
Directions	A419 Cirencester-Swindon; Kempsford is signed with Fairford. Right into village, past small village green; on right, through stone columns. Glass front door, by a fountain.

10% off stays of 3 or more nights. Stay 3 nights, 4th free, Oct-Apr.

Zehra I Williamson
Kempsford Manor, High Street,
Kempsford, Fairford GL7 4EQ
Tel   +44 (0)1285 810131
Mobile   +44 (0)7980 543882
Email   info@kempsfordmanor.com
Web   www.kempsfordmanor.com

Entry 227   Map 8

Gloucestershire

107 Gloucester Street

Slip through gates into a narrow courtyard of potted shrubs and honey-coloured Cotswold stone. This modest Georgian merchant's house is three minutes from the charming town centre yet blissfully quiet. Inside: buttery colours, well-loved antiques, soft uncluttered spaces. Restful, understated bedrooms are small, chic and spotless. Kitchen breakfasts overlook the sheltered garden — a verdant spot for relaxing in summer. For evenings, a creamy first-floor sitting room with a small log fire. Ethne and her ex-army husband are full of fun and good humour — very special.

Price	£80. Singles £55.
Rooms	2: 1 double, 1 twin.
Meals	Hotel 300 yds & restaurants 8-minute walk.
Closed	Rarely. (Enquire by email only in February.)
Directions	Directions on booking.

10% off stays of 2 or more nights.

Brendan & Ethne McGuinness
107 Gloucester Street,
Cirencester GL7 2DW
Tel   +44 (0)1285 657861
Mobile   +44 (0)7746 100789
Email   ethnemcg@onetel.com
Web   www.107gloucesterstreet.co.uk

Entry 228   Map 8

Gloucestershire

Lodge Farm

A plum Cotswolds position, a striking garden, a rolling programme of improvements, exceptional linen — there are plenty of reasons to stay. Then there are your flexible hosts, who can help wedding groups, give you supper en famille next to the Aga or something smart and candlelit round the dining room table: perfect for a house party. The sitting room has flowers, family photographs and lots of magazines; sometimes home-produced lamb for dinner, always excellent coffee at breakfast, homemade bread and their own free-range eggs. Peace and quiet lovers will delight, yet you are a short walk from Tetbury.

Price	£70–£80. Singles from £60. Family suite £95.
Rooms	4: 2 twins/doubles; 1 twin/double, 1 family suite sharing bath.
Meals	Dinner, 2-3 courses, £15–£25. Pub/bistro 2.5 miles.
Closed	Rarely.
Directions	From Cirencester A433 to Tetbury, right B4014 to Avening. After 250 yds, left onto Chavenage Lane. Lodge Farm 1.3 miles on right; left of barn on drive.

	Robin & Nicky Salmon
	Lodge Farm,
	Chavenage, Tetbury GL8 8XW
Tel	+44 (0)1666 505339
Mobile	+44 (0)7836 221457
Email	nsalmon.lodgefarm@btinternet.com
Web	www.lodgefarm.co.uk

Entry 229   Map 8

Gloucestershire

Drakestone House

A treat by anyone's reckoning. Utterly delightful people with wide-ranging interests (ex-British Council and college lecturing; arts, travel, gardening) in a manor-type house full of beautiful furniture. The house was born of the Arts and Crafts movement: wooden panels painted green, a log-fired drawing room for guests, handsome old furniture, comfortable proportions, good beds with proper blankets. The garden's massive clipped hedges, Monterey pines and smooth, great lawn are impressive, as is the whole place — and the views stretch to the Severn Estuary and Wales.

Price	£90. Singles £50.
Rooms	3: 1 twin/double, 1 double, 1 twin, each with separate bath/shower.
Meals	Dinner £35. BYO. Pub/restaurant under 1 mile.
Closed	Christmas & New Year.
Directions	B4060 from Stinchcombe to Wotton-under-Edge. 0.25 miles out of Stinchcombe village. Driveway on left marked, before long bend.

	Hugh & Crystal Mildmay
	Drakestone House,
	Stinchcombe, Dursley GL11 6AS
Tel	+44 (0)1453 542140

Entry 230   Map 8

Gloucestershire

The Moda House

A fine house and a big B&B, but one that retains a deeply homely feel; Duncan and Jo are hugely well-travelled and have filled it with pictures and artefacts from all over the world. Bedrooms differ (three are in a neat annexe) but all are cosy and well decorated with lovely colours, good fabrics, pocket sprung mattresses and bright bathrooms with thick towels. Breakfast is a truly local feast and will set you up for fabulous walks (you are a mile from the Cotswold Way), there's a basement sitting room with comfy armchairs and lots of books, and you have the bustling town to explore with its shops and restaurants.

Price	From £82. Singles from £65.
Rooms	11: 8 doubles, 3 singles.
Meals	Pubs/restaurants within 0.25 miles.
Closed	Rarely.
Directions	Exit M4 at junction 18. Follow A46 northbound. Turn left and follow A432 into town centre. House is at top of High Street.

Duncan & Jo MacArthur
The Moda House, 1 High Street,
Chipping Sodbury BS37 6BA
Tel +44 (0)1454 312135
Email enquiries@modahouse.co.uk
Web www.modahouse.co.uk

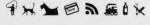

Entry 231 Map 3

Gloucestershire

Little Smithy

Minutes from the M4, the farming village is fairly quiet and your little cottage with mullioned windows completely private. Your front door opens into a hallway which runs the length of the building: at one end, the creamy twin with bright red bedspreads and sparkling bathroom next door, at the other, your L-shaped sitting room with an electric wood-burner. Upstairs is the comfy double and another smart bathroom; all is as neat as a pin. Joanna gives you breakfast in the main house, or on warm days in the garden: eggs from next door's hens, homemade bread and marmalade. Right on the Cotswold Way so perfect for walkers.

Price	£75. Singles £60.
Rooms	2: 1 double, 1 twin/double.
Meals	Pub/restaurant 1 mile.
Closed	Christmas & Easter.
Directions	Bath A46 north. Cross M4 signed Stroud, then almost immed. 1st turning on right. After Compass Inn, 2nd turning on right into village. Past church; house 1st on right after left-hand bend.

10% off stays of 2 or more nights. Free pick-up from local bus/train station.

Joanna Bowman
Little Smithy, Smithy House,
Tormarton, Badminton GL9 1HU
Tel +44 (0)1454 218412
Email richardbowman@uk2.net
Web www.littlesmithy.com

Entry 232 Map 3

Hampshire

Yew Tree House

A charming papier-mâché cat welcomes you at the front door, setting the tone for this artistic, tranquil house. The views, the house and the villagers are said to have inspired Dickens, who escaped London for the peace of the valley. The exquisite red brick was there 200 years before him; the rare dovecote, to which you may have the key, 300 years before that. Thoughtful hosts, interesting to talk to, have created a house of understated elegance: a yellow-ochre bedroom with Descamps bed linen, cashmere/silk curtains designed by their son, a view onto an enchanting garden, a profusion of flowers. Great value.

Price	£75. Singles by arrangement.
Rooms	2: 1 twin; 1 double with separate bath.
Meals	Pub in village.
Closed	Rarely.
Directions	From A30 west of Stockbridge for 1.5 miles, left at minor x-roads. After 2 miles left at T-junc. House on left at next junc. opposite Greyhound.

 Use your Sawday's Gift Card here.

Philip & Janet Mutton
Yew Tree House,
Broughton, Stockbridge SO20 8AA
Tel   +44 (0)1794 301227
Email   pandjmutton@onetel.com

Entry 233   Map 3

Hampshire

Sandy Corner

Stride straight onto open moorland from this smallholding on the edge of the New Forest – a good place for anyone who enjoys walking, cycling, riding, wildlife and the great outdoors. And there's plenty of room for wet clothes and muddy boots. You may hear the call of a nightjar in June, Dartford warblers nest nearby, hens cluck around the yard. Sue also keeps a horse, two cats, a few sheep. You have a little guest sitting room, fresh sunny bedrooms, your own spot in the garden and a marvellous, away-from-it-all feel. You can walk to one pub; others are nearby.

Price	From £78. Singles from £50.
Rooms	2 doubles.
Meals	Packed lunch £8. Pub within walking distance.
Closed	Rarely.
Directions	On A338, 1 mile S of Fordingbridge, at small x-roads, turn for Hyde & Hungerford. Up hill & right at school for Ogdens; left at next x-roads for Ogdens North; on right at bottom of hill.

Sue Browne
Sandy Corner,
Ogdens North, Fordingbridge SP6 2QD
Tel   +44 (0)1425 657295

Entry 234   Map 3

Hampshire

Vinegar Hill Pottery

A sylvan setting, stylish pottery, a young and talented family. The cobalt blues and rich browns of David's ceramics fill the old stables of a Victorian manor house. Take pottery courses (one hour to a long weekend) or just enjoy the creative Mexican-inspired décor. A narrow staircase spirals up to a modern loft: crisp whites, cathedral ceiling spiked with sunny windows, brilliant shower. The ground-floor garden suite has a patio, a sitting room, an unusual painted bed and optional children's beds. Lucy brings breakfast to your room. After which, stroll to the beach: stretch out and you almost touch the Isle of Wight.

Price	From £75. Singles from £60.
Rooms	2: 1 double, 1 suite (2 extra beds).
Meals	Pub/restaurant 0.25 miles.
Closed	Rarely.
Directions	A339 towards Christchurch. Left onto B3058. Next right into Manor Road, round bend into Barnes Lane. After Baptist church, Vinegar Hill is 3rd on right.

Lucy Rogers
Vinegar Hill Pottery,
Vinegar Hill, Milford on Sea SO41 0RZ
Tel +44 (0)1590 642979
Email info@davidrogerspottery.co.uk
Web www.davidrogerspottery.co.uk

Entry 235   Map 3

Hampshire

Bay Trees

Step in from the village street and you find yourself in a striking hall where the guest book perches on the music stand! Comfortable bedrooms are spotless and warm, with a hint of luxury; the double has French windows opening to a lush suntrap of a garden, a wonderful surprise, full of arbours and weeping willow and a brook at the end with a seat for two. Breakfasts are in gourmet style, served in the conservatory overlooking the magnolia. Robert, humorous and down-to-earth, makes you feel at ease the moment you arrive. The shingle beach with views to the Isle of Wight is a sprint away. *Min. two nights at weekends.*

Price	£80-£130. Singles from £50.
Rooms	4: 1 double, 1 four-poster; 1 triple, 1 single sharing bath (2nd room let to same party only).
Meals	Restaurants/pubs 100 yds.
Closed	Rarely.
Directions	From Lymington follow signs for Milford-on-Sea (B3058). On left, just past village green.

 10% off stays of 3 or more nights Mon-Thurs.

Robert Fry
Bay Trees,
8 High Street, Milford-on-Sea,
Lymington SO41 0QD
Tel +44 (0)1590 642186
Email rp.fry@virgin.net
Web www.baytreebedandbreakfast.co.uk

Entry 236   Map 3

Hampshire

Home Close

The setting is gorgeous, surrounded by the New Forest – walks start from the gate. The house, once a farm belonging to the Beaulieu estate, is now home to friendly Sally and Bob. You sleep in a sunshine-yellow bedroom overlooking the lovely garden, there are Lloyd Loom chairs for reading or TV, bottled water, proper milk, homemade shortbread. A generous breakfast, sometimes with home-baked bread, is taken in the pretty blue dining room at a solid oak table, from where you can watch the comings and goings of the birds beneath the arbour. Perfect for exploring the New Forest or a day trip to the Isle of Wight.

Price	From £80.
Rooms	1 double.
Meals	Packed lunch £7. Pubs/restaurants within 7 miles.
Closed	Christmas, New Year & occasionally.
Directions	M27 junc. 2. A326, then B3054 signed Beaulieu 1.1 miles from New Forest cattle grid, down gravel track signed Home Close & Vanguard. Left past cottage to gate.

	Sally Brearley
	Home Close,
	Hill Top, Beaulieu SO42 7YR
Tel	+44 (0)1590 612287
Email	homeclose@talktalk.net
Web	www.homeclosebedandbreakfast.co.uk

Entry 237   Map 3

Hampshire

Brymer House

Complete privacy in a B&B is rare. Here you have it, a 12-minute walk from town, cathedral and water meadows. Relax in your own half of a Victorian townhouse immaculately furnished and decorated and with a garden to match – all roses and lilac in the spring. Fizzy serves sumptuous breakfasts, there's a log fire in the guests' sitting room and fresh flowers abound – guests have been delighted. You are also left with an 'honesty box' so you may help yourselves to drinks. Bedrooms are small and elegant, with antique mirrors, furniture and bedspreads; bathrooms are warm and spotless. *Children over seven welcome.*

Price	£75-£85. Singles £54-£60.
Rooms	2: 1 double, 1 twin.
Meals	Pubs/restaurants nearby.
Closed	Christmas.
Directions	M3 junc. 9; A272 Winchester exit, then signs for Winchester Park & Ride. Under m'way, straight on at r'bout signed St Cross. Left at T-junc.

	Guy & Fizzy Warren
	Brymer House, 29-30 St Faith's Road,
	St Cross, Winchester SO23 9QD
Tel	+44 (0)1962 867428
Mobile	+44 (0)7762 201076
Email	brymerhouse@aol.com
Web	www.brymerhouse.co.uk

Entry 238   Map 4

Hampshire

Mulberry House

Deep into Jane Austen country, among ancient apple trees and rose bushes, is Mulberry House – the red-brick stable block of Old Alresford House. Peter and Sue are charming, and so is their home, filled with interesting pictures, fresh flowers and family photos. Private, quietly elegant guest rooms share a sitting room and kitchenette; the one in the eaves overlooks a pretty courtyard where a fountain plays. The dining room is elegant, but in fine weather you breakfast beneath the wisteria and vine-hung pergola on home-laid eggs and homemade jams. Comfortably English with a lovely garden.

Ethical Collection: Food. See page 420.

Price	£90. Singles £70.
Rooms	2: 1 double, 1 twin/double.
Meals	Pubs/restaurants within 15-minute walk.
Closed	Rarely.
Directions	M3 exit 9, signs to Alresford. In town centre, left onto B3046 to church on right. Then right into Colden Lane. House is 3rd on right through field gate.

	Sue & Peter Paice
	Mulberry House, Colden Lane,
	Old Alresford, Alresford SO24 9DY
Tel	+44 (0)1962 735518
Mobile	+44 (0)7801 931905
Email	suepaice@btinternet.com
Web	www.mulberryhousebnb.com

Entry 239 Map 4

Hampshire

The Threshing Barn

You are on the edge of the rolling Meon valley in South Downs National Park, the approach through hedge-lined lanes is bucolic and the beautifully restored barn sits on a conservation award-winning farm run by John. Choose between a colourful and homely double in the main house or independence in the glorious bothy – a beamed and light space with a big walk-in shower. Find flowers, good mattresses and feather and down pillows. Guests are greeted with tea, breakfast is a local or home-grown extravaganza (check out Emma's borage honey) and views are to one of the tallest village church spires in Hampshire. *Min. stay two nights.*

Price	£95. Singles £85.
Rooms	2: 1 double with separate bath. Bothy: 1 twin/double.
Meals	Packed lunch £7-£8. Pub 2 miles.
Closed	Rarely.
Directions	A272 Winchester to Petersfield. After A32 & A272 crossing, continue 0.8 miles towards Petersfield. Then left up Stocks Lane, 0.5 miles to the house.

 10% off stays of 2 or more nights Mon-Thurs. Bottle of wine in your room.

	Emma Bird
	The Threshing Barn,
	Stocks Lane, Privett GU34 3NZ
Tel	+44 (0)1730 828382
Mobile	+44 (0)7980 841154
Email	emmacbird@stocksfarmprivett.co.uk
Web	www.thethreshingbarn.co.uk

Entry 240 Map 4

Hampshire

Little Shackles

Gaze upon the pretty Arts and Crafts house from the comfort of the hammock or solar-heated pool: this is a charming place to stay. Rosemary advises on local gardens to visit (her own two acres are also special) and is the loveliest of hosts. Your bedroom has an elegant country air – firm beds with feather toppers, new armchairs and a new TV – and a spring-like bathroom with fluffy bathrobes and views to green fields. Breakfast is plentiful; dinner, at the lovely old drover's pub down the sleepy lane, is a simple treat. Within the South Downs National Park so the walks are marvellous, and Goodwood and Portsmouth are close.

Price	From £70. Singles from £40.
Rooms	2: 1 twin/double; 1 single sharing bath (2nd room let to same party only).
Meals	Packed lunch from £7. Pub 0.5 miles.
Closed	Rarely.
Directions	From London A3 take A272 junc. Petersfield, right at r'bout. 1st right into Kingsfernsden Ln, over level crossing, Reservoir Ln. Right into Harrow Ln. House 2nd on right.

Rosemary & Martin Griffiths
Little Shackles,
Harrow Lane, Petersfield GU32 2BZ
Tel   +44 (0)1730 263464
Email   martgriff@btinternet.com

Entry 241   Map 4

Hampshire

Mizzards Farm

The central hall is three storeys high, its vaulted roof open to the rafters. This is the oldest part of this lovely, wisteria-clad, mostly 16th-century farmhouse: kilims and fine antiques look splendid with old flagstones and wooden floors. There's a drawing room for musical evenings and an upstairs conservatory from which you can see the garden with its lake, outdoor chess and Harriet's sculptures. The four-poster is luxuriously kitsch with electric curtains, the other bedrooms are traditional and fresh. Come in the summer for occasional mini Glyndebournes on the lawn. *Children over eight welcome. Min. two nights.*

Price	£80-£90. Singles by arrangement.
Rooms	3: 1 double, 1 twin, 1 four-poster.
Meals	Pubs 0.5 miles.
Closed	Christmas & New Year.
Directions	From A272 at Rogate, turn for Harting & Nyewood. Cross humpback bridge; drive signed to right after 300 yds.

Harriet & Julian Francis
Mizzards Farm,
Rogate, Petersfield GU31 5HS
Tel   +44 (0)1730 821656
Email   francis@mizzards.co.uk

Entry 242   Map 4

Hampshire

Land of Nod

A 1939 house of character with hosts to match and one of the greatest gardens in the book... seven tended acres within 100 acres of woodland. There are azaleas and camellias, specimen trees, croquet, tennis, a white wisteria 40 years old – and orchids: Jeremy's passion. Breakfast in the chinoiserie dining room – the allegorical tableau is charming, the needlework on the walls dates from 1901. No sitting room, but bedrooms are spacious, with views over the garden; original baths have vast taps. Flexible breakfasts are locally sourced, with seasonal fruit and preserves from the garden. *Children over ten welcome.*

Hampshire

Weston Farm

Country life at its loveliest: a beautifully restored Georgian house and farm; fresh-laid eggs; a donkey and pony in the paddock, and generous, helpful hosts who will fetch you off the London train. Horse and hound wallpaper gallops over the hall, the sitting room has wood panelling, sash windows, a giant marble fireplace; and the family suite comes complete with rocking horse and kitchen. A footpath traces the 800-acre arable farm so roam free over water meadows. Stroll to the typical Hampshire village of Micheldever (thatched cottages, handsome church) for dinner – or it's eight miles to historic Winchester.

Price	From £80. Singles from £50.
Rooms	2: 1 twin; 1 twin with separate bath.
Meals	Restaurants 5-minute drive.
Closed	Rarely.
Directions	South on A3 to lights at Hindhead. Straight across & after 400 yds, right onto B3002. On for 3 miles. Entrance (signed) on right in a wood.

Bottle of wine in your room.

Price	£80. Family suite £120. Singles £50.
Rooms	4: 1 twin/double, 1 four-poster, 1 family suite & kitchen, 1 single,
Meals	Pub 1.5 miles.
Closed	Christmas.
Directions	M3 junc. 11 then A33 northbound. Left to Micheldever, then left at T-junc., 2nd left to Weston Colley. At bottom of hill Weston Farm on left.

Free pick-up from local bus/train station.

	Jeremy & Philippa Whitaker
	Land of Nod,
	Headley, Bordon GU35 8SJ
Tel	+44 (0)1428 713609
Email	pwhitaker100@hotmail.com

Entry 243 Map 4

	Laura Stevens
	Weston Farm, Weston Down Lane,
	Weston Colley, Winchester SO21 3AG
Tel	+44 (0)1962 774791
Mobile	+44 (0)7999 816417
Email	westonfarmbandb@googlemail.com
Web	www.westonfarmaccommodation.co.uk

Entry 244 Map 4

Hampshire

Little Cottage

Just 45 minutes from Heathrow but the peace is deep, the views are long and the wildlife thrives — watch fox and deer, hear the rare nightjar. Chris and Therese grow summer salads and soft fruits and give you superb home cooking; eat in a big conservatory filled with greenery. Guests have a lovely sitting room with an eclectic mix of modern and antique furniture, and a pretty terrace overlooks the garden; bedrooms are all ground-floor, fresh and light, the double has distant views. Perfect for walkers and those who seek solace from urban life but don't want to go too far. *Min. stay two nights at weekends. Over 12s welcome.*

Ethical Collection: Food. See page 420.

Price	£75–£90. Singles £50.
Rooms	3: 1 twin/double, 1 double, 1 single.
Meals	Dinner from £15. Pub 1.5 miles.
Closed	Christmas, New Year & occasionally.
Directions	B3011 from A30 in Hartley Wintney for 1.5 miles. Cottage on left, down a small track then fork left.

 10% off room rate.

Chris & Therese Abbott
Little Cottage, Hazeley Heath,
Hartley Wintney, Hook RG27 8LY
Tel +44 (0)1252 845050
Mobile +44 (0)7721 462214
Email info@little-cottage.co.uk
Web www.little-cottage.co.uk

Entry 245   Map 4

Herefordshire

Bunns Croft

The timbers of the medieval house are probably 1,000 years old. Little of the structure has ever been altered and it is an absolute delight: stone floors, rich colours, a piano, dogs, books and cosy chairs — all give a homely, warm feel. Cruck-beamed bedrooms are snugly small, the stairs are steep — this was a yeoman's house — and the twin's bathroom has its own sweet fireplace. The countryside is 'pure', too, with 1,500 acres of National Trust land five miles away. Anita is charming, loves to look after her guests, grows her own fruit and vegetables and makes fabulous dinners. Just mind your head.

Ethical Collection: Food; Community. See page 420.

Price	£70–£80. Singles £35.
Rooms	4: 1 twin; 1 double, 2 singles, sharing bath (let to same party only).
Meals	Dinner, 3 courses, £25. Pub 5 miles.
Closed	Rarely.
Directions	From Leominster, A49 towards Ludlow; 4 miles to village of Ashton, then left. House on right behind postbox after 1 mile.

Anita Syers-Gibson
Bunns Croft,
Moreton Eye, Leominster HR6 0DP
Tel +44 (0)1568 615836

Entry 246   Map 7

Herefordshire

Staunton House

This handsome Georgian rectory with light, colourful and well-proportioned rooms brims with beautiful furnishings. The original oak staircase leads to peaceful bedrooms with comfortable beds; the blue room looks onto garden and pond. It's a house that matches its owners – quiet, traditional and country-loving. Wander through the lovely garden, drive to Hay or Ludlow, stride some ravishing countryside, play golf near Offa's Dyke; return to Rosie and Richard's lovely home to relax in their drawing room before enjoying a delicious dinner in the elegant dining room. You will be well tended here.

Price	From £80. Singles from £50.
Rooms	2: 1 double, 1 twin/double.
Meals	Dinner, 2-3 courses, £20-£25. Pub/restaurant 2.5 miles.
Closed	Rarely.
Directions	A44 Leominster-Pembridge; right to Shobdon. After 0.5 miles, left to Staunton-on-Arrow; at x-roads, over into village. House opp. church, with black wrought-iron gates.

Rosie & Richard Bowen
Staunton House, Staunton-on-Arrow,
Pembridge, Leominster HR6 9HR

Tel	+44 (0)1544 388313
Mobile	+44 (0)7780 961994
Email	rosbown@aol.com
Web	www.stauntonhouse.co.uk

Entry 247   Map 7

Herefordshire

Garnstone House

Come for peace and quiet in the Welsh Marches, good food and lovely, humorous, down-to-earth hosts. The atmosphere is easy, and the furniture a lifetime's accumulation of eclectic pieces and pictures and prints of horses, hounds and country scenes. After dinner and good conversation, climb the picture-lined stairs to a comfortingly carpeted bedroom – either a twin or a double – and a bathroom that is properly old-fashioned. Delicious breakfasts, good dinners and a stunning garden to explore – the variety and colour of the springtime flowers are astonishing and the clematis is a glory.

Price	From £80. Singles from £45.
Rooms	2: 1 double, 1 twin, each with separate bath.
Meals	Dinner from £25. Pub/restaurant 1 mile.
Closed	Rarely.
Directions	A480 from Hereford; after 10 miles, right onto B4230 for Weobley. After 1.75 miles, right onto level tarmac private road; 2nd on left over cattle grid.

Free pick-up from local bus/train station.

Dawn & Michael MacLeod
Garnstone House,
Weobley HR4 8QP

Tel	+44 (0)1544 318943
Email	macleod@garnstonehouse.co.uk
Web	www.garnstonehouse.co.uk

Entry 248   Map 7

Herefordshire

Hall's Mill House

Quiet lanes bring you to this most idyllic spot — a stone cottage in a light and open valley. The sitting room is snug with wood-burner and sofas but the kitchen is the hub of the place — delicious breakfasts and dinners are cooked on the Aga. Grace, chatty and easy-going, obviously enjoys living in her modernised mill house. Rooms are small, fresh, with exposed beams and slate sills; only the old mill interrupts the far-reaching, all-green views. Drift off to sleep to the sound of the Arrow burbling by — a blissful tonic for walkers and nature lovers. Great value, too. *Children over four welcome.*

Price	£55-£60. Singles £27.50-£30.
Rooms	3: 1 double; 1 double, 1 twin, sharing bath.
Meals	Dinner from £15. Pub/restaurant 3 miles.
Closed	Christmas.
Directions	A438 from Hereford. After Winforton, Whitney-on-Wye & toll bridge, sharp right for Brilley. Left fork to Huntington, over x-roads & next right to Huntington. Next right into 'No Through Road', then 1st right.

Grace Watson
Hall's Mill House,
Huntington, Kington HR5 3QA
Tel   +44 (0)1497 831409

Entry 249   Map 7

Herefordshire

Winforton Court

Dating from 1500, the Court is dignified in its old age: undulating floors, great oak beams, thick walls, a long gallery for family parties. It is a dramatic, colourful home with exceptional timber-framed bedrooms; one room has an Indian-style bathroom and roll top bath, the sumptuous suite has a sitting area with sofas. Choose a book from the small library and relax by a warming log fire in the elegant guest sitting room; all is immaculate. Your hosts are delightful and generous: decanters of sherry, bedside chocolates, delicious breakfasts. Visit Hay, walk down to the Wye, relax in the splendid garden. *Fishing can be arranged.*

Price	£90-£115. Singles from £75.
Rooms	3: 1 double, 1 four-poster, 1 four-poster suite.
Meals	Pub/restaurant 2-minute walk.
Closed	20-30 December.
Directions	From Hereford, A438 into village. Past Sun Inn, house on left with a green sign & iron gates.

Bottle of local cider or chocolates for birthday, honeymoon or anniversary.

Jackie Kingdon
Winforton Court,
Winforton HR3 6EA
Tel   +44 (0)1544 328498
Email   jackie@winfortoncourt.co.uk
Web   www.winfortoncourt.co.uk

Entry 250   Map 7

Herefordshire

Tinto House

Bang in the centre of Hay-on-Wye, opposite the clock tower, amid a sea of bookshops, this beautiful Georgian townhouse brims with period features and original art. John and Karen have decorated their home with love: in the dining room, John's eye-catching paintings set off oak antiques, bookshelves, a fireplace; bedrooms bear mementos of France; one room holds art exhibitions. The garden, on the Wye's banks, is resplendent with roses and sculptures. Breakfast on local sausages and compotes from home-grown fruit before hitting the Brecon Beacons or Hay's independent shops. Perfect for lovers of outdoor and armchair pursuits.

Price	£80-£90. Singles £55-£75.
Rooms	4: 2 doubles, 1 twin; 1 double with separate bath.
Meals	Packed lunch £5. Pub/restaurant 100 yds.
Closed	Christmas & New Year.
Directions	From Hereford A438 towards Brecon. After 19 miles left at Clyro to Hay (1 mile). Cross river; right at T-junc. House 100 yds on right facing clock tower.

	Karen Clare
	Tinto House, 13 Broad Street, Hay-on-Wye HR3 5DB
Tel	+44 (0)1497 821556
Mobile	+44 (0)7985 559355
Email	tintohouse@tiscali.co.uk
Web	www.tinto-house.co.uk

Entry 251 Map 7

Herefordshire

Lower House

A luxuriant garden in a magical valley; strike out for the Black Mountains from the door. The house, itself a forest of old timber, is almost lost within the garden. It is old, but restored with affection. Stairs twist and creak, the unexpected awaits you. Irresistible bedrooms are panelled or timber-clad; bathrooms are new. There's a handsome room downstairs where you eat breakfast (plentiful, delicious), play the piano or read by the fire. Nicky and Pete are kind and generous, steeped in good taste and this exquisite project, next to Offa's Dyke path and on the Welsh border. One of the best! *Minimum stay two nights.*

Ethical Collection: Environment; Food. See page 420.

Price	From £90.
Rooms	2: 1 double; 1 double with separate bath/shower.
Meals	Pubs/restaurants in Hay-on-Wye, 1 mile.
Closed	Rarely.
Directions	East through Hay on B4348 for Bredwardine. On the edge of Hay, right into Cusop Dingle; 0.75 miles, old mill house on left; drive on right, across stone bridge over stream.

	Nicky & Peter Daw
	Lower House, Cusop Dingle, Hay-on-Wye HR3 5RQ
Tel	+44 (0)1497 820773
Mobile	+44 (0)7779 480783
Email	nicky.daw@btinternet.com
Web	www.lowerhousegardenhay.co.uk

Entry 252 Map 7

Herefordshire

Ty-Mynydd

Six miles over open heathland from Hay-on-Wye, it is a remote approach up the mountainside to Ty-Mynydd, and this renovated, stone-flagged farmhouse is absolutely gorgeous. Sheep graze the hillside, the views are simply the best and the garden is colourful, informal, delightful. Turn on the taps and taste water straight from your hosts' own mountain stream; awake to delicious bacon and eggs produced in the fields around you (this is a working organic farm). The lovely young family give you two sweetly restful rooms on the ground floor, one with 'that view', and a simple country bathroom. The sunsets are magical.

Ethical Collection: Environment; Food.
See page 420.

Price	From £85. Singles £60.
Rooms	2 doubles sharing bath (2nd room let to same party only).
Meals	Pubs 6-8 miles.
Closed	Christmas & New Year.
Directions	From Hay on A438, 1st left after Swan Hotel; 6 miles uphill to open heath under Hay Bluff; 2nd right signed Capel Y Ffin; 1 mile, signed.

N Spenceley
Ty-Mynydd,
Llanigon, Hay-on-Wye HR3 5RJ
Tel   +44 (0)1497 821593
Mobile +44 (0)7896 020459
Email   nikibarber@tiscali.co.uk
Web   www.tymynydd.co.uk

Entry 253   Map 7

Herefordshire

Ladywell House

Snuggling in the Golden Valley, wrapped by ancient oaks and a deep peacefulness, a wonderful place to relax. The whitewashed Edwardian dower house is welcoming and informal with understated good taste: soft colours, family paintings, antiques. The four-poster bedroom is regal, the twin fresh in blues and creams, and bathrooms are stylish and spoiling (one with a corner spa bath). A superb breakfast, using local or organic ingredients and homemade bread, is usually served in the conservatory; enjoy afternoon tea and cakes, or drinks, in the garden's Breeze House on summer days. Sarah and Charles are warm and generous hosts.

Ethical Collection: Environment; Food.
See page 420.

Price	From £70. Singles from £55.
Rooms	2: 1 four-poster; 1 twin with separate bath.
Meals	Bistro 5-minute drive. Pub 12-minute drive.
Closed	Occasionally.
Directions	From A465 Hereford to Abergavenny, B4348 to Hay-on-Wye. Go 6.5 miles then left to Michaelchurch Escley & Vowchurch. After approx. 1 mile house opposite tall fir tree.

Charles & Sarah Drury
Ladywell House,
Turnastone, Vowchurch HR2 0RE
Tel   +44 (0)1981 550235
Mobile +44 (0)7970 510110
Email   sarah@ladywellhouse.com
Web   www.ladywellhouse.com

Entry 254   Map 7

Herefordshire

Caradoc Court

Down the long drive, past the grand pillars and the Wellingtonia pines, to a lovely Jacobean manor, former seat of the Viscounts Scudamore. In 2009 the Handbys arrived, created four uncluttered, soft-carpeted bedrooms for guests and are mindfully making their mark on the place. Be wowed by impressive fireplaces and mullioned windows, massive oak roof trusses and polished sleigh beds, billiard room, ballroom and 12 wooded, landscaped acres, high on a bluff overlooking the Wye. The vistas are superb, the peace is restorative, the breakfasts are exemplary and there's a civilised pub at the end of the drive.

Price	From £95. Singles £75-£90.
Rooms	4: 3 doubles, 1 twin.
Meals	Pub 500 yds.
Closed	November-February.
Directions	From Ross-on-Wye, A49 to Hereford. After 0.5 miles, right to Sellack. Follow lane for 2 miles to Lough Pool pub. Entrance gates to drive just past pub, on right.

John Handby
Caradoc Court,
Sellack, Ross-on-Wye HR9 6LS
Tel   +44 (0)1989 730257
Email kathy@caradoccourt.co.uk
Web   www.caradoccourt.co.uk

Entry 255   Map 7

Herefordshire

Rock Cottage

Birds, books and beautiful Black Mountain views highlighted by morning sun, turning to an inky black line at dusk; the cottage glows. There's an instant feeling of warmth and friendliness as you step into the snug hall; find rich autumnal colours, old rugs, a big wood-burner and comfy sitting rooms. Local art and photos line the walls, bedrooms have sumptuous beds, perfect linen and garden posies. You eat (very well) at the communal oak table, or out on the pretty terrace. Thoughtful Chris and Sue will take you to hear the dawn chorus and there are food and literary festivals, bookshops and walks galore.

Price	£65-£85. Singles from £45.
Rooms	2 doubles.
Meals	Packed lunch £6. Dinner, 3 courses, £20. Pub/restaurant within 5 miles.
Closed	Christmas & New Year.
Directions	Hereford A465. After approx. 4.5 miles right onto B4348 to Vowchurch; left then 1st left signed 'St Margaret's & Church'. Pass church, down hill. Cottage 2nd on left. Park in space on right.

Chris & Sue Robinson
Rock Cottage, Newton St Margarets,
Hereford HR2 0QW
Tel   +44 (0)1981 510360
Email robinsrockcottage@googlemail.com
Web   www.rockcottagebandb.co.uk

Entry 256   Map 7

Herefordshire

Park View

Drop down into the Wye valley, up the smart drive to arrive at a large wing of this Grade II*-listed manor house. Find airy rooms with lots of interesting art, toasty wood-burners and views over the pine-clad hills. The bedroom is simply done with white linen on a comfortable bed. Your well-travelled, cultured hosts are keen cooks so full English choices are varied and the coffee is good; the cosy dining room is brimming with books. An arbour of vines, flowers and an avenue of crab apple will draw you out into the peaceful garden; walk along the Wye, explore the Marches, Brecon Beacons and the cathedral city of Hereford.

Price	£80–£90. Singles £65.
Rooms	1 double.
Meals	Dinner, 2-3 courses, £15–£25. Pub/restaurant within 5 miles.
Closed	Christmas & New Year.
Directions	A465 Hereford to Abergavenny. Right onto B4349 to Clehonger; 3 miles then right to Eaton Bishop. Thro' village, then right at Lane Head. Small lane to private driveway; house at end.

10% off room rate Mon–Thurs. 10% off stays of 2 or more nights.

Liz & Patrick Myles
Park View,
Eaton Bishop, Hereford HR2 9QE
Tel +44 (0)1981 250521
Email patrickmyles52@aol.com

Entry 257 Map 7

Herefordshire

Burghill Grange

A big, happy, friendly, family house. Harriet and John have sandblasted beams, waxed elm floors, uncovered some fine 18th-century ceilings and put in three smart bathrooms. Your sitting room is cosy – bright with fire, bold fabrics and interesting books; enjoy home-laid eggs, fresh bread, delicious coffee and sausages from Ludlow while looking over the peaceful garden and pond. A first-floor double is calm and uncluttered, the others beamed and large with great views to church tower and orchards; bathrooms have chunky roll tops, big towels and organic bubbles and creams. Handy for Hay, golf, antiques and the Brecons.

Ethical Collection: Food; Community. See page 420.

Price	From £75. Singles from £35.
Rooms	3: 1 double; 1 twin/double with separate shower; 1 twin with separate bath.
Meals	Occasional dinner £20. Pubs/restaurants 1-4 miles.
Closed	Rarely.
Directions	A4103 north of Hereford, then A4110 north to Cannon Pyon. After 2 miles, after Portway sign, left to Burghill. After Burghill sign, house 1st on left.

10% off stays of 2 or more nights. Free pick-up from local bus/train station. Late checkout (12pm).

Harriet Gordon
Burghill Grange,
Burghill, Hereford HR4 7SE
Tel +44 (0)1432 761016
Mobile +44 (0)7525 215414
Email enquiries@burghillgrange.com
Web www.burghillgrange.com

Entry 258 Map 7

Herefordshire

Moor Court Farm

The buildings, about 500 years old, ramble and enfold both gardens and guests. Buff Orpingtons potter and cluck, there are sheep in the fields, owls and bats in the oast house, geese in the yard and all feels deeply rural. This authentic idiosyncratic farmhouse is efficiently managed by Elizabeth, busy farmer's wife, and Peter; bedrooms are cottagey, the four-poster one has views to the Malvern Hills. Elizabeth cooks for the shoots and her traditional British dinners are made from the best local produce: enjoy home-produced meat and home-grown vegetables. Hampton Court Gardens and Eastnor Castle are just a short drive.

Price	From £70. Singles £45.
Rooms	3: 1 four-poster, 2 twins.
Meals	Dinner, 3 courses, from £19.
Closed	Rarely.
Directions	From Hereford, east on A438. A417 into Stretton Grandison; 1st right past village sign, through Holmen Park. Bear left. House on left.

Elizabeth & Peter Godsall
Moor Court Farm,
Stretton Grandison, Ledbury HR8 2TP
Tel   +44 (0)1531 670408
Email elizabeth@moorcourtfarm.co.uk
Web   www.moorcourtfarm.co.uk

Entry 259   Map 7

Herefordshire

Grendon Manor

The best of traditional meets modern country living: this 16th-century manor house is a super mix of the very old and very new. A working sheep and cattle farm is wrapped around it and you can walk over fields and down to a pretty Norman church. Jane is easy company and looks after you well. Guests in their own wing will rejoice in bedrooms with old beams, crisply comfortable linen and new bathrooms, while the guest sitting room downstairs has marvellous dark oak panelling, rich colours and glowing lamps. A farmhouse-tasty breakfast sets you up for beautiful Herefordshire walks, and Ludlow is close.

Price	From £90. Singles £50.
Rooms	3: 2 doubles, 1 twin.
Meals	Dinner £25 (groups only). Pub/restaurant 2 miles.
Closed	Rarely.
Directions	A44 through Bromyard. House 4 miles in the village of Bredenbury. Past Bredenbury Arms pub, 2nd drive on the left 200 yds on.

Jane Piggott
Grendon Manor,
Bredenbury, Bromyard HR7 4TH
Tel   +44 (0)1885 482226
Email jane.piggott@btconnect.com
Web   www.grendonmanor.co.uk

Entry 260   Map 7

Isle of Wight

Northcourt

A Jacobean manor with matchless grounds: 15 acres of terraced gardens, exotica and subtropical flowers – nature's paradise. The house is magnificent too, huge but a lived-in home, its big comfortable guest bedrooms in two wings. The formal dining room has separate tables; breakfast is served here and includes homemade bread and jams, garden fruit and honey and local produce. There's a snooker table in the library, a chamber organ in the hall and a grand piano in the vast music room. Groups are welcome and John offers garden tours. The peaceful village is in lovely downland, and you can walk from the garden to the Needles.

Price	£65–£105. Singles £47.50–£67.50.
Rooms	6 twins/doubles.
Meals	Pub 3-minute walk through gardens.
Closed	Rarely.
Directions	From Newport, into Shorwell; down steep hill, under rustic bridge & right opp. thatched cottage. Signed. From Brighstone left on bend after Crown Inn & village shop.

 15% off stays of 4 or more nights.

John & Christine Harrison
Northcourt,
Shorwell PO30 3JG

Tel	+44 (0)1983 740415
Mobile	+44 (0)7955 174699
Email	christine@northcourt.info
Web	www.northcourt.info

Entry 261   Map 4

Isle of Wight

Gotten Manor

Miles from the beaten track and bordered by beautiful stone barns, your separate wing in this unique Saxon house has a relaxed simplicity and shabby chic style – more funky than posh. Romantic bedrooms have limewashed walls, wooden floors, beams, soft lighting and sofas – hop up a steep open stair and through a low doorway to get to one. You sleep on a French rosewood bed and you bathe in a roll top tub in the room – wallow by candlelight with a glass of wine. The garden bursts with magnificent fruit trees; Caroline's breakfasts include smoked salmon and smoothies. Informal, rustic and peaceful. *Minimum stay two nights at weekends.*

Ethical Collection: Environment; Food. See page 420.

Price	£80–£100. Singles by arrangement.
Rooms	2 doubles.
Meals	Pub 1.5 miles.
Closed	Rarely.
Directions	0.5 miles south of Chale Green on B3399. After village, left at Gotten Lane. House at end of lane.

Caroline Gurney-Champion
Gotten Manor,
Gotten Lane, Chale PO38 2HQ

Tel	+44 (0)1983 551368
Mobile	+44 (0)7746 453398
Email	as@gottenmanor.co.uk
Web	www.gottenmanor.co.uk

Entry 262   Map 4

Kent

Hartlip Place

The house resonates with a faded, funky grandeur. Family portraits and mahogany pieces, a drawing room to die for, an antique table shimmering with hyacinths, sash windows with sweeping views, happy dogs, chirpy peacocks and hens, a garden intricate and special. After a candlelit dinner, up the circular stair to a colonial-style bedroom (or delightful four-poster) with garden views, decanter for sherry, old-fashioned bathroom and – big treat – real winter fire. A friendly home in a peaceful spot with lots to do on the doorstep: Sissinghurst Gardens, Canterbury Cathedral, Leeds Castle and more. *Children over 12 welcome.*

Price	From £90. Singles £50.
Rooms	2: 1 four-poster; 1 twin/double with separate bath.
Meals	Dinner £25. Pub 1 mile.
Closed	Christmas & New Year.
Directions	From Dover, M2 to Medway Services. Into station, on past pumps. Ignore no exit signs. Left at T-junc., 1st left & on for 2 miles. Left at next T-junc. House 3rd on left.

3 nights for 2 Mon-Thurs.

Sophie & Richard Ratcliffe
Hartlip Place,
Place Lane, Sittingbourne ME9 7TR

Tel	+44 (0)1795 842323
Mobile	+44 (0)7990 971614
Email	hartlipplace@btinternet.com
Web	www.hartlipplace.co.uk

Entry 263   Map 5

Kent

Dadmans

Once the dower house to Lynsted Park, Dadmans sits in a parkland setting with nearby orchards and grazing cattle and sheep. Your breakfast eggs are laid by rare-breed hens and there is local produce for dinner, served in the dining room on gleaming mahogany or in the Aga-warmed kitchen. Lovely bedrooms have patterned fabrics, indulgent beds, fresh flowers and good bathrooms. Outside there are ancient trees, walled gardens and lots of newly planted species including a nuttery; Doddington Place with its gardens and summer opera is a five-minute drive. *Over fours welcome. Minimum two nights at weekends April-Sept.*

Price	£85. Singles by arrangement.
Rooms	2: 1 twin; 1 double with separate bath.
Meals	Dinner, 4 courses, £35. Supper from £15. Pubs/restaurants nearby.
Closed	Rarely.
Directions	M20 junc. 8, then east on A20; left in Lenham towards Doddington. At The Chequers in Doddington, left; house 1.7 miles on left before Lynsted.

Free pick-up from local bus/train station.

Amanda Strevens
Dadmans,
Lynsted, Sittingbourne ME9 0JJ

Tel	+44 (0)1795 521293
Mobile	+44 (0)7931 153253
Email	amanda.strevens@btopenworld.com
Web	www.dadmans.co.uk

Entry 264   Map 5

Kent

Bunkers Hill

You are high on the North Downs, in this AONB, surrounded by sheep and fine views. Nicola, immensely kind and keen for guests to feel at home, gives you breakfast – eggs from her hens – in a delightful garden room with a variety of colourful plants. Nicola loves her garden and there is a summerhouse tucked away at the bottom with an enchanting outlook. Find an oak-panelled sitting room, cosy with a wood-burner, and one big guest bedroom, pretty with pale colours, period furniture and lovely garden views; the bathroom has a shower and Victorian cast-iron bath. Glorious gardens lie close by.

Price	£80. Singles £55.
Rooms	1 twin with separate bath & shower.
Meals	Pub within walking distance.
Closed	November-February.
Directions	From M20 junc. 8, A20 east for Ashford. At Lenham, left to Warren St. On for 1 mile. Harrow pub on right. Bear left. After 300 yds, 3-way junc. sharp left. House 4th on left.

Nicola Harris
Bunkers Hill,
Lenham
ME17 2EE
Tel   +44 (0)1622 858259

Entry 265   Map 5

Kent

Porch House

Rolling fields and cherry orchards, a porch smothered in roses, a view of the church: some of the treats in store at this 15th-century hall house. Step in to find more: a great big inglenook and numerous beams, rich deep curtains and rug-strewn floors, Victorian prints and books galore. Howard and Tony know how to make you feel at home, give you breakfasts to remember and delicious bedrooms above — one with a roll top bath and a canopied, twist-column bed. A winding brick path leads to a pretty orchard; beyond is Faversham with its market and creek. Canterbury and Whitstable are close. A great find. *Children over eight welcome.*

Price	£79-£95. Singles £55-£65.
Rooms	3: 2 doubles, 1 twin.
Meals	Pub 100 yds.
Closed	Rarely.
Directions	M2, junc. 6 to Faversham. At T-junc. left on to A2. Left after 0.25 miles, turn to Eastling. Porch House on right before you get to Carpenter Arms pub.

Howard Carter
Porch House,
The Street, Eastling,
Faversham ME13 0AY
Tel   +44 (0)1795 890980
Email   stay@porchhousebandb.co.uk
Web   www.porchhousebandb.co.uk

Entry 266   Map 5

Kent

The Linen Shed

A weatherboard house with a winding footpath to the front door and a pot-covered veranda out the back: sit here and nibble something delicious and homemade while you contemplate the pretty garden with its gypsy caravan. Vickie, wreathed in smiles, has created a 'vintage' interior: find wooden flooring, reclaimed architectural pieces, big old roll tops, a mahogany loo seat. Bedrooms (two up, one down) are painted in the softest colours, firm mattresses are covered in fine linen, cotton or linen dressing gowns wait patiently in the smart bathrooms. Food is seriously good here, and adventurous – try a seaside picnic hamper!

Ethical Collection: Food. See page 420.

Price	From £75. Singles from £60.
Rooms	3: 2 doubles with separate bath/shower; 1 double sharing bath.
Meals	Dinner from £25. Picnic hamper from £15. Pub/restaurant 300 yds.
Closed	Rarely.
Directions	M2, junc. 7; A2 for Canterbury. 1st immediate turnoff (100 yds) for Boughton, after 1 mile at T-junc. left. After 1 mile, left at phone box. House further along.

🧳 10% off stays of 2 or more nights. Free pick-up from local bus/train station.

Vickie Hassan
The Linen Shed, 104 The Street,
Boughton-under-Blean,
Faversham ME13 9AP
Tel +44 (0)1227 752271
Email bookings@thelinenshed.com
Web www.thelinenshed.com

🐈 🐕 🛜 🚂 👶 ✕

Entry 267   Map 5

Kent

Hoo Farmhouse

Jane and Nicolas are keen shrimpers – let them take you to Minnis Bay and cook your catch for supper! Passionate about the coastline and the area, Jane is also a generous hostess, baking cakes for your arrival and giving you greengages and flowers from the garden. Bedrooms are big and sunny and have Georgian skirting boards and elegant sash windows; new bathrooms have soaps from Provence. The large Georgian-fronted house, surrounded on three sides by garden and rosy-brick outbuildings, has pale classic colours within, a breakfast conservatory, a drawing room with a fire – and a cathedral down the road.

Ethical Collection: Food. See page 420.

Price	£90. Singles £65.
Rooms	3: 2 twins/doubles; 1 double with separate bath.
Meals	Supper, 2 courses, £12.50. Dinner, 3 courses, £25. Pub 1 mile.
Closed	Rarely.
Directions	A28 from Canterbury to Sarre, then A253 to Ramsgate. 4th exit at Monkton r'bout onto Willets Hill. Left at mini r'bout. House 0.75 miles on left.

Jane Irwin
Hoo Farmhouse,
Monkton Road, Minster,
Ramsgate CT12 4JB
Tel +44 (0)1843 821322
Email stay@hoofarmhouse.com
Web www.hoofarmhouse.com

🛜 🚂 👶 👋 ✕

Entry 268   Map 5

Kent

7 Longport

A delightful, unexpected hideaway bang opposite the site of St Augustine's Abbey and a five-minute walk to the Cathedral. You pass through Ursula and Christopher's elegant Georgian house to emerge in a pretty courtyard, with fig tree and rambling rose, to find your self-contained cottage. Downstairs is a cosy sitting room with pale walls, tiled floors and plenty of books, and a clever, compact wet room with mosaic tiles. Then up steep stairs to a swish bedroom with crisp cotton sheets on a handmade bed and views of magnolia and ancient wisteria. You breakfast in the main house or in the courtyard on sunny days. Perfect.

Ethical Collection: Food. See page 420.

Price	£90. Singles £60.
Rooms	Cottage: 1 double & sitting room.
Meals	Restaurants 5-minute walk.
Closed	Rarely.
Directions	Follow ring road around Canterbury. Signs for Sandwich A257, at St George's r'bout turn for Dover. After 300 yds left for Sandwich. At mini r'bout, left; house on left just before corner. No parking; public car park nearby.

💼 10% off stays of 2 or more nights.

🎁 Use your Sawday's Gift Card here.

Ursula & Christopher Wacher
7 Longport,
Canterbury CT1 1PE
Tel   +44 (0)1227 455367
Email   info@7longport.co.uk
Web   www.7longport.co.uk

🐕 🔊 🚂 ✕

Entry 269   Map 5

Kent

14 Westgate Grove

Slap bang in the city, overlooking the river Stour and within strolling distance of the cathedral… step through the understated door and you will be astonished. Pippa is an interior designer, her husband an architect, and bedrooms are cool, smooth and fresh with good lighting, smart fabrics and pretty flowers. Bathrooms dazzle with rain showers, Brazilian black slate and the fluffiest of towels; don't feel guilty – it's rainwater heated by solar panels. On warm days you breakfast in the rosy-walled garden with its ancient vines, olives, lemons, mimosa; for cooler evenings there is an outdoor fireplace. Lovely.

Price	£80–£100.
Rooms	2: 1 double; 1 double with separate bath.
Meals	Pub/restaurant 50 yds.
Closed	Rarely.
Directions	Centre of Canterbury, on river by the Westgate Towers.

Pippa Clague
14 Westgate Grove,
Canterbury CT2 8AA
Tel   +44 (0)1227 769624
Mobile   +44 (0)7815 107032
Email   pippa@clague.plus.com

🔊 🚂 ✕

Entry 270   Map 5

Kent

Great Weddington

The listed house of perfect proportions was built by a Sandwich brewer of ginger beer. The décor is delicious, the bedrooms desirable and cosy, the bathrooms snug and spotless, and Katie fills the rooms with flowers; she also arranges the flowers for Canterbury Cathedral. Dinner is followed by coffee and chocolates in the drawing room — rich fabrics, shelves of books, fine watercolours, much-loved antiques. Outside, stunning hedges and lawns and a terrace for tea in the summer. An enchanting home in a farmland setting, and the area hums with history. *Minimum stay two nights at weekends April-September. Pets by arrangement.*

Price	£100-£120. Singles £85-£120.
Rooms	2 twins/doubles.
Meals	Dinner (occasionally), 4 courses, £37.50 (not Sunday).
Closed	Christmas & New Year.
Directions	From Canterbury, A257 for Sandwich. On approach to Ash, stay on A257 (do not enter village), then 3rd left at sign to Weddington. House 200 yds down on left.

Katie & Neil Gunn
Great Weddington,
Ash, Canterbury CT3 2AR
Tel   +44 (0)1304 813407
Email   greatweddington@hotmail.com
Web   www.greatweddington.co.uk

Entry 271   Map 5

Kent

Park Gate

Peter and Mary are a generous team and their conversation is informed and easy. Behind the wisteria-clad façade are two sitting rooms (one with chesterfield, one with woodburner), ancient beams and polished wood. Bedrooms are freshly comfortable with gorgeous views over the garden to the fields beyond; bathrooms gleam, meals are delicious. More magic outside: croquet, tennis and thatched pavilions, wildlife and roses and a sprinkling of sheep to mow the paddock. The house has a noble history: Sir Anthony Eden lived here and Churchill visited during the war. Great value, and convenient for the Channel Tunnel.

Price	£80. Singles £40.
Rooms	3: 2 twins/doubles; 1 single with separate shower.
Meals	Dinner, 3 courses, £25. Pubs/restaurants 1 mile.
Closed	Christmas, New Year & January.
Directions	A2 Canterbury to Dover road; Barham exit. Through Barham to Elham. After Elham sign 1st right signed Park Gate 0.75 miles. Over brow of hill; house on left.

Bottle of wine with dinner on first night.

Peter & Mary Morgan
Park Gate,
Elham, Canterbury CT4 6NE
Tel   +44 (0)1303 840304
Email   marylmorgan@hotmail.co.uk

Entry 272   Map 5

Kent

West End House

The very smart red-bricked Georgian house, formerly the village surgery, is now a gorgeous retreat; there's a deeply peaceful and rural feel, yet you are near to Dover and Canterbury. You have complete independence in the spacious suite at the 'North End' of the house: a pretty bedroom with a checked throw on the comfortable bed, a bathroom with scented goodies, a cottagey sitting room and a little orchard garden. Lovely easy-going Lynne gives you homemade cake when you arrive, and delicious breakfasts (including smoked salmon and scrambled eggs) in an elegant family dining room with views over the garden.

Price	£80–£95. Singles £60–£65.
Rooms	1 suite for 2 with sitting room & kitchen.
Meals	Dinner, 3 courses, £25. Pub 800 yds.
Closed	Christmas & New Year.
Directions	A2 towards Dover. Follow signs for Coldred. With the green on left, take right fork for Eythorne. House is on left after village sign.

Bottle of wine. Checkout at 12pm.

Lynne Backhouse
West End House, Coldred Road,
Eythorne, Canterbury CT15 4BE
Tel +44 (0)1304 830594
Mobile +44 (0)7881 597077
Email lynne_backhouse@yahoo.co.uk
Web www.westendhousekent.co.uk

Entry 273 Map 5

Kent

Orchard Barn

Alison knows how to spoil (big beds, bread from the mill, home-grown soft fruit, homemade jams), David knows the wildlife, and they both love doing B&B. The big beautiful barn has been sympathetically restored, its middle section left open to create a stunning covered courtyard: find soaring beams, a comfortable leather sofa, fresh flowers. You get two snug, carpeted bedrooms up in the eaves – pale beams, bright colours, and a sweet bath (or shower) room. A delightful village, the ancient port of Sandwich nearby and egrets, kingfishers, swallows and squirrels a walk away. Superb. *Children over seven welcome.*

Ethical Collection: Environment; Food; Community. See page 420.

Price	£70–£85. Singles from £50.
Rooms	2: 1 double, 1 twin/double.
Meals	Pubs/restaurants within 1.5 miles.
Closed	20 December–3 January.
Directions	A258 Sandwich to Deal. 1st right after Worth sign into Felderland Lane; 0.5 miles concealed entrance on left, opp. black barn.

10% off stays of 3 or more nights.
10% off room rate Mon–Thurs.

David & Alison Ross
Orchard Barn,
Felderland Lane, Worth CT14 0BT
Tel +44 (0)1304 615045
Mobile +44 (0)7950 599304
Email orchardbarnworth@gmail.com
Web www.orchardbarn-worth.co.uk

Entry 274 Map 5

Kent

Beaches

A proper seaside townhouse on The Strand, facing Walmer Green and the sea. But no fierce landlady inside – just cheery Rosie and two sleek, cool bedrooms, one on the ground floor, one on the first. Both are light, bright and fresh, dressed mainly in pale colours but with colourful headboards and cushions, and with comfy chairs for admiring views. Bathrooms are funky in a nautical way, there's a super little garden for breakfast on sunny days, and good restaurants close by. Start your day with eggs benedict, cinnamon brioche, fresh croissants, good coffee. The perfect English seaside treat. *Minimum stay two nights for singles.*

Price	£85-£95. Singles £68.
Rooms	2 doubles.
Meals	Breakfast or picnic brunch for the beach. Pubs/restaurants 0.5 miles.
Closed	Last 2 weeks in July.
Directions	From Deal station or town centre, south along Victoria Road passing Deal Castle. Then on to The Strand which opens onto Walmer Green. House opposite bandstand.

Rosanna Lillycrop
Beaches, 34 The Strand,
Walmer, Deal CT14 7DX
Tel +44 (0)1304 369692
Mobile +44 (0)7752 720022
Email enquiries@beaches.uk.com
Web www.beaches.uk.com

Entry 275   Map 5

Kent

Kingsdown Place

Wow. A huge white villa set in stunning terraced gardens running down to the sea; on clear days you can see France! Tan has renovated both house and garden with panache: works of modern art festoon the walls, statues lurk and all is contemporary inside. Upstairs are neat bedrooms: one four-poster with long views, and, up a spiral staircase in the loft, a fabulous, very private bedroom with a sitting room and terrace. All have Conran mattresses and white linen. Breakfast on scrambled eggs and smoked salmon or the full works; take it outside on the terrace in good weather. Seaside chic.

Price	£95-£120. Singles from £75.
Rooms	3: 1 double & sitting room; 1 double, 1 four-poster each with separate bath & sitting room.
Meals	Packed lunch £10. Dinner £25. Restaurant 500 yds. Pub 0.5 miles.
Closed	Christmas & New Year.
Directions	Through Kingsdown village towards sea; at high flint wall on right, turn right, through gateway, then 3rd gateway on left.

 Bottle of wine with dinner on first night. Local food/produce in your room.

Tan Harrington
Kingsdown Place,
Upper Street, Kingsdown CT14 8EU
Tel +44 (0)1304 380510
Email tan@tanharrington.com

Entry 276   Map 5

Kent

Alkham Court Farmhouse

An enchanting lane leads up, up to the farm: the glorious Kent valleys unfurl below. Wendy and Neil, locals born and bred, have built the house from scratch and opened it to share with all those lucky enough to stay. Luscious large bedrooms, two on the ground floor, have embroidered throws, big mattresses, private entrances, sherry, chocolates and fresh flowers. Wake to farmers' market breakfasts and homemade muffins in a panorama-filled, toasty-warm 'Oak Room' from which you may never move, so deep are its seductions. Hens potter, cats purr, dogs doze, a hot tub burbles and Canterbury is close. *Minimum stay two nights.*

Price	£105–£125.
Rooms	3 doubles.
Meals	Packed lunch £7. Simple supper £5. Restaurant 0.5 miles.
Closed	Rarely.
Directions	M20 London to Dover. Past junc. 13; after tunnel in hill, left. Left at r'bout, then 1st left into Alkham Valley Rd. 2 miles, right into Meggett Lane. House just before top of hill, on right.

	Wendy Burrows
	Alkham Court Farmhouse, Meggett Lane, Alkham, Dover CT15 7DG
Tel	+44 (0)1303 892056
Email	wendy.burrows@alkhamcourt.co.uk
Web	www.alkhamcourt.co.uk

Entry 277 Map 5

Kent

Woodmans

No traffic noise, just blissful peace – and you're no more than a short hop to Canterbury. Your cosy ground-floor bedroom has its own entrance via a lovely garden with long views. Tuck into local bacon and eggs (from Sarah's own rescued hens) in the breakfast room with its old pine table, dresser and flowers – or decide to be lazy and let Sarah bring it to your room. You can eat delicious dinner here too, perhaps after some hearty walking on the Wye Downs with its magnificent Chalk Crown and far-reaching views to Dungeness and the coast. *Babies welcome; small cot and high chair available.*

Price	£75. Singles £40.
Rooms	1 double.
Meals	Dinner, 3 courses, £24.50. Packed lunch £6.50. Pub/restaurant 1 mile.
Closed	Rarely.
Directions	From M20, junc. 9. Signed Wye & Kennington A28. Right for Wye, over level crossing, thro' village. At x-roads left to Canterbury. Hassell St 2nd on left; house 4th on left with signed gate.

 Late checkout (12pm). Bottle of house wine with dinner if requested.

	Sarah Rainbird
	Woodmans, Hassell Street, Hastingleigh, Ashford TN25 5JE
Tel	+44 (0)1233 750250
Mobile	+44 (0)7836 505575
Email	sarah.rainbird@googlemail.com

Entry 278 Map 5

Kent

Stowting Hill House

A classic manor house in an idyllic setting, close to Canterbury and the North Downs Way. This warm, civilised home mixes Tudor beams with Georgian proportions, there's a huge conservatory full of greenery, a guest sitting room with sofas and log fire, and breakfasts fresh from the Aga. Traditional bedrooms are carpeted and cosily furnished. Your charming, country-loving hosts welcome you with tea and flowers from the garden – a perfect summer spot with its lawns, tree-lined avenue and stone obelisk. You are ten minutes from the Chunnel but this is worth more than one night. *Children over ten welcome.*

Price	£90–£95 Singles £65.
Rooms	2: 1 twin/double, 1 twin.
Meals	Dinner from £30. Pub 1 mile.
Closed	Christmas & New Year.
Directions	M20 junc. 11, B2068 north. After 4.6 miles, sharp left opposite Jet garage. House at bottom of hill on left, after 1.7 miles. Left into drive.

💼 10% off stays of 2 or more nights.

Richard & Virginia Latham
Stowting Hill House,
Stowting, Ashford TN25 6BE
Tel +44 (0)1303 862881
Email vjlatham@hotmail.com
Web www.stowtinghillhouse.co.uk

🐱 🛜 🚒 🐕 🐂 🎑 ⚔

Entry 279   Map 5

Kent

The Old Rectory

On a really good day (about once every five years) you can see France. But you'll be more than happy to settle for the superb views over Romney Marsh, the Channel in the distance. The big, friendly house, built in 1850, has impeccable, elegant bedrooms and good bathrooms; the large, many-windowed sitting room is full of books, pictures and flowers from the south-facing garden. Marion and David are both charming and can organise transport to Ashford International for you. It's remarkably peaceful – perfect for walking (right on the Saxon Shore path), cycling and birdwatching. *Children over ten welcome.*

Price	£70–£80. Singles £50.
Rooms	2: 1 twin; 1 twin with separate bath/shower.
Meals	Pubs within 4 miles.
Closed	Christmas & New Year.
Directions	M20, exit 10 for Brenzett & Hastings on A2070. After 6 miles, right for Hamstreet; immed. left; in Hamstreet, left B2067. After 1.5 miles, left (Ash Hill); 700 yds on right.

Marion & David Hanbury
The Old Rectory,
Ruckinge, Ashford TN26 2PE
Tel +44 (0)1233 732328
Email oldrectory@hotmail.com
Web www.oldrectoryruckinge.co.uk

🐱 🛜 🚒 🎑 ⚔

Entry 280   Map 5

Kent

Lamberden Cottage

Down a farm track find two 1780 cottages knocked into one, with flagstone floors, a cheery wood-burner in the guest sitting room and welcoming Beverley and Branton. There's a traditional country-cottage feel with pale walls, thick oak beams, soft carpeting and very comfortable bedrooms (the twin has a child's bedroom adjoining); views from all are across the Weald of Kent. Wander the lovely gardens to find your own private spot, sip a sundowner on the terrace, eat well in the family dining room on home-grown-vegetables and fruit. Near to Sissinghurst, Great Dixter and many historic places.

Kent

The Tower House

Peacefully back from the road, a stroll from the antique shops of Tenterden, is a delightful Georgian house with a turreted tower, an Edwardian folly. The box-lined path to the door sets the tone: this is a very well-cared for and hospitable home. Pippa collects vintage china, Mike is the gardener, both delight in meeting people and ensure your stay is happy. Deeply comfortable bedrooms, the biggest at the back, have antique iron beds and romantic white furnishings, flowers and delicious linen. A sofa'd guest sitting room, a gazebo in the garden, homemade blackcurrant jelly at breakfast, Sissinghurst a short drive. Perfect!

Price	From £75. Singles from £55.
Rooms	2: 1 double; 1 twin with adjoining room for children.
Meals	Dinner £22. Pub 1 mile.
Closed	Christmas & New Year.
Directions	From Tenterden A28 to Hastings. 2.5 miles Rolvenden. 2.5 miles to junc. Å268 right to Sandhurst. 300 yds Sandhurst sign on left. 20 yds right down farm track. House 80 yds on left.

Price	£70–£90. Singles £60.
Rooms	2: 1 double; 1 double with separate shower.
Meals	Pubs/restaurants 200 yds.
Closed	Christmas.
Directions	Junc. 8 on M20 to Sutton Valence, then Tenterden. Tower House on right (Tower very visible).

	Beverley & Branton Screeton
	Lamberden Cottage, Rye Road,
	Sandhurst, Cranbrook TN18 5PH
Tel	+44 (0)1580 850743
Mobile	+44 (0)7768 462070
Email	thewalledgarden@lamberdencottage.co.uk
Web	www.lamberdencottage.co.uk

	Pippa Carter
	The Tower House,
	27 Ashford Road, Tenterden TN30 6LL
Tel	+44 (0)1580 761920
Email	pippa@towerhouse.biz
Web	www.towerhouse.biz

Kent

Pullington Barn

Up a private drive and straight in to a vast, beamed expanse of bright light, warm colours, beautiful pictures and a cheery welcome from Gavin and Anne in their converted barn. There are endless books to choose: settle in the comfortable drawing room with its grand piano. Or sit in the pretty south-facing garden on a fine day; on the other side, views from the orchard spread over oast houses and church spires. Bedrooms (one on the ground floor) are both a good size with comfortable mattresses, co-ordinated bed linen and feather pillows. You breakfast soundly on local goodies; stride out for lovely country walks from the door.

Price	From £75. Singles £50.
Rooms	2: 1 double, 1 twin.
Meals	Pub/restaurant 0.5 miles.
Closed	Christmas.
Directions	A228 out of Tunbridge Wells. A21 to The Weald Garden of England r'bout. A262 to Sissinghurst. Right to Benenden. Final directions on booking.

10% off room rate Mon–Thurs.

Gavin & Anne Wetton
Pullington Barn,
Benenden TN17 4EH
Tel   +44 (0)1580 240246
Mobile   +44 (0)7849 759929
Email   anne@wetton.info
Web   www.wetton.info/bandb

Entry 283   Map 5

Kent

Ramsden Farm

A truly interesting and comfortable house, with south-facing views across the Wealds; charming Sally has renovated these former farm buildings with flair. Unhurried breakfasts are eaten in the huge kitchen with a lemon-coloured Aga and floor to ceiling glass doors opening on to a wooden deck; spill outside on warm days. After a hearty walk you can doze in front of a tree-devouring inglenook; find lovely sunny bedrooms too, with more of that view from each, tip-top mattresses and hand embroidered duvet covers. Sparkling bathrooms have Travertine marble and underfloor heating. Spoiling. *Self-catering in cottage.*

Price	From £80.
Rooms	3: 1 double, 1 twin; 1 double with separate bath.
Meals	Pub 1 mile.
Closed	Rarely.
Directions	From Benenden on B2086 towards Rolvenden, Dingleden Lane on right after 1 mile. House is 3rd on left.

Lift to and from local pub or restaurant. A bottle of Sally's famous Benenden Sauce.

Sally Harrington
Ramsden Farm,
Dingleden Lane, Benenden TN17 4JT
Tel   +44 (0)1580 240203
Email   sally@ramsdenfarmcottage.co.uk
Web   www.ramsdenfarmcottage.co.uk

Entry 284   Map 5

Kent

Barclay Farmhouse

Lynn's breakfasts are fabulous: fresh fruits, warm croissants, banana bread, eggs en cocotte. The weatherboarded guest barn may be in perfect trim but has a been-here-for-ever feel; you have a country-cosy dining room for breakfast or playing cards, a patio for summer, a big peaceful garden, a bird-happy pond. Gleaming bedrooms have brocade bedspreads, French oak furniture, chocolates, slippers, flat-screen TVs; shower rooms are in perfect order. Couples, honeymooners, garden lovers – many would love it here (but no children: the pond is deep). Warm-hearted B&B, and glorious Sissinghurst nearby. *Minimum stay two nights at weekends in high season.*

Price	£90. Singles from £65.
Rooms	Barn: 3 doubles.
Meals	Pubs/restaurants 1 mile.
Closed	Rarely.
Directions	From Biddenden centre, south on A262: Tenterden road. 0.7 miles, bear right (signed Par3 Golf, Vineyard & Benenden). Immed. on right.

Chilled local water, a bottle of local wine for repeat bookers and lifts to local restaurants.

Lynn Ruse
Barclay Farmhouse, Woolpack Corner, Biddenden TN27 8BQ
Tel   +44 (0)1580 292626
Email   info@barclayfarmhouse.co.uk
Web   www.barclayfarmhouse.co.uk

Entry 285   Map 5

Kent

Merzie Meadows

You get your own suite in this lovely ranch-style house with huge windows, pergolas groaning with climbers, and a Mediterranean-style swimming pool in the twittering garden. Pamela is just as light and bright: she keeps horses and hens and gives you locally sourced breakfasts. Your bedroom has a contemporary, uncluttered feel and is beautifully dressed in pale colours with pretty fabrics and a super bed, your own sitting room looks onto the garden and the bathroom is sleek with Italian marble and plump towels. All is peaceful; garden and nature lovers will adore it here. *Minimum stay two nights at weekends April-September.*

Price	£95-£99.
Rooms	1 suite for 2-3.
Meals	Pub 2.5 miles.
Closed	Mid-December to February.
Directions	A229 Maidstone to Hastings road, then B2079 for Marden. 1st right into Underlyn Lane, 2.5 miles, large Chainhurst sign, right onto drive.

Free pick-up from local train station (& drop-off, if spending day in London).

Use your Sawday's Gift Card here.

Pamela Mumford
Merzie Meadows, Hunton Road, Marden, Maidstone TN12 9SL
Tel   +44 (0)1622 820500
Mobile   +44 (0)7762 713077
Email   merziemeadows@me.com
Web   www.merziemeadows.co.uk

Entry 286   Map 5

Kent

Reason Hill

Brian and Antonia's 200-acre fruit farm is perched on the edge of the Weald of Kent, with stunning views over orchards and oast houses. The farmhouse has 17th-century origins (low ceilings, wonky floors, stone flags) and a conservatory for sunny breakfasts; colours are soft, antiques gleam and the mood is relaxed. The roomy twin has a bay window and armchairs, the pretty double looks over the garden. Come in spring for the blossom, summer for the fresh fruit and veg from the garden and anytime for a break – the Greensand Way runs along the bottom of the farm, you are close to Sissinghurst Castle and 45 minutes from the Channel Tunnel.

Price	From £80.
Rooms	3: 1 twin; 1 double with separate shower, 1 single sharing shower (let to same party only).
Meals	Pubs within 1 mile.
Closed	Christmas & New Year.
Directions	From Maidstone A229 for Hastings. After 4.5 miles, right at lights on B2163. In Coxheath, left up Westerhill Rd, 0.2 miles then right into private road; through fruit trees to Reason Hill.

Brian & Antonia Allfrey
Reason Hill,
Linton, Maidstone ME17 4BT

Tel	+44 (0)1622 743679
Mobile	+44 (0)7775 745580
Email	antonia@allfrey.net
Web	www.reasonhill.co.uk

Entry 287   Map 5

Kent

22 Lansdowne Road

Built in 1861, the house in leafy Tunbridge Wells "has never been as Victorian as it is now". So says Harold, whose devotion to Victoriana knows no bounds. Deep colours, rich velvets, marble tables, authentic wallpapers, tasselled lamps, portraits of Queen Victoria, tea and scones by the fire… be prepared to take a serious step back in time. Bedrooms are simple in comparison: ruched chintz in the ground-floor double, damask in the twin below – and a door to the conservatory. Bathrooms have large mirrors and brand new fittings, breakfast is a locally sourced spread. Those in search of heritage will marvel. *Off-road parking.*

Price	£80–£120. Singles £80.
Rooms	3: 1 double, 1 twin/double; 1 studio with shower & kitchenette.
Meals	Dinner, 2 courses, £30. Pubs/restaurants within 5-minute walk.
Closed	January.
Directions	From A21 to Tonbridge A26 to T. Wells centre. Grosvenor Rd one-way system left onto Victoria Rd. Onto Garden Rd, right onto Lansdowne Rd.

 Bottle of wine with dinner on first night.

Harold Brown
22 Lansdowne Road,
Tunbridge Wells TN1 2NJ

Tel	+44 (0)1892 533633
Mobile	+44 (0)7714 264489
Email	haroldmbrown@hotmail.com
Web	www.thevictorianbandb.com

Entry 288   Map 5

Kent

Swan Cottage

A delightful Georgian townhouse in Tunbridge Wells, just near the Pantiles with its covered walkways between shops, coffee houses and spas. Your genial host is an artist, his studio can be seen through the glass wall in the open-plan dining room and his engaging pen and ink drawings dot every wall. Bedrooms have plenty of space, are comfortable and contemporary with big sash windows and fresh flowers; bathrooms are roomy, light and white, one with rooftop views. In summer there's a little patio for local sausages and eggs at a pink table under the magnolia tree. And the High Street is at the bottom of the road.

Price	£85. Singles £50.
Rooms	2: 1 twin/double; 1 single with separate bath.
Meals	Pubs/restaurants 200 yds.
Closed	Rarely.
Directions	From railway station follow High Street for 300 yds, left up Little Mt Sion. House faces you at top of hill. Parking in garage at back of house on request.

6 greeting cards of your choice drawn by your host David Gurdon.

Use your Sawday's Gift Card here.

David Gurdon
Swan Cottage, 17 Warwick Road,
Tunbridge Wells TN1 1YL
Tel   +44 (0)1892 525910
Mobile   +44 (0)7775 897427
Email   swancot@btinternet.com
Web   www.swancottage.co.uk

Entry 289   Map 5

Kent

40 York Road

A smart Regency townhouse, slap bang in the centre of Royal Tunbridge Wells and a five-minute walk from the delightfully preserved Pantiles. Patricia will enjoy cooking for you; in another life she served up delights for hungry skiers coming off the French mountains. A gentle presence, she leaves you to come and go as you please; guests have a comfortable sitting room and bright, spotless bedrooms that are quieter than you may think. In the summer you will breakfast (deliciously) in the pretty courtyard garden before wandering into town for the cluster of great little shops and restaurants. Truly excellent. *Over 12s welcome.*

Price	From £74. Singles from £44.
Rooms	2 twins/doubles.
Meals	Supper £13. Dinner, 4 courses with wine, £25. Picnic available. Pub/restaurant nearby.
Closed	23 December-2 January.
Directions	From M25 junc. 5 onto A21, then A26 through Southborough to Tunbridge Wells. Sign for Lewes, then 4th road left. Halfway along, on left. Car parks nearby, from £3.50 per 24 hours.

Bottle of wine with dinner on first night.

Patricia Lobo
40 York Road,
Tunbridge Wells TN1 1JY
Tel   +44 (0)1892 531342
Email   yorkrd@uwclub.net
Web   www.yorkroad.co.uk

Entry 290   Map 5

Kent

Charcott Farmhouse

The 1750 tile-hung brick farmhouse is very much a family home; if you don't come expecting an immaculate environment you should enjoy it here. You share a pretty sitting room in the old bakehouse with the original beams and bread oven, and bedrooms are simple and unfussy, with traditional fabrics and country views. Ginny is charming while Nicholas – a tad eccentric for some – is highly knowledgeable about the area and a brilliant chef. Breakfast is an unrushed, happy affair with heaps of homemade bread and marmalade and free-range eggs from the family flock. You can come and go as you please.

Lancashire

Challan Hall

The wind in the trees, the boom of a bittern and birdsong. That's as noisy as it gets. On the edge of the village, delightful Charlotte's former farmhouse overlooks woods and Lake Haweswater; deer, squirrels and Leighton Moss Nature Reserve are your neighbours. The Cassons are well-travelled and the house, filled with a colourful mish-mash of mementos, is happily and comfortably traditional. Expect a sofa-strewn sitting room, a smart red and polished-wood dining room and two freshly floral bedrooms. Morecambe Bay and the Lakes are on the doorstep – come home to lovely views and stunning sunsets.

Price	From £65. Singles from £50.		Price	£70. Singles from £40.
Rooms	3: 2 twins; 1 twin with separate bath.		Rooms	2: 1 twin/double; 1 twin/double with separate bath.
Meals	Pub 5-minute walk.		Meals	Packed lunch available. Pubs 1 mile.
Closed	Rarely.		Closed	Rarely.
Directions	B2027 0.5 miles north of Chiddingstone Causeway. Equidistant between Tonbridge & Edenbridge. Look for signs to Greyhound pub.		Directions	M6 exit 35 to Carnforth, past railway station to Warton. Turn left signed Silverdale. After 2.5 miles T-junc., turn right, past golf club on left. Further 1 mile, house on right.

Sherry & biscuits in your room; homemade jam or marmalade to take home. Free pick-up from local bus/train station.

	Nicholas & Ginny Morris Charcott Farmhouse, Charcott, Leigh, Tonbridge TN11 8LG		**Charlotte Casson** Challan Hall, Silverdale LA5 0UH
Tel	+44 (0)1892 870024	Tel	+44 (0)1524 701054
Mobile	+44 (0)7508 683985	Mobile	+44 (0)7790 360776
Email	charcottfarmhouse@btinternet.com	Email	cassons@btopenworld.com
		Web	www.challanhall.co.uk

Entry 291   Map 5

Entry 292   Map 11

Lancashire

Northwood

A super stretch of golden beach with sand dunes is just across the road and delightful Lytham is a couple of miles away. The Victorian façade conceals light, lofty rooms mixing vintage and modern: bold wallpaper on odd walls, huge displays of flowers, original artwork. Your hosts happily find babysitters, advise on restaurants (then drive you there) and offer you maple syrup pancakes at breakfast, along with other treats. Bedrooms are generous: find coir carpets, baskets of plump blankets and towels, lovely colours and DVDs to watch on wet days. The whole place has an informal, warm and happy family vibe.

Price	£80. Family £90. Singles from £75.
Rooms	2: 1 double, 1 double/family room.
Meals	Restaurants 5-minute walk.
Closed	Christmas & New Year.
Directions	M6 exit 32 then M55 to Blackpool. Follow signs for Lytham St Annes then St Annes. Head for the promenade.

Free pick-up from local train station. Fridge full of beverages. Late checkout.

Shannon Kuspira
Northwood,
24 North Promenade,
St Annes on Sea FY8 2NQ
Tel +44 (0)1253 782356
Email skuspira@hotmail.com
Web www.24northwood.co.uk

Entry 293   Map 11

Lancashire

Peter Barn Country House

Wild deer roam and the views are fabulous – this is the Ribble Valley, an AONB that feels like a time-locked land. In the former 18th-century tithe barn, where old church rafters support a big yet cosy guest sitting room, find plump sofas, log fire and flat-screen TV. Bedrooms, too, are on the top floor – nicely private. The Smiths couldn't be more helpful and breakfast is a feast: jams and muesli are homemade, stewed fruits are from the gardens. Step outside: Jean has transformed a field into a riot of colour and scent, there are pretty corners, a meandering stream and water lilies bask in still pools. *Min. stay two nights.*

Price	£66-£74. Singles £40.
Rooms	3: 1 double, 1 twin/double; 1 double with separate bath.
Meals	Restaurants/pubs 1.5 miles.
Closed	Christmas & New Year.
Directions	M6 junc. 31, A59 to Clitheroe. Through Clitheroe to Waddington. Through village 0.5 miles, left on Cross Lane for 0.75 miles, past Colthurst Hall, house on left.

10% off stays of 3 or more nights.

Jean & Gordon Smith
Peter Barn Country House,
Cross Lane/Rabbit Lane,
Waddington, Clitheroe BB7 3JH
Tel +44 (0)1200 428585
Email jean@peterbarn.co.uk
Web www.peterbarn.co.uk

Entry 294   Map 12

Leicestershire

The Gorse House

Passing cars are less frequent than passing horses – this is a peaceful spot in a pretty village. The lasting impression of this 17th-century cottage is of lightness and space. There's a fine collection of paintings and furniture, and oak doors lead from dining room to guest sitting room. Country style bedrooms are simply done, the largest with three views; bathrooms are a little dated. The garden was designed by Bunny Guinness, the stables accommodate up to six horses and it's a stroll to a good pub dinner. The house is filled with laughter and the Cowdells are terrific hosts who absolutely love having guests to stay.

Price	From £60. Singles £35.
Rooms	3: 1 double, 1 family for 3. Stable: 1 triple & kitchenette.
Meals	Packed lunch £5. Pub 75 yds.
Closed	Rarely.
Directions	From A46 Newark-Leicester; B676 for Melton. At x-roads, straight for 1 mile; right to Grimston. There, up hill, past church. House on left, just after right-hand bend at top.

R L Cowdell
The Gorse House,
33 Main Street, Grimston,
Melton Mowbray LE14 3BZ
Tel   +44 (0)1664 813537
Email   cowdell@gorsehouse.co.uk
Web   www.gorsehouse.co.uk

Entry 295   Map 9

Leicestershire

Curtain Cottage

A pretty village setting for this cottage on the main street, next door to Sarah's interior design shop. You have your own entrance by the side and through a large garden, which backs onto fields with horses and the National Forest beyond. A conservatory is your sitting room: wicker armchairs, wooden floors, a contemporary take on the country look. Bedrooms are light and fresh, linen from The White Company on sumptuous beds, slate-tiled bathrooms, stunning fabrics. Breakfast is anything, anytime, full English with eggs from the hens or fresh fruit and croissants from the local shop – all is delivered to you. Perfect privacy.

Price	£85. Singles £60.
Rooms	2: 1 double, 1 twin.
Meals	Pubs/restaurants 150 yds.
Closed	Rarely.
Directions	Gravel driveway to left of Barkers Interiors Design Showroom on Main Street. From car park, access to cottage thro' gate into garden at rear of showroom.

 Bottle of wine in your room.

 Use your Sawday's Gift Card here.

Sarah Barker
Curtain Cottage,
92-94 Main Street,
Woodhouse Eaves LE12 8RZ
Tel   +44 (0)1509 891361
Email   sarah@curtaincottage.co.uk
Web   www.curtaincottage.co.uk

Entry 296   Map 8

Leicestershire

The Grange

Behind the mellow brick exterior (Queen Anne in front, Georgian at the back) is a warm family home. Log fires brighten chilly days and you are greeted with kindness and generosity by Mary and Shaun, whose young family includes two sweet dogs. Big, beautifully quiet bedrooms, one in the attic, are hung with strikingly unusual wallpapers and furnished with excellent beds and pretty antiques, bathrooms are simple yet impeccable and there's a fireplace in the big, flagstoned hall decorated with sporting prints and deeds. The garden has a treehouse and is large enough to roam.

Price	£80. Singles £50.
Rooms	2: 1 twin, 1 double.
Meals	Pubs/restaurants 0.5-1.5 miles.
Closed	Christmas & New Year.
Directions	M1 exit 20; A4304 towards Market Harborough. 1st left after Walcote marked 'Gt Central Cycle Ride'; 2 miles, then right into Kimcote, pass church on left. On right after Poultney Lane.

🧳 10% off room rate Mon-Thurs. 10% off stays of 2 or more nights.

Shaun & Mary Mackaness
The Grange,
Kimcote LE17 5RU
Tel +44 (0)1455 203155
Mobile +44 (0)7808 242530
Email shaunandmarymac@hotmail.com
Web www.thegrangekimcote.co.uk

Entry 297 Map 8

Lincolnshire

Brook House

This two-storey stable conversion in warm stone is all yours, set in its own courtyard with pretty filled pots, seating and statues. Beyond is farmland as far as the eye can see. There's a fresh, stylish feel to the sitting room with its Farrow & Ball 'matchstick' walls, tumbled limestone floors, underfloor heating and your own fridge. Up thick biscuit carpet is a spacious semi-galleried bedroom with white cane furniture, sloped ceiling, pretty fabrics and, from the bath, sunset views. Julian and Jenny have created a magical garden which is yours to explore – stoke up with a hearty breakfast first. Wonderful.

Price	£92. Singles £70.
Rooms	Stables: 1 double & sitting/ dining room.
Meals	Pubs/restaurants from 2 miles.
Closed	Christmas.
Directions	A1 north of Stamford; left just after South Witham exit, signed North Witham & Gunby. House is last in village, around corner and up hill on right.

🧳 Local food/produce in your room. Late checkout (12pm).

Julian & Jenny McAlpine
Brook House,
Gunby, Grantham NG33 5LF
Tel +44 (0)1476 860010
Email jennifermcalpine@aol.com
Web www.honeyandmcalpine.co.uk

Entry 298 Map 9

Lincolnshire

Belvoir Vale Cottage

The Vale of Belvoir is gloriously quiet and you're 200 yards from the Viking Way. Kind generous Norman and Suzie have restored two old roadside cottages, charmingly; the emphasis is on warmth, lovely colours, fresh flowers beautifully arranged, delicious food and gorgeous views – over the garden to Belvoir Castle. Bedrooms and bathrooms are a good size and have thick carpets and new windows to pull in the sun, big comfy beds, fluffy towels, great showers. Start the day with a full English or oak-smoked haddock with poached eggs; you'll be ridiculously, delightfully spoiled. *Children welcome if rooms let to one party.*

Price	£80–£95. Singles from £50.
Rooms	3: 1 twin/double & sitting room; 1 twin/double, 1 double.
Meals	Packed lunch available. Pubs/restaurants 1.2 miles.
Closed	Rarely.
Directions	A52 Nottingham-Grantham. At Sedgebrook x-roads, turn for Stenwith & Woolsthorpe. After 1.5 miles cross double bridges – private car park 300 yds.

Local Belvoir cordials in room. Free pick-up from local bus/train station.

Suzie & Norman Davis
Belvoir Vale Cottage,
Stenwith, Woolsthorpe-by-Belvoir,
Grantham NG32 2HE
Tel +44 (0)1949 842434
Email reservations@belvoirvale-cottage.co.uk
Web www.belvoirvale-cottage.co.uk

Entry 299   Map 9

Lincolnshire

Churchfield House

The little house was built in the sixties; inside glows with character and charm. Bridget is an interior decorator whose eye for detail and sense of fun will delight you. A snug bedroom sports fresh checks in creams and greens, firm mattress, down pillows, interesting pictures, even a gilt-trimmed copy of a Louis XIV chair. The bathroom is small but spotless, and there's a conservatory mood to the warm red, stone-tiled dining room, where glass doors open to a large, lush garden in summer. You're close to a good golf course, Bridget cooks and chats with warmth and humour – this is a gem.

Price	£60. Singles £40.
Rooms	1 twin with separate bath.
Meals	Dinner, 2 courses, from £18. Pubs/restaurants 3 miles.
Closed	Christmas & New Year.
Directions	A607 Grantham to Lincoln road. On reaching Carlton Scroop, 1st left for Hough Lane. Last house on left.

Bridget Hankinson
Churchfield House,
Carlton Scroop,
Grantham NG32 3BA
Tel +44 (0)1400 250387
Email info@churchfield-house.co.uk
Web www.churchfield-house.co.uk

Entry 300   Map 9

Lincolnshire

The Barn

Simon and Jane, the nicest people, have farmed for 30 years and love having guests to stay. Breakfasts are entirely local or homemade, home-grown and delicious; there are endless extras and nothing is too much trouble. In this light-filled barn conversion find old beams, new walls and good antiques; a brick-flanked fireplace glows and heated floors keep toes warm. Above the high-raftered main living/dining room is a comfy, good-sized double; in the adjoining stables, two further rooms, a crisp feel, sparkling showers, restful privacy. Views are to sheep-dotted fields and the village is on a 25-mile cycle trail.

Price	£70. Singles £50.
Rooms	3: 1 double, 1 twin/double; 1 single with separate bath/shower.
Meals	Supper, 2 courses, £17.50. Dinner, 3 courses, £25. BYO. Pubs in village & 2 miles.
Closed	Rarely.
Directions	Midway between Lincoln & Peterborough. From A15, in Folkingham, turn west into Spring Lane next to village hall; 200 yds on right.

10% off stays of 2 or more nights Mon–Thurs (November to March).

Simon & Jane Wright
The Barn, Spring Lane,
Folkingham, Sleaford NG34 0SJ
Tel   +44 (0)1529 497199
Mobile +44 (0)7876 363292
Email   sjwright@farming.co.uk
Web   www.thebarnspringlane.co.uk

Entry 301   Map 9

Lincolnshire

The White House

The smart wisteria-clad Georgian house stands right by the village green of this conservation village. Victoria and David, passionate about the place, have filled the rooms with gorgeous things: interesting books in the library, etchings, watercolours, a fine moulded fireplace, and English and Chinese porcelain. Each bedroom, too, is striking; one has an antique four-poster canopied in green silk and a sweet single room next door. Bathrooms are fresh and appealing. There are winter fires in the sitting rooms, afternoon tea in the pretty walled garden and your hosts can also suggest good places for eating out.

Price	£70. Singles from £40.
Rooms	2: 1 twin/double; 1 four-poster with separate bath (adjoining room if required).
Meals	Pub/restaurant in village.
Closed	Rarely.
Directions	A15 to Folkingham. Market Place on the main road. Turn left & park in the parking area nearly in front of the house. House on left of the village green.

A box of excellent Hansen's Chocolate House chocolates for stays of 2 or more nights.

Victoria & David Strauss
The White House, 25 Market Place,
Folkingham, Sleaford NG34 0SE
Tel   +44 (0)1529 497298
Email   victoria.strauss@btinternet.com
Web   www.bedandbreakfastfolkingham
           lincolnshire.co.uk

Entry 302   Map 9

Lincolnshire

Brills Farm

There aren't many hills in Lincolnshire, but Sophie and Charlie's early Georgian farmhouse is at the top of one of them. Built of warm brick, near a Roman settlement site, it shines with country elegance and charm, subtle colours and antique furniture. The drawing and dining rooms, filled with fresh flowers, overlook the valley, the beautiful, airy bedrooms have goose down duvets and lovely linen. The Whites are a delightful, young couple with a flourishing family (Sophie is a professional cook and event rider), enthusiastic and hospitable they will give you innovative dinners, and bacon from their own pigs. *Children over 12 welcome.*

Price	£90–£100. Singles £55–£60.
Rooms	3: 2 doubles, 1 twin/double.
Meals	Supper £20. Dinner £30. Packed lunch £10. Pubs 5-minute drive.
Closed	Christmas & New Year.
Directions	A46 Newark-Lincoln. Exit Brough, Norton Disney & Stapleford. Right at T-junc.; 0.5 miles; 1st left onto lane; 0.75 miles; wide gravel entrance, on right before hill (unsigned).

10% off room rate Mon–Thurs, excluding July and August.

Charles & Sophie White
Brills Farm, Brills Hill,
Norton Disney, Lincoln LN6 9JN
Tel   +44 (0)1636 892311
Mobile   +44 (0)7947 136228
Email   admin@brillsfarm-bedandbreakfast.co.uk
Web   www.brillsfarm-bedandbreakfast.co.uk

Entry 303   Map 9

Lincolnshire

Ryelands House

Farmer Mike and charming Caroline built this large red-brick and slate house on their land and are much committed to the Countryside Stewardship programme; hang out of your bedroom window to watch waders, even deer, round the nearby pond. Inside is warm with underfloor heating, and spacious. Your bedroom has a boutique hotel feel in shades of cream and brown, while two beautifully-lit sitting rooms are smoothly uncluttered and have comfortable armchairs. Pedal along those lovely flat lanes after breakfast, head to Lincoln and its cathedral or Horncastle for antiques; walk to the local pub for excellent bar food.

Price	From £75. Singles from £50.
Rooms	1 twin/double & sitting room.
Meals	Supper from £10 (Monday only). Packed lunch from £5. Restaurant 0.5 miles.
Closed	Christmas & New Year.
Directions	A15 Lincoln, Sleaford turn. Left at Mere onto B1178 for 3 miles; over staggered x-roads into Potterhanworth. At T-junc. right for 100 yds; left onto Barff Road, 0.5 miles, driveway on left.

Michael & Caroline Norcross
Ryelands House, Barff Road,
Potterhanworth, Lincoln LN4 2DU
Tel   +44 (0)1522 793563
Mobile   +44 (0)7977 590375
Email   norcross@ukfarming.co.uk
Web   www.ryelands-house.co.uk

Entry 304   Map 9

Lincolnshire

Baumber Park

Lincoln red cows and Longwool sheep surround this attractive rosy-brick farmhouse – once a stud that bred a Derby winner. The old watering pond is now a haven for frogs, newts and toads; birds sing lustily. Maran hens conjure delicious eggs and charming Clare, a botanist, is hugely knowledgeable about the area. Bedrooms are light and traditional with mahogany furniture; two have heart-stopping views. Guests have their own wisteria-covered entrance, sitting room with a log fire, dining room with local books and the lovely garden to roam. This is good walking, riding and cycling country; seals and rare birds on the coast.

Price	From £70. Singles from £40.
Rooms	3: 2 doubles; 1 twin with separate bath.
Meals	Pubs 1.5 miles.
Closed	Christmas & New Year.
Directions	From A158 in Baumber take road towards Wispington & Bardney. House 300 yds down on right.

Home-grown produce, as in season and available.

Use your Sawday's Gift Card here.

Clare Harrison
Baumber Park,
Baumber, Horncastle LN9 5NE
Tel   +44 (0)1507 578235
Mobile +44 (0)7977 722776
Email   mail@baumberpark.com
Web   www.baumberpark.com

Entry 305   Map 9

Lincolnshire

The Grange

Wide open Lincolnshire farmland on the edge of the Wolds. This immaculately kept farm has been in the family for five generations; an award-winning farm trail helps you explore. Laze to birdsong, catch the sun setting by the trout lake, relax with a book before the fire in a dining room whose elegant Georgian windows are generously draped. Sarah is young and energetic and gives you delicious homemade cake on arrival and home-laid eggs at breakfast. Comfortable bedrooms have spick and span bath or shower rooms and fabulous views that stretch to Lincoln Cathedral. A delightful couple running good farmhouse B&B.

Price	From £68. Singles from £45.
Rooms	2 doubles.
Meals	Supper from £18. Dinner, 2 courses, from £25. BYO. (No meals during summer.) Pub/restaurant 1 mile.
Closed	Christmas & New Year.
Directions	Exit A157 in East Barkwith at War Memorial, into Torrington Lane. House 0.75 miles on right after sharp right-hand bend.

10% off room rate Mon-Thurs.

Use your Sawday's Gift Card here.

Sarah & Jonathan Stamp
The Grange, Torrington Lane,
East Barkwith LN8 5RY
Tel   +44 (0)1673 858670
Mobile +44 (0)7951 079474
Email   sarahstamp@farmersweekly.net
Web   www.thegrange-lincolnshire.co.uk

Entry 306   Map 9

Lincolnshire

The Manor House

One guest's summing up reads: "Absolutely perfect — hostess, house, garden and marmalade." Delightful Ann — interested in horses, food, photography, people — makes you feel immediately at home. You have the run of downstairs: all family antiques, fresh flowers and space. Chintzy, carpeted bedrooms have dreamy views of the lovely sweeping gardens and duck-dabbled lake; dinners are adventurous and delicious: game casserole, ginger meringue bombe... Perfect stillness at the base of the Wolds and a pretty one-mile walk along the route of the old railway that starts from the front door. Very special, great value.

Price	From £70. Singles £50.
Rooms	2: 1 double, 1 twin.
Meals	Dinner from £20. BYO. Pub/restaurant 2 miles.
Closed	Christmas.
Directions	From Wragby A157 for Louth. After approx. 2 miles, at horse road sign, right. Red postbox & bus shelter at drive entrance, before graveyard.

Ann Hobbins
The Manor House,
West Barkwith LN8 5LF

Tel	+44 (0)1673 858253
Mobile	+44 (0)7751 891274

Entry 307   Map 9

Lincolnshire

Knaith Hall

This intriguing place, medieval church at its gate, dates from the 16th century. Lawns slope down to the river Trent; daffodils, lambs, a passing barge and waterfowl pattern the serenity. And the skyscapes are terrific; at night, a distant power station shines, enhancing that 'great rurality of taste' referred to in Pevsner. Indoors, diamond-paned windows, a domed dining room and fine furniture are softened by an easy décor and log fire — bring your jumpers in winter! Bedrooms are large with comfortable beds; wake to breakfast with award-winning sausages. An appealing family house, with friendly hosts and a relaxed atmosphere.

Price	From £70. Singles from £40.
Rooms	2: 1 double with separate shower, 1 twin with separate bath.
Meals	Dinner, 3 courses with wine, £20. Pub 4 miles.
Closed	Rarely.
Directions	Knaith 3 miles south of Gainsborough on A156 Lincoln-Gainsborough road. After Knaith signs, look for white gateposts on west side with sign for St Mary's Church.

Free pick-up from local train station.

John & Rosie Burke
Knaith Hall,
Knaith, Gainsborough DN21 5PE

Tel	+44 (0)1427 613005
Mobile	+44 (0)7796 881328
Email	rosemary@knaith.com

Entry 308   Map 9

Lincolnshire

The Manor House

At the end of a neatly raked gravel drive, a new manor house with wide views and stunning sunsets over the peaceful Trent valley. The Days have farmed in the village since 1898 and look after you with rich warm comfort and friendly ease. Rooms have opulent curtains with chintzy roses, period furniture and rural art. Beautiful gardens are awash with summer roses, ducks on the pond, horses in the paddock, sunny patios – one in front of the annexe is for guests' exclusive use. You can fish for carp in the lake, shooting can be arranged and there are music and art festivals, antique fairs and walks in abundance.

Price	£70. Singles £45.
Rooms	2: 1 double. Annexe: 1 twin/double with kitchenette.
Meals	Supper from £15. Pub/restaurant 3.5 miles.
Closed	Christmas & New Year.
Directions	A15 from Lincoln for 17.1 miles. Left on to Gainsthorpe Rd, right on to B1398 to Scunthorpe, then left for Manton. Down hill, right at bottom. 50 yds before end of road, gravel driveway on left.
	10% off stays of 2 or more nights. Late checkout (12pm).

	Judy Day
	The Manor House,
	Manton, Gainsborough DN21 4JT
Tel	+44 (0)1652 649508
Email	enquiries@manorhouse bedandbreakfast.co.uk
Web	www.manorhousebedandbreakfast.co.uk

Entry 309   Map 13

Lincolnshire

The Old Farm House

Hidden in the Lincolnshire Wolds, an 18th-century, ivy-covered house – and Nicola's father still farms the fields beyond the ha-ha. The stone-flagged, terracotta-washed hall gives a hint of warm colours to come; creamy walls show off tawny fabrics, prints and antiques; the beamed sitting/breakfast room has a big, rosy brick inglenook fireplace and tranquil views. Such a welcoming, tucked-away place, hopping with pheasant but just an easy drive from shops, golf and racing in the nearby towns. Excellent value, good plentiful food, and perfect if you fancy privacy and space. *Children over eight welcome.*

Price	£80. Singles £55.
Rooms	3: 2 doubles, 1 triple.
Meals	Pub 2 miles.
Closed	Christmas, New Year & occasionally.
Directions	M180 exit 5 from north; A18 signed Louth. Past airport; 2.5 miles after junc. of A46 right signed Hatcliffe. House third on right, before village.

	Nicola Clarke
	The Old Farm House, Low Road,
	Hatcliffe, Grimsby DN37 0SH
Tel	+44 (0)1472 824455
Mobile	+44 (0)7818 272523
Email	clarky.hatcliffe@btinternet.com
Web	www.oldfarmhousebandbgrimsby.com

Entry 310   Map 13

London

20 Bywater Street

In a quiet, pretty cul-de-sac off the fashionable King's Road, a delightful pastel-coloured house and a welcoming B&B. Caroline and Richard give you a light, quiet bedroom downstairs, with a deep green carpet and a wicker chair, fresh flowers, lots of magazines and books and a digital radio. The private shower room is next door with fluffy towels and good toiletries. Breakfast on freshly squeezed juice, fruit, muesli, croissants, muffins and more across the hall in the kitchen/conservatory, a cheery room that swims in morning sun, with doors opening onto a flower filled Yorkstone patio garden. The best of London laps at the door.

Price	From £115.
Rooms	1 double with separate shower.
Meals	Continental breakfast. Pubs/restaurants/cafes nearby.
Closed	Occasionally.
Directions	Tube: Sloane Square 6-minute walk (down King's Road, 6th street on right). Parking available locally.

	Caroline & Richard Heaton-Watson
	20 Bywater Street,
	Chelsea, London SW3 4XD
Email	caheatonw@aol.com
Web	www.20bywaterstreet.com

Entry 311   Map 22

London

90 Old Church Street

In a quiet street facing the Chelsea Arts Club is an enticing, contemporary haven. Softly spoken Nina is passionate about the arts, knows Chelsea inside out and takes real pleasure in looking after her guests. Antique shop spoils stand alongside more modern delights, the attention to detail is amazing and there are plentiful bunches of flowers. A lush carpet takes you up to the second floor and your super-private, surprisingly peaceful and deliciously designed bedroom and bathroom. Breakfast – fruit platters, yogurt and croissants – is shared with Nina in the kitchen. We love No. 90 – and the little black poodles!

Price	From £115. Singles from £100.
Rooms	1 double.
Meals	Continental breakfast £10. Restaurants nearby.
Closed	Occasionally.
Directions	Tube: South Kensington.

	Nina Holland
	90 Old Church Street,
	Chelsea, London SW3 6EP
Tel	+44 (0)20 7352 4758
Mobile	+44 (0)7831 689167
Email	ninastcharles@btinternet.com
Web	www.chelseabedbreakfast.com

Entry 312   Map 22

London

37 Trevor Square

A three-minute walk from Hyde Park or Harrods – a fabulous find. The square is peaceful, private and exquisite, so find a pretty corner and enjoy. Margaret runs an interior design company – rather successfully, by the look of things – and serves a superb full English breakfast in the kitchen/diner; there's also a small conservatory you are welcome to use. Bedrooms (one downstairs has an enormous bed and a little patio) have goose down pillows, cashmere duvets, electric blankets and a mini fridge; slip on your robe, listen to some music or watch a DVD – it's all here. Blissful luxury in the middle of Knightsbridge.

Price	From £180. Singles £100.
Rooms	3: 1 twin/double; 1 double, 1 twin sharing shower (let to same party only).
Meals	Restaurants 200 yds.
Closed	Occasionally.
Directions	Tube: Knightsbridge. Nearest car park £25 for 24 hrs (closed overnight).

Margaret & Holly Palmer
37 Trevor Square,
Knightsbridge, London SW7 1DY
Tel +44 (0)20 7823 8186
Email margaret@37trevorsquare.co.uk
Web www.37trevorsquare.co.uk

Entry 313   Map 22

London

6 Oakfield Street

This district dates from the mid-1660s and local historian Simon has maps to prove it; their road is the second smallest in London. Hospitable Margaret and Simon, language, art and Egypt lovers, live in a stylish 1860s house with a beautiful roof mural (hers), a marble-topped table in the dining room and a collection of Egyptian prints. There's an open-plan feel to the kitchen, and a roof terrace where you can sit in summer. Bedrooms are at the top of the house: the twin is little but, being at the back, is silent at night; the double has a big wooden bed and an antique armoire. Stroll to restaurants on Hollywood Road.

Price	£90. Singles £70.
Rooms	2: 1 double, 1 twin.
Meals	Restaurants nearby.
Closed	Occasionally.
Directions	Tube: Earl's Court 12-minute walk. South Kensington 20-minute walk or 5-minute bus ride on 14 or 414. Nearest car park £25 for 24 hrs.

Margaret & Simon de Maré
6 Oakfield Street,
Little Chelsea, London SW10 9JB
Tel +44 (0)20 7352 2970
Mobile +44 (0)7990 844008
Email margaretdemare@googlemail.com
Web www.athomeinnchelsea.com

Entry 314   Map 22

London

15 Delaford Street

A pretty Victorian, terraced Fulham home, inside all charming and spacious. In a tiny, sun-trapping courtyard you can have continental breakfast in good weather – tropical fruits are a favourite and the coffee is very good; a second miniature garden bursts with life at the back. The bedroom, up a spiral staircase, looks down on it all. Expect perfectly ironed sheets on a comfy bed, a quilted throw, books in the alcove, a sunny bathroom and fluffy white towels. The tennis at Queen's is in June and on your doorstep. Tim and Margot – she's from Melbourne – are fun, charming and happy to pick you up from the nearest tube.

Price	£90. Singles £65.
Rooms	1 double.
Meals	Restaurants nearby.
Closed	Occasionally.
Directions	Tube: West Brompton. Parking free eves & weekends; otherwise pay & display. 74 bus to West End nearby.

 Late checkout (12pm). Free pick-up from local bus/train station.

Margot & Tim Woods
15 Delaford Street,
Fulham, London SW6 7LT
Tel   +44 (0)20 7385 9671
Email   woodsmargot@hotmail.co.uk

Entry 315   Map 22

London

35 Burnthwaite Road

Near Queen's Club and Wimbledon for tennis and Fulham Broadway's tube, a sweet terraced house on the sunny side of the street. A fresh aqua carpet ushers you up to a bright bedroom on the second floor, and a spotless white bathroom squeezed under the eaves. It's as peaceful as can be. No sitting room but a rather smart dining table for breakfast – croissants, cereals, fresh fruit salad. A traditional and civilised feel prevails, thanks to lovely family pieces, fine china, touches of chintz – and friendly Diana who helps you plan your day. Buses to Piccadilly and Westminster, a stroll to the Thames, all of London at your feet.

Price	From £80. Singles from £65.
Rooms	1 twin/double.
Meals	Pubs/restaurants within walking distance.
Closed	Rarely.
Directions	Tube: Fulham Broadway 6-minute walk. Parking pay & display. Bus: 211, 414, 14.

Diana FitzGeorge-Balfour
35 Burnthwaite Road,
Fulham, London SW6 5BQ
Tel   +44 (0)20 7385 8081
Mobile   +44 (0)7831 571449
Email   diana@dianabalfour.co.uk
Web   www.dianabalfour.co.uk

Entry 316   Map 22

London

21 Barclay Road

The grand piano is a magnet for conductors and music professors from around the world. Delightful Charlotte and Adrian host lively social music evenings; Charlotte, who does something unspeakably high-powered by day, happily advises the best outings. You pretty much get the run of the house: a large sitting room with an open fire, tiny but beautifully laid out bedrooms, a decanter of sherry and sparkling bathrooms – one has a rain shower and tub. Help yourself to a light breakfast and good strong coffee before setting off to tour London. Bring your instrument... a great city find. *Use of grand piano by arrangement.*

Price	From £95. Singles £75.
Rooms	2: 1 double; 1 double with separate bathroom.
Meals	Food & music evenings occasionally. Restaurants 2-minute walk.
Closed	Occasionally.
Directions	Tube: Fulham Broadway 2-minute walk. Parking free 8pm-9am & all Sunday. 9am-8pm pay & display.

 Pancake and waffle breakfast by arrangement.

Charlotte Dexter,
21 Barclay Road,
Fulham, London SW6 1EJ
Tel   +44 (0)20 7384 3390
Mobile   +44 (0)7767 420943
Email   info@barclayhouselondon.com
Web   www.barclayhouselondon.com

Entry 317   Map 22

London

8 Parthenia Road

Caroline, an interior designer, mixes the sophistication of the city with the feel of the countryside and her handsome big kitchen is the engine-room of the house. It leads through to a light breakfast room with doors onto a pretty brick garden with chairs and table – hope for fine days. The house is long and thin, Fulham style, and reaches up to a big sloping-ceilinged bedroom in the eaves, cosy, sunny and bright. A remarkably quiet place to stay in an accessible part of town, near the King's Road with all its antique and designer shops, and Chelsea Football ground.

Price	£90-£130. Singles from £75.
Rooms	1 twin/double.
Meals	Continental breakfast. Restaurants nearby.
Closed	Rarely.
Directions	Tube: Parsons Green 4-minute walk. Parking £17.60 per day in street (free Mon-Sat 5pm-9am & all day Sun). Bus: 22, 2-minute walk.

Caroline & George Docker
8 Parthenia Road,
Fulham, London SW6 4BD
Tel   +44 (0)20 7384 1165
Email   dockercaroline@gmail.com

Entry 318   Map 22

London

39 Brookville Road

You are in the throng of vibrant Fulham with its quirky boutiques and antique shops, and a short walk to the King's Road, but these pretty pastel-coloured terraced houses are remarkably quiet inside. Musical Leah enjoys having guests: you breakfast on a sweet roof terrace with views, or at a long wooden table in the peachy dining room with tapestry chairs. Bedrooms are filled with lovely things: a buddha lamp, an antique walnut table, thick woven bedspreads and original art; beds are dressed well and duvets are duck down. One bathroom has achurch arch mirror and the other a large, ornately framed, mirror. Super restaurants are a stroll away. *Children over six welcome.*

Price	£80–£90.
Rooms	3: 1 double; 1 double, 1 twin sharing shower.
Meals	Pubs/restaurants within 0.25 miles.
Closed	Rarely.
Directions	Within 5-minute walk of Parsons Green tube station.

Leah Shellim
39 Brookville Road,
Parsons Green, London SW6 7BH
Tel +44 (0)20 7381 2093
Mobile +44 (0)7833 962199
Email leah492@btinternet.com
Web www.thevillesbedandbreakfast.co.uk

Entry 319 Map 22

London

Esmond Road

In a suburb of London long favoured by artists is a neat brick Victorian house framed by a beautiful maple; inside is a stylish and contemporary home. Warm gentle Ragini – life coach and relaxed B&Ber – welcomes you in. Find cream marble floors, a fabulous kitchen, Indian art on the walls and the scent of fresh lilies. All feels spacious, generous and calm, and there's a sweet garden behind. Bedrooms are upstairs: fresh, snug, with waffle robes and goose down; breakfast is vegetarian and delicious. Chiswick House, Kew and the river are wonderfully close, and the 94 bus whisks you straight to Piccadilly!

Price	£65–£100.
Rooms	2: 1 double; 1 double with shared bath.
Meals	Dinner £15. Pubs/restaurants 5-minute walk.
Closed	Rarely.
Directions	5-minute walk from Turnham Green underground station; across park, right on street with red postbox.

 10% off room rate Mon-Thurs. Meet at Turnham Green station. Late checkout (12pm).

Ragini Annan
Esmond Road,
Chiswick, London W4 1JG
Tel +44 (0)20 8747 1014
Mobile +44 (0)7973 327662
Email raginiannan@yahoo.co.uk

Entry 320 Map 22

London

31 Rowan Road

Terrific value for money in Brook Green: two private studios – one under the eaves with a big comfy bed, a window seat, and a bathroom with a deep cast-iron bath from which you can gaze out at the birds – the other (larger, more contemporary in style) on the lower ground floor, with its own wisteria-clad entrance. Continental breakfast is popped into your fridge the night before. Or join in with family life in a pink bedroom with books and hats, and a teenager's bedroom – and take breakfast in the pretty conservatory with Vicky and Edmund. There's a garden full of blossom and super restaurants close by.

Price	£50–£105. Extra person £15.
Rooms	4: 2 doubles sharing bath; 2 studios, each with twin/double, bath/shower & kitchen/ette. Extra bed available.
Meals	Continental breakfast. Pubs/restaurants 2 minutes.
Closed	Occasionally.
Directions	Tube: Hammersmith. Off-street parking £15 a day.

Vicky & Edmund Sixsmith
31 Rowan Road, Brook Green,
Hammersmith, London W6 7DT

Tel	+44 (0)20 8748 0930
Mobile	+44 (0)7966 829359
Email	vickysixsmith@btconnect.com
Web	www.abetterwaytostay.co.uk

Entry 321   Map 22

London

26 Hillgate Place

You are in luxurious, bohemian Notting Hill: a movie at the Coronet, a pint at the Windsor Castle, the best Thai at the Churchill and the chic-est shops. Whatever you do, roll back to Hilary and Maryo's relaxed and lived-in home for a bit of eastern spice: Indian textiles, old teak dressers, the odd wooden elephant, wildly colourful art (Hilary paints). The bigger double has a Indo-Caribbean influence and shares a bathroom up a flight of stairs; the smaller is smarter with a sofa and a claw-foot bath. Both rooms come with bathrobes and small fridge, and there are two gardens to look out on, one on a roof.

Price	£80–£98. Singles £70–£80.
Rooms	2: 1 double; 1 double sharing family bath.
Meals	Pubs/restaurants nearby.
Closed	Occasionally.
Directions	Tube: Notting Hill Gate 5-minute walk.

Bottle of champagne for stays of 2 or more nights.

Hilary Dunne & Maryo Josef
26 Hillgate Place,
Notting Hill Gate, London W8 7ST

Tel	+44 (0)20 7727 7717
Email	hilary.dunne@virgin.net
Web	www.26hillgateplace.co.uk

Entry 322   Map 22

London

101 Abbotsbury Road

The area is one of London's most desirable and Sunny's family home is opposite the borough's loveliest park, with open-air opera in summer. The whole top floor is generally given over to visitors. Warm, homely bedrooms are in gentle yellows and greens, with pale carpets, white duvets, pelmeted windows and a pretty dressing table for the double. The bathroom, marble-tiled and sky-lit, shines. You are well placed for Kensington High Street, Olympia, Notting Hill, Portobello Market, Kensington Gardens, the Albert Hall, Knightsbridge and Piccadilly! Relax, unwind, feel free to come and go. *Children over ten welcome.*

Price	From £110. Singles from £55.
Rooms	2: 1 double, 1 single, sharing bath.
Meals	Continental breakfast. Pubs/restaurants 5-minute walk.
Closed	Occasionally.
Directions	Tube Central line: Holland Park 7-minute walk. Off-street parking sometimes available.

Sunny Murray
101 Abbotsbury Road,
Holland Park, London W14 8EP
Tel   +44 (0)20 7602 0179
Mobile +44 (0)7768 362562
Email   sunny.murray@googlemail.com

Entry 323   Map 22

London

Fleet River Bakery Rooms

Meet real Londoners, not tides of tourists, in the narrow streets of this vibrant, interesting part of town. Your handsome, city-sharp studio is above the bustling bakery/cafe: nip downstairs for breakfast — excellent fresh food and coffee. You have a kitchen cum living area with polished wooden floor, sofa, and seriously comfortable bed. All new and good-looking in a refreshingly frill-free way and surprisingly quiet. People-watch through the long sash windows, cook up some local market produce or head out for a bundle of good restaurants — Covent Garden, Bloomsbury and the West End are all an easy walk.

Price	£115. Singles £84.
Rooms	4 studios: 1 double & kitchenette each.
Meals	Lunch in café downstairs, from £6.50. Packed lunch £7.50.
Closed	Rarely.
Directions	From Holborn tube: left from the main exit, down Kingsway, 2nd lane on left (Twyford Place). House on right at the end (corner of Twyford Place & Gate St).

Lucy Clapp
Fleet River Bakery Rooms, 71 Lincoln's
Inn Fields, Holborn, London WC2A 3JF
Tel   +44 (0)20 7691 1457
Mobile +44 (0)7966 267401
Email   rooms@fleetriverbakery.com
Web   www.fleetriverbakery.com

Entry 324   Map 22

London

30 King Henry's Road

Shops, restaurants and sublime views of Primrose Hill are a five-minute stroll from this interesting 1860s house; walls are covered in a lifetime collection of watercolours, drawings and maps. Your room on the top floor has a comfortable brass bed, a sisal floor, fine pieces of furniture, a wall of books, digital TV and a smart new bathroom. Breakfast on homemade bread and jams, bagels, croissants, yogurts and fresh fruit salad in the large kitchen/dining room with a big open fire and garden views. There's open-air theatre in Regent's Park in summer; Carole and Ted know London well and will happily advise.

Price	£110. Singles £80.
Rooms	1 double.
Meals	Pubs/restaurants 2-minute walk.
Closed	Occasionally.
Directions	Tube: Chalk Farm 5-minute walk. Free parking weekends, ticket parking nearby.

Carole & Ted Cox
30 King Henry's Road,
Primrose Hill, London NW3 3RP
Tel   +44 (0)20 7483 2871
Mobile +44 (0)7976 389350
Email   carole.l.cox@gmail.com

Entry 325   Map 22

London

66 Camden Square

A modern, architect designed house made of African teak, brick and glass. Climb wooden stairs under a glazed pyramid to light-filled, Japanese-style bedrooms with low platform beds, modern chairs and private sitting room/study. Sue and Rodger have travelled widely so there are pictures, photographs and ethnic pieces everywhere – and a burst of colour from Peckam the parrot. Share their lovely open-plan dining space overlooking a verdant bird-filled courtyard at breakfast – a delicious start to the day. Cool Camden's bustling market is close, along with theatres, restaurants, bars and zoo. *Children by arrangement.*

Price	£100. Singles £60.
Rooms	2: 1 double; 1 single sharing bath (2nd room let to same party only).
Meals	Pubs/restaurants nearby.
Closed	Occasionally.
Directions	Tube: Camden Town or Kentish Town. Parking free at weekends; meters during week. 10 minutes by taxi from St Pancras Eurostar Terminal.

Sue & Rodger Davis
66 Camden Square,
Camden Town, London NW1 9XD
Tel   +44 (0)20 7485 4622
Email   rodgerdavis@btopenworld.com

Entry 326   Map 22

London

Arlington Avenue

This 1848 townhouse is a real find – from here you can follow the canal up to Islington. Inside you find a world of books and art; immaculate bedrooms are colourful and filled with pictures, etchings and pretty furniture, with views over several gardens to the back. The grey marble bathroom might be shared now and then, and is two flights down, but if you don't mind that, you've struck gold. Shop locally, eat picnic suppers in the red and gold dining room, chill drinks in the fridge. You help yourself to breakfast in a lemon coloured country style kitchen; this is laissez-faire B&B and fantastic value.

Price	£45–£65. Singles £40–£55.
Rooms	2: 1 double; 1 single sharing bath.
Meals	Pubs/restaurants 100 yds.
Closed	Rarely.
Directions	Equal distance from Angel and Old Street tubes (15-minute walk). 2 minutes for bus stop to City, St Pauls, Tate Modern (City 5 minutes). 7 minutes to bus stop for West End (West End 20 minutes). Limited parking (by arrangement).

Late checkout (12pm). Discounts for longer stays.

Thomas Blaikie
Arlington Avenue,
Islington, London N1 7AX

Mobile	+44 (0)7711 265183
Email	thomas@arlingtonavenue.co.uk
Web	www.arlingtonavenue.co.uk

Entry 327   Map 22

London

26 Florence Street

There's a dramatic vibrancy to Valerie's home, just off Upper Street with its restaurants, and right by the Almeida and Sadler's Wells theatres. The Victorian house is stuffed with oriental, French and Italian pieces; your basement bedroom is filled with light and character. A feast of beautiful scenes and stories, every angle of Valerie's interior design merits applause; walls, doors and much of the furniture are ragged, sponged and stencilled in the colourful style of the Bloomsbury set; the conservatory has John Soane perspectives and Arabian Nights lanterns, screens and exotic plants. *Children over 12 welcome. Min. two nights.*

Price	£115. Singles £85–£95.
Rooms	1 double with separate shower (extra single available, so occasional share).
Meals	Pubs/restaurants nearby.
Closed	Occasionally.
Directions	From Highbury & Islington tube, right out of station. Down Upper Street, past Town Hall. Left immed. before Shell garage. Free overnight & weekend parking (Sat 6.30pm); otherwise meters & car parks.

Valerie Rossmore
26 Florence Street,
Islington, London N1 2FW

Email	valerie.rossmore@googlemail.com
Web	www.valerierossmore.co.uk

Entry 328   Map 22

London

26 Montefiore Street

Step into a hall of rich golds and yellows to find an elegant yet comfortable bolthole, with a little garden full of birds where you can have breakfast in the summer. This artisan house is in a quiet street and brims with books. Your bedroom has white bed linen and velour dressing gowns; go down a few steps to the fresh, chic bathroom with fluffy towels, bath oils and lotions. No sitting room but there are wicker chairs in a corner of the library/dining room looking out on to the pretty garden. Walk to Battersea Arts Centre, and Battersea Park with its festivals and art fairs; not far from Chelsea Flower Show too.

Price	From £110. Singles from £80.
Rooms	1 double with separate bath/shower (1 single in attached study, suitable for a child).
Meals	Restaurants 300 yds.
Closed	Occasionally.
Directions	Bus: 452 & 137, 12 minutes to Sloane Sq. Tube: Clapham Common. Train: Queenstown Rd & Battersea Park, 2 & 4 min Victoria & Waterloo. Parking: day pass £5 (free 5.30pm-9.30am Mon-Fri, all day Sat, Sun).

	D Porter
	26 Montefiore Street,
	Battersea, London SW8 3TL
Tel	+44 (0)20 7720 0939
Email	bedandbreakfast.london.sw8@gmail.com

Entry 329 Map 22

London

20 St Philip Street

Come to retreat from the frenzy of city life. In the 1890 Victorian cottage all is peaceful and calm and Barbara looks after you beautifully. The dining room, with the odd oriental piece from past travels, is where you have your full English breakfast – unusual for London – and across the hall is the elegant sitting room, with gilt-framed mirrors, sumptuous curtains, and a piano. Upstairs is a bright and restful bedroom with pretty linen and a cloud of goose down. The large, sparkling bathroom next door is all yours – fabulous. Nothing has been overlooked and the tiny courtyard garden is a summer oasis.

Price	From £110. Singles from £80.
Rooms	1 double with separate bath & shower.
Meals	Pubs/restaurants 200 yds.
Closed	Occasionally.
Directions	Rr'way stations (6-min ride Waterloo, 3-min ride Victoria). Or 137 & 452 bus (Sloane Sq) & 156 (Vauxhall) tubes 10 mins. Parking max 4 hrs (£2 per hr) or £10 day ticket, 9.30-5.30 Mon-Fri., otherwise free.

	Barbara Graham
	20 St Philip Street,
	Battersea, London SW8 3SL
Tel	+44 (0)20 7498 9967
Email	stay@bed-breakfast-battersea.co.uk
Web	www.bed-breakfast-battersea.co.uk

Entry 330 Map 22

London

28 Old Devonshire Road

Keen gardeners will love it here, in a surprisingly quiet part of Balham close to the leafy common: Georgina's award-winning plot is brimming with colour and scent. Take breakfast out here on sunny days, or in the orange dining room with its long wooden table, marble fireplace and watercolours. Your bedroom is peaceful and cosy with a brand new bed, flowers from the garden and lots of books; also a flat-screen TV. A very spacious bathroom has a good shower, smart waffle robes and more interesting art. You are near to a plethora of restaurants. *French & Italian spoken. Minimum stay two nights.*

London

The Coach House

A rare privacy: you have your own coach house, separated from the Notts' home by a stylish terracotta-potted courtyard with Indian sandstone paving and various fruit trees (peach, pear, nectarine). Breakfast in your own sunny kitchen, or let Meena treat you to a full English in hers (she makes great porridge, too). The lovely big attic bedroom has beams, cream curtains, rugs on polished wood floors; the brick-walled ground-floor twin is pleasant and airy; both look over the peaceful garden. Urban but bucolic – just perfect as a romantic retreat, or a family getaway. *Minimum three nights; two nights January & February.*

Price	£95. Singles £70.
Rooms	1 double.
Meals	Pubs/restaurants 500 yds.
Closed	Rarely.
Directions	Old Devonshire Road is a turning off Balham High Road, which is part of the A24 London to Dorking road. 5-minute walk from Balham mainline and tube stations. Visitors' parking permits available £5 per day.

 Discounts for longer stays.

🎁 Use your Sawday's Gift Card here.

Georgina Ivor
28 Old Devonshire Road,
Balham, London SW12 9RB
Tel   +44 (0)20 8673 7179
Mobile   +44 (0)7941 960199
Email   georgina@balhambandb.co.uk
Web   www.balhambandb.co.uk

Entry 331   Map 22

Price	£95–£190.
Rooms	Coach House: 1 family room for 2-3; 1 twin with separate shower. Same-party bookings only.
Meals	Pub/restaurant 200 yds.
Closed	Occasionally.
Directions	From r'bout on south side of Wandsworth Bridge, south down Trinity Rd on A214. At 3rd set of lights, 1.7 miles on, left into Upper Tooting Park. 4th left into Marius Rd, then 3rd left.

Meena & Harley Nott
The Coach House, 2 Tunley Road,
Balham, London SW17 7QJ
Tel   +44 (0)20 8772 1939
Email   coachhouse@chslondon.com
Web   www.coachhouse.chslondon.com

Entry 332   Map 22

London

108 Streathbourne Road

It's a handsome house in a conservation area that manages to be both elegant and cosy. The cream-coloured double bedroom has an armchair, a writing desk, pretty curtains and a big comfy walnut bed; the twin is light and airy. The dining room overlooks a secluded terrace and garden and there are newspapers at breakfast. You can eat in – David, who works in the wine trade, always puts a bottle on the table – or out, at one of the trendy new restaurants in Balham. A friendly city base on a quiet, tree-lined street – maximum comfort, delicious food and good value for London. Delightful. *Minimum stay two nights.*

London

38 Killieser Avenue

On a quiet leafy street, the Haworths have brought country-house chic to South London. Philip and Winkle have filled their elegant Victorian townhouse with stunning fabrics, warm sunny colours and treasures from far-flung travels. The house glows, the garden is ravishing, breakfasts are delicious (so are the scones!) and bedrooms are spacious: fine linen, lambswool throws, waffle robes, the scent of roses. Few people do things with as much natural good humour as Winkle, whose passions are cooking, gardening and garden history. Transport is close and you can be in Victoria in 15 minutes. *Garden tours & cream tea courses.*

Price	£95-£100. Singles £80-£85.
Rooms	2: 1 double with separate bath; 1 twin sharing bath (let to same party only).
Meals	Dinner £35. Restaurants 5-minute walk.
Closed	Occasionally.
Directions	Tube: Tooting Bec 7-minute walk. 319 bus from Sloane Square. Free parking weekends, otherwise meters or £5 daily.

Price	From £98. Singles from £70.
Rooms	2: 1 twin; 1 single with separate bath.
Meals	Dinner £30-£35.
Closed	Occasionally.
Directions	5-minute walk from Streatham Hill station (15 minutes to Victoria); 15-minute walk from Balham tube.

	Mary & David Hodges
	108 Streathbourne Road,
	Balham, London SW17 8QY
Tel	+44 (0)20 8767 6931
Email	davidandmaryhodges@gmail.com
Web	www.streathbourneroad.com

	Winkle Haworth
	38 Killieser Avenue,
	Streatham Hill, London SW2 4NT
Tel	+44 (0)20 8671 4196
Email	winklehaworth@hotmail.com
Web	www.thegardenbedandbreakfast.com

Entry 333   Map 22

Entry 334   Map 22

London

24 Fox Hill

This part of London is full of sky, trees and wildlife; Pissarro captured on canvas the view up the hill in 1870 (the painting is in the National Gallery). There's good stuff everywhere – things hang off walls and peep over the tops of dressers; bedrooms are stunning, with antiques, textiles, paintings and big, firm beds. Sue, a graduate from Chelsea Art College, employs humour and intelligence to put guests at ease and has created a special garden, too. Tim often helps with breakfasts. Frogs sing at night, woodpeckers wake you in the morning, in this lofty, peaceful retreat. *Victoria is 20 minutes by train.*

Price	£90–£120. Singles £50.
Rooms	3: 1 twin/double; 1 double, 1 twin sharing shower.
Meals	Dinner £35. Pubs/restaurants 5-minute walk.
Closed	Rarely.
Directions	Train: Crystal Palace (7-minute walk). Underground: East London line. Collection possible. Good buses to West End & Westminster.

Jar of house preserve in room. Free pick-up from local station. Bottle of house wine with dinner.

Sue & Tim Haigh
24 Fox Hill,
Crystal Palace, London SE19 2XE
Tel   +44 (0)20 8768 0059
Email suehaigh@hotmail.co.uk
Web   www.foxhill-bandb.co.uk

Entry 335   Map 22

London

113 Pepys Road

Anne is Chinese, well-travelled, loves this house, loves her guests, and is a trained Cordon Bleu cook; convivial breakfast can be English or oriental. The house overlooks the first landscaped park of its kind in south-east London; at night you see a carpet of lights. There are hats on the hat stand, batiks on the walls, orchids (Anne's passion). The downstairs room has a huge bed, bamboo blinds, a kimono for the bathroom; our favourites are upstairs, airy, bright, overlooking the garden (the magnolias are majestic). It's a ten-minute walk downhill to buses, tubes and trains… and blissfully quiet for London.

Price	From £100. Singles from £75.
Rooms	3: 1 double, 1 twin/double; 1 twin with separate bath.
Meals	Dinner from £35. BYO. Restaurant 0.5 miles.
Closed	Rarely.
Directions	Directions on booking.

Anne Marten
113 Pepys Road,
New Cross, London SE14 5SE
Tel   +44 (0)20 7639 1060
Email annemarten@pepysroad.com
Web   www.pepysroad.com

Entry 336   Map 22

London

16 St Alfege Passage

The approach is along the passage between the Hawksmoor church and its graveyard, away from the village's hubbub. At the end of the lane is a 'cottage' set about with greenery, lamp posts and benches. Inside, a cup of tea and flapjack await you in the eccentrically furnished (stuffed cat on dentist chair, huge parasol) sitting room. Bedrooms are cosy and colourful, with double beds (not huge) that positively encourage intimacy. Breakfast is in the basement, another engagingly furnished room awash with character. Robert, an actor, is easy, funny, chatty – and has created an unusual and attractive place.

Price	£90-£125. Singles from £80.
Rooms	3: 1 four-poster, 1 double, 1 single.
Meals	Pubs/restaurants 2-minute walk.
Closed	Rarely.
Directions	3-minute walk from Greenwich train & Docklands Light Railway station or Cutty Sark DLR station. Parking free from 5pm (6pm Sundays) to 9am.

Nicholas Mesure & Robert Gray
16 St Alfege Passage,
Greenwich, London SE10 9JS
Tel   +44 (0)20 8853 4337
Email info@st-alfeges.co.uk
Web   www.st-alfeges.co.uk

Entry 337   Map 22

Middlesex

Middle Cottage

What a find! A terrific spot right next to the Thames: Jonathan and Sarah have an eye for detail and do things well; you have your own, very private space in one half of their early Victorian cottages. Your light, upstairs sitting room has a dazzling collection of art and sculpture, chunky glass shelves full of design magazines and a soft grey sofa for reading. Your bedroom (not huge) is crisp and uncluttered with excellent lighting and blindingly white sheets; the funky bathroom is toasty with underfloor heating. Browse the newspapers over a robust breakfast; you can stroll to great shops and restaurants.

Price	From £110. Singles from £95.
Rooms	1 double. (Sofabed in sitting room.)
Meals	Pub/restaurant 20 yds.
Closed	Rarely.
Directions	Follow Teddington High Street towards the river. Middle Cottage sits within a terrace of 3, beside the footbridge near Teddington Lock.

Jonathan & Sarah Barker
Middle Cottage,
12 Ferry Road, Teddington TW11 9NN
Tel   +44 (0)20 8973 0777
Mobile   +44 (0)7775 803664
Email   sarah@middlecottage.org
Web   www.middlecottage.org

Entry 338   Map 22

Norfolk

The Merchants House

The oak four-poster – a beauty – came with the house. Part of the building (1400) is the oldest in Wells; in those days, the merchant could bring his boats up to the door. Liz and Dennis know the history, and happily share it. Inside is warm, friendly, inviting: the mahogany shines, the bathrooms sparkle, there are papers for breakfast, books to borrow and pretty sash windows overlooking salt marshes. As for Wells, it is on the famous Coastal Path, has a quay bustling with sailing boats and 16 miles of sands. Birdwatch by day, dine out at night – easy when you're in the centre. Breakfasts are a treat.

Price	£80. Singles £55.
Rooms	2: 1 four-poster, 1 double.
Meals	Pubs/restaurants 300 yds.
Closed	November–January.
Directions	B1105 from Fakenham to Wells-next-the-Sea, then follow signs to beach & quay. House is 150 yds west of the quay.

	Elizabeth & Dennis Woods The Merchants House, 47 Freeman Street, Wells-next-the-Sea NR23 1BQ
Tel	+44 (0)1328 711877
Mobile	+44 (0)7816 632742
Email	denniswoods@talktalk.net
Web	www.the-merchants-house.co.uk

Entry 339   Map 10

Norfolk

Glebe Farmhouse

Two miles south of Burnham, and a five-minute stroll from post office and delightful pub, is a charming farmhouse with a sun-drenched terrace and a pretty garden. Mary and Jeremy give you TV-free bedrooms that are large, peaceful and cosy, a log fire in the family sitting room that you are welcome to share and wonderful breakfasts in the big bright farmhouse kitchen. How lovely to come home to books, paintings, flowers and well-cushioned sofas after a wild walk on Holkham Beach… and a real fire in one bedroom, for a modest extra charge.

Price	From £75. Singles from £40.
Rooms	2: 1 double, 1 twin/double. Extra fold-up bed for child & cot.
Meals	Pub 5-minute walk.
Closed	Rarely.
Directions	A148 King's Lynn to Cromer, north onto B1355 just west of Fakenham. 6.5 miles to North Creake. Right after red phone box, then 300 yds. On right.

	Mary & Jeremy Brettingham Smith Glebe Farmhouse, Wells Road, North Creake, Fakenham NR21 9LG
Tel	+44 (0)1328 730133
Email	enquiries@glebe-farmhouse.co.uk
Web	www.glebe-farmhouse.co.uk

Entry 340   Map 10

Norfolk

1 Leicester Meadows

Up among 13 acres of wild meadow and woodland – not another building in sight. It's all so relaxed and unhurried: barn owls roosting in the outhouse, hens strutting the garden, geese pottering up from the pond. The 19th-century cottages, once the home of workers on the Holkham estate, have been imaginatively restored and enlarged. (Bob was an architect, Sara an art teacher; both are immensely friendly and helpful.) Polished wood and old brick are topped with bright rugs; paintings and ceramics engage the eye; steep stairs take you up to the bedrooms – one large, contemporary and elegant, the other cosy and fun.

Price	From £65. Singles from £50.
Rooms	2: 1 double, 1 twin/double. (Additional small room available.)
Meals	Supper from £18. Pub 1 mile.
Closed	Rarely.
Directions	Off A148 near Fakenham; B1355 dir. Burnham Market. In S. Creake, left by flint bus shelter, right into Avondale Rd; 1 mile, taking left fork. At bottom of hill, house set back 100 yds on left.

Bob & Sara Freakley
1 Leicester Meadows,
South Creake, Fakenham NR21 9NZ
Tel +44 (0)1328 823533
Email rf@freakley.com
Web www.leicestermeadows.com

Entry 341   Map 10

Norfolk

Manor House

Eclectic African art and enormous photos of wildlife decorate this elegant, early Victorian manor house just 20 minutes from the coast. Lorna is great fun and loves to share her interesting home; she moved here from Cape Town and has named the spacious, luxurious bedrooms after her favourite African haunts. Glamorous bathrooms are spotless and come complete with snazzy scents and towelling slippers. Breakfast is Aga cooked: organic sausages and bacon, croissants, eggs from the hens. Birdwatchers and walkers love it here; bring your horse too and Lorna will ride with you on the sandy north Norfolk beaches.

Price	£79-£137. Family suite £137.
Rooms	4: 2 doubles, 1 suite, 1 family suite for 4.
Meals	Packed lunch £5-£10. Supper, 2 courses, £15. Pub 200 yds.
Closed	Rarely.
Directions	From Fakenham A1067 for 5 miles, then right to G. Ryburgh. On entering village, cross bridge. Manor House on right behind brick & flint wall. Automatic gates.

Bottle of wine in your room.

Lorna Ward
Manor House, Station Road,
Great Ryburgh, Fakenham NR21 0DX
Tel +44 (0)1328 829788
Email manorhousenorfolk@gmail.com
Web www.northnorfolkbandb.co.uk

Entry 342   Map 10

Norfolk

The Close

A large, creeper-clad, Victorian house in the middle of the village, with a smooth lawn, mature trees, curved herbaceous border and a stream (source of the river Wensum). Bedrooms, one with a garden view, are large, light and airy, with a mix of antique and contemporary furniture, flowers, comfortable sofas with floral cushions; shower rooms are spotlessly tiled. You breakfast on home-baked bread and the local butcher's finest at a huge mahogany table in the dining room. Val and Rory know their patch well, so do ask: this is wonderful walking countryside and you are near the coast; Sandringham and Houghton, too.

Price	From £85. Singles £70.
Rooms	2 doubles.
Meals	Pub/restaurant 200 yds.
Closed	Rarely.
Directions	King's Lynn A148 to Fakenham. After 12 miles, through East Rudham. Right immed. after village opp. church. House 100 yds on right. Map provided on booking.

Valerie McGouran
The Close,
Station Road, East Rudham PE31 8SU
Tel   +44 (0)1485 528925
Email rorymcgouran@hotmail.com
Web   www.closenorfolk.com

Entry 343   Map 10

Norfolk

Bagthorpe Hall

Ten minutes from Burnham Market, yet here you are immersed in peaceful countryside. Tid is a pioneer of organic farming and the stunning 700 acres include a woodland snowdrop walk. Gina's passions are music, dance and gardens and she organises open days and concerts for charity. Theirs is a large, elegant house with a fascinating hall mural chronicling their family life; bedrooms – one with a tiny en suite shower room – have big comfy beds and lovely views. Breakfasts are delicious with local sausages and bacon, homemade jams and raspberries from the garden. Birdwatching, cycling and walking are all around. *Stabling available.*

Price	£80-£85. Singles £50.
Rooms	3: 1 double; 1 double with separate bath; 1 twin with separate shower.
Meals	Pubs/restaurants 2 miles.
Closed	Rarely.
Directions	King's Lynn A148 to Fakenham. In East Rudham, The Crown on right; next left signed Bagthorpe Rd. Continue 3.5 miles to Bagthorpe. Past cottages, farm on left, wood on right, white gates on right set back from trees. At top of drive.

Gina & Tid Morton
Bagthorpe Hall, Bagthorpe,
Bircham, King's Lynn PE31 6QY
Tel   +44 (0)1485 578528
Mobile +44 (0)7979 746591
Email   enquiries@bagthorpehall.co.uk
Web   www.bagthorpehall.co.uk

Entry 344   Map 10

Norfolk

Meadow House

Hand-made oak banisters, period furniture: this new-build is beautifully traditional. Breakfast is served in the lovely large drawing room, where you find a warm, sociable atmosphere with squashy sofas and comfy chairs for anytime use. One bedroom is cosy and chintzy, one is larger and more neutral; brand-new bathrooms gleam. Amanda knows B&B, does it well, and plans to grow vegetables once her land is tamed. There are footpaths from the door and plenty to see, starting with Walpole's Houghton Hall, a short walk. A bucolic setting for a profoundly comfortable stay, perfect for country enthusiasts.

Price	£70. Singles £40.
Rooms	2 twins/doubles.
Meals	Packed lunch £5-£7. Pub in village.
Closed	Rarely.
Directions	From King's Lynn, A148 for Cromer. 3 miles after Hillington, 2nd of 2 turnings right to Harpley (no signpost) opp. Houghton Hall sign. 200 yds on; over x-roads, house 400 yds on left.

	Amanda Case
	Meadow House,
	Harpley, King's Lynn PE31 6TU
Tel	+44 (0)1485 520240
Mobile	+44 (0)7890 037134
Email	amandacase@amandacase.plus.com
Web	www.meadowhousebandb.co.uk

Entry 345 Map 10

Norfolk

Litcham Hall

For the whole of the 19th century this was Litcham's doctor's house; the Hall is still at the centre of the community. The big-windowed guest bedrooms look onto stunning gardens with yew hedges, a lily pond and herbaceous borders. This is a thoroughly English home with elegant proportions – the hall, drawing room and dining room are gracious and beautifully furnished, and there's a large sitting room for guests. The hens lay the breakfast eggs, the garden fills the table with soft fruit in season and John and Hermione are friendly and most helpful. Close to Fakenham, Burnham Market and the coast. *Children & pets by arrangement.*

Price	£70-£90. Singles by arrangement.
Rooms	3: 2 doubles; 1 twin with separate bath.
Meals	Pub/restaurant 3 miles.
Closed	Christmas.
Directions	From Swaffham, A1065 north for 5 miles, then right to Litcham on B1145. House on left on entering village. Georgian red-brick with stone balls on gatepost.

10% off room rate Mon-Thurs. 10% off stays of 2 or more nights.

	John & Hermione Birkbeck
	Litcham Hall,
	Litcham, King's Lynn PE32 2QQ
Tel	+44 (0)1328 701389
Email	hermionebirkbeck@hotmail.com
Web	www.litchamhall.co.uk

Entry 346 Map 10

Norfolk

The Old Rectory

A stately place indeed: a venerable English rectory replete with period furniture, art, history, well-bred hosts (he shoots, she rides) and, in the expansive grounds, a ruined chapel, lake, croquet lawn and pool. Breakfast is served on the terrace in summer. You dine by candlelight on local game and the kitchen garden's offerings, then settle in the Georgian drawing room by the rocking horse. Sleep in the Coach House where plush beds have beautiful linen, warm throws and beaded cushions; dogs can stay in the stables. A rare chance to experience the best of British country life. *Riding & shooting can be arranged.*

Price	£85–£105. Singles £65–£85.
Rooms	Coach House: 1 double, 1 twin/double, 1 twin.
Meals	Dinner, 2 courses, £25; 3 courses, £35. Pub 1 mile. Restaurant 5 miles.
Closed	Rarely.
Directions	From Stone Ferry bypass, take road to Oxborough. 0.5 miles before Oxborough Hall, right down Ferry Road. House is 0.5 miles on left.

Veronica de Lotbiniere
The Old Rectory, Ferry Road,
Oxborough, King's Lynn PE33 9PT

Tel	+44 (0)1842 814215
Mobile	+44 (0)7769 687599
Email	onky.del@btinternet.com
Web	www.oldrectoryoxboroughbandb.co.uk

Entry 347 Map 9

Norfolk

Carrick's at Castle Farm

A comfortable, and jolly, mix of farmhouse B&B – rare-breed cattle, tractors, a large, warm-bricked house – and a rather swish interior. Both Jean and John are passionate about conservation and the protection of wildlife, and here you have absolute quiet for birdwatching, fishing, shooting or walking; recover in the drawing room with its books and lovely river views from long windows. Bedrooms are large, light and well thought-out with great bathrooms and binoculars, food is home-grown or local, and there is coffee and cake, or wine, when you arrive. The pretty garden leads down to the river Wensum and a footpath.

Ethical Collection: Environment; Food; Community. See page 420.

Price	£90–£95. Singles £60–£65.
Rooms	4: 2 doubles, 1 twin/double; 1 twin/double with separate bath.
Meals	Dinner, 3 courses, £25. BYO. Pub 0.5 miles.
Closed	Rarely.
Directions	Norwich A47 to Dereham (don't go into Dereham). B1147 to Swanton Morley. In village, take Elsing Road at Darby's pub; farm drive 0.5 miles on left.

 10% off room rate Mon–Thurs. 10% off stays of 2 or more nights.

 Use your Sawday's Gift Card here.

Jean Wright
Carrick's at Castle Farm, Castle Farm,
Swanton Morley, Dereham NR20 4JT

Tel	+44 (0)1362 638302
Email	jean@castlefarm-swanton.co.uk
Web	www.carricksatcastlefarm.co.uk

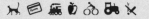

Entry 348 Map 10

Norfolk

Norfolk Courtyard

Walk straight in through French doors to your own, underfloor-heated room in the courtyard; privacy from the main house where young and friendly Simon and Catherine live. The rooms are decorated in soft colours, mattresses are perfect, cotton sheets are smooth and your handsome bathroom has limestone tiles — all rather luxurious. A table in the corner is beautifully laid for your continental breakfast (take it outside on good days) and you have a fridge to cool a bottle. There is a big attic room in one barn where you can play table tennis or read a book. Stunning walks await on the coast. *Minimum stay two nights (peak season).*

Norfolk

Stable Cottage

In the park of a privately owned village, one of Norfolk's finest Elizabethan houses, Heydon Hall. In the Dutch-gabled stable block, fronted by Cromwell's Oak, is this cottage — fresh, sunny and enchanting. Each room is touched by Sarah's warm personality and love of beautiful things; seagrass floors and crisp linen, toile de Jouy walls and pretty china. Bedrooms are cottagey and immaculate, there are fresh fabrics, baskets of treats in the bathrooms (one has a roll top bath) and delicious food on your plate (golden yolked eggs from Sarah's own hens and fruit from the kitchen garden). 20 minutes from the coast.

Price	£70-£85. Singles from £50.
Rooms	4: 3 doubles, 1 twin.
Meals	Pub/restaurant 0.5 miles.
Closed	Rarely.
Directions	From Fakenham take Norwich road for 10 minutes. Take Foulsham turning at the large water tower. House is first on left.

Price	£80. Singles £45.
Rooms	2 twins/doubles.
Meals	Occasional dinner, 3 courses, £20. BYO. Pub 1 mile.
Closed	Christmas.
Directions	From Norwich, B1149 for 10 miles. 2nd left after bridge, for Heydon. 1.5 miles, right into village, over cattle grid, into park. Pass Hall on left, cottage in front of you; left over cattle grid and into stable yard.

 Chilled bottle of wine. Late checkout (12pm).

Simon & Catherine Davis
Norfolk Courtyard,
Westfield Farm, Foxley Road,
Foulsham, Dereham NR20 5RH
Tel   +44 (0)1362 683333
Email   info@norfolkcourtyard.co.uk
Web   www.norfolkcourtyard.co.uk

Sarah Bulwer-Long
Stable Cottage,
Heydon Hall,
Heydon NR11 6RE
Tel   +44 (0)1263 587343
Mobile +44 (0)7780 998742

Entry 349   Map 10

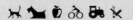

Entry 350   Map 10

Norfolk

Burgh Parva Hall

Sunlight bathes the Norfolk longhouse on summer afternoons; the welcome from the Heals is as warm. The listed house is all that remains of the old village of Burgh Parva, deserted after the Great Plague. It's a handsome house and warmly inviting... old furniture, rugs, books, pictures and Magnet the terrier-daschund. Large guest bedrooms face the sunsets and the garden annexe makes a sweet hideaway, especially in the summer. Breakfast eggs are from the garden hens, vegetables are home-grown, fish comes fresh from Holt and the game may have been shot by William. Settle down by the fire and tuck in.

Price	£65-£85. Singles from £40.
Rooms	3: 1 double, 1 twin; 1 twin with separate bath.
Meals	Dinner £23. BYO. Pub/restaurant 4 miles.
Closed	Rarely.
Directions	Fakenham A148 for Cromer. At Thursford B1354 for Aylsham. Just before Melton, speed bumps, left immed. before bus shelter, signed St Mary's church.1st house on right after farmyard.

Judy & William Heal
Burgh Parva Hall,
Melton Constable NR24 2PU
Tel   +44 (0)1263 862569
Email judyheal@dsl.pipex.com

Entry 351   Map 10

Norfolk

Holly Lodge

The whole place radiates a lavish attention to detail, from the spoilingly comfortable beds to the complimentary bottle of wine. It's perfect for those who love their privacy: these three snug guest 'cottages' have their own entrances as well as smart iron bedsteads and rugs on stone tiles, neat little shower rooms and tapestry-seat chairs, and books, music and TVs. Enjoy the Mediterranean garden with pond and decking in summer, the handsome conservatory and the utter peace. Your hosts are delightful: ex-restaurateur Jeremy who cooks enthusiastically, ethically and with panache, and Canadian-raised Gill.

Price	£90-£120. Singles £70-£100.
Rooms	3 cottages for 2.
Meals	Dinner, 3 courses with wine, £19.50. Pubs/restaurants 1 mile.
Closed	Rarely.
Directions	From Fakenham A148, Fakenham-Cromer road; 6 miles; left at Crawfish pub. Signs to Thursford Collection, past village green; 2nd drive on left.

 10% off stays Sun-Thurs. Bottle of wine in your room.

Jeremy Bolam
Holly Lodge,
Thursford Green NR21 0AS
Tel   +44 (0)1328 878465
Email info@hollylodgeguesthouse.co.uk
Web   www.hollylodgeguesthouse.co.uk

Entry 352   Map 10

Norfolk

Cleat House

A fantastic welcome in a peaceful street, a short walk from town and beach. This attractive late-Victorian seaside villa, built for a London merchant, has been sumptuously renovated inside. Bedrooms have original fireplaces and sash windows, upbeat fabrics and original art, and a warm inviting mix of antique and traditional. The guest sitting room comes with an honesty bar, games, books, DVDs and guides – set off for Holkham or Sandringham! Rob and Linda greet you with homemade treats and serve a tasty breakfast at separate tables – try Linda's hot dish of the day. You're beautifully cared for here. *Min. two nights at weekends.*

Price	£85–£130. Singles £70–£100.
Rooms	3: 2 suites; 1 suite with separate bath.
Meals	Pubs/restaurants within 0.5 miles.
Closed	Occasionally.
Directions	Off A148 onto A1082, at r'bout left, then right into Church St. 1st left into The Boulevard, 2nd left into North St. Montague Rd at the end of North St.

Bottle of wine in your room. 10% off stays of 2 or more nights Mon-Thur (Nov-Apr).

Rob & Linda Ownsworth
Cleat House, 7 Montague Road,
Sheringham NR26 8LN
Tel   +44 (0)1263 822765
Mobile +44 (0)7557 356952
Email   roblinda@cleathouse.co.uk
Web   www.cleathouse.co.uk

Entry 353   Map 10

Norfolk

Incleborough House

A listed, mellow-bricked 17th-century house in a beautiful walled lawned garden full of birds – 300 yards from the sea. Nick and Barbara have done a terrific restoration job and give you sumptuous bedrooms with huge beds, beautiful linen, super views, shining contemporary bathrooms, chocolates and wine. There's a drawing room for tea and cakes, with an open fire and books to read, and breakfast in the conservatory is an absolute treat – try slow-baked marmalade ham with poached eggs. The local walks are fabulous, and they do an excellent winter theatre package. *Min. two nights at weekends; check for late availability.*

Price	£165–£210. Singles £123.75–£157.50.
Rooms	4: 3 doubles; 1 suite with separate bathroom.
Meals	Light supper, with wine, £25. Restaurant 100 yds.
Closed	Rarely.
Directions	From Sheringham head for Cromer. In East Runton, 1st right into Felbrigg Road. House 200 yds on left behind oak trees.

10% off room rate Mon-Thurs. Bottle of wine in your room.

Nick & Barbara Davies
Incleborough House, Lower Common,
East Runton, Cromer NR27 9PG
Tel   +44 (0)1263 515939
Mobile +44 (0)7738 241672
Email   enquiries@incleboroughhouse.co.uk
Web   www.incleboroughhouse.co.uk

Entry 354   Map 10

Norfolk

The Old Rectory

Conservation farmland all around; acres of wild heathland busy with woodpeckers and owls; the coast two miles away. Relax in the spacious drawing room of this handsome 17th-century rectory and friendly family home, set in four acres of grounds. Fiona loves to cook and bakes her bread daily, food is delicious, seasonal and locally sourced, jams are homemade. Comfortable bedrooms have *objets* from diplomatic postings and the spacious suite comes with mahogany furniture and armchairs so you can settle in with a book. Super views, friendly dogs, tennis in the garden and masses of space.

Price	From £55. Singles £35.
Rooms	2: 1 suite; 1 double with separate bath & shower.
Meals	Dinner from £15. Pubs 2 miles.
Closed	Rarely.
Directions	From Norwich A1151 for Stalham. Just before Stalham, left to Happisburgh. Left at T-junc.; 3 miles; 2nd left after E. Ruston church, signed byway to Foxhill. Right at x-roads; 1 mile on right.

10% off room rate Mon-Thurs.

Peter & Fiona Black
The Old Rectory,
Ridlington NR28 9NZ
Tel   +44 (0)1692 650247
Mobile +44 (0)7774 599911
Email blacks7@gmail.com
Web   www.oldrectory.northnorfolk.co.uk

Entry 355   Map 10

Norfolk

Manor Farmhouse

A family buzz and candlelight in the farmhouse where you eat, peace in the 17th-century barn where you stay. All rooms lead off its charming, stylish, vaulted sitting room with cosy winter fire. You have a modern four-poster and a tiny shower on the ground floor, then two narrow staircases to two beautifully dressed bedrooms upstairs – small, quirky, fun, with a tucked-up-in-the-roof feel. Come for a sunny courtyard, billiards in the old stable, fresh flowers, lovely hosts, gorgeous food – and you may come and go as you please. Great value, a perfect rural retreat. *Children over seven welcome.*

Price	From £50. Singles from £40.
Rooms	3: 1 double, 1 twin/double, 1 four-poster.
Meals	Dinner, 3 courses, £17.50. BYO. Pubs 1 mile.
Closed	Christmas & New Year.
Directions	From Norwich, A1151 & A149 almost to Stalham. Left Walcott. At T-junc. left; 1 mile on, right H'burgh. Next T-junc., right. Next T-junc., left. Road bends right, sign by wall.

10% off stays of 4 nights Mon-Thurs. Norfolk handmade soap.

David & Rosie Eldridge
Manor Farmhouse,
Happisburgh NR12 0SA
Tel   +44 (0)1692 651262
Email manorathappisburgh@hotmail.com
Web   www.northnorfolk.co.uk/manorbarn

Entry 356   Map 10

Norfolk

Sutton Hall

Sweep up a gravel drive to a red-brick Victorian country house, in quiet parkland near the Norfolk Broads and coast. Sue serves eggs freshly laid by running hens, tomatoes from the kitchen garden, and knobbly apples from an orchard where deer and ducks roam free… breakfast on the terrace, or in a chandelier'd dining room with bay windows to the morning sun. Rooms are in keeping with the home's comfortable elegance – tall sash windows, a four-poster, fireplace, power showers, an extra bed for children; a Chinese screen adorns the high-ceilinged sitting room. Spend the day on the Broads with the binoculars.

Ethical Collection: Food. See page 420.

Price	From £90. Singles from £70.
Rooms	2 doubles. Extra child bed and cot.
Meals	Packed lunch from £6. Pubs/restaurant 1.5 miles.
Closed	Rarely.
Directions	A47 E of Norwich, A1064 at Acle, then B1152 to A149. Left dir. North Walsham, Stalham, 1st right into Sutton, then 1st right, 1st left and 2nd right into Hall Rd.

 10% off room rate Mon-Thurs. Free pick-up from local bus/train station. Late checkout (12pm).

	Sue Berry
	Sutton Hall,
	Hall Road, Sutton, Norwich NR12 9RX
Tel	+44 (0)1692 584888
Mobile	+44 (0)7977 575788
Email	enquiries@suttonhallnorfolk.co.uk
Web	www.suttonhallnorfolk.co.uk

Entry 357   Map 10

Norfolk

Sloley Hall

A grand and gracious yellow-brick Georgian house with formal gardens, tree-studded parkland and glorious views from every window. It has also been beautifully renovated, with flagstoned floors, Persian rugs, gleaming circular tables and vases of garden-grown flowers. Your hosts are delightful – Barbara and Simon were married here and are charmingly easy-going and helpful. A huge light-flooded dining room is perfect for breakfast; the drawing room is comfy and uncluttered with a marble fireplace and long views. Bedrooms are large and elegant with sumptuous bed linen, and generous bathrooms glow with warmth.

Price	£70-£90. Singles from £50.
Rooms	3: 1 suite; 1 double with separate shower; 1 twin with separate bath. Child bed available.
Meals	Pubs/restaurants 2-4 miles.
Closed	January-February.
Directions	From Norwich ring road, B1150 through Coltishall & Scottow. Right after Three Horseshoes pub (byway to Sloley); across staggered junc., 1st drive on right.

 10% off room rate Mon-Thurs. Free pick-up from local bus/train station.

	Barbara Gorton
	Sloley Hall,
	Sloley, Norwich NR12 8HA
Tel	+44 (0)1692 538582
Mobile	+44 (0)7748 152079
Email	babsgorton@hotmail.com
Web	www.sloleyhall.com

Entry 358   Map 10

Norfolk

38 St Giles

No expense spared here in this high-ceilinged, elegantly windowed town house: silk curtains in ravishing colours, handmade mattresses, plump goose down pillows and duvets, sumptuous linen, bathrobes, smart gadgetry, and thick towels in gorgeous bathrooms with L'Occitane treats. Breakfast on freshly baked croissants, porridge with caramelised apples, fruit and yogurt, or the full works – much will be locally sourced by Jeanette and William. Leave the car behind: you are slap bang in the right place here for languid strolls to the theatre, cathedral, historic market, interesting shops and good restaurants.

Price	£110–£160. Singles £90–£120.
Rooms	5: 3 doubles, 1 suite, 1 single.
Meals	Packed lunch £5. Light supper from £5. Pub/restaurant 50 yds.
Closed	23–27 December.
Directions	From inner ring road in Norwich, up Grape's Hill and at roundabout turn left onto St Giles Street. House is 200 yds down hill on right.

10% off stays of 2 or more nights.

Jeanette Bennett &
William Cheeseman
38 St Giles,
St Giles Street, Norwich NR2 1LL
Tel   +44 (0)1603 662944
Email   booking@38stgiles.co.uk
Web   www.38stgiles.co.uk

Entry 359   Map 10

Norfolk

The Buttery

Down a farm track, a treasure: your own thatch-and-flint octagonal dairy house perfectly restored by local craftsmen and as neat as a new pin. You get a jacuzzi bath, a little kitchen and a fridge stocked with delicious bacon and ground coffee so you can breakfast when you want; take it to the sun terrace in good weather. The sitting room is terracotta-tiled and has a music system, a warming fire and a sofabed for those who don't want to tackle the steep wooden stair to the snug bedroom on the mezzanine. You can play a game of tennis, and walk from the door into peaceful parkland and woods. Lovely!

Price	£80–£100.
Rooms	Cottage: 1 double, sitting room & small kitchen.
Meals	Pub 10-minute walk.
Closed	Rarely.
Directions	From A47 Barnham Broom & Weston Longville x-roads, south towards Barnham Broom. After 150 yds, 1st farm track on right. Left at T-junc., left again, house on left.

Bottle of wine.

Deborah Meynell
The Buttery,
Berry Hall, Honingham,
Norwich NR9 5AX
Tel   +44 (0)1603 880541
Email   thebuttery@paston.co.uk
Web   www.thebuttery.biz

Entry 360   Map 10

Norfolk

Washingford House

Tall octagonal chimney stacks and a Georgian façade give the house a stately air. In fact, it's the friendliest of places to stay and Paris gives you a delicious, locally sourced breakfast including plenty of fresh fruit. The house, originally Tudor, is a delightful mix of old and new. Large light-filled bedrooms have loads of good books and views over the four-acre garden, a favourite haunt for local birds. Bergh Apton is a conservation village seven miles from Norwich and you are in the heart of it; perfect for cycling, boat trips on the Norfolk Broads and the twelve Wherryman's Way circular walks. *Over 12s welcome.*

Price	£65-£75. Singles £35-£45.
Rooms	2: 1 twin/double; 1 single with separate bath.
Meals	Pubs/restaurants 4-6 miles.
Closed	Christmas.
Directions	A146 from Norwich to Lowestoft for 4 miles. Right after Gull Pub, signed Slade Lane. First left, then left at T-junc. for 1 mile. Straight over x-roads; house on left past post office.

Bottle of wine in your room. 10% off stays of 3 or more nights Mon-Thurs.

Paris & Nigel Back
Washingford House, Cookes Road, Bergh Apton, Norwich NR15 1AA
Tel   +44 (0)1508 550924
Mobile   +44 (0)7900 683617
Email   parisb@waitrose.com
Web   www.washingford.com

Entry 361   Map 10

Norfolk

Sallowfield Cottage

In a beautifully remote part of Norfolk is a hospitable house crammed with treasures: gorgeous prints and paintings, polished family pieces, leather fender seats by the drawing room fire. One bedroom, not huge but handsome, has a Regency-style canopied bed and decoration to suit the house (1850); another room is on the ground floor. Drift into the garden to find hedged rooms and a jungly pond with a jetty on which you breakfast (deliciously): magical in spring and summer. Caroline gives you the best, her lovely lurchers add to the charm, and if you have friends locally she can do lunch for up to ten. *Over nines welcome.*

Price	£70. Singles £45.
Rooms	3: 1 double, 1 twin; 1 double with separate bath.
Meals	Lunch £15. Dinner from £25. Pub 2.5 miles.
Closed	Christmas & New Year.
Directions	A11 Attleborough-Wymondham, Spooner Row sign. Over x-roads beside Three Boars pub. 1 mile; left at T-junc. to Wymondham for 1 mile. Rusty barrel on left, turn into farm track.

Caroline Musker
Sallowfield Cottage, Wattlefield, Wymondham, Norwich NR18 9NX
Tel   +44 (0)1953 605086
Mobile   +44 (0)7778 316616
Email   caroline.musker@tesco.net
Web   www.sallowfieldcottage.co.uk

Entry 362   Map 10

Norfolk

Rushall House

Plenty of treats to be had in this light and bright Victorian rectory: blue-shelled eggs for breakfast, homemade cake for tea, and radios, books and sofas in the double bedrooms. The wood-burner warm sitting room is classically decorated with a contemporary touch, airy bedrooms have pale walls, rich fabrics and a grand mix of colours and textiles (Jane's vintage furniture and fabrics are for sale in the courtyard studio). Walk or cycle after breakfast – it's good flat countryside and there are plenty of restorative pubs. Jane and Martin are relaxed hosts, and children will love collecting the eggs.

Ethical Collection: Food. See page 420.

Price	From £70. Singles from £45.
Rooms	3: 1 double; 1 double, 1 twin sharing bath/shower.
Meals	Dinner £23. BYO. Pubs/restaurants 0.5-3 miles.
Closed	Rarely.
Directions	Turn off A140 at r'bout to Dickleburgh; right at village store. After two miles pass Lakes Rd & Vaunces Lane, on right. Shortly after z-bend sign, house on right.

Free pick-up from local bus/train station.

Martin Hubner & Jane Gardiner
Rushall House, Dickleburgh Road,
Rushall, Diss IP21 4RX
Tel   +44 (0)1379 741557
Email   janegardineruk@aol.com
Web   www.rushallhouse.co.uk

Entry 363   Map 10

Norfolk

Home Farmhouse

A big yellow Jacobean farmhouse that stands in a couple of deeply rural acres. John and Anne rebuilt the house, removing the front wall to refit seasoned oak. Outside, birdsong fills the air; inside, the drawing-room fire crackles with gusto. A grandfather clock chimes in the hall, you can pick up the daily papers and sink into a sofa. John, a military historian, cooks breakfast (eggs from resident hens, apple juice from local orchards), while Anne whisks up delicious dinners. Smart bedrooms are wonderfully comfy with crisp linen, fresh flowers and interesting books. There are stables for horses and secure bike storage, too.

Price	£100. Singles £50.
Rooms	2: 1 double, 1 twin/double.
Meals	Dinner, 2 courses with cheese, £22.
Closed	Rarely.
Directions	A11 for Norwich, then A1075 to Shipdham. In village 1st right, signed Cranworth. 2nd left; house 1st on left.

Anne & John Smales
Home Farmhouse,
Letton, Thetford IP25 7PS
Tel   +44 (0)1362 820502
Email   anne@homefarmhouseletton.co.uk
Web   www.homefarmhouseletton.co.uk

Entry 364   Map 10

Northamptonshire

Bridge Cottage

A truly restful place: sip a glass of wine on the decking down by the Willowbrook; rolling green countryside envelops you, the cattle are drinking peacefully, kingfishers flash by and you may see a red kite (borrow some binoculars). Inside find beautiful bedrooms with sloping ceilings, the purest cotton sheets and proper blankets; bathrooms are thickly towelled and full of lovely lotions and bubbles. Rules are few, breakfast is local and scrumptious and served in the friendliest kitchen facing that heavenly view, there's a tranquil conservatory for a quiet read, and Judy and Rod look after you very well indeed.

Price	From £89. Singles from £50.
Rooms	4: 1 double, 2 twins; 1 double with separate bath.
Meals	Pub/restaurant in village.
Closed	Rarely.
Directions	From south A1 to Peterborough junc. A605 signed Oundle & Northampton for 4 miles. At 1st r'bout right thro' Fotheringhay, then Woodnewton. House 1st on left on bridge.

Judy Colebrook
Bridge Cottage, Oundle Road,
Woodnewton, Peterborough PE8 5EG

Tel	+44 (0)1780 470860
Mobile	+44 (0)7979 644864
Email	enquiries@bridgecottage.net
Web	www.bridgecottage.net

Entry 365   Map 9

Northamptonshire

Colledges House

Huge attention to comfort here, and a house full of laughter. Liz clearly derives pleasure from sharing her 300-year-old stone thatched cottage, immaculate garden, conservatory and converted barn with guests. Sumptuous bedrooms have deep mattresses with fine linen, sparkling bathrooms are a good size. The house is full of interesting things: a Jacobean trunk, a Bechstein piano, mirrors and pictures, pretty china, bright fabrics, a beautiful bureau. Cordon Bleu dinners are elegant affairs – and great fun. Stroll around the conservation village of Staverton – delightful. *Children over eight & babes in arms welcome.*

Price	£90-£98. Singles £67.50-£69.50.
Rooms	4: 1 single; 1 double with separate bath. Cottage: 1 double, 1 twin.
Meals	Dinner, 3 courses, £32. Pub 4-minute walk.
Closed	Rarely.
Directions	From Daventry, A425 to Leamington Spa. 100 yds past Staverton Park Conference Centre, right into village, then 1st right. Keep left, & at 'Give Way' sign, sharp left. House immed. on right.
	10% off stays of 2 or more nights for double occupancy only.

Liz Jarrett
Colledges House, Oakham Lane,
Staverton, Daventry NN11 6JQ

Tel	+44 (0)1327 702737
Mobile	+44 (0)7710 794112
Email	liz@colledgeshouse.co.uk
Web	www.colledgeshouse.co.uk

Entry 366   Map 8

Northamptonshire

The Vyne

Weighed down by wisteria, this 16th-century cottage rests in a honey-hued conservation village on the cusp of Oxfordshire. Beams and wonky lines abound; rooms are filled with good antiques and eclectic art. The spacious twin is enchanting, tucked under the rafters, its beds decorated in willow-pattern chintz, its walls glinting with gilded frames; the double has a Georgian four-poster and a sampler-decorated bathroom that's a quick flit next door. Warm and charming, Imogen not only works in publishing but is a dedicated gardener and Cordon Bleu cook – enjoy supper in her sunny secluded garden. *Babies welcome.*

Price	£75. Singles from £45.
Rooms	2: 1 twin; 1 four-poster with separate bath.
Meals	Supper £20. Dinner £30. BYO. Pub 2-minute walk.
Closed	Christmas & New Year.
Directions	M40 exit 11. A422 to Northampton, left onto B4525. 2 miles, left to Thorpe Mandeville. 3 miles, left to Culworth. After Culworth, right to Eydon.

Free pick-up from local bus/train station.

Imogen Butler
The Vyne, High Street,
Eydon, Daventry NN11 3PP
Tel   +44 (0)1327 264886
Mobile +44 (0)7974 801475
Email   imogen@ibutler2.wanadoo.co.uk

Entry 367   Map 8

Northamptonshire

The Coach House

Sunlight and flower-scent fill this sprawling, rosy-brick home. Originally a coach house and stables, it's now a series of elegant light-filled rooms wrapped round a central courtyard; you can breakfast out on sunny days. Sarah's eye for colour shows in the design of her large gardens, and her clever mix of modern and traditional furnishings. Bedrooms ooze country-house luxury with fine cotton, fluffy towels and glossy magazines; the first-floor family room has a magnificent shower room, the ground floor twin opens onto a private terrace. Play tennis, visit Woburn and Stowe, or have a day out at Silverstone.

Price	£80-£90. Singles £55.
Rooms	3: 1 double, 1 twin, 1 family room.
Meals	Packed lunch on request. Pub/restaurant within 5 miles.
Closed	Rarely.
Directions	From A43 dual carriageway, A5 North for Hinckley. After 1.1 miles sharp left to Duncote. First house on left, 300 yds, 2nd gate.

Good bottle of wine for stays of 2 nights.

Sarah Baker Baker
The Coach House,
Duncote, Towcester NN12 8AQ
Tel   +44 (0)1327 352855
Mobile +44 (0)7875 215705
Email   sarahbb54@gmail.com

Entry 368   Map 8

Northumberland

Matfen High House

Bring the wellies – and jumpers! You are 25 miles from the border and the walking is a joy. Struan and Jenny are amusing company, love sporting pursuits and will drive you to Matfen Hall for dinner. The sturdy stone house of 1735 is a lived-in, pretty place to stay: the en suite bedrooms have fine fabrics and good pictures, the bathrooms are stocked with fluffy towels and the drawing room promises books and choice pieces. Enjoy local bacon and sausages at breakfast, with Struan's marmalade and bread warm from the oven. The countryside is stunning, Hadrian's Wall and the great castles (Alnwick, Bamburgh) beckon.

Price	£70-£75. Singles £40.
Rooms	4: 1 double, 1 twin; 1 double, 1 twin sharing bath.
Meals	Packed lunch £4.50. Restaurant 2 miles.
Closed	Rarely.
Directions	A69 at Heddon on the Wall, onto B6318; 500 yds, right to Moorhouse; right at next junc. signed Brewery & visitor centre; past Hadrian Pet Hotel; 300 yds, right, opp. cottages.

10% off room rate Mon-Thurs.

Struan & Jenny Wilson
Matfen High House,
Matfen, Corbridge NE20 0RG
Tel +44 (0)1661 886592
Email struan@struan.enterprise-plc.com

Entry 369   Map 12

Northumberland

Bog House

It's too quiet for some townies – and thank goodness! If you've had it with bustle, bury yourself in the depths of Northumberland, two miles from Hadrian's Wall. Here is an immaculate barn conversion that's mercifully free from the usual modern furniture; what you have is a contemporary, airy feel and an open-raftered space stuffed with antiques. Rosemary has created a stunning place. Breakfast can be later at weekends and sausages are local, bread is freshly baked. The peace here is total; you have your own entrance and may come and go as you please. An indulgent, wonderful retreat. *Over 12s welcome. Broadband available.*

Price	£90. Singles £50.
Rooms	2: 1 twin; 1 double with separate bath.
Meals	Dinner £25. Pubs/restaurants 15-minute drive.
Closed	Rarely.
Directions	A68; 3 miles north of Corbridge, right onto B6318. After 3.5 miles, left signed Moorhouse. On for 1 mile, right; left to Bog House after 1 mile. Last farm on left.

Bottle of wine with dinner on first night. Packed lunch for two.

Use your Sawday's Gift Card here.

Rosemary Stobart
Bog House,
Matfen NE20 0RF
Tel +44 (0)1661 886776
Mobile +44 (0)7850 375535
Email rosemary.stobart@btinternet.com
Web www.boghouse-matfen.co.uk

Entry 370   Map 16

Northumberland

The Hermitage

A magical setting, three miles from Hadrian's wall, in a house full of friendship and comfort. Through ancient woodland, up the drive, over the burn and there it is: big, beautiful and Georgian. Interiors are comfortable country-house, full of warmth and charm; bedrooms, carpeted, spacious and delightful, are furnished with antiques, paintings and superb beds; bathrooms have roll top baths. Outside are lovely lawns, a walled garden, wildlife, and breakfasts on the terrace in summer. Katie – who was born in this house – looks after you brilliantly. *Guests back please by 11pm. Over sevens & babes in arms welcome.*

Price	From £85. Singles from £50.
Rooms	3: 1 double, 1 twin; 1 twin with separate bath.
Meals	Pub 2 miles.
Closed	October-February.
Directions	7 miles north of Corbridge on A68. Left on A6079 for 1 mile, then right through lodge gates with arch. House 0.5 miles down drive.

Simon & Katie Stewart
The Hermitage,
Swinburne, Hexham NE48 4DG
Tel   +44 (0)1434 681248
Email   katie.stewart@themeet.co.uk

Entry 371   Map 16

Northumberland

The Old Vicarage

Come for the tiny village, the ancient church, and a gentler way of life in this stone built, wisteria-covered former vicarage. Light pours in to an elegant drawing room with large open fire, chintzy chairs and sofa, soft rugs, beautiful antique furniture and pictures. Bedrooms are comfortingly traditional, with crisp white sheets, squishy pillows, thick curtains and white bathrooms. Margaret gives you a grand breakfast in a toasty warm conservatory overlooking the garden; wander down to the river or to have a peek at the church, which dates from 1080! Newcastle, Alnwick Garden and stunning beaches are all a short drive away.

Price	£65-£85. Singles £50.
Rooms	3: 1 double; 1 twin, 1 single sharing bath.
Meals	Dinner, 3 courses with wine, £25. Pub 1 mile.
Closed	Christmas, New Year & Easter.
Directions	6 miles west of Morpeth on B6343, towards Scots Gap and Cambo.

10% off room rate.

Margaret Smart
The Old Vicarage,
Hartburn, Morpeth NE61 4JB
Tel   +44 (0)1670 772562
Email   margiecook2001@yahoo.co.uk

Entry 372   Map 16

Northumberland

Shieldhall

The guest rooms are in the charming 18th-century farm buildings, each with its own entrance. Stephen and his sons make and restore antique furniture and rooms are named after the wood used within: Elm, Oak, Mahogany, Pine. Bathrooms are spacious, there's a beautiful sitting room/library and you pop across the courtyard for meals in the main house – once home to the family of Capability Brown. Celia is friendly and attentive and loves cooking, so ingredients are often organic or locally sourced; there's also a secret bar and a small but interesting wine list. Peaceful, hospitable B&B – with fine views.

Price	£80. Singles £60.
Rooms	3: 1 double, 1 twin, 1 four-poster.
Meals	Dinner, 4 courses, £28. Pub 7 miles.
Closed	Rarely.
Directions	From Newcastle A696 for Jedburgh. 5 miles north of Belsay, right onto B6342. On left after 500 yds (turn into front courtyard).

Guided tour of antique furniture restoration workshops & advice on related subjects.

Celia & Stephen Robinson-Gay
Shieldhall,
Wallington, Morpeth NE61 4AQ

Tel	+44 (0)1830 540387
Email	stay@shieldhallguesthouse.co.uk
Web	www.shieldhallguesthouse.co.uk

Entry 373   Map 16

Northumberland

Thistleyhaugh

Enid thrives on hard work and humour, her passions are pictures, cooking and people and if she's not the perfect B&B hostess, she's a close contender. Certainly you eat well – local farm eggs at breakfast and their own beef at dinner. Choose any of the five large, lovely bedrooms and stay the week; they are awash with old paintings, silk fabrics and crisp white linen. But if you do tray downstairs, past the log fire and the groaning table, there are 720 acres of organic farmland to discover and a few million more of the Cheviots beyond that. Wonderful hosts, house and region.

Price	£90. Singles £60-£85.
Rooms	5: 3 doubles, 1 twin, 1 single.
Meals	Dinner, 3 courses, £25. Pub/restaurant 2 miles.
Closed	Christmas, New Year & January.
Directions	Leave A1 for A697 for Coldstream & Longhorsley; 2 miles past Longhorsley, left at Todburn sign; 1 mile to x-roads, then right; on 1 mile over white bridge; 1st right, right again, over cattle grid.

Henry & Enid Nelless
Thistleyhaugh,
Longhorsley, Morpeth NE65 8RG

Tel	+44 (0)1665 570629
Email	thistleyhaugh@hotmail.com
Web	www.thistleyhaugh.co.uk

Entry 374   Map 16

Northumberland

East Hepple Farmhouse

In the farmhouse sitting room, a wood-burner blazes away in winter. The double, too, has a sitting room, with an original cast-iron range and shelves groaning with books — bibliophile heaven. The peace is so deep in the Coquet valley that you may sleep until the whiff of sizzling local bacon hits your nostrils. Beds are firm, old pine pieces pretty, pillows feathery soft and views over the river to the Simonside hills abundant. Joan and Brian are expert at looking after you, will drive you to dinner and guide you the next day to the beaches, Cragside, Alnwick Castle and fabulous walking. To stay is a treat. *Fishing can be arranged nearby.*

Price	£70–£75. Singles from £50.
Rooms	2: 1 double & sitting room; 1 twin sharing bath (let to same party only).
Meals	Packed lunch £5. Pubs/restaurants 2.5 miles.
Closed	Rarely.
Directions	West from Rothbury on B6341. Thro' Thropton to Hepple, pass church on left; next right, then immediate hard right into driveway.

Bottle of wine in your room.

Use your Sawday's Gift Card here.

Joan & Brian Storey
East Hepple Farmhouse,
Hepple, Rothbury NE65 7LH
Tel +44 (0)1669 640221
Email joanstorey@coquetdale.net
Web www.easthepplefarm.co.uk

Entry 375 Map 16

Northumberland

Alnham Farm

Delve deep into the glorious sheep-dotted hills and valleys of the Northumberland National Park to find Jenny's handsome Georgian farmhouse and a dollop of urban chic in bedrooms and bathrooms. Walkers will be in heaven: set off with a tummy full of farmhouse porridge, home-reared sausages and bacon or a smashing Craster kipper. Spot whirling buzzards, the elusive red squirrel, otters if you are lucky; return to the crispest linen, gleaming mahogany, fresh flowers, and a power shower or a soak in a free-standing tub (bubbles and lotions provided). Castles, deep dunes and long white beaches are an easy drive.

Price	£80. Singles £50.
Rooms	2: 1 double, 1 twin/double with separate bathroom.
Meals	Pub/restaurant 7 miles.
Closed	December–February.
Directions	From Whittingham, over bridge left to Netherton; 3.5miles right to Little Ryle & left passing Unthank Farm. Left at T-junc. & down front drive before 1st cottage on left.

Picnic and map for walkers. Bottle of wine in your room.

Jenny Sordy
Alnham Farm,
Alnwick NE66 4TJ
Tel +44 (0)1669 630210
Email jenny@alnhamfarm.co.uk
Web www.alnhamfarm.co.uk

Entry 376 Map 16

Northumberland

Courtyard Garden

In the county town of Northumberland, with its grand castle and innovative gardens, step directly off the pavement and enter a courtyard surrounded by shrubs and pretty pots; sit out here on sunny days and sip a glass of something cool. Bedrooms (one overlooking the church, the other the garden) are traditional and immaculate; bathrooms, one with a roll top bath, have original wooden floors, thick towels. Friendly Maureen gives you breakfast in the comfortable sitting room at a round Georgian table underneath the window. Explore the town on foot, stride along white beaches, discover more castles; history is all around you.

Northumberland

Bilton Barns

A solidly good farmhouse B&B whose lifeblood is still farming. The Jacksons know every inch of the countryside and coast that surrounds their 1715 home; it's a pretty spot. They farm 400 acres of mixed arable land that sweeps down to the coast yet always have time for guests. Dorothy takes pride in creating an easy and sociable atmosphere – three couples who were introduced to each other one weekend now return for reunions! Bedrooms are big, carpeted, fresh and comfortable, a conservatory leads onto the garden and there's an airy guests' sitting room with an open fire and views to the sea.

Price	From £70. Singles from £50.
Rooms	2: 1 double, 1 twin/double.
Meals	Pub/restaurant within 300 yds.
Closed	Rarely.
Directions	A1, Alnwick turnoff A1068. Over roundabout; left at next roundabout B6346. Prudhoe Street 1st left. Pass police station; house opposite St Paul's Church.

  Free pick-up from local train station. Organic skin care products.

	Maureen Mason
	Courtyard Garden,
	10 Prudhoe Street, Alnwick NE66 1UW
Tel	+44 (0)1665 603393
Email	maureenpeter10@btinternet.com
Web	www.courtyardgarden-alnwick.com

Entry 377   Map 16

Price	£75-£80. Singles £38-£65.
Rooms	3: 1 double, 1 twin, 1 four-poster.
Meals	Packed lunch £4-£6. Pub/restaurant 2 miles.
Closed	Christmas & New Year.
Directions	From Alnwick, A1068 to Alnmouth. At Hipsburn r'bout follow signs to station & cross bridge. 1st lane to left, 0.3 miles down drive.

	Brian & Dorothy Jackson
	Bilton Barns,
	Alnmouth, Alnwick NE66 2TB
Tel	+44 (0)1665 830427
Mobile	+44 (0)7939 262028
Email	dorothy@biltonbarns.com
Web	www.biltonbarns.com

Entry 378   Map 16

Northumberland

Laundry Cottage

History lovers, peace seekers and observers of nature will mellow further in this glorious spot overlooking the Cheviot hills. On arrival enjoy cake and tea with evening sun – in the sun room, or in the garden on warm days. Douse yourself in one of Ginia's hiker's breakfasts, stride through iron age forts and the remains of Saxon palaces or visit long white beaches; return to Welsh slate. floors, wood-burners, squishy sofas, feather and down on deep mattresses and fluffy towels. The feel is light and airy, Peter and Ginia are amiable hosts and the super garden is filled with roses in summer.

Price	£64. Singles £45.
Rooms	2: 1 double, 1 twin.
Meals	Dinner £16–£20. Pub/restaurant 5 miles.
Closed	Rarely.
Directions	Out of Wooler on the Chatton road (B6348). A few miles on, turn left over narrow bridge to East Horton.

💼 £18 off stays of 3 or more nights Mon–Thurs.

Peter & Ginia Gadsdon
Laundry Cottage,
East Horton, Wooler NE71 6EZ
Tel   +44 (0)1668 215383
Email   peter@gadsdon.me.uk
Web   www.laundry-cottage-bnb.co.uk

🧍 🐕 🐈 🍴

Entry 379 Map 16

Northumberland

Broome

A totally surprising one-storey house, full of beautiful things. It is an Aladdin's cave and sits in the middle of a coastal village with access to miles of sandy beaches. The garden/breakfast room is its hub and has a country cottage feel; enjoy locally smoked kippers here, award-winning 'Bamburgh Bangers' and home-cured bacon from the village butcher. There's also a sun-trapping courtyard full of colourful pots for breakfasts in the sun. Guests have a cheerful sitting/dining room and bedrooms with fresh flowers and good books. Mary is welcoming and amusing and has stacks of local knowledge.

Price	£100–£110. Singles £70.
Rooms	2: 1 double, 1 twin, sharing bath/shower (2nd room let to same party only).
Meals	Pubs/restaurants 2-minute walk.
Closed	1 November–1 April.
Directions	From Newcastle north on A1; right for Bamburgh on B1341. To village, pass 30mph sign & hotel; 1st right at Victoria Hotel. House 400 yds on right.

Mary Dixon
Broome,
22 Ingram Road, Bamburgh NE69 7BT
Tel   +44 (0)1668 214287
Mobile   +44 (0)7956 013409
Email   mdixon4394@aol.com

🐕 🍴

Entry 380 Map 16

Northumberland

West Coates

Slip through the gates of this Victorian townhouse and you're in the country. Two acres of leafy gardens, with pretty spots to relax, belie the closeness of Berwick's centre. From the lofty ceilings and sash windows to the soft colours, paintings and gleaming furniture, the house has a calm, ordered elegance. Bedrooms have antiques and garden views; two have roll top baths; fruit, homemade cakes, flowers welcome you. Warm, friendly Karen is a stunning cook, inventively using local produce and spoiling you; she runs a cookery school here too. The coastline is stunning and there are castles and country houses galore to visit.

Nottinghamshire

Compton House

Two minutes from Newark's antique shops and ancient market, seek out this terraced Georgian townhouse where the mayor once lived. Naturally elegant, and overlooking Fountain Gardens, the sunny drawing room has a marble fireplace; Lisa and Mark have filled the place with lovely personal touches. Rooms are named after friends, from plush red-gold Judy's room to Harry's bijou single; the best is Cooper's, with a four-poster bed, a roll top bath through a draped archway and a wall hand-painted by a local artist. Pad down to the sunny basement for Mark's feast of a breakfast. Hotel comforts but a truly personal feel.

Price	£90–£120. Singles from £60.		Price	£90. Singles from £65.
Rooms	3: 1 double, 1 twin/double; 1 twin/double with separate bath/shower.		Rooms	7: 2 doubles, 1 twin/double, 2 twins, 1 four-poster; 1 single with separate shower.
Meals	Dinner £35. Pub/restaurant 15-minute walk.		Meals	Packed lunch £6. Buffet lunch £15. Dinner, 2 courses, from £25. Pub/restaurant 0.5 miles.
Closed	Christmas & New Year.		Closed	Occasionally Christmas.
Directions	From A1 take A6105 into Berwick. House 300 yds on left. Stone pillars at end of drive. Train station 10-minute walk.		Directions	Nottingham, A52; join A46 N to Newark. At r'about, 2nd exit. Right at lights, left at next lights then 1st right. House on left.

🧳	10% off room rate Mon–Thurs. Free pick-up from local bus/train station.		🧳	Free pick-up from local bus/train station.

	Karen Brown West Coates, 30 Castle Terrace, Berwick-upon-Tweed TD15 1NZ		**Mark & Lisa Holloway** Compton House, 117 Baldertongate, Newark NG24 1RY
Tel	+44 (0)1289 309666	Tel	+44 (0)1636 708670
Mobile	+44 (0)7814 281973	Mobile	+44 (0)7817 446485
Email	karenbrownwestcoates@yahoo.com	Email	info@comptonhousenewark.com
Web	www.westcoates.co.uk	Web	www.comptonhousenewark.com

Entry 381   Map 16

Entry 382   Map 9

Nottinghamshire

Willoughby House

Past the village pub, through a gate, this three-storey brick farmhouse reflects its owners' skilful interior design. The house brims with tokens of its 18th century past, like meat hooks in the scullery-turned-sitting room, but feels ever so smart. Bedrooms are large and comfortable: climb up to Harry's room with its brass bed and toy soldiers over the fireplace; Edward's and George's share raftered loft space and a swish bathroom. Sarah rustles up delicious meals in a dining room embraced by poppy red walls and shutters. Get out on hikes or bikes; round the little village, or Southwell and Newark are close.

Price	£75–£95. Singles £55–£65.
Rooms	4: 1 twin/double; 1 double, 1 twin/double sharing bath (same party only); 1 double with separate bath/shower.
Meals	Dinner, 2 courses, from £20. Packed lunch £7.50. Pub 3-minute walk; restaurants within 1.5 miles.
Closed	Christmas & occasionally.
Directions	1.5 miles off A1, Cromwell & Norwell exit. At Cromwell left Norwell, 1.5 miles. House opp. school lane on corner of Willoughby Court.

25% off stays of 4 nights.

Andrew & Sarah Nesbitt
Willoughby House, Main Street,
Norwell, Newark NG23 6JN
Tel   +44 (0)1636 636266
Mobile   +44 (0)7789 965352
Email   willoughbybandb@aol.com
Web   www.willoughbyhousebandb.co.uk

Oxfordshire

Uplands House

Come to be spoiled at this 'farmhouse' built in 1875 for the Earl of Jersey's son. Renovated by a talented couple, it's elegant and sumptuously furnished; expect large light bedrooms, crisp linen, thick towels and long bucolic views from the Orangery where you have tea and cake. Relax here with a book as the sounds and scents of the pretty garden waft by, or chat to charming Poppy while she creates delicious dinner — a convivial occasion enjoyed with your hosts. Breakfast is Graham's domain — try smoked salmon with scrambled eggs and red caviar. You're well placed for exploring but you'll find it hard to leave.

Price	£90–£160. Singles £60–£90.
Rooms	3: 1 double; 1 twin/double, 1 four-poster, each with separate bath.
Meals	Dinner, 2–4 courses, £20–£30. Pub 1.25 miles.
Closed	Rarely.
Directions	M40 junc. 11; thro' Banbury, A422 towards Stratford. Thro' Wroxton; just after 'Upton House' National Trust sign, right single lane drive marked 'Uplands Farm'. 1st drive on right to house.

Use your Sawday's Gift Card here.

Poppy Cooksey & Graham Paul
Uplands House,
Upton, Banbury OX15 6HJ
Tel   +44 (0)1295 678663
Mobile   +44 (0)7836 535538
Email   poppy@cotswolds-uplands.co.uk
Web   www.cotswolds-uplands.co.uk

Oxfordshire

Buttslade House

Choose between a gorgeous ground-floor retreat across the courtyard, or a very pretty twin in the 17th-century farmhouse with barns and stables. The guest sitting room is a clever melody of ancient and contemporary styles: Spanish art, antique sofas, velvet cushions. Beds have seriously good mattresses, feather and down pillows and crisp white linen; bathrooms are smart and sparkling – one with a Victorian roll top. Diana is lovely and will pamper you or leave you, there's a blissful garden to stroll through, breakfast is a feast of fruits and homemade bread and it's a hop to the village pub. A fun and stylish treat.

Price	£80. Singles £50.
Rooms	2: 1 double; 1 twin with separate bath.
Meals	Dinner, 3 courses, £25. Lunch £7. Pub 100 yds.
Closed	Rarely.
Directions	From B4035 look for signs to Wykham Arms. Buttslade is 2nd house beyond pub, going down the hill.

 10% off room rate Mon-Thurs. 10% off stays of 3 or more nights.

Diana Thompson
Buttslade House, Temple Mill Road,
Sibford Gower, Banbury OX15 5RX
Tel   +44 (0)1295 788818
Email   janthompson50@hotmail.com
Web   www.buttsladehouse.co.uk

Entry 385   Map 8

Oxfordshire

Gower's Close

All the nooks, crannies and beams you'd expect from an ancient thatched cottage in a Cotswold village… and more besides: good food, lively conversation and lots of inside information about gardens to visit. Judith is a keen gardener who writes books on the subject (her passion for plants is evident from her own glorious garden) and her style and intelligence are reflected in her home. Pretty, south-facing and full of sunlight, the sitting room opens onto the garden and terrace. Bedrooms are light, charming and cottagey; the twin is at garden level. A thoroughly relaxing place to stay.

Price	£75-£80. Singles £50.
Rooms	2: 1 double, 1 twin.
Meals	Dinner, 4 courses, £28 (min. 4 people). Pub/restaurant 100 yds.
Closed	Christmas & New Year.
Directions	In Sibford Gower, 0.5 miles south off B4035 between Banbury & Chipping Campden. House on Main Street, same side as church & school.

Judith Hitching & John Marshall
Gower's Close,
Sibford Gower, Banbury OX15 5RW
Tel   +44 (0)1295 780348
Mobile   +44 (0)7776 231588
Email   judith@gowersclose.co.uk
Web   www.gowersclose.co.uk

Entry 386   Map 8

Oxfordshire

Minehill House

Bump your way up the track (mind the car!) to the top of a beautiful hill and a gorgeous family farmhouse with views for miles and young, energetic Hester to care for you. Children will adore the ping-pong table and the trampoline; their parents will enjoy the gleaming old flagstones, vibrant contemporary oils, wood-burning stove and seriously sophisticated food. Rest well in the big double room with its verdant leafy wallpaper and stunning views, and a cubby-hole door to extra twin beds; bathrooms are sparklingly clean and spacious. Bracing walks straight from the door.

Price	£95. Singles from £50. Family £135.
Rooms	1 double/family.
Meals	Dinner, 3 courses, £35. Supper £20. BYO. Packed lunch available. Pubs 1-5 miles.
Closed	Christmas & New Year.
Directions	From Banbury B4035 to Brailes; after 10 miles take road left signed Hook Norton; 0.5 miles, right onto unmarked uphill farm track to house.

Hester & Ed Sale
Minehill House,
Lower Brailes, Banbury OX15 5BJ
Tel   +44 (0)1608 685594
Mobile   +44 (0)7890 266441
Email   hester@minehillhouse.co.uk
Web   www.minehillhouse.co.uk

Entry 387   Map 8

Oxfordshire

Home Farmhouse

This 400-year-old house is charming, with low ceilings, inglenook fireplaces and winding stairs. All rooms are faded and brimming with character: the drawing room is elegant and beamed and pretty bedrooms are decorated with antiques and old-fashioned chintz. Comfortable beds have good mattresses and traditional blankets; bathrooms are small and a little dated. Enjoy independence in the simple barn room with its mixture of time-worn furniture and own entrance up old stone steps. The family's travels are evident all over and it's all so laid-back you'll find it hard to leave. The dogs are delightful too – Samson and Goliath.

Price	£84. Singles £54.
Rooms	3: 1 double, 1 twin/double. Barn: 1 twin/double.
Meals	Dinner £28. Supper £20. Pub 100 yds.
Closed	Christmas.
Directions	M40 junc. 10, A43 for Northampton. After 5 miles, left to Charlton. There, left & house on left, 100 yds past Rose & Crown.

 Fruit, chocolates, flapjacks in room. 10% off room rate Mon-Thurs.

Rosemary & Nigel Grove-White
Home Farmhouse,
Charlton, Banbury OX17 3DR
Tel   +44 (0)1295 811683
Mobile   +44 (0)7795 207000
Email   grovewhite@lineone.net
Web   www.homefarmhouse.co.uk

Entry 388   Map 8

Oxfordshire

The Old Post House

Great natural charm in the 17th-century Old Post House, where shiny flagstones, rich dark wood and mullion windows combine with warm fabrics, deep sofas and handsome furniture. Bedrooms are big, with antique wardrobes, oak headboards and a comforting old-fashioned feel. The walled gardens are lovely – rich with espaliered fruit trees, and with a pool for sunny evenings. Christine, a well-travelled ex-pat, has a springer spaniel and an innate sense of hospitality; her breakfasts are delicious. There's village traffic but your sleep should be sound. Deddington is delightful. *Children over 12 welcome.*

Price	£85. Singles £55.
Rooms	3: 1 twin/double; 1 double with separate bath, 1 four-poster with separate shower.
Meals	Occasional dinner. Pubs/restaurants in village.
Closed	Rarely.
Directions	A4260 Oxford to Banbury. In Deddington, on right next to cream Georgian house. Park opposite.

Free pick-up from local bus/train station.

Christine Blenntoft
The Old Post House,
New Street, Deddington OX15 0SP

Tel	+44 (0)1869 338978
Mobile	+44 (0)7713 631092
Email	kblenntoft@aol.com
Web	www.oldposthouse.co.uk

Entry 389   Map 8

Oxfordshire

Hawk Hill House

Generous parkland and gardens lead to tailored fields, happy dogs and the odd grazing horse. Sensible, hospitable, relaxed Alison gives guests floral traditional bedrooms in a big extended house full of corridors and separate stairs – a refuge for busy lives. Expect china, chintz, feathery pillows and hand-held showers, privacy, tranquillity and a livery for visiting steeds, and an inviting family kitchen for fruit crumbles and shepherd pies; there's a more formal dining room if you prefer. It's a 20-minute walk over the fields to a brilliant pub in Great Tew — and heaps more beyond.

Price	£80.
Rooms	3: 1 double, 1 twin; 1 double with separate bath.
Meals	Supper, 2-3 courses, £17.50-£25. Pub/restaurants 2-3 miles.
Closed	Rarely.
Directions	Oxford & Banbury to Deddington, then B4031 towards Chipping Norton. Through Hempton, and down steep hill, then left to Nether Worton. Only house in village on right hand side.

James & Alison Kerr-Muir
Hawk Hill House, Nether Worton,
Chipping Norton OX7 7AP

Tel	+44 (0)1608 683355
Mobile	+44 (0)7710 353224
Email	hawkhillhouse@gmail.com
Web	www.hawkhill-house.co.uk

Entry 390   Map 8

Oxfordshire

Rectory Farm

A general sense of peaceful order pervades at this solid, big house set in a manicured lawn. Inside find large, light bedrooms, floral and feminine, with bold chintz bed covers, draped kidney-shaped dressing tables, thick mattresses; some have garden views, others face the farm buildings. Sink into comfy sofas flanking a huge fireplace in the drawing room, breakfast on local bacon and sausage with free-range eggs, stroll the pretty garden, or grab a rod and try your luck on one of the trout lakes. Elizabeth knows her patch well; walkers can borrow maps, and she can point the way to lovely shops for the dedicated.

Price	£90-£100. Singles £65-£75.
Rooms	3: 1 double, 1 twin/double; 1 twin/double with separate bath.
Meals	Pub/restaurant 1.5 miles.
Closed	December/January.
Directions	A44 out of Chipping Norton towards Moreton-in-the-Marsh. After 1.5 miles right into Salford. Right at pub, then immediate left uphill past green on right. Left into drive for Rectory Farm, continue 200 yds then left.
🧳	10% off stays of 3 or more nights. Free trout fishing if staying 2 or more nights.

Elizabeth Colston
Rectory Farm,
Salford, Chipping Norton OX7 5YY

Tel	+44 (0)1608 643209
Mobile	+44 (0)7866 834208
Email	enquiries@rectoryfarm.info
Web	www.rectoryfarm.info

Entry 391 Map 8

Oxfordshire

Upper Court Farm

In a peaceful, gently hilly spot in the Cotswolds, the super smart Edwardian farmhouse comes with groomed gardens and 30 acres for Chloë's horses – bring yours! A dressage rider, she and Tim are interesting hosts and their home is laden with good quality fabrics, country art and family pieces. Choose from a top-floor bedroom or your own flat; each has madly comfortable beds, pretty covers, smart bathrooms and drenching showers. Tim is a foodie and breakfast is generous and local; people come for miles for Slatters, an organic shop in the village. Relax in the rose garden with a drink – two sweet dogs will join you.

Price	£80-£90. Singles £60-£70.
Rooms	2: 1 double; 1 suite with kitchenette.
Meals	Pub/restaurant 2 miles.
Closed	Christmas & Boxing Day.
Directions	From Chipping Norton A361 south, after approx. 3 miles 2nd left to Chadlington. After 0.5 miles, 1st drive on the left.

Chloë Robson
Upper Court Farm, Mill End,
Chadlington, Chipping Norton OX7 3NY

Tel	+44 (0)1608 676296
Mobile	+44 (0)7717 571792
Email	chloe.uppercourt@gmail.com

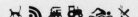

Entry 392 Map 8

Oxfordshire

Fox House

In idyllic stonewalled little Holwell is a big stylish house on a corner – the old village school. Welcoming Susan, who is in the antiques business, gives you two super sitting rooms (one with a friendly wood-burner, the other with a barn window and a heated flagstone floor), and three immaculately cosy bedrooms (one double downstairs) and serves delectable breakfasts on pretty blue china and jams and juices from the orchard. The garden is open and leads to pasture and horses, the countryside is delicious in every season and footpaths radiate from the door. The Cotswolds at its finest!

Price	£80–£125. Singles from £65.
Rooms	3: 1 double; 1 twin, 1 double sharing bath (let to same party only).
Meals	Packed lunch £6. Dinner, 3 courses, £25. Pubs/restaurants 2 miles.
Closed	Christmas.
Directions	A361 south from Burford over A40. Right at sign for Cotswold wildlife park, then right signed Holwell. First house left on corner.

Special homemade extra breakfast choices. 10% off room rate Mon-Thurs.

	Susan Blacker
	Fox House,
	Holwell, Burford OX18 4JS
Tel	+44 (0)1993 823409
Email	foxhouse-rooms@btconnect.com
Web	www.foxhouse-rooms.co.uk

Entry 393   Map 8

Oxfordshire

Manor Farmhouse

Helen and John radiate pleasure and good humour in this old Cotswold stone farmhouse, once part of the Blenheim estate (a short walk down the lane). Find comfortable, traditional living with good prints and paintings, venerable furniture and nothing cluttered or overdone. Shallow, curvy, 18th-century stairs lead up to the pretty double; the small bedroom has a challenging spiral stair to a cobbled courtyard. Breakfast is by the stone fireplace and ancient dresser. On warm days have tea in a sheltered corner by the fig tree and pots, and wander in the lovely garden; the village is quiet yet close to Oxford.

Price	£75–£80. Singles from £70.
Rooms	2 doubles sharing shower (let to same party only).
Meals	Pub within walking distance.
Closed	Christmas.
Directions	A44 north from Oxford's ring road. At r'bout, 1 mile before Woodstock, left onto A4095 into Bladon. Last left in village; house on right, on 2nd bend in road, with iron railings.

	Helen Stevenson
	Manor Farmhouse, Manor Road,
	Bladon, Woodstock OX20 1RU
Tel	+44 (0)1993 812168
Email	helstevenson@hotmail.com
Web	www.oxtowns.co.uk/woodstock/ manor-farmhouse

Entry 394   Map 8

Oxfordshire

Rectory Farm

Come for the happy vibe. It's relaxed here and you are welcomed with tea and homemade shortbread by Mary Anne. The date above the entrance stone reads 1629; the bedrooms, spotless and light, have beautiful arched mullion windows. The huge twin with ornate plasterwork overlooks the garden and church, the pretty double is cosier and both have good showers and big fluffy towels. A herd of Red Ruby Devon cattle are Robert's pride and joy; the family have farmed for generations and you can buy the beef. Excellent breakfast coffee and sometimes their own bacon too; it's a treat to stay. *Min. two nights at weekends & high season.*

Price	£85. Singles £60.
Rooms	2: 1 double, 1 twin.
Meals	Pub 2-minute walk.
Closed	Mid–December to mid-January.
Directions	From Oxford, A420 for Swindon for 8 miles & right at r'bout, for Witney. Over 2 bridges, immed. right by pub car park. After 1 mile right at T-junc.; drive on right, past church.

 10% off stays of 3 or more nights Mon–Thurs.

Mary Anne Florey
Rectory Farm,
Northmoor, Witney OX29 5SX
Tel   +44 (0)1865 300207
Mobile   +44 (0)7974 102198
Email   pj.florey@farmline.com
Web   www.oxtowns.co.uk/rectoryfarm

Entry 395   Map 8

Oxfordshire

Oxford University

Oxford at your fingertips – at a fair price. In the city's ancient heart are Wadham and Keble; in leafy North Oxford is small friendly St Hugh's. Keble's sleeping quarters, functional though a good size, stand in stark contrast to the neo-gothic grandeur of its dining hall – pure Hogwarts! Wadham's hall, medieval, soaring, is yet more glorious – with top breakfasts. Its student-simple bedrooms are reached via crenellated cloisters and lovely walled gardens; ask for a room facing the beautiful quad. At St Hugh's: three residences (one historic), a student bar, romantic gardens and a 15-minute walk into town. *12 colleges in total.*

Price	Doubles £88-£110. Twins £60-£100. Singles £30-£75.
Rooms	Wadham: 250. St Hugh's: 200. Keble: 320. All with twins & singles, some with family rooms. Some share showers.
Meals	Breakfast included. Keble: occasional supper £10.20. Restaurants 2-15 minutes' walk.
Closed	Mid-Jan to mid-March; May/June; Oct/Nov; Christmas. A few rooms available throughout year.
Directions	Website booking. On-request parking at St Hugh's & Lady Margaret Hall.

University Rooms
Oxford University,
Oxford
Web   www.oxfordrooms.co.uk

Entry 396   Map 8

Oxfordshire

Willow Cottage

You are a short step from a village with an excellent pub (return across fields with a torch). Or treat yourself to dinner at Le Manoir aux Quat'Saisons. Katrina's delicious thatched cottage sits down a quiet lane. Through your own entrance find a guest dining room with armchairs by the old range, interesting prints and paintings, an eclectic mix of antiques and contemporary furniture. Bedrooms are warm, comfortable and stylish with views over the garden; shower rooms (not huge) are brand new and deeply smart. Breakfast, unhurried and bristling with local produce, sets walkers up for the Chiltern Way and the Ridgeway.

Oxfordshire

Brook Barn

Not your average country B&B, but a swish interior of light oak, soaring rafters, lots of light and space, and well-travelled charming owners. Bedrooms are of the boutique-hotel breed: good lighting, lots of space for sitting, and beds that you want to climb into there and then; bathrooms vary in size but all have enormous towels and lovely lotions and potions. Breakfast at a time to suit you, either on your terrace, or in the beamed dining room; all is sourced locally and the mushrooms are home-grown. Grab a book, stroll round the garden, or find a sofa to flop into downstairs – this is a place to relax.

Price	£80. Singles £55.
Rooms	2 doubles.
Meals	Packed lunch £7. Pubs/restaurants 0.5 miles.
Closed	Rarely.
Directions	M40 junc. 7, left off slip road. 5.5 miles to pub on right, after 0.5 miles right to Denton. On for 2 miles, pass right turn to Cuddesdon, take next right, 'Brookside only'. House 200 yds on right.

10% off room rate Mon-Thurs.

Price	£100-£225. Singles £80-£135.
Rooms	5: 4 doubles; 1 twin/double with separate bath/shower.
Meals	Dinner from £18.50. Packed lunch £10.50-£19.50. Pub/restaurant 2 miles.
Closed	Christmas.
Directions	Ashbury road out of Wantage. Left to Letcombe Regis, round right-hand bend, 400 yds after cream house, drive on left.

Bottle of wine with dinner on first night.

Katrina Sheldon
Willow Cottage,
Denton, Oxford OX44 9JG
Tel   +44 (0)1865 874728
Email   katrinasheldon@aol.com
Web   www.willowcottage.info

Entry 397   Map 8

Sarah-Jane & Mark Ashman
Brook Barn,
Letcombe Regis, Wantage OX12 9JD
Tel   +44 (0)1235 766502
Email   info@brookbarn.com
Web   www.brookbarn.com

Entry 398   Map 3

Oxfordshire

Fyfield Manor

A fabulous house in Oxfordshire (once owned by Simon de Montfort) with vast water gardens and a water wheel for eco underfloor heating, created by the Browns. From the grand wood-panelled hall enter a beamed dining room with high-backed chairs, brass rubbings, a wood-burner and a pretty 12th-century arch; you breakfast on eggs from the hens, garden fruit, organic bacon. Charming bedrooms have views, slippers and comfortable sofas. Oxford Park & Ride is nearby, there's walking from the door and delightful Christine has wangled you a free glass of wine in the local pub if you walk or cycle to get there! Superb. *Over 10s welcome.*

Ethical Collection: Environment. See page 420.

Price	£70-£80. Singles £50-£60.
Rooms	2: 1 twin/double; 1 family room with sofabed & separate bath.
Meals	Pubs within 1 mile.
Closed	Rarely.
Directions	Exit 6 from M40, then B4009 to Benson. Left to Benson village. Thro' village for 0.5 mile dir. Ewelme. 8 foot wall immed. after cream house on right. Thro' gates at end of wall to main house.

25% discount on pilates or Alexander Technique lesson.

	Christine Brown
	Fyfield Manor,
	Benson, Wallingford OX10 6HA
Tel	+44 (0)1491 835184
Email	chris_fyfield@hotmail.co.uk
Web	www.fyfieldmanor.co.uk

Entry 399   Map 4

Rutland

Old Rectory

Jane Austen fans will swoon. This elegant 1740s village house was used as Mr Collins's 'humble abode' by the BBC: you breakfast in the beautiful dining room that was 'Mr Collins's hall', and you can sleep in 'Miss Bennett's bedroom'. Victoria is the archetypal English woman – feisty, fun and gregarious – and looks after you beautifully with White Company linen in chintzy old-fashioned bedrooms and (not swish) bathrooms, fruit from the lovely garden and Aga-cooked bacon and eggs. You are near to some pleasant market towns and lovely walking and riding country. Don't forget the smelling salts!

Price	£85. Singles £45.
Rooms	2: 1 twin; 1 double with separate bath.
Meals	Pubs within 3 miles.
Closed	Rarely.
Directions	5 miles NE of Oakham, through Ashwell. Or 7 miles west of A1 from Stretton.

10% off room rate Mon-Thurs.
10% off stays of 2 or more nights.

Use your Sawday's Gift Card here.

	Victoria Owen
	Old Rectory,
	Teigh, Oakham LE15 7RT
Tel	+44 (0)1572 787681
Mobile	+44 (0)7717 223678
Email	torowen@btinternet.com
Web	www.teighbedandbreakfast.co.uk

Entry 400   Map 9

Shropshire

Tybroughton Hall

Off a winding country lane, surrounded by 40 acres of grassland, find a pretty white listed farmhouse and a wonderful welcome from Daisy, her family and two dear dogs. Step into the hallway with its polished antique table and bright garden flowers and you know you've made the right choice: this is a house to unwind in. After a day's hiking or biking, bliss to return to bedrooms cosy and comfortable – the traditional double with its country view or the large lovely twin. Breakfasts are worth getting up for: Tim makes the preserves, bees make the honey, hens lay the eggs and the pigs (five beauties!) provide the bacon.

Price	£75-£80. Singles £50-£55.
Rooms	2: 1 double; 1 twin with separate bath.
Meals	Dinner £20-£25. Pub 4 miles.
Closed	Rarely.
Directions	From Whitchurch A525 (Wrexham). After 3.6 miles right at crossroads at top of hill (Malpas, Tybroughton). Continue for 1.1 miles, then left. After 0.3 miles 1st house on right.

10% off stays of 2 or more nights.

	Daisy Woodhead Tybroughton Hall, Tybroughton, Whitchurch SY13 3BB
Tel	+44 (0)1948 780726
Mobile	+44 (0)7850 395885
Email	daisy.woodhead@btinternet.com

Entry 401   Map 7

Shropshire

Pinfold Cottage

Heart-warming B&B in a beautiful spot with lots of books, a parrot called Polly and vintage games and toys to add to the merry clutter. Walls are covered in illustrations and some lovely paintings, bedrooms are calm, simple and charming, but the biggest treat is Sue. Generous with her time, spirit and home cooking, she makes her own muesli with fruits and nuts from the garden. Natural sounds are provided by the well-fed birdlife and the trickle of the stream that meanders through the enchanting garden. Breakfasts are healthy and delicious and you'll revel in the peace. Superb value.

Price	£60. Singles £40.
Rooms	2: 1 double, 1 single, each with separate shower. Extra bath available.
Meals	Dinner, 3 courses, from £15. Packed lunch £7. Restaurant 0.5 miles.
Closed	Rarely.
Directions	From Oswestry, A483 from A5 for Welshpool. 1st left to Maesbury; 3rd right at x-roads with school on corner; 1st house on right.

	Sue Barr Pinfold Cottage, Newbridge, Maesbury, Oswestry SY10 8AY
Tel	+44 (0)1691 661192
Email	suebarr100@hotmail.com

Entry 402   Map 7

Shropshire

The Isle

History buffs and nature lovers will delight: these 800 acres are almost enfolded by the River Severn; drive through lion-topped stone pillars to the house, built in about 1682 and extended later. Charming Ros and Edward are truly hands-on: all wood for fires is grown on the estate which also provides eggs, bacon, ham and vegetables – so you eat well! Flop in front of a huge fire in the drawing room with Chinese rug, family antiques and sublime views. Peaceful bedrooms are large and light with pocket-sprung memory mattresses and snazzy, upmarket bathrooms. Super walks, rides and fishing on the estate.

Price	£75–£90. Singles £50–£60.
Rooms	3: 2 doubles; 1 twin with separate bath.
Meals	Packed lunch £5. Dinner £20. Pub/restaurant 4.3 miles.
Closed	Rarely.
Directions	From Shrewsbury signs for Oswestry & Bicton (B4380). At Four Crosses pub right into Isle Lane. After 0.5 mile drive thro' pillars with lions. Follow B&B signs.

10% off room rate Mon-Thurs.
10% off stays of 2 or more nights.

Use your Sawday's Gift Card here.

Ros & Edward Tate
The Isle,
Bicton, Shrewsbury SY3 8EE
Tel   +44 (0)1743 851218
Mobile +44 (0)7776 257286
Email   ros@isleestate.co.uk
Web   www.the-isle-estate.co.uk

Entry 403   Map 7

Shropshire

Brimford House

Beautifully tucked under the Breidden Hills, farm and Georgian farmhouse have been in the Dawson family for four generations. Views stretch all the way to the Severn; the simple garden does not try to compete. Bedrooms are spotless and fresh: a half-tester with rope-twist columns and Sanderson fabrics, a twin with Victorian wrought-iron bedsteads, a double with a brass bed, a big bathroom with a roll top bath. Liz serves you farm eggs and homemade preserves at breakfast, and there's a food pub just down the road. Sheep and cattle outdoors, a lovely black lab in, and wildlife walks from the door. Good value.

Price	£60–£75. Singles £40–£60.
Rooms	3: 2 doubles, 1 twin.
Meals	Packed lunch £4.50. Pub 3-minute walk.
Closed	Rarely.
Directions	From Shrewsbury A458 Welshpool road. After Ford, right onto B4393. Just after Crew Green, left for Criggion. House 1st on left after Admiral Rodney pub.

Bottle of sparkling wine, minimum 2-night stay.

Liz Dawson
Brimford House,
Criggion, Shrewsbury SY5 9AU
Tel   +44 (0)1938 570235
Mobile +44 (0)7801 100848
Email   info@brimford.co.uk
Web   www.brimford.co.uk

Entry 404   Map 7

Shropshire

Hardwick House

On a quiet street in the heart of Shrewsbury, this fine Georgian house has been in Lucy's family for generations. The dining room with oak panelling and huge fireplace is a lovely space to breakfast on locally sourced produce and homemade bread; vases of garden flowers are dotted all around this cheerful, family home. Bedrooms are traditional and comfortable with pretty china tea cups; bathrooms are old-fashioned. The walled garden is fabulous; take tea in the splendid 18th-century summerhouse. Birthplace of Darwin, this is a fascinating historic town; walk to the abbey, castle, theatre, festivals and great shops. Lucy is delightful.

Shropshire

Whitton Hall

Down a long private drive with fields on either side is a lovely 18th-century farmhouse, elegant but not intimidating, with a sense of timelessness. A large open hallway with a warming fire is a comfortable, peaceful space for relaxing with a book. You breakfast in the dining room, on local muesli, bread, marmalades and jams, milk from their Jersey cows, soft fruit from their garden, sausages and bacon from down the road. Up a stunning staircase are peaceful, light and large bedrooms, with graceful, country house furniture and long views to glorious gardens. Unwind in the peace. *Over 12s welcome.*

Price	£75–£95. Singles £55–£65.
Rooms	2: 1 twin/double, 1 twin.
Meals	Pubs/restaurants 150 yds.
Closed	Christmas & New Year.
Directions	Follow signs to town centre. House near St Chad's church. Train: left out of station & up the hill. Staight down Pride Hill, then up into St John's Hill.

Late checkout (12pm). Local produce in your room.

Lucy Whitaker
Hardwick House,
12 St John's Hill,
Shrewsbury SY1 1JJ
Tel +44 (0)1743 350165
Email gilesandlucy@btinternet.com
Web www.hardwickhouseshrewsbury.co.uk

Entry 405   Map 7

Price	From £75. Singles from £45.
Rooms	2: 1 double, 1 twin, each with separate bath & shower.
Meals	Supper £20. Packed lunch available. Restaurant 1.5 miles.
Closed	Christmas & New Year.
Directions	From Shrewsbury bypass (A5), B4386 to Westbury. Rght at x-roads opposite Lion pub, Immediate left, 50 yds on, left for Vennington. After 0.75 miles, drive on left; house at end, on right.

Christopher & Gill Halliday & Kate Boscawen
Whitton Hall,
Westbury, Shrewsbury SY5 9RD
Tel +44 (0)1743 884459
Mobile +44 (0)7974 689629
Email accommodation@whittonhall.com

Entry 406   Map 7

Shropshire

Meole Brace Hall

Charles takes B&B to a new state of excellence: come to be spoilt in a heavenly house. The quintessence of English period elegance, it's a sumptuous home rich with polished mahogany and eye-catching wallpapers and fabrics. Bedrooms have comfortable sofas and flat-screen TVs; the Blue Room has an elegant half-tester bed. Sit on the terrace overlooking the manicured gardens: a stream trickles down to the willow pond, a second pond with lion fountains is home to koi carp. All this under the watchful eye of Dolly, the friendly Patterdale cross terrier. A 25-minute stroll from town – but it feels a million miles away.

Shropshire

Lawley House

A lovely calm sense of the continuity of history and family life emanates from this large, comfortable Victorian home. Jackie and Jim are delightful hosts and great fun. Bedrooms welcome you with flowers, books, duck down pillows – and stupendous views of the Stretton Hills, even from bed. Tuck into a generous breakfast in the dining room, elegant with family portraits and a grand piano you are welcome to play. Enjoy long hilltop views from the spectacular conservatory or the garden – lush with lupins, sweet peas, delphiniums and 50 types of rose that bloom in profusion. *Children over 12 welcome.*

Price	From £79. Singles from £59.
Rooms	3: 2 doubles, 1 twin.
Meals	Restaurants 1 mile.
Closed	Rarely.
Directions	A5 & A49 junc. (south of bypass), signs to centre. Over 1st mini r'bout, 2nd exit at next; 2nd left into Upper Rd; 150 yds on at bend, left & immed. right into Church Lane. Drive at bottom on left.

Price	£60-£80. Singles £40-£55.
Rooms	3: 1 double, 2 twins/doubles.
Meals	Pub/restaurant 1.5 miles.
Closed	Christmas & New Year.
Directions	From Shrewsbury, south on A49. Ignore turn in Dorrington, keep on for 3 miles. 0.5 miles before Leebotwood, right to Smethcott. Follow signs uphill for 2 miles; drive on left just before Smethcott.

 10% off room rate Mon-Thurs.

	Charles Hathaway
	Meole Brace Hall,
	Shrewsbury
	SY3 9HF
Tel	+44 (0)1743 235566
Email	hathaway@meolebracehall.co.uk
Web	www.meolebracehall.co.uk

	Jackie & Jim Scarratt
	Lawley House,
	Smethcott,
	Church Stretton SY6 6NX
Tel	+44 (0)1694 751236
Email	jscarratt@onetel.com
Web	www.lawleyhouse.co.uk

Entry 407   Map 7

Entry 408   Map 7

Shropshire

The Manor House

House, garden and owner have bags of character: clever Caroline, an interior designer, gives you lots of space to roam. Find ancient beams and salvaged panels, the odd contemporary painting or ceramic, a glowing wood-burner, and bright splashes of colour. Your bedroom is lovely, with a sloping ceiling, fresh white walls and a bang-up-to-date bathroom – all chubby towels and Jo Malone potions. Peaceful breakfasts overlooking the bird-filled garden will set you up for anything and there are plenty of hearty walks from the door, or nearby Ludlow and Church Stretton to explore.

Price	£100. Singles £90.
Rooms	1 double.
Meals	Packed lunch £10. Dinner from £25. BYO. Pub/restaurant 100 yds.
Closed	Christmas & New Year.
Directions	From Ludlow, left off A49 into Church Stretton, up to staggered crossroads, then right. Past schools on right, into All Stretton. Past Yew Tree pub, next council road left, by phone box & postbox & immed. left into drive.

Free drop-off within 10 mile radius. Fair trade chocolate in your room.

Caroline Montgomery
The Manor House,
All Stretton SY6 6JU
Tel   +44 (0)1694 724508
Mobile   +44 (0)7908 722470
Email   caro@manorhouseallstretton.co.uk
Web   www.manorhouseallstretton.co.uk

Entry 409   Map 7

Shropshire

Hannigans Farm

High on the hillside, a mile up the drive, the views roll out before you – stunning. Privacy and peace are yours in the converted dairy and barn across the flower-filled yard. Big, carpeted, ground-floor rooms have comfy beds and sofas; one has views that roll towards the setting sun. In the morning Fiona and Alistair, delightful, easy-going and fun, serve you home eggs, sausages from their own pigs and honey from their bees in the book-lined dining room of their farmhouse. Feel free to take tea in the garden with its little hedges and manicured lawns; you'll feel restored in this quiet Shropshire corner.

Price	£75. Singles by arrangement.
Rooms	2 twins.
Meals	Pub 1.25 miles.
Closed	Rarely.
Directions	From Bridgnorth, A458 to Shrewsbury. 0.5 miles after Morville, right onto stone road & follow signs for 1 mile, to farm.

Bowl of fruit in your room.

Use your Sawday's Gift Card here.

Fiona Thompson
Hannigans Farm,
Morville, Bridgnorth WV16 4RN
Tel   +44 (0)1746 714332
Email   hannigansfarm@btinternet.com
Web   www.hannigans-farm.co.uk

Entry 410   Map 7

Shropshire

The Old Rectory

With its own spring water, horses, dogs and slow pace this Georgian rectory is comfortable country living at its best. Izzy and Andy are charming and interesting and give you scones and tea by the fire in a drawing room full of family photos, plump sofas and books. Elegant bedrooms have fluffy hot water bottles; smart bathrooms have scented lotions in pretty bottles, robes and slippers. Candlelit dinner will often be fish or game with garden vegetables; breakfast is local and leisurely with homemade granola and jams. There's a bootroom for muddy feet and paws, stabling and seven acres to roam. *Pets sleep in bootroom.*

Shropshire

The White Cottage

A narrow road three miles from Bishop's Castle snakes past fields of placid sheep, through farm gates, to the White Cottage and a lovely welcome from Tim and Mary. This is B&B with a difference: your very own stone bothy – once used by drovers – now a light, warm and inviting suite, bright with art and stylish touches. A member of Shropshire's 'Buy Local, Eat Local' scheme, Mary delivers a breakfast basket to your patio deck – or will cook you something scrumptious in her kitchen: scurry up to the cottage for scrambled eggs or devilled kidneys. All around you are country sounds and bucolic beauty.

Price	From £80. Singles from £65.		Price	£80.
Rooms	2: 1 double, 1 twin/double.		Rooms	Bothy: 1 double & kitchen/ dining area.
Meals	Dinner, 3 courses, £25. Packed lunch £10. Pubs 1.25-4 miles.		Meals	Pubs/restaurants 3 miles.
Closed	Rarely.		Closed	Occasionally.
Directions	From Ludlow B4117 dir. Cleobury Mortimer. After 0.5 miles left onto B4364. After 6 miles right at 3 Horse Shoes pub. Straight on for 1.25 miles. Drive on right by red letter box.		Directions	From Bishop's Castle, A488 towards Clun. Pass through Colebatch. At next staggered crossroads right. After 0.5 miles, signed gate on right.

 Bottle of wine with dinner on first night.

 10% off room rate Mon-Thurs. Late checkout (12pm).

	Isabel Barnard The Old Rectory, Wheathill WV16 6QT			**Mary Wraith** The White Cottage, Golden Grove, Acton, Bishop's Castle SY9 5LD
Tel	+44 (0)1746 787209		Tel	+44 (0)1588 630330
Email	enquiries@theoldrectorywheathill.com		Email	staying@thewhitecottageacton.co.uk
Web	www.theoldrectorywheathill.com		Web	www.thewhitecottageacton.co.uk

Entry 411   Map 7

Entry 412   Map 7

Shropshire

The Birches Mill

Just as a mill should be, tucked in the nook of a postcard valley. It ended Gill and Andrew's search for a refuge from the city, and it's a treat to share its seclusion and beauty; all you hear is the river. Fresh breezy bedrooms in the 17th-century part have elegant brass beds, goose down duvets and fine linen – one keeps the original long roll top bath – while the new stone and oak extension blends beautifully and has become a big attractive twin. Happy hens provide the breakfast eggs. Gill and Andrew are affable hosts in a stunning valley of meadowland and woods. *Children over 12 welcome.*

Shropshire

Clun Farm House

These young relaxed owners make a great team. Susan gives you homemade marmalade at breakfast and seasonal produce at dinner; Anthony helps you discover the secrets of the village and the heavenly hills. Both are enthusiastic collectors of country artefacts and have filled their listed 15th-century farmhouse with eye-catching things; the cowboy's saddle by the old range echoes Susan's roots. Bedrooms have aged and oiled floorboards, fun florals and bold walls; bathrooms are small and simple. Walk Offa's Dyke and the Shropshire Way; return to a cosy wood-burner, a warm smile and a delicious dinner. Good value.

Price	£82–£92. Singles by arrangement.
Rooms	3: 1 double, 1 twin; 1 double with separate bath.
Meals	Packed lunch £6. Pub 3 miles.
Closed	November–March.
Directions	From Clun A488 for Bishops Castle. 1st left, for Bicton. 2nd left for Mainstone, then narrow winding lane for 1.5 miles. Up bank to farm, then 1st right for Burlow. House at bottom of hill on left by river.

5% off stays Mon-Thurs.

Price	From £75. Singles by arrangement.
Rooms	2: 1 double (with extra bunk bed room); 1 twin/double with separate shower.
Meals	Dinner from £25. Packed lunch £4. Pubs/restaurants nearby.
Closed	Occasionally.
Directions	A49 from Ludlow & onto B4368 at Craven Arms, for Clun. In High St on left 0.5 miles from Clun sign.

Gill Della Casa & Andrew Farmer
The Birches Mill,
Clun SY7 8NL

Tel	+44 (0)1588 640409
Email	birchesmill@btinternet.com
Web	www.birchesmill.co.uk

Entry 413   Map 7

Anthony & Susan Whitfield
Clun Farm House, High Street,
Clun, Craven Arms SY7 8JB

Tel	+44 (0)1588 640432
Mobile	+44 (0)7885 261391
Email	susanwhitfield@talk21.com
Web	www.clunfarmhouse.co.uk

Entry 414   Map 7

Shropshire

Hopton House

Karen looks after her guests wonderfully and even runs courses on how to do B&B! Unwind in this fresh and uplifting converted granary with old beams, high ceilings and a sun-filled dining/sitting room overlooking the hills. The bedroom above has its own balcony; those in the barn, one up, one down, each with its own entrance, are as enticing: beautifully dressed beds, silent fridges, good lighting, homemade cakes. Bathrooms have deep baths (and showers) — from one you can lie back and gaze at the stars. Karen's breakfasts promise Ludlow sausages, home-laid eggs, fine jams and homemade marmalade.

Ethical Collection: Environment; Food.
See page 420.

Price	From £105.
Rooms	3: 1 double. Barn: 2 doubles.
Meals	Restaurant 3 miles.
Closed	19-27 December.
Directions	A49 Craven Arms exit, B4368 west. After 1 mile, left signed Hopton Heath. At Hopton Heath x-roads, right over bridge, follow road right. House 2nd on left.

 Local food/produce in your room.

Use your Sawday's Gift Card here.

	Karen Thorne
	Hopton House,
	Hopton Heath, Craven Arms SY7 0QD
Tel	+44 (0)1547 530885
Email	info@shropshirebreakfast.co.uk
Web	www.shropshirebreakfast.co.uk

Entry 415   Map 7

Shropshire

Brick House Farm

From the roadside this looks unexceptional, but once through the gates and into the farmyard with strutting chickens you can see the black and white checked side of this freshly-painted 16th-century longhouse. In the guest sitting room David has kept the walls simple white, restored beams and red tiles, and found a hidden fireplace; warm yourself here on a comfy sofa with a good book. Sleep soundly on smart mattresses, soak in a deep Villeroy & Boch bath, tuck into home-grown lamb for supper at a smart table. The garden seeps into unspoilt countryside with peaceful, grazing horses.

Price	£75.
Rooms	2: 1 double, 1 twin/double, each with separate bath.
Meals	Dinner, 4-5 courses, £25. BYO. Restaurant 4 miles.
Closed	Rarely.
Directions	On A4110, from Leintwardine; house 1st on left, with sandy coloured render, opposite church.

 3rd night half price for stays starting on a Sunday, Monday or Thursday.

	David Watson
	Brick House Farm, Adforton,
	Leintwardine, Craven Arms SY7 0NF
Tel	+44 (0)1568 770870
Email	info@adforton.com
Web	www.adforton.com

Entry 416   Map 7

Shropshire

Lower Buckton Country House

You are spoiled here in house-party style; Carolyn – passionate about Slow Food – and Henry, are born entertainers. Kick off with homemade cake in the drawing room with its oil paintings, antique furniture and old rugs; return for delicious nibbles when the lamps and wood-burner are flickering. Dine well at a huge oak table (home-reared pork, local cheeses, dreamy puddings), then nestle into the best linen and the softest pillows; bedrooms feel wonderfully restful. This is laid-back B&B: paddle in the stream, admire the stunning views, find a quiet spot with a good book. Great fun! *Cookery courses. Stabling for horses.*

Ethical Collection: Food; Community. See page 420.

Price	£90.
Rooms	3: 2 doubles; 1 twin/double with separate bath.
Meals	Dinner, 4 courses, £35. BYO wine. Pub/restaurant 4 miles.
Closed	Rarely.
Directions	South through Leintwardine; after 0.25 miles right A4113. At Walford right at x-roads down narrow lane for Buckton. Over river, 2nd house on left, entrance by village green; white gate with postbox in wall.

Home-grown vegetable goodie bag. Free pick-up from local bus/train station.

Henry & Carolyn Chesshire
Lower Buckton Country House,
Buckton, Leintwardine SY7 0JU
Tel +44 (0)1547 540532
Mobile +44 (0)7960 273865
Email carolyn@lowerbuckton.co.uk
Web www.lowerbuckton.co.uk

Entry 417   Map 7

Shropshire

Upper Buckton

You can't help being bowled over by the beautiful setting and the grandeur of the place. In lush gardens that slope peacefully down to millstream, meadows and river, this Georgian house, complete with heronry and point-to-point course, stands on a motte and bailey site. Convivial dinners, preceded by drinks in the drawing room, are delicious: Yvonne's cooking using local produce is upmarket and creative, Hayden's wine list is a treat. Retire to large bedrooms with huge beds made to perfection (proper blankets, lovely linen). Marvellous for walkers returning from a day in the glorious Welsh Borders. *Children by arrangement.*

Price	£84–£110. Singles £57–£65.
Rooms	3: 1 double, 1 twin/double; 1 twin/double with separate bath.
Meals	Dinner, 4 courses, £30. Pub/restaurant 2 miles.
Closed	Rarely.
Directions	From Ludlow, A49 to Shrewsbury. At Bromfield, A4113. Right in Walford for Buckton, on to 2nd farm on left. Large sign on building.

Guided tour of the heronry when appropriate. 10% off stays of 2 or more nights.

Hayden & Yvonne Lloyd
Upper Buckton, Leintwardine,
Craven Arms, Ludlow SY7 0JU
Tel +44 (0)1547 540634
Email ghlloydco@btconnect.com
Web www.upperbuckton.co.uk

Entry 418   Map 7

Shropshire

Walford Court

Come for a break from clock-watching and a spot of fresh air. Large bedrooms delight with the comfiest mattresses on king-size beds, scented candles, books, games and double-end roll top baths – one under a west facing window. Aga-cooked breakfasts include eggs from 'the ladies of the orchard'; candlelit dinners may be served outside on fine evenings. Wander through apple, plum and pear trees, find a motte and bailey, strike out for a long hike. Craig and Debbie are thoughtful and hugely keen on wildlife (you get binoculars) and this is the perfect place to bring a special person – and a bottle of champagne.

Ethical Collection: Environment; Food. See page 420.

Price	£75–£85. Singles £65–£75.
Rooms	3: 1 double; 2 doubles each with sitting room.
Meals	Dinner, 2-3 courses, £15–£25. Packed lunch available. Lunch in the tea room. Pubs/restaurants 1-3 miles.
Closed	Christmas & Boxing Day.
Directions	A49 N of Ludlow; A4113 Knighton. Thro' Leintwardine; right Walford. There, left for Presteigne, then immed. left. Signs to Walford Court Tea Room.

Local food/produce in room. Homemade muffins to take away.

Debbie & Craig Fraser
Walford Court, Walford,
Leintwardine, Ludlow SY7 0JT
Tel   +44 (0)1547 540570
Email   info@romanticbreak.com
Web   www.romanticbreak.com

Entry 419   Map 7

Shropshire

35 Lower Broad Street

You're almost at the bottom of the town, near the river and the bridge. Elaine's terraced Georgian cottage is spotless and cosy; her office doubles as a sitting area for guests with leather armchairs and desk space for workaholics. Upstairs are two good-sized doubles with a country crisp feel, king-size beds and a pretty blue and white bathroom. Walkers, shoppers, antique- and book-hunters can fill up on homemade potato scones, black pudding, organic eggs and good coffee before striding out to explore. This is excellent value B&B: comfortable, clean and can be enjoyed without a car. Perfect for two couples.

Ethical Collection: Food; Community. See page 420.

Price	£70. Singles £45.
Rooms	2: 1 double & sitting room; 1 double sharing bath (let to same party only).
Meals	Pubs/restaurants 100 yds.
Closed	Rarely.
Directions	Right out of railway station, 200 yds to lights. Left onto Corve St, then up to top of hill. At lights, right & follow to Broad St; thro' arch into Lower Broad St. On right towards bottom.

Free pick-up from local train station. Fruit in bedroom.

Use your Sawday's Gift Card here.

Elaine Downs
35 Lower Broad Street,
Ludlow SY8 1PH
Tel   +44 (0)1584 876912
Mobile   +44 (0)7980 037576
Email   a.downs@tesco.net
Web   www.ludlowbedandbreakfast.blogspot.com

Entry 420   Map 7

Shropshire

Rosecroft

A pretty, quiet, traditional house with charming owners, well-proportioned rooms, an elegant sitting room and not a trace of pomposity. Breakfasts are huge enough to set you up for the day: Pimhill organic muesli, smoked or unsmoked local bacon, black pudding, delicious jams. The garden is a delight to stroll through – in summer you can picnic here – while serious walkers are close to the Welsh borders. Bedrooms and bathrooms are polished to perfection; there are fresh flowers, plenty of interesting books, home-baked cakes when you arrive. The village has a super pub and Ludlow is close by. *Children over 12 welcome.*

Price	£70-£75. Singles £50-£55.
Rooms	2: 1 double; 1 double with separate bath.
Meals	Packed lunch £4. Pub 200 yds.
Closed	Rarely.
Directions	Between Ludlow & Leominster on A49, turn onto B4362 at Woofferton. After 1.5 miles, left into Orleton. Past school & small green, house on right, opp. vicarage.

Free pick-up from local bus/train station. 3 nights for 2, 1 October to 20 March.

Gail Benson
Rosecroft,
Orleton, Ludlow SY8 4HN
Tel +44 (0)1568 780565
Email gailanddavid@rosecroftorleton.co.uk
Web www.stmem.com/rosecroft

Entry 421   Map 7

Shropshire

Timberstone Bed & Breakfast

The house is young and engaging – as are Tracey and Alex, new generation B&Bers. Come for charming bedrooms – two snug under the eaves, two in the smart oak-floored extension – roll top baths, pretty fabrics, thick white cotton, beams galore... and reflexology, massage or a sauna in the garden studios; Tracey, once in catering, is a reflexologist. In the warm guest sitting/dining room find art, books, comfy sofas and glass doors onto the terrace. Breakfasts are special with eggs from the roaming hens, local bacon, croissants; have a delicious supper here, or head for Ludlow and its clutch of Michelin stars.

Ethical Collection: Environment; Food. See page 420.

Price	£90-£100. Singles £50-£90.
Rooms	5: 2 doubles, 1 double with sofabed, 1 family. Summerhouse: 1 double (summer only).
Meals	Dinner, 3 courses, £25. Pubs/restaurants 5 miles.
Closed	Rarely.
Directions	B4364 Ludlow-Bridgnorth. After 3 miles, right to Clee Stanton; on for 1.5 miles; left at signpost to Clee Stanton; 1st house on left.

Late checkout (12pm). 10% off room rate Mon-Thurs.

Use your Sawday's Gift Card here.

Tracey Baylis & Alex Read
Timberstone Bed & Breakfast,
Clee Stanton, Ludlow SY8 3EL
Tel +44 (0)1584 823519
Mobile +44 (0)7905 967263
Email timberstone1@hotmail.com
Web www.timberstoneludlow.co.uk

Entry 422   Map 7

Shropshire

Cleeton Court

Rare peace: a tiny lane leads to this part 14th-century farmhouse, immersed in the countryside with views over meadows and heathland. You have your own entrance, and the use of the pretty drawing room, elegantly comfortable with sofas and a log fire. Beamed bedrooms are delightfully furnished, one with a magnificent, chintzy four-poster and a vast bathroom; recline in the cast-iron bath with a glass of wine, gaze on views from the window as you soak. Bring your boots: the walking is superb, and charming Ros gives you a smashing, locally sourced breakfast to get you going. *Children over five welcome.*

Price	From £70. Singles £45–£50.
Rooms	2: 1 twin/double, 1 four-poster.
Meals	Packed lunch on request. Pubs/restaurants 1.5–4 miles.
Closed	Christmas & New Year.
Directions	From Ludlow, A4117 for Kidderminster for 1 mile; left on B4364 for Cleobury North; on for 5 miles. In Wheathill, right for Cleeton St Mary; on for 1.5 miles; house on left.

10% off stays of 3 or more nights.

Rosamond Woodward
Cleeton Court,
Cleeton St Mary, Ludlow DY14 0QZ
Tel   +44 (0)1584 823379
Mobile +44 (0)7778 903136
Email   roswoodward@talktalk.net
Web   www.cleetoncourt.co.uk

Entry 423   Map 7

Somerset

West Liscombe

Down deep Devon lanes, then up, up, up to the remote farmhouse encircled by footpaths and bridle paths, breezes and green views. Heaven! Inside is comfy, cheery, chintzy and English to the core. Deborah, true country lady and Cordon Bleu cook, was born to do B&B; she runs the Pony Club and welcomes all. The grandfather clock tick-tocks in the sitting room, the silver shines, the log-burner glows, and the guest bedrooms, with books, great beds and posies of flowers, are well-groomed and inviting. Sheep roam the drive, the garden stretches down the valley, Exmoor is 600 yards, the sea is 11 miles.

Price	From £75. Singles £45.
Rooms	2: 1 double; 1 twin with separate bath.
Meals	Lunch £7.50. Dinner £20. Pub 5 miles.
Closed	Rarely.
Directions	In East Anstey village pass school on left; continue 1 mile to Waddicombe, up hill for 50 yds. Postbox in wall, turn right; house 500 yds.

Robert & Deborah Connell
West Liscombe,
Waddicombe, Dulverton TA22 9RX
Tel   +44 (0)1398 341282
Email   deborahconnell@btinternet.com

Entry 424   Map 2

Somerset

Emmetts Grange

A superb landscape high on the moor with 900 acres of moorland asking to be discovered – the rugged real deal. This listed country house, at the end of a long drive, is well-loved and lived-in; be greeted by a fox head in the hall and a portrait of an ancestor in wig and ermine. Easy-going, kind Tom and Lucy have boys, dogs, ponies, hens, and raise Red Devon cattle; they are knowledgeable about the area and Lucy is keen on studying the family's genealogy. Bedrooms and bathrooms are large and comfortable with an old-fashioned but bright and colourful feel. Tom is the cook and, not surprisingly, is pretty keen on the local beef.

Price	£80–£120. Singles from £50.
Rooms	4: 2 twins/doubles, 1 twin, 1 four-poster.
Meals	Dinner, 3 courses, £30. Pub 2 miles.
Closed	Christmas, New Year & occasionally.
Directions	M5 exit 27. A361 towards South Molton. 25 miles then right to A399 Ilfracombe. 1 mile, right towards Simonsbath. 6 miles, entrance to Grange on right.

10% off stays of 2 or more nights.

Tom & Lucy Barlow
Emmetts Grange,
Simonsbath, Minehead TA24 7LD
Tel   +44 (0)1643 831138
Mobile   +44 (0)7773 239797
Email   mail@emmettsgrange.co.uk
Web   www.emmettsgrange.co.uk

Entry 425   Map 2

Somerset

North Wheddon Farm

Pootle through the vibrant green patchwork of Exmoor National Park and bowl down a pitted track to land in Blyton-esque bliss – a classic Somerset farmyard, crackling with geese and hens, round which is the gentleman farmer's house. Bedrooms are airy and comfortable with grand views, books, fresh flowers and small, but neat-as-a-pin bathrooms. Bring children and they will be in heaven, with eggs to collect and pigs to pat, or come just for yourself and a bit of indulgence. Food is 'River Cottage' style and much is home-reared, the walking is fabulous for miles and kind Rachael sends you off with a thermos of tea.

Price	£75–£80. Singles £38.50.
Rooms	3: 1 double, 1 twin/double; 1 single with separate bath.
Meals	Dinner, 3 courses, £24. Cold/hot packed lunch £7.50–£9.75. Pub 0.25 miles.
Closed	Rarely.
Directions	From Minehead A396 to Wheddon Cross. Pass pub on right & Moorland Hall on left. North Wheddon is next driveway on right. Satnav not reliable.

Rachael Abraham
North Wheddon Farm,
Wheddon Cross TA24 7EX
Tel   +44 (0)1643 841791
Email   rachael@go-exmoor.co.uk
Web   www.northwheddonfarm.co.uk

Entry 426   Map 2

Somerset

Glen Lodge

High brick walls and tumbling gardens in the Victorian tanner's house give way to the warm embrace of a wood-burning stove and a giddy rush of intriguing artwork – one painting is by an elephant! Polished oak floors are dotted with oriental rugs, bedrooms are immaculate, bay windows gaze on the Bristol Channel. Meryl and David care about sustainable living – feast on American home baking and fruit from their 21 acres: all is recycled, composted and enjoyed. Surrounded by the woods and wilds of Exmoor National Park yet a short stroll from popular Porlock, you'll revel in comfort, warmth and their passion for life.

Price	£90. Singles £60.
Rooms	5: 3 doubles; 1 double, 1 twin each with separate bath.
Meals	Packed lunch £8. Dinner £30. Pub/restaurant 0.5 miles.
Closed	Christmas & New Year.
Directions	From Minehead, A39 to Porlock; on entering town, left at church into Parsons Street 0.5 miles up. Left over bridge. Gate to house in front.

 10% off stays Mon–Thurs. Free pick-up from local bus/train station.

	Meryl Salter
	Glen Lodge,
	Hawkcombe, Porlock TA24 8LN
Tel	+44 (0)1643 863371
Mobile	+44 (0)7749 326009
Email	glenlodge@gmail.com
Web	www.glenlodge.net

Entry 427   Map 2

Somerset

Higher Orchard

A little lane tumbles down to the centre of lovely old Dunster. The village is a two minute-walk yet here you have open views of fields, sheep and sea. Exmoor footpaths start behind the house and Janet encourages explorers, by bike or on foot; ever helpful and kind, she is a local who knows the patch well. The 1860s house keeps its Victorian features, bedrooms are quiet and simple and the double has a view to Blue Anchor Bay and Dunster castle and church. All is homely, with stripped pine, cream curtains, fresh flowers, garden fruit and home-laid eggs for breakfast. *Children & pets by arrangement.*

Ethical Collection: Environment; Food. See page 420.

Price	£70. Singles from £35.
Rooms	3: 1 double, 2 twins/doubles.
Meals	Packed lunch from £3.50. Restaurants 2-minute walk.
Closed	Christmas.
Directions	From Williton, A39 for Minehead for 8 miles. Left to Dunster. There, right fork into 'The Ball'. At T-junc. at end of road, right. House 75 yds on right.

10% off stays Mon–Fri. Lifts to walking start points. Free pick-up.

	Janet Lamacraft
	Higher Orchard,
	30 St George's Street, Dunster TA24 6RS
Tel	+44 (0)1643 821915
Mobile	+44 (0)7896 464420
Email	lamacraft@higherorchard.fsnet.co.uk
Web	www.higherorchard-dunster.co.uk

Entry 428   Map 2

Somerset

The Old Priory

The 12th-century priory leans against its church, with a rustic gate, a walled garden, a tumble of flowers. Both house and hostess are dignified, unpretentious and friendly. Here are old oak tables, flagstones, wood panelling, higgledy-piggledy corridors and large bedrooms in the softest colours. But an ancient English house in a sweet Somerset village needs a touch of pepper and relaxed, cosmopolitan Jane adds her own special flair with artistic touches here and there, and books and dogs for company. Peaceful spots and scents in the lovely garden, Dunster Castle above on the hill and gentle walks from the door.

Ethical Collection: Food. See page 420.

Price	£90. Singles by arrangement.
Rooms	3: 1 twin, 1 four-poster; 1 double with separate shower.
Meals	Pubs/restaurants 5-minute walk.
Closed	Christmas.
Directions	From A39 into Dunster, right at blue sign 'Unsuitable for Goods Vehicles'. Follow until church; house adjoined.

Free pick-up from Dunster station. Jar of Exmoor honey & free-range eggs (when available).

	Jane Forshaw
	The Old Priory,
	Priory Green, Dunster TA24 6RY
Tel	+44 (0)1643 821540
Web	www.theoldpriory-dunster.co.uk

Entry 429 Map 2

Somerset

The Old House

Coleridge is said to have stayed here, and been inspired by the walks; but if the muse fails to strike you, bedrooms are in a private wing and elegant comforts abound. The enormous Coleridge Suite has a sofa, good books, an open fire, views to the beautiful garden and a sleigh bed; nip across your own landing to the bathroom, freshly decorated in blue and white. Sarah's Room is feminine, pink and pretty with white armchairs. Amiable Manor serves breakfast in the dining room or garden: soft fruits, full English, or smoked salmon and scrambled eggs. The quiet village has a bistro and bracing walks are in every direction.

Price	£75-£85. Singles from £60.
Rooms	2: 1 twin/double; 1 suite with separate bath.
Meals	Pub/bistro 50 yds.
Closed	Rarely.
Directions	M5, Bridgwater junc.; follow A39 towards Minehead 8 miles. Left into Nether Stowey; after 300 yds right into courtyard of house.

	Manor & Ann Scourfield
	The Old House,
	Nether Stowey TA5 1LJ
Tel	+44 (0)1278 732392
Email	scourfieldfam@yahoo.co.uk
Web	www.theoldhouse-quantocks.co.uk

Entry 430 Map 2

Somerset

Parsonage Farm

The Quantock Hills are wonderful for walking and cycling, with the Coleridge Way starting down the lane. In this 17th-century farmhouse relaxed hosts give you easy comfort with quarry floors, books, a cosy log-fired sitting room and spacious bedrooms with tranquil country views. Suki, from Vermont, has turned a stable into a studio – her pots and paintings add charm to the décor. Breakfast by the fire is a feast: homemade bread and jam, eggs from the hens, juice from the orchard, porridge and pancakes with maple syrup. Relax in the beautiful walled kitchen garden; there's an outdoor wood-fired pizza oven too! *Over twos welcome.*

Ethical Collection: Environment; Food; Community. See page 420.

Price	£60–£80. Singles £45–£65.
Rooms	3: 1 double (extra sofabed), 1 twin/double (extra sofabed); 1 double sharing bath.
Meals	Supper £10. Dinner, 2-3 courses, £20–£25. Pub/restaurant 1 mile.
Closed	Christmas.
Directions	A39 Bridgwater-Minehead. 7 miles on, left at Cottage Inn for Over Stowey; 1.8 miles; house on right after church. Signed car park.

 10% off room rate Mon-Thurs. Free pick-up from local bus/train station. Late checkout (12pm).

Susan Lilienthal
Parsonage Farm,
Over Stowey, Nether Stowey TA5 1HA
Tel +44 (0)1278 733237
Mobile +44 (0)7928 368836
Email suki@parsonfarm.co.uk
Web www.parsonfarm.co.uk

Entry 431 Map 2

Somerset

Cothelstone Manor

A gloriously grand manor quite without stuffiness, on the edge of Exmoor, gazing up to the Quantock Hills. Nigel and Finny, naturally friendly, invite you into their family home. Inside, find elegant rooms, logs burning in the galleried hall, family photos, art and beautiful antiques; all gleams. Bedrooms have pretty views through mullion-leaded windows, immaculate linen and comfortable bathrooms with fluffy towels and flowers. Wake to Sunday church bells and breakfasts of local bacon and sausages, homemade jams and eggs from hens who roam the walled gardens. The Coleridge Way is on the doorstep.

Price	£98. Singles £75.
Rooms	2 doubles (extra bed available).
Meals	Picnic hamper £10. Pub within 2 miles.
Closed	Rarely.
Directions	M5 junc.25. A358 towards Minehead. At turning to Bishops Lydeard, up through village for approx. 1.5 miles. House signed.

Nigel & Finny Muers-Raby
Cothelstone Manor,
Cothelstone, Taunton TA4 3DS
Tel +44 (0)1823 433480
Mobile +44 (0)7709 434411
Email finny@cothelstonemanor.co.uk
Web www.cothelstonemanor.co.uk

Entry 432 Map 2

Somerset

Bashfords Farmhouse

A feeling of warmth and happiness pervades this exquisite 17th-century farmhouse in the Quantock hills. The Ritchies love doing B&B – after 18 years! – and interiors have a homely feel with well-framed prints, natural fabrics, comfortable sofas, and a sitting room with inglenook, sofas and books. Bedrooms are pretty, fresh and large and look over the cobbled courtyard or open fields. Charles and Jane couldn't be nicer, know about local walks (the Macmillan Way runs by) and love to cook: local meat and game, tarte tatin, homemade bread and jams. A delightful garden rambles up the hill; the pub is just a minute away.

Price	£70. Singles £40.
Rooms	3: 1 twin/double; 1 twin/double with separate shower; 1 twin with separate bath.
Meals	Dinner £27.50. Supper £22.50. Pub 75 yds.
Closed	Rarely.
Directions	M5 junc. 25. A358 for Minehead. Leave A358 at West Bagborough turning. Through village for 1.5 miles. Farmhouse 3rd on left past pub.

Charles & Jane Ritchie
Bashfords Farmhouse,
West Bagborough, Taunton TA4 3EF
Tel +44 (0)1823 432015
Email info@bashfordsfarmhouse.co.uk
Web www.bashfordsfarmhouse.co.uk

Entry 433 Map 2

Somerset

Rock House

Tucked away in an AONB, near the Quantocks and Exmoor, this elegant Georgian house hides behind a tall hedge in a sleepy village. Deborah greets her guests with impeccable manners and scrumptious biscuits; take tea in the drawing room where fresh flowers are beautifully arranged and there are books to read. Bedrooms are well-presented and full of thoughtful touches like fresh milk and a torch; bathrooms have generous towels and Molton Brown lotions. The Rock House fry-up will set you up for miles of walking, or a quick stroll to the top of the pretty garden with its croquet lawn. *Children & pets by arrangement.*

Price	From £80. Singles from £50.
Rooms	2: 1 twin/double; 1 double (extra single bed) with separate bath.
Meals	Pub 100 yds.
Closed	Christmas.
Directions	M5 exit 25, signs to A358 Minehead. Left to Halse. Rock House in middle of village, near the pub.

Christopher & Deborah Wolverson
Rock House,
Halse, Taunton TA4 3AF
Tel +44 (0)1823 432956
Mobile +44 (0)7720 928951
Email dwolverson@rockhousesomerset.co.uk
Web www.rockhousesomerset.co.uk

Entry 434 Map 2

Somerset

Causeway Cottage

Robert and Lesley are ex-restaurateurs, so guests heap praise on their food, most of which is sourced from a local butcher and fishmonger; charming Lesley is an author, runs cookery courses and once taught at Prue Leith's. This is the perfect, pretty Somerset cottage, with an apple orchard and views to the church across a cottage garden and a field. The bedrooms are light, restful and have a country-style simplicity with their green check bedspreads, white walls and antique pine furniture; guests have their own comfortable sitting room. Easy access to the M5 yet with a rural feel. Very special. *Children over ten welcome.*

Price	£78. Singles by arrangement.
Rooms	3: 1 double, 2 twins.
Meals	Supper from £25. Pub/restaurant 0.75 miles.
Closed	Christmas.
Directions	From M5 junc. 26, West Buckland road for 0.75 miles. 1st left just before stone building. Bear right; 3rd house at end of lane, below church.

Lesley & Robert Orr
Causeway Cottage,
West Buckland, Taunton TA21 9JZ

Tel	+44 (0)1823 663458
Email	causewaybb@talktalk.net
Web	www.causewaycottage.co.uk

Entry 435   Map 2

Somerset

Frog Street Farm House

Through a pastoral landscape, past green paddocks and fine thoroughbreds, to a beautiful longhouse set in pretty secluded gardens surrounded by 130 acres. Its heart dates back to 1436 and its renovation is remarkable, highlighting beamed ceilings, Jacobean panelling and open fireplaces. Louise and David, brimful of enthusiasm for both house and guests, give you four exquisite bedrooms in French country style, one with its own sitting room – very romantic. Louise happily does evening meals and hosts small house parties with ease. After a day out, return to great leather sofas and a wood-burning stove. What value!

Price	From £90. Singles from £70. Suite from £140.
Rooms	4: 3 doubles, 1 family suite for 4.
Meals	Dinner, 3 courses, £25. Pubs within 2.5 miles.
Closed	Rarely.
Directions	A358 to Illminster. 1st exit to Hatch Beauchamp. At Hatch Inn left into Station Rd. Left after 0.5 miles; over humpback bridge, Frog St Farm in front.

10% off room rate Mon-Thurs.

Louise & David Farrance
Frog Street Farm House,
Hatch Beauchamp, Taunton TA3 6AF

Tel	+44 (0)1823 481883
Mobile	+44 (0)7811 700789
Email	frogstreet@hotmail.com
Web	www.frogstreet.co.uk

Entry 436   Map 2

Somerset

Pyle House

Swoop down onto a buttermilk yellow lodge with landscaped gardens hugged by Somerset's rolling green fields: it's so well renovated you'd never guess it was an 1800s hunting lodge for Whitestaunton Estate. Past the flagstoned hallway, discover a house of pristine paintwork, valley views, swish bathrooms and immaculate bedrooms. Madeleine loves to cook so expect a breakfast worthy of the fine china it comes on; Michael's pride and joy are his fossil finds – proof of the area's antiquity. It's perfect for walkers: kick boots into the drying room, browse through maps, stroll to the pub for a meal. *Children over ten welcome.*

Price	From £70. Singles £45.
Rooms	3: 1 suite, 1 twin/double (with sofabed);1 double with separate shower.
Meals	Pub/restaurant 0.5 miles.
Closed	Christmas & New Year.
Directions	From Chard A30 for Honiton. After 4 miles, right for Howley. Take 2nd right through stone pillars, signed Pyle, to cream house at end of drive.

Free pick-up from local bus/train station.

Madeleine Berry
Pyle House,
Whitestaunton, Chard TA20 3DZ
Tel +44 (0)1460 239268
Email info@pylehouse.co.uk
Web www.pylehouse.co.uk

Entry 437   Map 2

Somerset

Huntstile Organic Farm

Catapult yourself into country life in the foothills of the Quantocks; make that connection between the rolling green hills, the idyllic munching animals and the delicious, organic food on your plate; here it is understood. Lizzie and John buzz with energy in this gorgeous old house with Jacobean panelling and huge walk-in fireplaces, two sitting rooms, sweet and cosy rustic bedrooms, a café, and a restaurant serving their own meat, eggs and vegetables. House parties, weddings, team building, a stone circle for hand-fasting ceremonies – all come under Lizzie's happy and efficient umbrella. And there are woodlands to roam.

Ethical Collection: Environment; Food; Community. See page 420.

Price	From £85. Singles from £60.
Rooms	7: 3 doubles; 1 twin/double sharing bath; 1 family room. Apartment: 1 double, 1 twin with sitting room.
Meals	Dinner, 3 courses, £20-£25. Packed lunch £5-£7.50. Pub/restaurant 3 miles.
Closed	22 December-7 January.
Directions	M5 junc. 24, North Petherton. Before village right to Goathurst and Broomfield. Take 2nd right to Goathurst. House 1 mile on right.

10% off room rate Mon-Thurs. Bottle of organic wine with stays of 2 nights.

Lizzie Myers
Huntstile Organic Farm,
Goathurst, Bridgwater TA5 2DQ
Tel +44 (0)1278 662358
Email huntstile@live.co.uk
Web www.huntstileorganicfarm.co.uk

Entry 438   Map 2

Somerset

Blackmore Farm

Come for atmosphere and architecture: the Grade I-listed manor-farmhouse is remarkable. Medieval stone walls, a ceiling open to a beamed roof, ecclesiastical windows, a fire blazing in the Great Hall. Ann and Ian look after guests and farm (900 acres plus dairy) with equal enthusiasm. Furnishings are comfortable not lavish, bedrooms are cavernous and the oak-panelled suite (with secret stairway intact) takes up an entire floor. Breakfast at a 20-foot polished table in the carpeted but baronial Great Hall, store your bikes in the chapel, visit the calves in the dairy. A rare place. *Farm shop on site.*

Price	£100. Singles £50.
Rooms	4: 1 double, 1 twin, 1 four-poster, 1 suite.
Meals	Pubs/restaurants 5-minute walk.
Closed	Rarely.
Directions	From Bridgwater, A39 west around Cannington. After 2nd r'bout, follow signs to Minehead; 1st left after Yeo Valley creamery; 1st house on right.

 10% off room rate Mon-Thurs.

Use your Sawday's Gift Card here.

	Ann Dyer
	Blackmore Farm,
	Cannington, Bridgwater TA5 2NE
Tel	+44 (0)1278 653442
Email	dyerfarm@aol.com
Web	www.dyerfarm.co.uk

Entry 439   Map 2

Somerset

Church Cottage

Partly clothed in English garden and with views to the church, this 400-year-old cottage has wooden beams, low ceilings and wonky walls. Ignore the modern house on the other side of the road and restore your senses with neutral colours, soft cushions, a flash of Thompson gazelle skin, the whiff of woodsmoke and floppy roses on a scrubbed table. Caroline rustles up a fine breakfast in her calm kitchen; relax in the charming walled garden or sitting room. Bedrooms are simple and comfy – pine furniture, good linen; the Potting Shed is a private, sweet nest for two. Miles of walking straight from the door.

Price	£75-£90. Singles £65-£80.
Rooms	2: 1 double. Potting Shed: 1 double.
Meals	Pubs 1 mile.
Closed	Rarely.
Directions	M5 exit 23 to A39. 7 miles; left to Shapwick. Cottage on left next to church.

10% off stays of 3 or more nights Mon-Thurs.

	Caroline Hanbury Bateman
	Church Cottage, Station Road,
	Shapwick, Bridgwater TA7 9NH
Tel	+44 (0)1458 210904
Mobile	+44 (0)7875 598155
Email	c.hanbury.bateman@btinternet.com
Web	www.churchcottageshapwick.co.uk

Entry 440   Map 3

Somerset

Edington House

Step back in time into this rambling, ancient English country house, where twists and turns link panelled rooms replete with silk curtains, portraits, fireplaces, chandeliers, objets d'art. Families will love exploring the countless sitting and dining rooms and large sweeping gardens: discover a pool, tennis court, Georgian summerhouse, kitchen garden, orchard and ponies. Your easy-going, well-travelled hosts (she Austrian, he English) want guests to enjoy it all. Bedrooms are just as grandiose, with draped floral fabrics, antiques and patterned wallpapers. Inge is a serious cook and suppers are a highlight.

Somerset

The Lynch Country House

Peace, seclusion and privacy at this immaculate Regency house in lush Somerset. First-floor bedrooms are traditionally grand, attic rooms are small but bright; those in the coach house have a more modern feel. Deep warm colours prevail, fabrics are flowery and carpets soft green. You'll feel as warm as toast and beautifully looked after. A stone staircase goes right to the top where the observatory lets in a cascading light; the flagged hall, high ceilings, long windows and private tables at breakfast create a country-house hotel feel. A lovely garden has a pond, wildlife and a terrace from which to drink it all in.

Price	£110–£130. Singles £120.
Rooms	3: 1 four-poster, 1 double, 1 family suite for 3-4.
Meals	Dinner, 4 courses, £35. Supper, 2 courses, £20. Pub/restaurant 1 mile.
Closed	Christmas.
Directions	Leave M5 junc. 23, A30 dir. Glastonbury. After 4 miles left signed Edington. Left at crossroads in village; house immediately on left behind high wall.

🧳 10% off room rate Mon-Thurs. 10% off stays of 2 or more nights.

Price	£75–£110. Singles £65–£75.
Rooms	9: 1 double, 1 twin, 2 four-posters; 1 double (extra single bed) with separate bath. Coach house: 3 doubles, 1 twin.
Meals	Sunday lunch from £15 (bookings only). Restaurants 5-minute walk.
Closed	Rarely.
Directions	From London, M3 junc. 8, A303. At Podimore r'bout A372 to Somerton. At junc. of North St & Behind Berry.

	Inge Sprawson
	Edington House,
	Edington TA7 9JS
Tel	+44 (0)1278 722238
Email	inge@edingtonhouse.co.uk
Web	www.edingtonhouse.co.uk

	Mike McKenzie
	The Lynch Country House,
	4 Behind Berry, Somerton TA11 7PD
Tel	+44 (0)1458 272316
Email	enquiries@thelynchcountryhouse.co.uk
Web	www.thelynchcountryhouse.co.uk

🚶🐦🐕🛶📷📶🛁🏊♿🍴

🚶🐦👤🛶📷📶🚂🍾🍴

Somerset

Barwick Farm House

A 17th-century farmhouse sitting in ten acres of organically managed land dotted with Dorset sheep, hens and horses. Charming Angela and Robin have limewashed walls in vibrant colours, restored ancient elm boards and exposed the sandstone fireplace lintels in this interesting house full of open fires, books and flowers. Roomy bedrooms have good cotton sheets, comfortable beds and a mishmash of styles; one bathroom, painted bubble-gum pink, has a free-standing bath and views over fields. Wake to birdsong and the sizzle of good local bacon; excellent walking and cycling start from the door and there are gardens to visit.

Ethical Collection: Environment; Food. See page 420.

Price	£60-£75. Singles from £35.
Rooms	2: 1 double, 1 family suite for 4.
Meals	'Early Bird' packed breakfasts also available. Restaurant 100 yds.
Closed	Rarely.
Directions	A37 to Dorchester; 0.25 miles outside Yeovil, 1st exit off r'bout (opp. Red House pub) following signs to Little Barwick House restaurant. House in fork of road.

 Home-grown produce. Free pick-up from local bus/train station.

	Angela Nicoll
	Barwick Farm House,
	Barwick, Yeovil BA22 9TD
Tel	+44 (0)1935 410779
Mobile	+44 (0)7967 385307
Email	info@barwickfarmhouse.co.uk
Web	www.barwickfarmhouse.co.uk

Entry 443   Map 3

Somerset

Yarlington House

A mellow Georgian manor surrounded by impressive parkland, romantic rose gardens, apple tree pergola and laburnum walk. Your hosts are friendly and flexible, artists with an eye for quirky detail; Carolyn's embroideries are everywhere. Something to astound at every turn: fine copies of 18th-century wallpapers, elegant antiques, statues with hats atop and tremendous art. Traditional bedrooms with glorious garden views and proper 50s bathrooms have a faded charm. Enjoy a full English breakfast, grape juice from the glasshouse vines, log fires and lovely local walks. Surprising, unique. *Children by arrangement.*

Price	£120. Singles £60.
Rooms	2: 1 double, 1 twin.
Meals	Pubs/restaurants within 0.5 miles.
Closed	25 July-23 August.
Directions	From Wincanton take A371 to Castle Cary. After Holbrook House take 2nd left, then 3rd right (both signed Yarlington). First stone gateposts on left.

 Use of studio area and tour of house & garden. 10% off room rate Mon-Thurs.

	Charles and Carolyn de Salis
	Yarlington House,
	Yarlington, Wincanton BA9 8DY
Tel	+44 (0)1963 440344
Email	carolyn.desalis@yarlingtonhouse.com

Entry 444   Map 3

Somerset

Rectory Farm House

Lavinia has showered love and attention on her early Georgian house and garden in a landscape that has changed little since the 18th century. Beams, sash windows, wood fires and high ceilings are the backdrop for polished family furniture and delightfully arranged flowers. Good-sized bedrooms in restful colours have starched linen, fluffy bathrobes and binoculars for watching the wildlife; the beautiful, peaceful garden draws deer, badgers, foxes, hares. Breakfast is so local it could walk to the table – and includes homemade marmalade and jams. A lovely summery place – and only a mile off the A303!

Price	From £90. Singles from £65.
Rooms	3: 1 double; 1 twin/double, 1 double sharing bath (let to same party only).
Meals	Dinner £30. Pub 0.5 miles.
Closed	Christmas & New Year.
Directions	From the east, exit A303 on to B3081 for Bruton. After 1 mile, left into Rectory Lane. House 0.25 miles on right.

Michael & Lavinia Dewar
Rectory Farm House, Charlton Musgrove, Wincanton BA9 8ET
Tel +44 (0)1963 34599
Mobile +44 (0)7775 651868
Email l.dewar@btconnect.com
Web www.rectoryfarmhouse.com

Entry 445   Map 3

Somerset

Bratton Farmhouse

A gorgeous old (1600) house around which strut hens and happy Jacob sheep. Intelligent and generous Suellen has created contemporary, warm interiors and the bedrooms are a joy. One, in the main house, has oak-panelled walls, bucolic views and a vast bed with old French embroidered linen. Another, in a newly converted studio across the courtyard, gives you complete independence with your own stylish sitting room made cosy with a wood-burner; lovers can laze till late in a huge nest of feather and down. Good books and art surround you, breakfasts are delicious and imaginative, and walks are from the door.

Ethical Collection: Food. See page 420.

Price	From £80. Singles from £65.
Rooms	3: 2 doubles, each with separate bath/shower. Studio: 1 twin/double & sitting room.
Meals	Lunch £10. Dinner, 3 courses, £25. Packed lunch £5. Pub 2 miles.
Closed	Rarely.
Directions	A303 then A371 signed Wincanton & Castle Cary. Follow signs to Castle Cary. After approx. 2.5 miles, right to Bratton Seymour. House 0.4 miles on right.
	10% off stays Mon-Thurs. Local food. Late checkout (12pm). Bottle of wine with dinner.

Suellen Dainty
Bratton Farmhouse, Bratton Seymour, Wincanton BA9 8BY
Tel +44 (0)1963 32458
Mobile +44 (0)7780 848567
Email sdainty52@googlemail.com
Web www.brattonfarmhouse.co.uk

Entry 446   Map 3

Somerset

The Cottage

An old farmworker's house, modernised and freshly spruced, stands proud in verdant countryside. Long views from the clipped garden drift into the distance; warm Sue (plus cute Jack Russells) greets you. You sleep in the extension to the front of the house; a double with views down the valley, a twin with check curtains. Both have comfy beds, book-filled shelves, homely touches and peacefulness. Breakfast is a leisurely affair of local bacon and eggs. Lounge about in the Beggs' living room filled with good furniture and family photos or tramp off on an inspiring walk: Leland trail, MacMillan Way... you're spoilt for choice.

Price	£70. Singles from £45.
Rooms	2: 1 twin/double; 1 twin/double with separate bath.
Meals	Dinner £25. Packed lunch £5. Pub/restaurant 1 mile.
Closed	Christmas & rarely.
Directions	Maggs Lane east off the A371, halfway between Wincanton and Shepton Mallet.

 10% off room rate Mon-Thurs. Lifts & pick-ups to walking start/finish points.

Susan Begg
The Cottage,
Ansford Park Farm, Ansford Park,
Maggs Lane,
Castle Cary BA7 7JJ
Tel +44 (0)1963 351066
Email beggsusan@tiscali.co.uk

Entry 447   Map 3

Somerset

Westbrook House

David is an interior designer; Keith does gardens – hence this blend of good taste and style in a revamped 1870s house with generous, well-tended grounds. Wander through a young orchard, spot unusual plants, sit on stone benches or a sunny patio; a wildlife meadow contrasts with clipped lawns. Inside, every object has a story (your hosts are full of smiles and stories too): tapestries from India, a mirrored cabinet from an officer's mess, ornate brass lanterns. Light floods into the dining room as you breakfast on local treats – all the while absorbing the peace of this tranquil hamlet, where cows amble calmly down the lane.

Price	From £95. Singles £65.
Rooms	3: 1 double, 1 twin; 1 double with separate bath.
Meals	Dinner £30. Pub/restaurant 4 miles.
Closed	Rarely.
Directions	From Glastonbury A361 to Shepton Mallet. After 2 miles, right for W. Bradley. Signed for W. Bradley; at fork in road, right for Baltonsborough. House on left.

Keith Anderson & David Mendel
Westbrook House,
West Bradley, Glastonbury BA6 8LS
Tel +44 (0)1458 850604
Email mail@westbrook-bed-breakfast.co.uk
Web www.westbrook-bed-breakfast.co.uk

Entry 448   Map 3

Somerset

Chalice Hill House

You can see St John's spire poking out over the treetops: vibrant Glastonbury buzzes just below. Fay's contemporary artistic flair mingles naturally with the classical frame of this Georgian house, where grand mirrors, wooden floors, gentle colours and loads of books create an interesting feel. The bedrooms are enchanting, not at all understated: carved oak Slavic sleigh beds, embroidered Indian cotton bedspreads and views of the dovecote, wedding cake tree and Chalice Hill beyond. Weekend breakfasts are leisurely, served with panache (and optional chilli jam!). Exotic, comfortable elegance, a beautiful garden and a lovely hostess.

Price	£110. Singles £80.
Rooms	3: 2 doubles, 1 twin.
Meals	Pubs/restaurants 5-minute walk.
Closed	Rarely.
Directions	From top of Glastonbury High Street, right; 2nd left into Dod Lane. Past Chalice Hill Close; right into driveway.

10% off room rate Mon-Thurs.

Fay Hutchcroft
Chalice Hill House,
Dod Lane, Glastonbury BA6 8BZ
Tel   +44 (0)1458 830828
Email   mail@chalicehill.co.uk
Web   www.chalicehill.co.uk

Entry 449   Map 3

Somerset

Chindit House

Inside this light and elegant Edwardian mansion you will find fine architectural features, charming furniture, fresh flowers, vibrant paintings and compelling sculptures. There are long views over garden and town from the large, light sitting room; bedrooms have spoilingly serious mattresses, good art, thick curtains and sleek, contemporary bathrooms. Breakfast, with speciality breads, is enormous and locally sourced. Peter, a sculptor, and Felicity, an art consultant, are easy-going and fun. You are a short hop from the town with its lively mix of exotic shops and colourful characters.

Price	£100-£125. Singles £70-£85.
Rooms	4: 2 doubles; 2 singles with shared bath (let to same party only).
Meals	Pubs/restaurants 500 yds.
Closed	Rarely.
Directions	In the centre of Glastonbury. Left at top of High Street on to Wells Road. House is about 200 yds along on left – just before corner with St Edmunds Road.

10% off room rate Mon-Thurs.
Bottle of wine in your room.
Late checkout (12pm).

Peter Smith & Felicity Wright
Chindit House,
23 Wells Road, Glastonbury BA6 9DN
Tel   +44 (0)1458 830404
Mobile   +44 (0)7855 034495
Email   enquiries@chindit-house.co.uk
Web   www.chindit-house.co.uk

Entry 450   Map 3

Somerset

Upper Crannel Farm Barn

Your views, across sheep and the lush flat Levels, reach to both Glastonbury and Wells; birds wing across a vast, silent sky. Phoebe has created a magical place: up you climb to the first floor of the barn, into a huge sitting room with a vast medieval painted fireplace. Each room is a work of art, with stacks of it on the walls – the kitchen is handsome and seductive, the bedroom is generous and richly clad. Breakfast will be left for you to cook when you want, you can walk across fields to climb Glastonbury Tor and Wells is just five miles. This house is a treat, and Phoebe is too. *Min. two night stay.*

Somerset

The Coach House

Take a glass of wine to your private courtyard and absorb the peace; or picnic in the lush gardens. In the hamlet of Dulcote, a mile from Wells, is a converted coach house flooded with light, full of character and with the latest mod cons. Downstairs, a black and white zebra theme plays; upstairs (white walls, snowy duvets, soft carpets, high beams) are views that reach to the Mendips. And then there's Karen, full of ideas for your stay, who leaves delicious goodies in your fridge so you can breakfast in your jim-jams. For romantic couples or a girls' weekend, this is B&B at its most luxurious – and so private!

Price	£140.
Rooms	1 double with sitting room & kitchen (extra beds available).
Meals	Pubs/restaurants 2.5 miles.
Closed	Rarely.
Directions	A39 north of Glastonbury towards Wells. From r'bout by hospital go approx. 0.3 miles. At lollipops sharp left; follow single track. After one mile small bridge straight ahead and entrance to long tree-lined drive.

Local food/produce in your room.
10% off room rate Mon-Thurs.

Phoebe Judah
Upper Crannel Farm Barn,
Glastonbury BA6 9AD
Tel +44 (0)1458 831758
Email phoebe.judah@btinternet.com

Entry 451   Map 3

Price	£95.
Rooms	Coach House: 1 double, 1 twin & sitting room, sofabeds, kitchen, shower (same party only).
Meals	Pubs within 2 miles.
Closed	Rarely.
Directions	Directions on booking.

Karen Smallwood
The Coach House, Little Fountains,
Dulcote, Wells BA5 3NU
Tel +44 (0)1749 678777
Mobile +44 (0)7789 778880
Email stay@littlefountains.co.uk
Web www.littlefountains.co.uk

Entry 452   Map 3

Somerset

Manor Farm

Hens, ducks and geese stroll around the pond and the peace is supreme. And there's a magical view of the cathedral: you can walk to Wells across the fields. Ros, a geologist and keen walker, looks after guests with immense kindness and is happy for folk to linger. The house is ancient and much loved (massive low beams, creaking floorboards), packed with books, pictures and a comfy mishmash of furniture; a log fire warms the garden suite in winter and French windows open to a walled garden, illuminated at night. Water comes from the spring, breakfast can be a different treat each day – in the lovely conservatory in summer. Bliss.

Price	£75–£95. Singles from £45.
Rooms	4: 1 suite & sitting room; 2 doubles; 1 twin/double with separate bath/shower;
Meals	Packed lunch & light meals from £5. Pubs/restaurants 1 mile.
Closed	Rarely.
Directions	From Wells, A371 for Shepton Mallet for 1 mile; left onto B3139. In Dulcote, left at stone fountain. House on right after Manor Barn.
🧳	Free pick-up from local bus/train station. 10% off stays of 4 or more nights.
🎁	Use your Sawday's Gift Card here.

Rosalind Bufton
Manor Farm,
Dulcote, Wells BA5 3PZ
Tel   +44 (0)1749 672125
Mobile   +44 (0)7597 021708
Email   rosalind.bufton@talktalk.net
Web   www.wells-accommodation.co.uk

Entry 453   Map 3

Somerset

Hillview Cottage

Don't tell too many of your friends about this place! It's an unpretentious ex-quarryman's cottage presided over by Catherine, a warm-spirited and cultured host who makes fresh coffee, tells you about the area and can even show you around Wells Cathedral (she's an official guide). This is a comfy tea-and-cakes family home with rugs on wooden floors, antique quilts, an old Welsh dresser and elevated views. The bedrooms have a French feel, the bathroom has an armchair for chatting, and there's a friendly sitting room with an open fire. Glorious walks and excellent value. *Self-catering in Garden Studio.*

Price	From £70. Singles from £35.
Rooms	2: 1 twin/double; 1 twin sharing bath (2nd room let to same party only).
Meals	Pubs 5-minute walk.
Closed	Rarely.
Directions	From Wells A371 to middle of Croscombe. Right at red phone box & then immed. right into lane. House up on left after 0.25 miles. Straight ahead into signed drive.
🧳	Escorted walks. Tour of Wells Bishop's Palace. Late checkout (12pm).

Michael & Catherine Hay
Hillview Cottage, Paradise Lane,
Croscombe, Wells BA5 3RN
Tel   +44 (0)1749 343526
Mobile   +44 (0)7801 666146
Email   cathyhay@yahoo.co.uk

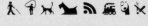

Entry 454   Map 3

Somerset

numbertwelve

Simple pleasures: after a day exploring England's smallest city or the Mendip Hills, return to tea on the balcony and sunlight glinting on Wells Cathedral. Cathy's family house is spacious, secluded, fantastically located, with a private guest wing. Settle on huge sofas around the sitting room fire; snuggle in new king beds; awaken to Cathedral bells, a south-facing view over the lovely walled garden and kedgeree or corned beef hash. Cathy's art studio is next door and she'll help connect you to the local community: tiny Wells – a five-minute walk – bustles with markets, music, art and life.

Price	£80–£95. Singles £60–£80.
Rooms	2 doubles.
Meals	Pub 0.25 miles. Restaurant 0.5 miles.
Closed	Rarely.
Directions	From Bristol A39, 1st left into College Rd. Round into North Rd, house 150 yds on right. Train station 20-minute drive, bus station 15-minute walk.

Cathy Charles
numbertwelve,
12 North Road, Wells BA5 2TJ
Tel +44 (0)1749 679406
Mobile +44 (0)7980 881861
Email stay@numbertwelve.info
Web www.numbertwelve.info

Entry 455   Map 3

Somerset

Stoberry House

Super swish B&B in this old coach house surrounded by 26 acres of parkland, but within walking distance of Wells; Frances has thought of everything to soothe you: bedrooms are sumptuous and spoiling – all differently styled, and most are in the main house, but there's one little love nest in a cottage. Bathrooms are vamped up and spacious. Breakfast is enormous: fresh fruit, porridge, boiled eggs with soldiers, prunes and berries, ham and salami, pancakes with grilled bacon, whatever you desire. Work it off with a stroll around the gorgeous gardens, and return to a choice of sitting rooms – one 40-foot long.

Ethical Collection: Community. See page 420.

Price	£75–£125. Singles £65–£97.50.
Rooms	3: 2 doubles, 1 twin/double.
Meals	Pubs/restaurants 0.5 miles.
Closed	Rarely.
Directions	A39 from Bristol, enter Wells, left into College Rd. Immediately left into Stoberry Park, follow track to Stoberry House at top of park.

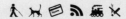 Use your Sawday's Gift Card here.

Frances Young
Stoberry House,
Stoberry Park, Wells BA5 3LD
Tel +44 (0)1749 672906
Email stay@stoberry-park.co.uk
Web www.stoberry-park.co.uk

Entry 456   Map 3

Somerset

Beryl

A lofty, mullioned, low-windowed home – yet light, bright and devoid of Victorian gloom. Every bedroom has a talking point – an extravagantly draped four-poster, an original bath clad in mahogany reached by a tiny private stair... The flowery rooms in the attic have a 'gothic revival' feel, thanks to arched doorways. Holly and her devoted staff serve delicious breakfasts in the sunny dining room, and drinks in the richly elegant drawing room. A jewellery boutique is run by her daughter in the Coach House. The old walled garden is full of flowers, roses, ancient figs and espaliered apples; the wonders of Wells lie just below.

Price	£85–£140.
Rooms	10: 2 doubles, 1 twin, 2 twins/doubles, 2 four-posters, 2 family rooms (1 with four-poster); 1 double with separate shower.
Meals	Pubs/restaurants within 1 mile. Kitchenette.
Closed	Christmas.
Directions	Wells B3139 Radstock. Signs to Horringtons; after church left, Hawkers Lane, by bus pull in. At top of lane, past Beryl sign; 500 yds to main gate.

10% off room rate Sun-Thurs.

Holly Nowell
Beryl,
Wells BA5 3JP
Tel   +44 (0)1749 678738
Email   stay@beryl-wells.co.uk
Web   www.beryl-wells.co.uk

Entry 457   Map 3

Somerset

Burnt House Farm

Lovers of modern art, clean lines, pale wood and clever lighting will be thrilled, and nature lovers – you are in a deeply rural valley with no roads, and acres of ancient woodland to explore. David, an architect, and charming Elizabeth have transformed their farmhouse into a cool, clean space: tea and cake when you arrive, relaxed breakfasts in a light, slate-floored room with an ash table and contemporary fireplace, big bedrooms with fabulous views in the softest creams, thick mattresses, squishy pillows and a gleaming new bathroom or shower. This feels remote but you are near to Bath, Wells and mystical Glastonbury.

Price	£80–£85. Family £130.
Rooms	3: 1 twin/double; 1 double, 1 twin sharing bath (let to same party only).
Meals	Pub/restaurant 2 miles.
Closed	Christmas & Boxing Day.
Directions	From Bristol A37 to Shepton Mallet and Yeovil until after Gurney Slade. Down hill, then right at chevron posts. Right at Fern Cottage to Burnt House Farm.

10% off room rate Mon-Thurs.

David & Elizabeth Parry
Burnt House Farm, Burnthouse Drove,
Windsor Hill, Shepton Mallet BA4 4JQ
Tel   +44 (0)1749 840185
Email   stay@burnthousedrove.co.uk
Web   www.burnthousedrove.co.uk

Entry 458   Map 3

Somerset

Pennard House

Splendid Pennard has been in Susie's family since the 1600s – a comfortably lived-in home with bedrooms as big as any we've seen. Discover a library and billiard room, a drawing room and dining room, and, upstairs, old-fashioned bedrooms with a mix of furniture, fine linen and beautiful views. The gardens are stunning with terraces leading on to sweeping lawns, roses, mature trees, a grass tennis court and a Victorian spring-fed swimming pool (swim with the newts!). The Georgian Coach House has been converted into a venue for weddings and conferences, and you're free to roam 60 tranquil acres of orchards, meadows and woods.

Price	£90. Singles from £45.
Rooms	4: 1 double, 2 twins; 1 twin/double with separate bath/shower.
Meals	Pub 2 miles.
Closed	Rarely.
Directions	From Shepton Mallet south on A37, through Pylle, over hill & next right to East Pennard. After 500 yds, right & follow lane past church to T-junc. at very top. House on left.

Free pick-up from local bus/train station.

Martin & Susie Dearden
Pennard House,
East Pennard, Shepton Mallet BA4 6TP
Tel   +44 (0)1749 860266
Mobile   +44 (0)7770 751357
Email   susie@pennardhouse.com

Entry 459   Map 3

Somerset

Broadgrove House

Down a long, private lane with views towards Alfred's Tower and Longleat, tranquillity: a 17th-century stone house with a walled cottage garden. Inside is just as special. Beams, flagstones and inglenook fireplaces have been sensitively restored; rugs, pictures, comfy sofas and polished antiques add warmth and serenity. The twin, at the end of the house, has its own sitting room. Breakfast on homemade and farmers' market produce before exploring Stourhead, Wells, Longleat. Sarah, engaging, well-travelled and a great cook, looks after guests and horses with enthusiasm. *Shooting available. Children by arrangement.*

Price	From £80. Singles £50.
Rooms	2: 1 twin & sitting room; 1 double with separate bath.
Meals	Pub/restaurant 1 mile.
Closed	Christmas.
Directions	Directions on booking.

10% off room rate Mon-Thurs.

Sarah Voller
Broadgrove House,
Leighton, Frome BA11 4PP
Tel   +44 (0)1373 836296
Mobile   +44 (0)7775 918388
Email   broadgrove836@tiscali.co.uk
Web   www.broadgrovehouse.co.uk

Entry 460   Map 3

Somerset

Claveys Farm

For the artistic seeker of inspiration, not those who thrill to standardised luxury. Fleur is a talented artist, Francis works for English Heritage, both have a passion for art, gardening and lively conversation. Rugs are time-worn, panelling and walls are distempered with natural pigment, bedrooms are better than simple, bathrooms old. From the Aga-warm kitchen of this lived-in, historic farmhouse come eggs from the hens, oak-smoked bacon from Fleur's rare-breed pigs and homemade bread and jams. Acres of fields, footpaths and woodland for long walks, and a garden for children to adore. Bring your woolly jumpers!

Ethical Collection: Food. See page 420.

Price	£70. Singles £50.
Rooms	2: 1 double/family; 1 twin with separate bath (shared with owner sometimes).
Meals	Dinner, 3 courses, £25. BYO. Packed lunch £7. Pub in village.
Closed	Rarely.
Directions	At Mells Green on Leigh-on-Mendip road SW from Mells (NGR ST718452). Past red phone box; house last on right before speed de-restriction signs. If lost, Mells PO, by village pond, has map outside.

	Fleur & Francis Kelly
	Claveys Farm,
	Mells, Frome BA11 3QP
Tel	+44 (0)1373 814651
Mobile	+44 (0)7968 055398
Email	bandb@fleurkelly.com

Entry 461   Map 3

Somerset

The Cyder Barn

Somerset cider was once pressed in this cute stone barn — now hugged by honeysuckle. Its beamed cathedral ceiling and new windows enclose a bijou studio for two. Pure pizzazz: spot-lit stone walls, dashing pinks, browns and terracottas on a king-size bed overhung by striped kilims, a swish wet room, and a gravel terrace and table in mature gardens alive with birds and bright colours. Step over to the main farmhouse for breakfast among art and antiques (for dinner, a good restaurant is opposite). Roger will relate the area's history and Jackie can show you her jewellery studio; both are happy, humorous and relaxed.

Price	£80.
Rooms	Barn: 1 twin/double.
Meals	Restaurant opposite.
Closed	Rarely.
Directions	Cottage & barn on Frome-Whatley road: 2nd house on right, past Whatley Village sign.

Free pick-up from local bus/train station.

	Jackie Truman
	The Cyder Barn, Park Farm Cottage,
	Whatley, Frome BA11 3JU
Tel	+44 (0)1373 836703
Mobile	+44 (0)7721 579814
Email	rwtrumanstamps.jtruman@virgin.net

Entry 462   Map 3

Somerset

The Old Vicarage

The vicarage sits at the foot of Jack and Jill's hill in a sleepy Mendip village. Your room has its own courtyard entrance and comfy sitting room, goose down on an antique French bed, beautiful carpets designed by Lizzy and a limestone wet room. Your hosts are informal and friendly and their home exudes charm: a medieval stone floor in the hall, old flagstones, flowers, wood-burners and a pretty kitchen. Hens potter in the garden, carp laze in the canal pond; breakfast when you want on a full English, garden compotes and delicious coffee. National Trust gems and splendid walking on the Colliers Way will keep you busy.

Price	£95.
Rooms	1 double & sitting room.
Meals	Pub 100 yds.
Closed	Christmas, two weeks in August & occasionally.
Directions	The Old Vicarage is at the centre of Kilmersdon opposite the church. The village is on the B3139 off the A362 Radstock to Frome road.

Elizabeth Ashard
The Old Vicarage, Church Street,
Kilmersdon, Radstock BA3 5TA

Tel	+44 (0)1761 436926
Email	lizzyashard@btinternet.com
Web	www.theoldvicaragesomerset.co.uk

Entry 463   Map 3

Somerset

Flint House

Off a village lane, up a sweeping drive, is an elegant 18th-century home with a private chapel. Smart yet relaxed, it's a perfect mix: a sophisticated sitting room with low valley views, a roaring fire in the snug. Be seduced by the Mendips in your modern-classic bedroom with roll top bath; and a cosy twin for a larger party. Breakfast treats await on the summer veranda, from pancakes to poached plums. Take to the tennis court or sit under wisteria, cake in hand, and gaze on the noble garden – Jacquie is loving its restoration. Pop to a local or arrange dinner with your relaxed hosts. Walks galore – and Bath irresistibly near.

Price	From £85. Singles £60.
Rooms	2: 1 double; 1 twin sharing shower (let to same party only).
Meals	Dinner, 3 courses, £20–£25. Picnic lunch £8. Afternoon tea £4. Pubs 10-minute walk.
Closed	Rarely.
Directions	Radstock A367 to Shepton Mallet. At r'bout B3139 to Frome, take right signed Holcombe. At village shop left into Common Lane. House after chapel on left through green gates.

10% off 2nd night.
Bottle of wine.

Jacquie Hamshaw Thomas
Flint House, Common Lane,
Holcombe, Radstock BA3 5DS

Tel	+44 (0)1761 232419
Mobile	+44 (0)7723 031378
Email	htsuk@btconnect.com
Web	www.flinthousebandb.co.uk

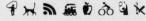

Entry 464   Map 3

Somerset

The Post House

Four centuries old and listed, this was Chewton Mendip's post office; now it's a delightful home with a sunny feel. Smiling, stylish Karen loves meeting new people — make the most of her and John's knowledge of Bath, Bristol and Wells. After a day's exploring, return to fresh, warm, lovely bedrooms and bathrooms furnished in gentle greys and creams. Huge flagstones cover the oldest part downstairs, there's a big stone fireplace in the Old Bakery Cottage and the odd low beam; pale walls display charming sketches from an artist friend, much of the furniture is French country, and a Gallic-rustic mood prevails.

Price	£80.
Rooms	3: 1 double; 1 double with separate bathroom. The Old Bakery Cottage: 1 double.
Meals	Pub 0.5 miles.
Closed	Rarely.
Directions	Situated 0.5 miles south of Chewton Mendip centre. The Post House can be found on left hand side heading south on A39. Private parking and entrance are found at rear of property.

Karen Price
The Post House, Bath Way,
Chewton Mendip, Wells BA3 4NS
Tel   +44 (0)1761 241704
Email   info@theposthousebandb.co.uk
Web   www.theposthousebandb.co.uk

Entry 465   Map 3

Somerset

Harptree Court

A gorgeous Georgian house that has been in Charles' family for generations. Inside all is elegant and grand, but this is very much a family home; there's a welcoming log fire in the hall and Charles and Linda are charming and relaxed. The interior gleams with flowers, art and polished wood, and the dining room looks onto the beautiful garden; warm, sunny bedrooms have delicate fabrics, china pieces and antiques, and bathrooms sparkle. An excellent breakfast of garden fruits, local honey and sausages sets you up for a walk in the grounds: acres of parkland with ponds, an ancient bridge, carpets of spring flowers. A peaceful delight.

Ethical Collection: Food; Community.
See page 420.

Price	£95–£120.
Rooms	4: 3 doubles, 1 twin/double.
Meals	Pub 300 yds.
Closed	Rarely.
Directions	Turn off A368 onto B3114 towards Chewton Mendip. After approx. 0.5 miles, right into drive entrance, straight after 1st x-roads. Left at top of drive.

Linda Hill
Harptree Court,
East Harptree, Bristol BS40 6AA
Tel   +44 (0)1761 221729
Mobile   +44 (0)7970 165576
Email   bandb@harptreecourt.co.uk
Web   www.harptreecourt.co.uk

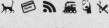

Entry 466   Map 3

Somerset

The Tithe Barn

You are in a quiet, well-kept village surrounded by softly rolling hills, but the joys of Bath and Bristol are a short drive. Down a narrow lane with lawns and orchard on either side, find Stephen and Pauline's pinky-red stone 15th-century tithe barn. Step up the spiral staircase leading to a gallery to the roomy, simple bedrooms; there are views from both rooms over the lovely garden and bathrooms have fine toiletries. You breakfast well in the conservatory: smoked salmon, local sausages and bacon, home-laid eggs, delicious homemade jams, honey from the garden. There are smart new stables for your horse, too.

Ethical Collection: Food; Community. See page 420.

Price	£70–£100. Singles £70–£90.
Rooms	2 doubles.
Meals	Pubs/restaurants 2 miles.
Closed	Rarely.
Directions	From Chew Magna on B3130, right after about 2 miles at little white cottage in middle of road. Right in village to Sandy Lane. House 200 yds on right.

   Free grazing if you bring your horse on holiday. 10% off room rate Mon–Thurs.

Stephen & Pauline Croucher
The Tithe Barn, Sandy Lane,
Stanton Drew, Bristol BS39 4EL
Tel +44 (0)1275 331887
Email stephen.jcroucher@btinternet.com
Web www.thetithebarnsomerset.co.uk

Entry 467   Map 3

Somerset

Burrington Farm

Can this really be ten minutes from Bristol airport? High in the Mendips, it is blissfully quiet and rural, with fabulous views. A narrow lane takes you to Ros and Barry's 15th-century longhouse – and the kindest of welcomes. Inside are rugs and flagstones, books, paintings and fine old furniture. Guests have a cosy low-beamed sitting room and bedrooms are charming; you'll need to be nimble to negotiate ancient steps and stairs. For those who prefer a bit more privacy there's a lovely family room in a separate green oak barn – stunningly converted. The garden is enchanting and you are free to roam. *Airport pick-up offered.*

Price	£80–£120.
Rooms	4: 1 double, 1 family; 2 doubles sharing bath (let to same party only).
Meals	Pub 10-minute walk.
Closed	Christmas.
Directions	A368 Bath to Weston-super-Mare, between Blagdon and Churchill. Take Burrington village sign, on to square with school on right. House 4th on left after Parish Rooms, immed. after Stable Cottage.

Yatton station pick-up. 10% off stays of 2 or more nights Mon–Thurs.

Use your Sawday's Gift Card here.

Barry & Ros Smith
Burrington Farm,
Burrington BS40 7AD
Tel +44 (0)1761 462127
Mobile +44 (0)7825 237144
Email unwind@burringtonfarm.com
Web www.unwindatburringtonfarm.co.uk

Entry 468   Map 3

Somerset

Barton Drove Cottage

Come for the views – on a clear day you can see the Black Mountains. The pretty cottage extension is tucked into the hill so the first-floor drawing room opens directly to the terrace. All is polished and spotless inside: pretty bedrooms have patterned rugs on soft carpets, goose down and crisp linen, fresh flowers, gleaming bathrooms and a loo with a view. Charming, child-friendly, Sarah gives you bacon and sausages from Mendip piggies, eggs from her hens, soft fruit from the garden and maybe pheasant casserole for supper. Roe deer in the field, primroses in the woods, wonderful walking on Wavering Down.

Ethical Collection: Food. See page 420.

Price	£70. Singles £35.
Rooms	2: 1 double; 1 twin with separate bath.
Meals	Dinner from £17.50. Packed lunch £5. Pub 1 mile.
Closed	Rarely.
Directions	From A38 0.5 miles up Winscombe Hill. When road begins to descend, left between houses onto unmade track. Cottage 100 yds on the left.

10% off room rate Mon-Thurs. 3-course dinner for the price of 2 courses.

	Sarah Gunn
	Barton Drove Cottage,
	Winscombe Hill,
	Winscombe BS25 1DJ
Tel	+44 (0)1934 842373
Email	sarahgunn2000@hotmail.com
Web	www.bartondrovecottage.com

Entry 469   Map 3

Somerset

Church House

Feel happy in this warm Georgian rectory with sweeping views over gardens, seaside homes and the dramatic Bristol channel. Tony and Jane are great fun, enormously generous and love what they do. Bedrooms are large, pristine and indulgent with goose down duvets as soft as a cloud, swish modern bathrooms, huge towels and thoughtful extras like fluffy hot water bottles and scrumptious biscuits. Breakfasts are a grand feast of eggs from their hens, organic sausages and homemade preserves, all served on delightful china at a long mahogany table. Take the whole house and be cosseted – great for large gatherings.

Price	From £80. Singles from £60.
Rooms	5: 4 doubles, 1 twin.
Meals	Pubs 400 yds.
Closed	Rarely.
Directions	M5 junc. 21, follow signs for Kewstoke. After Old Manor Inn on right, left up Anson Rd. At T-junc. right into Kewstoke Rd. On for 1 mile; church on right; drive between church & church hall.

10% off room rate Mon-Thurs. Free pick-up from local bus/train station.

	Jane & Tony Chapman
	Church House,
	27 Kewstoke Road, Kewstoke,
	Weston-super-Mare BS22 9YD
Tel	+44 (0)1934 633185
Email	churchhouse@kewstoke.net
Web	www.churchhousekewstoke.co.uk

Entry 470   Map 2

Staffordshire

Stoop House Farm

Step through a rosy arch from this enchanting 18th-century farmhouse: the view across garden, fields and valley will bowl you over. Inside, oak beams, heated flagged floors, a cast-iron range, a bedroom shot through with olive and gold. In this thriving conservation village (with lovely pub), the farm draws on the latest in green design, while two Andalusian horses share the grounds with sheep, pigs and poultry – expect superb eggs at breakfast! Your warm, lovely hosts, she a midwife, he a climber, share their passion for the outdoors with their guests – and the Peak District National Park lies at your feet.

Price	From £80. Singles £60.
Rooms	1 suite & sitting room.
Meals	Pub 1-minute walk.
Closed	Rarely.
Directions	From Leek A523 towards Ashbourne. At crossroads left B5053. Thro' Onecote, up hill then 2nd right signed Butterton. Thro' village past shop on right, 200 yds, then right fork. House 2nd on right.

Bottle of wine in your room.

Andrea Evans
Stoop House Farm,
Butterton,
Leek ST13 7SY
Tel +44 (0)1538 304486
Email bnfrench@yahoo.co.uk
Web www.stoophousefarm.co.uk

Entry 471 Map 8

Staffordshire

Martinslow Farm

High up in the Peaks, lost to the world with the most amazing, uninterrupted views, this listed 300-year-old farmhouse once sheltered donkeys… the accommodation has since stepped up a gear. The sitting room is warm and inviting with beams, log-burner and muted chintz. Peaceful, refurbished bedrooms in the stable block have a country, cosy feel; the Tack Room has mahogany beds and the rooms can interconnect for families. Diana and Richard love country pursuits, dogs and good company. Perfect tranquillity, a sheltered patio for great views, and delicious locally sourced food. *Children over nine welcome.*

Price	From £95. Singles £60.
Rooms	Stables: 1 double, 1 twin.
Meals	Dinner, 3 courses, £27.50. Supper £20. Pub 5-minute walk.
Closed	Rarely.
Directions	A523 Leek-Ashbourne. At Winkhill, signs to Grindon. Over x-roads, left at T-junc.; 300 yds; house on right below lane.

£5 off stays of 3 or more nights.

Richard & Diana Bloor
Martinslow Farm,
Winkhill,
Leek ST13 7PZ
Tel +44 (0)1538 304500
Email richard.bloor@btclick.com
Web www.martinslowfarm.co.uk

Entry 472 Map 8

Staffordshire

Manor House

A working rare-breed farm in an area of great beauty, a Jacobean farmhouse with oodles of history. Behind mullioned windows is a glorious interior crammed with curios and family pieces, panelled walls and wonky floors... hurl a log on the fire and watch it roar. Three rooms have four-posters; one bathroom flaunts rich red antique fabrics. Chris and Margaret are passionate hosts who serve perfect breakfasts (eggs from their own hens, sausages and bacon from their pigs and home-grown tomatoes) and give you the run of a garden resplendent with plants, vistas, tennis, croquet, two springer spaniels and one purring cat. Heaven.

Ethical Collection: Food. See page 420.

Price	£60-£75. Singles £38-£50.
Rooms	4: 3 four-posters, 1 double.
Meals	Pub/restaurant 1.5 miles.
Closed	Christmas.
Directions	From Uttoxeter, B5030 for Rocester. Beyond JCB factory, left onto B5031. At T-junc. after church, right onto B5032. 1st left for Prestwood. Farm 0.75 miles on right over crest of hill, through arch.

10% off stays of 2 or more nights.

Chris & Margaret Ball
Manor House, Prestwood,
Denstone, Uttoxeter ST14 5DD
Tel +44 (0)1889 590415
Mobile +44 (0)7976 767629
Email cm_ball@yahoo.co.uk
Web www.towersabovetherest.com

Entry 473 Map 8

Suffolk

Pavilion House

A conservation village surrounded by chalk grassland – famous for its flora, fauna and butterflies; marked walks are straight from this 16-year-old red-brick house. Friendly Gretta teaches cooking and you are in for a treat: homemade cake, enormous breakfasts with her own bread and jams, proper dinners or simple suppers. Sleep peacefully in traditional, comfortable bedrooms (one up, two down) with crisp linen and radios. There's a guest sitting room too: English comfort with an oriental feel, parquet floors, antiques, original drawings, a cosy log-burner. Wander the superb garden. Newmarket and Cambridge are close.

Price	£70. Singles £40-£50.
Rooms	3: 1 double, 1 twin/double, 1 single each with separate bath/shower.
Meals	Lunch from £10. Dinner from £25. BYO. Pub 1.5 miles.
Closed	Christmas.
Directions	4 miles south of Newmarket. A1304, over r'bout with horse statue, further 1.5 miles, then left to Dullingham. Pavilion House 1st on right after 1 mile. Train station 400 yds.

Bottle of wine in your room.

Gretta & David Bredin
Pavilion House, 133 Station Road,
Dullingham, Newmarket CB8 9UT
Tel +44 (0)1638 508005
Email gretta@thereliablesauce.co.uk
Web www.pavilionhousebandb.co.uk

Entry 474 Map 9

Suffolk

The Old Vicarage

Up the avenue of fine horse chestnut trees to find just what you'd expect from an old vicarage: a Pembroke table in the flagstoned hall, a refectory table sporting copies of *The Field*, a piano, silver pheasants, a log fire that warms the sitting room and homemade cake on arrival. The house is magnificent, with huge rooms and passageways. Comfy mattresses are dressed in old-fashioned counterpanes, and the double has hill views. Weave your way through the branches of the huge copper beech to the garden that Jane loves; she grows her own vegetables, keeps hens and cooks a fine breakfast. *Children over seven welcome.*

Price	£80. Singles £50.
Rooms	2: 1 double; 1 twin with separate bath. Extra single room off double (let to same party only).
Meals	Dinner £20. BYO. Packed lunch £6. Pub 1 mile.
Closed	Christmas.
Directions	Cambridge, A1307 Haverhill. Left Withersfield; T-junc., left. Almost 3 miles on, high yew hedge; 'Concealed Entrance' sign on left, sharp turn into drive.

Bottle of wine for stays of 3 or more nights.

Jane Sheppard
The Old Vicarage,
Great Thurlow, Newmarket CB9 7LE
Tel   +44 (0)1440 783209
Mobile   +44 (0)7887 717429
Email   s.j.sheppard@hotmail.co.uk

Entry 475   Map 9

Suffolk

The Old Manse Barn

A large, lush loft apartment in sleepy Suffolk; this living/eating/sleeping space of blond wood, white walls and big windows has an urban feel yet overlooks glorious countryside. Secluded from the main house, in a timber-clad barn, the style is thrillingly modern: leather sofas, glass dining table, stainless steel kitchenette. Floor lights dance off the walls, CD surround-sound creates mood and you can watch the stars from your bed. Homemade granola, local bread and ham in the fridge – breakfast when you like. There's peace for romance, solitude for work, a garden to sit in and friendly Sue to suggest the best pubs.

Price	From £70.
Rooms	Apartment: 1 double & kitchenette.
Meals	Pubs within walking distance.
Closed	Rarely.
Directions	A134 towards Bury St Edmunds & Sudbury; A1141 Lavenham, left after 1.4 miles towards Cockfield & Stowmarket; house 1.2 miles on right.

Late checkout (12pm). Local food/produce in your room.

Sue & Ian Jones
The Old Manse Barn, Chapel Road,
Cockfield, Bury St Edmunds IP30 0HE
Tel   +44 (0)1284 828120
Mobile   +44 (0)7931 753996
Email   bookings@theoldmansebarn.co.uk
Web   www.theoldmansebarn.co.uk

Entry 476   Map 10

Suffolk

16 Bolton Street

The house is 15th century and rests on a quiet street in lovely, bustling Lavenham: part medieval, part Tudor, this is one of England's showpiece towns. Heavy beams, low doorways, books, magazines, fresh flowers and gentle hosts create a warm happy feel; steep oak stairs lead to fresh, cosy bedrooms where patchwork quilts, colourful cushions and handmade curtains abound. Gillian likes nothing better than to spoil her guests with breakfasts of local sausages and bacon, potato cakes, very special mushrooms and fresh fruit. A delightful, relaxed, generous place to stay. *Minimum stay two nights at weekends.*

Price	£80–£90.
Rooms	2: 1 twin/double, 1 double.
Meals	Pubs/restaurant within walking distance.
Closed	Rarely.
Directions	From the market square in Lavenham, pass The Great House Restaurant, then left into Bolton Street. Long pink house at bottom on right. Park outside to unload; Gillian will help with parking.

Gillian de Lucy
16 Bolton Street,
Lavenham CO10 9RG

Tel	+44 (0)1787 249046
Mobile	+44 (0)7747 621096
Email	gdelucy@aol.com
Web	www.guineahouse.co.uk

Entry 477   Map 10

Suffolk

Milden Hall

Over five generations of Hawkins have lived in this seemingly grand 16th-century hall farmhouse with its smooth wooden floors, enormous windows and vast fireplaces. Bedrooms that range from big to huge are elegantly old-fashioned and filled with fascinating tapestries, wall hangings and lovely furniture. Juliet is a passionate conservationist, full of ideas for making the most of the surrounding countryside, on foot or by bicycle. Expect delicious home-grown bacon, sausages, bantam eggs and compotes for breakfast in the sunny living room, warmed by a wood-burner in the winter. *Self-catering Barn for large groups.*

Ethical Collection: Environment; Food; Community. See page 420.

Price	£65–£90. Singles from £45.
Rooms	3: 2 twins, 1 double/family room, with separate shared bath & 2nd wc.
Meals	Occasional supper from £20. BYO. Pubs/restaurants 2–3 miles.
Closed	Rarely.
Directions	Lavenham, A1141 for Monks Eleigh. After 2 miles, right to Milden. At x-roads, right, Sudbury B1115. Hall's long drive 0.25 miles on left. Train to Sudbury 7 miles; bus runs past drive.

Christopher & Juliet Hawkins
Milden Hall,
Milden, Lavenham CO10 9NY

Tel	+44 (0)1787 247235
Email	hawkins@thehall-milden.co.uk
Web	www.thehall-milden.co.uk

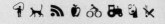

Entry 478   Map 10

Suffolk

Hill House

Nayland is a charming village and this apricot-coloured, listed house sits on a quiet lane. Enter an unusual tunnel hall with flagstones, rugs and fresh flowers, to find a beamed drawing room and an elegant dining room. There are well-polished antiques, good art, and creamy colours dotted with bright chintz; smart, fresh bedrooms have good views over the pretty garden and you get a choice of pillows. Pauline happily shares her home with you and provides generous Aga breakfasts — with homemade bread and preserves. Good walks abound in Constable country; Beth Chatto gardens nearby. *Minimum stay two nights at weekends in summer.*

Price	From £75. Singles from £40.
Rooms	2: 1 twin/double; 1 double with separate bath.
Meals	Pub/restaurant a short walk.
Closed	Christmas & New Year.
Directions	Enter village from A134 into Bear St. Past T-junction into Birch St. 100 yds turn left, house 70 yds uphill on right.

Free pick-up from local station.

Pauline & David Heigham
Hill House,
Gravel Hill, Nayland CO6 4JB
Tel   +44 (0)1206 262782
Email   heighamhillhouse@hotmail.com
Web   www.heighamhillhouse.co.uk

Entry 479   Map 10

Suffolk

West Lodge

This beautifully mellowed brick 1600s coach house has the original huge front door and stunning views from the garden over Dedham Vale. There's a comfortable snug for guests with pinky, terracotta walls and a red sofa; go up your own staircase to simple, light and airy bedrooms and old-fashioned, compact bathrooms. Friendly Penny, and ex-chef Paul, will give you local bacon and sausages and very good dinners in a colourful dining room stuffed full of gleaming antiques and silver — or on balmy evenings in the summer house, maybe with a cocktail up inthe trees first. *Babes in arms & over eights welcome. French & Spanish spoken.*

Price	£70-£75. Singles £50.
Rooms	3: 2 doubles, 1 family suite.
Meals	Dinner, 3 courses, £22.50. Pub/restaurant 140 yds.
Closed	Rarely.
Directions	From A12 exit for B1070, at junc. left towards East Bergholt. At Carriers Arms pub (0.8 miles) right. At post office (0.4 miles), right into Cemetery Lane. Entrance to house 80 yds on left.

10% off stays of 3 or more nights. Bottle of wine with dinner on first night.

Paul & Penny Lewis
West Lodge, The Street,
East Bergholt, Colchester CO7 6TF
Tel   +44 (0)1206 299808
Mobile   +44 (0)7886 075369
Email   westlodgebandb@talktalk.net
Web   www.westlodge.uk.com

Entry 480   Map 10

Suffolk

Poplar Farm House

Only a few miles from Ipswich but down a green lane, this rambling farm house has a pretty, whitewashed porch and higgledy-piggledy roof. All light, elegant and spacious with wonderful flowers, art, sumptuous soft furnishings (made by Sally) and quirky sculptures; expect comfortable beds, laundered linen and smart bathrooms. Sally is relaxed and friendly and will give you eggs from her handsome hens, homemade bread, veg from the garden on an artistically laid table. Play tennis, swim, steam in the sauna or book one of Sally's arts and crafts courses, then wander in the woods beyond with beautiful dogs Shale and Rune.

Price	£65. Singles £45.
Rooms	3: 2 doubles, 1 twin, sharing 2 bath/shower rooms. Yurt: 1 double.
Meals	Dinner, 3 courses, £15–£25. Packed lunch £7. Pub 1 mile.
Closed	Rarely.
Directions	From Ipswich A1214 signed Colchester. After 2 miles at Holiday Inn turn right (at lights) onto A1071, signed Hadleigh. Poplar Lane is immediately on left. House first on right.

Reductions for stays of 2 or more nights. Free pick-up from local bus/train station.

Sally Sparrow
Poplar Farm House, Poplar Lane,
Sproughton, Ipswich IP8 3HL
Tel   +44 (0)1473 601211
Mobile   +44 (0)7950 767226
Email   sparrowsally@aol.com
Web   www.poplarfarmhousesuffolkbb.eu

Suffolk

Aldham Mill

Roses dance over the red-brick mill, a river tinkles past, Suffolk history abounds. The Burton family saved the listed mill from dereliction, and the inside teems with family treasures: open fires, fine china, lace-edged towels, tip-top wool and horsehair mattresses. Children love the granary games room with ping pong — worthy of an Enid Blyton novel. Breakfast on homemade bread and marmalade, local eggs and bacon, then stroll among the snowdrops; Lady Burton opens her gardens for charity in summer. A whisper of a bygone age, and a wonderful, traditional launch pad for Constable country. *Stair lift to single room.*

Price	From £70. Singles £40.
Rooms	2: 1 twin; 1 single with separate bath.
Meals	Pub/restaurants 0.5 miles.
Closed	Christmas & rarely.
Directions	A1071 to Hadleigh. Down High St to end, then right signed Aldham & Elmsett. After 0.5 miles road crosses Hadleigh bypass. Mill immed. on left (don't go to Aldham village). Trains to Ipswich, 10 miles; Colchester 8 miles.

Priscilla Burton
Aldham Mill, Aldham Mill Hill,
Hadleigh, Ipswich IP7 6LE
Tel   +44 (0)1473 822486
Email   priscillaburton@btinternet.com

Suffolk

The Old Rectory

Through the front door to a generously proportioned and flagstoned hall and a smiling welcome from Christopher. Archways lead down the corridor to the library (cosy with maps, books and open fire) and a tall elegant staircase leads to spacious bedrooms, one with delightful bow windows and a view of the sea. There are sash windows and shutters, pelmets and antiques, heaps of good books. Outside: 20 acres of woodlands, meadows, paddocks, croquet lawn and vegetable garden (walled and wonderful). Walks galore on the Deben Peninsula, music at Snape Maltings; it's Suffolk at its best and peace reigns supreme.

Suffolk

Melton Hall

There's more than a touch of theatre to this beautiful listed house. The dining room is opulent red; the drawing room, with its delicately carved mantelpiece and comfortable sofas, has French windows to the terrace. There's a four-poster in one bedroom, an antique French bed in another (occasional road noise) and masses of fresh flowers and books. The garden includes an orchid and wildflower meadow: a designated County Wildlife Site. River walks, the coast and the Saxon burial site Sutton Hoo are close. Generous Cindy, her delightful children, little dog Snowball and cats Bea and Bubbles, all give a great welcome.

Price	£75. Singles £50.	Price	£105-£130. Singles from £60.
Rooms	3: 2 doubles, 1 twin. Extra bed available.	Rooms	3: 1 double; 1 double, 1 single sharing bath.
Meals	Dinner, 3 courses, £30. Supper, 2 courses, £20. Pub 5-minute walk.	Meals	Dinner, 1-3 courses, £19-£38. BYO. Pubs/restaurants nearby.
Closed	Occasionally.	Closed	Rarely.
Directions	From A12 Woodbridge bypass A1152. After railway line at r'bout, B1083 for 7 miles to Alderton. Driveway on left after 30mph & Alderton signs.	Directions	From A12 Woodbridge bypass, exit at r'bout for Melton. Follow for 1 mile to lights; there, right. Immediately on right.

	Christopher Langley The Old Rectory, Alderton, Woodbridge IP12 3DE		Lucinda de la Rue Melton Hall, Woodbridge IP12 1PF
Tel	+44 (0)1394 410003	Tel	+44 (0)1394 388138
Email	clangley@keme.co.uk	Mobile	+44 (0)7775 797075
Web	www.oldrectoryaldertonbandb.co.uk	Email	cindy@meltonhall.co.uk
		Web	www.meltonhall.co.uk

Entry 483   Map 10

Entry 484   Map 10

Suffolk

Grange Farm

The tennis court and garden are surrounded by a 12th-century listed otter-filled moat – this is a glorious old place. Ancient stairs rise and fall all over the 13th-century house, there are sloping floors and honey-coloured beams and a lovely dining room that was once the dairy. Bedrooms are large, comfortable and traditional; the sitting room is cosy with baby grand, log fire, fresh flowers, books, puzzles and games, and the views are to a garden full of birds. Delightful Elizabeth spoils you with homemade cake, local honey, own bread and homemade marmalade for breakfast. Good value, great fun.

Price	£68. Singles £34.
Rooms	2: 1 twin/double, 1 twin, sharing bath.
Meals	Pub 2-mile walk.
Closed	December-March.
Directions	A1120 (Yoxford to Stowmarket) to Dennington. B1116 north for approx. 3 miles. Farm on right 0.9 miles north of Owl's Green & red phone box.

 Half a bottle of wine or Aspall apple juice in room on arrival.

	Elizabeth Hickson
	Grange Farm, Dennington,
	Framlingham, Woodbridge IP13 8BT
Tel	+44 (0)1986 798388
Mobile	+44 (0)7774 182835
Web	www.grangefarm.biz

Entry 485   Map 10

Suffolk

Bealings House

A picture postcard of a setting and a large, beautifully proportioned, Georgian house sitting high in mature parkland. Charming Selina and Jonathan give the whole thing an unpretentious feel and you are encouraged to make yourself at home — among family memorabilia, grand marble fireplaces, Irish linen, well-trodden floorboards, fading Persian rugs, first-class antiques, gilt-framed landscape paintings and bursts of dried flowers. Bedrooms and bathrooms are fearfully old-fashioned and you may need to bring an extra jumper if you are a pampered city-dweller. Quirky, with wonderful grounds.

Price	From £70. Singles from £50.
Rooms	3: 1 double, 1 twin each with separate bath/shower. Apartment: 1 double, sitting room, kitchen & separate bath.
Meals	Pub/restaurant 1 mile.
Closed	Rarely.
Directions	From Ipswich A12 N. At Woodbridge r'bout, N on A12; after 150 yds left at Seckford Hall Hotel sign. After 1 mile left at T-junc. at bottom of hill; then 1st right. Entrance immed. on right.

	Selina & Jonathan Peto
	Bealings House,
	Great Bealings, Woodbridge IP13 6NP
Tel	+44 (0)1394 382631
Email	jonathanpeto@btinternet.com
Web	www.bealingshouse.co.uk

Entry 486   Map 10

Suffolk

Church House

A short hop from riverside Woodbridge and musical Snape Maltings, between a conservation churchyard and a history-rich field, is something different and unusual: a customised house of gentle colours and textures, home to an architect and a designer. From the hand-carved, wood-reclaimed porch to the lovely wildlife garden, there's a feeling of warmth and delight. Under the eaves: two jewel-bright bedrooms full of books and fresh flowers. In the kitchen: a big farmhouse table laid for beautiful breakfasts. And, a short walk away, "the best gastropub in East Anglia". Brilliant!
Children over eight welcome.

Price	£70–£80. Singles £60–£70.
Rooms	2: 1 twin/double; 1 twin with separate bath/shower.
Meals	Pub 1 mile.
Closed	Rarely.
Directions	From A12 at Woodbridge take B1079 dir. Grundisburgh. After approx. 4 miles double bend round Burgh church. House opp. the Clopton parish sign.

Sally Pirkis
Church House,
Clopton, Woodbridge IP13 6QB
Tel   +44 (0)1473 735350
Email   sallypirkis@gmail.com
Web   www.churchhousebandbsuffolk.co.uk

Entry 487   Map 10

Suffolk

Flindor Cottage

In deepest Suffolk where the night skies are magnificent is a timber-framed bolthole that pampers your rotten. This 16th-century cottage has expanded over the years and now has the feel of a small country house: old timbers, bold colours, low ceilings, a smart garden. The bedroom, hidden away at the back, has its own entrance and brims with wonders: exposed beams, bowls of fruit, a huge sleigh bed, a claw-foot bath as deep as the sea. There are maps for walkers, fresh flowers, books galore. Tanya's delicious breakfasts deliver local eggs, hot croissants, fresh fruit and lashings of coffee or tea. A treat.

Price	£100. Singles £85.
Rooms	1 double.
Meals	Pub 200 yards.
Closed	Christmas & New Year.
Directions	A14 to Needham Market, then A140 north and A1120 east. South onto B1077 after 7 miles. In village, pass windmill, then left into The Street. On left just after pub.

Mark & Tanya Felton
Flindor Cottage,
The Street, Framsden IP14 6HG
Tel   +44 (0)1473 890058
Email   tanya@flindor.com
Web   www.flindorcottage.co.uk

Entry 488   Map 10

Suffolk

Haughley House

A timber-framed medieval manor in three acres of garden overlooking farmland. The attractive village is in a conservation area, and your hosts, the Lord of the Manor and his wife, are accomplished cooks and passionate about organic food; they produce their own beef, game, eggs, vegetables and soft fruits. Breakfast is an Aga-cooked feast of homemade bread, Suffolk cured bacon and black pudding, fresh juices and compote; delicious dinners are served in an elegant, silk-lined dining room. You'll find genuine country-house style here with tea and homemade cake on arrival, pretty wallpapers, flowers and a welcoming fire in the hall.

Price	£90–£100. Singles £60–£65.
Rooms	3: 2 doubles, 1 twin.
Meals	Dinner, 3 courses, £28. Restaurants 12 miles.
Closed	Rarely.
Directions	From A14 exit 49, follow signs to Haughley. Fork left at village green, house 100 yds on left.

🧳 Bottle of wine with dinner on 1st night. 10% off stays of 2 or more nights Sun–Thur (not bank holidays).

Jeffrey & Caroline Bowden
Haughley House,
Haughley IP14 3NS
Tel +44 (0)1449 673398
Email bowden@keme.co.uk
Web www.haughleyhouse.co.uk

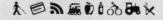

Entry 489 Map 10

Suffolk

Oak House

A wonderful, higgledy-piggledy Suffolk pink farmhouse – and owners who love good food and adventure. Inside creaks with medieval character: lead windows, crooked stairs, low carved ceilings, inglenook fireplaces, a roll top bath, a bread oven (Tom plans pizzas). With Kathy's 60s Royal Doulton and dazzling colours you're in for some fun. Outside: fruit trees, trampoline, an unfenced pond (wild swimming?) and a pheasant that breakfasts with Kathy's chickens. Over a candlelit dinner in the 15th-century kitchen (a sitting room in progress), ask what treats hide in these quiet surroundings, from walks and castles to camels.

Price	£55–£90. Singles from £45. Child £10.
Rooms	2: 1 double; 1 double with separate bath.
Meals	Dinner, 3 courses, £18–£24. BYO. Packed lunch £5.
Closed	Rarely.
Directions	A14 at Stowmarket take B1113 dir. Finningham and Botesdale for 6 miles; 1 mile beyond Finningham, right into Mill St for Gislingham. House 1 mile on left.

🧳 10% off room rate.

Kathy Brooke
Oak House,
Mill Street, Gislingham IP23 8JT
Tel +44 (0)1379 788959
Email kathy@oakhousesuffolk.co.uk
Web www.oakhousesuffolk.co.uk

Entry 490 Map 10

Suffolk

Mallard Manor

Your slightly quackers host, Ida, waddled far and wide for a suitable spot to start dabbling in B&B. She finally alighted on this place which had been built by a local MP – no expenses spared – before hastily being put up for sale. Standing on the deck, it's easy to see what propelled your hostess here: water, vast expanses of it. At night, dive on to super comfy beds with goose down duvets and plump feather pillows. Morning time and Ida lays on a super breakfast of duck eggs for her happy brood of guests. They flock from all corners of the world – particularly Russia and Scandinavia, lured by the temperate climate.

Price	A large bill.
Rooms	22.
Meals	Breakfast only. The Fat Duck is close.
Closed	Occasionally in winter.
Directions	Turn right, then left, then right, then slip behind the first bullrushes on the left.

	Ida Down
	Mallard Manor,
	Gressingham, Orpington QUA CK1
Tel	(0) 22 22 22 22
Email	Idadown@qk.qk
Web	www.webfeet.qk

Entry 491   Map 100

Suffolk

Sandpit Farm

Idyllic views of the wide Alde valley from this deeply comfortable, listed farmhouse. The river borders their 20 acres of beautiful meadows, orchard, gardens, tennis court, ponds and remains of brick-lined moat. Be charmed by family antiques and portraits, easy colour schemes, some beams and open fires, and every cossetting thing in the pretty bedrooms, one with its own sitting room. Susie and her Aga will cook a scrumptious breakfast of homemade and local produce. Near the coast, Snape for concerts, great birdwatching, walks and cycling. Peaceful and so relaxing. *Painting classes possible.*

Price	£65–£80. Singles from £50.
Rooms	2: 1 double, 1 twin.
Meals	Pub/restaurant 1.5 miles.
Closed	Rarely.
Directions	From A1120, Yoxford to Stowmarket, east to Dennington; take B1120, Framlingham. First left; house 1.5 miles on left.

 Home-grown produce in season to take home. 5% off stays of 3 or more nights.

	Susie Marshall
	Sandpit Farm,
	Bruisyard, Saxmundham IP17 2EB
Tel	+44 (0)1728 663445
Email	smarshall@aldevalleybreaks.co.uk
Web	www.aldevalleybreaks.co.uk

Entry 492   Map 10

Suffolk

Willow Tree Cottage

Seductively near RSPB Minsmere, medieval castles, fabulous walks and the glorious coast; and Edwardian Southwold with its pier and sandy beach. The evening sun pours into the back of this contemporary cottage with butter yellow walls; you are on the edge of the village but all is quiet with an orchard behind and a bird-filled garden for tea. No sitting room, but easy chairs in your bedroom face views, your bed is carefully dressed and the bathroom sparkles. Caroline is a good cook and breakfast is large (try her kedgeree). Snape Maltings, for music lovers, is just four miles away. *Minimum two nights at weekends.*

Price	£65–£68. Singles £45–£50.
Rooms	1 double.
Meals	Pub/restaurant 1.5 miles.
Closed	Rarely.
Directions	1.5 miles north of Saxmundham on B1121 & 100 yds north off turning to Kelsale. Belvedere Close on left immediately after Cloutings Close, behind White Gables.

 Free pick-up from local bus/train station.

Caroline Youngson
Willow Tree Cottage,
3 Belvedere Close, Kelsale,
Saxmundham IP17 2RS
Tel   +44 (0)1728 602161
Email   cy@willowtreecottage.me.uk
Web   www.willowtreecottage.me.uk

Entry 493   Map 10

Suffolk

Dunan House

You may get wild mushrooms for breakfast and new-laid eggs, homemade bread and marmalade. This is a relaxed and lovely place to stay, with entertaining hosts and a lively décor: Ann is a potter and her artistry is apparent. Bedrooms are upbeat and attractive, with woven rugs and imaginative and decorative touches, while the delightful family room in the eaves has its own little sitting/sleeping room and long views. It is wonderfully close to the sea with views over the marshes to the river Alde — and beyond. *Min. two nights at weekends; three on bank holidays. See website for availability calendar.*

Price	From £75. Singles from £65.
Rooms	3: 1 twin/double, 1 double, 1 family room.
Meals	Pubs/restaurants 7-minute walk.
Closed	Christmas.
Directions	From A1094 drive towards town from r'bout. First right towards hospital, through 'Private Road' gate. House 100 yds on left, opp. tennis courts.

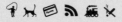 10% off stays of 2 or more nights, Sun–Thurs (not July–Sept & bank holidays).

Simon Farr & Ann Lee
Dunan House,
41 Park Road,
Aldeburgh IP15 5EN
Tel   +44 (0)1728 452486
Email   dunanhouse@btinternet.com
Web   www.dunanhouse.co.uk

Entry 494   Map 10

Suffolk

Arch House

Arch House stands in three acres of garden, meadow and woodland, in easy reach of Snape Maltings and Aldeburgh, the Minsmere bird reserve and the sea. It is also home to the delightful and fun-loving Araminta who offers complementary therapies, welcomes children and is happy to babysit. The décor is traditional, the bedrooms colourful, and the elegant drawing/dining room has a boudoir grand piano and a warming log fire. Araminta is a fabulous cook and you eat well in the large farmhouse kitchen by the wood-burner: bacon and sausages are local, vegetables and fruit are home-grown and organic. Wonderful value, too.

Ethical Collection: Food. See page 420.

Price	£55-£70. Singles £30.
Rooms	2: 1 double; 1 twin with separate bath.
Meals	Dinner from £15. BYO. Pub 200 yds.
Closed	Rarely.
Directions	From A12, A1094 into Aldeburgh. Left at r'bout onto B1122 to Leiston. On left, 0.5 miles after Aldringham sign.

 Free pick-up from local bus/train station. Late checkout (12pm).

Araminta Stewart
Arch House,
Aldeburgh Road,
Aldringham IP16 4QF
Tel   +44 (0)1728 832615
Email   amintys@aol.com
Web   www.archhouse-aldeburgh.com

Entry 495   Map 10

Suffolk

The Old Methodist Chapel

This converted listed Victorian chapel is full of atmosphere, warm colours and beautiful stained glass windows. Bedrooms have their own entrance and are charming — one, with access to conservatory and courtyard garden, has pale walls, oak floors and beams; the flag-floored Retreat Room sports bright rugs and bedcovers from far-flung places. The chapel is comfortably, cosily cluttered and Jackum is easy-going and interesting. Potions and lotions by your bath, videos, DVDs and music in your room, books and flowers in every corner, and an organic breakfast with famous bacon from Peasenhall. *Minimum stay two nights.*

Price	£75-£100. Singles £50-£75.
Rooms	2: 1 twin; 1 double with separate bath.
Meals	Restaurant directly opposite. Pubs/restaurants within walking distance.
Closed	Occasionally.
Directions	From A12 in Yoxford, A1120 signed Peasenhall & Stowmarket. Chapel 200 yds on right.

Free pick-up from local bus/train station. Bottle of wine for 3 or more nights.

Jackum Brown
The Old Methodist Chapel,
High Street,
Yoxford IP17 3EU
Tel   +44 (0)1728 668333
Email   browns@chapelsuffolk.co.uk
Web   www.chapelsuffolk.co.uk

Entry 496   Map 10

Suffolk

Church Farmhouse

This lovely Elizabethan farmhouse is in a quiet hamlet by an ancient thatched church, but the bird sanctuary at Minsmere, Southwold, Snape Maltings, music and the coast are near for lovely days out. Characterful Sarah, well-travelled and entertaining, is also an excellent cook, so breakfast will be a treat, and occasional dinners are well worth staying in for. Bedrooms are restful and painted in soft colours; beds are supremely comfortable and well dressed in laundered white cotton. There are peaceful views, fresh flowers, lots of books and a calm atmosphere. *Children over 12 welcome. Min. two nights at weekends.*

Price	From £85. Singles from £50.
Rooms	3: 1 double, 1 twin; 1 double with separate bath.
Meals	Dinner £24–£28. Pub/restaurants within 4 miles.
Closed	Christmas.
Directions	A12 for Wangford; left signed Uggeshall; house 1 mile on left before church.

Sarah Lentaigne
Church Farmhouse,
Uggeshall, Southwold NR34 8BD
Tel	+44 (0)1502 578532
Mobile	+44 (0)7748 801418
Email	uggeshalljupp@btinternet.com
Web	www.uggeshall.fsnet.co.uk

Entry 497   Map 10

Suffolk

Valley Farm

Soaps and sweeties in baskets, walking and cycle route maps on tap, DVDs for your TVs: some of the personal touches you'll find at this delightfully unpretentious B&B. The soft brick farmhouse in a lovely corner of Suffolk sits in two acres of new landscaped garden, with a play area for children, a field for kite flying and a wonderful indoor solar-heated pool, shared with the self-catering guests. You get jams from their fruits for breakfast – Jackie and Andrew have a passion for real food – and two friendly and comfortable carpeted bedrooms, each with a spotless new shower. *Minimum stay two nights at weekends.*

Price	£70–£90. Singles £70–£90.
Rooms	2: 1 double, 1 family room for 3-4.
Meals	Pub 1.2 miles.
Closed	Rarely.
Directions	From A144 at Halesworth, B1123 signed Holton & Southwold. Fork left at Holton, on to school, then left. Valley Farm 0.25 miles on left.

 Free pick-up from local bus/train station. 1 hour per day exclusive use of pool.

Jackie Circus
Valley Farm, Bungay Road,
Holton, Halesworth IP19 8LY
Tel	+44 (0)1986 874521
Email	mail@valleyfarmholton.co.uk
Web	www.valleyfarmholton.co.uk

Entry 498   Map 10

Surrey

Greenaway

An enchanting cottage in an idyllic corner of Chiddingfold. People return time and again – for the house (1545), the garden with dovecote, vegetables, flowers and hens, the glowing interiors, and Sheila and John. The sitting room is inviting with rich colours and textures, and the turning oak staircase leads to bedrooms that are cosy and sumptuous at the same time. Bathrooms are bliss, with deep roll top tubs. Come for gorgeous countryside and walks on the Greensand Way... who would guess London and the airports were so close? Delicious English B&B; readers are full of praise.

Price	£90–£115. Singles from £65.
Rooms	3: 1 double; 1 double, 1 twin sharing bath.
Meals	Hotels within walking distance.
Closed	Rarely.
Directions	A3 to Milford, then A283 for Petworth. At Chiddingfold, Pickhurst Road off green. House 3rd on left, with large black dovecote.

Sheila & John Marsh
Greenaway, Pickhurst Road,
Chiddingfold GU8 4TS
Tel +44 (0)1428 682920
Email jfmarsh@gotadsl.co.uk

Entry 499 Map 4

Surrey

Lower Eashing Farmhouse

A homely place with a lovely walled garden and super hosts; Gillian, who speaks French, German and Spanish, enjoys welcoming people from all over the world. The house, 16th to 19th century, has exposed timbers, books and bold colours. The dining room is red; the guest sitting room – with open fire and fascinating artefacts from around the world – is big enough for a small company meeting, or a wedding group. Your hosts, who are great fun, run an efficient and caring ship. In the walled garden, sipping tea, the distant rumble of the A3 reminds you how well placed you are for Gatwick and Heathrow.

Price	From £80. Singles from £50.
Rooms	4: 1 twin/double; 1 twin/double with separate bath/shower; 2 singles sharing shower.
Meals	Pub 300 yds.
Closed	Occasionally.
Directions	A3 south. 5 miles after Guildford, Eashing signed left at service station. Third house on left behind white fence.

Free pick-up from local bus/train station.

David & Gillian Swinburn
Lower Eashing Farmhouse,
Lower Eashing, Godalming GU7 2QF
Tel +44 (0)1483 421436
Email davidswinburn@hotmail.com

Entry 500 Map 4

Surrey

High Edser

Ancient wattle and daub, aged timbers and bags of character – it really does ramble. Built in 1532, High Edser sits in 2.5 acres of smooth lawns beyond which lie the village and the Surrey hills. But, unlike many houses of a certain age, this one is light and inviting and has the sort of family clutter that makes you feel at home. Bedrooms are full of character; Patrick and Carol leave you plenty of space to gently unfurl. The carved wooden fireplace in the stone-flagged dining room is spectacular, and there's a snug study just for guests. Very peaceful in an AONB, yet close to both airports.

Price	£65–£75. Singles £30–£40.
Rooms	3: 1 double; 1 double, 1 twin, sharing bath.
Meals	Pub/restaurant 300 yds.
Closed	Rarely.
Directions	From A3, 1st exit after M25, for Ripley. Through Ripley & West Clandon, over dual c'way (A246) onto A25. 3rd right to Shere. There, right to Cranleigh. House 5 miles on left, 1 mile past The Windmill.

 10% off room rate Mon-Thurs. 10% off stays of 2 or more nights.

 Use your Sawday's Gift Card here.

Patrick & Carol Franklin Adams
High Edser, Shere Road,
Ewhurst, Cranleigh GU6 7PQ
Tel   +44 (0)1483 278214
Mobile   +44 (0)7775 865125
Email   carol@highedser.co.uk
Web   www.highedser.co.uk

Entry 501   Map 4

Surrey

Blackbrook House

A large Victorian house sitting in lawns and garden and with a wide gravel drive; this has a rural feel but you are less than two miles from the centre of Dorking. Emma and Rae, both easy-going, give you a super little sitting room with a hidden TV and space to make a cup of tea; both bedrooms are spacious, smart and feminine with floral fabrics, deep pocket sprung mattresses and good linen, bathrooms are tip-top. Breakfast is beautifully presented with cereals and fruit or the full Monty. Walk it off over lawns, shrubs and woods – or strike out further over National Trust land.

Price	£85–£90. Singles from £55.
Rooms	2 doubles.
Meals	Pub 0.5 miles.
Closed	Christmas & New Year.
Directions	R'bout outside Dorking A24 intersects A25. A24 0.5 miles. Left into Blackbrook, signed. 1 mile until Plough pub. Turn into pub & up track. House 3rd on left.

Emma & Rae Burdon
Blackbrook House,
Blackbrook, Dorking RH5 4DS
Tel   +44 (0)1306 888898
Mobile   +44 (0)7880 723512
Email   blackbrookbb@btinternet.com
Web   www.blackbrookhouse.org.uk

Entry 502   Map 4

Surrey

Old Great Halfpenny

It feels as rural as Devon, yet you are perfectly placed for airports and easy access to London, with Guildford a few minutes away. The 16th-century farmhouse sits on a country lane beneath the Pilgrim's Way. Beyond Michael's immaculate gardens roll the Surrey Hills; there are stunning views from every room and glorious walks start from the door. You have your own entrance up fairly steep steps to lovely bedrooms which Alison, an interior designer, has made beautiful with fine fabrics and antique French beds. Wake to the smell of home-baked bread; in summer you breakfast on the terrace. Special.

Price	£85–£95. Singles from £65.
Rooms	2 doubles, each with separate bath.
Meals	Pub 0.5 miles.
Closed	Rarely.
Directions	From London, exit A3 before Guildford, signed Burpham. From here 2 miles to house. Ring for detailed directions.

Michael & Alison Bennett
Old Great Halfpenny, Halfpenny Lane,
St Martha, Guildford GU4 8PY
Tel   +44 (0)1483 567835
Mobile +44 (0)7768 745765
Email   bennettbird@gmail.com

Entry 503   Map 4

Surrey

Swallow Barn

A squash court, coach house and stables, once belonging to next-door's manor, have become a home of old-fashioned charm. Full of family memories and run very well by Joan, the B&B is excellently placed for Windsor, Wisley and golf courses; close to both airports, too. Lovely trees in the garden, fields and woods beyond, a paddock and a summer pool... total tranquillity, and you can walk to the pub. None of the bedrooms is huge but the beds are firm, the garden views are pretty and the downstairs double has its own sitting room. Breakfasts are both generous and scrumptious. *Children over eight welcome.*

Price	From £80. Singles from £45.
Rooms	3: 1 double & sitting room; 1 twin with separate shower. Apple Store: 1 twin.
Meals	Pub/restaurant 0.75 miles.
Closed	Rarely.
Directions	From M25, exit 11, A319 into Chobham. Left at T-junc.; left at mini r'bout onto A3046. After 0.7 miles, right between street light & postbox. House 2nd on left.

Joan Carey
Swallow Barn, Milford Green,
Chobham, Woking GU24 8AU
Tel   +44 (0)1276 856030
Mobile +44 (0)7768 972904
Email   swallowbarn@web-hq.com
Web   www.swallow-barn.co.uk

Entry 504   Map 4

Sussex

Church Gate

Janie has added a conservatory and huge, sunny, Aga kitchen to her 1930s house; she greets with afternoon tea, rustles up tasty home eggs at breakfast, and may even treat guests to home-baked bread or croissants, served on the terrace in summer. The house is adorned with Nigerian musical instruments and Janie's photographs; bedrooms in the separate cottage are fresh with low windows looking onto the garden, lovely soaps in the bath and shower rooms, driftwood lamps in the airy flagstoned sitting room. Set off for nearby Chichester with its theatre and shops, or pretty Itchenor, a mecca for sailors.

Ethical Collection: Food. See page 420.

Price	From £90. Singles from £70.
Rooms	Cottage: 1 double, 1 twin & sitting room.
Meals	Pub within 1 mile.
Closed	Often in the winter months.
Directions	From A27 at Chichester A286 Witterings; 5 miles; at r'bout bear right onto B2179. 0.5 miles right to Itchenor. 1 mile, house opposite church.

Bottle of wine in your room. Local food/produce in your room.

Janie Impey
Church Gate,
Itchenor,
Chichester PO20 7DL
Tel   +44 (0)1243 514700
Email   janie.allen@btinternet.com
Web   www.chichesterbandb.co.uk

Entry 505   Map 4

Sussex

Itchenor Park House

The Duke of Richmond reportedly built Itchenor Park for his French mistress in 1783; it's a listed Georgian house in beautiful formal gardens on a 700-acre farmed estate. It is remote and utterly peaceful, and a path across the fields brings you to Chichester harbour for boat trips and sailing bustle. There are great walks to the beach, too, and around the village. You stay in a cosy self-contained apartment in the wing with a sitting room, kitchenette and wood-burner. And you may enjoy the lovely little walled garden, sheltered from the winds. Susie leaves you breakfast in the fridge. *Ask about body & soul detox breaks.*

Price	From £95. Singles from £60.
Rooms	Apartment: 1 twin/double & sitting room with sofabed & kitchenette.
Meals	Continental breakfast in fridge. Pub 5-minute walk.
Closed	Rarely.
Directions	A27 at Chichester onto A286 towards the Witterings. At Birdham, right at garage onto B2179; 500 yds, right to Itchenor. Driveway on left past church, signed.

Late checkout (12pm). Local food/produce in your room.

Susie Green
Itchenor Park House,
Itchenor,
Chichester PO20 7DN
Tel   +44 (0)1243 512221
Mobile   +44 (0)7718 902768
Email   susie.green@lineone.net

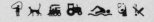

Entry 506   Map 4

Sussex

The Old Manor House

Wild flowers in jugs, old wooden floors and beams, pretty cottagey curtains: Judy's manor house near Chichester has bags of character and she is friendly and chatty. Originally constructed round a big central fireplace, the rooms are all refreshingly simple allowing the original features to shine. Sweet bedrooms up steep stairs have seagrass floors, limed furniture and a skylark or chiff chaff on the doors. Enjoy breakfast by the wood-burner in the dining room: fresh fruit smoothies and an organic full English. Great for horse racing, castle visiting, sailing, theatre and festivals; fantastic walks on the south downs, too.

Price	From £85.
Rooms	3: 2 doubles; 1 double sharing shower room with owner.
Meals	Pub/restaurant 500 yds.
Closed	Christmas.
Directions	From Arundel, A27 west to Fontwell r'bout. Then A29 towards Bognor Regis, along Westergate Street. House on left with large forecourt.

Judy Wolstenholme
The Old Manor House,
Westergate Street, Westergate,
Chichester PO20 3QZ
Tel   +44 (0)1243 544489
Email   judy@veryoldmanorhouse.com
Web   www.veryoldmanorhouse.com

Entry 507   Map 4

Sussex

Lordington House

Croquet on the lawn in summer, big log fires and woolly jumpers in winter, brilliant food all year round. On a sunny slope of the Ems valley, life ticks by peacefully as it has always done…The house is vast and impressive, a lime avenue links the much-loved garden with the AONB beyond and friendly guard dog Shep looks on. The 17th-century staircase is a glory, the décor is engagingly old-fashioned: Edwardian beds with firm mattresses and floral covers, carpeted Sixties-style bathrooms, toile wallpaper on wardrobe doors. A privilege to stay in a house of this age and character! *Over fives welcome. Dogs by arrangement.*

Price	From £95. Singles from £47.50.
Rooms	4: 1 double; 1 twin/double with separate bath/shower; 1 double, 1 single sharing bath/shower.
Meals	Dinner £25. Packed lunch from £6. Pub 1 mile.
Closed	Rarely.
Directions	Follow B2146 from Walderton. After 0.5 miles, turn right entering the village thro' white railings. Lordington House up long drive on right.
	Free pick-up from local pubs or stations.

Mr & Mrs Hamilton
Lordington House,
Lordington,
Chichester PO18 9DX
Tel   +44 (0)1243 375862
Email   hamiltonjanda@btinternet.com

Entry 508   Map 4

Sussex

West Marden Farmhouse

Bowl down a gentle valley in the South Downs to find a 16th-century farmhouse with beautiful Sussex granaries and barn; the Edney family has farmed the land for generations. Your delightful, helpful hosts, committed to the environment, give guests a sitting/dining room with a huge old fireplace, comfortable sofas, oak floor and French windows to the garden. Upstairs are beamed bedrooms with a luxurious feel and fabulous bathrooms (free-standing baths, swish showers) bursting with aromatic soaps and oils. Breakfasts are delicious, the walking is great, Goodwood is a 20-minute drive. *Minimum stay two nights at weekends.*

Price	From £115.
Rooms	2: 1 twin/double, 1 double.
Meals	Pub 75 yds.
Closed	Occasionally.
Directions	West Marden Farmhouse is in centre of village opposite Noredown Way.

 Lifts to local walking start points.

Carole Edney
West Marden Farmhouse,
West Marden, Chichester PO18 9ES
Tel   +44 (0)2392 631761
Email carole.edney@btinternet.com
Web   www.westmardenfarmhousebandb.co.uk

Entry 509   Map 4

Sussex

Lyndale House

Come to feel spoiled in a pretty 18th-century merchant's house right in the centre of Midhurst; Trina and David are relaxed and thoughtful and look after you well. Their home is filled with antiques and family heirlooms, and an interesting collection of antique maps reveals all the places they've lived. Cordon Bleu-trained Trina is passionate about good food; breakfasts and dinners are local and organic. Bedrooms are light and fresh, one overlooks the church; bathrooms are smart and sparkling. Sit in the sunny walled garden with a book. A great spot for bikers and hikers. *Min. two nights during Goodwood & Cowdray.*

Price	From £85. Singles from £75.
Rooms	2: 1 double; 1 twin/double with separate bath/shower.
Meals	Packed lunch from £8. Dinner from £20. Pubs/restaurants 50 yds.
Closed	Rarely.
Directions	From Petersfield A272 to Midhurst, approx. 10 miles. At mini roundabout straight on, then 3rd left. House opposite war memorial and church.

 Homemade chocolates in your room. 10% off stays of 2 or more nights.

Trina Duncan
Lyndale House,
Church Hill, Midhurst GU29 9NX
Tel   +44 (0)1730 813362
Email trinadad48@aol.com
Web   www.lyndalehousebandb.co.uk

Entry 510   Map 4

Sussex

Redford Cottage

In a tiny hamlet, a friendly home with much-loved books and very kind hosts. The immense inglenook dates back to 1510 and the garden suite opens to undulating lawns; it is cosy, old-worldly, floral and private, and its sitting room comes with a wood-burner. The barn has the woody spaciousness of a ski chalet and is perfect for friends... old rugs, new pine, games, views and (up steep open stairs) beds tucked under a sloped ceiling. The silence is filled with birdsong and you are surrounded by woodland, wildlife and the rolling South Downs. Breakfasts in the conservatory are a treat. *Minimum stay three nights during Goodwood.*

Price	From £95. Singles from £65.
Rooms	3: 1 suite. Barn: 2 twins/doubles & sitting room.
Meals	Pub/restaurant 2.5 miles.
Closed	Christmas.
Directions	On old A3, north from Petersfield, at Hill Brow right for Rogate, left after 300 yds to Milland. Follow lane through woods for 6 miles; right for Midhurst & Redford. On right, 150 yds beyond Redford sign.

Caroline & David Angela
Redford Cottage,
Redford, Midhurst GU29 0QF
Tel +44 (0)1428 741242
Email redfordcottage@btinternet.com

Entry 511   Map 4

Sussex

73 Sheepdown Drive

Strolling distance from lovely Petworth, in a cul-de-sac with outstanding valley views, is a modern but traditional tile-hung house with a gorgeous little garden. Friendly charming Angela, vice-president of the National Gardens Scheme, knows all there is to know about the gardens of Sussex. Bedrooms are fresh and simple, with well-dressed beds and good pictures. You take breakfast at a superb Jacobean oak table and can soak up the sunshine from the comfort of the conservatory; then walk down through fields to the pub in Byworth for supper. Handy for Chichester's Theatre, Goodwood and the treasures of Petworth House.

Price	From £60. Singles from £40.
Rooms	2 twins sharing bath & shower.
Meals	Pub/restaurant 10-minute walk.
Closed	Christmas & New Year.
Directions	From Petworth on A283. Sheepdown Drive east of town centre.

Angela Azis
73 Sheepdown Drive,
Petworth GU28 0BX
Tel +44 (0)1798 342269

Entry 512   Map 4

Sussex

Fitzlea Farmhouse

A wooded track leads to the beautiful, mellow, 17th-century farmhouse with tall chimneys and a cluster of overgrown outbuildings – a sensational house in a breathtaking setting. Wood-panelled walls and ancient oak beams, a vast open fireplace, mullioned windows and deep sofas create a mood of relaxed country charm. Maggie gives you a delicious locally sourced breakfast in her Aga-warm kitchen; in spring, the scent of bluebells wafts through open doors. A winding staircase leads to comfortable timbered bedrooms which overlook fields, rolling lawns and woodland where you can stroll in peace. *Children by arrangement.*

Price	£65-£90. Singles by arrangement.
Rooms	3: 1 family room; 1 double, 1 twin, sharing bath.
Meals	Packed lunch available. Pubs/restaurants 2 miles.
Closed	Rarely.
Directions	Directions on booking.

	Maggie Paterson
	Fitzlea Farmhouse,
	Selham,
	Petworth GU28 0PS
Tel	+44 (0)1798 861429

Entry 513   Map 4

Sussex

Riverhill Lodge

Views, views and more views over gorgeous National Park, from this handsome red-brick house with early Georgian origins. A sunny, airy sitting room with open fire and elegant cream and pink sofas, looks onto the well-planted garden; you breakfast copiously in a cosy terracotta-coloured dining room – cheerful Chris and Jenny serve up homemade bread, eggs from local hens and smoked bacon. Bedrooms are newly prettified in pale, neutral colours, with fresh fabrics and deep mattresses; bathrooms are sleekly up-to-date and toasty warm, with the thickest towels. Walk from the house for miles; the peace and quiet is palpable.

Price	£85-£125.
Rooms	2: 1 double, 1 twin/double.
Meals	Pub 0.75 miles.
Closed	Christmas & occasionally Easter.
Directions	From Petworth go east, past Welldiggers pub on right. 0.5 miles, then left. As road ceases to be a green 'tunnel' (before house on left) take right. Beech hedge on right.

	Christopher & Jenny Leaver
	Riverhill Lodge,
	Riverhill, Fittleworth,
	Pulborough RH20 1JY
Tel	+44 (0)1798 343872
Email	bookings@riverhilllodge.co.uk
Web	www.riverhilllodge.co.uk

Entry 514   Map 4

Sussex

Linacre Lodge

On the edge of the small village of Rudgwick, and originally part of the Baynards Park Estate, this late Victorian lodge house is a relaxed and friendly home. The kitchen is full of historic, Italian James Bond posters and unusual little chairs are found throughout: Laura is a collector and loves having people to stay. Smart, pretty bedrooms include elderflower cordial, flowers, sweets and magazines; one has its own sitting room with children's books and games. There's a huge choice at breakfast: full English or continental. Chris and Laura are keen walkers – borrow maps, order a packed lunch and set off from the door. *Dogs £5.*

Price	From £85. Singles from £70. Child (over 2) £10.
Rooms	2: 1 double; 1 double & sitting room.
Meals	Packed lunch £6.50. TV supper (pizza, salad & popcorn) £12.50. Pub/restaurant 2 miles.
Closed	Christmas & New Year.
Directions	A281 Guildford to Horsham. Into Rudgwick, past King's Head pub on right; 2nd left on sharp right bend onto Baynard's Lane. House about 0.5 miles on right.

 10% off room rate Mon–Thurs.

Laura Anstead
Linacre Lodge,
Baynards, Rudgwick,
Horsham RH12 3AD
Tel +44 (0)1403 823522
Email chrisandlaura@linacrelodge.co.uk
Web www.linacrelodge.co.uk

Entry 515 Map 4

Sussex

The Hyde Granary

A 1,000-acre estate, where roe deer roam and the odd buzzard circles above. The granary stands at the end of a one-mile drive, alongside a coach house and clock tower, in the shadow of the big house. Airy interiors are just the ticket: timber frames, exposed walls, beams in the dining room and a drying room for walkers. Bedrooms are uncluttered and have a country feel: one has a claw-foot bath, the other is in the eaves. Margot, a homeopath, can realign your back after a long journey, and does super breakfasts. There's a small garden for sundowners in summer, you can walk to the village and Gatwick is close.

Price	£80. Singles £45.
Rooms	2: 1 double; 1 double with separate bath/shower.
Meals	Pub 1.7 miles.
Closed	Christmas & New Year.
Directions	Leave village for Crawley on B2114. Pass through 30mph zone, then 1st left up drive onto Hyde Estate. Follow drive for 1 mile. Keep left at houses; house on right.

 10% off stays of 2 or more nights.

Margot Barton
The Hyde Granary,
The Hyde, London Road, Handcross,
Haywards Heath RH17 6EZ
Tel +44 (0)1444 401930
Email margot@thehydegranary.com
Web www.thehydegranary.com

Entry 516 Map 4

Sussex

Sussex Prairies

A wonderfully friendly, family farm: Paul and Pauline designed the showcase six-acre garden and look after the Shetland sheep, rare-breed pigs and chickens; Pauline is a bundle of creativity inside the farmhouse they built together – her mother sells homemade cakes and farm-reared meat in the tea shop. All are committed to green living. Sleep in country-chic rooms dotted with funky objets d'art, wake to the cock's crow and descend to the light dining room for eggs, sausages and fruit from the farm. Brighton is close, the South Downs on your doorstep. All who love great gardens, good food and fun company will be in clover.

Price	From £105. Singles from £90.
Rooms	3: 2 doubles, 1 twin.
Meals	Restaurant 0.25 miles, pub 1.5 miles.
Closed	Rarely.
Directions	20 minutes N of Brighton, via M23 & A23; via B2116 (Wheatsheaf Rd) north & to the east of Henfield. House on right. Nearest train station Hassocks, 15-minute taxi.

10% off stays of 2 or more nights Mon-Thurs.

Pauline McBride
Sussex Prairies,
Morlands Farm, Wheatsheaf Road,
Henfield BN5 9AT
Tel   +44 (0)1273 495902
Email   morlandsfarm@btinternet.com
Web   www.sussexprairies.co.uk

Entry 517   Map 4

Sussex

The Grange

There's a time-worn feel to this dreamy home. Books are stuffed into shelves, walls are decorated with years of paintings and carved African hippos guard the stairs. The mainly-Queen-Anne rectory in a secluded spot beside the church feels wonderfully timeless with its oak stairs, antique swords, ancient tapestry and comfy old-fashioned sitting room (all yours). Bedrooms are traditional and have lovely views over the garden; there's a small single room attached to one. Few modern innovations here but Bunny looks after you beautifully and there's marvellous walking in Ashdown Forest: this is Pooh Bear country.

Price	From £75. Singles £50.
Rooms	2: 1 double & sitting room (with single room attached); 1 double with separate bath.
Meals	Pubs/restaurant 200 yds.
Closed	Occasionally.
Directions	In the centre of Hartfield, take road (Church Street) between The Haywagon & The Anchor pubs. Pass church on left; house is beyond church, on left.

Bunny & James Murray Willis
The Grange,
Hartfield
TN7 4AG
Tel   +44 (0)1892 770259
Email   bunnymw@hotmail.co.uk

Entry 518   Map 5

Sussex

Old Whyly

Breakfast in a light-filled, chinoiserie dining room – there's an effortless elegance to this manor house, once home to one of King Charles's Cavaliers. Bedrooms are atmospheric, one in French style. The treats continue outside with a beautiful flower garden annually replenished with 5,000 tulips, a lake and orchard, a swimming pool and a tennis court – fabulous. Dine under the pergola in summer: food is a passion and Sarah's menus are adventurous with a modern slant. Glyndebourne is close so make a party of it and take a divine 'pink' hamper, with blankets or a table and chairs included. Sheer bliss.

Price	£95–£135. Singles by arrangement.
Rooms	3: 2 twins/doubles; 1 twin/double with separate bath.
Meals	Dinner, 3 courses, £32.50. Hampers £35. Pub/restaurant 0.5 miles.
Closed	Rarely.
Directions	0.5 miles past Halland on A22, south from Uckfield; 1st left off Shaw r'bout towards E. Hoathly; on for 0.5 miles. Drive on left with postbox; central gravel drive.

Sarah Burgoyne
Old Whyly,
London Road,
East Hoathly BN8 6EL
Tel   +44 (0)1825 840216
Email   stay@oldwhyly.co.uk
Web   www.oldwhyly.co.uk

Entry 519   Map 5

Sussex

Netherwood Lodge

The whiff of the log fire, the scent of fresh flowers and a smattering of chintz over calm, uncluttered interiors will please you in this single-storey coach house: engaging Margaret may give you homemade cake or scones in an elegant sitting room with views over the pretty garden. Cosy bedrooms are beautifully dressed and chic with wool carpets, silk and linen curtains, oak furniture and gloriously comfortable beds. You eat well, much is locally sourced and homemade for the flexible, award-winning breakfasts. This is a quiet part of East Sussex, ideal for walking, National Trust properties and Glyndebourne.

Ethical Collection: Food. See page 420.

Price	From £100. Singles from £80.
Rooms	2: 1 twin; 1 double with separate bath.
Meals	Pub/restaurant 1 mile.
Closed	Rarely.
Directions	A22 towards Eastbourne. Left at Golden Cross between BP garage and antique shop. 0.5 miles, right at T-junc. then sharp right into unmade lane. House 2nd on left.

Local food/produce on your departure.

Margaret Clarke
Netherwood Lodge,
Muddles Green, Chiddingly,
Lewes BN8 6HS
Tel   +44 (0)1825 872512
Email   netherwoodlodge@hotmail.com
Web   www.netherwoodlodge.co.uk

Entry 520   Map 5

Sussex

Hailsham Grange

Come for elegance and ease. Noel welcomes you into his lovely Queen 'Mary Anne' home (1701-1705) – set back from the road in a town where they still hold two cattle markets a week. No standing on ceremony here, despite the décor: classic English touched with chinoiserie in perfect keeping with the house. Busts on pillars, swathes of delicious chintz, books galore and bedrooms a treat: a sunny double and a romantic four-poster. Summery breakfasts are served on the flagged terrace, marmalades and jams on a silver salver. The town garden, with its box parterre and bank of gothic summerhouse, is an equal joy.

Price	£105–£140. Singles from £80.
Rooms	4: 1 double, 1 four-poster. Coach house: 2 suites.
Meals	Pub/restaurant 300 yds.
Closed	Rarely.
Directions	From Hailsham High St, left into Vicarage Rd. House 200 yds on left. Park in adjacent coach yard.

Use your Sawday's Gift Card here.

Noel Thompson
Hailsham Grange,
Hailsham BN27 1BL
Tel   +44 (0)1323 844248
Email   noel@hgrange.co.uk
Web   www.hailshamgrange.co.uk

Entry 521   Map 5

Sussex

Ocklynge Manor

On top of a peaceful hill, a short stroll from Eastbourne, find tip-top B&B in an 18th-century house with an interesting history – ask Wendy! Now it is her home, and you will be treated to home-baked bread, delicious tea time cakes and scrummy jams – on fine days you can take it outside. Creamy carpeted, bright and sunny bedrooms, all with views over the lovely walled garden, create a mood of relaxed indulgence and are full of thoughtful touches: dressing gowns, DVDs, your own fridge. Breakfasts are superb and there's a chintzy, comfy sitting room just for guests: this is a very spoiling, nurturing place.

Price	From £90. Singles from £50.
Rooms	3: 1 twin, 1 suite for 3; 1 double with separate shower.
Meals	Pub 5-minute walk.
Closed	Rarely.
Directions	From Eastbourne General Hospital, over r'bout on A2021. 1st right to Kings Avenue; up hill to T-junc. Cream house faces you on right.

Wendy Dugdill
Ocklynge Manor,
Mill Road, Eastbourne BN21 2PG
Tel   +44 (0)1323 734121
Mobile   +44 (0)7979 627172
Email   ocklyngemanor@hotmail.com
Web   www.ocklyngemanor.co.uk

Entry 522   Map 5

Sussex

St Benedict

The grand seaside villa, in a conservation area, has been meticulously restored by Stephen using the original 1880 floor plan. Lovers of Victoriana will swoon: find hand-printed wallpapers, gleaming mahogany, Persian rugs, Dutch marquetry furniture, coal fires in winter, decorative objects and artwork galore. Bedrooms are all extremely comfy with brass beds, eiderdowns and Victorian linen; wake to a full English, kedgeree or local kippers, served in the family dining room from a working dumb waiter. Relax in a sumptuous drawing room or borrow a book from the lovely library and head for a summerhouse tea in the walled garden.

Price	£90. Singles £60.
Rooms	3 doubles each with separate bath.
Meals	Dinner £25. Packed lunch £10. Pub/restaurant 0.5 miles.
Closed	Rarely.
Directions	From Hastings, west A27 Marine Parade until London Rd, St L. on Sea. Right (signed London) away from sea. Take 5th on left, just before disused church. At top of hill, over junc. beside St John's Church, house 100 yds, on left.

Free pick-up from local bus/train station. 25% off stays of 2 or more nights.

	Stephen Groves
	St Benedict, 81 Pevensey Road,
	St Leonards on Sea TN38 0LR
Tel	+44 (0)1424 434973
Email	stephen.groves@zen.co.uk
Web	www.victorian-bed-and-breakfast.com

Entry 523   Map 5

Sussex

Swan House

Effortless style drifts through the beamed rooms of this boutiquey B&B in a 1490s bakery, from a roaring inglenook fireplace to an honesty bar in a mock bookcase – all run by relaxed creative hosts Brendan and Lionel. Bedrooms hold surprises: Elizabethan frescoes, an old pulley for bags of flour, a window seat, seashell mosaics and handmade soaps. Step out into lively Old Hastings, wander down to see fishing boats tucked in for the night or find an antiques bargain. Seagulls herald the new day: pick a morning paper; breakfast like kings on organic croissants and local kippers (dinners also on request). Unique.

Price	£115-£145. Singles £70-£95.
Rooms	4: 3 doubles, 1 suite.
Meals	Restaurants 2-minute walk.
Closed	Christmas.
Directions	In Hastings Old Town, close to the seafront, a 20-minute walk from Hastings town centre and train station.

25% off room rate Mon-Thurs.

	Brendan McDonagh
	Swan House,
	1 Hill Street, Hastings TN34 3HU
Tel	+44 (0)1424 430014
Email	res@swanhousehastings.co.uk
Web	www.swanhousehastings.co.uk

Entry 524   Map 5

Sussex

Appletree Cottage

An enviable position facing south for this old hung-tile farmer's cottage, covered in roses, jasmine and wisteria; views are over farmland towards the coast at Fairlight Glen. Jane will treat you to tea and cake when you arrive – either before a warming fire in the drawing room, or in the garden in summer. Both bedrooms are sunny, spacious, quiet and traditional, one with gorgeous garden views. Breakfast well on apple juice from their own apples, homemade jams and marmalade, local bacon. Perfect for walkers with a footpath at the front gate, but birdwatchers will be happy too, and you are near the steam railway at Bodiam.

Price	£80. Singles £50.
Rooms	2: 1 twin; 1 double with separate bath.
Meals	Pub/restaurant 0.5 miles.
Closed	Rarely.
Directions	A21 towards Hastings. Left at B2089 towards Rye. 0.25 miles beyond Cripps Corner left at Beacon Lane. Right at farm track at top of hill – house is 1st on left (second drive).

 10% off stays of 2 or more nights.

	Jane & Hugh Willing
	Appletree Cottage, Beacon Lane, Staplecross, Robertsbridge TN32 5QP
Tel	+44 (0)1580 831724
Email	appletree.cottage@hotmail.co.uk
Web	www.appletreecottagestaplex.com

Entry 525   Map 5

Sussex

Wellington House

A stroll away from the gardens of Great Dixter is a warm, comfortable, charming B&B. Behind the Victorian red-brick façade the Brogdens have worked an informal magic, giving guests a cosy sitting room and two big peaceful bedrooms above. These are creamy-walled and carpeted, with comfy mattresses, antique bed linen, pristine shower rooms and good toiletries. Fanny is passionate about food, bakes her own bread, grows her own peaches – a treat; Vivian is a charmer. Visit Bodiam by river boat, comb Camber Sands, explore Rye, revel in Dixter… and return to tea and homemade cakes in the garden.

Price	£90. Singles £60.
Rooms	2 doubles.
Meals	Dinner, 3 courses, from £25 (min 4); 2 courses, £22. Pubs within 2 miles.
Closed	Christmas & New Year.
Directions	Follow brown tourist signs in Northiam village for Great Dixter House & Gardens to Dixter Rd. House at main road end, next to opticians.

Late checkout.

	Fanny & Vivian Brogden
	Wellington House, Dixter Road, Northiam, Rye TN31 6LB
Tel	+44 (0)1797 253449
Mobile	+44 (0)7989 928236
Email	fanny@frances14.freeserve.co.uk
Web	www.wellingtonhousebandb.co.uk

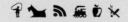

Entry 526   Map 5

Sussex

Boonshill Farm

A glorious farmhouse with a duck pond, brick and weatherboard outbuildings, flouncing flower beds and charming Lisette, a garden designer from London. Large bedrooms have big wide floor boards and inviting beds, decorative gates for headboards, reclaimed windows for mirrors and a delicious rusticity. Bathrooms could appear in *Country Living* (and have!); views are green from every window. Outside are acre of lawns, a wildflower garden, hens and handsome Berkshire pigs; organic breakfasts are outstanding. A bucolic retreat ten minutes from Rye, in rolling Sussex hills: open the door and walk for miles.

Price	£80-£110. Singles £50-£80. Child £20.
Rooms	2: 1 double, 1 twin. Extra child bed.
Meals	Pub 1 mile.
Closed	Rarely.
Directions	Grove Lane opposite The Bell in Iden. Down lane for 1 mile, then left immediately before oast house, down track. Go past Boonsfield Farm; Boonshill at end of track, on left, white gate.

Lisette Pleasance
Boonshill Farm,
Grove Lane, Iden, Rye TN31 7QA

Tel	+44 (0)1797 280533
Mobile	+44 (0)7706 054787
Email	boonshillfarm@yahoo.co.uk
Web	www.boonshillfarm.co.uk

Entry 527   Map 5

Sussex

Kester House

For all those who fancy a taste of 17th-century England, here's a friendly B&B rich with history. Derek and Monique are loving their new venture, in a half-timbered village house in a lovely conservation area. Settle in by the big inglenook (a treat in winter), surf the house laptop, sink into an easy chair. Up the steep stair are low doorways and cosy bedrooms with iPod docks and silk cushions, the suite with a pitched beamed ceiling, the four-poster with deep rich colours. Delicious American pancakes and burritos vie with full English at breakfast, served at the big friendly table. Civilised, and great fun.

Price	£80-£105. Singles from £60.
Rooms	3: 1 four-poster en suite; 1 double, 1 suite for 2, each with separate bathroom.
Meals	Pub 150 yds.
Closed	Rarely.
Directions	M25 & A21 junc. 5. Head south on A21 to Hastings; left to Sedlescombe B2244. On entering village house on right opposite Bridge Antiques.

10% off stays of 2 or more nights. Bottle of wine in your room.

Derek & Monique Wright
Kester House, The Street,
Sedlescombe, Battle TN33 0QB

Tel	+44 (0)1424 870035
Email	service@kesterhouse.co.uk
Web	www.kesterhouse.co.uk

Entry 528   Map 5

Warwickshire

Hardingwood House

Close to Birmingham and the NEC and with a theatrical, Tudor feel. Denise, warm and delightful, spoils guests with big bedrooms, dressing rooms, good linen and deep gold-tapped baths. There are books, flowers, antique clocks and plush sofas; a wood-burner warms the sitting room; dark timbers and reds and pinks abound. The 1737 barn is immaculate inside and out: the kitchen gives onto a stunning patio, while bedrooms have views to garden or fields. Breakfast is delicious: homemade bread and muesli, local sausages, bacon and jams. Much rural charm – and there's a self-catering cottage for two if you like your independence.

Price	£80. Singles from £60.
Rooms	3: 1 double, 2 twins.
Meals	Pub 1 mile.
Closed	Rarely.
Directions	M6 junc. 4; A446 for Lichfield. Into right lane & 1st exit towards Coleshill. From High St, into Maxstoke Lane. After 4 miles, right. 1st drive on left.

	Denise Owen
	Hardingwood House,
	Hardingwood Lane, Fillongley,
	Coventry CV7 8EL
Tel	+44 (0)1676 542579
Email	denise@hardingwoodhouse.fsnet.co.uk

Entry 529   Map 8

Warwickshire

Park Farm House

Fronted by a circular drive, the warm red-brick farmhouse is listed and old – it dates from 1655. Linda is friendly and welcoming, a genuine B&B pro, giving you an immaculate guest sitting room filled with pretty family pieces. The bedrooms sport comfortable mattresses, mahogany or brass beds, blankets on request, bathrobes, fresh flowers and magazines. A haven of rest from the motorway (morning hum only) this is in the heart of a working farm yet hugely convenient for Birmingham, Warwick, Stratford and Coventry. You may get their own beef at dinner and the vegetables are home-grown.

Price	From £79. Singles from £48.
Rooms	2: 1 double, 1 twin.
Meals	Dinner, 3 courses, from £25. Supper £19. Pub/restaurant 1.5 miles.
Closed	Rarely.
Directions	M6 & M69 exit 2; B4065 through Ansty to Shilton; left at lights & next left. Over bridge, right to Barnacle; through village. Left at brick wall signed Spring Road. House at end of drive, over cattle grid.

	Linda Grindal
	Park Farm House,
	Barnacle, Shilton,
	Coventry CV7 9LG
Tel	+44 (0)2476 612628
Web	www.parkfarmguesthouse.co.uk

Entry 530   Map 8

Warwickshire

Mows Hill Farm

From the chocolate labradors in the flagstoned kitchen to the cattle munching in their stalls this late-Victorian farmhouse is a proper working farm of 1,300 acres that has been in the family for generations. Lynda and Edward give you an elegant and comfortable sitting and dining room with field views, loads of books and magazines, family portraits and an open fire. Breakfast on homemade bread and jams, fruit salad, home-reared bacon, just-laid eggs – in the conservatory looking onto the garden in the summer. Bedrooms have cotton sheets, armchairs for flopping and cosy bathrobes. A warm, family home. *Children over ten welcome.*

Price	£80-£90. Singles from £55.
Rooms	2: 1 twin/double; 1 double with separate bath.
Meals	Pub/restaurant 3 miles.
Closed	Rarely.
Directions	A3400 Hockley Heath; B4101 (Spring Lane); left into Umberslade Rd. At 2nd triangle, keep right & onto Mows Hill Rd; 0.25 miles on right.

10% off room rate Mon-Thurs.

Lynda Muntz
Mows Hill Farm,
Mows Hill Road, Kemps Green,
Tanworth in Arden B94 5PP
Tel   +44 (0)1564 784312
Email mowshill@farmline.com
Web   www.b-and-bmowshill.co.uk

Warwickshire

Shrewley Pools Farm

A charming, eccentric home and fabulous for families, with space to play and animals to see: sheep, bantams and pigs. A fragrant, romantic garden, too, and a fascinating house (1640), all low ceilings, aged floors and steep stairs. Timbered passages lead to large, pretty, sunny bedrooms (all with electric blankets) with leaded windows and polished wooden floors and a family room with everything needed for a baby. In a farmhouse dining room Cathy serves sausages, bacon, and eggs from the farm, can do gluten-free breakfasts and is happy with teas for children. Buy a day ticket and fish in the lake.

Price	From £55. Singles from £45.
Rooms	3: 1 family room (& cot); 1 twin, 1 single sharing bath (let to same party only).
Meals	Packed lunch £5. Child's high tea £5. Pub/restaurant 1.5 miles.
Closed	Christmas.
Directions	From M40 junc. 15, A46 for Coventry. Left onto A4177. 4.5 miles to Five Ways r'bout. 1st left, on for 0.75 miles; signed, opp. Farm Gate Poultry: track on left.

10% discount for members of armed forces. Free pick-up from local bus/train station.

Cathy Dodd
Shrewley Pools Farm,
Five Ways Road, Haseley,
Warwick CV35 7HB
Tel   +44 (0)1926 484315
Email cathydodd@hotmail.co.uk
Web   www.shrewleypoolsfarm.co.uk

Warwickshire

Machado Gallery

Artists and artisans have lived in this red-brick village house since 1746 – and it has never looked finer. Sue, a well-travelled sculptor and designer, has spent 21 happy years filling her home with art and natural light: skylights gulp sunshine into the fire-warmed sitting room; carved Russian windows frame daylight; bedrooms – one with a private patio, another a Juliet balcony – have pretty linen and super bathrooms. Wake to espresso coffee and homemade bread, then sit out by the garden pond or browse the studio gallery. The village pubs are close; Warwick, the Cotswolds and Stratford-on-Avon beckon.

Price	£70–£95. Singles from £50.
Rooms	3: 2 doubles, 1 twin/double.
Meals	Packed lunch & clotted cream tea available. Pub 50 yds. Restaurant 100 yds.
Closed	Occasionally.
Directions	M40 junc. 15, A429 to Stow for 1 mile. Left into Barford Village. Cross Norman bridge & mini r'bout under the cedar tree. House 10 yds on left.

 Singles 3 nights for 2 Sun–Thurs.

Sue Machado
Machado Gallery, 9 Wellesbourne Road, Barford, Warwick CV35 8EL
Tel +44 (0)1926 624061
Web www.machadogallery.co.uk

Entry 533   Map 8

Warwickshire

Oxbourne House

Hard to believe the house is new, with its beamed ceilings, fireplaces and antiques. Bedrooms are fresh, crisp, cosy and cared for, the family room with an 'in the attic' feel; lighting is soft, beds excellent, bath and shower rooms attractive and warm, and views far-reaching. In the garden are tennis, sculpture and Graeme's rambler-bedecked pergola. Wake to birdsong and fresh eggs from their own hens; on peaceful summer nights, watch the dipping sun. Posy and Graeme are hugely likeable and welcoming and the excellent village pub is just down the road. A most comforting place to stay. *Dogs by arrangement.*

Ethical Collection: Food; Community. See page 420.

Price	£70–£90. Singles from £50.
Rooms	3: 1 double, 1 family room; 1 twin/double with separate bath.
Meals	Dinner from £20. Pub 5-minute walk.
Closed	Rarely.
Directions	A422 from Stratford-upon-Avon for Banbury. After 8 miles, right to Oxhill. Last house on right on Whatcote Road.

 10% off stays of 3 or more nights.

 Use your Sawday's Gift Card here.

Graeme & Posy McDonald
Oxbourne House,
Oxhill, Warwick CV35 0RA
Tel +44 (0)1295 688202
Mobile +44 (0)7753 661353
Email graememcdonald@msn.com
Web www.oxbournehouse.com

Entry 534   Map 8

Warwickshire

Stamford Hall

Soft hills and lines of poplars bring you to the high, pretty red-brick Georgian house with a smart hornbeam hedge. James, whose art decorates the walls, and Alice look after you impeccably but without fuss. You have a generous sitting room overlooking the garden, with gleaming furniture, early estate and garden etchings, and pastel blue sofas. Peaceful bedrooms are on the second floor and both have charm: soft wool tartan rugs on comfy beds, calming colours, attractive fabrics, restful outlooks. Wake to home-baked soda bread and Alice's full English; walk it off in open countryside or head for Stratford.

Price	£80. Singles £50–£60.
Rooms	2: 1 double, 1 twin.
Meals	Pub 1 mile.
Closed	Christmas & occasionally.
Directions	From x-roads on Fosse Way B4455 & A422 head north on B4455 signed Leicester for 1 mile. Right at x-roads signed Pillerton. After 200 yds, right fork, after another 200 yds right after aluminium barns.

James & Alice Kerr
Stamford Hall,
Fosse Way, Ettington,
Stratford-upon-Avon CV37 7PA

Tel	+44 (0)1789 740239
Email	jk@jameskerr.co.uk
Web	www.stamfordhall.co.uk

Entry 535   Map 8

Warwickshire

The Bakehouse

Red-bricked and mellow on the outside, a lavishly romantic bolthole within. Find beautifully upholstered armchairs, a rose-soft sofa laden with tapestry cushions, an embellished repro mirror with a fun French flourish, plentiful glossy mags and little gilt-framed pictures, and a wood-burner that belts out the heat... and that's just the sitting room. The bedroom is spacious and light, with immaculate carpeting, dark beams and a view onto the neighbouring farmyard and gardens. There's a tiny courtyard for guests and Shoshana is warm and generous. Comfort, character and style, minutes from Stratford and its theatres.

Price	From £95.
Rooms	1 double (extra single available on mezzanine).
Meals	Restaurant/pub next door.
Closed	Rarely.
Directions	From Stratford-upon-Avon, Shipston road then right to Broadway B4632 for 3 miles. Signed Lower Quinton on left.

Shoshana Kitchen
The Bakehouse, Magdalen House,
The Green, Lower Quinton,
Stratford-upon-Avon CV37 8SG

Tel	+44 (0)1789 721792
Email	info@cotswoldbakehouse.co.uk
Web	www.cotswoldbakehouse.co.uk

Entry 536   Map 8

Warwickshire

Cross o' th' Hill Farm

Stratford in 12 minutes on foot, down a footpath across a field: from the veranda you can see the church where Shakespeare is buried. There's been a farm on this rural spot since before Shakespeare's time but part of the house is Victorian. Built around 1860, it's full of light, with wall-to-ceiling sash windows, glass panelling in the roof, large uncluttered bedrooms and smart, newly decorated bathrooms. The garden, full of trees and birds, dates from the same period – there's even a sunken croquet lawn. Decima grew up here; she and David are gentle hosts, and passionate about art and architecture.

Ethical Collection: Food. See page 420.

Price	£90-£95. Singles £65-£70.
Rooms	3: 2 doubles; 1 double with separate bath/shower.
Meals	Pubs/restaurants 20-minute walk.
Closed	20 December-23 February.
Directions	From Stratford south on A3400 for 0.5 miles, 2nd right on B4632 for Broadway Rd for 500 yds. 2nd drive on right for farm.

	Decima Noble
	Cross o' th' Hill Farm,
	Broadway Road,
	Stratford-upon-Avon CV37 8HP
Tel	+44 (0)1789 204738
Email	decimanoble@hotmail.com
Web	www.crossothhillfarm.com

Entry 537   Map 8

Warwickshire

Sequoia House

A cat snoozes by the Aga in this smart Victorian townhouse – an easy stroll from Stratford and a civilised base for exploring Shakespeare country. Step into a pretty tiled hallway and discover high ceilings, deep bays, generous landings, handsome flagstones, a homely sitting room. The easy-going Evanses (Welsh-born) downsized from the hotel they used to run here, and are happy to treat just a few guests: trouser presses and piles of towels mingle with fine old furniture in immaculate rooms. A walkway runs past cricket grounds straight into town. Hotel touches but a warmly personal welcome, and so wonderfully convenient.

Price	£125. Singles £85.
Rooms	6 doubles.
Meals	Pub/restaurant 100 yds.
Closed	Christmas & New Year.
Directions	From M40 (junc. 15) to Stratford (signed). Enter town, then signed A3400 Shipston. Cross River Bridge, then 2nd exit off traffic island. House 100 yds on right.

 10% off stays of 2 or more nights Sun-Thurs.

	Jean Evans
	Sequoia House,
	51 Shipston Road,
	Stratford-upon-Avon CV37 7LN
Tel	+44 (0)1789 268852
Email	reservations@sequoia-house.co.uk
Web	www.sequoia-house.co.uk

Entry 538   Map 8

Warwickshire

Marston House

A generous feel pervades this lovely family home; Kim's big friendly kitchen is the hub of the house. She and John are easy-going and kind and there's no standing on ceremony. Feel welcomed with tea on arrival, delicious breakfasts, oodles of interesting facts about what to do in the area. The house, with solar electricity, is big and sunny; old rugs cover parquet floors, soft sofas tumble with cushions, sash windows look onto the smart garden packed with birds and borders. Bedrooms are roomy, traditional and supremely comfortable. A special, peaceful place with a big heart, great walks from the door and Silverstone a short hop.

Ethical Collection: Environment; Food; Community. See page 420.

Price	£85-£100. Singles from £60.
Rooms	2: 1 twin/double with separate bath; 1 twin/double with separate shower.
Meals	Supper, 3 courses, £29.50. Dinner £35 (min. 4). Pub 5-minute walk.
Closed	Rarely.
Directions	M40 exit 11. From Banbury, A361 N 7 miles; Byfield village sign, left Twistle Lane; on to Priors Marston – down hill; 5th house on left with cattle grid, after S-bend.

Bottle of wine with dinner on first night.

Kim & John Mahon
Marston House,
Byfield Road, Priors Marston,
Southam CV47 7RP
Tel   +44 (0)1327 260297
Email   kim@mahonand.co.uk
Web   www.ivabestbandb.co.uk

Entry 539   Map 8

Warwickshire

Yew Tree Farm

Pristine gravel courtyard, softly weathered stone, mullioned windows, pleached limes: a charming and beautiful house. Colefax and Fowler'd rooms brim with exquisite china, portraits and furniture; the gleaming dining table is acres long. The pretty twin room in the attic is particularly full of chintzy character, the mahogany four-poster room is beautifully done and the bathrooms are smart and new, with a power shower in one. Relax in the top-floor sitting room. Outside, pheasants strut around formal gardens full of sweet peas. Visit the Whichford potteries, return to creature comforts and visual delights.

Price	£105. Singles £55.
Rooms	3: 1 four-poster, 1 twin, 1 single each with separate bath.
Meals	Pub 0.5 miles.
Closed	Rarely.
Directions	Chipping Norton, Great Rollright. Third turning to Whichford. Then 1st turning to Ascott. Down hill and straight into drive.

Susan Hereford
Yew Tree Farm,
Ascott,
Shipston-on-Stour CV36 5PP
Tel   +44 (0)1608 684115
Email   susanhereford@tiscali.co.uk
Web   www.yewtreeascott.co.uk

Entry 540   Map 8

Warwickshire

The Old Manor House

An attractive 16th-century manor house with beautiful landscaped gardens sweeping down to the river Stour. The beamed double has oak furniture and a big bathroom; the old-fashioned twin and single are in a private wing. There is a large and elegant drawing and dining room whose antiques, contemporary art and open fire are for visitors to share. Jane prepares first-class breakfasts, and in warm weather you can have tea on the terrace: pots of tulips in spring, old scented roses in summer, meadow land beyond. A comfortable, lived-in family house with Stratford and the theatre close by. *Children over seven welcome.*

Price	From £90. Singles from £50.
Rooms	3: 1 double with separate bath; 1 twin, 1 single sharing bath (2nd room let to same party only).
Meals	Restaurants nearby.
Closed	Rarely.
Directions	From Stratford, A422 for 4 miles for Banbury. After 4 miles, right at r'bout onto A429 for Halford. There, 1st right, down hill on Queen's Street. House with black & white timbers straight ahead after 150 yds.

Jane Pusey
The Old Manor House,
Halford, Shipston-on-Stour CV36 5BT
Tel   +44 (0)1789 740264
Mobile +44 (0)7786 467916
Email   info@oldmanor-halford.fsnet.co.uk
Web   www.oldmanor-halford.co.uk

Entry 541   Map 8

Warwickshire

Salford Farm House

Beautiful within, handsome without. Thanks to subtle colours, oak beams and lovely old pieces, Jane has achieved a seductive combination of comfort and style. A flagstoned hallway and an old rocking horse, ticking clocks, beeswax, fresh flowers: this house is well-loved. Jane was a ballet dancer, Richard has green fingers and runs a fruit farm and farm shop nearby – you may expect meat and game from the Ragley Estate and delicious fruits in season. Bedrooms have a soft, warm elegance and flat-screen TVs, bathrooms are spotless and welcoming, views are to garden or fields. Wholly delightful.

Ethical Collection: Food; Community.
See page 420.

Price	£90. Singles £55.
Rooms	2 twins/doubles.
Meals	Dinner £25. Restaurant 2.5 miles.
Closed	Rarely.
Directions	A46 from Evesham or Stratford; exit for Salford Priors. On entering village, right opp. church, for Dunnington. House on right, approx. 1 mile on, after 2nd sign on right for Dunnington.

Jane & Richard Beach
Salford Farm House,
Salford Priors, Evesham WR11 8XN
Tel   +44 (0)1386 870000
Email salfordfarmhouse@aol.com
Web   www.salfordfarmhouse.co.uk

Entry 542   Map 8

Wiltshire

The Priory

This is a good city apartment in a partly Jacobean house on the main street; having its own entrance it will suit those who like independence. A quiet conservatory-style bedroom – overlooking the pretty courtyard garden – has chintz curtains, bulging book shelves, interesting art, gleaming furniture and a large comfortable sofa; the bathroom is spotless. Wake to birdsong, and a generous continental breakfast served at a large table in the Aga-warmed kitchen. Not sophisticated but a cosy, unusual base if you're visiting Salisbury – and you can do it all on foot. *Minimum stay two nights. Free parking.*

Price	From £85. Singles from £65.
Rooms	1 twin.
Meals	Pub/restaurant 100 yds.
Closed	Rarely.
Directions	Enter town's one-way system. From north side of Market Square right into Brown St. Through 2 sets of lights; house on left, set back from road.

	Sarah Credland
	The Priory,
	95 Brown Street, Salisbury SP1 2BA
Tel	+44 (0)1722 502337
Email	credland@btopenworld.com
Web	www.theprioreybedandbreakfast.co.uk

Entry 543   Map 3

Wiltshire

85 Exeter Street

You are so central here that you can wander into town on foot (having parked by the house or walked from the station). Susan's Georgian house, facing the cathedral close, is on a main road but the bedrooms sit very quietly at the back and the upstairs drawing room has a lovely view of the spire. Enjoy a good breakfast of fresh fruit, local bacon and sausages, and homebaked bread downstairs at one big table. Bedrooms are simple and traditional: William Morris curtains, a five-foot bed and a shower cabinet in one, a single bed with a spare roll-out bed in the other. Good, solid city B&B. *French & German spoken.*

Price	From £80. Singles from £65.
Rooms	2: 1 double; 1 twin with separate bath/shower.
Meals	Pubs/restaurants nearby.
Closed	Rarely.
Directions	Ring road round Salisbury to south of city; past r'bout to Southampton; at next r'bout (Exeter St r'bout), 3rd exit on to Exeter St (signed Old George Mall). No 85 near city centre. Park opp. house; ask for permit on arrival.
🧳	Bottle of wine in your room.

	Susan Orr-Ewing
	85 Exeter Street,
	Salisbury SP1 2SE
Tel	+44 (0)1722 417944
Mobile	+44 (0)7904 814408
Email	info@85exeterstreet.co.uk
Web	www.85exeterstreet.co.uk

Entry 544   Map 3

Wiltshire

The Mill House

In a tranquil village next to the river is a house surrounded by water meadows and wilderness garden. Roses ramble, marsh orchids bloom and butterflies shimmer. This 12-acre labour of love is the creation of ever-charming Diana and her son Michael. Their home, the time-worn 18th-century miller's house, is packed with country clutter – porcelain, foxes' brushes, ancestral photographs above the fire – while bedrooms are quaint and flowery, with firm comfy beds; organic breakfasts are served at small tables. Diana has lived here for many many years, and has been doing B&B for 27 of them! *Children over six welcome.*

Price	From £90. Singles from £65.
Rooms	5: 3 doubles, 1 family room; 1 twin with separate bath.
Meals	Pub 5-minute walk.
Closed	Rarely.
Directions	From A303 take B3083 at Winterbourne Stoke to Berwick St James. Go through village, past Boot Inn & church. Turn left into yard just before the sharp left bend. Coming from A36 (B3083), house 1st on right.

Diana Gifford Mead &
Michael Mertens
The Mill House,
Berwick St James, Salisbury SP3 4TS
Tel   +44 (0)1722 790331
Web   www.millhouse.org.uk

Entry 545   Map 3

Wiltshire

Little Langford Farmhouse

A rare treat to have your milk fresh from the cow – the Helyers have pedigree cattle. The bedrooms of this rather grand Victorian-gothic farmhouse are large and pretty with period furniture and crisp linen; there are impressive countryside views, a baby grand and a billiard room. Everything is elegant and polished yet cosy, and terrace doors are thrown open for delicious al fresco breakfasts in summer. The farm, part of which is an SSSI, is treasured for glorious walks, wild flowers and butterflies, there's croquet on the lawn and the Helyers are immensely welcoming. *Min. two nights at weekends. Children by arrangement.*

Price	£80-£84. Singles £60-£70.
Rooms	3: 1 double, 1 twin/double; 1 twin with separate shower.
Meals	Pub/restaurant 1.75 miles.
Closed	November-February.
Directions	Exit A303 junc. A36, Salisbury. 2 miles; right for The Langfords. In Steeple L, right for Hanging L. At T-junc. opp. village hall, left for Little Langford. House 0.75 miles on left.

  10% off stays of 3 or more nights.

Use your Sawday's Gift Card here.

Patricia Helyer
Little Langford Farmhouse,
Little Langford,
Salisbury SP3 4NP
Tel   +44 (0)1722 790205
Email bandb@littlelangford.co.uk
Web   www.littlelangford.co.uk

Entry 546   Map 3

Wiltshire

Dowtys

A beautifully converted Victorian dairy farm with fabulous views over the Nadder valley. Peaceful, private, stylish bedrooms, one on the ground floor, have original beams, antiques and big Vi-Spring beds; bathrooms are perfect. The sunny guest sitting room has a contemporary feel too, with its wood-burner, heated floors and sliding doors to the garden. Have delicious breakfast in the old milking parlour, now the dining room, or on the terrace, sit beneath the espaliered limes in the lovely garden, dip into the National Trust woods. Footpaths start from the gate and your charming hosts will help you with all your plans.

Price	£75–£85. Singles from £55.
Rooms	3: 1 double & sitting room; 1 double, 1 twin each with separate bath/shower.
Meals	Packed lunch on request. Pub 0.25 miles.
Closed	Christmas & New Year.
Directions	B3089 approaching Dinton from east (Barford St Martin). Take 1st turn right after village sign & 30mph, signed Wylye. 100 yds; 1st right up Dowtys Lane to house.

10% off stays of 3 or more nights Mon-Thurs.

Di & Willi Verdon-Smith
Dowtys,
Dowtys Lane, Dinton,
Salisbury SP3 5ES
Tel   +44 (0)1722 716886
Email   dowtys.bb@gmail.com
Web   www.dowtysbedandbreakfast.co.uk

Entry 547   Map 3

Wiltshire

Old Stoke

As pretty as thatched cottages come. This lovely old farmhouse is edged by an AONB filled with birdsong and wildlife, yet you are close to Salisbury. Guests have a book-filled sitting room with Dorset cream walls and pretty chairs and sofas to collapse onto: upstairs are fresh bedrooms with bright fabrics on headboards and window cushions, feathery beds and sparkling bathrooms. Tracie is charming and cooks well; good wholesome food using eggs from her own hens, vegetables from the garden and delicious flapjacks or cake for tea. Stroll down the fecund garden to a meadow and the river. *Children over eight welcome.*

Price	£65–£75. Singles from £45.
Rooms	2: 1 twin/double; 1 double with separate bath.
Meals	Dinner £17.50–£22.50. Packed lunch £6. Pub 1 mile.
Closed	December-February.
Directions	SW from Salisbury on A354; right at Coombe Bissett dir. Bishopstone. 2nd left after White Hart, signed Stoke Farthing. In hamlet, sharp bend to right, 2nd house on left. Parking to left of house.

Bottle of wine with dinner on first night.

Tracie Pickford
Old Stoke,
Stoke Farthing, Broad Chalke,
Salisbury SP5 5ED
Tel   +44 (0)1722 780513
Email   stay@oldstoke.co.uk
Web   www.oldstoke.co.uk

Entry 548   Map 3

Wiltshire

Manor Farm

Two children, two cats, 22 chickens, 250 sheep, a burgeoning young garden and a greenhouse to die for: Katie looks after it all with energy and good humour, and goes the extra mile for her guests. Dating from the 1600s, it's a house with a history – and today combines luxury with simplicity. Be cheered by an elegant sitting room with a real fire, a suite with thick feather pillows and a big comfy bed, a bathroom with taupe towels and Neal's Yard bubbles, a breakfast, delivered to your private quarters, of local and home-grown delights, an iPod dock and DVDs on request. And there's a room to store your bicycles and boots!

Price	£85. Singles £60.
Rooms	1 suite.
Meals	Supper tray £20. Packed lunch £10. Pub within walking distance.
Closed	Christmas & lambing time.
Directions	A354 Coombe Bissett, 1st right to Broadchalke. 5 miles to village. Left opp. pub, 0.25 miles, church on right. Road bends 90° right. On apex straight on, then left. House 2nd left.

🧳 Bottle of wine in your room.

Katie Jowett
Manor Farm,
Broad Chalke, Salisbury SP5 5DW
Tel +44 (0)1722 780230
Email info@manorfarmbroadchalke.co.uk
Web www.manorfarmbroadchalke.co.uk

Entry 549   Map 3

Wiltshire

The Duck Yard

Independence with your own terrace, your own entrance and your own sitting room. Peaceful too, at the end of the lane, with a colourful cottage garden, a summerhouse and roaming hens and ducks. Harriet makes wedding cakes, looks after guests and cheerfully rustles up fine meals at short notice; breakfasts promise delicious homemade bread. Your carpeted bedroom and aquamarine bathroom are tucked under the eaves; below is a sitting room cosy with wood-burner, books and old squashy sofas, leading to a terrace. Good for walkers – maps are supplied and you may even borrow a dog. *Reflexology available: book in advance.*

Price	£70-£80. Singles £55.
Rooms	1 twin/double & sitting room.
Meals	Dinner, 3 courses, £25. Packed lunch £7. Pub 2 miles.
Closed	Christmas & New Year.
Directions	A303 to Wylye, then for Dinton. After 4 miles left at x-roads, for Wilton & Salisbury. On for 1 mile, down hill, round sharp right bend, signed Sandhills Rd. 1st low red brick building on left. Park in space on left.

🧳 25% off room rate Mon-Thurs. Late checkout (12pm).

Harriet & Peter Combes
The Duck Yard, Sandhills Road,
Dinton, Salisbury SP3 5ER
Tel +44 (0)1722 716495
Mobile +44 (0)7729 777436
Email harriet.combes@googlemail.com

Entry 550   Map 3

Wiltshire

Manor Farm

Could this be everyone's idea of a country B&B? A lovely old mellow-stone farmhouse (1500s) in a quaint little village with delightful, friendly hosts, three gorgeous dogs and a huge organic vegetable garden. Inside, it is family-friendly not spanking-smart, comfortable, colourful and easy-going. Your quarters at one end of the house have a big family room on the floor above the guest breakfast/sitting room; family pictures and photographs bring the walls to life, boots huddle discreetly behind a screen, two lived-in sofas lie in wait. You can even book a flight in Bertie's microlight for a different view of Wiltshire.

Price	From £70. Singles from £45.
Rooms	1 family room with separate bath.
Meals	Packed lunch £5-£8. Pub within 3 miles.
Closed	Christmas.
Directions	From London & Stonehenge, A303. After A350 junc. pass Esso garage, turn immediately left, then sharp right signed West Knoyle. House 1st on right at bottom of hill.

10% off room rate Mon–Thurs.

Frances & Bertie Grotrian
Manor Farm,
West Knoyle, Warminster BA12 6AG

Tel	+44 (0)1747 830380
Email	bertiegrotrian@yahoo.co.uk
Web	www.englishfarmhouse.co.uk

Entry 551   Map 3

Wiltshire

Oaklands

A comfortable townhouse, a south-facing garden, two dear dogs and a lovely old Silver Cross pram sitting under the stairs. It was the first house in Warminster to have a bathroom; the bathrooms have multiplied since and the interiors have had a delightful makeover – easy to see why this spacious 1880s house has been in the family forever. Andrew and Carolyn, relaxed and charming, serve delicious breakfasts in the beautiful new conservatory at the drawing room end. Bedrooms, desirable and welcoming, overlook churchyard and trees; fresh fabrics, soft colours, cosy bathroom, family antiques. And restaurants are a stroll.

Price	£65-£85. Singles from £55.
Rooms	3: 2 doubles, 1 twin/double (rooms can interconnect).
Meals	Occasional dinner (min. 4 guests). Pub/restaurant 0.5 miles.
Closed	Christmas & rarely.
Directions	From Warminster centre direction Salisbury. On right, opp. end of St John's churchyard.

10% off room rate.

Carolyn & Andrew Lewis
Oaklands, 88 Boreham Road,
Warminster BA12 9JW

Tel	+44 (0)1985 215532
Mobile	+44 (0)7850 158302
Email	apl1944@yahoo.co.uk
Web	www.stayatoaklands.co.uk

Entry 552   Map 3

Wiltshire

The Old School House

Charmingly cluttered, sparklingly clean, this 1860 village house is filled with light, beautiful objects and lovely pieces of furniture. Find a comfy chair in the snug with its loaded book shelves on art, gardening and travel – Darea's passions. Your chintzy bedrooms (the double is larger) have wooden arched beams, excellent mattresses and a newly decorated bathroom with oatmeal tiles. Breakfast is in the smart kitchen with its humming black Aga: good sausages and bacon, local eggs. A little south-facing courtyard has colourful pots and a bench for idle gazing; Stonehenge, Longleat and Stourhead beckon.

Price	£70-£80. Singles £40-£50.
Rooms	2: 1 double, 1 twin sharing bath (let to same party only).
Meals	Pub 500 yds.
Closed	Rarely.
Directions	From London exit 303 at first Wylye turn off signed A36 Warminster, Salisbury. Right fork, right at T-junc., then immediate left into Wylye village. Past pub, church & shop & house immediately after.

Darea Browne
The Old School House,
Wylye, Warminster BA12 0QR
Tel +44 (0)1985 248228
Email dareabrowne@aol.com

Wiltshire

Puckshipton House

An intriguing name, Puckshipton: it means Goblin's Barn. The house is deep in the lush countryside of the Vale of Pewsey, reached by a long tree-lined drive. You stay in the Georgian end, with a private entrance that leads to a Regency-blue hall. Rooms are stylish and uncluttered, an attractive mix of old and new with good beds, crisp linen and bathrooms that are cossetting, one with a roll top bath. The dining and sitting rooms have wood-burners both. James, a forester, and Juliette have young children, a walled garden and a thatched hen house from which to fetch your breakfast egg.

Ethical Collection: Environment; Food.
See page 420.

Price	£80. Singles £50.
Rooms	2: 1 four-poster; 1 twin/double with separate bath/shower.
Meals	Pubs/restaurant 5-minute drive.
Closed	Christmas.
Directions	Devizes A342 towards Rushall; left to Chirton, right to Marden & through village. On for 0.25 miles; right into private drive.

10% off stays of 3 or more nights. Flexible check in & checkout.

Juliette & James Noble
Puckshipton House,
Beechingstoke, Pewsey SN9 6HG
Tel +44 (0)1672 851336
Web www.puckshipton.co.uk

Wiltshire

Copes Cottage

Sarah says her pretty thatched cottage "has a smile on its face"; it has a wildflower meadow too, and far-reaching views over the Vale of Pewsey. Arrive for tea and cake in Sarah's friendly Aga kitchen. Breakfast is in a dining room full of warm colours, flowers, books, glowing lamps and blue and white china. You have a choice of bedrooms – one with beams, antique bed and adjoining space for children, the other more modern and airy; the rustic sitting room is in a converted barn with comfy sofas and table tennis. Set out for forest and downland walks, ancient monuments, Salisbury Cathedral; look for crop circles in summer.

Price	£80. Singles £50.
Rooms	2: 1 double (with extra double room, let to same party only); 1 double with separate bath/shower.
Meals	Pub/restaurant 3 miles.
Closed	Rarely.
Directions	A346 Marlborough to Burbage. At roundabout 4th exit towards Pewsey on B3087. Left into village. After 200 yds, right into Harris Lane. Cottage at end.

Sarah Townsend-Rose
Copes Cottage, Harris Lane,
Easton Royal, Pewsey SN9 5LX
Tel   +44 (0)1672 810427
Email   sarahtrose@hotmail.com
Web   www.copescottage.co.uk

Entry 555   Map 3

Wiltshire

Westcourt Farm

Rozzie and Jonny left London to restore a medieval, Grade II* cruck truss hall house (beautifully) amid wildflower meadows, hedgerows, ponds, geese and hens. Delightful people, they love to cook and can spoil you rotten. Rooms are freshly decorated, crisp yet traditional, the country furniture is charming and the architecture fascinating. Bedrooms have comfortable beds and fine linen, bathrooms are spot-on, there's a lovely light drawing room and a barn for meetings and parties. Encircled by footpaths and fields, Westcourt is the oldest house in a perfect village, two minutes from a rather good pub.

Price	£80. Singles £50.
Rooms	2: 1 twin; 1 double.
Meals	Pub/restaurant in village.
Closed	Rarely.
Directions	A338 Hungerford-Salisbury; after 4 miles signed Shalbourne; through village & fork left at pub; 150 yds, 2nd drive on right.

Jonny & Rozzie Buxton
Westcourt Farm,
Shalbourne, Marlborough SN8 3QE
Tel   +44 (0)1672 871399
Email   rozzieb@btinternet.com
Web   www.westcourtfarm.com

Entry 556   Map 3

Wiltshire

Fisherman's House

Ducks shoot the rapids of the Kennet river as it flows past the lawns of this exquisitely situated home — bliss to sit out here with binoculars on a warm day. Built in 1812 it looks every inch a doll's house, but charming Heather adds a deft human touch. Elegant breakfasts are served in the Edwardian style conservatory, there's a delightful guests' sitting room with an open fire and, upstairs, three sumptuously decorated bedrooms that face the garden and river; time slips by effortlessly here. Many people come to visit the crop and stone circles and Bath and Marlborough are a hop away. *Fly fishing can be arranged.*

Price	£85. Singles £40-£50.
Rooms	3: 1 double; 1 twin, 1 single sharing bath.
Meals	Lunch/packed lunch from £5. Pub 500 yds.
Closed	Rarely.
Directions	From Hungerford, A4 for Marlborough. After 7 miles, right for Stitchcombe, down hill (bear left at barn) & left at T-junc. On entering village, house 2nd on left.

	Heather Coulter
	Fisherman's House,
	Mildenhall, Marlborough SN8 2LZ
Tel	+44 (0)1672 515390
Mobile	+44 (0)7785 225363
Email	heathercoulter610@btinternet.com
Web	www.fishermanshouse.co.uk

Entry 557   Map 3

Wiltshire

Poulton Grange

A big new purpose-built family farmhouse with geothermal underfloor heating and enormous Georgian-style windows: views soar over the Marlborough hills. Deborah and James, the loveliest hosts, give you delicious local breakfasts in the Aga-warm kitchen or the dining room with its Arts & Crafts dresser. Admire the views from a sitting room with a dash of family comfort and a quirky combination of old and new furniture. South-facing bedrooms are large, light and extremely peaceful, with smart bathrooms and Cole & Lewis goodies. It may feel remote but it's a short hop from Marlborough's lovely shops and pubs.

Price	£100. Singles £70.
Rooms	2 twins/doubles.
Meals	Dinner, 2 courses, £20. Pub/restaurant 2 miles.
Closed	Rarely.
Directions	In Marlborough, down hill to The Green. Left into St Martins. Past Tin Pit & white gates & railings on left. Left dir. Rabley & Poulton, under railway bridge then immed. left into drive.

Bottle of champagne for stays of 2 or more nights. Experience helping with lambing during April.

	Deborah & James Sheppard
	Poulton Grange,
	Poulton, Marlborough SN8 2LN
Tel	+44 (0)1672 516888
Mobile	+44 (0)7786 958712
Email	sheppard@poultongrange.com
Web	www.poultongrange.com

Entry 558   Map 3

Wiltshire

Overtown Manor

It's just a few miles from the centre of Swindon, but this listed manor house is still part of a working farm, tucked into quiet countryside. Feel swish in an elegant, duck-egg blue drawing room with ornate plaster work, marble fireplace and lofty sash windows overlooking gardens and pool. You'll eat like a lord in the impressive dining room: Nancy is a chef and chooses produce locally sourced or home-grown. Large light bedrooms are classic country-house style, with views; bathrooms are new, tiled in stone and heated to perfection. Explore quaint villages and stone circles, try clay pigeon shooting; all is possible.

Price	£95. Singles £65.
Rooms	3 twins/doubles.
Meals	Dinner, 2-3 courses, £15-£25. Pub within 5 miles.
Closed	Rarely.
Directions	M4 junc.15 Marlborough. After 1 mile, right B4005 Chiseldon, just before petrol station. Cont. to mini r'bout, Patriots Arms pub on left; 2nd exit B4005. At T-junc. right. 100 yds, left signed Overtown. Cont. to x-roads; on left.

	Nancy Lawson
	Overtown Manor,
	Wroughton, Swindon SN4 0SH
Tel	+44 (0)1793 814737
Mobile	+44 (0)7887 597090
Email	nancy@overtownmanor.co.uk
Web	www.overtownmanor.co.uk

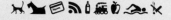

Entry 559   Map 3

Wiltshire

Westhill House

A large Regency house in the centre of this market town; you are on the edge of the marvellous Cotswolds. Vivacious Brenda, well-travelled and a collector of art, has filled her home with bold colours, eclectic paintings, beautiful glass and ceramics; the elegant drawing room has an open fire and the dining room is dramatically red. Bedrooms come in creams and blues, beds are new, wine glasses and corkscrew await; bathrooms are contemporary and indulgent with fluffy towels. Be greeted with tea and cake, try French toast with fruit and maple syrup for breakfast, or full English. Marked walking trails run from the door.

Price	£75-£105. Singles £60-£90.
Rooms	3 doubles.
Meals	Pubs/restaurants within 5 miles.
Closed	Rarely.
Directions	Exit 15 off M4, A419 to Cirencester. Take A361 Burford, Highworth exit. Left at lights in Highworth onto Cricklade Road. House on right immed. after Oak Drive. Black wrought-iron gate.

 10% off room rate Mon-Thurs. Free pick-up from local bus/train station.

	Brenda Haywood
	Westhill House,
	Cricklade Road, Highworth SN6 7BL
Tel	+44 (0)1793 764219
Email	info@westhillhouse.net
Web	www.westhillhouse.net

Entry 560   Map 3

Wiltshire

Winkworth Farm

You have the mellow stone farmhouse to yourselves, so this is perfect for a family party; your hosts look after you with friendly ease and live in the attached wing. Find a pleasing mix of old and new upstairs and down: pretty fabrics, old beams, gleaming wooden floors, log fires, well-dressed beds and smart bathrooms. This working organic Cotswold farm has been in the Newman family for over a century and Jeremy and Melanie run functions in the beautifully restored barns. Visit pretty Malmesbury (of 'Tamworth Two' fame!) with its Norman abbey and gardens, browse the antique shops in Tetbury, wander in Westonbirt Arboretum.

Price	£100–£120.
Rooms	3: 2 doubles; 1 family room with separate bath.
Meals	Packed lunch £5. Pub 4 miles.
Closed	Rarely.
Directions	From Malmesbury B4042 for Wootton Bassett. Left to Lea. In Lea, right opp. school. House along drive through fields, 1 mile from road.

 10% off stays of 2 or more nights.

	Jeremy & Melanie Newman
	Winkworth Farm,
	Lea, Malmesbury SN16 9NH
Tel	+44 (0)1666 823499
Email	info@winkworthfarm.com
Web	www.winkworthfarm.com

Entry 561   Map 3

Wiltshire

Bullocks Horn Cottage

Up a country lane is this hidden-away house which the delightful Legges have turned into a haven of peace. Liz loves fabrics and flowers and mixes them with flair, Colin has painted a mural for the conservatory, bright with plants and wicker sofa. Super bedrooms, both twins, have lovely views; the sitting room has a log fire, fine antiques, big comfy sofas, and the garden is so special it's appeared in magazines. Organic veg and herbs from the garden and local seasonal food make an appearance at dinner which, on balmy nights, you may eat under the arbour, covered in climbing roses and jasmine. *Children over 12 welcome.*

Ethical Collection: Food. See page 420.

Price	From £85. Singles from £45.
Rooms	2: 1 twin; 1 twin with separate bath.
Meals	Dinner £20–£25. BYO. Pub 1.5 miles.
Closed	Christmas.
Directions	From A429, B4040 through Charlton, past Horse & Groom. 0.5 miles, left signed 'Bullocks Horn No Through Road'. On to end of lane. Right then 1st on left.

	Colin & Liz Legge
	Bullocks Horn Cottage,
	Charlton, Malmesbury SN16 9DZ
Tel	+44 (0)1666 577600
Email	bullockshorn@clara.co.uk
Web	www.bullockshorn.co.uk

Entry 562   Map 3

Wiltshire

Manor Farm

The road through the sleepy Wiltshire village brings you to a Queen Anne house with a *petit château* feel, enfolded by a tranquil walled garden with wild flower meadow, groomed lawns and... hens! Inside is as lovely; watercolourist Clare is a perfectionist behind the scenes and is charming. Comfortable and elegant bedrooms have well dressed sash windows; one has soft-painted panelled walls hung with good pictures. Scrumptious, all-organic breakfasts are served in a butter-yellow kitchen; the eclectically furnished drawing room, shared among guests, has a real fire and a delightful lived-in, family feel.

Price	£90. Singles £50.
Rooms	2 doubles.
Meals	Pubs within 3 miles.
Closed	Christmas & New Year.
Directions	M4 exit 17. North on A429 for Malmesbury, right on B4042. Right after 3 miles to Little Somerford. Past pub, right at crossroads, 50 yds on, house behind tall wall.

10% off room rate Mon-Thurs.

Clare Inskip
Manor Farm, Little Somerford,
Chippenham SN15 5JW
Tel   +44 (0)1666 822140
Mobile   +44 (0)7970 892344
Email   clareinskip@hotmail.com

Entry 563   Map 3

Wiltshire

Manor Farm

Farmyard heaven in the Cotswolds. A 17th-century manor farmhouse in 550 arable acres; horses in the paddock, dozing dogs in the yard, tumbling blooms outside the door and a perfectly tended village, with duck pond, a short walk. Beautiful bedrooms are softly lit, with muted colours, plump goose down pillows and the crispest linen. Breakfast in front of the fire is a banquet of delights, tea among the roses is a treat, thanks to charming, welcoming Victoria; she will arrange a table for dinner at the pub too. This is the postcard England of dreams, with Castle Combe, Lacock, grand walking and gardens to visit. *Over 12s welcome.*

Price	From £84. Singles from £46.
Rooms	3: 2 doubles; 1 twin with separate bath.
Meals	Pub nearby.
Closed	Rarely.
Directions	From M4 A429 to Cirencester (junc. 17). After 200 yds, 1st left for Grittleton; there, follow signs to Alderton. Farmhouse near church.

Victoria Lippiatt-Onslow
Manor Farm,
Alderton, Chippenham SN14 6NL
Tel   +44 (0)1666 840271
Mobile   +44 (0)7721 415824
Email   victoria.lippiatt@btinternet.com
Web   www.themanorfarm.co.uk

Entry 564   Map 3

Wiltshire

The Coach House

In an ancient hamlet a few miles north of Bath, an impeccable conversion of an early 19th-century barn. Bedrooms are fresh and cosy with sloping ceilings, while the pale drawing room is elegant with porcelain, antiques and striking floral displays. Sliding glass doors lead to a south-facing patio, then to a well-groomed croquet lawn bordered by flowers, with vegetable garden, tennis court, woodland and paddock. Helga and David are delightful and give you homemade jams and marmalade at breakfast. The splendours of Bath and the charm of Castle Combe are an easy drive; golfers, too, should be happy.

Price	£70–£80. Singles £35–£45.
Rooms	2: 1 double with separate bath/shower; 1 twin/double sharing bath (let to same party only).
Meals	Dinner, 3 courses, from £20. Pubs/restaurants 1 mile.
Closed	Rarely.
Directions	From M4 junc. 17, A350 for Chippenham. A420 to Bristol (east) & Castle Combe. After 6.3 miles, right into Upper Wraxall. Sharp left opp. village green; at end of drive.

10% off room rate Mon–Thurs. Late checkout (12pm).

Helga & David Venables
The Coach House, Upper North Wraxall, Chippenham SN14 7AG
Tel   +44 (0)1225 891026
Email   david@dvenables.co.uk
Web   www.upperwraxallcoachhouse.co.uk

Entry 565   Map 3

Wiltshire

The Little House

Set in a quintessential Cotswold village, mellow-stoned and listed, Little House greets you with a parquet'd hallway, two lively dogs and coffee and cakes from lovely host Carolyn. The interiors are warmly informal, while the fine furniture testifies to Richard's auctioneer eye. Very comfortable bedrooms – a vaulted twin, a four-poster reached up an outside stair – come with spotless tongue'n'groove bathrooms, crisp bedding and decadent towels; all lead off a pretty, guest-friendly courtyard garden. The French-windowed, often fire-lit dining room is where you are treated to homemade/farmshop breakfasts; no wonder guests return!

Price	£65–£80. Singles from £40.
Rooms	3: 1 twin, 1 double & sitting room, 1 four-poster.
Meals	Pubs within walking distance.
Closed	Rarely.
Directions	M4 junc. 17, dir. Chippenham. Right onto A350, on 3rd r'bout right onto A420. Left to Biddestone. House on right just before road bends to left in the village.

Bottle of wine in your room.

Carolyn Madley
The Little House, Cuttle Lane, Biddestone, Chippenham SN14 7DF
Tel   +44 (0)1249 712831
Email   carolynmadley@btinternet.com
Web   www.littlehouse.2day.ws

Entry 566   Map 3

Wiltshire

Glebe House

The rogues' gallery of photographs up the stairs says it all: Glebe House is quirky and fun. Friendly Ginny spoils guests rotten with pressed linen and sociable dinners served on Wedgewood china. Charming, cosy and comfortable are the bedrooms, one with an Indian theme; delightful is the drawing room with its landscape oils, Bechstein piano and rugs from all over Asia; settle into the sofa and roast away by the fire. Breads, marmalades and jams are homemade, beautiful views shoot off down the valley, the garden is alive with hundreds of birds and Mr Biggles (the grey parrot) chats by the Aga.

Ethical Collection: Environment; Food; Community. See page 420.

Price	£80. Singles £45.
Rooms	2: 1 double, 1 twin.
Meals	Dinner, 3 courses, from £25 (BYO). Pub 4 miles.
Closed	Christmas.
Directions	From Devizes-Chippenham A342. Follow Chittoe & Spye Park. On over crossroads onto narrow lane. House 2nd on left.

 10% off stays of 2 or more nights. Bottle of wine with dinner on first night.

Ginny Scrope
Glebe House,
Chittoe, Chippenham SN15 2EL
Tel   +44 (0)1380 850864
Mobile   +44 (0)7767 608841
Email   gscrope@aol.com
Web   www.glebehouse-chittoe.co.uk

Entry 567   Map 3

Wiltshire

Cadwell Hill Barn

Elizabeth is a dynamo at interior design and gardens. The result: a stunningly converted barn hugged by exuberant greenery and packed with interesting fabrics, lampshades, paintings and hand-made chandeliers. Arrive for tea and cake in the sunny raftered upstairs sitting room, or down in the dining area with its inglenook fireplace, Persian rugs and elegant, cosy feel. Bedrooms are calm, soft spaces, one with its own sitting room; bathrooms have underfloor heating and walk-in showers. Countryside rolls into the distance, the local village has a lively community and though five minutes from the M4 it's a peaceful spot.

Price	£80-£100. Singles £50.
Rooms	4: 1 double, 1 suite; 1 double, 1 single sharing separate bath (let to same party only).
Meals	Pub/restaurant 2 miles.
Closed	Christmas.
Directions	M4, A46 towards Bath, junc. 18. About 1 mile, then left signed West Littleton. Through village, pass green and St James' church, then on for further 0.3 miles; house on right.

Elizabeth Edwards
Cadwell Hill Barn,
West Littleton, Chippenham SN14 8JE
Tel   +44 (0)1225 891122
Mobile   +44 (0)7787 305500
Email   maesdewi1@gmail.com
Web   www.cadwellhillbarn.co.uk

Entry 568   Map 3

Wiltshire

The Limes

Through the electric gates, past the gravelled car park and the pretty, box-edged front garden and you arrive at the middle part of a 1620 house divided into three. The beams, stone mullions and leaded windows are charming, and Ellodie is an exceptional hostess. Immaculate, comfortable bedrooms have pretty curtains and fresh flowers, smart bathrooms have good soaps and thick towels, logs glow in the grate, and breakfasts promise delicious Wiltshire bacon, prunes soaked in orange juice and organic bread. You are on the main road leading out of Melksham – catch the bus to Bath from right outside the door.

Price	From £78. Singles £50–£55.
Rooms	3: 2 twins/doubles, 1 single.
Meals	Dinner £23–£28. BYO. Packed lunch £6. Pub 1.5 miles.
Closed	Rarely.
Directions	Leave Melksham on A365 to Bath. After Victoria Motors, sharp right at 1st entrance, brown gates will open slowly. Park on right, follow path to house.

10% off stays Mon–Thurs & for 3-night stays over a weekend.

Ellodie van der Wulp
The Limes, Shurnhold House,
Shurnhold, Melksham SN12 8DG
Tel   +44 (0)1225 790627
Mobile   +44 (0)7974 366892
Email   eevanderwulp@gmail.com

Entry 569   Map 3

Worcestershire

Abbots Grange

A magical manor awash with history, ancient Cotswold stone, atmosphere and deep comfort. Admire the oak panelling, mullioned windows, beautiful rugs and bedrooms with antique four-posters; sink into sumptuous red and gold sofas in the breathtaking Great Hall and enjoy a welcome cream tea. Topsy runs Huffkins, her own craft bakery and tearooms, so breakfast's breads, cakes and patisserie are all made here. She and her sister Faith look after you very well. Read in quiet spaces, wander down to the brook; the picture-perfect village has boutiques and galleries while great houses and gardens are close by.

Price	£100–£150. Singles £80–£130.
Rooms	3: 2 four-posters; 1 four-poster with separate bath.
Meals	Pub/restaurant 50 yds.
Closed	Rarely.
Directions	From Evesham A44 dir. Broadway. From the village green & High Street turn into Church Street. After 30 yds, right onto gravel drive leading to house.

Bottle of our house Champagne for stays of 3 or more nights.

Topsy Taee
Abbots Grange,
Broadway WR12 7AE
Tel   +44 (0)20 8133 8698
Email   rooms@abbotsgrange.com
Web   www.abbotsgrange.com

Entry 570   Map 8

Worcestershire

Harrowfields

Tucked just off the high street is a compact cottage that's massively comfortable and stylish too: contemporary colours and old beams, great books and a homely feel. Your bedroom is large enough to lounge in with a good sofa, an antique brass bed, crisp linen and a cosy wood-burner; the spoiling continues in a shower room with comfy robes. Susie and Adam (who cooks) are natural and charming, hens cluck around the delightful garden, breakfast is local and seasonal, you can walk for miles or just to the pub. Romantic couples will be in heaven; uncork the wine, light the fire, turn up the music.

Worcestershire

The Birches

Thoughtful Katharine is attentive; Edward puts you at ease humming a jolly tune. Come and go as you please from this self-contained annexe, spotless and contemporary. French windows lead to a pretty terrace, then to a charming garden opening to fields and views of the Malverns. Though the house is easily accessible, the tranquillity is sublime; plenty of spots to sit and ponder the view back to the timber-framed house. Hens pottering on the lawn lay eggs for breakfast, served – in your room – with local bacon and sausages, and bread from Ledbury's baker. Wander further for abundant leafy walks and lovely Regency Malvern.

Price	£75. Singles from £60.
Rooms	1 double.
Meals	Pubs in village.
Closed	Rarely.
Directions	Enter Eckington from Bredon (M5 junc. 9). Turn 1st right by village shop. House on left before Anchor pub.

 Free pick-up from local bus/train station.

 Use your Sawday's Gift Card here.

Susie Alington & Adam Stanford
Harrowfields, Cotheridge Lane,
Eckington WR10 3BA
Tel   +44 (0)1386 751053
Email   susie@harrowfields.co.uk
Web   www.harrowfields.co.uk

Entry 571   Map 8

Price	£70. Singles £50.
Rooms	1 double.
Meals	Pub/restaurant 0.3 miles.
Closed	Rarely.
Directions	From Ledbury A449, signed Malvern. After 1 mile right onto A438. After 3 miles, crossroads; left, then after 1 mile right into Birts Street. House on right after 0.25 miles.

 10% off room rate Mon-Thurs.

Katharine Litchfield
The Birches, Birts Street,
Birtsmorton, Malvern WR13 6AW
Tel   +44 (0)1684 833821
Mobile   +44 (0)7875 458441
Email   katharine-thebirches@hotmail.co.uk
Web   www.the-birchesbedandbreakfast.co.uk

Entry 572   Map 8

Worcestershire

Bidders Croft

Completely rebuilt in 1995 from 200-year-old bricks, this solid house with its newly-fitted solar panels, has oak-framed loggias and an enormous conservatory where you eat overlooking the garden, orchard, newly-planted vineyard and the Malvern Hills. Traditional bedrooms with padded headboards and dressing tables are warm and comfortable; bathrooms shine. Bill and Charlotte give you a log fire, books and magazines in the drawing room and an Aga-cooked breakfast with home-produced eggs and fruits; enjoy a bottle of Bill's perry on the terrace. The hills beckon walkers, the views soar and the Malvern theatres are a short drive.

Price	£80-£95. Singles £50-£55.
Rooms	2: 1 twin with separate bath; 1 double with separate shower.
Meals	Pub/restaurant 250 yds.
Closed	Christmas & New Year.
Directions	From Upton-upon-Severn, A4104 dir. Little Malvern & Ledbury. After 3 miles, pass The Inn at Welland on right; drive is 250 yds on left, house signed.

 Bottle of vintage Cava for bookings of 2 or more nights.

 Use your Sawday's Gift Card here.

Bill & Charlotte Carver
Bidders Croft,
Welland, Malvern WR13 6LN
Tel   +44 (0)1684 592179
Mobile +44 (0)7763 055366
Email   carvers@bidderscroft.com
Web   www.bidderscroft.com

Entry 573   Map 8

Worcestershire

Old Country Farm

Ella's passion for this remote, tranquil place – and the environment in general – is infectious. She believes the house was once home to a Saxon chief. Certainly, it has beams dating from 1400; now it's a rambling mix of russet stone and colour-washed brick, with a warm and delightfully cluttered kitchen, wooden floors, lovely rugs. Friendly bedrooms are simple and rustic; one has a beautiful oak bed, duck your head in another. Ella's parents collected rare plants and the garden is full of hellebores and snowdrops; roe deer and barn owls flit in the surrounding woods. A wonderful retreat for nature lovers and walkers.

Ethical Collection: Environment; Food.
See page 420.

Price	£65-£90. Singles £35-£55.
Rooms	3: 1 double; 1 double with separate bath; 1 double with separate shower.
Meals	Pubs/restaurants 3 miles.
Closed	Rarely.
Directions	From Worcester A4103 for 11 miles; B4220 for Ledbury. After leaving Cradley, left at top of hill for Mathon, right for Coddington; house 0.25 miles on right.

Ella Grace Quincy
Old Country Farm,
Mathon, Malvern WR13 5PS
Tel   +44 (0)1886 880867
Email   ella@oldcountryhouse.co.uk
Web   www.oldcountryhouse.co.uk

Entry 574   Map 8

Worcestershire

The Hayloft

Beams galore — and photos too. Dennis is a photographer and your bedroom walls are lined with his colourful works; you get a jolly comfortable bed, posh robes, snazzy bathrooms with candles, plump towels and views across rolling fields. All is peaceful here: wake to a sizzling full English from cheery Maureen, with proper black pudding and homemade jams. You are near the Wychavon Way and the Droitwich Canal for walking, boating and birdwatching, but you could just pootle round the garden which slides down the hill into the countryside, or bubble gently in the hot tub. Excellent value, hearty suppers, lovely people.

Price	£70-£80. Singles from £45.
Rooms	3: 2 doubles; 1 double with separate bath.
Meals	Dinner, 2-3 courses, £15-£20. Packed lunch £5. Pubs/restaurants 2-3 miles.
Closed	Rarely.
Directions	From Droitwich take the A442 Kidderminster road. After approximately 1 mile turn left into Doverdale Lane. Upper Hall is half a mile on right on the hill top.

Dennis's expert advice on digital cameras and Photoshop editing techniques. 10% off stays of 2 or more nights.

Maureen & Dennis Alton
The Hayloft, Upper Hall,
Hampton Lovett, Droitwich WR9 0PA
Tel +44 (0)1905 772819
Mobile +44 (0)7533 056398
Email maureen@hayloftbandb.com
Web www.hayloftbandb.com

Entry 575 Map 8

Yorkshire

Broomhead

High in the ancient county of Hallamshire, amid curlews and skylarks and 6,000 acres of National Park, is the renovated stable block of Broomhead Hall. This warm, light, contemporary conversion is home to a lovely young family, passionate about the land and their responsibility for it. After a day of trout fishing or picnicking beside Ewden Beck, bliss to come home to a cosy soothing bedroom with cowparsley print walls, a bed heaped with pillows and breathtaking views. A fire-warmed snug rammed with books, a huge oil painting of the grouse moor up high, eggs from their hens at breakfast: it's fabulous.

Ethical Collection: Community. See page 420.

Price	£80. Singles £50.
Rooms	1 twin/double.
Meals	Packed lunch £5. Pub/restaurant 2.5 miles.
Closed	Rarely.
Directions	A616 past Stocksbridge. Left signed Bradfield. Follow road for about 2.5 miles. Broomhead 1st farm on left after steep hairpin bend and bridge.

Late checkout (12pm).

Catherine Rimington Wilson
Broomhead,
Bolsterstone, Sheffield S36 4ZA
Tel +44 (0)1142 882161
Email catherine_heaton@yahoo.co.uk

Entry 576 Map 12

Yorkshire

Sunnybank

A Victorian gentleman's residence just a short walk up the hill from the centre of bustling *Last of the Summer Wine* Holmfirth, still with its working Picturedrome cinema (touring bands too), arts and folk festivals, restaurants and shops. Attentive hosts look after you well when the Whites are away. Big peaceful bedrooms are a fresh mix of contemporary, Art Nouveau and Art Deco pieces, caramel cream velvets and silks, spoiling bathrooms and lovely views. A full choice Yorkshire breakfast will set you up for a lazy stroll round the charming gardens, or a brisk yomp through rural bliss. *Min. stay two nights at weekends.*

Price	£70–£110. Singles from £55.
Rooms	3: 2 doubles, 1 twin/double (with extra single bed).
Meals	Dinner, 3 courses, £25. Dinner, 2 courses, £20. Packed lunch £12. Pubs/restaurants 500 yds.
Closed	Rarely.
Directions	A6024 signed Glossop out of Holmfirth centre. Then right into Upperthong Lane. House is first drive on right after St John's Church.

 Bottle of wine with dinner on first night.

Peter & Anne White
Sunnybank, 78 Upperthong Lane,
Holmfirth HD9 3BQ
Tel   +44 (0)1484 684065
Email info@sunnybankguesthouse.co.uk
Web   www.sunnybankguesthouse.co.uk

Entry 577   Map 12

Yorkshire

Thurst House Farm

This solid Pennine farmhouse, its stone mullion windows denoting 17th-century origins, is English to the core. Your warm, gracious hosts give guests a cosy and carpeted sitting room with an open fire in winter; bedrooms are equally generous, with inviting brass beds, lovely antique linen and fresh flowers. Outside: clucking hens, two friendly sheep and a hammock in a garden with beautiful views. Tuck into homemade bread, marmalade and jams at breakfast, and good traditional English dinners, too — just the thing for walkers who've trekked the Calderdale or the Pennine Way. *Over eights welcome. Alternative therapy rooms.*

Price	£80. Singles by arrangement.
Rooms	2: 1 double, 1 family room.
Meals	Dinner, 4 courses, £25 (BYO). Packed lunch £5. Restaurants within 0.5 miles.
Closed	Christmas & New Year.
Directions	Ripponden on A58. At brown Beehive sign, right up Royd Lane 100 yds before lights; right at T-junc. opp. Beehive Inn; on for 1 mile. House on right, gateway on blind bend, reverse in.

David & Judith Marriott
Thurst House Farm, Soyland,
Ripponden, Sowerby Bridge HX6 4NN
Tel   +44 (0)1422 822820
Mobile +44 (0)7759 619043
Email   judith@thursthousefarm.co.uk
Web   www.thursthousefarm.co.uk

Entry 578   Map 12

Yorkshire

Ponden House

Bump your way up to Brenda's sturdy house, high on the wild Pennine Way. The spring water makes wonderful tea and the house hums with interest and artistic touches. Comfy sofas are jollied up with throws, there are homespun rugs and hangings, paintings, plants and a piano. Feed the hens, plonk your boots by the Aga, chat with your lovely leisurely hostess as she turns out fab home cooking; food is a passion. Bedrooms are exuberant but cosy, it's great for walkers and there's a hot tub under the stars (bookable by groups in advance). Good value with a lived-in, homely feel.

Price	£70–£75. Singles from £45.
Rooms	3: 2 doubles; 1 twin sharing bath.
Meals	Occasional dinner, 3 courses, £18. Packed lunch £6. Pub/restaurant 1 mile.
Closed	Rarely.
Directions	From B6142 for Colne. Pass through Stanbury village, then past Old Silent Inn. Access by Ponden reservoir.

	Brenda Taylor
	Ponden House,
	Stanbury, Haworth BD22 0HR
Tel	+44 (0)1535 644154
Email	bjt@pondenhouse.co.uk
Web	www.pondenhouse.co.uk

Entry 579 Map 12

Yorkshire

Pickersgill Manor Farm

A sparkling welcome, immaculate bedrooms, spectacular views. So you'll forgive the ramshackle yard: this is a working farm! The handsome new farmhouse stands high on the moors, criss-crossed by the Millennium Way. Lisa seduces you with Italian coffee and homemade cake, then shows you the rest: lovely big bedrooms; a guest sitting room with books, games and wood-burning stove; bathrooms with Neal's Yard potions and stacks of white towels. Delicious breakfasts are for walkers – sausages from their pigs, eggs from their hens – and are fun. If you time it right, you'll be cuddling new-born lambs.

Price	£75. Singles £55.
Rooms	2: 1 double, 1 family.
Meals	Supper £13. Packed lunch £7. Afternoon tea £7. Pub/restaurant 1.5 miles.
Closed	Rarely.
Directions	A65 from Ilkley, then A6034 to Silsden Moor. On top of hill right into Cringles Lane. After 1.5 miles, left into Low Lane. After 0.5 miles, left when you see B&B sign.

	Lisa Preston
	Pickersgill Manor Farm,
	Low Lane, Silsden Moor BD20 9JH
Tel	+44 (0)1535 655228
Email	pickersgillmanorfarm@btinternet.co.uk
Web	www.pickersgillmanorfarm.co.uk

Entry 580 Map 12

Yorkshire

Braythorne Barn

Great independence here with your own entrance. Inside are paintings, fine furniture, colourful fabrics and rugs; floors are light oak, windows and doors are hand-crafted and sunlight dances around the rooms. Bedrooms are small but understatedly luxurious with beautiful rafters, glorious views, a fresh country feel. Bathrooms have Molton Brown toiletries and plump towels; the guest sitting room is gorgeous. Visit charming Harrogate or walk the Priests Way. Hens in the field, great breakfasts – perhaps brandy-soaked fruit compote... a rural idyll with a contemporary twist. *Children over 12 welcome. Minimum two nights.*

Price	£85–£95. Singles from £60.
Rooms	2: 1 twin; 1 double with separate shower.
Meals	Pubs/restaurants 2-4 miles.
Closed	Rarely.
Directions	From Pool-in-Wharfedale, A658 over bridge towards Harrogate. 1st left to Leathley; right opp. church to Stainburn (1.5 miles). Bear left at fork; house next on left.

	Petrina Knockton
	Braythorne Barn,
	Stainburn, Otley LS21 2LW
Tel	+44 (0)113 284 3160
Mobile	+44 (0)7866 372488
Email	trina@braythornebarn.co.uk
Web	www.braythornebarn.co.uk

Entry 581   Map 12

Yorkshire

Brandymires

The Wensleydale hills lie framed through the windows of the time-warp bedrooms; no TV, no fuss, just calm. In the middle of the National Park, this is a glorious spot for walkers. Gail and Ann bake their own bread, make jams and marmalade, and their delicious well-priced dinners, served at your own table, are prepared with fresh local produce. Bedrooms share bathrooms over two floors. Two rooms, not in their first flush of youth, have four-posters; all have views. If you're arriving by car, take the 'over-the-top' road from Buckden to Hawes – stunning. A friendly, characterful place. *Min. two nights. Over eights welcome.*

Ethical Collection: Food. See page 420.

Price	£56. Singles £33.
Rooms	3: 1 twin, 2 four-posters, sharing 2 bath/shower rooms (one room only per floor can be let on request).
Meals	Dinner, 4 courses, £19.50 (not Thursday). Pubs/restaurant 5-minute walk.
Closed	November-February.
Directions	300 yds off A684, on road north out of Hawes, signed Muker & Hardraw. House on right.

	Choice of any bottle of wine from list with first dinner.

	Gail Ainley & Ann Macdonald
	Brandymires,
	Muker Road, Hawes DL8 3PR
Tel	+44 (0)1969 667482

Entry 582   Map 12

Yorkshire

Hill Top

Books, magazines, bath essences, biscuits by the bed – and the charming, warm and welcoming Christina. Her pretty, listed, limestone farmhouse dates from 1820 and is deceptively big. Ivory walls are a perfect foil for some good furniture and paintings; the sitting room overlooks the charming garden and has a cosy fire. Bedrooms are comfy and conventional; food is fresh, interesting and as homemade as possible. Far-reaching views over rolling countryside in this AONB where waterfalls, moorland and castles beckon. Handy for Scotland or the south. *Babes in arms & children over ten welcome.*

Price	£80. Singles £40.
Rooms	2: 1 twin; 1 twin sharing bath (let to same party only).
Meals	Dinner, 2-3 courses, £17.50-£22.50. Pub/restaurant 1.5 miles.
Closed	Christmas & New Year.
Directions	From Scotch Corner west on A66. Approx. 7 miles on, down hill. Left to Newsham. Through village; 2nd left opp. sign on right for Helwith. House on right, name on gate.

	Christina Farmer
	Hill Top,
	Newsham, Richmond DL11 7QX
Tel	+44 (0)1833 621513
Email	plow67@btinternet.com

Entry 583   Map 12

Yorkshire

Manor House

It's the handsomest house in the village. Annie – warm, intelligent, fun – invites you in to spacious interiors elegantly painted and artfully cluttered. Tall shuttered windows and a big open fire, candles in glass sconces and heaps of flowers, soft wool carpets and charming fabrics: a genuinely relaxing family home. Bedroom are a treat, one with green views on two sides and a bathroom with a French country feel; fittings are vintage but spotless. Stride the Dales or discover Georgian Richmond, a hop away; return to a simple delicious supper, with veg from the garden and eggs from the hens. *Note: peacocks in village!*

Price	£95. Singles £50.
Rooms	2: 1 double; 1 twin/double with separate bath.
Meals	Supper, 2 courses, £20. BYO. Pubs 1 mile.
Closed	Christmas.
Directions	From A1, A66 Scotch Corner towards Brough. After 5 miles, slip road to Ravensworth. In village, right at Bay Horse pub; up steep hill to x-roads then right. In Gayles, left at telephone box into Middle St. House 3rd on left.
	Late checkout (12pm).

	Annabel Burchnall
	Manor House, Middle Street,
	Gayles, Richmond DL11 7JF
Tel	+44 (0)1833 621578
Email	annieburchnall@hotmail.com

Entry 584   Map 12

Yorkshire

Cliffe Hall

What remains is the Victorian section of an earlier mansion, added by Richard's family in 1858. Inside is a beautifully proportioned and charming family home: huge reception rooms, plasterwork ceilings, acres of sofas, family portraits, floor to ceiling shelves of books. Bedrooms are large, sunny, traditional and uncontrived, bathrooms carpeted and twin beds super-comfy; large windows look onto the glorious grounds that run down to the river Tees. Breakfast on local organic bread and eggs and seasonal fruit from the garden. A special place with a soft, timeless grandeur and a big welcome.

Ethical Collection: Food; Community.
See page 420.

Price	From £90. Singles from £50.
Rooms	2 twins/doubles, each with separate bath.
Meals	Pub 1 mile.
Closed	Rarely.
Directions	From A1, exit 56. North for 4.2 miles on B6275. Into drive (on left before Piercebridge); 1st right fork. Darlington Station 7 miles.

	Caroline & Richard Wilson
	Cliffe Hall,
	Piercebridge, Darlington DL2 3SR
Tel	+44 (0)1325 374322
Mobile	+44 (0)7785 756380
Email	petal@cliffehall.co.uk

Entry 585   Map 12

Yorkshire

Rawcar Farm

There's no doubt you've arrived at a farm! Apart from the bucolic setting and the agricultural paraphernalia, friendly owners Jane and Ian may well greet you fresh from tending their beloved Dexters. But this characterful homestead takes 'farmstay' to a new level, and without an ounce of chintz. The two bedrooms are classy, a modern-vintage mix with fabulous fluffy-towelled bathrooms and far-reaching views across trampable countryside; the Coast to Coast trail runs past the farm drive. Enjoy Jane's own bread for breakfast and home-reared beef for dinner, served in an impressive, vaulted dining room: the food is a wow.

Price	£100–£110.
Rooms	2 twins/doubles.
Meals	Dinner from £22. Pubs/restaurants 2.5 miles.
Closed	November–March.
Directions	Northallerton to A167; left at r'bout to B6271 dir. Yafforth, Scorton & Richmond. Right to Streetlam after 4 miles. After 1 mile left to Whitwell & Ellerton. Rawcar 2nd farm on right.

 10% off stays of 2 or more nights.

	Jane McBretney
	Rawcar Farm,
	Danby Wiske, Northallerton DL7 0AL
Tel	+44 (0)1325 378297
Email	jmcbretney@btinternet.com
Web	www.rawcar.co.uk

Entry 586   Map 12

Yorkshire

Lovesome Hill Farm

Who could resist home-reared lamb followed by apple crumble cake? This is a working farm and the Pearsons the warmest people imaginable; even in the mayhem of the lambing season they greet you with delicious cakes and Yorkshire tea. Their farmhouse is as unpretentious as they are: chequered tablecloths, cosy bedrooms (four in the old granary, one in the cottage) with garden and hill views, and a Victorian-style sitting room. Wake to tasty breakfasts of home-laid eggs and homemade bread and jams. You have easy access to the A167 and are brilliantly placed for the Moors and Dales. Good for walkers, families, business people.

Price	£74–£84. Singles £42–£50. Gate Cottage: from £84.
Rooms	5: 1 twin, 1 double, 1 family room, 1 single. Gate Cottage: 1 double.
Meals	Dinner, 2 courses, £18–£25. BYO. Packed lunch £5. Pub 4 miles.
Closed	Rarely.
Directions	From Northallerton, A167 north for Darlington for 4 miles. House on right, signed.

Tour of the working farm.

John & Mary Pearson
Lovesome Hill Farm,
Lovesome Hill, Northallerton DL6 2PB
Tel   +44 (0)1609 772311
Email lovesomehillfarm@btinternet.com
Web   www.lovesomehillfarm.co.uk

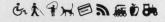

Entry 587   Map 12

Yorkshire

Mill Close

Country-house B&B in a tranquil spot among fields and woodland; spacious, luxurious and with your own entrance through a flower-filled conservatory. Beds are large and comfortable, there's a grand four-poster with a spa bath, lovely linen and sconces for flickering candle light. Be spoiled by handmade chocolates, fluffy robes, even your own 'quiet' fridge. An elegant, pretty blue and cream sitting room has an open fire – but you are between the National Park and the Dales so walks are a must. Start with one of Patricia's famous breakfasts: bacon and sausages from the farm, smoked haddock or salmon, homemade jams. Bliss.

Price	£80–£95. Singles £45–£65.
Rooms	3: 2 doubles, 1 four-poster.
Meals	Pubs/restaurants 2 miles.
Closed	Christmas & New Year.
Directions	Follow the brown tourist signs from the village of Patrick Brompton on A684. Farm is 1 mile from village.

Bottle of wine for stays of 3 or more nights.

Patricia Knox
Mill Close,
Patrick Brompton, Bedale DL8 1JY
Tel   +44 (0)1677 450257
Email pat@millclose.co.uk
Web   www.millclose.co.uk

Entry 588   Map 12

Yorkshire

Braithwaite Hall

Immerse yourself in fascinating history at this working hill farm in the gorgeous Dales; the house belongs to the National Trust and parts go back to 1301. Lovely, unfussy Charles and Vicky farm hundreds of acres but look after you with substantial breakfasts (eggs from their hens, homemade bread and jams) and super bedrooms with long views and fine furniture. The house is worth exploring: an oak staircase dating back to 1667, stone flagging, wood panelling, enormous fireplaces. The village is tickety-boo pretty, Richmond is near, and you straddle the pretty Dales and the wild Moors for bracing walks and birdwatching.

Price	£70–£100. Singles £65.
Rooms	3: 1 double, 1 four-poster; 1 twin with separate bath.
Meals	Pub 1.5 miles.
Closed	December–February.
Directions	A6108 Leyburn towards Middleham, then towards East Witton. Braithwaite 1.5 miles on left, heading east, from the top of village green.

Free fishing on our own river. Bottle of wine for stays of 2 or more nights.

Charles & Vicky Duffus
Braithwaite Hall,
East Witton, Leyburn DL8 4SY
Tel   +44 (0)1969 640287
Email   info@braithwaitehall.co.uk
Web   www.braithwaitehall.co.uk

Entry 589   Map 12

Yorkshire

Park House

The soundtrack could be *Perfect Day*: a scenic drive, delicious cake on arrival, undisturbed peace in the converted estate house – partly built with stone from next door's stunning Cistercian Jervaulx Abbey, owned by your hosts. Antique gems stand out among leather bucket chairs, splashes of colour brighten a neutral palette, guest bedrooms are luxurious. Try Carol's bacon, egg and maple crumpets for breakfast – the menu lists local suppliers. Leave pets and children at home but take boots and binoculars for the glorious scenery of Wensleydale: an AONB and a fitting backdrop to a perfect country stay.

Price	From £75. Singles from £65.
Rooms	4: 3 doubles, 1 twin.
Meals	Packed lunch £9.50. Restaurant 1.25 miles.
Closed	Rarely.
Directions	House is midway between Masham & Leyburn, about 25 minutes off A1. Full directions given on booking.

Entrance to Jervaulx Abbey. Taxi service to & from local award-winning restaurant.

Ian & Carol Burdon
Park House,
Jervaulx, Masham, Ripon HG4 4PH
Tel   +44 (0)1677 460184
Mobile +44 (0)7730 983439
Email   ba123@btopenworld.com
Web   www.jervaulxabbey.com

Entry 590   Map 12

Yorkshire

Low Sutton

Judi's biscuits are a sweet welcome, Steve has a twinkle in his eye: they're B&B pros. Wood fires in the vast dining/sitting room and cosy snug burn fuel from their own copse; good insulation and underfloor heating keep the homely rooms comfy. Curl up in a soft white robe with a book, or wallow in the sparkling bathrooms – one is solar-heated (more greenie points!). There are six acres to explore with ponies, sheep, dogs and chickens; taste the fruit keen cook Judi jams up for breakfast and expect good dinners with veggies from the garden. Country delights from abbeys to markets are in easy reach.

Ethical Collection: Environment; Food.
See page 420.

Price	£70. Singles £50.
Rooms	2 doubles.
Meals	Packed lunch £5. Dinner £20. Pub/restaurant 1.5 miles.
Closed	Rarely.
Directions	From Ripon A6108 through Masham towards Leyburn. 1.5 miles outside Masham left into Sutton Lane. House 0.25 miles on left.

 10% off stays of 2 or more nights. Home-produced gift to take away.

Judi Smith
Low Sutton,
Masham, Ripon HG4 4PB
Tel +44 (0)1765 688565
Mobile +44 (0)7821 600521
Email info@lowsutton.co.uk
Web www.lowsutton.co.uk

Entry 591 Map 12

Yorkshire

Lawrence House

A classically elegant, comfortable house run with faultless precision by John and Harriet – former wine importer and interior decorator respectively. The house is listed, and Georgian, the garden is formal, flagged and herbaceous, the position – by the back gate to Fountains Abbey and Studley Royal, overlooking long meadow and parkland – is supreme. There's a linen-sofa'd drawing room just for guests, and the promise of a very good dinner. Bedrooms and bathrooms are in a private wing: light, well-proportioned, full of special touches. Relaxed, peaceful and timeless. *Golf, riding & clay pigeon shooting can be arranged.*

Price	£120. Singles £80.
Rooms	2: 1 twin/double, 1 twin.
Meals	Dinner £30. Pub/restaurant 1 mile.
Closed	Christmas & New Year.
Directions	A1 to Ripon. B6265 & Pateley Bridge road for 2 miles. Left into Studley Roger. House last on right.

John & Harriet Highley
Lawrence House,
Studley Roger, Ripon HG4 3AY
Tel +44 (0)1765 600947
Email john@lawrence-house.co.uk
Web www.lawrence-house.co.uk

Entry 592 Map 12

Yorkshire

Mallard Grange

Perfect farmhouse B&B. Hens, cats, sheepdogs wander the garden, an ancient apple tree leans against the wall, guests unwind and feel part of the family. Enter the rambling, deep-shuttered 16th-century farmhouse, cosy with well-loved family pieces, and feel at peace with the world. Breakfast is generous – homemade muffins, poached pears with cinnamon and a sizzling full Monty. A winding steep stair leads to big, friendly bedrooms, two cheerful others await in a converted 18th-century smithy and Maggie's enthusiasm for this glorious area is as genuine as her love of doing B&B. *Minimum stay two nights at weekends.*

Price	£75-£99. Singles from £70.
Rooms	4 twins/doubles.
Meals	Pubs/restaurants 10-minute drive.
Closed	Christmas & New Year.
Directions	B6265 from Ripon for Pateley Bridge. Past entrance to Fountains Abbey. House on right, 2.5 miles from Ripon.

Jar of homemade jam or 6 free-range eggs for stays Mon-Thurs.

Maggie Johnson
Mallard Grange,
Aldfield, Ripon HG4 3BE
Tel   +44 (0)1765 620242
Mobile +44 (0)7720 295918
Email   maggie@mallardgrange.co.uk
Web   www.mallardgrange.co.uk

Entry 593   Map 12

Yorkshire

The Old Rectory

Once the residence of the Bishops of Whitby this elegant rectory has a comfortable lived-in air. Both Turner and Ruskin stayed here and probably enjoyed as much good conversation and comfort as you will. Bedrooms are pretty, traditional and with grand views; the drawing room is classic country house with a fine Venetian window and an enticing window-seat. The graceful, deep pink dining room looks south over a large garden of redwood and walnut trees – some are 300 years old. Caroline will give you a generous breakfast; wander at will to find an orchard, tennis court and croquet lawn. *Children over three welcome.*

Price	From £70. Singles from £40.
Rooms	2: 1 double with separate bath & dressing room; 1 twin/double with separate bath & shower.
Meals	Pub opposite.
Closed	Rarely.
Directions	Take A168 (Northallerton road) off A19; over r'bout; left into village; house opp. pub, next to church.

10% off stays of 2 or more nights Mon-Thurs.

Tim & Caroline O'Connor-Fenton
The Old Rectory,
South Kilvington, Thirsk YO7 2NL
Tel   +44 (0)1845 526153
Mobile +44 (0)7981 329764
Email   ocfenton@talktalk.net

Entry 594   Map 12

Yorkshire

Shallowdale House

Phillip and Anton have a true affection for their guests so you will be treated like angels. Sumptuous bedrooms dazzle in yellows, blues and limes, acres of curtains frame wide views over the Howardian Hills, bathrooms are gleaming and immaculate. Breakfast on the absolute best; fresh fruit compote, dry-cured bacon, homemade rolls – and walk it off in any direction straight from the house. Return to an elegant drawing room, with a fire in winter, and an enticing library. Dinner is out of this world and coffee and chocolates are all you need before you crawl up to bed. Bliss. *Children over 12 welcome.*

Ethical Collection: Food. See page 420.

Price	£99.50-£125. Singles £80-£95.
Rooms	3: 2 twins/doubles; 1 double with separate bath/shower.
Meals	Dinner, 4 courses, £37.50. Pub 0.5 miles.
Closed	Christmas & New Year.
Directions	From Thirsk, A19 south, then 'caravan route' via Coxwold & Byland Abbey. 1st house on left, just before Ampleforth.

	Anton van der Horst & Phillip Gill Shallowdale House, West End, Ampleforth YO62 4DY
Tel	+44 (0)1439 788325
Email	stay@shallowdalehouse.co.uk
Web	www.shallowdalehouse.co.uk

Entry 595   Map 12

Yorkshire

Cundall Lodge Farm

Ancient chestnuts, crunchy drive, sheep grazing, hens free-ranging. This four-square Georgian farmhouse could be straight out of Central Casting. Homely rooms of damask sofas and bright wallpapers have views to Sutton Bank's White Horse or the river Swale, spotless bedrooms are inviting – family furnishings, fresh flowers, Roberts radios – and tea and oven-fresh cakes welcome you. This is a working farm and the breakfast table groans with free-range eggs, homemade jams and local bacon. The garden and river walks guarantee peace, and David and Caroline are generous and delightful. *Children over ten welcome.*

Ethical Collection: Food; Community. See page 420.

Price	£80-£95.
Rooms	3: 2 doubles; 1 twin/double.
Meals	Packed lunch £5. Pubs/restaurants 2 miles.
Closed	Christmas & January.
Directions	Exit junc. 49 A1(M) onto A168 (Thirsk). Turn off 1st junc. for Cundall. Turn right at the Crab & Lobster. 2 miles on left.

 10% off stays Mon-Thurs.

	Caroline Barker Cundall Lodge Farm, Cundall, York YO61 2RN
Tel	+44 (0)1423 360203
Mobile	+44 (0)7773 494260
Email	enquiries@cundall-lodgefarm.co.uk
Web	www.cundall-lodgefarm.co.uk

Entry 596   Map 12

Yorkshire

The Chantry

The Chantry is a listed building in a village setting, lived in by Diana and Nigel – warm, humorous and engaging. A member of the Slow Food movement in York, and half Lebanese by birth, Diana reflects her culture in her cooking; her big ramshackle kitchen is the heart of this house. Bedrooms have space and high ceilings and an old-fashioned décor while bathrooms are swisher; the mood is comfy, warm, authentic, historic, and ever so gently eccentric. Pull yourself away from the suntrap terrace and sally forth into town: York, history-rich, is a sturdy walk (or a 20-minute bike ride) away.

Price	£80. Singles £60.
Rooms	2: 1 double, 1 twin.
Meals	Dinner £25. Pubs 200 yards, restaurant 0.5 miles.
Closed	Rarely.
Directions	From York take Bishopthorpe Road. Enter Bishopthorpe, left into Chantry Lane after Bishopthorpe Palace. Last house on right.

10% off stays of 2 or more nights.

Diana Naish
The Chantry, Chantry Lane,
Bishopthorpe, York YO23 2QF
Tel   +44 (0)1904 709767
Mobile   +44 (0)7850 912203
Email   diananaish@athomecatering.
         freeserve.co.uk

Yorkshire

Corner Farm

Coffee and scones on arrival? You get a lovely welcome here! This peaceful farmhouse is so well insulated it's snug and warm even on the coldest day. With York so close and stunning estates nearby, this is a cosy nest from which to explore the area – or just the village pub. Bathrooms are swish and bedrooms are light, fresh and comfortable: cast-iron beds, fine sheets, cute satin cushions. Much-loved Dexters graze on six acres – Tim and Sharon are aiming for self-sufficiency – and apples from the orchard are pressed for your breakfast, flexibly served and with lots of choice, including home-laid eggs.

Price	£80. Singles £50.
Rooms	2: 1 double, 1 twin.
Meals	Packed lunch £4. Pub 100 yds.
Closed	Rarely.
Directions	From York A1079 (6.5 miles). Through two roundabouts, at Kexby left. then on for 0.9 miles. Left for Low Catton, then into village. House 0.8 miles on right.

10% off stays of 2 or more nights.

Sharon Stevens
Corner Farm,
Low Catton, York YO41 1EA
Tel   +44 (0)1759 373911
Mobile   +44 (0)7711 440796
Email   info@cornerfarmyork.co.uk
Web   www.cornerfarmyork.co.uk

Yorkshire

The Mount House

A dollop of stylish fun in the rolling Howardian Hills (an AONB), Kathryn and Nick's redesigned village house is light, airy and filled with gorgeous things – from good antiques to splashy modern art and fresh flowers. The ground-floor twin with white cast-iron beds has its own cosy book-filled sitting room; the sunny upstairs double has views across the roof tops to open countryside. Kathryn, an excellent cook, will spoil you at breakfast – supper too, if you wish – sometimes in the pretty garden. Discover Nunnington Hall, Castle Howard, old market towns and great walking; only 20 minutes from York too. Super.

Price	From £90. Singles from £55.
Rooms	2: 1 double; 1 twin & sitting room.
Meals	Dinner, 2-4 courses, £20-£35. BYO. Pub/restaurant 200 yds.
Closed	Rarely.
Directions	North from York, left off A64 through Flaxton & Sheriff Hutton. Follow signs to Terrington. First gateway on right after sharp right bend as you enter village.

A supper with wine when staying 3 or more nights Mon-Thurs.

Kathryn Hill
The Mount House,
Terrington, York YO60 6QB

Tel	+44 (0)1653 648206
Email	mount.house@clayfox.co.uk
Web	www.howardianhillsbandb.co.uk

Entry 599   Map 13

Yorkshire

Hunters Hill

The moors lie behind this elegant farmhouse, five yards from the National Park, in farmland and woodland with fine views; the position is marvellous and you can walk from the door. The house is full of light and flowers; bedrooms are pretty but not overly grand, and look onto valley or church. The lovely lived-in drawing room displays comfortable old sofas, paintings and fine furniture; rich colours, hunting prints and candles at dinner create a warm and cosy feel. The family has poured a good deal of affection into this tranquil house and the result is a home that's happy, charming and remarkably easy to relax in... Wonderful.

Price	£80. Singles from £50.
Rooms	2: 1 double; 1 twin/double with separate bathroom.
Meals	Dinner, 3 courses, £35. Pub/restaurant 10-minute walk.
Closed	Rarely.
Directions	From A170 to Sinnington. On village green, keep river on left, fork right between cottages, sign to church. Up lane, bearing right up hill. House past church beyond farm buildings.

Jane Otter
Hunters Hill,
Sinnington, York YO62 6SF

Tel	+44 (0)1751 431196
Email	ejorr@tiscali.co.uk

Entry 600   Map 13

Yorkshire

No. 54

The welcome tea and homemade cakes set the tone for your stay; this is a happy place. No 54 was once two cottages on the Duncombe estate; now it's a single house and Lizzie has made the most of the space. Buttermilk walls, be-rugged flagged floors, country furniture, open fires and a stylish lack of clutter. A single-storey extension has been fashioned into three extra bedrooms around a secluded courtyard. Thoughtful extras – a Roberts radio, fresh milk, hot water bottles – make you feel looked after, and the breakfasts will fuel the most serious of walks. Make a house party and bring your friends!

Price	£90.
Rooms	3: 2 doubles, 1 twin.
Meals	Restaurants 10-minute walk.
Closed	Christmas & New Year.
Directions	A170 to Helmsley; right at mini r'bout in centre, facing The Crown; house 500 yds along A170, on right.

Lizzie Would
No. 54,
Bondgate, Helmsley YO62 5EZ
Tel   +44 (0)1439 771533
Email   lizzie@no54.co.uk
Web   www.no54.co.uk

Entry 601   Map 13

Yorkshire

West View Cottage

In a village packed with thatched houses is Valerie's – gorgeous, 17th-century and fronted by cottage flowers, with a bench at the side to take advantage of the views; they reach for miles. The hall is high-raftered with a stunning chandelier, the little dining room has exquisite oak panelling; there's no sitting room but a sofa in your bedroom, reached via the patio, beautifully self-contained. Fabulous curtains, an ornate brass bed, a funky bathroom – comfortable luxury in an unusual space. History and abbeys abound, the North Yorks Moors lie across the field, and bright friendly Valerie knows the area inside out.

Price	£80–£90. Singles £59.
Rooms	1 double.
Meals	Pubs/restaurants 2 miles.
Closed	Rarely.
Directions	Helmsley A170 towards Pickering. After 1 mile, left towards Pockley. House on right, 1 mile from A170.

Valerie Lack
West View Cottage,
Pockley, Helmsley YO62 7TE
Tel   +44 (0)1439 770526
Email   westview.cottage@btinternet.com
Web   www.westviewcottage.info

Entry 602   Map 13

Yorkshire

Brickfields Farm

Down a long peaceful track but just a stone's throw from bustling Kirkbymoorside is this walker's paradise. Friendly Janet sends you off to the North Yorks Moors with maps and information – and a tasty breakfast, served at separate tables in the conservatory overlooking guinea fowl and sheep. Bedrooms are in the main house or in the long low barn or converted cow shed, and all are lovely; a French vintage bed, antiques, heavy curtains, sprung mattresses, fresh flowers, a hidden fridge. Bathrooms have big open showers, thick towels and generous lotions and bubbles. *Not suitable for children.*

Yorkshire

Union Place

A listed Adam Georgian townhouse – elegance epitomised. Lofty well-proportioned rooms with polished floors and cornices and fireplaces intact are delightfully dotted with sophisticated, quirky objets: bead-and-embroidery lampshades and chandeliers, bone china, a small mirrored Indian ceramic child's dress – and your urbane host Richard's accomplished paintings. Bedrooms, one painted duck egg blue, one green with floral wallpaper, are beautiful, with lots of lace and fine linen; the claw-foot roll top in the shared bathroom cuts a dash. Breakfast is unbeatable... then it's off to explore the North York Moors. Superb.

Price	£90–£130.		Price	£55–£65.
Rooms	7: 1 twin. Barn: 4 suites. Cow shed: 1 suite, 1 four-poster suite.		Rooms	2 doubles sharing bath.
Meals	Pub/restaurant 1 mile.		Meals	Pubs/restaurants within walking distance.
Closed	Rarely.		Closed	Christmas.
Directions	A170 east from Thirsk to Kirkbymoorside; continue past roundabout for 0.5 miles. Right into Kirkby Mills, signed. House 1st right along small lane.		Directions	On the outskirts of Whitby on the A174 (Whitby to Middlesbrough) approx. 100 yds from Harrison's Garage.

🧳	6 breakfast eggs: extra fresh, free-range.		🧳	10% off stays of 2 or more nights. Free pick-up from local bus/train station.

	Janet Trousdale Brickfields Farm, Kirkby Mills, Kirkbymoorside YO62 6NS			**Richard & Jane Pottas** Union Place, 9 Upgang Lane, Whitby YO21 3DT
Tel	+44 (0)1751 433074		Tel	+44 (0)1947 605501
Email	janet@brickfieldsfarm.co.uk		Email	pottas1@btinternet.com
Web	www.brickfieldsfarm.co.uk		Web	www.unionplacewhitby.co.uk

Entry 603   Map 13

Entry 604   Map 13

Yorkshire

Thorpe Hall

Arrive and listen: nothing, bar the wind in the trees and the odd seagull; the eye gathers glimmering sea and mighty headland, the final edge of the moors. Are there still smugglers? The wonderful house smells of polish and flowers, the panelled drawing room breathes history. Angelique, a delight, has furnished it all, including her TV-free bedrooms, with an eclectic mix of old and new and some fun (a framed transport caff poster in the breakfast room). She's hung contemporary art on ancient walls and has made a veg patch with young Phoebe. David helps with breakfast when he's not globetrotting. The very opposite of stuffy.

Price	£80–£90.
Rooms	7: 3 doubles; 3 doubles, 1 twin sharing separate bath & shower rooms.
Meals	Pub wlthin 0.25 miles.
Closed	Occasionally.
Directions	Scarborough, A171 Whitby. After 15 miles right at junc. for Fylingthorpe & Robin Hood's Bay. In centre of Fylingthorpe, right onto Middlewood Lane, house on left before ford.

Late checkout (12pm).

Angelique Russell
Thorpe Hall,
Middlewood Lane, Fylingthorpe,
Whitby YO22 4TT
Tel   +44 (0)1947 880667
Email   thorpehall@googlemail.com
Web   www.thorpe-hall.co.uk

Entry 605   Map 13

Yorkshire

Holly Croft

Huge kindness and thoughtful touches (hot water bottles, lifts to the pub, cake and tea on arrival) make this special. The décor is in Edwardian style, the rooms are scented with flowers and polish, the clock ticks, the comforts are indisputable. The double has a textured silk headboard with matching curtains, there are bathrobes in fitted wardrobes, big showers and generous breakfasts – own jams, Yorkshire teas, kippers if you choose – served at the gleaming mahogany table. After a bracing cliff-top walk return to a homely open-fired sitting room overlooking the lovely garden. Wonderful Whitby is 20 minutes away.

Price	£75–£80. Singles £55–£60.
Rooms	2: 1 twin/double; 1 double with separate bath.
Meals	Dinner by arrangement (4+ only). Pub 600 yds.
Closed	Rarely.
Directions	A171 from Scarborough to Whitby; at Scalby x-roads, by tennis courts, take road on right. Signed 500 yds on right.

10% off room rate Mon-Thurs. Free pick-up from local bus/train station.

Use your Sawday's Gift Card here.

John & Christine Goodall
Holly Croft,
28 Station Road, Scalby,
Scarborough YO13 0QA
Tel   +44 (0)1723 375376
Email   christine.goodall@tesco.net
Web   www.holly-croft.co.uk

Entry 606   Map 13

Yorkshire

Crown House

The Firths have renovated their Victorian townhouse in chic New England style. Colours are muted, art is contemporary, stripes and new pieces blend with antiques and there is always something quirky to catch the eye. Luxurious ground-floor bedrooms have books, music, DVDs, jelly beans and fabulous bathrooms. Barbara is passionate about the area and is an amazing host: you'll find maps, smart suppers and breakfasts of black pudding, Whitby kippers, muffins... or continental in your room. The road is busy but inside all is quiet, graceful and relaxed and you're a walk away from town, theatre, stunning Italian gardens and sea.

Price	£100-£110. Singles from £70.
Rooms	2: 1 double, 1 twin/double.
Meals	Dinner £30. Pub/restaurant 200 yds.
Closed	Rarely.
Directions	A64 to Scarborough; right at lights immed. after B&Q into Queen Margaret's Rd. At traffic lights right. House on left on corner of Belvedere Road and Filey Road.

10% off stays of 2 or more nights Mon-Thurs. 20% off stays of 3 or more nights.

	Barbara Firth
	Crown House,
	20 Filey Road,
	Scarborough YO11 2TU
Tel	+44 (0)1723 375401
Email	barbara@crownhousescarborough.co.uk
Web	www.crownhousescarborough.co.uk

Entry 607   Map 13

Yorkshire

Flamborough Rigg Cottage

Even in the North York Moors it's rare to find a spot so remote – rarer still to find such luxury in an 1820s farmhouse set in fields of lambs. Philip and Caroline know how to delight guests with brilliant bathrooms, crisp linen, delicious meals from home-grown produce. They've melded modern touches with handsome antiques, like contemporary art around a grandfather clock in the vaulted dining room – it works. One bedroom has a sitting area; the others have French doors to an orchard garden; all gaze over hills that cry out for walking. Dogs are welcome, Whitby coast is ten miles, and there's fine food and company to round off the day.

Price	From £85. Singles £65.
Rooms	3: 2 doubles, 1 double & sitting room.
Meals	Supper platter £15. Pub 2 miles.
Closed	Rarely.
Directions	Leave Pickering passing the Steam Railway towards Newton-upon-Rawcliffe and Stape. Go through Newton in to Stape. 500 yards past phone box turn left, keep left. House 4th property along.

Late checkout (12pm).

	Philip & Caroline Jackson
	Flamborough Rigg Cottage,
	Middlehead Road, Stape,
	Pickering YO18 8HR
Tel	+44 (0)1751 475263
Email	enquiries@flamboroughriggcottage.co.uk
Web	www.flamboroughriggcottage.co.uk

Entry 608   Map 13

Yorkshire

Rectory Farmhouse

Walk from the door straight onto the North Yorkshire Moors; it's a brisk 30-minute stride across fields to the Steam Railway too. Michael and Heather have been here since 1997 – along with dogs, horses, a flock of sheep and bountiful hens. There's a relaxed, homely vibe with comfortable sofas and an open fire; enjoy homemade cakes and tea or sherry in the guest lounge, a proper Yorkshire dinner and hearty breakfast in the dining room. Comfy bedrooms have fluffy bathrobes, flowers, pretty cushions and throws. Excellent value, and superb for walking, biking and riding. *Over eights welcome. Minimum stay two nights.*

Price	From £60. Singles £40.
Rooms	4: 1 double, 1 twin. Apartment: 1 double, 1 twin sharing separate bath (let to same party only).
Meals	Dinner, 2 courses, £15. BYO. Pub in village.
Closed	Christmas & New Year.
Directions	From A169 take Lockton & Levisham road. Once through Lockton, look for house sign after 0.75 miles on right, in Levisham.

Bottle of wine in your room. Late checkout (12pm).

Michael & Heather Holt
Rectory Farmhouse,
Levisham, Pickering YO18 7NL
Tel   +44 (0)1751 460491
Mobile   +44 (0)7971 625898
Email   info@rectoryfarmlevisham.co.uk
Web   www.rectoryfarmlevisham.co.uk

Entry 609   Map 13

Yorkshire

The Wold Cottage

Drive through mature trees, and a proper entrance with signs, to an elegant Georgian Manor house in 300 glorious acres; arrive for tea in the warm and welcoming guest lounge. The dining room has heartlifting views across the landscaped gardens, and there are gorgeous original features: fanlights, high ceilings and broad staircases. Bedrooms are sumptuous and comfortable with lots of thoughtful extras: fluffy bathrobes, chocolates and biscuits. You are warmed by straw bale heating, food is local and delicious: an award-winning Yorkshire breakfast sets you up for discovering RSPB Bempton Cliffs and the unspoilt Wolds.

Ethical Collection: Environment; Food. See page 420.

Price	£100–£120. Singles £60–£75.
Rooms	6: 2 doubles, 2 twins. Barn: 1 family room, 1 double.
Meals	Supper £25. Wine from £12.95.
Closed	Rarely.
Directions	A64 onto B1249. Through Foxholes to Wold Newton. In village, take road between pond & pub; signed on right.

Local food/produce and water in your room. Free pick-up from local bus/train station.

Derek & Katrina Gray
The Wold Cottage,
Wold Newton, Driffield YO25 3HL
Tel   +44 (0)1262 470696
Mobile   +44 (0)7811 203336
Email   katrina@woldcottage.com
Web   www.woldcottage.com

Entry 610   Map 13

Yorkshire

Village Farm

Tucked behind houses and shops, this was once the village farm with land stretching to the coast. Now the one-storey buildings overlooking a courtyard are large bedrooms in gorgeous colours with luxurious touches. Chrysta, fresh from London, is living her dream and looks after you well: baths are deep, beds crisply comfortable, heating is underfoot. Delicious breakfasts are served at wooden tables in a cheerful light room with a contemporary feel; dinner is candlelit and locally sourced. Stride the cliffs, watch birds at Flamborough Head or make for Spurn Point – remote and lovely. *Dogs £5.*

Price	£75. Singles £60. Child (over 4) £15.
Rooms	3: 1 twin/double, 2 family rooms for 4.
Meals	Dinner, 3 courses, £17.50. Pubs/restaurants within 20 yds.
Closed	Rarely.
Directions	A165 Beverley to Bridlington. At Beeford x-roads, right onto B1249 to Skipsea. Pass church on left, at x-roads straight across to Back Street. On right, opp. pub.

 Take dinner with us during your stay and get a free bottle of wine with your meal.

Chrysta Newman
Village Farm, Back Street,
Skipsea, Driffield YO25 8SW
Tel +44 (0)1262 468479
Mobile +44 (0)7973 340562
Email villagefarmskipsea@yahoo.com
Web www.villagefarmskipsea.co.uk

Entry 611　Map 13

Yorkshire

Low Penhowe

With the Turners at the helm, you are on a safe ship. They see to everything so perfectly – the crispness of the breakfast bacon, the freshness of the eggs from their hens, the homemade bread, the bowls of flowers, the fire in the guest drawing room. Traditional, comfortable bedrooms face south and overlook the garden – lap up the views in summer while birds soar and twitter, Christopher's Highland cattle peer over the fence and the chickens strut and scratch. Castle Howard and the North Yorks Moors are in front of you and all around are abbeys, castles, rivers, ruins and woods. *Children over ten welcome.*

Ethical Collection: Environment; Food; Community. See page 420.

Price	£80–£99. Singles £65.
Rooms	2: 1 double; 1 twin/double with separate bath.
Meals	Packed lunch £6. Pubs 1.5 miles.
Closed	Christmas & New Year.
Directions	A64 at Whitwell on the Hill, right for Kirkham. Over crossing & Derwent, pass Kirkham Priory & Stone Trough Inn. Right at T-junc., left for Burythorpe, over x-roads, 700 yds; right up drive.

 Bottle of house wine for a minimum 2-night stay.

Christopher & Philippa Turner
Low Penhowe,
Burythorpe, Malton YO17 9LU
Tel +44 (0)1653 658336
Mobile +44 (0)7900 227000
Email lowpenhowe@btinternet.com
Web www.bedandbreakfastyorkshire.co.uk

Entry 612　Map 13

Yorkshire

Dowthorpe Hall

Caroline is lovely, cooking is her passion and she trawls the county for the best; fish and seafood from Hornsea, Dexter beef, game from the local shoot; her fruits and veg are home-grown. All is served in a sumptuous Georgian dining room by flickering candlelight, after which you retire to a comfortable drawing room; this is a marvellously elegant, and happy, house. Sleep peacefully on a luxurious mattress, wake to the aroma of bacon, sausages, eggs and home-baked bread. There are acres of gorgeous garden to roam – orchards, pathways, potager and pond – and a trio of historic houses to visit.

Price	£80-£90. Singles £50.
Rooms	2: 1 twin/double; 1 double with separate bath.
Meals	Dinner £25. Pubs 0.25-5 miles.
Closed	Rarely.
Directions	North on A165 for Bridlington, through Ganstead & Coniston. On right, white railings & drive to Dowthorpe Hall.

1 night free for stays of 5 or more nights. Bottle of wine with dinner on 1st night.

John & Caroline Holtby
Dowthorpe Hall,
Skirlaugh, Hull HU11 5AE
Tel   +44 (0)1964 562235
Email john.holtby@farming.co.uk
Web   www.dowthorpehall.com

Entry 613   Map 13

Guernsey

Seabreeze

Maggie's house – the most southern on Guernsey – comes with enormous views: Herm and Sark glistening in the water under a vast sky. The breakfast terrace is hard to beat, there are sofas in the conservatory, cliff-top paths for fabulous walks, a beach for picnics in summer. The house started life as HQ for French pilots flying seaplanes in WWI; these days warm, rustic interiors make for a great island base. It's not grand, just very welcoming with rooms that hit the spot: pretty linen, bathrobes, super showers, fresh flowers. You can hire bikes locally, then spin up the lane to a Michelin-starred restaurant. Brilliant.

Price	£70-£80. Singles from £40.
Rooms	3: 1 twin/double, 1 single; 1 twin/double & kitchen.
Meals	Pubs/restaurants 500 yds & 0.5 miles.
Closed	Rarely.
Directions	South from St Peter Port for 3 miles. Through Fermain village, then left at lights for Jerbourg Point. Keep left at Hotel Jerbourg and last house on right along cliff top lane, keeping sea on left.

Late checkout (12pm). Free pick up from airport or harbour.

Maggie Talbot-Cull
Seabreeze, La Moye Lane,
Route De Jerbourg, St Martin GY4 6BN
Tel   +44 (0)1481 237929
Email seaplane@mail.com
Web   www.guernseybandb.com

Entry 614   Map 4

Scotland

Aberdeenshire

Cairness House

A Palladian mansion, one of Scotland's finest, a bona fide jaw-dropper. Julio and Khalil rescued the house from neglect; water was pouring through the roof, 120 windows needed repair. It is a work in progress, open to the public, its interior refurbishment faithful to original drawings. Wander and find Doric columns, marble busts, a Georgian kitchen and Masonic stonework influenced by the Temple of Solomon. Stately bedrooms are vast, there are walls of books and an open fire in the morning room: tea and cake are served on arrival. Also: an arboretum of specimen trees and a five-acre kitchen garden. Worth the detour.

Price	£100–£130.
Rooms	3: 2 four-posters; 1 four-poster with separate bath.
Meals	Supper, 3 courses, £30. Dinner £50.
Closed	Rarely.
Directions	Leave A90 seven miles south of Fraserburgh for St Combs on B3033. House signed left after two miles.

10% off stays of 2 or more nights.

Julio Soriano-Ruiz &
Khalil Hafiz Khairallah
Cairness House,
Lonmay, Fraserburgh AB43 8XP
Tel   +44 (0)1346 582078
Email   info@cairnesshouse.com
Web   www.cairnesshouse.com

Entry 615   Map 19

Aberdeenshire

Balwarren

Thirty acres at the end of a farm track, a field of Highland cattle, mixed woodland, ancient dykes, a lochside full of birdlife, a herb garden with 200 varieties and a burn you may follow down the hill. Hazel and James, warm, friendly, quietly passionate about green issues, came to croft 25 years ago and the whole place is a delight: cathedral roof, shiny wooden floors, cashmere blankets, sparkling bathrooms and log fires. Enjoy superb breakfasts and dinners: eggs from their hens, homemade marmalade and jams, beef from their cattle. A beautiful, uplifting and peaceful place in glorious countryside. *Cream teas £3.50.*

Ethical Collection: Environment; Food.
See page 420.

Price	£68–£85. Singles £45–£50.
Rooms	2: 1 twin, 1 double.
Meals	Dinner, 3 courses, £25. Pub/restaurant 10 miles.
Closed	Rarely.
Directions	North from Aberchirder on B9023. Right at Lootcherbrae (still B9023); 2nd left for Ordiquhill. After 1.7 miles, right at farm track opp. Aulton Farm; last croft up track.

10% off stays of 2 or more nights. Bottle of wine with dinner on first night.

Hazel & James Watt
Balwarren,
Ordiquhill,
Banff AB45 2HR
Tel   +44 (0)1466 751688
Email   balwarrenbedandbreakfast@gmail.com
Web   www.balwarren.com

Entry 616   Map 19

Aberdeenshire

Old Mayen

Follow narrow lanes crowded by beech trees and hedges, through high rolling hills to a beautiful house with a river coursing along the unspoilt valley below. Find immaculate country-house style in elegant bedrooms with window seats, pretty chintzes, plumped cushions and spoiling bathrooms; there's a book-filled sitting room and candlelit dinners by a winter fire. Fran and Jim are infectiously enthusiastic and kind, breakfasts are a moveable feast (outside in good weather) and the garden hums with birds. A fine retreat for tired and jaded souls – and there are castles, distilleries and gardens to visit.

Price	£90. Singles £50.
Rooms	2: 1 double; 1 double with separate shower.
Meals	Dinner £25. Supper, 2 courses, £18. Restaurant 12 miles.
Closed	Rarely.
Directions	From A96, A97 to Banff. After crossing river Deveron (9 miles), left onto B9117; 3 miles, on left behind thick beech hedge.

10% off stays of 2 or more nights.

James & Fran Anderson
Old Mayen,
Rothiemay,
Huntly AB54 7NL
Tel   +44 (0)1466 711276
Email   oldmayen@hotmail.co.uk

Entry 617   Map 19

Aberdeenshire

Lynturk Home Farm

The stunning drawing room, with pier-glass mirror, baby grand and enveloping sofas, is reason enough to come; the food, served in a candlelit, deep-sage dining room, is delicious, with produce from the farm. You're treated as friends here and your hosts are delightful. It's peaceful, too, on the Aberdeenshire Castle Trail. The handsome farmhouse has been in the family since 1762 and you can roam the surrounding, rolling, 300 acres. Inside: flowers, polished furniture, Persian rugs, family portraits and supremely comfortable bedrooms. "A blissful haven," says a reader. *Fishing, shooting & golf breaks.*

Price	From £90. Singles £50.
Rooms	3: 1 double, 2 twins/doubles.
Meals	Dinner, 4 courses, £30. Pub 1 mile.
Closed	Rarely.
Directions	20 miles from Aberdeen on A944 (towards Alford); thro' Tillyfourie, then left for Muir of Fowlis & Tough; after Tough, 2nd farm drive on left, signed.

 Bottle of wine with dinner on first night. Late checkout (12pm).

John & Veronica Evans-Freke
Lynturk Home Farm,
Alford
AB33 8DU
Tel   +44 (0)1975 562504
Mobile +44 (0)7773 389793
Email   lynturk@hotmail.com

Entry 618   Map 19

Aberdeenshire

Ardneidly Steading

Near a conservation village in rugged open countryside, the granite former steading conceals an entrancing interior. Walls are white or café au lait, timbers are reclaimed, and art, antiques and textiles add personality; there's a designer wood-burner in the split-level living room and games for the grandchildren. Mandy and Colin make their own jams, grow their own food and create perfect breakfasts on the Aga; Mandy loves house, garden and guests in equal measure. Two peaceful bedrooms, simple and stylish, are up a private stair; bathrooms are delicious. Wildlife, biking, hiking, castles by the hatful. Heaven!

Price	£80. Singles £55.
Rooms	2: 1 double, 1 twin.
Meals	Supper £20. Packed lunch from £7.50. Pub/hotel 1 mile.
Closed	Rarely.
Directions	From Aberdeen, A944 west; 2 miles past Dunecht right. Follow signs to Monymusk. Through village. After 0.5 miles, left at crossroads. House second on left.

For a stay of 3 nights, having supper every night, the third night's supper is free.

Colin & Mandy Hamilton
Ardneidly Steading,
Monymusk AB51 7HX
Tel   +44 (0)1467 651222
Mobile   +44 (0)7821 259700
Email   info@ardneidlysteading.co.uk
Web   www.ardneidlysteading.co.uk

Entry 619   Map 19

Aberdeenshire

Woodend House

Elegant riverside living at a fishing lodge by the river Dee – one of the most magnificent settings in Scotland. Outside, a wild, wonderful garden; inside, beautiful wallpapers, fabrics and rugs. The dining hall and drawing room have dreamy river views, the large bedrooms ooze comfort and more views, and the bathrooms have cast-iron baths and fine toiletries. Food is locally sourced and seasonal: summer porridge with walnuts and fruit, homemade bread, seriously good dinners with home-grown vegetables. All this, and a fishing hut and a secure rod room for salmon and sea trout fishing in season. *Minimum stay two nights.*

Price	£110. Singles £80.
Rooms	3: 1 double, 1 twin; 1 twin with separate bath.
Meals	Dinner, 4 courses, £30. Packed lunch £5-£10. Pub 2 miles.
Closed	Christmas, New Year & occasionally.
Directions	4 miles west of Banchory on A93. Entrance to drive on south side of road, just west of Backhill of Trustach.

Miranda & Julian McHardy
Woodend House,
Trustach, Banchory AB31 4AY
Tel   +44 (0)1330 822367
Mobile   +44 (0)7812 142728
Email   miranda.mchardy@woodend.org
Web   www.woodend.org

Entry 620   Map 19

Aberdeenshire

Lys-na-Greyne House

Peace, tranquillity and a natural welcome – one of the loveliest places in this book. Expect a sweeping stair, sun-streamed rooms, log fires and the most comfortable beds in Scotland. Your room may be huge – two are; one with a dressing room and a balcony, all with family antiques, bathrobes, fine linen… and views of river, field, forest and hill where osprey and lapwing glide. Meg picks fruit and flowers from a garden that borders the river Dee and her food is delicious; David is an enthusiastic naturalist and can advise on walking and wildlife. Nearby, golf, fishing and castles by the hatful.

Ethical Collection: Community. See page 420.

Price	£90–£100.
Rooms	3: 2 twins/doubles; 1 twin/double with separate bath/shower. Extra shower available.
Meals	Pub/bistro 1 mile.
Closed	Rarely.
Directions	From Aboyne, A93 west for Braemar. Just before 30mph sign, left down Rhu-na-Haven Rd. House 400 yds on, 4th gateway on right.

💼 Fresh flowers in room.

David & Meg White
Lys-na-Greyne House,
Rhu-na-Haven Road, Aboyne AB34 5JD
Tel   +44 (0)1339 887397
Email meg.white@virgin.net

Entry 621   Map 19

Angus

Rottal Lodge

A single track road winds beneath snow-topped mountains, buzzards soar above: Glen Clova has a remote and special beauty. Approach the 1911 shooting lodge and there is Jemima, full of smiles. Hens share the sun with a labrador; inside all is comfort and warmth. Find charming carpeted bedrooms with valences and tartan bedspreads, a library with a wood-burning stove, candle sconces and big peachy sofas and exquisite views down the glen. There's an honesty tray in the drawing room, trout in the loch and Jemima will cook salmon if you catch one. This is Scotland's 'Walking Kingdom' and you are in the heart of it.

Price	£120. Singles £80.
Rooms	4: 1 double; 1 twin with separate bath/shower; 1 twin, 1 double sharing bath.
Meals	Pub/restaurant 2.5 miles.
Closed	Christmas & New Year.
Directions	Heading for Glen Clova, go through Dykehead; approx. 3 miles, then right signed Rottal Lodge. Over bridge; after approx. 3 miles large white house on right, at end of drive, signed.

💼 10% off stays of 2 or more nights. Late checkout (12pm).

Jemima Ward
Rottal Lodge,
Glen Clova, Kirriemuir DD8 4QT
Tel   +44 (0)1575 550279
Email jemimaward@rottal.org.uk

Entry 622   Map 19

Angus

Newtonmill House

The house and grounds are in perfect order; the owners are warm, charming and discreet. This is a little-known part of Scotland, with glens and gardens to discover; fishing villages, golf courses and deserted beaches, too. Return to a cup of tea in the sitting room or summerhouse, a wander in the lovely walled garden, and a marvellous supper of local produce; Rose grows 20 varieties of potato and her hens' eggs make a great hollandaise! Upstairs are crisp sheets, soft blankets, feather pillows, fresh flowers, homemade fruit cake and warm sparkling bathrooms with thick towels. Let this home envelop you in its warm embrace.

Price	£96–£115. Singles from £60.
Rooms	2: 1 twin; 1 double with separate bath.
Meals	Dinner, £23–£32. BYO. Packed lunch £10. Pub 3 miles.
Closed	Christmas.
Directions	Aberdeen-Dundee A90, turning marked Brechin & Edzell B966. Heading towards Edzell, Newtonmill House is 1 mile on left, drive marked by pillars and sign.

10% off stays of 2 or more nights Nov-May.

Use your Sawday's Gift Card here.

Rose & Stephen Rickman
Newtonmill House,
Brechin DD9 7PZ
Tel   +44 (0)1356 622533
Mobile   +44 (0)7793 169482
Email   rrickman@srickman.co.uk
Web   www.newtonmillhouse.co.uk

Entry 623   Map 19

Argyll & Bute

Achamore House

No traffic jams here, tucked between the mainland and Islay. Despite its grandeur – turrets, Arts & Crafts doors, plasterwork ceilings – Achamore is not stuffy and neither is Don, your American host. A coastal skipper, he can take you to sea, or over to other islands in his boat. Find warm wood panelling and light-washed rooms, huge bedrooms with shuttered windows, oversize beds, heavy antiques; all have iPods and music. You get the run of the house – billiard room, library, large lounge, TV room (great for kids). With 50 acres of gardens and a quiet beach it's ideal for big parties or gatherings.

Price	£90–£130. Singles from £35.
Rooms	9: 2 doubles, 1 family room; 2 doubles sharing bath; 2 twins/doubles sharing bath; 2 singles sharing bath.
Meals	Pub/restaurant 1 mile.
Closed	November-February.
Directions	Uphill from ferry landing, turn left at T-junc.; 1 mile, stone gates on right, signed; house at top of drive.

Free pick-up from ferry port.

Don Dennis & Emma Rennie
Achamore House,
Isle of Gigha PA41 7AD
Tel   +44 (0)1583 505400
Email   gigha@atlas.co.uk
Web   www.achamorehouse.com

Entry 624   Map 14

Argyll & Bute

Corranmor House

A radiant setting on the Ardfern peninsula. Barbara and Hew are as committed to their guests as they are to their 400-acre farm – and are charming and interesting in equal measure. In a formal red dining room sparkling with silver they treat you to goose, mutton and lamb from the farm, or fish from local landings. Breakfasts too are delicious. Simple, old fashioned bedrooms are exceptionally private – the neat double, with kitchen, across the courtyard, the small suite with the cosy log-fired sitting room. Wander and admire; the eye always comes to rest on the water and boats of Loch Craignish and the Sound of Jura.

Price	£80–£135. Singles £50.
Rooms	2: 1 double & sitting room; 1 family suite & sitting room.
Meals	Dinner, 3 courses, £30; with lobster £45. Pubs/restaurants 0.75 miles.
Closed	1–29 December; 4th week of August.
Directions	From A816, B8002 to Ardfern, & through village; 0.75 miles past church, long white house high on right. Right by Heron's Cottage, up drive.

Hew & Barbara Service
Corranmor House,
Ardfern, Lochgilphead PA31 8QN
Tel   +44 (0)1852 500609
Email   corranmorhouse@aol.com

Entry 625   Map 14

Argyll & Bute

Melfort House

Enter a wild landscape of hidden glens, ancient oak woods and rivers that tumble to a blue sea. Find a big beautiful house with views straight down the loch, aglow with exquisite fabrics and polished antiques, fine oak floors and paintings and prints. Bedrooms have upholstered beds in soft plaids, delicious colours, superb views; bathrooms have huge towels and locally made soaps. Yvonne and Matthew are brilliant at looking after you: fresh fruit at breakfast, Stornoway black pudding, chilli omelettes, tattie scones or kedgeree. Sally forth with boots or bikes, come home to a dram and a roaring log fire. Argyll at its finest.

Price	£95–£120. Singles from £70. £15 for sofabed.
Rooms	3: 2 twins/doubles, 1 suite.
Meals	Dinner, 3 courses, from £30. Packed lunch £7. Pub/restaurant 400 yds.
Closed	Rarely.
Directions	From Oban take A816 south, signed Campbeltown. After 14 miles, go thro' Kilmelford, then right to Melfort. Follow road & bear right after bridge.

Yvonne & Matthew Anderson
Melfort House,
Kilmelford, Oban PA34 4XD
Tel   +44 (0)1852 200326
Mobile +44 (0)7795 438106
Email   relax@melforthouse.co.uk
Web   www.melforthouse.co.uk

Entry 626   Map 14

Argyll & Bute

Glenmore

An easy-going, old-fashioned home with no need to stand on ceremony. The house was built in the 1800s but it's the later 30s additions that set the style: carved doorways, red-pine panelling, dark furniture, Art Deco pieces, oak floors and a curvy stone fireplace. Alasdair's family has been here for 150 years and many family antiques remain. One of the huge doubles is arranged as a suite with a single room and a sofabed; bath and basins are chunky 30s style with chrome plumbing. From the organic garden and the house there are magnificent views of Loch Melfort with its bobbing boats; you're free to come and go as you please.

Price	£85–£100. Family suite £85–£160. Singles £50–£65.
Rooms	2: 1 family suite; 1 double with separate bath/shower.
Meals	Pub 0.5 miles, restaurant 1.5 miles.
Closed	Christmas & New Year.
Directions	From A816 0.5 miles south of Kilmelford; then on to Glenmore. House signed (both directions). Past Lodge House at bottom of drive; on for 0.25 miles to big house.

Free pick-up from local bus/train station. Bottle of wine in your room.

Melissa & Alasdair Oatts
Glenmore,
Kilmelford, Oban PA34 4XA
Tel   +44 (0)1852 200314
Mobile   +44 (0)7786 340468
Email   oatts@glenmore22.fsnet.co.uk
Web   www.glenmorecountryhouse.co.uk

Entry 627   Map 17

Argyll & Bute

Ardtorna

Come for perfect comfort and uninterrupted views of loch and mountain. These thoughtful, professional hosts are happy to share their new, open-plan, eco-friendly house where contemporary Scandinavian and Art Deco styles are cleverly blended with homely warmth. Sink into a bedroom with a wall of glass for those wow views – and homemade tablet, a wet room or jacuzzi, Molton Brown treats. Flowers and jauntily coloured coffee pots decorate the oak table in the stunning dining room: food is home-baked and delicious. Argyll brims with historical sites and walks; return to watch the sun go down over the Morvern hills. Fabulous.

Price	£80–£150. Singles from £80.
Rooms	4 twins/doubles.
Meals	Room service supper £10–£20. Pub/restaurant 3 miles.
Closed	Rarely.
Directions	From Oban A828 over Connel bridge; north for 4 miles. House on right on hill, 0.5 miles before Sealife Sanctuary.

Bottle of wine in your room for stays of 2 or more nights. Free pick-up from local bus/train station.

Karen Webster
Ardtorna,
Mill farm, Barcaldine, Oban PA37 1SE
Tel   +44 (0)1631 720125
Email   info@ardtorna.co.uk
Web   www.ardtorna.co.uk

Entry 628   Map 17

Argyll & Bute

Ardnacross Farm

The Forresters' Aberdeen Angus cattle farm borders Mull's stunning coastline, where eagles, whales, red deer and otters leap, swoop, breach and soar. The farmhouse is wonderfully homely: the dining room with a huge antique table and open fire; the guest room (reached by private stairs) with a pretty patterned bedspread and floral curtains. The Scottish breakfast with Ardnacross eggs and porridge is hearty. Tobermory has everything from very good fish and chips and pleasant restaurants to an excellent theatre and festival; you can catch a boat trip to Iona or Staffa too. A beautiful slice of island Scotland.

Price	£70.
Rooms	1 double.
Meals	Pubs/restaurants 5 miles.
Closed	Christmas & New Year.
Directions	15 miles from Craignure & 11 miles from Fishnish ferry terminals. Right from either on Tobermory road. House halfway between Salen and Tobermory on right.

Picnic lunch using local & farm produce.

	Rory & Penelope Forrester
	Ardnacross Farm,
	Aros, Isle of Mull PA72 6JS
Tel	+44 (0)1680 300262
Email	enquiries@ardnacross.com
Web	www.holidaycottages-mull.co.uk

Entry 629   Map 17

Argyll & Bute

Strongarbh House

High on the hill overlooking the pretty houses of Tobermory – and its bay, bursting with boats in summer – is a big friendly Victorian villa. Step in to find beautiful proportions and a calm, sophisticated décor: designers Jane and Adrian have created a truly original retreat. Find Paris '68 posters and chic tables in the breakfast room, sofas and whisky in the library, afternoon teas in the art gallery. After a gorgeous day driving around Mull, return to a striking four-poster or a view of the sea; rooms are stocked with iPod docks, coffee machines, crisp linen, and are refreshingly TV-free. *Over 12s welcome.*

Price	£90-£135. Singles £65-£110.
Rooms	4 doubles.
Meals	Pubs/restaurants 500 yds.
Closed	January & February.
Directions	From Tobermory Main Street, left up Back Brae. Right at hairpin. Left at Western Isles Hotel. Stay left at fork by white house. House at end of road.

Bottle of wine in your room.

	Jane Wilde & Adrian Lear
	Strongarbh House,
	Tobermory, Isle of Mull PA75 6PR
Tel	+44 (0)1688 302319
Email	stay@strongarbh.com
Web	www.strongarbh.com

Entry 630   Map 17

Argyll & Bute

Meall Mo Chridhe

Caring owners, exquisite food and a welcome sight amid the savage beauty of Britain's most westerly village. The warm ochre walls of this listed Georgian manse peep through wooded gardens across the Sound to Mull. Rooms are beautiful – French antiques, a wood stove, roll top baths – but it's the food that draws most to this far-flung spot. What David magics from his 45-acre smallholding (a bit of everything that grows, grunts, bleats or quacks) Stella transforms into feasts. Dine on spiced mackerel, minted lamb, hazelnut meringue; and duck eggs at breakfast. A gem buried in spectacular, wild walking country.

Price	£103-£204. Singles £51.50-£102.
Rooms	3 doubles.
Meals	Dinner £44. Pub 0.25 miles.
Closed	Rarely.
Directions	Left from Corran Ferry, 8 miles south of Fort William. Through Strontian to Salen, then on B8007 to Kilchoan. House approx. 0.5 miles on right.

	Stella & David Cash
	Meall Mo Chridhe,
	Kilchoan, Acharacle PH36 4LH
Tel	+44 (0)1972 510238
Mobile	+44 (0)7730 100639
Email	enquiries@westcoastscotland.co.uk
Web	www.westcoastscotland.co.uk

Entry 631   Map 17

Ayrshire

Heughmill

Five acres of fields and lawn with free-range hens that kindly donate for breakfast and views to the sea. The house is just as good, surrounded by old stone farm buildings, with climbing roses and a small burn tumbling through. Inside, a lovely country home with tapestries in an airy hall, an open fire in the sitting room and a terrace that sits under a vast sky. Country-house bedrooms are stylishly homely. Two have the view, one has an old armoire, another comes with a claw-foot bath; all have delightful art. Julia sculpts, Mungo cooks breakfast on the Aga. Rural Ayrshire waits, yet you are close to the airport.

Price	£65-£80. Singles on request.
Rooms	3: 2 twins/doubles, 1 twin.
Meals	Pubs/restaurants within 2 miles.
Closed	Christmas & New Year.
Directions	3 miles south of Kilmarnock, turn east down B730 for Tarbolton. After 0.75 miles, right onto narrow road signed Ladykirk. House is 250 yds on right.

	Mungo & Julia Tulloch
	Heughmill,
	Craigie, Kilmarnock KA1 5NQ
Tel	+44 (0)1563 860389
Email	mungotulloch@hotmail.com
Web	www.stayprestwick.com

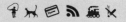

Entry 632   Map 14

Clackmannanshire

Kennels Cottage

Live the dream: tour Scotland by classic car. Sandy does Triumphs, Austin Healeys, convertible Beetles. Tanya spoils you, with big crisp beds, huge towels, elegant blinds, orchids and oriental touches. The old gamekeeper's cottage is a stunningly fresh, stylish and immaculate place, all white walls, white sofas, books, paintings and the odd flash of gold. In the morning, feast on local bacon, Fair Trade coffees and eggs from their hens served at one convivial table. Take a picnic to the garden, wander through what was the Dollarbeg estate, replete with pheasant and deer... totally unwind. *Ask about mini tour of Scotland package.*

Price	£70–£80. Singles £50.
Rooms	3 doubles.
Meals	Packed lunch £10. Pub 2 miles.
Closed	December/January.
Directions	From Dollar take B913 towards Blairingone. House 2 miles from Dollar just before Blairingone.

 3 nights for price of 2 Mon-Thurs. 10% off mini tour package (classic car hire plus b&b).

	Tanya Worsfold & Sandy Stewart
	Kennels Cottage,
	Dollarbeg, Dollar FK14 7PA
Tel	+44 (0)1259 742186
Email	tanya.worsfold@btinternet.com
Web	www.guesthousescotland.co.uk

Entry 633   Map 15

Dumfries & Galloway

The House on the Shore

Impossible not to be wowed by this incredible shoreline setting with views across the Solway Firth. The 1,250-acre estate has been in Jamie's family for generations; he and Sheri are excellent hosts and love their dower house with its rich and varied woodland and wildlife, formal gardens and stupendous views. Grand but with a family feel, this is old country house style at its best with rugs on polished floors, paintings, open fires and fresh flowers. The farm produces its own meat, an enormous walled kitchen garden is being restored, and a peach tree fruits abundantly; you'll eat well. Very special.

Price	£80–£100. Singles £40–£60.
Rooms	2: 1 double, 1 twin.
Meals	Dinner, 3 courses, £25 (BYO). Pub/restaurant 2 miles.
Closed	Rarely.
Directions	A710 Dumfries towards Dalbeatie. Left in Kirkbean. First right, second left at top of hill, 0.5 miles down private drive then left to the house.

Bottle of wine in your room.

	Jamie & Sheri Blackett
	The House on the Shore,
	Arbigland, Kirkbean, Dumfries DG2 8BQ
Tel	+44 (0)1387 880717
Email	sheri@arbigland.com
Web	www.arbiglandestate.co.uk

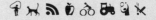

Entry 634   Map 11

Dumfries & Galloway

Chipperkyle

Sink into the sofas without worrying about creasing them; this beautiful Scottish-Georgian family home has not a hint of formality, and the sociable Dicksons put you at your ease. Sitting and dining rooms connect through a large arch; there are family pictures, rugs on wooden floors and a log fire. Upstairs: good linen, striped walls, flowered curtains, armchairs, lots of books and windows with views – this wonderful house just gets better and better. There are 200 acres, dogs, cats, donkeys and hens (children can collect the eggs!), and you can walk, play golf, visit gardens, sail or cycle – in magnificent countryside.

Dumfries & Galloway

Byreburnfoot House

Tucked away down a gravelled drive on the banks of the salmon-rich Esk, this pretty Victorian forester's house combines traditional charm with modern comforts. Airy rooms and wooden floors offset antique pieces – grandfather clock, writing desk, chandeliers – within an elegant rural décor: cushioned bay windows, fashionable florals. Beds are big, the linen is trimmed and the views are sublime. Warm hosts Bill and Lorraine are keenly green-fingered, and their 1.5 acres of orchards, flower-fringed lawns and organic kitchen garden are deliciously productive. Stay a few days and become part of the scenery. *Fabulous fishing.*

Price	£96. Discounts for children.
Rooms	2: 1 double; 1 twin with separate bath/shower. Cot available.
Meals	Dinner available for groups. Pub 3 miles.
Closed	Christmas.
Directions	A75 Dumfries ring road for Stranraer. Approx. 12 miles to Springholm & right to Kirkpatrick Durham. Left at x-roads, after 0.8 miles, up drive on right by white lodge.

🧳 Late checkout (12pm). 50% off 4th night.

🎁 Use your Sawday's Gift Card here.

Willie & Catriona Dickson
Chipperkyle, Kirkpatrick Durham,
Castle Douglas DG7 3EY
Tel   +44 (0)1556 650223
Mobile +44 (0)7917 730009
Email   special_place@chipperkyle.co.uk
Web   www.chipperkyle.co.uk

Entry 635   Map 11

Price	£80–£90. Singles £55.
Rooms	3: 2 doubles; 1 twin/double with separate bath.
Meals	Dinner, 3 courses, £25. Packed lunch from £7.50. Pub/restaurant 5 miles.
Closed	Rarely.
Directions	From Carlisle (M6 junc. 44) on A7 north. Signs for Canonbie, then cross river Esk at traffic lights and turn immed. left. House on right, about 1 mile further.

🧳 Bottle of wine with dinner on first night. Late checkout (12pm).

Bill & Loraine Frew
Byreburnfoot House,
Canonbie DG14 0XB
Tel   +44 (0)1387 371209
Mobile +44 (0)7764 194901
Email   bill.napierfrew@ukf.net
Web   www.byreburnfoot.co.uk

Entry 636   Map 15

Dumfries & Galloway

Knockhill

Fabulous Knockhill: stunning place, stunning position, a country house full of busts and screens, oils and mirrors, chests and clocks, rugs and fires. In the intimate drawing room, full of treasures, floor-to-ceiling windows look down the wooded hill. Fine stone stairs lead to country-house bedrooms that are smart yet homely: headboards of carved oak or padded chintz, books and views. Come for a grand farming feel and delicious Scottish meals; the Morgans are the most unpretentious and charming of hosts. Mellow, authentic, welcoming – an enduring favourite.

Price	£88–£90. Singles £54–£64.
Rooms	2: 1 twin; 1 twin with separate bath.
Meals	Dinner £26. Pub 5 miles.
Closed	Rarely.
Directions	From M74 junc. 19, B725 for Dalton. Right by church in Ecclefechan, signed Hoddam Castle. After 1.2 miles right at x-roads towards Lockerbie. 1 mile on, right at stone [not whitewashed] lodge cottage. At top of long drive.

Yda & Rupert Morgan
Knockhill,
Lockerbie DG11 1AW
Tel   +44 (0)1576 300232
Mobile +44 (0)7813 944107
Email   morganbellows@yahoo.co.uk

Entry 637   Map 15

Dumfries & Galloway

Applegarth House

Here is an old peaceful manse at the top of the hill, right next door to the church, with a 12th-century motte; the views from the pretty garden stretch for miles around. The house is a good size, with original pine floors and sweeping stairs. Off the large and light landing are three comfortable bedrooms with shuttered windows and glorious garden and country views. Let the tawny owls lull you to sleep then wake to freshly stewed fruits and excellent porridge. There are paths to wander through the flower beds, statues to admire and endless wildlife; a perfect stop off point for a trip north or south.

Price	£88–£90. Singles from £55.
Rooms	3: 2 twins; 1 double with separate bath.
Meals	Supper, 2 courses, £22. BYO. Hotel restaurant 1.5 miles.
Closed	Rarely.
Directions	M74 junc. 17 Lockerbie, B7076 Johnstonebridge. 1st right after 1.5 miles; after 100 yds left over m'way bridge. After 1 mile, right at T-junc., then 2nd left to church. Next to church. Don't use satnav.

10% off stays of 2 or more nights. Free pick-up from local bus/train station.

Frank & Jane Pearson
Applegarth House,
Lockerbie DG11 1SX
Tel   +44 (0)1387 810270
Mobile +44 (0)7732 127779
Email   jane@applegarthtown.demon.co.uk

Entry 638   Map 15

Edinburgh

7 Gloucester Place

A cantilevered staircase in walnut and mahogany, a soaring hand-painted cupola: the classic Georgian townhouse is five minutes from Princes Street. Rooms are cosy yet immaculate, sprinkled with paintings and decorative things from travels to far-flung places. Bedrooms are comfy, traditional and well-stocked with books and radio (and there are Z-beds for children). Bag the south-facing double with its stunning Art Deco bathroom and garden views. Naomi is pretty relaxed and happy to chat to you about the local music and art scene, or to leave you in peace. An interesting and hospitable place to unwind.

Price	£90–£120. Singles from £60.
Rooms	3: 1 double; 1 double with separate bath; 1 double with separate shower. Extra child beds.
Meals	Pubs/restaurants 300 yds.
Closed	Christmas & rarely.
Directions	From George St (city centre), down Hanover St, across Queen St at lights. Left into Heriot Row, right onto India St, then left.

Naomi Jennings
7 Gloucester Place,
Edinburgh EH3 6EE
Tel +44 (0)131 225 2974
Mobile +44 (0)7803 168106
Email naomijennings@hotmail.com
Web www.stayinginscotland.com

Entry 643   Map 15

Edinburgh

10 London Street

A Roman X marks this special spot: a beautiful Georgian terraced house in Edinburgh's world heritage New Town, home to descendants of Scots author John Gibson Lockhart. Step into a family home of period elegance and charming informality: accept a sherry by the fire in the sash-windowed drawing room (with baby grand piano), chat with Pippa and Hugh over breakfast bagels, sleep undisturbed in 'Beauregard' with its lovely views and paintings. Or pick 'Gibson' for its off-courtyard privacy and self-catering option. The best of Edinburgh is a stroll away, good buses zip you further afield, but at night-time all is quiet.

Price	£100–£120.
Rooms	2 doubles (one with self-catering option).
Meals	Pub/restaurant 500 yds.
Closed	Rarely.
Directions	In the centre of Edinburgh, 10-minute walk from Edinburgh Waverly (main train & bus station, airport bus terminal station).

 Late checkout (12pm).

Pippa Lockhart
10 London Street,
Edinburgh EH3 6NA
Tel +44 (0)131 556 0737
Email pippa@hjlockhart.co.uk
Web www.londonstreetaccommodation.co.uk

Entry 644   Map 15

Edinburgh

Geraldsplace

Elegant Georgian 'New Town'... so splendid and handsome it's a World Heritage Site. Gerald – enthusiastic, charming, a B&B pro – lives on one of its finest streets in a lower ground floor flat of character, comfort and colour. Be treated to DVDs and books in the hall, a laptop with fast broadband, home-baked bread, locally smoked salmon, a decanter of Scotch in each room. Bedrooms have cosiness, warmth, fine fabrics, excellent art; ask for the room with the view. There's a patio to share, a private garden opposite, a perfect location and, of course, Gerald, your brilliantly well-informed, up-to-the-minute host.

Price	£89-£119 (additional supplement during festivals).
Rooms	2 twins/doubles.
Meals	Restaurants within 3-minute walk.
Closed	Rarely.
Directions	10 minutes' walk from air, train, tram, bus & coach terminals at city centre. East end of Princes Street.

Gerald Della-Porta
Geraldsplace, 21b Abercromby Place,
Edinburgh EH3 6QE
Tel   +44 (0)131 558 7017
Email   gerald11@geraldsplace.com
Web   www.geraldsplace.com

Entry 645   Map 15

Edinburgh

22 Royal Circus

Step from an elegant cobbled crescent in Georgian New Town into another world: of Aga-cooked breakfasts, landscaped gardens and a farmhouse kitchen you're welcome to share. Well-travelled Kirsty has filled her listed, William Playfair-designed basement flat with bold reds and yellows, family art and Indian treasures. Choose the romantic Moroccan-style en suite or the larger, brighter family room. Young fruit trees and carved garden furniture dot the grounds; seasoned botanists can trot to the Botanic Garden; shoppers can walk to Princes Street through World Heritage streets of delis, cafés, restaurants. Charming!

Price	£89-£119 (additional supplement during festivals).
Rooms	2: 1 double; 1 family room with separate bath.
Meals	Pubs/restaurants 2-minute walk.
Closed	Christmas & New Year.
Directions	10-minute walk from city centre or within walking distance to Stockbridge. House on the north side facing south.

 Bottle of wine in your room. 10% off room rate Mon-Thurs.

Kirsty MacGregor
22 Royal Circus,
Edinburgh EH3 6SS
Tel   +44 (0)1312 261303
Email   stay@22royalcircus.co.uk
Web   www.22royalcircus.co.uk

Entry 646   Map 15

Edinburgh

11 Belford Place

Guests love Susan's modern townhouse quietly tucked away in a private road above the Water of Leith. A golden retriever wags his welcome in the wooden-floored entrance, a picture-lined staircase winds upward. In summer, New Zealand flax bursts into flower in an exquisite sloping garden. Handsome rooms offer china cups and floral spreads; dazzling bathrooms have Molton Brown goodies. Taste Stornoway black pudding at the gleaming breakfast table along with fresh fruit, homemade jams and more. You hear owls at night yet you're a hop from the city, with free parking and a bus stop nearby. *Minimum stay two nights in August.*

Price	£70–£120.
Rooms	3: 1 double, 2 twins/doubles.
Meals	Pub 200 yds. Restaurants 10-minute walk.
Closed	Christmas.
Directions	From city centre to Belford Rd; Belford Pl 1st left after Travelodge Hotel. House down hill opp. Edinburgh Sports Club. Free parking. No 13 bus passes top of lane to city centre.

Bottle of wine and chocolates in your room on arrival.

Susan Kinross
11 Belford Place,
Edinburgh EH4 3DH

Tel	+44 (0)131 332 9704
Mobile	+44 (0)7712 836399
Email	suekinross@blueyonder.co.uk

Entry 647   Map 15

Edinburgh

12 Belford Terrace

Leafy trees, a secluded garden, a stone wall and, beyond, a quiet riverside stroll. On the doorstep of the Modern Art and Dean galleries with Edinburgh's theatres and restaurants just a 15-minute walk, this Victorian end terrace, beside Leith Water, oozes an easy-going elegance, helped by Carolyn's laid-back but competent manner. Garden level bedrooms have their own entrance and are big and creamy with stripy fabrics, antiques, sofas and huge windows. (The single has a *Boys Own* charm.) Carolyn spoils with crisp linen, books and biscuits and a delicious, full-works breakfast. After a day in town, relax on the sunny terrace.

Price	£70–£100. Singles from £40.
Rooms	3: 1 double, 1 twin/double; 1 single with separate shower.
Meals	Pub/restaurants within 10-minute walk.
Closed	Christmas.
Directions	From Palmerston Place through 2 sets of lights, downhill on Belford Rd past the Travelodge. Immediately left is Belford Terrace. Limited free parking, 2-minute drive.

Fresh flowers and bottle of wine in your room.

Carolyn Crabbie
12 Belford Terrace,
Edinburgh EH4 3DQ

Tel	+44 (0)131 332 2413
Email	carolyncrabbie@blueyonder.co.uk

Entry 648   Map 15

Edinburgh

Wallace's Arthouse Scotland

The apartment door swings open to a world of white walls, smooth floors, modern art, acoustic jazz, and smiling Wallace with a glass of wine – well worth the three-storey climb up this old Assembly Rooms building. Your host – New York fashion designer and arts enthusiast, Glasgow-born, not shy – has created a bright, minimalist space sprinkled with humour and casual sophistication. Bedrooms capture light and exude his inimitable style; the kitchen's narrow bar is perfect for a light breakfast. Leith is Edinburgh's earthy side with its docks and noisy street life, but fine restaurants abound and the centre is close. Memorable.

Price	£95. Singles £85.
Rooms	2 doubles.
Meals	Pubs/restaurants 10 yds.
Closed	Christmas Eve & Christmas Day.
Directions	From Princes St, follow Leith Walk to the foot and left along Gt. Junction St. Then 1st right along Henderson St to Water of Leith traffic lights. Right along Bernard St; at the next lights right into Constitution St.

10% off room rate Mon–Thurs. Late checkout (12pm).

Wallace Shaw
Wallace's Arthouse Scotland,
41-4 Constitution Street,
Edinburgh EH6 7BG
Tel   +44 (0)131 538 3320
Email   cawallaceshaw@mac.com
Web   www.wallacesarthousescotland.com

Entry 649   Map 15

Edinburgh

2 Fingal Place

An elegant house on a Georgian terrace. The leafy park lies opposite (look upwards to Arthur's Seat). Bustling theatres, shops and the university are a stroll away, yet this is a very quiet house. Your hostess is sometimes away so you may be looked after by a housekeeper, but when at home Gillian can help plan your trips – or cater for celebrations and graduations with lunch and dinner; it's entirely flexible. Downstairs at garden level bedrooms have mahogany antique beds, floral curtains and bathrooms with good towels. Noodle the Llasa Apso and Gillian's cat will welcome you. *Parking metered 8.30-5.30pm weekdays.*

Price	£80–£115 (£90–£130 during Festival). Singles from £55 (from £65 during Festival).
Rooms	2: 1 twin (with single room attached), 1 twin.
Meals	Pubs/restaurants 100 yds.
Closed	22–27 December.
Directions	From centre, Lothian Rd to Tollcross (clock) & Melville Drive. At 2nd major lights, right into Argyle Place; immed. left into Fingal Place.

Gillian Charlton-Meyrick
2 Fingal Place,
The Meadows, Edinburgh EH9 1JX
Tel   +44 (0)131 667 4436
Mobile   +44 (0)7880 705022
Email   gcmeyrick@fireflyuk.net
Web   www.fingalplace.co.uk

Entry 650   Map 15

Edinburgh

20 Blackford Road

A 20-minute stroll from the Royal Mile is a substantial Victorian house with relaxed hosts and a touch of old-world luxury. From a cushioned window seat you gaze onto a lovely wildlife-filled walled garden where you can eat out on a warm day; breakfasts, though not cooked, are superb and include homemade breads and fruit. Bedrooms, one up, one down, are tranquil and serene, with delicately papered walls and lush toile de Jouy; the drawing room, with comfortable cream sofas, soft lights, a drinks tray and beautiful books, is elegant yet cosy. A happy, charming place to stay. *Minimum stay two nights in July & August.*

Price	£75–£100. Singles from £65.
Rooms	2: 1 twin/double, 1 twin, each with separate bath.
Meals	Restaurants 300 yds.
Closed	Christmas & New Year.
Directions	A720 city bypass, take Lothianburn exit to city centre. Continue for 2.5 miles on Morningside Rd; right into Newbattle Terrace; 2nd left into Whitehouse Loan. Immed. right into Blackford Road. House at end on left.

John & Tricia Wood
20 Blackford Road,
Edinburgh EH9 2DS

Tel	+44 (0)131 447 4233
Mobile	+44 (0)7930 452945
Email	enquiries@grangebandb.co.uk
Web	www.grangebandb.co.uk

Edinburgh

1 Albert Terrace

A warm-hearted home with a lovely garden, an American hostess and two gorgeous Siamese cats. You are 20 minutes by bus from Princes Street yet the guests' sitting room overlooks pear trees and clematis and the rolling Pentland Hills. Cosy up in the winter next to a log fire; in summer, take your morning paper onto the terrace above the sunny garden. Books, fresh flowers, interesting art and ceramics and – you are on an old, quiet street – utter, surprising peace. Bedrooms are colourful, spacious and bright, one with an Art Deco bathroom and views over the garden. Clarissa is arty, easy, generous and loves having guests.

Price	£80–£95. Singles £55.
Rooms	3: 1 double; 1 double, 1 single sharing bath.
Meals	Pubs/restaurants nearby.
Closed	Rarely.
Directions	From centre of Edinburgh, A702 south, for Peebles. Pass Churchill Theatre (on left), to lights. Albert Terrace 1st right after theatre. Metered parking on street, but non-metered area nearby.

Clarissa Notley
1 Albert Terrace,
Edinburgh EH10 5EA

Tel	+44 (0)131 447 4491
Email	canotley@aol.com

Edinburgh

Craigbrae

Half a mile down a narrow winding lane and you reach a traditional stone farmhouse, with huge windows overlooking fields. The house has been recently renovated so there's a lovely new bathroom in New England style and bedrooms that ooze tranquillity and thoughtful touches. Your hosts are hospitable and great fun; the drawing room is warm, cosy and homely; there are books, china, family pieces and good oil paintings. Edinburgh is 15 minutes by train from the village, the airport 12 minutes by taxi or car. And there's a pretty garden that catches the sun with plenty of places to sit.

Price	£80–£100. Singles from £40.
Rooms	3: 1 double; 2 twins/doubles sharing 2 bath/shower rooms.
Meals	Pubs/restaurants 2 miles.
Closed	Christmas.
Directions	Directions on booking and on website.

Louise & Michael Westmacott
Craigbrae,
Kirkliston, Edinburgh EH29 9EL

Tel	+44 (0)131 331 1205
Email	louise@craigbrae.com
Web	www.craigbrae.com

Entry 653   Map 15

West Lothian

Highfield House

Although much of it is grand, there's a relaxed feel to this 18th-century manse house, where Jillian and Hugh enjoy having guests. Treat yourself to a quiet time in the large, light sitting room with family photos, books and paintings, comfy sofas by the fire and a sunny window seat. Bedrooms are softly painted in yellows and blues, beds have good mattresses and bathrooms are spotless. Breakfast on old favourites, or haggis and black pudding, in a dining room with oodles of sunlight and Hugh's oil-clad ancestors watching; home cooking in the evening is candlelit and cosy – or catch the train into town. *Dogs extra charge.*

Price	£76–£80. Singles £50.
Rooms	2 twins/doubles.
Meals	Packed lunch £6. Dinner £15-£25. Pub/restaurant 3 miles.
Closed	Christmas.
Directions	A71 from Edinburgh. 5 miles beyond city bypass left onto B7031 to Kirknewton. Next right then cross railway line. House is on left at top of hill.

 10% off stays of 2 or more nights. Bottle of wine in your room.

Jillian & Hugh Hunter Gordon
Highfield House,
Kirknewton EH27 8BJ

Tel	+44 (0)1506 881489
Email	jill@hunter-gordon.co.uk
Web	www.highfield-h.co.uk

Entry 654   Map 15

East Lothian

Inveresk House

Cromwell stayed here, and plotted his siege of Edinburgh Castle; the house oozes history. The magnificent main rooms are furnished with ornate antiques, squashy sofas in chintzes, flowers, gilt, mirrors, seriously gorgeous rugs and Alice's own vibrant art. Bedrooms and bathrooms, on the expected scale, come with vintage radiators, huge beds, good old-fashioned comfort. Musicians will be happy – there is a baby grand. Come for Inveresk (a conservation village), golf (the course at Musselburgh is the oldest in the world), interesting conversation and history by the hatful. Edinburgh is a bus hop away.

Price	£100–£120. Family room £140. Singles £65.
Rooms	3: 1 double, 1 twin, 1 family room.
Meals	Pubs/restaurants in Musselburgh.
Closed	Rarely.
Directions	From Edinburgh, A199 (A1) to Musselburgh. There, signs to Inveresk. At top of Inveresk Brae, sharp right into cul-de-sac. 2nd opening on right, opp. gates with GM on them, bear right past cottages to house.

10% off stays of 2 or more nights.

Alice & John Chute
Inveresk House, 3 Inveresk Village,
Musselburgh EH21 7UA
Tel   +44 (0)131 665 5855
Mobile +44 (0)7931 950566
Email   chute.inveresk@btinternet.com
Web   www.invereskhouse.com

Entry 655   Map 15

East Lothian

Glebe House

A treasure of a home – and host! A perfect Georgian family house with all the well-proportioned elegance you'd expect, it is resplendent with original features – fireplaces, arched glass, long windows – that have appeared more than once in interiors magazines. Bedrooms are light and airy with pretty fabrics and lovely linen. The beach is a stone's throw away, views are leafy-green, golfers have over 21 courses to choose from. There's also a fascinating sea bird centre close by – and you are 30 minutes from Edinburgh: regular trains bring you to the foot of the castle.

Price	From £100. Singles by arrangement.
Rooms	3: 1 double, 1 four-poster; 1 twin with separate bath.
Meals	Restaurants 2-minute walk.
Closed	Christmas & New Year.
Directions	From Edinburgh, A1 for Berwick. Left onto A198, follow signs into North Berwick. Right into Station Rd signed 'The Law', to 1st x-roads; left into town centre; house on left behind wall.

Gwen & Jake Scott
Glebe House,
Law Road, North Berwick EH39 4PL
Tel   +44 (0)1620 892608
Mobile +44 (0)7973 965814
Email   gwenscott@glebehouse-nb.co.uk
Web   www.glebehouse-nb.co.uk

Entry 656   Map 16

East Lothian

Eaglescairnie Mains

Wildlife thrives: eight acres of conservation headland have been created and wildflower meadows planted on this 350-acre working farm... you'd never guess Edinburgh was so close. The Georgian farmhouse sits in lovely gardens, its peace uninterrupted. There's a traditional conservatory for locally sourced breakfasts, a perfectly gracious drawing room (coral walls, rich fabrics, log fire) for wintery nights, and beautiful big bedrooms full of books and kind extras. Barbara is warm and charming, Michael's commitment to the countryside is wide-ranging; follow signed farm walks to the pub in Gifford.

Ethical Collection: Environment; Community. See page 420.

Price	£70–£80. Singles from £45.
Rooms	3: 2 doubles, 1 twin.
Meals	Pub 1 mile.
Closed	Christmas.
Directions	From A1 at Haddington, B6368 south for Bolton & Humbie. Right immed. after traffic lights on bridge. 2.5 miles on through Bolton, at top of hill, left for Gifford. Entrance 0.5 miles on left.

Barbara & Michael Williams
Eaglescairnie Mains,
Gifford, Haddington EH41 4HN

Tel	+44 (0)1620 810491
Mobile	+44 (0)7713 333193
Email	williams.eagles@btinternet.com
Web	www.eaglescairnie.com

Entry 657   Map 16

Fife

Blair Adam

If staying in a place with genuine Adam features is special, how much more so in the Adam family home! They've been in this corner of Fife since 1733: John laid out the walled garden, son William was a prominent politician, Sir Walter Scott used to come and stay... you may be similarly inspired. The house, in a swathe of parkland and forest overlooking the hills and Loch Leven, has big, comfortable light-flooded rooms filled with intriguing contents, and superb walks from the door. The pretty bedroom is on the ground floor and you eat with your friendly hosts in the dining room, with coffee by the fire after dinner.

Price	From £100. Singles from £50.
Rooms	1 twin.
Meals	Dinner, with wine, £25. Restaurants 5 miles.
Closed	December/January.
Directions	From M90 exit 5, take B996 south for Cowdenbeath. Right for Maryburgh, through village, right through pillars onto a long drive, under bridge, then 0.5 miles on up to house.

10% off stays of 2 or more nights.

Keith & Elizabeth Adam
Blair Adam,
Kelty KY4 0JF

Tel	+44 (0)1383 831221
Mobile	+44 (0)7986 711099
Email	adamofblairadam@hotmail.com

Entry 658   Map 15

Fife

Greenlaw House

With superb views towards the Lomond Hills, Debbie's bright, warm converted farm steading will please you the moment you step in. The oak-floored sitting room has Afghan rugs, sofas around a log-burner, a grand piano; step onto the decked area for summer sun. In all the rooms is a medley of modern and antique, and fascinating art. The ground-floor bedroom has a lovely old chest and books; the more lived-in upstairs one has the view. Debbie loves to cook: kedgeree, porridge with cream, organic eggs, local honey. Falkland Palace, hunting haunt of the Stuart kings, is close; there are wonderful walks and sea eagles soar.

Price	£70-£85. Singles £40-£50.
Rooms	2: 1 double; 1 double with separate bath.
Meals	Dinner £20-£30. Restaurants 15-minute drive.
Closed	Christmas & New Year.
Directions	B937 north off A91, at Trafalgar junc. turn towards Newburgh. After exactly 1 mile right onto tarmac road. Third house at top.

10% off stays of 2 or more nights. Late checkout (12pm).

Debbie Butler
Greenlaw House,
Braeside, Collessie, Cupar KY15 7UX
Tel   +44 (0)1337 810236
Email   butlerjackson@googlemail.com
Web   www.greenlawhouse.com

Entry 659   Map 15

Fife

Kinkell

An avenue of beech trees patrolled by guinea fowl leads to the house. If the sea views and the salty smack of St Andrews Bay air don't get you, step inside and have your senses tickled. The elegant drawing room has two open fires, rosy sofas, a grand piano – gorgeous. Bedrooms and bathrooms are immaculate, sunny and warm. There's great cooking too; Sandy and Frippy excel in the kitchen and make full use of local produce. From the front door head down to the beach, walk the wild coast, jump on a quad bike, try your hand at clay pigeon shooting. All this and wonderful hosts. *Online booking available.*

Price	£90. Singles from £55.
Rooms	3 twins/doubles.
Meals	Dinner £30. Restaurants in St Andrews, 2 miles.
Closed	Rarely.
Directions	From St Andrews, A917 for 2 miles for Crail. Driveway in 1st line of trees on left after St Andrews.

Use your Sawday's Gift Card here.

Sandy & Frippy Fyfe
Kinkell,
St Andrews KY16 8PN
Tel   +44 (0)1334 472003
Mobile   +44 (0)7836 746043
Email   fyfe@kinkell.com
Web   www.kinkell.com

Entry 660   Map 16+19

Highland

The Grange

A Victorian townhouse with its toes in the country: the mountain hovers above, the loch shimmers below and the garden slopes steeply to great banks of rhododendrons. Bedrooms, the one in the turret with a sumptuous new bathroom, are large, luscious, warm and inviting: crushed velvet, beautiful blankets, immaculate linen – all ooze panache. Expect decanters of sherry, ornate cornices, a Louis XV bed and a superb suite with contemporary touches. Elegant breakfasts are served at glass-topped tables; Joan's warm vivacity and love of B&B means guests keep coming back. And just a 10-minute walk into town.

Price	£116–£120.
Rooms	3: 2 doubles, 1 suite.
Meals	Restaurants 12-minute walk.
Closed	Mid-November to March.
Directions	A82 Glasgow-Fort William; 1 mile after 30mph sign into Fort William, turn right up Ashburn Lane, next to Ashburn guesthouse. House on left at top.

 50% off 4th night.

Joan & John Campbell
The Grange,
Grange Road, Fort William PH33 6JF
Tel +44 (0)1397 705516
Email info@thegrange-scotland.co.uk
Web www.thegrange-scotland.co.uk

Entry 661　Map 17

Highland

Arisaig House

Imposing Arisaig – a 19th-century industrialist's highland fantasy – sits in a walkers' paradise; the views to Skye are to die for. In former days it was a hotel; now Sarah, who has known Arisaig all her life, revels in returning house and gardens to their former glory. The sitting room is bright with Sanderson sofas, portraits and paintings and a huge open fire, and bedrooms are spacious and charming, with comfortable furniture and updated bathrooms. Lovely generous Sarah, passionate Slow Food member, serves breakfasts, high teas and dinners at the long oak table: don't miss the Stornoway black pudding!

Price	£100–£150. Singles £75.
Rooms	8 twins/doubles.
Meals	Dinner, 3 courses, from £25. Pub/restaurant 3 miles.
Closed	Rarely.
Directions	Just off A830 Fort William to Mallaig road. 3 miles east of Arisaig & 1 mile from Beasdale Station. House well signed. Inverness, Glasgow & Edinburgh airports within 3.5 hours.

 10% off stays of 2 or more nights. Bottle of wine in your room.

Sarah Winnington-Ingram
Arisaig House,
Arisaig PH39 4NR
Tel +44 (0)1687 450730
Email sarahwi@arisaighouse.co.uk
Web www.arisaighouse.co.uk

Entry 662　Map 17

Highland

Tigh An Dochais

An arresting, award-winning, 'see-through' house, quite unlike its neighbours, on a strip of land between the busy town road and the rocky shoreline, with stunning views out the back across the bay to mountains and islands. Huge windows and a cathedral ceiling allow light to flood in to an oak-floored sitting room with a wood-burner and modern art. Gliding glazed doors in crisp luxurious bedrooms open to larchwood verandas – and the shore! Bathrooms are toasty underfoot. Neil meets, greets, cooks, bakes: try black pudding from Stornoway at breakfast; superb fish, shellfish and game for supper. Irresistible B&B.

Price	£85–£90. Singles £70–£75.
Rooms	3: 2 doubles, 1 twin/double.
Meals	Dinner, 4 courses, £22–£25. BYO. Packed lunch £5. Pub/restaurant 200 yds.
Closed	Rarely.
Directions	Leave Skye Bridge & follow A87 to Broadford. After 6 miles pass Hebridean Hotel on left, house is 200 yds further up A87 on right.

	Neil Hope
	Tigh An Dochais,
	13 Harrapool, Isle of Skye IV49 9AQ
Tel	+44 (0)1471 820022
Email	hopeskye@btinternet.com
Web	www.skyebedbreakfast.co.uk

Entry 663   Map 17

Highland

The Berry

Drive through miles of spectacular landscape then bask in the final approach down a winding single-track road to Allt-Na-Subh – just five houses overlooking the loch. Joan, who is friendly and kind, prepares delicious meals in her Rayburn-warmed kitchen – the hub of this character-filled house. Inside is fresh and light with stylish bedrooms – one up, one down; the sitting room has a log fire and stunning views. Eat fish straight from the boats, stride the hills and spot golden eagles, red deer and otters. The perfect place for naturalists and artists, or those seeking solace. A hidden gem. *Minimum stay two nights at weekends.*

Price	£70. Singles from £35.
Rooms	2: 1 double with separate shower; 1 double sharing bath.
Meals	Dinner, 3 courses with wine, £30. Packed lunch £7. Pub 3 miles.
Closed	Rarely.
Directions	From A87 at Dornie follow signs for Killilin, Conchra & Salachy. House 2.7 miles on left.

	Joan Ashburner
	The Berry, Allt-Na-Subh,
	Dornie, Kyle of Lochalsh IV40 8DZ
Tel	+44 (0)1599 588259

Entry 664   Map 17

Highland

Duncraig Castle

The original owner built the station at Duncraig purely to bring his friends to the castle; Suzanne, open and friendly, is just as keen to share her grand country house. Wood fires blaze, stunning views are of open sea and high mountain, and the rooms are vast. Expect tartan carpet, tiger skins, dark wood panelling and floor to ceiling windows; suits of armour and heraldic pennants hang theatrically on your route to the dining room. Bedrooms are huge, comfortable and velvety with whisky, glasses and shortbread set by all the well-made beds. Walks are marvellous, and you can eat freshly caught langoustines at Plockton Inn.

Price	From £109. Singles from £80.
Rooms	3 doubles.
Meals	Pub/restaurant 1.9 miles.
Closed	November-March (open by arrangement for larger parties).
Directions	From Stromeferry direction follow A890; take right signed Achmore & Plockton. Follow road 3.6 miles. Duncraig Castle signed on right after Duncraig Nursery.

5% off second and subsequent nights.

Suzanne Hazeldine
Duncraig Castle,
Plockton IV52 8TZ
Tel   +44 (0)1599 544295
Mobile   +44 (0)7702 736513
Email   suzanne@duncraigcastle.co.uk
Web   www.duncraigcastle.co.uk

Entry 665   Map 17

Highland

Aurora

The perfect spot for walkers and climbers (single-track roads, lochs, rivers and mountains) and the perfect B&B for groups: three smart, uncluttered bedrooms have flexible sleeping arrangements and spick and span shower rooms. The guest sitting room is light and airy with binoculars, books to borrow, maps and a small fridge for your wine – stay put for glorious sunsets and views to Harris. Breakfast time is generously bendy; good seasonal food is important here and you eat round a big table. There's a drying room and bike storage, but those wanting to relax will love it here too. *Minimum stay two nights. Over 12s welcome.*

Ethical Collection: Environment; Food.
See page 420.

Price	£76-£96. Singles £50-£96.
Rooms	3: 1 double, 2 twins/doubles (extra single bed).
Meals	Packed lunch £6. Pub/restaurant within 0.5 miles.
Closed	November-March.
Directions	From Inverness A9 north, signed 'Wester Ross Coastal Trail'. Left at Garve A832. Left at Kinlochewe A896. In Shieldaig at Heron sign 1st right; house 4th on left.

Packed lunch first full day.

Ann Barton
Aurora,
Shieldaig, Torridon IV54 8XN
Tel   +44 (0)1520 755246
Email   info@aurora-bedandbreakfast.co.uk
Web   www.aurora-bedandbreakfast.co.uk

Entry 666   Map 17

Highland

Tanglewood House

Down a steep drive through stunning landscape to this modern, curved house on the shore of Loch Broom – and distant views of the old fishing port of Ullapool. The drawing room is filled with antiques, fine fabrics, original paintings, flowers and a grand piano; bask in the views from the floor-to-ceiling window. Bedrooms are delightful: bold colours, crisp linen, proper bath tubs with fluffy towels. Anne's son, Julian, an ex-London chef, is linking up with local producers making the dinners at this 'gastro-B&B' even more special. Explore the wild garden then stroll to the rocky private beach for a swim in the loch. Superb.

Price	From £96. Singles from £76.
Rooms	3: 1 double, 2 twins.
Meals	Dinner, 4 courses, from £36. BYO. Pubs 1 mile.
Closed	Christmas, New Year & Easter.
Directions	Just outside Ullapool from Inverness on A835, left immed. after 4th 40mph sign. Take cattle grid on right & left fork down to house.

	Anne Holloway
	Tanglewood House,
	Ullapool IV26 2TB
Tel	+44 (0)1854 612059
Email	anne@tanglewoodhouse.co.uk
Web	www.tanglewoodhouse.co.uk

Entry 667   Map 17

Highland

The Old Ferryman's House

This former ferryman's house is small, homely and delightful, just yards from the river Spey with its spectacular mountain views. Explore the countryside or relax in the garden with a tray of tea and homemade treats; plants tumble from whisky barrels and pots and you can spot red squirrels. The sitting room is cosy with a wood-burning stove and lots of books (no TV). Generous Elizabeth, a keen traveller who lived in the Sudan, cooks delicious and imaginative meals: herbs and some veg from the garden, eggs from her hens, heathery honeycomb, homemade bread and preserves. An unmatched spot for explorers, and very good value.

Price	£58. Singles £29.
Rooms	3: 1 double, 1 twin, 1 single, all sharing 1 bath & 2 wcs.
Meals	Dinner, 3 courses, £21. BYO. Packed lunch £6.50.
Closed	Occasionally in winter.
Directions	From A9, follow main road markings through village, pass golf club & cross river. Or turn off B970 to Boat of Garten. House on left, just before river.

	Elizabeth Matthews
	The Old Ferryman's House,
	Boat of Garten PH24 3BY
Tel	+44 (0)1479 831370

Entry 668   Map 18

Highland

Rehaurie Cottage

You are steeped in history here, surrounded by woodland, castles, cairns and ancient battlefields. This 19th-century woodcutter's cottage is mercifully free of tartan; instead find clean lines, neutral colours and a contemporary feel. Spacious bedrooms are at either side of the house, one in cool greys with its own sitting room, the other in pretty rose-pink and cream with a private feel; both have sparkling, well-designed bathrooms. Sylvia and Chris, lovely people, give you an ample breakfast in the dining room which leads to a veranda; walks from the door are stunning. Discover jazz and Highland games in Nairn.

Price	£70–£95. Singles £55–£60.
Rooms	2 doubles (1 with sitting room), each with separate bath/shower.
Meals	Packed lunch £6. Supper from £12.50. Pub 5 miles.
Closed	Rarely.
Directions	From Inverness A96 to Nairn; A939 to Grantown. Continue for 1.5 miles past Littlemill, then right signed Cawdor, 6 miles. Cottage on left after 200 yds.

 15% off October–March (not Easter, Christmas, & New Year).

Sylvia Price
Rehaurie Cottage,
Nairn IV12 5JD
Tel   +44 (0)1309 651322
Mobile +44 (0)7513 974276
Email   stay@rehaurie.co.uk
Web   www.rehaurie.co.uk

Entry 669   Map 18

Highland

The Farmhouse

This freshly painted Victorian cottage is up a tree-lined driveway. Barbara's new home glows with art, antique rugs, a dazzling chandelier and French linen curtains; the kitchen has a magnificent dresser stocked with colourful pottery and comfortable armchairs in a warm spot by the wood-burner. The master bedroom sports smart linen, large feather pillows and a spotless bathroom. You get great home baking, and Barbara's creative energy will soon transform the garden, too. Highland views and the wildlife are spectacular, the mountain air is clean; this is a great escape.

Ethical Collection: Food. See page 420.

Price	£75–£80. Singles from £55.
Rooms	2: 1 double; 1 twin with separate bath.
Meals	Dinner, 3 courses, from £30. Pub 3.5 miles.
Closed	Christmas & New Year.
Directions	From Inverness follow signs to Beauly. After approx. 8 miles, right to Kirkhill. Follow road signed Beauly. House 1 mile on right.

 Late checkout (11am).

Barbara Turner
The Farmhouse,
Kirkhill, Beauly IV5 7PF
Tel   +44 (0)1463 831379
Mobile +44 (0)7411 059838
Email   mlbtuk@googlemail.com

Entry 670   Map 18

Highland

Craigiewood

The best of both worlds: the remoteness of the Highlands (red kites, wild goats) and Inverness just four miles. The landscape surrounding this elegant cottage exudes a sense of ancient mystery augmented by these six acres – home to woodpeckers, roe deer and glorious roses. Inside, maps, walking sticks, two cats and a lovely, family-home feel – what you'd expect from delightful owners. Bedrooms, old-fashioned and cosy, overlook a garden reclaimed from Black Isle gorse. Gavin is experimenting with solar panels, and runs garden tours: he can take you off to Inverewe, Attadale, Cawdor and Dunrobin Castle. Warm, peaceful, special.

Price	£76–£90. Singles £40–£50.
Rooms	2 twins.
Meals	Pub 2 miles.
Closed	Christmas & New Year.
Directions	A9 north over Kessock Bridge. At N. Kessock junc. left to r'bout to Kilmuir. After 0.25 miles, right to Kilmuir; left at top of road. Pass Drynie Farm, then right; house 1st left.

 Use your Sawday's Gift Card here.

Araminta & Gavin Dallmeyer
Craigiewood,
North Kessock, Inverness IV1 3XG
Tel   +44 (0)1463 731628
Mobile   +44 (0)7831 733699
Email   2minty@craigiewood.co.uk
Web   www.craigiewood.co.uk

Entry 671   Map 18

Highland

Knockbain House

This is a well-loved farm, its environmental credentials supreme, and David and Denise are warm and interesting. A beautiful setting, too: landscaped gardens, a 700-acre farm (cows, lambs, barley) and rolling countryside stretching to Cromarty Firth. A grandfather clock ticks away time to relax, by floor-to-ceiling windows and a wood-burner in the antiques-filled sitting room; over a breakfast or dinner of home-grown foods; with a drink on the pond-side terrace; in bedrooms with new bathrooms and stunning views. Revel in the birds, walks and your hosts' commitment to this glorious unspoilt nature. *Babes in arms & over tens welcome.*

Price	£70–£90. Singles from £35.
Rooms	2: 1 double, 1 twin.
Meals	Dinner, 3 courses, £25. Packed lunch £5. Pubs/restaurants 1 mile.
Closed	Rarely.
Directions	From Dingwall, A834 past County Buildings & police station. After 200 yds, first left Blackwells Street. Narrow road to farm road, 300 yds then over cattle grid up driveway.

David & Denise Lockett
Knockbain House,
Dingwall IV15 9TJ
Tel   +44 (0)1349 862476
Mobile   +44 (0)7736 629838
Email   davidlockett@avnet.co.uk
Web   www.knockbainhouse.co.uk

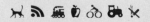

Entry 672   Map 18

Highland

Wemyss House

The peace is palpable, the setting overlooking the Cromarty Firth is stunning. Take an early morning stroll and spot buzzards, pheasants, rabbits and roe deer. The deceptively spacious house with sweeping maple floors is flooded with light and fabulous views, big bedrooms are warmly decorated with Highland rugs and tweeds, there's Christine's grand piano in the living room, Stuart's handcrafted furniture at every turn, and a sweet dog called Bella. Aga breakfasts include homemade bread, preserves and eggs from happy hens. Dinners are delicious; Christine and Stuart are wonderful hosts.

Ethical Collection: Food. See page 420.

Price	From £90.
Rooms	3: 2 doubles, 1 twin.
Meals	Dinner £35. Restaurants 15-minute drive.
Closed	Rarely.
Directions	From Inverness, A9 north. At Nigg r'bout, right onto B9175. Through Arabella; left at sign to Hilton & Shandwick; right towards Nigg; past church; 1 mile, right onto private road. House on right.

Bottle of wine with dinner on first night.

Use your Sawday's Gift Card here.

Christine Asher & Stuart Clifford
Wemyss House,
Bayfield, Tain IV19 1QW
Tel   +44 (0)1862 851212
Mobile   +44 (0)7759 484709
Email   stay@wemysshouse.com
Web   www.wemysshouse.com

Entry 673   Map 18

Highland

St Callan's Manse

Fun, laughter and conversation flow in this warm and happy home. You share it with prints, paintings, antiques, sofas, amazing memorabilia, three dogs, nine ducks, 14 hens and 1,200 teddy bears of every size and origin. Snug bedrooms have pretty fabrics, old armoires, flower-patterned sheets and tartan blankets; your sleep will be sound. Caroline cooks majestic breakfasts and dinners; Robert, a fund of knowledgeable anecdotes, can arrange just about anything. All this in incomparable surroundings: 60 acres of sheep-strewn land plus glens, forests, buzzards, deer and the odd golden eagle. A gem. *Dogs by arrangement.*

Price	£80. Singles £65.
Rooms	2: 1 double with separate bath; 1 double with separate shower.
Meals	Dinner, 2-4 courses, £16-£25. BYO. Pub/restaurant in village, 1.5 miles.
Closed	March & occasionally.
Directions	From Inverness, A9 north. Cross Dornoch bridge. 14 miles on, A839 to Lairg. Cross small bridge in Rogart; sharp right uphill, for St Callan's church. House 1.5 miles on, on right, next to church.

Free pick-up from local bus/train station. Local food/produce in your room. Late checkout (12pm).

Robert & Caroline Mills
St Callan's Manse,
Rogart IV28 3XE
Tel   +44 (0)1408 641363
Email   caroline@rogartsnuff.me.uk

Entry 674   Map 21

Moray

Westfield House

Sweep up the drive to the grand home of an illustrious family: Macleans have lived here since 1862. Inside find polished furniture and burnished antiques, a tartan-carpeted hall, an oak stair hung with ancestral oils. John farms 500 acres while Veronica cooks sublimely; dinner is served at a long candelabra'd table, with vegetables from the vegetable garden. A winter fire crackles in the guest sitting room, old-fashioned bedrooms are warm and inviting (plump pillows, fine linen, books, lovely views), the peace is deep. A historic house in a perfect setting, run by the most charming people.

Price	£90. Singles from £45.
Rooms	3: 1 twin; 1 twin with separate bath & shower; 1 single with separate bath.
Meals	Supper, 2 courses, £20. Dinner, 3 courses, £25. Pub 3 miles.
Closed	Rarely.
Directions	From Elgin, A96 west for Forres & Inverness; after 2.5 miles, right onto B9013 for Burghead; after 1 mile, signed right at x-roads. Cont. to 'Westfield House & Office'.

	John & Veronica Maclean
	Westfield House,
	Elgin IV30 8XL
Tel	+44 (0)1343 547308
Email	veronica.maclean@yahoo.co.uk
Web	www.westfieldhouseelgin.co.uk

Entry 675   Map 18

Perth & Kinross

Grenich Steading

Perched above silvery Loch Tummel is Lindsay's award-winning renovation of a once derelict barn. Inside, blue-and-white Portuguese tiles, lots of ornaments and books and a wood-burning stove. All yours are a kitchen, dining and sitting room: you can self-cater if you choose (minimum one week). Gaze upon mountain-to-loch views, climb the hills, walk the glens or visit the theatre at Pitlochry – there's so much to do you'll barely be inside. Lindsay nurtures both garden and guests, and her Scottish deerhound and cocker spaniel are welcoming too. The sunsets are fabulous. *Over eights welcome. Min. two nights at weekends May-Oct.*

Price	From £80. Singles £60.
Rooms	2: 1 double; 1 twin sharing bath & sitting room (2nd room let to same party only).
Meals	Dinner, with wine, £30 (Oct-Mar only). Pub 0.75 miles.
Closed	Rarely.
Directions	From A9 north of Pitlochry for Killiecrankie. Left, B8019 for Tummel Bridge to Loch Tummel Inn. After 0.75 miles, right at sign, then up forestry road for 0.5 miles.

	Lindsay Morison
	Grenich Steading, Strathtummel,
	Tummel Bridge, Pitlochry PH16 5RT
Tel	+44 (0)1882 634332
Mobile	+44 (0)7502 199163

Entry 676   Map 15+18

Perth & Kinross

Beinn Bhracaigh

Here is a solid Victorian villa, with later wings, built for an Edinburgh family in the 1880s, when Pitlochry was hailed as the Switzerland of the North. Ann and Alf, generous hosts, have swept through with the cream paint and all is spanking new. Expect soft lighting, gleaming wooden floors, silk flowers, bowls of pot pourri and scented candles. The lounge is comfy and has an honesty bar with over 50 malt whiskies, good-sized bedrooms have excellent mattresses, padded headboards and views to the Tummel Hills, bathrooms are all new with thick towels and lovely lotions. Breakfast is a huge, imaginative feast.

Ethical Collection: Food. See page 420.

Price	£75-£95. Singles from £60.
Rooms	10: 4 doubles, 6 twins/doubles.
Meals	Dinner £22.50-£30 (special group occasions only). Pubs/restaurants within 10-minute walk.
Closed	23-28 December.
Directions	From A9, turn for Pitlochry. Under railway bridge, then right at scout hut & up East Moulin Road. 2nd left into Higher Oakfield; house almost immediately on left.

Ann & Alf Berry
Beinn Bhracaigh, 14 Higher Oakfield,
Pitlochry PH16 5HT
Tel   +44 (0)1796 470355
Mobile +44 (0)7708 668436
Email   info@beinnbhracaigh.com
Web   www.beinnbhracaigh.com

Entry 677   Map 15+18

Perth & Kinross

Rock House

Prepare to fall hopelessly in love. Hard to know here, high above Loch Tay, whether the views are more beautiful outside or in. The cathedral ceiling in the sitting room allows light to soar upwards, there's a striking collection of modern art and an unfussy style: white sofas, painted furniture, and, here and there, a bit of quirky fun or a perfect antique. Sleep deeply in beds piled with linen cushions, soft woollen throws and cotton ticking, wake to grape and mint salad, Irish bread, kedgeree or anything else you want… Roland and Penny are passionate about their house, the land, and real food. *Minimum stay two nights.*

Price	£127. Singles £88.
Rooms	2 doubles.
Meals	Dinner, 2-3 courses, £25-£35. Packed lunch £12. Pub/restaurant 2.2 miles.
Closed	Rarely.
Directions	From Aberfeldy, A827 dir. Kenmore. At Loch Tay where main road turns sharp right, cont. along narrow road signed Acharn. Follow loch side for 2.2 miles. At top of hill, house on right.

Roland & Penny Kennedy
Rock House, Achianich,
Kenmore, Aberfeldy PH15 2HU
Tel   +44 (0)1887 830336
Email   rockhouse@lochtay.co.uk
Web   www.lochtay.co.uk

Entry 678   Map 15+18

Perth & Kinross

Essendy House

Down a tree-lined drive blazing with colour in the autumn, Tess and John's charming country house is surrounded by lochs, castles and serenity. Inside is cosy and comfortable with warm fires, flowers, porcelain, Italianate murals and an unusual collection of family artefacts. Traditionally furnished bedrooms have antiques, good linen, garden views and silk or floral touches. Enjoy hearty breakfasts and suppers in the huge dining room or family kitchen; the terrace is heaven in summer. There's lots to do: visit cathedral and theatre, hike Macbeth's Birnham Hill, play golf, ski, fish and admire the swooping ospreys.

Perth & Kinross

Inchyra House

Sweep up through mature parkland to a gorgeous welcome from Caroline and James, and Flint the Scottish deerhound. Here is 18th grandeur, all grace and charm with a fire blazing in the hall. Elegant doubles are classically decorated: 'Yellow' has the edge with lawn views but 'Blue' is gracious too, with a chaise longue and vintage lace; Nettle has a charmingly old-fashioned French feel. Set off for Perth or a round of golf, return for tea and scones in the splendid drawing room with parkland views. Or slope off to the library with its open fire: wherever you are, you'll feel beautifully at home.

Price	£90. Singles £45.
Rooms	2: 1 double, 1 twin.
Meals	Packed lunch £5. Supper, 2 courses, £20. Pub/restaurant 2 miles.
Closed	Christmas & New Year. February/March.
Directions	A93 Perth to Blairgowrie. At Blairgowrie, left to B947. Two miles, over bridge with rusty green railings, uphill after bridge, drive at summit on right, white railings.

10% off stays of 2 or more nights.

Price	£130-£140. Singles £90.
Rooms	3: 1 twin; 1 double, 1 twin each with separate bath.
Meals	Pub 0.5 miles. Restaurants 4 miles.
Closed	Christmas & New Year.
Directions	A90 towards Dundee. After 4 miles take exit to Glencarse and St Madoes. Keep left. Gates 150 yds on left opposite Linden Garden Centre.

10% off stays of 2 or more nights. Late checkout (12pm).

	John Monteith
	Essendy House,
	Blairgowrie PH10 6QY
Tel	+44 (0)1250 884260
Mobile	+44 (0)7841 121538
Email	johnmonteith@hotmail.com
Web	www.essendy.org

Entry 679   Map 15+18

	Caroline & James Hoyer Millar
	Inchyra House,
	Glencarse, Perth PH2 7LU
Tel	+44 (0)1738 860210
Email	caroline@hoyers.demon.co.uk
Web	www.inchyra.com

Entry 680   Map 15

Perth & Kinross

Old Kippenross

What a setting! Old Kippenross rests in 150 peaceful acres of gorgeous park and woodland overlooking the river Allan — spot red squirrels and deer, herons, dippers and otters. The 15th-century house has a Georgian addition and an air of elegance and great courtesy, with its rustic white-vaulted basement, and dining room and sitting room strewn with soft sofas and Persian rugs. Sash-windowed bedrooms are deeply comfortable, warm bathrooms are stuffed with towels. Susan and Patrick (an expert on birds of prey) are welcoming, the food is good and there's a croquet lawn in the walled garden. *Over tens welcome. Dogs by arrangement.*

Price	£96–£98. Singles £63–£64.
Rooms	2: 1 double, 1 twin/double (with adjoining single room, let to same party only).
Meals	Dinner £28. BYO. Pub 1.5 miles.
Closed	Rarely.
Directions	M9 exit 11, B8033 for Dunblane. 500 yds, right over dual c'way, thro' entrance by stone gatehouse. Down drive, 1st fork right after bridge. House along gravelled drive.

💼 Bottle of wine with dinner on first night. Salmon & trout fishing on river Allan, by arrangement.

Susan & Patrick Stirling-Aird
Old Kippenross,
Dunblane FK15 0LQ
Tel   +44 (0)1786 824048
Email   kippenross@hotmail.com

Entry 681   Map 15

Perth & Kinross

Mackeanston House

They grow their own organic fruit and vegetables in the walled garden, make their own preserves, bake their own bread. Likeable and energetic — Fiona a wine buff and talented cook, Colin a tri-lingual guide — your hosts are hospitable people whose 1690 farmhouse combines informality and luxury in peaceful, central Scotland. Light-filled bedrooms have pretty fabrics, fine antiques, TVs and homemade cake. Roomy bathrooms have robes and a radio; one has a double shower (with a seat if you wish it). Dine by the log fire in the dining room, or in the conservatory with views to Stirling Castle. *Local & battlefield tours.*

Price	£96–£100. Singles £58–£60.
Rooms	2: 1 double, 1 twin/double.
Meals	Dinner £30. Pub 1 mile.
Closed	Christmas.
Directions	From M9, north, junc. 10 onto A84 for Doune. After 5 miles, left on B826 for Thornhill. Drive on left after 2.2 miles, right off farm drive.

💼 Bottle of wine on 1st night of minimum 2-night stay (dinner, b&b).

Fiona & Colin Graham
Mackeanston House,
Doune, Stirling FK16 6AX
Tel   +44 (0)1786 850213
Mobile   +44 (0)7921 143018
Email   info@mackeanstonhouse.co.uk
Web   www.mackeanstonhouse.co.uk

Entry 682   Map 15

Scottish Borders

Skirling House

An intriguing house with 1908 additions, impeccably maintained. The whole lovely place is imbued with the spirit of Scottish Arts & Crafts, augmented with Italianate flourishes. Colourful blankets embellish chairs; runners soften flagged floors; the carvings, wrought-ironwork and rare Florentine ceiling are sheer delight. Upstairs, superb comfort holds sway: carpets and rugs, window seats and wicker, fruit and flowers. Bob cooks the finest local produce, Isobel shares a love of Scottish contemporary art and both look after you beautifully. Outside: 25,000 trees have been planted and grand walks from the door.

Price	£100–£130. Singles £60–£85.
Rooms	5: 3 doubles, 1 twin, 1 twin/double.
Meals	Dinner £32. Pubs/restaurants 2 miles.
Closed	Christmas & January/February.
Directions	From Biggar, A702 for Edinburgh. Just outside Biggar, right on A72 for Skirling. Big wooden house on right opp. village green.

10% off room rate Mon–Thurs. Late checkout (12pm).

Bob & Isobel Hunter
Skirling House,
Skirling, Biggar ML12 6HD

Tel	+44 (0)1899 860274
Email	enquiry@skirlinghouse.com
Web	www.skirlinghouse.com

Entry 683   Map 15

Scottish Borders

Fauhope House

Near to Melrose Abbey and the glorious St Cuthbert's Walk, this solid 1890s house is immersed in bucolic bliss. Views soar to the Eildon Hills through wide windows with squashy seats; all is luxurious, elegant, fire-lit and serene with an eclectic mix of art. Bedrooms are warm with deeply coloured walls, thick chintz, pale tartan blankets and soft carpet; bathrooms are modern and pristine. Breakfast is served with smiles at a flower-laden table and overlooking those purple hills. A short walk through the garden and over a footbridge takes you to the interesting town of Melrose, with shops, restaurants and its own theatre.

Price	From £90. Singles from £60.
Rooms	3 twins/doubles.
Meals	Pub/restaurant 0.5 miles.
Closed	Rarely.
Directions	From A7, through Gattonside; at end of village, left onto Monkswood Rd, right onto private drive.

Ian & Sheila Robson
Fauhope House,
Gattonside, Melrose TD6 9LY

Tel	+44 (0)1896 823184
Mobile	+44 (0)7816 346768
Email	info@fauhopehouse.com

Entry 684   Map 15

Scottish Borders

Whitehouse Country House

A proud avenue of trees leads to Angela and Roger's 19th-century dower house in the heart of the Borders. This is hunting, fishing and shooting territory, with big views and warm Scottish hospitality. Enjoy the river walk, watch deer sniffing the air and swans rising against the sky. Then retreat to the airy drawing room with roaring fire. Angela's cooking is heavenly – maybe game or their own smoked salmon in a spacious dining room. Traditional, comfortable bedrooms and bathrooms are a good size with glorious views. In the morning, surrender to a Scottish Borders Best Breakfast 2010!

Ethical Collection: Food. See page 420.

Price	From £90. Singles from £55.
Rooms	3: 1 double, 2 twins.
Meals	Dinner £22-£29. Supper tray £10. Packed lunch £7. Pub 3 miles.
Closed	Rarely.
Directions	A68 from Edinburgh to St. Boswells. From M6 at Carlisle, A7 to Hawick, then A698 & A68 to St. Boswells. From St. Boswells B6404 to turning on right for Whitehouse.

10% off room rate including meals (pay before you stay).

Angela & Roger Tyrer
Whitehouse Country House,
St Boswells, Melrose TD6 0ED
Tel   +44 (0)1573 460343
Mobile   +44 (0)7877 800582
Email   staying@whitehousecountryhouse.com
Web   www.whitehousecountryhouse.com

Entry 685   Map 16

Scottish Borders

New Belses Farm

Once lost by Lord Lothian in a game of backgammon, this Georgian farmhouse is safe in current hands. Delightful Helen divides her time between helping on the farm, gardening and caring for pets, fan-tail doves, hens (fox permitting), family and guests. Bedrooms glow in a harmony of old paintings, lush chintzes and beautiful antiques, beds are extra long, towels snowy white and breakfasts come complete with free-range sausages and eggs from the farm. It's like home, only better. Discover great Border towns, stunning abbeys, fishing on the Tweed. Enjoy an excellent dinner locally then back to plump sofas by the log fire. Heaven.

Ethical Collection: Food. See page 420.

Price	From £90.
Rooms	2: 1 double, 1 twin.
Meals	Pubs/restaurants 5-7 miles.
Closed	Christmas.
Directions	From Jedburgh, A68 for Edinburgh. Left after 3.5 miles to Ancrum; B6400 Ancrum to Lilliesleaf road; right after 4 miles, down drive (signed).

Local food/produce in your room.

Peter & Helen Wilson
New Belses Farm,
Ancrum, Jedburgh TD8 6UR
Tel   +44 (0)1835 870472
Mobile   +44 (0)7710 277020
Email   wilson699@totalise.co.uk

Entry 686   Map 16

Scottish Borders

Lessudden

A treat to stay in a great and historic tower house in the heart of the Scottish Borders. Your generous hosts give you big cosy bedrooms (one with an old-fashioned bathroom, one with hill views), and a spacious sitting room with fine old rugs, heaps of books and a log fire. Memorable meals are served at a polished oak refectory table beneath the gaze of Sir Walter Scott's uncle and aunt, who used to live here. The 1680s white-stone stairwell is unique, the décor is traditional and homely, the living is relaxed and Alasdair and Angela care for their guests as open-heartedly as they do their cats, dogs, horses and hens.

Ethical Collection: Environment; Food; Community. See page 420.

Price	£100. Singles £70.
Rooms	2: 1 double; 1 twin with separate bath.
Meals	Dinner, 3-4 courses, £25. Pub 0.5 miles.
Closed	Rarely.
Directions	North on A68 to St Boswells. Right opp. Buccleuch Arms Hotel, on through village; left up drive immed. beyond turning to golf course.

10% off stays of 3 or more nights.

Alasdair & Angela Douglas-Hamilton
Lessudden,
St Boswells TD6 0BH
Tel   +44 (0)1835 823244
Email alasdaird@lineone.net
Web   www.lessudden.com

Entry 687   Map 16

Scottish Borders

Kirkbank House

Come for wonderful panoramas past wisteria'd walls over pretty-as-a-picture Paxton to the Cheviot Hills. Newly transformed by cosmopolitan hosts John and Lena, the 1760 house is now a boutiquey B&B freshly furnished with finds from their time in Asia: bright Thai silk throws, Buddha sculptures, ornamental orchids, yoga mats, and a Chinese altar/washstand in the L'Occitane-fresh bathroom; the results are stunning. John is an accomplished cook (dinners are a delight) and photographer; his work complements modern art on the walls. Huge beds, turned-down top-notch linen and chocs on the pillow: fabulous.

Price	£95-£120.
Rooms	3: 1 double, 1 twin/double; 1 double with separate bath/shower.
Meals	Dinner, 3 courses, £25. Packed lunch £8. Pub 200 yds.
Closed	Rarely.
Directions	From A1 Berwick-upon-Tweed bypass take B6461 signed Kelso, right to Paxton after 4 miles, then right at Cross Inn, follow private road and signs to Kirkbank.

10% off stays of 2 or more nights. Free pick-up from local bus/train station.

Lena Tomnay
Kirkbank House,
Paxton, Berwick upon Tweed TD15 1TE
Tel   +44 (0)1289 386534
Mobile +44 (0)7890 292545
Email info@kirkbankhouse.co.uk
Web   www.kirkbankhouse.co.uk

Entry 688   Map 16

Stirling

Quarter

This stately 1750s house commands views across Stirling's lush countryside and comes complete with crunching gravel drive and original ceiling dome. It was owned by the same family for generations until Pippa arrived, taking over its high ceilings, period features, sash windows. Pad your way upstairs to three comfortable bedrooms and bathrooms, brightened with a floral touch. Breakfast is a grand affair at a polished table; pecking hens provide the eggs and Pippa is determined to restore the kitchen garden to its former glory. The house is cocooned in extensive grounds and you've easy access to Stirling, Edinburgh and Perth. *Dogs by arrangement.*

Price	£90. Singles £50.
Rooms	3: 1 double, 1 twin/double, 1 twin.
Meals	Pub/restaurant 4 miles.
Closed	Christmas.
Directions	Stirling, exit 9 off the M9. From roundabout take A872 towards Denny, after exactly 2 miles turn left (200 yds past Wellsfield Farm) through grey pillars up to house.

 Fruit and fresh flowers in your room. Free pick-up from local bus/train station.

	Pippa Maclean
	Quarter,
	Denny FK6 6QZ
Tel	+44 (0)1324 825817
Email	pippa@edmonstone.com
Web	www.quarterstirling.com

Entry 689   Map 15

Stirling

The Moss

Rozie loves fishing and Jamie keeps bees; they live in a charming listed house full of lovely things and are great hosts. Outside are 28 acres where deer prune the roses, pheasants roam and a garden seat sits with its toes in the water. Generous bedrooms are very private in their own wing and have big beds with feather pillows, books, flowers and long views to pastures and moorland. Expect walking sticks and the bell of HMS Tempest in the porch, rugs in the hall and smart sofas in the log-fired drawing room. Breakfast comes fresh from the Aga and is delivered to a big oak table, from which there are yet more views.

Price	£90. Singles £45.
Rooms	3: 1 twin; 2 doubles sharing bath (2nd room let to same party only).
Meals	Pubs/restaurants within 2 miles.
Closed	Rarely.
Directions	4 miles west of Blanefield. Half a mile after Beech Tree Inn turn left off A81. After 300 yds, over bridge, 1st entrance on left.

	Jamie & Rozie Parker
	The Moss,
	Killearn G63 9LJ
Tel	+44 (0)1360 550053
Mobile	+44 (0)7787 123599
Email	themoss@freeuk.com

Entry 690   Map 15

Stirling

Blairhullichan

So much to do in the Trossachs National Park: woodland walks, cycle tracks, even your own fishing bay on the edge of Loch Ard and a private island to wade out to for picnics. The tranquil house sits high on a slope with fabulous loch views from the drawing room — comfortable with window bay, fireplace and stacks of books. Reassuringly old-fashioned bedrooms have new mattresses and crisp linen; bathrooms have good towels and lotions. Be charmed by the 'Highlands in miniature' — plus resident labradors and welcoming Bridget, who gives you a grand breakfast and the best of her local knowledge. *Minimum stay two nights.*

Price	£75-£80. Singles £40.
Rooms	4: 1 double, 1 twin; 2 doubles each with separate bath/shower.
Meals	Dinner, with wine, £25-£35. Restaurant 10 miles.
Closed	Rarely.
Directions	A81 to Aberfoyle; then onto B829 to Kinlochard; on for 4.5 miles, pass Macdonald Hotel; left at red phone box; bumpy road, on for 0.5 miles. Ignore 'Water Dept No Entry' sign. On left, signed.

Bottle of wine with dinner on first night. Late checkout (12pm).

John & Bridget Lewis
Blairhullichan,
Kinlochard, Aberfoyle FK8 3TN
Tel   +44 (0)1877 387341
Email jablewis@aol.com
Web   www.blairhullichan.net

Entry 691   Map 15

Stirling

Cardross

Dodge the lazy sheep on the long drive to arrive (eventually!) at a sweep of gravel and lovely old Cardross, in a gorgeous setting with its 15th-century tower. Bang on the enormous old door and either Archie or Nicola (plus labradors and Jack Russells) will usher you in. And what a delight it is; light and space, long views, exquisite furniture, wooden shutters, towelling robes, fresh flowers, crisp linen, a cast-iron period bath — and that's just the bedrooms. It all feels warm, kind and generous, the drawing room is vast, the house is filled with character and the Orr Ewings can tell you all the history. *Young people over 14 welcome.*

Price	£100-£110. Singles £65-£70.
Rooms	2: 1 twin; 1 twin with separate bath.
Meals	Occasional dinner £28. Pub/restaurant 2.5 miles.
Closed	Christmas & New Year.
Directions	A811 Stirling-Dumbarton to Arnprior; B8034 towards Port of Menteith; 2 miles, then cross Forth over humpback bridge. Drive with yellow lodge 150 yds from bridge on right. 1st exit on right from drive.

10% off stays of 2 or more nights.

Sir Orr Ewing
Cardross,
Port of Menteith, Kippen FK8 3JY
Tel   +44 (0)1877 385223
Email cardrossestate@googlemail.com
Web   www.cardrossholidayhomes.com

Entry 692   Map 15

Broad Bay House

In a wild landscape, 21st-century sophistication and style. Built in 2007, the house rises on graceful flights of decking above the beach. On an otherwise deserted shore, there is a villa right next door – but it disappears the moment you're inside. A stunning hall leads to a vaulted living room, whose windows face the waves on three sides... wow! More intimate boutique hotel than B&B – subtle lighting, oak doors, original art – Broad Bay House has been designed with sheer, unadulterated comfort in mind. Ian and Marion are considerate, generous, flexible hosts and the food, served at candlelit tables, is heavenly.

Pairc an t-Srath

Richard and Lena's lovely home overlooks the beach at Borve, another absurdly beautiful Harris view. Inside, smart simplicity abounds: wooden floors, white walls, a peat fire, colourful art. Airy bedrooms fit the mood perfectly: trim carpets, chunky wood beds, Harris tweed throws, excellent shower rooms (there's a bathroom, too, if you want a soak). Richard crofts, Lena cooks, perhaps homemade soup, venison casserole, wet chocolate cake with raspberries. Views from the dining room tumble down hill, so expect to linger over breakfast. You'll spot otters in the loch, while the standing stones at Callanish are unmissable.

Price	£145–£180.		Price	£100. Singles from £50.
Rooms	4: 2 doubles, 2 twins/doubles.		Rooms	4: 2 doubles, 1 twin, 1 single.
Meals	Dinner, 3 courses, £35. Packed lunch £10. Pub/restaurant 7 miles.		Meals	Dinner, 3 courses, £35. Restaurant 3 miles, pub 7 miles.
Closed	Rarely.		Closed	Rarely.
Directions	A867 from Stornoway towards Barvas & Ness. On edge of Stornoway, right onto B895. After 6 miles, house on right, between Back & Gress.		Directions	South from Tarbet ferry and first house on left in village; or north from Leverburgh ferry and last house on right.

 Use your Sawday's Gift Card here.

	Ian Fordham		Lena & Richard MacLennan
	Broad Bay House, Back,		Pairc an t-Srath,
	Stornoway, Isle of Lewis HS2 0LQ		Borve, Isle of Harris HS3 3HT
Tel	+44 (0)1851 820990	Tel	+44 (0)1859 550386
Email	stay@broadbayhouse.co.uk	Email	info@paircant-srath.co.uk
Web	www.broadbayhouse.co.uk	Web	www.paircant-srath.co.uk

Entry 693   Map 20

Entry 694   Map 20

Kinloch

Meander across the flower-filled machair to
the wide open spaces of South Uist – home
to waders, hen harriers, corncrakes and
talkative Wegg. The house, built 20 years ago,
is comfy with books, photos, easy chairs,
pictures and angling paraphernalia.
Bedrooms – the upstairs double the best –
have patchwork and pine and a general junk-
shop chic; views across the loch are
enormous, sunrises are spectacular. Wegg
loves cooking, especially barbecued fish and
game; his breakfasts and dinners are sociable
occasions and you are surrounded by a clever
acre of garden. Nature lovers will adore it.
Shoes off at the front door!

Price	£84. Singles £42.
Rooms	3: 1 twin/double; 1 twin/double, 1 single both with separate bath.
Meals	Dinner £22. Packed lunch £8. Restaurant 5 miles.
Closed	Rarely.
Directions	30 mins from Benbecula airport; 30 mins from Lochboisdale ferry; 45 mins from Lochmaddy.

	Wegg Kimbell
	Kinloch,
	Grogarry,
	Isle of South Uist HS8 5RR
Tel	+44 (0)1870 620316
Email	wegg@kinlochuist.com
Web	www.kinlochuist.com

Wales

Anglesey

Cleifiog

On a soft spring morning this could be Lake Garda. The bay view is spectacular, the masts of Beaumaris chink in the wind. Lovely Gill and gardening husband Laurie have taken over the running of this B&B and serve a delicious breakfast round the dining room table. All is stunning inside and out: the soft light, the scent of lilies, the smell of freshly brewed coffee. First it was a Georgian hospice, later a customs house; now the big, bright, elegant sitting room's panelling is offset by white linen sofas and pretty potted plants, and bedrooms are inviting with top-notch linen. Lap up the views and the beautiful sea air.

Price	£85-£95. Singles £55-£65.
Rooms	3: 2 twins/doubles, 1 suite.
Meals	Pub/restaurant 200 yards.
Closed	Christmas & New Year.
Directions	A55 over Britannia Bridge to Anglesey. Take A545 to Beaumaris. Past 2 left turns, house is 5th on left facing the sea. Bus stop outside.

Bottle of wine in your room.

Gill Beevers
Cleifiog,
Townsend, Beaumaris LL58 8BH
Tel   +44 (0)1248 811507
Email   enquiries@cleifiog.co.uk
Web   www.cleifiogbandb.co.uk

Entry 696   Map 6

Carmarthenshire

Sarnau Mansion

Listed and Georgian, the house has its own water supply. Play tennis and revel in 16 acres of beautiful grounds complete with pond, walled garden and woodland with nesting red kites. Bedrooms are simply furnished in heritage colours; bathrooms are big. The oak-floored sitting room with chesterfields has French windows onto the garden, the dining room is simpler with separate tables and there's good, fresh home cooking from Cynthia. One mile from the A40, you can hear a slight hum of traffic if the wind is from that direction. You are 15 minutes from the National Botanic Garden of Wales. *Children over five welcome.*

Price	£70-£80. Singles £50.
Rooms	3: 2 doubles, 1 twin.
Meals	Dinner, 3 courses, around £20. BYO. Pub 1 mile.
Closed	Rarely.
Directions	From Carmarthen A40 west for 4 miles. Right for Bancyfelin. After 0.5 miles, right into drive on brow of hill.

10% off stays of 4 or more nights.

Cynthia & David Fernihough
Sarnau Mansion, Llysonnen Road,
Bancyfelin, Carmarthen SA33 5DZ
Tel   +44 (0)1267 211404
Email   d.fernihough@btinternet.com
Web   www.sarnaumansion.co.uk

Entry 697   Map 6

Carmarthenshire

Plas Alltyferin

Wisteria-wrapped and, in parts, delightfully creaky, this Georgian family house sits in 270 beautiful acres. The breakfast room has the original panelling and the bedrooms have an old-fashioned charm. Not the place for you if you like spotlessness and state-of-the-art plumbing, but the views across the ha-ha to the Norman hill fort are timelessly lovely and the welcome is heartfelt. Gerard and Charlotte are the easiest, kindest and dog-friendliest of hosts. You're close to the National Botanical and Aberglasney gardens – and, most importantly, many lovely gastropubs! *Over tens welcome. Ballooning, shooting, fishing arranged.*

Price	£70-£80. Singles £35-£45.
Rooms	2: 1 twin; 1 twin with separate bath.
Meals	Pubs/restaurants within 2 miles.
Closed	September & occasionally.
Directions	From Carmarthen A40 east to Pont-ar-gothi. Left before bridge & follow narrow lane for approx. 2 miles keeping to right-hand hedge. House on right, signed. Call for precise details.

 10% off stays of 3 or more nights. Late checkout (12pm).

 Use your Sawday's Gift Card here.

Charlotte & Gerard Dent
Plas Alltyferin, Pont-ar-gothi,
Nantgaredig, Carmarthen SA32 7PF
Tel   +44 (0)1267 290662
Email   dent@alltyferin.co.uk
Web   www.alltyferin.co.uk

Entry 698   Map 6

Carmarthenshire

The Glynhir Estate

This fine old house on a Huguenot estate stands on the western edge of the Black Mountain. Outside: a waterfall, a two-acre kitchen garden, a brigade of chickens, and peacocks that patrol the grounds with panache. Inside, the house has spurned the urge to take itself too seriously and remains decidedly lived in. Find William Morris wallpaper in the dining room, lemon trees in the conservatory and old cabinets stuffed with interesting things in the sitting room. Country-house bedrooms fit the mood perfectly: smart and comfortable with excellent bathrooms. You can ride, walk, fish or visit Aberglasney Garden – just ask Katy.

Price	£80. Family room £98.50. Singles £50.
Rooms	4: 3 doubles, 1 family.
Meals	Dinner from £17.50. Pubs/restaurants 2 miles.
Closed	December-February.
Directions	M4 junc. 49, 2nd exit A483 for Ammanford. At 2nd traffic lights left to Llandybie, then 2nd right up Glynhir Road. After 1.2 miles house on right.

Katy Jenkins
The Glynhir Estate, Glynhir Road,
Llandybie, Ammanford SA18 2TD
Tel   +44 (0)1269 850438
Mobile   +44 (0)7810 864458
Email   enquiries@theglynhirestate.com
Web   www.theglynhirestate.com

Entry 699   Map 7

Carmarthenshire

Mandinam

On a heavenly bluff at the edge of the Beacons, beneath wheeling red kites and moody Welsh skies, lies Mandinam, the 'untouched holy place'. Delightful artistic Marcus and Daniella are its guardians, and they look after you as friends. Be charmed by bold rugs on wooden floors, weathered antiques, lofty ceilings, fires... and scrumptious meals in the red dining room. The serene four-poster room has a small gallery with a sofa; the large, rustic coach house room is plain with simple furnishings and shower, a wood-burner and a terrace. Watch the sun go down, revel in the peace and wonderful views.

Ethical Collection: Environment; Food; Community. See page 420.

Price	£70–£80. Singles by arrangement.
Rooms	2: 1 four-poster. Coach house: 1 twin/double. Self-catering in Shepherd's Hut.
Meals	Lunch or picnic from £7.50. Dinner, with wine, £25. Restaurants/pubs 2 miles.
Closed	Christmas.
Directions	Llangadog village shop, left; 50 yds, right Myddfai. Past cemetery, 1st right Llanddeusant; 1.5 miles, left through woods. Train: Llangadog.

Bottle of wine with dinner. Free pick-up from local train station.

Daniella & Marcus Lampard
Mandinam,
Llangadog SA19 9LA
Tel +44 (0)1550 777368
Email iolo@onetel.com
Web www.mandinam.com

Entry 700   Map 7

Carmarthenshire

The Drovers

The ice-cream pink Georgian townhouse looks good enough to eat – as do the leek and cheese cakes; Jill is a superb cook. A fabulous Welsh hospitality pervades this B&B, along with antiques, gas log fires and peaceful, cosy rooms. Downstairs areas are spacious, with a rambling hotel feel; sunny bedrooms are laced with books and Sanderson wallpapers; bathrooms come in contemporary white and cream, stocked with spoiling towels. Over breakfast (relaxed, delicious, locally sourced) you gaze through deep sash windows onto the town square; order a packed lunch and head for the hills. *Minimum stay two nights at weekends in high season.*

Price	£65–£80. Singles from £45.
Rooms	3: 2 doubles, 1 twin/double.
Meals	Dinner, 3 courses, £20. Packed lunch £5. Inns 50 yds.
Closed	Christmas & New Year.
Directions	In town centre, opposite the fountain.

10% off room rate Mon-Thurs.

Jill Blud
The Drovers,
9 Market Square, Llandovery SA20 0AB
Tel +44 (0)1550 721115
Email jillblud@aol.com
Web www.droversllandovery.co.uk

Entry 701   Map 7

Ceredigion

Ffynnon Fendigaid

Arrive through rolling countryside – birdsong and breeze the only sound; within moments you will be sprawled on a leather sofa admiring modern art and wondering how a little bit of Milan arrived here along with Huw and homemade cake. A place to come and pootle, with no rush; you can stay all day to stroll the fern-fringed paths through the acres of wild garden to a lake and a grand bench, or opt for hearty walking. Your bed is big, the colours are soft, the bathrooms are spotless and the food is local – try all the Welsh cheeses. Wide beaches are close by, red kites and buzzards soar above you. Pulchritudinous.

Price	From £72. Singles from £42.
Rooms	2 doubles.
Meals	Dinner, 2–3 courses, £18–£21. Pub 1 mile.
Closed	Rarely.
Directions	From A487 Cardigan & Aberystwyth coast road, take B4334 at Brynhoffnant towards Rhydlewis. 1 mile to junc. where road joins from right & lane to house on left.

Bottle of wine on first night (either at dinner or in your room).

Huw Davies
Ffynnon Fendigaid,
Rhydlewis, Llandysul SA44 5SR
Tel +44 (0)1239 851361
Mobile +44 (0)7974 135262
Email ffynnonf@btinternet.com
Web www.ffynnonf.co.uk

Entry 702   Map 6

Ceredigion

Broniwan

Carole and Allen keep cattle and chickens on their organic farm and their perfect kitchen garden is prolific. With huge warmth and a tray of cakes they invite you into their cosy, ivy-clad house. Downstairs find natural colours and the odd vibrant flourish of local art, a wood-burner and lots of books – a literary weekend can be arranged; upstairs bedrooms and bathrooms are simple and old-fashioned. The wonderful garden with views to the Preseli hills has a water lily pond and is full of birds. Food is delicious and home-grown, coastal paths are close, the National Botanic Garden of Wales and Aberglasney are a 45-minute drive.

Price	£66–£70. Singles £35.
Rooms	2: 1 double; 1 double with separate bath.
Meals	Dinner £25–£30. BYO. Restaurant 7–8 miles.
Closed	Rarely.
Directions	From Aberaeron, A487 for 6 miles for Brynhoffnant. Left at B4334 to Rhydlewis; left at post office & shop, 1st lane on right, then 1st track on right.

10% off stays of 2 or more nights.

Carole & Allen Jacobs
Broniwan,
Rhydlewis, Llandysul SA44 5PF
Tel +44 (0)1239 851261
Email broniwan@btinternet.com
Web www.broniwan.com

Entry 703   Map 6

Conwy

Pengwern Country House

The steeply wooded Conwy valley snakes down to this stone and slate gabled property set back from the road in Snowdonia National Park. Inside has an upbeat traditional feel: a large sitting room with floor-to-ceiling bay windows and pictures by the Betws-y-Coed artists who once lived here. Settle with a book by the wood-burner; Gwawr and Ian know just when to chat and when not. Bedrooms have rough plastered walls, colourful fabrics and super bathrooms, one with a double-ended roll top and views of Lledr Valley. Breakfast on fruits, yogurts, herb rösti, soda bread – gorgeous. *Minimum stay two nights. Welsh spoken.*

Price	£72-£84. Singles from £62.
Rooms	3: 1 double, 1 four-poster, 1 twin/double.
Meals	Pubs/restaurants within 1.5 miles. Packed lunch £5.50.
Closed	Christmas & New Year.
Directions	From Betws-y-Coed, A5 towards Llangollen for 1 mile. Driveway on left, opposite small stone building.

	Gwawr & Ian Mowatt
	Pengwern Country House,
	Allt Dinas, Betws-y-Coed LL24 0HF
Tel	+44 (0)1690 710480
Mobile	+44 (0)7729 076926
Email	gwawr.pengwern@btopenworld.com
Web	www.snowdoniaaccommodation.co.uk

Entry 704   Map 7

Conwy

Maesmor Hall

Historic and grand, this old Welsh manor, gazing over Berwyn mountains, is surrounded by parkland, river and organically farmed acres. The furnishings and décor are classic country house with fine paintings, sculptures and china in comfortable elegant rooms; Johanna is friendly and you're welcomed as part of the family. Breakfast in the polished dining room might include scrambled eggs and pancetta, cockles and lavabread. Wander outside for croquet, tennis and rose garden, chat to Truffle the labrador. Come for open-air theatre in summer, peaches from the peach house and an array of wildlife and walks.

Price	£80-£100. Singles £60.
Rooms	3: 2 doubles, 1 twin.
Meals	Pubs/restaurants a short walk.
Closed	Christmas & New Year.
Directions	From Chester take Wrexham bypass, turn off for Llangollen & join A5, until Maerdy. Then left opp. Goat pub, over bridge, gates in front.

 10% off room rate Mon-Thurs. Bottle of wine in your room.

	Johanna Jackson
	Maesmor Hall,
	Maerdy, Corwen LL21 0NS
Tel	+44 (0)1490 460411
Email	maesmorhall@aol.com

Entry 705   Map 7

Denbighshire

Plas Efenechtyd Cottage

Efenechtyd means 'place of the monks' but there's nothing spartan about Dave and Marilyn's handsome brick farmhouse: breakfasts of local sausages, eggs from their hens, salmon fish cakes with mushrooms and homemade bread, are served at a polished table in the dining room with exotic wall hangings from Vietnam and Laos. Light bedrooms have a clear, uncluttered feel, excellent mattresses and good linen; bathrooms are surprisingly bling and warm as toast with plump towels. Motor or walk to Ruthin with its windy streets and interesting shops, or strike out for Offa's Dyke with a packed lunch; this is stunning countryside.

Flintshire

Plas Penucha

Swing back in time with polished parquet, tidy beams, a huge Elizabethan panelled lounge with books, leather sofas and open fire – a cosy spot for tea in winter. Plas Penucha – 'the big house on the highest point in the parish' – has been in the family for 500 years. Airy, old-fashioned bedrooms have long views across the garden to Offa's Dyke and one has a shower in the corner. The L-shaped dining room has a genuine Arts & Crafts interior; outside, rhododendrons and a rock garden flourish. Beyond is open countryside and St Asaph, with the smallest medieval cathedral in the country.

Price	From £65. Singles £45.
Rooms	3: 2 doubles, 1 twin.
Meals	Packed lunch £6. Pub 1.6 miles.
Closed	Rarely.
Directions	From Ruthin follow signs for Bala. Straight over mini roundabout onto B5105. Take 1st left after 1 mile. Right at T-junc.; house is 50 yds on right.

Price	From £68. Singles from £35.
Rooms	2: 1 double, 1 twin.
Meals	Dinner £19. Packed lunch £5. Pub/restaurant 2-3 miles.
Closed	Rarely.
Directions	From Chester, A55, B5122 left for Caerwys. 1st right into High St. Right at end. 0.75 miles to x-roads & left, then straight for 1 mile. House on left, signed.

Welsh cakes and a jar of our jam or marmalade to take home.

10% off stays of 2 or more nights. Late checkout (12pm).

	Dave Jones & Marilyn Jeffery Plas Efenechtyd Cottage, Efenechtyd, Ruthin LL15 2LP
Tel	+44 (0)7540 501009
Mobile	+44 (0)7540 501009
Email	info@plas-efenechtyd-cottage.co.uk
Web	www.plas-efenechtyd-cottage.co.uk

	Nest Price Plas Penucha, Peny Cefn Road, Caerwys, Mold CH7 5BH
Tel	+44 (0)1352 720210
Email	info@plaspenucha.co.uk
Web	www.plaspenucha.co.uk

Entry 706 Map 7

Entry 707 Map 7

Flintshire

Golden Grove

Huge, Elizabethan and intriguing – Golden Grove was built by Sir Edward Morgan in 1580. The Queen Anne staircase, oak panelling, faded fabrics and fine family pieces are enhanced by jewel-like colour schemes: rose-pink, indigo, aqua. In summer the magnificent dining room is in use; in the winter the sitting room fire counters the draughts. The two Anns are charming and amusing, dinners are delicious and the family foursome tend the garden – beautiful, productive and well-kept. They also find time for the sheep farm as well as their relaxed B&B. Many love staying here and return to this exceptional place.

Price	£110. Singles £65.
Rooms	3: 1 double; 1 double, 1 twin, each with separate bath.
Meals	Dinner £32. Pubs 2 miles.
Closed	November-February.
Directions	Turn off A55 onto A5151 for Prestatyn. At filling station before Trelawnyd, right. Branch left immed. over 1st x-roads; right at T-junc. Gates 170 yds on left.

Ann & Mervyn and
Ann & Nigel Steele-Mortimer
Golden Grove,
Llanasa, Holywell CH8 9NA
Tel   +44 (0)1745 854452
Email   golden.grove@lineone.net
Web   www.golden-grove-estate.co.uk

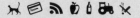

Entry 708   Map 7

Gwynedd

Abercelyn Country House

The 1729 rectory comes with rhododen-dron-rich grounds, an immaculate kitchen garden and a mountain stream. In spite of the rugged setting Abercelyn is a genteel retreat. Shutters gleam, logs glow and bedrooms are spacious and light with smart bathrooms and luscious views. You are well looked after: the drawing room overflows with outdoor guides, Ray orchestrates adventure trips to Snowdonia National Park and Lindsay cooks a great breakfast with eggs from their own hens. Bala Lake is a ten-minute stroll – or you can strike off round it for the whole 14 miles – bracing indeed! *Guided walks & canoeing.*

Ethical Collection: Environment; Food; Community. See page 420.

Price	£76-£90. Singles £55-£60.
Rooms	3: 2 doubles, 1 twin/double.
Meals	Pub 10-minute drive. Restaurant 15-minute walk; free return taxi service.
Closed	Rarely.
Directions	On A494 Bala-Dolgellau road, 1 mile from centre of Bala, opp. Llanycil Church. Bus service: Wrexham - Bala - Llanycil - Dolgellau - Bamouth.

Stay 4 or more nights for a guided walk (half day) with a mountain guide.

Ray & Lindsay Hind
Abercelyn Country House,
Llanycil, Bala LL23 7YF
Tel   +44 (0)1678 521109
Mobile   +44 (0)7867 778900
Email   info@abercelyn.co.uk
Web   www.abercelyn.co.uk

Entry 709   Map 7

Gwynedd

Bryniau Golau

Under clear skies, there are few more soul-lifting views: the long lake and miles of Snowdonia National Park. Each generous room is beautifully furnished – traditional with a contemporary twist, and more glorious views to the garden and lake. Katrina, friendly and adaptable, spoils you with open fires in the sitting room, goose down duvets on the beds, spa baths and underfloor heating; Peter cooks scrumptious and hearty breakfasts and dinners. Linger on the lawn, perhaps with a drink as the sun sets, and try your hand at fly fishing or white water rafting. A wonderful place for a house party – and the walking is superb.

Price	£80-£90. Singles £55-£65.
Rooms	3: 2 four-posters, 1 twin/double.
Meals	Dinner, 2-3 courses, £20-£25. Pubs/restaurants within 2 miles.
Closed	Rarely.
Directions	From Bala B4391; 1 mile, B4403 Llangower. Pass Bala Lake Hotel; look for sign showing left turn; 20 yds after tree, sign on right; left up hill, over cattle grid; 1st on right.

10% off room rate Mon-Thurs.
Bottle of wine in your room.

Katrina le Saux
Bryniau Golau,
Llangower, Bala LL23 7BT
Tel   +44 (0)1678 521782
Email   katrinalesaux@hotmail.co.uk
Web   www.bryniau-golau.co.uk

Entry 710   Map 7

Gwynedd

Bryn Mair House

From supremely indulgent rooms, experience the raw beauty of Wales' National Park. This handsome former rectory is lavish and stylish, with plump pillows, chandeliers, antique furniture and snug sitting areas – in stunning scenery just out of town. Tackle Snowdonia's walks and bike trails, browse the charming market town of Dolgellau or head eight miles to the coast. Everything here feels wonderfully generous: the mountains and private garden, the sink-into beds, the luxurious bathrooms, even Jan's warm, smiling friendliness and excellent breakfasts – come and enjoy the sensation of being spoilt!

Price	£90-£95. Singles £75.
Rooms	3: 2 doubles; 1 twin/double with separate bath.
Meals	Pub/restaurant 5-minute walk.
Closed	Christmas.
Directions	Leave A470 for Dolgellau, cross bridge into town. At T-junc. right, then 1st left. Across Springfield Rd, and 2nd right. At end of lane left, then right up the drive.

10% off stays of 2 or more nights.

Jan Ashley
Bryn Mair House,
Dolgellau LL40 1SR
Tel   +44 (0)1341 422640
Email   jan@janashley.wanadoo.co.uk
Web   www.brynmairbedandbreakfast.co.uk

Entry 711   Map 7

Gwynedd

The Old Rectory on the lake

The drive to get here is fantastic and the approach truly beautiful – The Old Rectory waits for you on the other side of the lake. The owners are full of enthusiasm for their fabulous B&B and spoil guests rotten – comfy beds with smooth cotton sheets, binoculars for bird spotting and luxurious baths. There are views from every window to the luminous lake, and you can climb Cadair Idris from the front door. Return, weak-limbed, to a delicious, home-cooked meal taken in the airy Orangery and... maybe a wallow in the hot tub under the stars sipping a glass of champagne. *Min. two nights at weekends; three on bank holidays.*

Price	£100. Singles £70.
Rooms	3 doubles.
Meals	Dinner, 4 courses, £30. Pub 4 miles.
Closed	Rarely.
Directions	A470 from Dolgellau. A487 from Cross Foxes Inn, then B4405 (signposted Tywyn). Follow along lakeside; turn right at end of lake and cont. 0.25 miles. House illuminated by blue lights at night.

 Use your Sawday's Gift Card here.

Ricky Francis
The Old Rectory on the lake,
Talyllyn LL36 9AJ

Tel	+44 (0)1654 782225
Mobile	+44 (0)7919 190445
Email	enquiries@rectoryonthelake.co.uk
Web	www.rectoryonthelake.co.uk

Entry 712 Map 7

Gwynedd

The Slate Shed at Graig Wen

Sarah and conservationist John spent months travelling in a camper looking for their own special place and found this lovely old Welsh slate cutting mill... captivated by acres of wild woods and stunning views. You'll feel at ease as soon as you step into their eclectic modern home with its reclaimed slate and wood, cosy wood-burners, books, games, snug bedrooms (one downstairs) and superb bathrooms. Breakfast communally on local eggs and sausages, honey from the mountainside, homemade bread and granola. Hike or bike the Mawddach Trail, climb Cadair Idris, wonder at the views... and John's chocolate brownies.

Price	£75-£130. Singles £55-£65.
Rooms	5: 4 doubles, 1 twin/double.
Meals	Packed lunch £6.50. Pub 5 miles.
Closed	Rarely.
Directions	From Dolgellau, A493 dir. Fairbourne & Tywyn. After 5 miles, postbox on right; continue on narrow road to brow of hill. House signed on right, 1 mile before Arthog. Ignore satnav.

10% off stays of 2 or more nights Mon-Thurs, excluding July & August.

Sarah Heyworth
The Slate Shed at Graig Wen,
Arthog LL39 1BQ

Tel	+44 (0)1341 250482
Email	hello@slateshed.co.uk
Web	www.slateshed.co.uk

Entry 713 Map 7

Gwynedd

Y Goeden Eirin

A little gem tucked between the sea and the mountains, an education in Welsh culture, and a great place to explore wild Snowdonia, the Llŷn peninsula and the dramatic Eifl mountains. Inside presents a cosy picture: Welsh-language and English books share the shelves, paintings by contemporary Welsh artists enliven the walls, an arty 70s décor mingles with sturdy Welsh oak in the bedrooms – the one in the house the best – and all bathrooms are super. Wonderful food is served alongside the Bechstein in the beamed dining room – the welcoming, thoughtful Eluned and John have created an unusually delightful space.

Ethical Collection: Environment; Food.
See page 420.

Price	£80–£100. Singles from £60.
Rooms	3: 2 doubles, 1 twin.
Meals	Dinner, 4 courses, £28. Wine from £14. Packed lunch £12. Pub/restaurant 0.75 miles.
Closed	Christmas, New Year & occasionally.
Directions	From Caernarfon onto Porthmadog & Pwllheli road. A487 thro' Bontnewydd, left at r'bout, signed Dolydd. House 0.5 miles on right, last entrance before garage on left.

 Bottle of wine with dinner on first night.

Use your Sawday's Gift Card here.

	John & Mrs Eluned Rowlands
	Y Goeden Eirin,
	Dolydd, Caernarfon LL54 7EF
Tel	+44 (0)1286 830942
Mobile	+44 (0)7708 491234
Email	john_rowlands@tiscali.co.uk
Web	www.ygoedeneirin.co.uk

Entry 714   Map 6

Monmouthshire

Allt-y-bela

It's a rare treat to come here. This beautiful late medieval farmhouse sits in its own secret valley and is reached down a narrow lane. Built between 1420 and 1599, Allt-y-bela is now perfectly presented for the 21st century. Here you'll find conviviality and warmth among soaring beams and period furniture. The dining room has an enormous log fire for delicious and social eating and there's a super farmhouse kitchen if you want to be more involved. Bedrooms soothe with limewashed walls, fabulous beds, no TV and stunning art. Peace, privacy and an amazing garden in deep yet accessible countryside. Exceptional.

Price	£125. £25 room supplement for one-night stay.
Rooms	2 doubles.
Meals	Farmhouse supper £30. Other meals by arrangement. Pubs/restaurants 3 miles.
Closed	Rarely.
Directions	A449 towards Usk, then B4235 to Chepstow. After 200 yds, unsigned right turn. Follow for 0.5 miles; left into 'No Through Road', follow for 0.5 miles.

	William Collinson & Arne Maynard
	Allt-y-bela,
	Llangwm Ucha, Usk NP15 1EZ
Mobile	+44 (0)7892 403103 (unreliable)
Email	bb@alltybela.co.uk
Web	www.alltybela.co.uk

Entry 715   Map 7

Monmouthshire

Penpergwm Lodge

On the edge of the Brecon Beacons, a large and lovely Edwardian house. Breakfast round the mahogany table, relax by the fire in the sitting room with books to read and piano to play. The Boyles have been here for years and pour much of their energy into three beautiful acres of parterre and potager, orchard and flowers. Bedrooms are gloriously traditional – ancestral portraits, embroidered bed covers, big windows, good chintz – with garden views; bathrooms are a skip across the landing. A pool and tennis for the sporty, two summer houses for the dreamy, a good pub you can walk to. Splendid, old-fashioned B&B.

Price	£75. Singles £45.
Rooms	2 twins, each with separate bath.
Meals	Pub within walking distance.
Closed	Rarely.
Directions	A40 to Abergavenny; at big r'bout on SE edge of town, B4598 to Usk for 2.5 miles. Left at King of Prussia pub, up small lane; house 200 yds on left.

Use your Sawday's Gift Card here.

Catriona Boyle
Penpergwm Lodge,
Abergavenny NP7 9AS
Tel   +44 (0)1873 840208
Email boyle@penpergwm.co.uk
Web   www.penplants.com

Entry 716   Map 7

Monmouthshire

Upper Red House

Head down the lane into deepest Monmouthshire and the meadows, orchards and woodland of Teona's organic farm. There are six ponds and miles of bushy hedges; bees, ponies, peafowl and wildlife flourish. The 17th-century house, restored from dereliction, has lovely views, flagstones and oak, limewashed walls and a magical feel. Up steep stairs are rustic bedrooms with beams, lots of books, no TV; the attic rooms get the best views of all. Bathrooms are simple, one has a huge old roll top tub. After a good vegetarian breakfast at the long kitchen table take a farm tour, explore Offa's Dyke or Wye Valley and revel in the silence.

Ethical Collection: Environment; Food; Community. See page 420.

Price	£75-£90. Singles £35-£45.
Rooms	4: 1 double en suite; 1 double, 2 singles sharing bath (let to same party only).
Meals	Vegetarian packed lunch £6. Pubs/restaurants 3.5 miles.
Closed	Rarely.
Directions	Monmouth B4233 through Rockfield to Hendre. Left after Rolls Golf Course entrance; after 1.5 miles 1st right; after 0.75 miles 1st left; at end of lane, house on right.

Free farm & wildlife tour.
Local food/produce in your room.
Late checkout (12pm).

Teona Dorrien-Smith
Upper Red House, Llanfihangel-Ystern-Llewern, Monmouth NP25 5HL
Tel   +44 (0)1600 780501
Email upperredhouse@mac.com
Web   www.upperredhouse.co.uk

Entry 717   Map 7

Pembrokeshire

Hayston

Calm, friendly dogs greet you in the courtyard of this attractive Pembrokeshire farmhouse surrounded by pretty bantams and barns. Nicky and Johnny's home is a relaxed place; rooms have a comfortable, faded grandeur and the garden has lovely spots to sit. Eat in the deep-red beamed dining room with books, flowers and a big log fire; supper is often local lamb or fish direct from the fisherman. Sleep in cottagey bedrooms in the house, one with a garden view, or up stone steps in your own sunny coach house. Castles, surfing championships, stunning beaches and brilliant coastal walks will bring you back.

Price	£75. Singles £40.
Rooms	3: 1 twin with separate bath; 1 single with shared bath (let to same party only). Coach house: 1 double.
Meals	Occasional dinner from £12. Pubs/restaurants 3 miles.
Closed	Christmas.
Directions	B4319 Pembroke to St Petrox. After 2nd right turn to St Twynnells, take 2nd left (no through road) signed Thorne Chapel. First farm on right.
💼	10% off stays of 2 or more nights.

Nicola Rogers
Hayston,
Merrion, Pembroke SA71 5EA
Tel   +44 (0)1646 661462
Email   haystonhouse@btinternet.com
Web   www.haystonfarmhouse.co.uk

Entry 718   Map 6

Pembrokeshire

Penfro

This is fun – idiosyncratic and a tad theatrical, rather than conventional and uniformly stylish. The Lappins' home is an impressive Grade II*-listed Georgian affair, formerly a ballet school. Judith is warm and friendly; her taste – she's also a WW1 expert – is eclectic verging on the wacky and she minds that guests are comfortable and well fed. You eat communally, and very well, at the big scrubbed table in the flagged Aga kitchen at garden level... the garden's big and beautiful so enjoy its conversational terrace and hammocks. And discuss which of the three very characterful bedrooms will suit you best, plumbing and all!

Ethical Collection: Food. See page 420.

Price	£69-£89. Singles from £49.
Rooms	3: 1 double; 1 double, 1 twin each with separate bath.
Meals	Dinner, 3 courses, £20. Packed lunch from £8. Pub 250 yds.
Closed	Rarely.
Directions	A4075 Pembroke; 2 miles to mini r'bout. Straight ahead, down hill, bear right. Right lane past castle; T-junc. bear right. Road widens by Chapel Pembroke Antique Centre. House on right.
💼	Penfro jam or similar. Subsequent visits of 2 or more nights £5 per night discount.

Judith Lappin
Penfro,
111 Main Street, Pembroke SA71 4DB
Tel   +44 (0)1646 682753
Mobile   +44 (0)7763 856181
Email   info@penfro.co.uk
Web   www.penfro.co.uk

Entry 719   Map 6

Pembrokeshire

Cresselly House

Imagine staying at the Georgian mansion of an old country friend – that's what it's like to stay at Cresselly. Step into a sunny square hall with a sweeping stair and the ancestors on the walls. Beeswax and lavender scent the air, cosy bedrooms are as grandly traditional as can be, new bathrooms sparkle and views swoop over the park. Choose to breakfast at the kitchen table, in the dining room or in your room; tuck into a simple supper with Hugh & Co (huge fun) or a gourmet feast à deux. The walking and riding are glorious, and there's amazing stabling for your horse: this is the heartland of the South Pembrokeshire Hunt.

Price	£150. Singles £95.
Rooms	4: 2 doubles, 2 twins.
Meals	Supper, 2 courses, £25-£55. Pub 1 mile.
Closed	Rarely.
Directions	A40 from Carmarthen, then A4075. After 0.5 miles left at r'bout. After 6 miles Cresselly village sign, at top of hill right dir. Cresswell Quay. After 200 yds right into drive.

🧳 10% off room rate Mon-Thurs. Bottle of wine in your room. Late checkout (12pm).

	Hugh Harrison-Allen
	Cresselly House,
	Cresselly, Kilgetty SA68 0SP
Tel	+44 (0)1646 651992
Email	info@cresselly.com
Web	www.cresselly.com

🐈 📖 📶 🐕 🚜 ✗

Entry 720   Map 6

Pembrokeshire

Furzehill Farm

Riding boots and hats by the door; hunting prints up the stairs; books, TV and L-shaped sofa in the sitting room; warmth and comfort in spades. After a peaceful night in a cosy carpeted bedroom (and perhaps a soak in a jacuzzi), wake to Paul's tasty breakfasts in the Aga-friendly kitchen – or at a pretty table by the sitting room window. With horses in the stables and an assortment of busy dogs, this is a relaxed place for families. Discover the heavenly walks and beaches of South Pembrokeshire, the bird-rich Cleddau Estuary and the unspoilt Cresselly Arms down the road, as authentic as a pub can be.

Ethical Collection: Environment; Food. See page 420.

Price	£55-£70. Family room £90. Singles from £30.
Rooms	3: 1 family for 3-4 (extra bed + cot) en suite; 1 double, 1 bunk-bed room, sharing separate bathroom & jacuzzi.
Meals	Dinner, 3 courses, £18. Supper from £12. Packed lunch £5. Pub/restaurant 3 miles.
Closed	Christmas.
Directions	A40 to Canaston Bridge; A4075 Pembroke. Right at Crosshands; after sharp bend, left Cresswell Quay; left at T-junc. for C. Quay; 2nd entrance on left.

🧳 10% off stays of 2 or more nights.

	Val Rees & Paul Higginson
	Furzehill Farm,
	Martletwy, Narberth SA67 8AN
Tel	+44 (0)1834 891480
Mobile	+44 (0)7887 592218
Email	val@furzehillfarm.com
Web	www.furzehillfarm.com

🐎 🐈 📶 🚐 🐕 🚜 ✗

Entry 721   Map 6

Pembrokeshire

Knowles Farm

The Cleddau estuary winds its way around this 1,000-acre organic farm — its lush grasses feed the cows that produce milk for the renowned Rachel's yogurt. Your hosts love the area, are passionate about its conservation and let you come and go as you please; picnic in the garden, wander through bluebell woods, discover a pond — dogs love it too! Gini rustles up scrumptious, candlelit dinners; food is fully organic or very local (five miles!). You have your own entrance to bedrooms which are old-fashioned but well-maintained, with comfy beds, fresh flowers and glorious views. Traditional, real-farmhouse B&B.

Price	From £70.
Rooms	3: 2 doubles; 1 twin with separate bath.
Meals	Supper from £12. Dinner, 4 courses, £22. (Not in school holidays.) Packed lunch £6. Pub 1.5 miles, restaurant 3 miles.
Closed	Rarely.
Directions	A4075 to Cresselly; turn right. Follow signs for Lawrenny to first x-roads; straight over; next x-roads right; 100 yds on left.

Virginia Lort Phillips
Knowles Farm,
Lawrenny SA68 0PX
Tel   +44 (0)1834 891221
Email   ginilp@lawrenny.org.uk
Web   www.lawrenny.org.uk

Entry 722   Map 6

Pembrokeshire

Boulston Manor

A lush descent through ancient woodland, with tantalising glimpses of open water, takes you to the ivy-clad 1790s house and a great place to stay. A country-house drawing room with veranda and Cleddau views is yours to use; soft sofas, horsey pictures, fresh flowers and a grand piano set the tone. Perfectly refurbished bedrooms and bathrooms are roomy and glamorous: yards of thick fabrics, dazzling white linen, stone fireplaces, marble tiling, and, in one, a jucuzzi with the grandest parkland views. Generous Jules and Rod are lively and fun, you will eat good, local food and there's miles of walking in the National Park.

Price	£60–£100.
Rooms	3 doubles.
Meals	Supper £20. Dinner from £25. Pub/restaurant 3 miles.
Closed	Rarely.
Directions	From Salutation Square (County Hotel) Haverfordwest, take Uzmaston Road past Popes Garage. Through Uzmaston, past Goodwood (signed Boulston). Continue for 1.5 miles and follow Boulston signs.

Roderick Thomas
Boulston Manor,
Haverfordwest SA62 4AQ
Tel   +44 (0)1437 764600
Email   info@boulstonmanor.co.uk
Web   www.boulstonmanor.co.uk

Entry 723   Map 6

Pembrokeshire

Pentower

Curl up with a cat and watch the ferries – or sometimes a porpoise – coasting to Ireland; French windows open onto the terrace and a glorious vista. Mary and Tony are welcoming; they've done an excellent restoration on the turreted 1898 house, keeping its quarry tiled floors, decorative fireplaces and impressive staircase. Spotless bedrooms are light and airy, with large showers; the Tower Room has the views. There's a tiled dining/sitting room for full English (or Welsh) breakfasts – also with views, a 'temple' in the garden for summer, Fishguard is a short stroll, and the stunning coastal path nearby.

Price	£80-£85. Singles £45.
Rooms	3: 2 doubles, 1 twin.
Meals	Packed lunch £5. Pubs/restaurants 500 yds.
Closed	Occasionally.
Directions	A40 to Fishguard town; at r'bout, 2nd exit onto Main Street. Before sharp left bend, right fork onto Tower Hill; 200 yds on, through house gates.

Homemade Welsh recipe cakes. Bottle of wine for stays of 2 or more nights.

Tony Jacobs & Mary Geraldine Casey
Pentower,
Tower Hill, Fishguard SA65 9LA
Tel +44 (0)1348 874462
Email sales@pentower.co.uk
Web www.pentower.co.uk

Entry 724   Map 6

Powys

Plas Uchaf Country Guest House

Sweep up the drive to this gracious Queen Anne house and marvel at spectacular views over the Tanat Valley. Inside, find a pleasing mix of old and new. Bedrooms with a smart hotel slant have pale carpet or polished old floors, glossy beds and striking wallpapers; you'll feel nicely independent in the garden room. Help yourself from the honesty bar in the cosy book-filled sitting room, from which French windows lead to a garden with reading spots and clucking hens. Chris is easy and chatty and he and Julie are keen cooks; dine well at linen-clad tables in the elegant dining room. Snowdonia National Park beckons.

Price	£70-£90. Singles £50-£52.
Rooms	6: 4 doubles, 1 twin/double; 1 twin with separate bath.
Meals	Dinner, 2-3 courses, £14.95. Packed lunch from £5. Pub 1.5 miles.
Closed	Rarely.
Directions	From Oswestry take A495 then B4396 dir. Bala. 500 yds through village of Llangedwyn, house on hill to right.

10% off room rate Mon-Thurs.

Chris Brown
Plas Uchaf Country Guest House,
Llangedwyn, Oswestry SY10 9LD
Tel +44 (0)1691 780588
Email info@plasuchaf.com
Web www.plasuchaf.com

Entry 725   Map 7

Powys

Ty Derw

Up on the hill, in southern Snowdonia, a Victorian quarryman's house with fine views across the valley. In late spring, wisteria colours its whitewashed face, while a terraced garden and Foel Dinas Hill rises behind. Inside, warm, homely interiors are just the ticket: a sitting room with books and games in case it rains; a pretty dining room for delicious breakfasts; four colourful bedrooms that fix you up after a day in the hills: piping hot water, comfy beds, pretty fabrics, blissful silence. Nick and Mair are kind, generous and brim with local knowledge. Nearby mountain-bike trails are out of this world.

Price	£72. Singles from £50.
Rooms	4: 3 doubles, 1 twin.
Meals	Dinner, 3 courses, £22.
Closed	Rarely.
Directions	North on A470 at its junction with A458. House signed left after 0.5 miles. Up track and on right.

10% off stays of 2 or more nights.

Nick & Mair Godley
Ty Derw, Dinas Mawddwy,
Machynlleth SY20 9LR
Tel +44 (0)1650 531318
Email enquiries@tyderw.co.uk
Web www.tyderw.co.uk

Entry 726   Map 7

Powys

Talbontdrain

Way off the beaten track, remote and wild, sits a white-painted stone farmhouse. The Cambrian mountains stretch to the south, the river Dovey lies in the vale below and kind Hilary knows all the walks and can sort special routes for you. She cooks a hearty breakfast too, and a good convivial supper, and gives you colourful bedrooms – not swish, but with everything you need. There are photographs of garden plants, a pianola, and furniture in such a mix of styles that it all gives a feeling of great informality. The peace is deep – even the cockerel stays quiet until a respectable time. Walkers will adore it.

Ethical Collection: Food. See page 420.

Price	£64–£76. Singles £32–£35.
Rooms	4: 1 double, 1 family room for 3; 1 twin/double, 1 single sharing shower.
Meals	Dinner, 2 courses, £18. Packed lunch £6.
Closed	Christmas & Boxing Day.
Directions	Leaving Machynlleth on A489, 1st right signed Forge. In Forge bear right to Uwchygarreg up 'dead end'. 3 miles, pass phone box on left, up steep hill. House on left at top.

Free entry to the Centre for Alternative Technology if staying 2 or more nights.

Hilary Matthews
Talbontdrain,
Uwchygarreg, Machynlleth SY20 8RR
Tel +44 (0)1654 702192
Email hilary@talbontdrain.co.uk
Web www.talbontdrain.co.uk

Entry 727   Map 7

Powys

The Old Vicarage

Come for vast skies, forested hills and quilted fields that stretch for miles. This Victorian vicarage is a super base: smart, welcoming, full of comforts. You get a log fire in a cosy sitting room, a super-smart dining room with long country views and fancy bedrooms that spoil you all the way. Tim's food is just as good. Local suppliers are noted on menus, but much is grown in the garden, where chickens run free. Resist laziness and take to the hills – the Kerry Ridgeway is on your doorstep as is Powis Castle – for glorious walking, then home and afternoon tea. *Children over 12 welcome.*

Ethical Collection: Environment; Food.
See page 420.

Price	£95. Singles £65.
Rooms	4: 1 twin/double, 2 doubles, 1 family suite.
Meals	Dinner, 3 courses, £30. Packed lunch available. Pub 4 miles.
Closed	Rarely.
Directions	A483, 3.5 miles from Newtown towards Llandrindod Wells, left on sharp right bend, house first on left.

25% off stays of 2 or more nights.

Tim & Helen Withers
The Old Vicarage,
Dolfor, Newtown SY16 4BN
Tel   +44 (0)1686 629051
Mobile   +44 (0)7753 760054
Email   tim@theoldvicaragedolfor.co.uk
Web   www.theoldvicaragedolfor.co.uk

Entry 728   Map 7

Powys

The Old Vicarage

Blessed are those who enter… especially devotees of Victoriana. The house, designed by Sir George Gilbert Scott, is a delight. Your host, charming and fun, ushers you in to a rich confection of colours, dark wood and a lifetime's collecting: splendid brass beds, cast-iron radiators, porcelain loos, sumptuous bedspreads and a garden with grotto, waterfall and rill. Dine by candle or gas light (the food is superb), ring the servants' bell for early morning tea. You are on the English side of Offa's Dyke: look north to the heavenly Radnorshire hills, south to all of Herefordshire. *Minimum stay two nights weekends & bank holidays.*

Price	From £98.
Rooms	3: 2 doubles, 1 twin/double.
Meals	Dinner, 4 courses, £34. Pub 10-minute drive.
Closed	Rarely.
Directions	B4355, between Presteigne & Knighton; in village of Norton, immed. north of church.

10% off stays of 2 or more nights (subject to availability).

Paul Gerrard
The Old Vicarage,
Norton, Presteigne LD8 2EN
Tel   +44 (0)1544 260038
Email   paul@nortonoldvic.co.uk
Web   www.oldvicarage-nortonrads.co.uk

Entry 729   Map 7

Powys

Rhedyn

Come here if you need to remember how to relax. Such an unassuming little place, but with real character and soul: great comfort too with exposed walls in the bedrooms, funky lighting, pocket sprung mattresses, lovely books to read, and calm colours; bathrooms are modern and delightfully quirky. But the real stars of this show are Muiread and Ciaran: wonderfully warm, enthusiastic and engaging, with a passion for good, local food and a desire for more self-sufficiency – pigs and bees are planned next. This is a totally tranquil place, with agreeable walks through the Irfon valley and bog snorkelling too!

Price	£75. Singles £65.
Rooms	3 doubles.
Meals	Dinner, 3 courses, £25. Packed lunch £7.50. Pub/restaurant 1 mile.
Closed	Rarely.
Directions	From Builth Wells follow A483 towards 'Garth'. Pass Cilmery village, Rhedyn signpost is one mile on right. House is in middle of field.

 Use your Sawday's Gift Card here.

Muiread & Ciaran O'Connell
Rhedyn,
Cilmery, Builth Wells LD2 3LH
Tel   +44 (0)1982 551944
Mobile   +44 (0)7768 717614
Email   info@rhedynguesthouse.co.uk
Web   www.rhedynguesthouse.co.uk

Entry 730   Map 7

Powys

Trericket Mill Vegetarian Guesthouse

Part guest house, part bunk house, all very informal – yet Grade II*-listed. The dining room has been created amid a jumble of corn-milling machinery: B&B guests, campers and bunkers pile in together to fill hungry bellies with Nicky and Alistair's delicious veggie food from a chalkboard menu. Stoves throw out heat in flagstoned living rooms with comfy chairs and books; bedrooms are simple pine affairs. Bookworms take note: the bookshops and festival of Hay are a short drive. Set out to explore on foot, horseback or bike – lovers of the outdoors looking for good value and a planet-friendly bias will be in heaven.

Ethical Collection: Environment; Food; Community. See page 420.

Price	£66–£75. Singles £43–£55.
Rooms	3: 2 doubles, 1 twin.
Meals	Dinner, 3 courses, £18.75. BYO. Simple supper £8.50. Pub/restaurant 2 miles.
Closed	Christmas & occasionally in winter.
Directions	12 miles north of Brecon on A470. Mill set slightly back from road, on left, between Llyswen & Erwood. Train to Llandrindod Wells; bus to Brecon every 2 hrs will drop at mill on request.

🧳 Bottle of wine in your room.

Alistair & Nicky Legge
Trericket Mill Vegetarian Guesthouse,
Erwood, Builth Wells LD2 3TQ
Tel   +44 (0)1982 560312
Email   mail@trericket.co.uk
Web   www.trericket.co.uk

Entry 731   Map 7

Powys

Hafod Y Garreg

A unique opportunity to stay in the oldest house in Wales – a fascinating, 1402 cruck-framed hall house, built for Henry IV as a hunting lodge. Informal Annie and John have filled it with a charming mix of Venetian mirrors, Indian rugs, pewter plates, gorgeous fabrics and oak furniture. Dine by candlelight in the fabulous dining room – maybe pheasant pie with chilli jam and hazelnut mash: delicious. Bedrooms are luxurious and comfortable with Egyptian cotton bed linen. Reach the Grade II*-listed house by a bumpy track across gated fields crowded with chickens, cats, goats… a special, secluded and relaxed place.

Price	£82. Singles from £75.
Rooms	2 doubles.
Meals	Dinner, 3 courses, £24. BYO. Pubs/restaurants 2.5 miles.
Closed	Christmas.
Directions	From Hay-on-Wye, A479 then A470 to B. Wells. Through Llyswen, past forest on left, down hill. Next left for Trericket Mill, then immed. right & up hill. Straight through gate across track to house.

Bottle of wine in your room.

Annie & John McKay
Hafod Y Garreg,
Erwood, Builth Wells LD2 3TQ
Tel   +44 (0)1982 560400
Email   john-annie@hafod-y.wanadoo.co.uk
Web   www.hafodygarreg.co.uk

Entry 732   Map 7

Powys

The Old Store House

Unbend here with agreeable books, chattering birds, and twinkling Peter, who asks only that you feel at home. Downstairs are a range-warmed kitchen, a sunny conservatory overlooking garden, ducks and canal, and a charmingly ramshackle sitting room with a wood-burner, sofas and a piano – no babbling TV. Bedrooms are large, light and spotless, with more books, soft goose down, armchairs and bathrooms with views. Breakfast, without haste, on toothsome scrambled eggs, local bacon and sausages, blistering coffee. Bliss – but not for those who prefer the comfort of rules. Walk into the hills from the back door. *Self-catering available.*

Price	£80. Singles £40.
Rooms	4: 3 doubles, 1 twin.
Meals	Packed lunch £4. Pub/restaurant 0.75 miles.
Closed	Rarely.
Directions	From Brecon, Abergavenny A40. After 1 mile, left for Llanfrynach B4558. Left, cross narrow stone bridge. House is 1.3 miles on right.

Pick-up from local bus/train station. Late checkout (12pm).

Peter Evans
The Old Store House,
Llanfrynach LD3 7LJ
Tel   +44 (0)1874 665499
Email   oldstorehouse@btconnect.com
Web   www.theoldstorehouse.co.uk

Entry 733   Map 7

Powys

Ty'r Chanter

Warmth, colour, children and activity: this house is fun. Tiggy welcomes you like family; help collect eggs, feed the lambs or the pony, drop your shoes by the fire. The farmhouse and barn are stylishly relaxed; deep sofas, tartan throws, heaps of books, views to the Brecon Beacons and Black Mountains. Bedrooms are soft, simple sanctuaries with Jo Malone bathroom treats. Children's rooms zing with murals; toys, kids' sitting room, sandpit – child heaven. Walk, fish, canoe, book-browse in Hay or stroll the estate. Homemade cakes, whisky to help yourself to: fine hospitality.

Price	£90. Singles £55.
Rooms	4: 1 double; 1 double with separate bath/shower; 2 children's rooms.
Meals	Packed lunch £8. Pub 1 mile.
Closed	Christmas.
Directions	From Crickhowell, A40 towards Brecon. 2 miles left at Gliffaes Hotel sign. 2 miles, past hotel, house is 600 yds on right.

	Tiggy Pettifer
	Ty'r Chanter,
	Gliffaes, Crickhowell NP8 1RL
Tel	+44 (0)1874 731144
Mobile	+44 (0)7802 387004
Email	tiggy@tyrchanter.com
Web	www.tyrchanter.com

Entry 734   Map 7

Powys

Llangattock Court

Built in 1690 and mentioned in Pevsner as an 'outstanding example of a country house in this style', this is indeed grand and sits in the middle of the sleepy village, surrounded by a large garden. Both bedrooms are a good size (one has a big French bed and a small shower room) with lovely antiques and a fresh feel; views from one soar across to the Black Mountains. Breakfast in style in the enormous dining room overlooked by framed relatives, stroll through the rose garden, visit a castle or historic house, walk to the local pub for dinner. Morgan is a painter; some of his paintings are on display.

Price	£50-£80. Singles £45.
Rooms	2: 1 double, 1 suite for 4 (four-poster & twin).
Meals	Restaurants/pubs within 1 mile.
Closed	Christmas & New Year; 1-2 weeks October.
Directions	A465, then B4777 to Gilwern. Signs to Crickhowell. In Legar, left at Vine Tree Inn. Pass Horse Shoe Inn on right; after 60 yds right; right again 50 yds beyond church signed Dardy. 1st on left.
	10% off room rate Mon-Thurs. Free pick-up from local bus/train station.

	Polly Llewellyn
	Llangattock Court,
	Llangattock, Crickhowell NP8 1PH
Tel	+44 (0)1873 810116
Email	morganllewellyn@btinternet.com
Web	www.llangattockcourt.co.uk

Entry 735   Map 7

Swansea

Blas Gwyr

Llangennith was once a well-kept secret – now walkers, riders, surfers and beach lovers of all ages flock. Tucked back from the bustling bay is an extended 1700s cottage with a boutique-hotel facelift. All is simple but stylish: bedrooms are modern and matching with tiled floors and contemporary paintings; bathrooms come with warm floors and fluffy towels. Everything from the bedspread to the breakfast is local: make sure you try the lavabread. After a day at sea, fling wet gear in the drying room and linger over a coffee on the front deck, or walk to the pub for a sun-kissed pint. Laid-back bliss. *Welsh spoken.*

Price	£110–£120.
Rooms	4: 1 double, 1 double (with sofabed), 1 twin/double, 1 suite for 2-4.
Meals	Packed lunch available. Dinner £27.50-£30 (selected weekends). Pub 150 yds.
Closed	Rarely.
Directions	M4 junc. 47, A483. Next 2 r'bouts, A484. Dual c'way then r'bout, 1st left, B4296. Right at lights. In Llangennith, pass pub; mini r'bout, right, then immed. right into car park.

10% off room rate Mon-Thurs.

Dafydd & Kerry James
Blas Gwyr, Plenty Farm,
Llangennith, Swansea SA3 1HU
Tel   +44 (0)1792 386472
Mobile   +44 (0)7974 981156
Email   info@blasgwyr.co.uk
Web   www.blasgwyr.co.uk

Entry 736   Map 2

Wrexham

Worthenbury Manor

Homemade bread and Hepplewhite! This is a good, solid house of generous proportions and your hosts live in part of it. Wallow in antique oak four-posters in rose-carpeted chandeliered bedrooms, full of comfort (books, games and flowers adding a cosy touch) and breakfast on fresh fruit (some from the garden) local bacon and sausages and award-winning marmalade. Ian, history buff and former chef, is thoughtful and looks after you properly; dinner is quite an occasion. The listed house is close to Chester yet in a quiet, birdsung setting; the original building was enlarged in the 1890s in the William and Mary revival style.

Price	£70–£85. Singles £40–£50.
Rooms	2: 1 four-poster; 1 four-poster with separate bath.
Meals	Dinner, 3 courses, £30. Lunch £18.
Closed	December-February.
Directions	Between A525 Whitchurch-Wrexham & A41 Whitchurch-Chester, on B5069 between Bangor-on-Dee (Bangor-is-y-coed) and Malpas. Manor on right before bridge.

3 nights for price of 2. Bottle of wine with dinner on first night.

Use your Sawday's Gift Card here.

Elizabeth & Ian Taylor
Worthenbury Manor,
Worthenbury LL13 0AW
Tel   +44 (0)1948 770342
Email   enquiries@worthenburymanor.co.uk
Web   www.worthenburymanor.co.uk

Entry 737   Map 7

Becoming a member of Sawday's Travel Club opens up hundreds of discounts, treats and other offers at over 700 of our Special Places to Stay in Britain and Ireland, as well as 50% discount on all Sawday's books.

Where you see the 💼 symbol in this book it means the place has a special offer for Club members. It may be money off your room price, a bottle of wine or a basket of home-grown produce. The offers for each place are within each entry and on our website. These were correct at the time of going to print, but owners reserve the right to change the listed offer. Latest offers for all places can be found on our website, www.sawdays.co.uk.

Membership is only £25 per year. To join the Travel Club visit www.sawdays.co.uk/bookshop/travel_club.

The small print

You must mention that you are a Travel Club member when booking, and confirm that the offer is available. Your Travel Club card must be shown on arrival to claim the offer. Sawday's Travel Club cards are not transferable. If two cardholders share a room they can only claim the offer once. Offers for Sawday's Travel Club members are subject to availability. Alastair Sawday Publishing cannot accept any responsibility if places fail to honour offers; neither can we accept responsibility if a place changes hands and drops out of the Travel Club.

Photo left: Mallard Grange, entry 593
Photo right: Nonsuch House, entry 108

Your passport to a choice of Special Places to Stay in Britain & Ireland

Sawday's Gift Cards can be used at a whole array of bed and breakfasts, hotels, self-catering places and pubs with rooms scattered across Britain and Ireland. You may fancy a night in a country house which towers majestically over the River Usk, or perhaps a weekend in a splendid Georgian mansion in the Cotswolds. Stay in a garret above a legendary London coffee house or sample a stunning barn conversion in the depths of Northumberland.

Wherever you choose as a treat for yourself, friends or a loved one we know it will be fun, unusual, maybe even eccentric and definitely life affirming. A perfect present.

Gift Cards are available in six denominations – £25, £50, £75, £100, £150 and £200, and come in attractive packaging, which includes a series of postcards and a printed booklet featuring all the participating places.

You can purchase Gift Cards at: www.sawdays.co.uk/gift-cards/ or you can order them by phone: +44(0)1275 395431.

You can also view the full list of participating places on our website www.sawdays.co.uk and search by this symbol: 🎁

Wheelchair-accessible

At least one bedroom and bathroom accessible for wheelchair users. Phone for details.

Channel Islands
Guernsey 614

England
Bedfordshire 8
Buckinghamshire 15
Cheshire 23
Cornwall 52 • 64 • 66
Cumbria 79
Derbyshire 98
Devon 108 • 114 • 146 • 147
Dorset 179
Essex 199
Gloucestershire 207 • 208 • 211 • 232
Hampshire 245
Herefordshire 253
Kent 277 • 285
Leicestershire 295
Norfolk 342 • 354
Oxfordshire 390
Shropshire 415
Somerset 439 • 448 • 453 • 457
Suffolk 482 • 496
Surrey 504
Warwickshire 533 • 534
Wiltshire 549 • 567
Yorkshire 580 • 587 • 603 • 607 • 610 • 611

Scotland
Argyll & Bute 628
Scottish Borders 683
Western Isles 693

Wales
Gwynedd 712, 713
Powys 725

Stay all day

Stay all day if you wish.

England
Bath & N.E. Somerset 3 • 5 • 6
Berkshire 10
Buckinghamshire 15
Cambridgeshire 17 • 18 • 19 • 20
Cheshire 22 • 24 • 25
Cornwall 27 • 28 • 29 • 30 • 31 • 32 • 37 • 38 • 40 • 43 • 44 • 46 • 47 • 49 • 50 • 51 • 52 • 56 • 57 • 62 • 67 • 68
Cumbria 70 • 71 • 74 • 77 • 79 • 80 • 81 • 85 • 89 • 90 • 92 • 93
Derbyshire 94 • 96 • 98 • 99
Devon 103 • 105 • 107 • 108 • 109 • 110 • 112 • 113 • 114 • 115 • 118 • 121 • 122 • 123 • 124 • 135 • 138 • 147 • 148 • 149
Dorset 153 • 155 • 156 • 159 • 163 • 166 • 168 • 169 • 170 • 171 • 178 • 179 • 180 • 182 • 183 • 185 • 187 • 188 • 189
Essex 194 • 195
Gloucestershire 200 • 201 • 204 • 205 • 206 • 208 • 214 • 216 • 217 • 218 • 219 • 220 • 221 • 224 • 227 • 229
Hampshire 235 • 236 • 241
Herefordshire 248 • 250 • 252 • 259 • 260
Kent 273 • 277 • 284 • 290
Lincolnshire 298 • 299 • 302
London 320 • 321 • 322 • 327 • 332 • 337
Middlesex 338
Norfolk 339 • 342 • 348 • 349 • 352 • 353 • 354 • 356 • 357 • 360 • 362
Northamptonshire 365 • 367 • 368
Northumberland 372 • 373 • 375 • 377
Nottinghamshire 382 • 383
Oxfordshire 384 • 385 • 393 • 396 • 397 • 399
Rutland 400

Quick reference indices

Shropshire 404 • 408 • 409 •
410 • 411 • 412 • 415 • 417 •
418 • 419 • 420 • 421 • 422 •
423
Somerset 425 • 426 • 427 •
428 • 429 • 430 • 431 • 433 •
434 • 436 • 438 • 439 • 441 •
443 • 444 • 446 • 447 • 449 •
450 • 451 • 452 • 453 • 454 •
456 • 457 • 459 • 462 • 464 •
465 • 466 • 470
Staffordshire 472 • 473
Suffolk 475 • 480 • 486 • 490 •
495 • 496
Surrey 502
Sussex 506 • 521 • 523 • 524 •
526
Warwickshire 533 • 537 •
539 • 541
Wiltshire 543 • 546 • 550 •
554 • 565
Worcestershire 571 • 572 • 574
Yorkshire 579 • 584 • 585 •
587 • 590 • 597 • 600 • 604 •
605 • 607 • 608 • 609 • 610

Scotland

Aberdeenshire 618 • 620 • 624 •
626 • 628 • 629 • 630 • 631
Ayrshire 632
Clackmannanshire 633
Dumfries & Galloway 636
Dunbartonshire 641
East Lothian 655 • 657 • 642 •
645 • 646 • 648 • 652
Fife 658 • 660
Highland 662 • 663 • 666 •
667 • 668 • 672 • 674
Perth & Kinross 676 • 677 • 679
Scottish Borders 683 • 685 •
686 • 688
Stirling 689 • 691
West Lothian 654
Western Isles 693

Wales

Anglesey 696
Carmarthenshire 697 • 698 •
699 • 700 • 701
Ceredigion 703

Flintshire 707 • 708
Gwynedd 709 • 710 • 711 •
712 • 713
Monmouthshire 715 • 716
Pembrokeshire 719 • 720
Powys 725 • 726 • 727 • 728 •
731 • 733 • 734
Wrexham 737

Singles

These places have a single
room OR rooms let to single
guests for half the double
room rate or under.

Channel Islands

Guernsey 614

England

Bath & N.E. Somerset 3 • 6 • 7
Cornwall 26 • 34 • 35 • 37 •
45 • 50 • 55
Cumbria 80 • 84 • 90
Devon 103 • 114 • 118 • 121 •
125
Dorset 158 • 162 • 172 • 173 •
174
Essex 195 • 196
Gloucestershire 200 • 205 •
218
Herefordshire 246 • 249 • 258
Kent 272
London 323
Norfolk 361
Northumberland 378
Shropshire 422
Somerset 426 • 439 • 443 •
444 • 454 • 459 • 469
Suffolk 478 • 484 • 485 • 495
Surrey 501
Sussex 508
Wiltshire 553 • 557 • 562 • 565
Worcestershire 575
Yorkshire 583 • 587 • 601

Scotland

Argyll & Bute 624 • 631

Quick reference indices

East Lothian 655
Edinburgh 642 • 648 • 652
Fife 658
Highland 662 • 668 • 671 • 672
Moray 675
Perth & Kinross 679
Stirling 689 • 690 • 691
Western Isles 694 • 695

Wales
Ceredigion 703
Flintshire 707
Pembrokeshire 718 • 721
Powys 727 • 733

On a budget
These places have a double
room for £70 or under

Channel Islands
Guernsey 614

England
Bath & N.E. Somerset 3 • 6
Bedfordshire 8
Cambridgeshire 19
Cornwall 37 • 38 • 45 • 48 •
61
Cumbria 71 • 77 • 78 • 81 •
82 • 88 • 89
Devon 102 • 103 • 104 • 105 •
111 • 112 • 116 • 118 • 121 •
122 • 125 • 126 • 130 • 134 •
141 • 142
Dorset 160 • 162 • 163 • 168 •
171 • 172 • 173 • 174 • 175 •
182 • 183 • 186 • 187
Essex 194 • 195 • 196 • 197
Gloucestershire 201 • 205 •
218 • 220 • 227 • 229
Hampshire 241
Herefordshire 246 • 249 • 254 •
256 • 259
Isle of Wight 261
Kent 274 • 280 • 282 • 291
Lancashire 292 • 294
Leicestershire 295

Lincolnshire 300 • 301 • 302 •
305 • 306 • 308 • 309
London 320 • 321 • 327
Norfolk 341 • 345 • 346 • 349 •
351 • 355 • 356 • 358 • 361 •
362 • 363
Northumberland 369 • 372 •
375 • 377 • 379
Oxfordshire 396 • 399
Shropshire 402 • 404 • 408 •
420 • 421
Somerset 428 • 431 • 433 •
437 • 443 • 447 • 454 • 461 •
467 • 469
Staffordshire 473
Suffolk 474 • 476 • 478 • 480 •
481 • 482 • 485 • 487 • 490 •
492 • 493 • 495 • 498
Surrey 501
Sussex 512 • 513
Warwickshire 532 • 533 • 534
Wiltshire 548 • 550 • 552 •
553 • 565 • 566
Worcestershire 572 • 574 • 575
Yorkshire 577 • 579 • 582 •
589 • 591 • 594 • 604 • 609

Scotland
Aberdeenshire 616
Argyll & Bute 629
Ayrshire 632
Clackmannanshire 633
East Lothian 657
Edinburgh 647 • 648
Fife 659
Highland 664 • 668 • 669 • 672

Wales
Carmarthenshire 697 • 698 •
700 • 701
Ceredigion 703
Denbighshire 706
Flintshire 707
Pembrokeshire 719 • 721 •
722 • 723
Powys 725 • 727 • 731 • 735
Wrexham 737

Quick reference indices

For many years Alastair Sawday Publishing has been 'greening' the business in different ways. Our aim is to reduce our environmental footprint as far as possible and with almost everything we do we have environmental implications in mind. In recognition of our efforts we won a Business Commitment to the Environment Award in 2005, a Queen's Award for Enterprise in the Sustainable Development category in 2006, and the Independent Publishers Guild Environmental Award in 2008.

The buildings

Beautiful as they were, our old offices leaked heat, used electricity to heat water and rooms, flooded spaces with light to illuminate one person, and were not ours to alter.

So in 2005 we created our own eco offices by converting some old barns to create a low-emissions building. Heating and

Photo left: Tom Germain
Photo right: Jackie King

lighting the building, which houses over 30 employees, now produces only 0.28 tonnes of carbon dioxide per year – a reduction of 35%. Not bad when you compare this with the six tonnes emitted by the average UK household. We achieved this through a variety of innovative and energy-saving building techniques, some of which are described below.

Insulation   By laying insulating board 90mm thick immediately under the roof tiles and on the floor, and lining the inside of the building with plastic sheeting, we are now insulated even for Arctic weather, and almost totally air-tight.

Heating We installed a wood pellet boiler from Austria in order to be largely fossil-fuel free. The heat is conveyed by water to all corners of the building via an underfloor system.

Water   We installed a 6,000-litre tank to collect rainwater from the roofs. This is pumped back, via an ultra-violet filter, to lavatories, shower and basins. There are also two solar thermal panels on the roof providing heat to the one hot-water cylinder.

Lighting   We have a mix of low-energy lighting – task lighting and up lighting – and have installed three sun pipes.

Electricity   Our electricity has long come from the Good Energy Company and is 100% renewable.

Materials Virtually all materials are non-toxic or natural, and our carpets are made from (80%) Herdwick sheep wool from National Trust farms in the Lake District.

Doors and windows Outside doors and new windows are wooden, double-glazed and beautifully constructed in Norway. Old windows have been double-glazed.

More greenery

Besides having a building we are proud of, and which is pretty impressive visually, too, we work in a number of other ways to reduce the company's overall environmental footprint.

- office travel is logged as part of a carbon sequestration programme, and money for compensatory tree planting donated to SCAD in India for a tree-planting and development project
- we avoid flying and take the train for business trips wherever possible
- car sharing and the use of a company pool car are part of company policy, with recycled cooking oil used in one car and LPG in the other
- organic and Fair Trade basic provisions are used in the staff kitchen and organic and/or local food is provided by the company at all in-house events
- green cleaning products are used throughout
- kitchen waste is composted on our allotment
- the allotment is part of a community garden – alongside which we keep a small family of pigs and hens

However, becoming 'green' is a journey and, although we began long before most companies, we realise we still have a long way to go.

Many of you may want to stay in environmentally friendly places. You may be passionate about local, organic or home-grown food. Or perhaps you want to know that the place you are staying in contributes to the community? To help you we have launched our Ethical Collection, so you can find the right place to stay and also discover how each owner is addressing these issues.

The Collection is made up of places going the extra mile, and taking the steps that most people have not yet taken, in one or more of the following areas:

• Environment Those making great efforts to reduce the environmental impact of their Special Place. We expect more than energy-saving light bulbs and recycling – in this part of the Collection you will find owners who make their own natural cleaning products, properties with solar hot water and biomass boilers, the odd green roof and a good measure of green elbow grease.

• Community Given to owners who use their property to play a positive role in their local and wider community. For example, by making a contribution from every guest's bill to a local fund, or running pond-dipping courses for local school children on their farm.

• Food Awarded to owners who make a real effort to source local or organic food, or to grow their own. We look for those who have gone out of their way to strike up relationships with local producers or to seek out organic suppliers. It is easier for an owner on a farm to produce their own eggs than for someone in the middle of a city, so we take this into account.

How it works

To become part of our Ethical Collection owners choose whether to apply in one, two or all three categories, and fill in a detailed questionnaire asking demanding questions about their activities in the chosen areas. You can download a full list of the questions at www.sawdays.co.uk/about_us/ethical_collection/faq/

We then review each questionnaire carefully before deciding whether or not to give the award(s). The final decision is subjective; it is based not only on whether an owner ticks 'yes' to a question but also on the detailed explanation that accompanies each 'yes' or 'no' answer. For example, an owner who has tried as hard as possible to install solar water-heating panels, but has failed because of strict conservation planning laws, will be given some credit for their effort (as long as they are doing other things in this area).

We have tried to be as rigorous as possible and have made sure the questions are demanding. We have not checked out the claims of owners before making our decisions, but we do trust them to be honest. We are only human, as are they, so please let us know if you think we have made any mistakes.

The Ethical Collection is still a new initiative for us, and we'd love to know what you think about it – email us at ethicalcollection@sawdays.co.uk or write to us. And remember that because this is a new scheme some owners have not yet completed their questionnaires – we're sure other places in the guide are working just as hard in these areas, but we don't yet know the full details.

Ethical Collection in this book
On the entry page of all places in the Collection we show which awards have been given.

A list of the places in our Ethical Collection is shown below, by entry number.

Environment
20 • 27 • 34 • 39 • 43 • 52 • 61 • 62 • 67 • 68 • 72 • 79 • 92 • 98 • 117 • 129 • 200 • 220 • 252 • 253 • 254 • 262 • 348 • 399 • 415 • 419 • 422 • 428 • 431 • 438 • 443 • 478 • 539 • 554 • 567 • 574 • 591 • 610 • 612 • 616 • 657 • 666 • 700 • 709 • 714 • 717 • 721 • 728 • 731

Food
4 • 25 • 27 • 35 • 39 • 43 • 52 • 61 • 62 • 67 • 68 • 72 • 76 • 89 • 93 • 98 • 100 • 103 • 107 • 108 • 117 • 118 • 119 • 125 • 136 • 140 • 147 • 148 • 149 • 151 • 176 • 189 • 200 • 209 • 220 • 239 • 245 • 246 • 252 • 253 • 254 • 258 • 262 • 267 • 268 • 269 • 274 • 348 • 357 • 363 • 415 • 417 • 419 • 420 • 422 • 428 • 429 • 431 • 438 • 443 • 446 • 461 • 466 • 467 • 469 • 473 • 478 • 495 • 505 • 520 • 534 • 537 • 539 • 542 • 554 • 562 • 567 • 574 • 582 • 585 • 591 • 595 • 596 • 610 • 612 • 616 • 666 • 670 • 673 • 677 • 685 • 686 • 687 • 700 • 709 • 714 • 717 • 719 • 721 • 727 • 728 • 731

Community
4 • 25 • 34 • 54 • 61 • 67 • 72 • 98 • 107 • 147 • 246 • 258 • 348 • 417 • 420 • 431 • 438 • 456 • 466 • 467 • 478 • 534 • 539 • 542 • 567 • 576 • 585 • 596 • 612 • 621 • 657 • 700 • 709 • 717

Ethical Collection online
There is stacks more information on our website, www.sawdays.co.uk. You can read the answers each owner has given to our Ethical Collection questionnaire and get a more detailed idea of what they are doing in each area. You can also search for properties that have awards.

Photo: Alec Studerus

Alastair Sawday's

Self-catering collection

Time away with your friends or family is precious, and when you are booking a whole week or more in one place you dare not get it wrong. To whom do you turn for advice and who on earth do you trust when the web is awash with advice from strangers? Our stunning self-catering collection satisfies an obvious need for impartial and trustworthy help. The criteria for inclusion are the same as for our books: we have to like the place and the owners. It has, quite simply, to be 'special'.

Cosy cottages, manor houses, tipis, châteaux, city apartments and more, in Britain and Europe

www.sawdays.co.uk/self-catering

Alastair Sawday has been publishing books for over 20 years finding Special Places to Stay in Britain and abroad. All our properties are inspected by us and are chosen for their charm and individuality and now with 25 titles to choose from there are plenty of places to explore. You can buy any of our books at a reader discount of 25%* on the RRP.

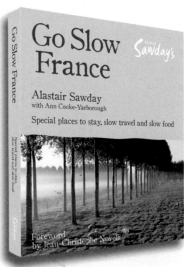

List of titles:	RRP	Discount price
British Bed & Breakfast	£15.99	£11.99
British Bed & Breakfast for Garden Lovers	£19.99	£14.99
British Hotels and Inns	£14.99	£11.24
Pubs & Inns of England & Wales	£15.99	£11.99
Venues	£11.99	£8.99
Cotswolds	£9.99	£7.49
Devon & Cornwall	£9.99	£7.49
Wales	£9.99	£7.49
Ireland	£12.99	£9.74
French Bed & Breakfast	£15.99	£11.99
French Self-Catering	£14.99	£11.24
French Châteaux & Hotels	£14.99	£11.24
French Vineyards	£19.99	£14.99
Paris	£9.99	£7.49
Green Europe	£11.99	£8.99
Italy	£14.99	£11.24
Portugal	£12.99	£9.74
Spain	£15.99	£11.99
Morocco	£9.99	£7.49
India	£11.99	£8.99
Go Slow England	£19.99	£14.99
Go Slow France	£19.99	£14.99
Go Slow Italy	£19.99	£14.99
Eat Slow Britain	£19.99	£12.99

*postage and packaging is added to each order

How to order:

You can order online at: www.sawdays.co.uk/bookshop/

or call: +44(0)1275 395431

We have indexed places under their
MAIN postal town. See maps for
clear positioning.

Aberfeldy	678
Aberfoyle	691
Abergavenny	716
Aboyne	621
Acharacle	631
Aldeburgh	494
Aldringham	495
Alford	618
All Stretton	409
Alnwick	376–378
Alresford	239
Ammanford	699
Ampleforth	595
Appleby-in-Westmorland	90
Arisaig	662
Arthog	713
Ashbourne	100–101
Ashburton	114–116
Ashford	279–280
Axminster	136–137
Aylesbury	13
Badminton	232
Bakewell	96
Bala	709–710
Bamburgh	380
Banbury	386–387
Banchory	620
Banff	616
Barnard Castle	193
Barnstaple	146–147
Bartlow	20
Bath	1–7
Battle	528
Beaminster	152
Beaulieu	237
Beauly	670
Beaumaris	696
Bedale	588
Benenden	283–284
Bere Regis	166
Berwick-upon-Tweed	381, 688
Betws-y-Coed	704
Biddenden	285
Bideford	140–141
Biggar	683
Bishop's Castle	412
Bisley	221
Blairgowrie	679
Blandford Forum	174–179
Boat of Garten	668
Bodmin	29–34
Bordon	243
Boscastle	27
Bournemouth	171
Bracknell	10
Braintree	197
Brampton	71
Brechin	623
Bridgnorth	410
Bridgwater	438–440
Bridport	154–156
Bristol	12, 466–467
Broadway	570
Bromyard	260
Buckfastleigh	113
Buckingham	14
Budleigh Salterton	132–133
Builth Wells	730–732
Burford	393
Burnham-on-Crouch	199

Burrington	468	Corwen	705
Bury St Edmunds	476	Coventry	529–530
Caernarfon	714	Cranbrook	281
Callington	65	Cranleigh	501
Camborne	40	Craven Arms	414–416
Cambridge	18	Crediton	138
Campsie Glen	640	Crickhowell	734–735
Canonbie	636	Cromer	354
Canterbury	269–272	Cupar	659
Carlisle	69–70	Darlington	585
Carmarthen	697–698	Dartmouth	107–109
Castle Cary	447	Daventry	366–367
Castle Douglas	635	Deal	275
Chagford	123	Deddington	389
Chale	262	Delabole	28
Chard	437	Denny	689
Cheltenham	211–219	Dereham	348–349
Chester	22–23	Dingwall	672
Chichester	505–509	Diss	363
Chiddingfold	499	Dolgellau	711
Chippenham	563–568	Dollar	633
Chipping Campden	205	Dorchester	157–164
Chipping Norton	390–392	Dorking	502
Chipping Sodbury	231	Dover	277
Christchurch	172	Driffield	610–611
Church Stretton	408	Droitwich	575
Cirencester	224–228	Dulverton	424
Clapton-on-the-Hill	210	Dumfries	634
Clitheroe	294	Dunblane	681
Clun	413	Dunster	428–429
Cockermouth	80	Dursley	230
Colchester	196, 480	East Barkwith	306
Coleford	200	East Hoathly	519
Colyton	134	East Mersea	195
Coniston	85	East Rudham	343
Corbridge	369	Eastbourne	522
Corfe Castle	167	Eckington	571

Edinburgh	642–653	Hayle	39
Edington	441	Haywards Heath	516
Elgin	675	Helmsley	601–602
Ely	16–17	Helston	48–52
Evesham	542	Henfield	517
Exeter	126–131	Hereford	256–258
Fairford	227	Hexham	371
Fakenham	340–342	Heydon	350
Falmouth	54–55	Highworth	560
Faversham	266–267	Holmesfield	95
Fishguard	724	Holmfirth	577
Fordingbridge	234	Holywell	708
Fort William	661	Honiton	135
Framsden	488	Hook	245
Fraserburgh	615	Hope Valley	94
Frome	460–462	Horncastle	305
Gainsborough	308–309	Horsham	515
Gartocharn	641	Hove	11
Gislingham	490	Hull	613
Glastonbury	449	Hungerford	9
Glastonbury	448–451	Huntly	617
Gloucester	202	Inverness	671
Godalming	500	Ipswich	481–482
Grantham	298–300	Isle of Gigha	624
Grimsby	310	Isle of Harris	694
Guildford	503	Isle of Lewis	693
Haddington	657	Isle of Mull	629–630
Hailsham	521	Isle of Skye	663
Halesworth	498	Isle of South Uist	695
Happisburgh	356	Jedburgh	686
Hartfield	518	Kelty	658
Hastings	524	Kendal	86–89
Haughley	489	Keswick	78–79
Haverfordwest	723	Kilgetty	720
Hawes	582	Killearn	690
Haworth	579	Kilmarnock	632
Hay-on-Wye	251–253	Kimcote	297

King's Lynn	344–347	Macclesfield	25
Kingsbridge	104	Machynlleth	726–727
Kingsbridge	105–106	Machynlleth	727
Kingsdown	276	Maidstone	286–287
Kington	249	Maldon	198
Kippen	692	Malmesbury	561–562
Kirkby Lonsdale	93	Malpas	24
Kirkby Stephen	91–92	Malton	612
Kirkbymoorside	603	Malvern	572–574
Kirknewton	654	Manningtree	194
Kirriemuir	622	Marlborough	556–558
Kyle of Lochalsh	664	Matfen	370
Launceston	63–64	Matlock	97–99
Lavenham	477–478	Melksham	569
Lawrenny	722	Melrose	684–685
Ledbury	259	Melton Constable	351
Lee	149	Melton Mowbray	295
Leek	471–472	Midhurst	510–511
Leintwardine	417	Milford on Sea	235
Lenham	265	Milton Keynes	15
Leominster	246–247	Minehead	425
Lewes	520	Modbury	102–103
Leyburn	589	Mold	707
Lincoln	303–304	Monmouth	717
Linton	19	Monymusk	619
Liskeard	61–62	Moreton-in-Marsh	206–208
Llandovery	701	Morpeth	372–374
Llandysul	702–703	Morwenstow	26
Llanfrynach	733	Musselburgh	655
Llangadog	700	Nairn	669
Lochgilphead	625	Narberth	721
Lockerbie	637–638	Nayland	479
London	311–337	Neston	21
Lostwithiel	60	Nether Stowey	430–431
Ludlow	418–423	Newark	382–383
Lymington	236	Newmarket	474–475
Lynton	148, 150	Newnham	201

Newton Abbot	117–121	Rogart	674
Newtown	728	Ross-on-Wye	255
North Berwick	656	Rothbury	375
North Molton	145	Ruthin	706
Northallerton	586–587	Rye	526–527
Norwich	357–362	Salisbury	180, 543–550
Oakham	400	Saltash	66–67
Oban	626–628	Sandy	8
Okehampton	139	Saxmundham	492–493
Orpington	491	Scarborough	606–607
Oswestry	402, 725	Shaftesbury	181–182
Otley	581	Sheffield	576
Oxford	396–397	Shepton Mallet	458–459
Padstow	38	Sherborne	187–192
Painswick	220	Sheringham	353
Pembroke	718–719	Shipston-on-Stour	540–541
Penrith	74–77	Shorwell	261
Penzance	45–47	Shrewsbury	403–407
Perth	680	Silsden Moor	580
Peterborough	365	Silverdale	292
Petersfield	241–242	Sittingbourne	263–264
Petworth	512–513	Sleaford	301–302
Pewsey	554–555	Somerton	442
Pickering	608–609	South Molton	144
Pitlochry	676–677	Southam	539
Plockton	665	Southwold	497
Poole	170	Sowerby Bridge	578
Porlock	427	St Andrews	660
Presteigne	729	St Annes on Sea	293
Privett	240	St Boswells	687
Pulborough	514	St Ives	41–44
Radstock	463–464	St Leonards on Sea	523
Ramsgate	268	St Martin	614
Richmond	583–584	Stirling	682
Ridlington	355	Stockbridge	233
Ripon	590–593	Stow-on-the-Wold	209
Robertsbridge	525	Stranraer	639

Stratford-upon-Avon	535–538	Wallingford	399
Stroud	222–223	Wantage	398
Sturminster Newton	183–186	Wareham	169
Swanage	168	Warminster	551–553
Swansea	736	Warwick	532–534
Swindon	559	Wells	452, 457, 465
Tain	673	Wells-next-the-Sea	339
Talyllyn	712	Weobley	248
Tanworth in Arden	531	West Barkwith	307
Taunton	432–436	Weston-super-Mare	470
Tavistock	124–125	Weymouth	165
Teddington	338	Wheathill	411
Tenterden	282	Wheddon Cross	426
Tetbury	229	Whitby	604–605
Tewkesbury	203–204	Whitchurch	401
The Lizard	53	Wigton	72–73
Thetford	364	Wimborne	173
Thirsk	594	Wincanton	444–446
Thursford Green	352	Winchester	238, 244
Tonbridge	291	Windermere	81–83
Torpoint	68	Winforton	250
Torquay	122	Winscombe	469
Torridon	666	Witney	395
Totnes	110–112	Woking	504
Towcester	368	Woodbridge	483–487
Truro	56–59	Woodhouse Eaves	296
Tunbridge Wells	288–290	Woodstock	394
Ullapool	667	Woolacombe	151
Ulverston	84	Wooler	379
Umberleigh	142–143	Worth	274
Usk	715	Worthenbury	737
Uttoxeter	473	Yeovil	443
Vowchurch	254	York	596–600
Wadebridge	35–37	Yoxford	496

① Highland

Highland

Wemyss House

② The peace is palpable, the setting overlooking the Cromarty Firth is stunning. Take an early morning stroll and spot buzzards, pheasants, rabbits and roe deer. The deceptively spacious house with sweeping maple floors is flooded with light and fabulous views, big bedrooms are warmly decorated with Highland rugs and tweeds, there's Christine's grand piano in the living room, Stuart's handcrafted furniture at every turn, and a sweet dog called Bella. Aga breakfasts include homemade bread, preserves and eggs from happy hens. Dinners are delicious; Christine and Stuart are wonderful hosts.

③ Ethical Collection: Food. See page 420.

St Callan's Manse

Fun, laughter and conversation flow in this warm and happy home. You share it with prints, paintings, antiques, sofas, amazing memorabilia, three dogs, nine ducks, 14 hens and 1,200 teddy bears of every size and origin. Snug bedrooms have pretty fabrics, old armoires, flower-patterned sheets and tartan blankets; your sleep will be sound. Caroline cooks majestic breakfasts and dinners; Robert, a fund of knowledgeable anecdotes, can arrange just about anything. All this in incomparable surroundings: 60 acres of sheep-strewn land plus glens, forests, buzzards, deer and the odd golden eagle. A gem. *Dogs by arrangement.*

④	Price	From £90.
⑤	Rooms	3: 2 doubles, 1 twin.
⑥	Meals	Dinner £35. Restaurants 15-minute drive.
⑦	Closed	Rarely.
⑧	Directions	From Inverness, A9 north. At Nigg r'bout, right onto B9175. Through Arabella; left at sign to Hilton & Shandwick; right towards Nigg; past church; 1 mile, right onto private road. House on right.

Price	£80. Singles £65.
Rooms	2: 1 double with separate bath; 1 double with separate shower.
Meals	Dinner, 2-4 courses, £16-£25. BYO. Pub/restaurant in village, 1.5 miles.
Closed	March & occasionally.
Directions	From Inverness, A9 north. Cross Dornoch bridge. 14 miles on, A839 to Lairg. Cross small bridge in Rogart; sharp right uphill, for St Callan's church. House 1.5 miles on, on right, next to church.

⑨ 🍷 Bottle of wine with dinner on first night.

🍷 Free pick-up from local bus/train station. Local food/produce in your room. Late checkout (12pm).

⑩ 🎁 Use your Sawday's Gift Card here.

Christine Asher & Stuart Clifford
Wemyss House,
Bayfield, Tain IV19 1QW
Tel +44 (0)1862 851212
Mobile +44 (0)7759 484709
Email stay@wemysshouse.com
Web www.wemysshouse.com

Robert & Caroline Mills
St Callan's Manse,
Rogart IV28 3XE
Tel +44 (0)1408 641363
Email caroline@rogartsnuff.me.uk

⑪ 🚶 🐕 📖 📶 🌿 ♿ ✂

🍴 🐕 📶 🚒 🌿 🚜 ✂

⑫ Entry 673 Map 18

Entry 674 Map 21